EARLY CHRISTIANITY IN CONTEXT

Editor
John M. G. Barclay

Editorial Board
Loveday Alexander, Troels-Engberg-Pedersen
Bart Ehrman, Joel Marcus, John Riches

Published under

LIBRARY OF NEW TESTAMENT STUDIES

287

formerly the Journal for the Study of the New Testament Supplement Series

Editor
Mark Goodacre

THE ORIGINAL GOSPEL OF THOMAS
IN TRANSLATION

With a Commentary and New English
Translation of the Complete Gospel

APRIL D. DeCONICK

t &t clark

Published by T&T Clark International
A Continuum imprint
The Tower Building, 11 York Road, London SE1 7NX
80 Maiden Lane, Suite 704, New York, NY 10038

www.tandtclark.com

British Library Cataloguing-in-Publication Data
A catalogue record for this book is available from the British Library

ISBN 0-5670-4382-7 (hardback)

Typeset by ISB Typesetting, Sheffield
Printed   in Great Britain by

To my *Doktorvater*

Jarl Fossum

and the *Religionsgeschichtliche Schule* you inspired in the States,

Charles Gieschen
Phil Munoa
Andrei Orlov
Kevin Sullivan

CONTENTS

PREFACE

The Original Gospel of Thomas in Translation began as a hundred-page interpretative appendix to my monograph, *Recovering the Original Gospel of Thomas: A History of the Gospel and Its Growth* (LNTSSup, 286; London: T&T Clark, 2005). As I wrote *Recovering* and the appendix, I realized that the appendix was becoming more extensive than I had originally intended. So at the good suggestion of my editor, John Barclay, before the publication of *Recovering*, I pulled the appendix and began to reshape it into a freestanding commentary and translation of the *Gospel of Thomas*. In the process of rewriting the appendix into a separate book, I tried to create a volume that could be read and understood on its own, a volume that would be a useful resource apart from *Recovering*. Having said this, however, its theoretical and substantive connection with *Recovering* should not be overlooked since its original purpose was to provide detailed support for the arguments and discussions in that monograph. So personally, I consider the two books 'sister' volumes that together provide a detailed picture of my reconstruction of the *Gospel of Thomas*, its history and growth.

Because of this connection, I begin *The Original Gospel of Thomas* in Chapter 1 by summarizing and synthesizing the discussions contained in *Recovering*. In Chapter 2, I provide for the first time a reconstruction of the earliest version of the Gospel, the Kernel *Thomas*, which I estimate dates to 30–50 CE. The translation and reconstruction of the Kernel should not be understood as the exact 'original' *Thomas*, only the best approximate possible given the sources and method available. I also provide in Chapter 3 a new translation of the complete *Gospel of Thomas*. To showcase the gradual accrual of material in the Kernel, I have given the Kernel sayings in regular type while the accretions are in *italic*.

I set up the commentary with separate entries for each logion. Each entry includes the same sections, although it should be noted that in cases where one or more of the categories did not apply, I did not retain the heading in that particular entry. Each entry begins with its English translation. It should be noted that, whenever a logion has both a Greek witness and a Coptic witness, I have attempted to incorporate the oldest reading into the English translation of the logion. Next the Greek fragment with its translation is presented, and then the Coptic text with its translation. I use the following signs in my transcriptions and translations to signal textual or translation problems or decisions:

    ( ) Parentheses are placed around words not in the manuscript but that the translation needs in order to capture the meaning of the Greek or Coptic.

  (( )) Double parentheses surround text where the translation is based on the Greek manuscript tradition rather than the Coptic.

[ ]   Square brackets indicate lacunae or effacement and their possible recon-
         structions.

[[ ]]   Double square brackets surround text where it has been emended. In
         these cases, the translation is based on a correction of an error perceived
         in the manuscript tradition.

<< >>   Double pointed brackets surround text where an alternative reading is
         presented based on a possible Aramaic text behind the Greek or Coptic.

.   Dots under letters indicate that only a part of a letter is visible in the
         manuscript and that the ink marks indicate the likelihood of this
         restoration

   In each entry under the label *ATTRIBUTION*, I have identified whether or not the
logion is from the Kernel Gospel or is a later accretion. The following section,
TEXT AND TRANSLATION ISSUES, focuses on problems with the text, emendations,
translation choices, and language issues. In the next section, *INTERPRETATIVE
COMMENT*, I provide my interpretation of the logion based on the understanding
of the Gospel that I mapped out in *Recovering* and summarized in Chapter 1 of
this volume. My interpretation does not contain references to the Gnostic
hermeneutic applied to the Gospel by numerous scholars for so many decades.
Instead it focuses on providing an alternative hermeneutic which sees the Gospel
as an example of early 'orthodox' Syrian religiosity. The *SOURCE DISCUSSION* for
each logion is meant to highlight various positions that have been argued over the
last fifty years as well as my own opinions. I have included in the entries
LITERATURE PARALLELS as well as charts detailing *AGREEMENTS WITH THE SYRIAN
GOSPELS, THE WESTERN TEXT AND THE DIATESSARON*. When identifying the parallel
sayings to the logia, in addition to my own knowledge of the ancient literature, I
found especially helpful W.D. Stoker, *Extracanonical Sayings of Jesus* (1989)
and M. Meyer, *The Gospel of Thomas* (1992). I have attempted to be as complete
as possible with the identification of parallels, although I recognize that there may
be some variants that I have missed. Because of the limited space for publication,
I have included only English translations of the parallels, but have referenced the
original language critical editions in a convenient *PRIMARY SOURCE BIBLIOGRAPHY*
so that the original language text can easily be found. There has been no attempt
to translate the biblical passages anew since they already exist in numerous translations. So the English translation of the biblical passages is taken from the standard RSV, although I have taken liberties with punctuation. Unfortunately, this
means that the language I have chosen to translate *Thomas*' version of sayings
that have New Testament parallels does not necessarily correspond to the RSV
translation, so the original language of the New Testament should be consulted
and compared with the Greek and Coptic of *Thomas*. The Greek New Testament
can be found in the standard edition of *Novum Testamentum Graece*. As for the
agreements with the Syrian Gospels, the Western Text, and the Diatessaron, these
were compiled from the earlier work of G. Quispel (1959; 1975e) and T. Baarda
(1983c). Each entry ends with a *SELECT BIBLIOGRAPHY* which highlights the
works that served as the basis for my discussion of the logion.

My transcriptions are based not only on previous scholars' work, but also on my own physical examination in the manuscripts. In late October 2004 while on Sabbatical leave from Illinois Wesleyan University, I flew to Boston, Oxford, and London to consult the Greek papyri fragments of the Gospel. I am indebted to the University which supported my travel and research odyssey with a generous faculty research grant. My gratitude extends to all the curators who kindly assisted me with the handling of the papyri: Ms Susan Halpert, Reference Librarian at the Houghton Library; Michael Boggan, Librarian in the Manuscripts Reading Room at the British Library; Dr Bruce-Benfield, Senior Assistant Librarian in the stately Duke Humfrey's Reading Room at the Bodleian Library. My thanks also to Professor Christopher Rowland of Oxford University, Queen's College, who hosted my delightful (and inspiring!) visit to Oxford.

In March 2005 while on Spring break, I travelled to Old Cairo to consult the Nag Hammadi manuscript of the Gospel which is housed in a wooden vault in the library of the Coptic Museum. I wish to thank especially Mm. Kamilia Makîam, Director of Manuscripts at the Coptic Museum, for her generous assistance with the Coptic manuscript. Many others aided my travel to Egypt and facilitated my application to examine the Coptic manuscript, and to these kind people I also wish to extend my thanks: Dr Zahi Hawas, Secretary General of the Supreme Council of Antiquities; Dr Phillip Halim, Director of the Coptic Museum; Mm. Amira Khattab, Deputy Director of Research and Government Relations for the American Research Center in Egypt; Dr Gawdat Gabra, former Director of the Coptic Museum. Professor Marvin Meyer of Chapman University and Professor Karen King of Harvard University gave me valuable advice regarding travel to Old Cairo and the Museum, for which I am grateful.

Birger Pearson kindly mentioned to me the work of J. Liebenberg (2001), which I did not know about when writing *Recovering*. The fact that Birger Pearson called my attention to Liebenberg's monograph has enriched this commentary, particularly my discussions of the Thomasine parables. Kevin Sullivan and Deirdre Dempsey were great conversation partners, particularly when it came to laying out the Aramaic and Syriac substratum of *Thomas*. David Cook graciously introduced me to T. Khalidi, *The Muslim Jesus*. Steve Patterson gave me helpful feedback regarding my views on *Thomas'* compositional history as I presented them in *Recovering*. I thought his discussion in 'Wisdom in Q and Thomas' had implications for the Gospel's compositional history, but the article was only meant to be a traditio-historical contribution. He remains sceptical about the compositional history of *Thomas*.

A word of thanks to my secretary and research assistant, Regina Linsalata, who collected and collated articles and books, and put together the bibliographies, and to my student assistant, Abigail Mohaupt, who compiled the indices. And thanks to my husband, Wade Greiner, who has spent countless hours discussing with me the *Gospel of Thomas* and asking me all the 'right' questions. His avid interest, support and encouragement mean more to me than I can express in words.

Finally, a note about the dedication to my *Doktorvater*, Jarl Fossum. When I told him that I wanted to write another book on the *Gospel of Thomas*, he asked me quite seriously, 'What more can be said about the *Gospel of Thomas*?' So this is for you, Jarl, and the *Religionsgeschichtliche Schule* you inspired in the States.

April DeConick
Assumption of the Blessed Virgin Mary, 2005

ABBREVIATIONS

AGJU	Arbeiten zur Geschichte des antiken Judentums und des Urchristentums
Aphr	Aphraates
Ar	Arabic New Testament
BCNH	Bibliothèque Copte de Nag Hammadi
BIFAO	*Bulletin de l'Institut français d'archéologie orientale*
Bo	Boharic New Testament
BZ	*Biblische Zeitschrift*
BZNW	Beihefte zur Zeitschrift für die neutestamentliche Wissenschaft
C	Old Syriac Curetonianus
Clem	Clement of Alexandria
Crum	W.E. Crum, *A Coptic Dictionary* (Oxford: Clarendon Press, 1939)
CSCO	I.B. Chabot, *et al.* (eds), Corpus scriptorum christianorum orientalium. (Paris, 1903–)
D	Codex Bezae
EPRO	Etudes preliminaries aux religions orientales dans l'empire romain
ETL	*Ephemerides theologicae lovanienses*
ExpTim	*Expository Times*
GCS	Die griechische christliche Schriftsteller der ersten [drei] Jahrhunderte
HDR	Harvard Dissertations in Religion
Hel	Heliand
HeyJ	*Heythrop Journal*
HR	*History of Religions*
HTR	*Harvard Theological Review*
JBL	*Journal of Biblical Literature*
JECS	*Journal of Early Christian Studies*
JJS	*Journal of Jewish Studies*
JRS	*Journal of Roman Studies*
JSJ	*Journal for the Study of Judaism in the Persian, Hellenistic, and Roman Periods*
JSNT	*Journal for the Study of the New Testament*
JSNTSup	*Journal for the Study of the New Testament*, Supplement
JTS	*Journal of Theological Studies*
LCL	Loeb Classical Library
LNTS	*Library of New Testament Studies*
LNTSSup	*Library of New Testament Studies*, Supplement
Mac	Pseudo-Macarius
Matt(H)	Hebrew Matthew
MGWJ	*Monatschrift für Geschichte und Wissenschaft des Judentums*
NHS	Nag Hammadi Studies
NHMS	Nag Hammadi and Manichaean Studies
NumenSup	*Numen,* Supplement
NTS	*New Testament Studies*

NovT	*Novum Testamentum*
NTSup	*Novum Testamentum,* Supplement
P	Peshitta
Pal	Palestinian Syriac Lectionary
PG	J.-P. Migne (ed.), *Patrologiae cursus completus: Series graeca* (162 vols; Paris, 1857–86)
PL	J.-P. Migne (ed.), *Patrologia cursus completus. Series prima [latina]* (221 vols; Paris, 1844–65)
REG	*Revue des études grecques*
RHR	*Revue de l'histoire des religions*
RSR	*Recherches de science religieuse*
S	Old Syriac Sinaiticus
Sa	Sahidic New Testament
SBL	Society of Biblical Literature
SBLSP	*Society of Biblical Literature Seminar Papers*
SBT	Studies in Biblical Theology
SC	Sources chrétiennes (Paris: Cerf, 1943–)
StEv	*Studia evangelica*
T^A	A. Sebastianus Marmardji, *Diatessaron de Tatien* (Beriut: Imprimerie Catholique, 1935).
T^{EC}	L. Leloir (ed. and trans.), *Éphrem de Nisibe: Commentaire de l'évangile concordant ou Diatessaron, traduit du syriaque et de l'arménien* (SC 121; Paris: Cerf, 1966).
T^L	E. Ranke (ed.), *Codex Fuldensis: Novum Testamentum latine interprete Hieronymo ex manuscripto Victoris Capuani* (Leipzig: Elwert, 1868).
T^N	D. Plooij, C.A. Phillips, *et al.*, *The Liège Diatessaron* (Verhandelingen der koninklijke Nederlandse Akademie van Wetenschappen, Afdeling Letterkunde 31.1-8; Amsterdam: 1929–70).
T^P	G. Messina, *Diatessaron Persiano* (BibOr 14; Rome: Pontifical Biblical Institute, 1951).
T^V	V. Todesco, 'Diatessaron Veneto', in *Il Diatessaron in Volgare Italiano* (Studi e Testi 81; Vatican City: Vatican Apostolic Library, 1938).
T^T	V. Todesco, 'Diatessaron Tuscano, 'in *Il Diatessaron in Volgare Italiano* (Studi e Testi 81; Vatican City: Vatican Apostolic Library, 1938).
T^{Pep}	M. Goates (ed.), *The Pepysian Harmony* (Early English Text Society 157; London: Miford, 1922).
TDNT	Gerhard Kittel and Gerhard Friedrick (eds), *Theological Dictionary of the New Testament* (trans. Geoffrey W. Bromiley; 10 vols; Grand Rapids: Eerdmans, 1964–76)
TF	Theologische Forschung
THB	Titus Bostra, *Contra Manicheaos*
TLZ	*Theologische Literaturzeitung*
TRu	*Theologische Rundschau*
TU	Texte und Untersuchungen
TUGAL	Texte und Untersuchungen zur Geschichte der altchristlichen Literatur
VC	*Vigiliae christianae*
VCSup	*Vigiliae christianae,* Supplement
WUNT	Wissenschaftliche Untersuchungen zum Neuen Testament
Zach	Zacharias Chrysopolitanus, *Commentary on the Latin Diatessaron*
ZNW	*Zeitschrift für die neutestamentliche Wissenschaft und die Kunde der älteren Kirche*

LIST OF ILLUSTRATIONS

Part I

THE *GOSPEL* IN TRANSLATION

Chapter 1

BOUNDARIES AND BASICS

Eight years ago in the prologue to *Seek To See Him*, I lamented the fact that an exhaustive commentary on the *Gospel of Thomas* did not exist, while scores of such commentaries continue to be written on New Testament texts. Other than religious bias, I fail to reason why this is the case, especially when we have before us a real gem, a 'found' early Christian Gospel that indeed may contain a kernel of Jesus' sayings pre-dating Quelle.

Although several smaller commentaries representing the interpretations of individual scholars have been released in the last decade, sadly, in my opinion, the most recent 'comprehensive' commentary to date was written by J. Ménard in 1975, nearly thirty years ago![1] At that time it represented the *status questionae* which had been worked out with great enthusiasm in manifold lectures and publications during the 1960s. Because *Thomas* speaks of the light within each individual while degrading the cosmos and the human body, brilliant scholars spilled much ink developing Gnostic interpretations for each of the logia. Ménard's commentary represented this academic consensus on *Thomas*, that this Gospel was written by a Gnostic author who revised Synoptic sayings of Jesus in order to convey an esoteric message to elite religionists.[2] Although a few voices at the time followed either G. Quispel's or H. Koester's lead, arguing that the Gospel retained early independent tradition, the majority of scholars whom Ménard represented felt that the Gospel was dependent, late and essentially irrelevant to the study of Christian origins.[3]

---

1.   Ménard (1975). For a range of recent commentaries offering individual interpretations, see Meyer (1992) which presents an historical view of the Gospel as an example of an ancient sapiential collection; Valantasis (1997) which provides an interpretation for a modern reader, emphasizing the original ascetic nature of the Gospel and possibilities for what this might mean to us today; Davies (2002) which offers a commentary to enhance the spirituality of the modern reader with little interest in historical issues.

2.   Cerfaux and Garitte (1957); Grant (1959); Wilson (1958/1959; 1960b); Bauer (1960); Grant with Freedman (1960); Schoedel (1960); Roques (1960a; 1960b); Smyth (1960); Cornélis (1961); Gärtner (1961); Haenchen (1961); Turner and Montefiore (1962); Bauer (1964); Vielhauer (1964); Schrage (1964a); Säve-Söderbergh (1967). The most recent attempt is that of Fieger (1991).

3.   Quispel (1957; 1958/1959; 1958; 1959; 1960; 1967a); Koester (1971).

1.1. *A Gnostic Gospel?*

Analysis of the Nag Hammadi documents alongside Patristic materials has challenged the traditionally held appeal to a generic Gnostic religiosity and Gnosticism as a religious movement, let alone *Thomas*' association with such a religion. It is becoming increasingly clear that 'Gnosticism' and its adjective 'Gnostic' are misnomers, that is they are not so much descriptors of historical realities as they are modern typological constructs.[4] What we are realizing is that our traditional understanding of Gnosticism and its corollaries summed up at Messina was built on our circular assumption that the characteristics held in common by 'deviant' groups in antiquity described a larger religiosity, an umbrella religion under which various deviants hovered.[5] Gnostic and Gnosticism came to represent a form of religiosity characterized by a negative view of the cosmos and human existence, a feeling of nihilism in contrast with the yearning for everything spiritual. As such, various traditions – Hermetic, apocalyptic, mystical, encratic – lost their distinctiveness and were subsumed under the Gnostic umbrella. Everything esoteric became Gnostic as if, by definition, orthodoxy was devoid of esoteric tendencies.

But this 'golden bough' is breaking. Analysis of the Nag Hammadi materials has revealed that the Hermetics were distinct from the Valentinians who were distinct from the Sethians who were distinct from the Simonians and so on. Their distinctiveness was not only in regard to their social boundaries and behaviours, but also their theological positions. There was not an umbrella religion called 'Gnosticism' in which these groups participated. So to continue to characterize the *Gospel of Thomas* 'Gnostic' is historically misleading, and its perpetuation ends in chasing a pink elephant. If scholars should continue inventing elaborate Gnostic interpretations of *Thomas*' logia, their endeavours will be nothing more than exercises in scholarly imagination and modern Gnostic eisegesis. Certainly it is fair to ask whether the *Gospel of Thomas* was written by a Valentinian (such as the *Gospel of Philip* was), or a Basilidian, or a Carpocratian, or a Naasene. But as I have argued in detail elsewhere, since *Thomas* intrinsically lacks any mythological or sociological references distinct to any of these forms of Christianity, this question leads us nowhere either.[6]

1.1.1. *An Alternative Solution*

In my opinion, this current state of knowledge requires a reexamination of the *Gospel of Thomas*, offering an alternative hermeneutic and commentary to the passé Gnostic, a hermeneutic and commentary that is sensitive to shifting Christian constituencies, is contextualized in historical realities, and is grounded in traditions located in specific geographical areas. This book is intended to be a contribution in that direction. Although it is still not the comprehensive encyclopedic

---

4. Williams (1996); Markschies (2003: 1–28); King (2003).
5. Bianchi (1967).
6. DeConick (1996: 3–27).

commentary I wish for, it is an attempt to read the *Gospel of Thomas* as a text echoing early Syrian religiosity instead of a Gospel written by and for some shadowy Gnostics. For all these reasons, I do not include extensive references to the Gnostic hermeneutic applied to the text over the years, but have focused my commentary on the alternative hermeneutic which I have developed more fully in the companion volume to this commentary, *Recovering the Original Gospel of Thomas: A History of the Gospel and Its Growth* (London: T&T Clark, 2005).

G. Quispel warned us decades ago that we needed to be more careful about describing early Syrian Christianity as if it should be similar to Roman Christianity, making texts like the *Pseudo-Clementines*, the apocryphal *Acts*, and the Thomasine literature appear deviant and 'Gnostic'. His warning is worth reprinting:

> Our students ought to know that Christianity has been interpreted in several ways, according to the genius of the peoples to whom it was entrusted: if Rome stressed the legal aspects of the new religion, and the Greeks developed the ontological interpretation of God and Christ, the Syrians were not interested in dogmatic strife, at least until Ephrem Syrus in the fourth century, and conceived their faith rather as a Way, a way of life.[7]

Has the contemporary move to 'novelize' the original Aramaic Christianity of James and the Mother Church in Jerusalem and to 'multiply' Christianity in Palestine given scholars licence to lose touch with orthodox Christianity that developed early on in Syria, an orthodoxy very different from that which simultaneously was growing in the West? Is the Academy returning to a modified but still hypercritical pre-World War II position advocated by Eduard Schwartz in 1932 that the Christian Jewish elements in texts like the *Pseudo-Clementines* – the hostility towards Paul, the primacy of James, and so on – are mythologies created by novelists who wished to legitimate the opinions of existing Christian congregations?[8]

Certainly it must be recognized that communal memory and the need to explain the present played a large part in the motivation and codification of the traditions. But, and here is where the Academy is on the verge of making a grave error, this process was not detached from the historical past and actual memories of the community. The presence of traceable traditions in our texts leads us forward to a historically plausible reconstruction of early Christianity. The Christianity in Syria as it emerges in our texts shows strong roots and ties with traditions from Jerusalem. Pauline traditions and hermeneutics generally were not developed by the early eastern Syrian community. Thus, the theology of the cross as Paul developed it and later the lawyers in the Roman Church, is not emphasized. This fact alone makes early Syrian texts look 'strange' to the Western eye. And I suspect, since the Western trained scholar has had need to legitimate his or her form of Christianity as the earliest and most authentic, the study of Syrian Christianity has been relegated to the deviant, the Gnostic, rather than heir to Jerusalem.

---

7. Quispel (1975d: 146).
8. Schwartz (1932).

1.1.2. *Characteristics of Early Syrian Christianity*

What do our texts tell us about the nature and characteristics of early Syrian Christianity? As A. Vööbus taught us long ago, Christianity in eastern Syria in the first couple of hundreds of years demanded celibacy and asceticism for admission into the Church.[9] The willingness to take on this renunciatory life fused with the Christian faith made admission to the Syrian Church possible. The larger Catholic Church particularly in the West did not favour this old position of the Syrian Christians, and consequently our historical memory of these people is of sectarians and even heretics. But the literary evidence from Nag Hammadi, the apocryphal *Acts*, the *Pseudo-Clementines*, the records of the Church Fathers, and so on, point to a form of Christianity in Syria which was encratic, honouring the solitary life over the marital. It was E. Peterson who first recognized the old Palestinian origins of these notions, tracing them back to a form of Christian Judaism which, like other forms of Judaism, taught about the two inclinations of the soul.[10] The evil inclination was identified with the sexual impulse and needed to be guarded against. For these Christians, baptism followed by daily washings and renunciations extinguished the desire and made it possible for the believer to restore his soul to the glorious prelapsarian Image of God.

This position on the solitary life appears to have shifted with Aphraates, whose writings show us that the demands of celibacy were eventually relaxed, reserved for the privileged class of the Syrian Church, the 'sons and daughters of the Covenant'. This shift occurred at a time when the Syrian Church was becoming more influenced by Roman theology and practices. It appears that only at this time in the history of Syrian Christianity were the married allowed full entrance into the Church.

As far as early Syrian theology is concerned, here the East does not meet the West either. In the early Syrian literature, the human being regains Paradise lost through his or her own effort of righteous living as revealed by Jesus, not through some act of atonement on Jesus' part. Over and over again through story after story, the Christian is taught that he or she must become as self-controlled as possible, particularly concentrating on overcoming desire and passions that lurk in the soul. He or she is taught through discourse and example that marriage should be abandoned in order to achieve the prelapsarian condition of 'singleness'. When this is done, gender differences are abolished and the believer can be united with his or her divine double in the 'bridal chamber'. This divine double, the person's new spouse, is in fact Jesus himself. In the literature, it is Judas Thomas (Judas the Twin) who becomes the metaphor for all believers since Jesus is described as his very own divine Twin.

1.1.3. *An Ancient 'Orthodox' Syrian Gospel*

This is the historical context for the Christianity described in the *Gospel of Thomas*. The sayings in this little book describe a mystical form of Christianity

---

9. Vööbus (1951); Vööbus (1960).
10. Peterson (1959: 209–35).

in which the believer worked not just to understand God, but to 'know' him in the deepest and most intimate sense. They wished to *experience* God immediately and directly. The Thomasine Christians teach us in their Gospel that the first step toward this Ultimate experience is to achieve a personal state of passionlessness. Complete control over their bodies garnered for them the condition necessary to storm the gates of Eden. So many sayings point to an encratic praxis, honouring the life of the solitary above all else (L. 4.1, 4.3, 11.2–4, 16.4, 21.1–4, 21.6–9, 22, 23.2, 27.1, 37, 49, 64.12, 75, 85, 101, 105, 106, 110, 111.2, 114). These Christians worked hard to recreate their bodies into the glorious Image of Adam through permanent celibacy. In the sayings, we find that they tried to imitate Jesus' crucifixion which they understood differently from Western Christians. To them, Jesus' crucifixion was the ultimate example of a person crucifying the flesh and its appetites (L. 55, 56, 58, 80, 87, 112). So they taught each other that it was necessary to 'fast from the world' and guard against temptations and worldliness (L. 27, 21.6–8, 110). With the intervention of the Holy Spirit received at baptism, they fought the apocalyptic battle internally, overpowering their inner demons (L. 21, 29, 70). These Christians appear to have placed great stock in the power of the eucharist, mentioning on several occasions the power of divine food and drink to render the person 'equal' to Jesus (L. 13, 61, 108).

Once the passionless body in imitation of Jesus had been achieved, the believer was encouraged to study and meditate on the words of Jesus (L. 1). Through this praxis, they sought revelation and vision. This God-Experience included journeys into the heavenly realms to see Jesus (L. 37) and worship before God's throne (L. 15). Knowledge of the passage through the spheres was memorized (L. 50) so that the believer could gaze upon God before death in order not to die (L. 59). In heaven, they would meet their divine doubles, their lost Images, their true selves (L. 84). They would directly encounter the Living God – God the Father and Jesus his Son. They believed that these experiences would bring about their complete and final transformation into their original bodies of Glory, so that they would no longer 'die'.

Again, there is nothing about this mystical spirituality that is 'heretical' or 'Gnostic' by traditional definitions. In fact, it appears to be a precursor of the spirituality of the Orthodox Church which grew out of the traditions of a mysticism of the heart. When the heart is indwelled by the Holy Spirit, the Orthodox believe that the soul can transform itself progressively into its glorious original Image. According to the Eastern Christian tradition this personal transformation is possible only because the glorious Image that was ours in the beginning has been *diminished* by Adam's decision, not lost. It is, in fact, recoverable. This personal transformation is achieved through the hard work of the individual who aligns his or her life with that of Jesus, imitating him. In addition, when the Orthodox Christian partakes of the eucharist, it is believed that he or she is ingesting a divine body and achieving 'at-one-ment' with God. The death of Jesus is not the focus of Orthodoxy. Rather it is the Incarnation when the human and divine united and the transformation of the human soul into the glorious 'original' Image was rekindled. In Orthodoxy, the believer is called to self-knowledge, renunciation of the flesh through temperance in marriage or the Eremitic life, spiritual warfare and purification of the passions, the path of virtue, contemplation and glorification through 'gnosis' and 'theoria', the great vision of God.[11]

Why has the spirituality of the *Gospel of Thomas* been so misunderstood by previous scholars? I dare say that it is the unfamiliarity of scholars of the West with the teachings of the Orthodox Church that have resulted in years of confusion and misdirection about the teachings contained in *Thomas*. The Western tradition is in love with Augustine and so teaches that Adam's sin completely severed the Image of God from the human being, leaving him dark, lost and helpless. Thus, Western thinkers believe the central act of Jesus was that of atonement for the sin of Adam through his torturous death on the Cross. This is reenacted in the eucharist, a sacrificial meal in which all believers reap vicarious benefit. Certainly this is not the teaching of the *Gospel of Thomas*, but it is the standard, the canon, by which the teachings of *Thomas* have been wrongly assessed for so many years. I hope in this volume to provide another standard by which to assess this Gospel as an 'orthodox' text from early Syrian Christianity.

1.2. *A Late Gospel?*

To say the least, there is much energy tied up in the question of dating this Gospel and its traditions. Scholars have been divided on this issue. Those arguing for independence are for earlier dates (50 to 140 CE) while those for dependence later dates (140 onwards). Many scholars wish to remain sceptical about the compositional history of *Thomas*. I have been very frustrated with this scepticism because I think if we remain in the dark about how this text came into its present form then we should not be using it to create theories about early Christianity or the historical Jesus. There appears to me to be the desire in many scholars' works, particularly those working in North America, to see *Thomas* as a church document, but one that reflects a very early form of Christianity, a sapiential Christianity unadulterated by cross theology or apocalyptic thinking. Further, there has been the tendency to identify this sapiential theology with Jesus' teaching, an identification which essentially has collapsed *Thomas'* theology into Jesus' theology, as if it has been forgotten that *Thomas'* theology is a church theology created by the community for communal reasons. In *Recovering,* I have reviewed these positions in some detail and have offered a new model for understanding the development of this Gospel, a model which is supported by studies in orality and rhetorical composition. The results of the application of my method has led to the identification of early sayings in *Thomas* which belonged to an old speech gospel from Jerusalem, as well as a set of late accretions.[12]

1.2.1. *The Kernel* Gospel of Thomas

This Kernel Gospel, as I call it, was composed of at least five speeches of Jesus and has affinities with Quelle. In fact, every Thomasine saying that has a parallel

---

11. For an introduction to the subject, see Spidlik (1986).
12. For details, refer especially to Chapter 3 (DeConick 2005).

with Quelle belonged to the Kernel Gospel. This represents over 50 per cent of the sayings belonging to the Gospel. Not even one Thomasine logion with a common Quelle variant can be located among the accretions! This provides independent confirmation, in my opinion, that the very strict methodology that I developed and applied to the Gospel in *Recovering* was successful distinguishing between earlier traditions and later accretions.

What I discovered while compiling my research in *Recovering* is that the *Gospel of Thomas* is neither early nor late, but both. It began as a smaller Gospel of sayings organized into a speech collection similar to the speech Gospels mentioned by Clement in the *Pseudo-Clementines*. The contents of the speeches point to their origin in the Jerusalem mission prior to 50 CE. The speeches were meant to be used in oral missionary settings where the orator 'stood in' for Jesus, reperforming his teachings. All five speeches were organized around eschatological themes, showcasing the urgency of the times, the premises of discipleship, and the need for exclusive commitment to Jesus. The Christology in the Kernel sayings is very old, pre-dating even Quelle. In the Kernel, Jesus is God's Prophet who exclusively speaks God's truth. He also is understood to have been exalted to the status of a great Angel whose main role is that of the Judge, casting fire upon the earth. These descriptors are comparable to those commonly associated with early Christian Judaism from Jerusalem.

1.2.2. Later Accretions in the *Gospel of Thomas*

It appears that this Kernel Gospel was taken to Syria very early in the mission of the Jerusalem Church. These words of Jesus left with the Syrian Christians quickly developed within an oral environment of reperformance. Between the years 50 and 120 CE, the Kernel was adapted during oral performances to the changing needs, demands and ideologies of the Christian community in Syria. Accretions gradually entered the speeches of Jesus and served to reconfigure older traditions and hermeneutics no longer relevant to the experience of the Syrian community. Chart 1, reproduced from *Recovering*, conveniently identifies the Kernel and accretive materials, and the approximate dates for the accrual of the later sayings.

As can be seen from this chart, logia accrued in response to Gentile interests that eventually came to dominate the community, a leadership crisis, the death of the eyewitnesses, and the development of Christology. But the main experience which led to the reconfiguration of the Gospel was the fact that the community's original eschatological expectations had been disconfirmed by its contemporary experience of the Non-Event. When the Kingdom did not come, rather than discarding their Gospel and closing the door of their church, the Thomasine Christians responded by reinterpreting Jesus' sayings. They believed that they had misunderstood previously Jesus' intent, that they had applied the wrong hermeneutics to his sayings. So they aligned their old traditions with their present experience by shifting their theology to the mystical and creating a new hermeneutic through which the old traditions could be reinterpreted. This response is visible in the way in which they reperformed their old Gospel. Initially between 60 and 100 CE, they added question and answer units and dialogues that addressed the subject directly.

New sayings and interpretative clauses accrued, logia that worked to instruct the Christian in the new theology and guide him or her hermeneutically through the Gospel.

This eschatological rift does not appear to have been completely solved with these initial measures because the accretions show that the community continued to address the crisis by developing an encratic regime and Hermetic hermeneutic that served to completely transform the imminent Kingdom into the immanent Kingdom. This shift is evident in the sayings that accrued in the Gospel between 80 and 120 CE, a time when the community believed in a fully present Kingdom, and tried to recreate among themselves a utopian community, the Garden of Eden. According to the content of these accretions, they thought that their church was Paradise on earth. They were Adam and Eve before the Fall. Through encratic performance and visionary experience, they came to believe that they had achieved the eschatological promises of God in the present. The grandest of these promises was the complete transformation of their bodies into the original luminous Image of God. In face of a communal memory crisis, the Non-Event became the fulfilment of the Event. Jesus' promise of the imminent End had been realized within the boundaries of their community. The Christian no longer waited for the End to arrive and Jesus to return to achieve the promises of the Eschaton. His or her transformation was achieved immediately through imitative performance and direct mystical apprehension of God and his Son.

1.3. *A Coptic Gospel?*

My translation of the complete *Gospel of Thomas* is not meant to be another translation of the fourth-century Coptic Gospel manuscript. Rather it incorporates the older Greek fragments into the translation, attempting to provide the earliest edition of the full Gospel possible based on the extant manuscripts. The Greek and Coptic transcriptions are based on my own physical examination of the manuscripts as well as previous scholars' work, beginning with the original publications of the Greek fragments by B.P. Grenfell and A.S. Hunt and ending with the recent critical editions put out by B. Layton, H. Attridge and H.-G. Bethge.[13]

1.3.1. *The Greek Oxyrhynchus Fragments*
P. Oxy. 654 is kept safely in the vault of the British Library as Papyrus 1531. It is written on the verso side of a survey list of various pieces of land. The list is in a cursive script coming from the late second or early third centuries. It was not an uncommon practice for literary documents to be written on the back of documentary papyri as is the case here. The scribal hand on the verso is quite beautiful and legible, a medium-size block script from the mid- to late third century. The leaf has been broken in half vertically, so that we have extant approximately half the page. The length of the line can be estimated to 30 letter spaces on average.

---

13. Grenfell and Hunt (1897); Blass (1897); Cersoy (1898); Grenfell and Hunt (1904); Hofius (1960); Marcovich (1969); Fitzmyer (1971); Mueller (1973); Layton (1989); Attridge (1989); Bethge (1997).

Chart 1. *Gradual Accrual of Logia*

		Kernel Gospel, 30–50 CE			
2	21.10	38.1	61.1	74	96.1–2
4.2–3	21.11	39	62.1	76	96.3
5	23.1	40	62.2	78	97
6.2–3	24.2	41	63.1–3	79	98
8	24.3	42	63.4	81	99
9	25	44.2–3	64.1–11	82	100.1–3
10	26	45	65.1–7	86	102
11.1	30	46.1–2a, c	65.8	89	103
14.4	31	47	66	90	104
15	32	48	68.1	91.2	107
16.1–3	33	54	69.2	92	109
17	34	55	71	93	111.1
20.2–4	35	57	72	94	
21.5	36	58	73	95	

Accretions, 50–60 CE
Relocation and Leadership Crisis

12
68.2

Accretions, 60–100 CE
Accommodation to Gentiles and Early Eschatological Crisis
(with shift to mystical dimension of apocalyptic thought)

3.1–3	18	37	51	60	88
6.1	20.1	38.2	52	64.12	91.1
14.1–3	24.1	43	53	69.1	113
14.5	27.2	50	59	70	

Accretions, 80–120 CE
Death of Eyewitnesses, Christological Developments and Continued Eschatological Crisis
(with incorporation of encratic and hermetic traditions)

Incipit	11.2–4	23.2	56	84	108
1	13	27.1	61.2–5	85	110
3.4–5	16.4	28	67	87	111.2
4.1	19	29	75	100.4	111.3
4.4	21.1–4	44.1	77	101	112
6.4–5	21.6–9	46.2b	80	105	114
7	22	49	83	106	

The scribe has included marks in the text that appear to function as orator's aids. Before or after each phrase 'Jesus said', the scribe has drawn a coronis. In addition, in the line following the coronis, the scribe has drawn a line above several letters, indicating the beginning of a new saying. These lines and the coronis function to draw the orator's eye to the page, aiding against the loss of place during recitation. This fragment contains words from the Incipit and L. 1–7.

P.Oxy. 655 is housed in the Houghton Library on the campus of Harvard University as SM 4367. It is a small single-sided fragment that has been pieced together under glass. So there are disparate breaks and lacunae to contend with. It contains words from L. 24, 36–39.

P. Oxy. 1 is in the care of the librarians at the stately Bodleian Library in Oxford. It is catalogued as MS. Gr. th. e. 7 (P) and can be viewed in the Duke Humfrey's Reading Room. This fragment is double-sided, written in a legible hand. Breaks in transcription are mainly due to erosion of the manuscript. The scribe included coronis marks occasionally, although he appears to have used them to fill odd spaces at the end of lines when he was not able to finish a word in that line. Words from L. 26–33 and 77.2–3 can be read.

My transcription and reconstruction of the Greek papyri varies significantly from Attridge's accepted one in Layton's critical edition. There were numerous instances where dotted letters in his transcription were not legible to my eye even under ultraviolet light, or at edges of lacunae or eroded surfaces. So in my transcription, I have placed dots under partial letters that can be reasonably determined while leaving others in brackets. I am also very cautious about letter space, especially with P.Oxy. 654 which gives us only about half the letters for each line. There are several lines that Attridge has reconstructed which, in my estimation, simply cannot be, due to the limits of the line.

1.3.2. *The Coptic Translation*

The Coptic manuscript belongs to the Nag Hammadi collection and is catalogued under special glass as Codex 2, leaves 32.10 to 51.28. The manuscript is housed in a wooden vault in the library of the Coptic Museum in Old Cairo. The manuscript is written in a beautiful Coptic hand and was carefully transcribed and corrected. The pages are almost wholly intact except for some damage on the outside edges and corners of the leaves. The damage occasionally interferes with the preservation of the letters, so some letter and word reconstruction of the broken papyri is necessary. I have tried to make these judgements as fairly as possible with great consideration for the letter space available.

As for my translation of the Coptic, whenever gender-inclusive translation does not compromise the integrity of the Coptic text, I have chosen to translate the masculine reference as indefinite or neuter. Whenever possible, I have tried to render idiomatic statements gracefully into English rather than literally.

1.3.3. *An Aramaic 'Original'*

I have tried in my English translation of the *Gospel of Thomas* to unlock some of the nuances of the Coptic language with the premise that the Coptic is a translation of a Greek manuscript which, itself, was probably a translation of a Semitic language 'original'. This premise is based on the examination of numerous Semitisms present in specific logia, particularly where the Greek and Coptic are best explained with a Semitic substratum. The champion of this position was A. Guillaumont whose early studies revealed two levels of tradition prior to the Greek and Coptic. The first and earliest is a Palestinian Aramaic, while the second and latest is a Syriac that has fused with the early Western Aramaic.[14]

W. Schrage, K.H. Kuhn and B. Dehandschutter have offered a qualifier to this opinion, maintaining that some of these Semitisms are explained best as biblicisms or Coptic idioms.[15] Even if they may be correct in some of the limited cases they present, these objections do not supplant the weight of the counter evidence. They do not overturn the fact that there remain a substantial number of Semitisms in *Thomas* (about half of the logia contain likely Semitisms) which cannot be explained on these grounds, expressions which occur frequently in other literature produced in Syria. Particularly noteworthy are those logia that contain Semitic syntax such as the expression 'fast from the world' found in L. 27. This expression is not native to Greek but is a Semitic construction and occurs frequently in Syriac literature.[16] The strongest evidence for a Semitic substratum, in my opinion, however, lies not with arguments about syntax but with translation errors. A fine example is L. 30, a particularly troublesome aphorism that makes no sense in the Coptic. The Greek is very fragmentary and scholars have struggled to understand the aphorism by reconstructing the Greek in such a way to make it sensible but completely different from the Coptic. My own analysis of the papyrus in the Bodleian Library, however, has led me to a reconstruction similar to the Coptic: 'Where there are three people, gods are there. Where there is one alone, [I say,] I am with him.' In this case, neither the Greek nor the Coptic makes sense, *but* the nonsense can be easily explained, as Guillaumont did years ago, by understanding 'gods' (θεοί) to be a mistranslation of a dialect variant of Elohim which is, of course, both a name of God in Judaism as well as the plural form 'gods'. This is a case where we are not dealing with a simple Semitism retained in a Greek or Coptic translation, but a translation error probably from an Aramaic 'original' into Greek.

In my judgement, the logia identified as indicative of a Semitic substratum include 48 logia, approximately 42 per cent of the 114 sayings.[17] I have charted these sayings (Chart 2 and Chart 3) according to their distribution in the Kernel Gospel or the accretive material. What is so remarkable to me is the identification of the Aramaic and Syriac substratum in the Kernel and accretions respectively. Across the Kernel sayings, with the exception of L. 9.2, 91.2 and 100.1 which are

---

14. Guillaumont (1958; 1960; 1962; 1981).

15. Schrage (1964b); Kuhn (1960); Dehandschutter (1975: 129–130).

16. Guillaumont (1962: 18–23); Baker (1965a).

17. This is a synthesis mainly of the work of Guillaumont (1958; 1960; 1962; 1981), Quispel (1957; 1958/1959; 1975b), Nagel (1969a), Baarda (1983a; 1992; 1994b), Baker (1965), Strobel (1963), Grobel (1962), Guey (1960), and Perrin (2002). For particular details, refer to the commentary in Part 2.

explained with reference solely to Syriac, an Aramaic substratum predominates. Except in these cases, references to Aramaic can or must explain the issues raised in the Kernel sayings. Could the Kernel Gospel have been composed in Aramaic? As for the accretions, the opposite appears to be the case. Except for L. 12.1 and 60.1 which are explained as Aramaisms, a Syriac substratum is dominant. References to Syriac can or must explain the issues raised in the accretions. Could the accretive material accruing later in the Gospel have been composed in Syriac? This appears to me to be the most plausible scenario given the evidence.

As for L. 12.1, it is important to recall that I had identified this saying as the earliest accretion, accruing in the Gospel between 50 and 60 CE. This early date would warrant an Aramaic substratum, rather than the later Syriac. In the case of L. 60.1, I had postulated in *Recovering* that this dialogue had been created from an earlier Kernel parable which was no longer recoverable. So it is not altogether surprising to me that an Aramaism would survive in this late dialogue. The fact that a couple of Syriasms are found in the Kernel also is not surprising to me, but supports the theory that the Kernel was originally written in Aramaic, the Western dialect of Palestine. Once it was taken to Syria, it was reperformed and adapted into Syriac, the dialect of the East. This conclusion is supported by the reconstructive work of N. Perrin who has argued recently that the Gospel's catchword organization might be better explained as a reflection of Syriac composition than Greek.[18] In my opinion, the evidence for Syriac composition was not at the 'original' level of the Gospel as Perrin argues, but reflects a recomposition of the Gospel, a dialect shift from Aramaic to Syriac that occurred as the Kernel was reperformed in the Syrian environment.

1.4. *A Dependent Gospel?*

In the 1970s, the work of the form-critic H. Koester began to shift perceptions about the age of the traditions within the *Gospel of Thomas* from the late second century to the mid-first century.[19] Although his position was not favoured at the time, it gradually gained prominence, especially in the United States. Koester and his students argued that, although the Gospel in its present form is 'gnosticized', form-critical analysis demonstrates that many of the sayings were contemporary with Quelle, preserved in forms often more 'primitive' than the Synoptics. In fact, they are best understood as variants independent of the New Testament Gospels. They were able to support these claims by appealing to the oral background of the text where variants of particular forms of sayings would be commonplace and deductions could be made about secondary developments by analysing parallel sayings.[20]

---

18. Perrin (2002).
19. Koester (1957; 1968; 1971).
20. Cf. Crossan (1973; 1983); Sellew (1985); Cameron (1986); Hedrick (1986; 1990; 1994b); Scott (1987; 1991); Stoker (1988); Patterson (1990: 77–123; 1993); Meyer (1992).

Chart 2. *Possible Semitisms in the Kernel Gospel*

Saying	Identification of possible Semitism
8.1–3	גבא or ܓܒܐ explains ⲤⲰ̄ⲦⲠ in *Thomas* and συλλέγειν in Matthew
9.1–5	'to fill one's hand' is Semitic expression; על is mistranslated into Greek Synoptics as 'along' while *Thomas* retains the Semitism, 'by' or 'on'; 'gathered them up', rather than 'devoured' as the Greek Synoptics have it, might be explained by ܠܩܛ which can mean 'to gather' or 'to pick up' as an animal might with its mouth
16.3	Semitic syntax preserved in *Thomas* in phrasing, 'there will be five people in a house, three will be against two and two against three...' since two clauses are juxtaposed instead of the first clause subordinated as a conditional clause
25.1–2	Reflexive use of 'as your own soul'; Synoptics have 'yourself'
30.1–2	Variant of 'Elohim' mistaken by Greek translator for plural 'theoi'
33.2–3	'to come in and to go out' is Semitic expression; 'a hiding place' (*Thomas*) and 'a cellar' (Luke) may derive from סתר
36.1–3	'from morning until evening' is Semitic expression meaning 'continuously'
39.1–2	קבל or שׁקל explains ϪⲒ in *Thomas* and ἤρατε in Luke
42	עבר explains expression 'be passersby'
44	'in heaven' is Semitic phrase meaning 'by God'
45.1–4	'which is in your heart' is Semitic expression
48	שׁלם explains 'to make peace' in *Thomas* and 'to agree' in Matthew
55.1–2	'become a disciple of mine' and the repetition of the possessive pronoun in 'his father...his mother...his brothers...his sisters' are Semitic constructions
61.1	'the one...the one' is explained as a literal translation of an Aramaic phrase הד...והד
69.2	ו explains that Matthew and Luke use ὅτι while *Thomas* Ⲱ̄ⲒⲚⲀ
72.1–3	חלק or פלג explains the expression 'divider'
76.1–2	The reflexive 'he purchased *for himself*' is Semitic expression
78.1–3	ⲀⲨⲰ is explained as a mistranslation of the Aramaic ו
79.1–3	ינק explains *Thomas*' 'the breast that nourished you' and Luke's 'the breasts that nursed you'
90.1–2	'lordship' in *Thomas* rather than Matthew's 'burden' explained as an Aramaic tendency
91.1–2	ܒܚܢ 'to test' or 'to examine' explains *Thomas*' Ⲡ̄ⲠⲒⲢⲀⲌⲈ and Luke's δοκιμάζειν
97.1–4	'on the road being distant' corresponds to בדרך רחקה; 'she did not realize it' may rest on either ידע or ראה or חזא, which can mean 'to comprehend' or 'to realize', 'to see' or 'to know'; ϨⲒⲤⲈ̄ may correspond to the Aramaic בישׁא
98.1–3	ⲀϥϪⲞⲦⲤ̄ Ⲛ̄ⲦϪⲞ is explained as the proleptic use of the pronoun common to Aramaic syntax
100.1–4	The Coptic, 'a piece of gold', is a mistranslation of ܕܝܢܪ which can refer to either the Roman *denarius* or a piece of gold or silver
102	'Woe to them, the Pharisees' is explained as Aramaic syntax
104.1–2	The parallelism, 'What sin have I committed? Or how have I been conquered?' is explained by either חוב or ܚܝܒ, which can mean both 'to be conquered' or 'to sin'.
107.1–3	צבי which can mean both 'to wish' or 'to delight in', may be behind ϮⲞⲨⲰϢⲔ, and explains why the Synoptics employ forms of the Greek χαίρειν, while *Thomas* has ⲞⲨⲰϢ.
109.1–3	'to go and plough' and 'he took that field and sold it' are Semitic expressions.

Chart 3. *Possible Semitisms in the Accretive Material*

Saying	Identification of possible Semitism
1	'to taste death' is commonly found in Semitic languages, meaning 'to die'
3.1–3	CⲰK ϨHTⸯ is explained by either נגד or ܢܓܕ, which mean both 'to draw' and 'to lead'. The translator erred in his rendering into Greek. Clearly the meaning is 'to lead'.
12.1	*Thomas* has 'Who will be great over us?' while the Greek and Syriac Synoptic accounts have 'the greatest'. This is explained by an Aramaic substratum
13.8	NCⲢⲰϨK attributes an incorrect masculine pronoun to the feminine antecedent KⲰϨT. This is explained as scribal error due to a distracted translator working with a Semitic original since 'fire' is feminine in Hebrew, Aramaic and Syriac
14.3	N̄NETⲘⲠⲦN̄Ⲁ is a Semitism, meaning 'yourselves'. The reflexive use of 'spirit' is peculiar to Syriac
16.4	MONⲀXOC is explained by its Syriac compliment ܝܚܝܕܝܐ
18.3	'to taste death' is commonly found in Semitic languages, meaning 'to die'
19.3	'to taste death' is commonly found in Semitic languages, meaning 'to die'
21.4	'to strip naked', is explained as a translation error since in Syriac the standard word meaning 'to disrobe', ܫܠܚ, also means 'to renounce'
27.1	The Syriac preposition ܠ may be responsible for both the accusative (Greek) and dative (Coptic) translations of 'to fast from the world' since it may signify either a direct or indirect object
27.2	σαββατίσητε τὸ σάββατον may be explained as a Greek translation of a Semitic expression (cf. תשבתו שבתכם in Lev. 23.32), 'to observe the Sabbath day as a Sabbath'
43.1–3	ⲀYⲰ is explained as a mistranslation of the Aramaic ו or Syriac ܘ
49.1–2	MONⲀXOC is explained by its Syriac compliment ܝܚܝܕܝܐ
56.1–2	Here we find ⲠⲦⲰMⲀ instead of CⲰMⲀ which is found in the doublet L. 80. This is explained as different translations of the same Aramaic term, פגר, or Syriac term, ܦܓܪ, meaning 'corpse' or 'body'. 'Has found' is explained as a mistranslation of either מצא or ܡܨܐ, meaning either 'to find' or 'to master'. 'The world does not deserve the person who…' is a Semitic expression
60.1–2	ⲀYCⲀMⲀⲢEITHC EϥϥI, is explained as an attempt to translate an Aramaic predicate participal construction; ⲠH ⲘⲠKⲰTE ⲘⲠEϨIEIB is explained as a mistranslation of the Syriac ܟܪ̈ܟ which can mean both 'to surround' and 'to bind'
75	MONⲀXOC is explained by its Syriac compliment ܝܚܝܕܝܐ
80	'The world does not deserve the person who…' is a Semitic expression
85.1–2	'The world does not deserve the person who…' and 'to taste death' are Semitic expressions
111.3	'The world does not deserve the person who…' is a Semitic expression.
113.1–4	'By waiting' in *Thomas* and 'with things to be observed' in Luke are explained by either נטר or ܢܛܪ since both carry this dual meaning
114.1–2	ϮNⲀCⲰK M̄MOC is explained by either נגד or ܢܓܕ, which mean both 'to draw' and 'to lead'. The translator erred in his rendering into Greek. Clearly the meaning is 'to lead'

1.4.1. *Independence Appeals*

Although Koester's appeal to oral tradition as the background of the logia forged new possibilities for understanding *Thomas*, very recent studies in orality and rhetoric have shown that this appeal to background was too narrow. As I have discussed in extensive detail in the sister volume, *Recovering*, the culture out of which *Thomas* emerged was one dominated by an oral consciousness in which composition occurred mainly in the field of oral performance. Orality was the preferred mode of composition and transmission.[21]

Generally, writing was limited to correspondence or state documents. Or preservation, reserved for times when the community felt their memory of the traditions was fading or threatened from the death of the eyewitnesses or disasters like war. Authors preferred to rely on memory and oral witnesses as sources for their compositions whenever possible, although actual texts would be consulted if the situation necessitated it.

When traditions were written down, the texts were used as storage sites and memory aids for the continued oral performance of the traditions. Often the traditions of teachers would be stacked in lists that functioned rhetorically to illicit an argument or to instruct. During the performance of the traditions, the recitation of the words fluctuated as the needs of the audience shifted as well as the purposes of the orator or teacher. Orators recomposed the text every time it was performed, elaborating, explaining, interpreting, shifting details, and so on.

This rich manner of transmission has consequences beyond the fact that multiple variants will be located within early Christian texts or that newer material, including interpretative material, will have accrued alongside older. It suggests what we have known for a long time. Simple observation of the manuscript tradition of the New Testament and extra-canonical texts reveals that multiple variations of the 'same' text existed, not identical versions. This fact can be ignored no longer, and the implications it has for the old model of source criticism upon which form and redaction criticisms depend must be faced. That is, the likelihood that Matthew and Luke used exactly the same copy of Quelle and Mark is nil.[22] Although careers have been built on the reconstruction of Quelle, its redactions and its modifications at the hands of Matthew and Luke, studies in orality suggest a much more complicated and messy picture, as J. Dunn has highlighted in his work as well.[23]

This is a picture that scholars generally do not like because it leads to uncertainties and probabilities rather than confidence. Without certainty of our sources, the well-loved demonstrations in Matthean and Lukan redaction of Quelle and Mark become little more than schoolhouse exercises.

This fact makes the arguments for *Thomas'* dependence much more difficult to maintain. Of course there are scholars on both sides of the issue with reasons all around. Those who have argued for independence cite as evidence the fact that the logia in *Thomas* do not follow the same sequence as the sayings in the Synoptics. That the Thomasine parables are not allegorized like their Synoptic counterparts. That form-critically the logia in *Thomas* belong to an earlier stage of tradition than the Synoptic parallels. That there is present Synoptic-like material that is not paralleled in the Synoptics. That there is an absence of redactional

---

21. See especially, Chapter 1 (DeConick, 2005).
22. Betz (1995: 42–44).
23. Dunn (2000: 294).

activity traceable to Synoptic hands. These statements in scholarly literature have become quite standardized and generally accepted.[24]

But are they accurate perceptions? In fact, there are a couple of clusters in *Thomas* where the sequencing is the same as we find in the Synoptics (cf. L. 16.1–2 and 16.3; 55.1 and 55.2; 65 and 66). There is at least one example of a parable that is allegorized (L. 21.1–4/21.5/21.6–7) and several more interpreted (L. 64.1–11/64.12; 65/66; 76.1–2/76.3) and possibly even rewritten into a dialogue (L. 60). There is plenty of secondary material and developed logia in *Thomas* including accretive dialogues, question and answer units, interpretative clauses and the like. Although *Thomas* contains unparalleled material, so too Matthew and Luke contain special material unparalleled in their sources. As for redactional activity, if one examines the parallels on the basis of the traditional schools of source, form and redaction criticisms, there is evidence for Lukan dependence in some logia. This is a point that even J. Sieber conceded in the conclusion of his much-referenced dissertation, although this point seems to have been passed over by most scholars using his book in order to validate arguments for independence.

1.4.2. *Dependence Appeals*

As for the scholars who have argued for dependence, their position is equally problematic. They began by making the mistake that parallels with Synoptic material are indicative of dependence. It was realized by the mid-1960s that parallel material is noteworthy but not determinative. It was W. Schrage's monograph that pointed the way. In *Das Verhältnis des Thomas-Evangeliums zur synoptischen Tradition und zu den koptischen Evangelienübersetzungen*, Schrage systematically worked through the logia and identified what he thought to be Synoptic redactional elements in *Thomas*' logia.[25] Since its publication, the only monograph of which I am aware that deals with these same issues was written in 1991 by M. Fieger.[26] Its analysis of the source issue appears to be dependent upon Schrage's monograph, including his synopticon of the Coptic parallels and Schrage's problematic thesis that the Coptic *Thomas* is dependent upon the Coptic version of the New Testament. Because Fieger's discussion is so dependent upon Schrage, I have reserved my overview of the issue mainly to Schrage and the few articles written by other scholars since his book, articles which have added various nuances to Schrage's standard arguments. I have also noted those points where Fieger offers new insights.

I have taken the same approach with J. Sieber's response to Schrage, his 1966 Claremont dissertation, *A Redactional Analysis of the Synoptic Gospels with regard to the Question of the Sources of the Gospel According to Thomas*.[27] Sieber has given us the most complete systematic response to the dependence argument

---

24. Cf. Montefiore (1960/1961: 335–338); Koester (1983); Crossan (1985: 37); Cameron (1986: 14–17); Fallon and Cameron (1988: 4219–24); Stoker (1988: 98); Neller (1989: 2–3); Hedrick (1989/90: 42–48, 52–56).

25. Schrage (1964a).

26. Fieger (1991).

27. Sieber (1966).

put forward by Schrage. Every scholar of whom I am aware since Sieber has relied on and referenced his position. So again, I have limited my discussion of the issue to Sieber, except when others have contributed a new nuance or alternative argument to the discussion. Although Sieber favours independence and scholars have relied on him in this regard, it should be correctly noted that he does concede the possibility for dependence in the case of L. 31, 39, 45, 56, 79 and 104, based on the presence of words that some scholars regard as traditionally redactional. All are from the Lukan hand. The central contribution made by Sieber, however, is his identification of the major flaw in the redactional appeal – the assumption that our literary sources are fixed and certain. This assumption does not take into account the fact that because our sources developed within an oral environment what we have traditionally earmarked 'redactional traces' might instead be evidence of source variation. In such a case, dependence and independence become very relative terms, and parallels between Luke and *Thomas* would point to a common tradition of saying variants rather than Lukan editorial remarks surfacing in *Thomas*.

1.4.3. *An Alternative Appeal*

My own investigation into the matter has conceived an even messier and more complicated picture, one which will not satisfy those who are looking for a definitive answer. If *Thomas* grew as a rolling corpus, one *could* argue that it is possible that the Kernel was initially dependent on the Synoptics to which additional material accrued at a later time. *But,* in order to demonstrate this theory, one is faced with the same persistent problems that have dogged the discussion previously: parallels are not determinative; redactional elements are difficult to maintain since the assumption that it relies on – that the Synoptic sources are fixed and certain – does not take into account the fact that the Synoptic sources developed within an oral environment, let alone the problems of secondary orality or scribal harmonization; at best, the most successful dependence appeals have been limited to a handful of sayings, relying on a very small amount of evidence.

There are a number of weighty reasons, however, why it is better to understand the Kernel to have been an early independent document that becomes secondarily developed. As I argued in *Recovering*, first and foremost, the content of the Kernel sayings reflects the early interests of the first Jerusalem church. This is particularly the case regarding its Prophet Christology, which presented Jesus' earthly role in connection with a line of Jewish prophets who came as models of righteousness and interpreters of the Law, who was to be greater than all other prophets including the Baptist, who would be the 'rejected cornerstone'. The imminent eschatology of the Kernel also aligns with the expectations of the Jerusalem church which taught the immediate coming of God's Judgement and Kingdom. Jesus would be responsible for bringing God's Judgement upon the world, since he had been exalted at his death to God's right hand as Yahweh's great Angel.

Second, as I detailed in *Recovering*, a study of the accretions shows that they served to reinterpret older traditions. These secondary adaptations map post-50 Christian concerns like the admission of Gentiles to the community and the delay of the Eschaton, suggesting that *the Kernel which is being adapted must be from an even earlier period of Christianity.* This adaptation of earlier material is undeniable in the construction of the dialogues, question-and-answer units, and the interpretative phrases. The questions and interpretative clauses are clearly secondary to the saying, not only in terms of retrospective (and sometimes disconnected) content, but also because versions of some of the sayings circulated in other imaginary contexts in early Christian literature. Literary criticism of these units shows a remarkable consistency in vocabulary and thematic characteristics, all of which are references to late-first- and early-second-century theological developments, like the encratic ideal and hermetic patterns. This adaptation of the earlier traditions is coherent with post-50 Christianity, and leads me to conclude that the Kernel being adapted is more likely earlier than this date, rather than later. In fact, *the adaptation of the earlier Kernel, in terms of the reshaping of the Christian communal memory, looks to me to be very complementary to the adaptation of earlier traditions evident in the composition of the Synoptic gospels and John in this same period.* So it should not surprise us that there is strong evidence favouring the Kernel's Aramaic and oral heritages.

1.4.3.1. *Reliance on Aramaic Traditions.* As I have covered in Section 1.3 above, the Kernel *Thomas* appears to have been composed in Aramaic. This suggests that it did not rely on the Greek Synoptics but Aramaic traditions from Jerusalem. In fact, as A. Guillaumont and others have pointed out, several parallels with Synoptic variants even suggest that *Thomas'* translation of the Aramaic into Greek took a different route than the translation of the Aramaic material into Greek in the pre-Synoptic sources (Chart 4, overleaf).

It is noteworthy that in all these instances, the translation variants are found in the Kernel sayings, not the accretions. So there is good evidence, in my opinion, that the Kernel is dependent upon pre-Synoptic Aramaic traditions which the Synoptics also may have relied upon, but in Greek translation.

1.4.3.2. *A Connection with the* Pseudo-Clementines *and Tatian.* To this evidence, it should be noted that clusters and hermeneutics of the sayings in the Kernel do not jive with the Synoptics, but with the *Pseudo-Clementines* which is claimed to be based on speeches of Jesus that were recited by Peter and recorded by a scribe in books for the Jerusalem mission (L. 38, 39, 40, 45, 46//*Rec.* 1.54, 59–60, 2.30; L. 92, 93, 94//*Rec.* 2.3, 3.1; L. 62.1, 62.2//*Hom.* 18.7–10, 13; L. 39 and 42//*Hom.* 2.9; L. 9, 10, 11, 14.4, 15//*Hom.* 11.2–7). Equally striking are the numerous single sayings that appear to have been interpreted in the Kernel speeches in ways very similar to the interpretations given in the *Pseudo-Clementines* (cf. L. 10//*Rec.* 6.4; L. 32//*Hom.* 8.4; L. 39.1–2//*Hom.* 18.15–16; L. 41.1–2//*Hom.* 18.16; L. 62.2//*Hom.* 18.3; L. 68.1//*Hom.* 12.29; L. 76.1–2//*Rec.* 3.62; L. 52.1–2//*Rec.* 1.59). In all these cases, the New Testament parallels do not show familiarity with the Kernel cluster or the hermeneutic. Again, it is noted that every Thomasine saying that has a distinctive parallel in the *Pseudo-Clementines* is a Kernel saying, not an accretion (L. 9, 16, 32, 39, 40, 54, 62, 64, 68, 76, 93, 95).

Chart 4. *Evidence for a Possible Pre-Synoptic Aramaic Substratum*

9.2	עַל is mistranslated into Greek in the Synoptics as 'along', while *Thomas* retains the reference to the Aramaic, 'by' or 'on'.
16.3	L. 16.3, against Luke 12.52, preserves Semitic syntax in its phrasing, 'there will be five people in a house, three will be against two and two against three...' Here, we have two clauses juxtaposed instead of the first clause subordinated as a conditional clause. The translator of Luke's Greek text did not understand the Semitic syntax and wrongly introduced διαμεμερίσμένοι in the first clause.
25.1–2	Reflexive use of 'as your own soul'; Synoptics have 'yourself'.
30.2–3	'a hiding place' (*Thomas*) and 'a cellar' (Luke) may derive from סתר.
39.1–2	קבל or שׁקל explains ϪΙ in *Thomas* and ἦρατε in Luke.
40.1–2	אבא may represent an Aramaic substratum, explaining 'Father' (*Thomas*) and 'my Father' (Matthew).
48	שׁלם explains 'to make peace' in *Thomas* and 'to agree' in Matthew.
69.2	ו explains that Matthew and Luke use ὅτι while *Thomas* ϢΙΝΑ.
79	ינק explains *Thomas* 'the breast that nourished you' and Luke's 'the breasts that nursed you'.
90	'lordship' in *Thomas* rather than Matthew's 'burden' explained as an Aramaic tendency.
107.1–3	צבי which can mean both 'to wish' or 'to delight in', may be behind ϮΟΥΟϢΚ, and explains why the Synoptics employ forms of the Greek χαίρειν, while *Thomas* has ΟΥΩϢ.

This striking agreement between the Kernel and the *Pseudo-Clementines* cannot be mere coincidence given the fact that other Syrian witnesses have knowledge of the later accretions. In the case of the *Liber Graduum*, L. 6, 18, 19, 22, 27, 37, 75, 85, 105, 106[28] at least are paralleled. Pseudo-Macarius' writings at least are familiar with L. 3, 11, 22, 27, 37, 51, 112, 113.[29] All of these are accretions.

This evidence leads me to wonder how sceptical as scholars we should remain regarding Clement's claim found in the *Pseudo-Clementines* that he was hired by James to follow Peter, listen to his speeches about Jesus' teachings, and record them in books for the Jerusalem mission. Given the recovery of the Kernel and the uncanny parallels in the *Pseudo-Clementines*, I think that this claim in fact may have some historical validity. Does the Kernel represent one of these speech books from Jerusalem? Did it or a very similar version influence the *Pseudo-Clementine* tradition? These possibilities become even more likely in my opinion when we also recognize that the parallels noted by both G. Quispel and T. Baarda between the Gospel and Tatian's *Diatessaron* occur at the level of the Kernel, not the accretions, with the exception of L. 113 (Quispel: 6, 8, 9, 16, 21, 25, 32, 33, 35, 36, 39, 40, 44, 45, 46, 47, 48, 55, 57, 63, 64, 66, 68, 74, 79, 86, 89, 90, 91, 94, 95, 96, 98, 100, 104, 109, 113; Baarda: 4, 8, 9, 10, 16, 20, 21, 26, 32, 33, 34, 35, 38, 39, 40, 44, 45, 46, 47, 48, 54, 55, 56, 57, 61, 63, 64, 65, 68, 69, 72, 73, 76, 78, 79, 86, 89, 91, 93, 94, 96, 99, 100, 104, 107, 113).[30] The bulk of this

28. Baker (1965/1966).

29. Quispel (1975f; 1967a); Baker (1964).

30. Both Quispel and Baarda have included L. 1 which they indicate parallels John 8.52. I do not find this parallel to be convincing so I have not included it in my discussion. See, Quispel (1959; 1975a); Baarda (1983c).

evidence weighs in favour of the likelihood that an early form of the *Gospel of Thomas* very similar to the Kernel, if not the Kernel itself, was known in Syria to Tatian and may have been one of the sources for the *Pseudo-Clementines.*

1.4.3.3. *Characteristics of Orally Transmitted Material.* All in all, it looks like the *Gospel of Thomas* began as an early speech book from the Jerusalem mission. It was composed in Aramaic and taken to Syria where it was developed along lines consistent with early Syrian Christianity. This means that the Kernel could easily contain pre-Synoptic traditions which later in time, after the Synoptic Gospels were written and distributed, became secondarily adapted to the Synoptic memory, as well as expanded with different material. If this scenario is accurate, it would mean that in the *Gospel of Thomas*, we would have both traces of independent 'original' orality or old multiforms, as well as traces of secondary orality or memories of Synoptic wording that accrued as the sayings were retold and re-remembered after the Synoptics were written and were beginning to gain prominence. In very simple terms, what started as an independent Kernel in the mid-first century may have become a dependent Gospel in the early second century by the time its composition was completed. To make things even more complicated, we must face the fact that when the *Gospel of Thomas* was translated into Greek and then into Coptic, the translation choices and phrasing may have been affected by scribal memories of the Synoptic tradition or secondary scribal adaptation.

The big question that comes to the forefront is one that I am not sure I can offer any definitive answer. How can we distinguish between 'original' oral multiforms, secondary orality, secondary scribal adaptation, and direct literary dependence? Our biggest obstacle may be that not enough experimental research has been conducted on the problem. R. McIver and M. Carroll have made the only experimental examination of the problem I know of.[31] They conclude that direct literary dependence is evident in cases where the same sixteen or more words are found in exact sequence, with the exception of aphorisms, poetry, or lyrics which tend to be remembered and repeated with very little variation. Characteristics of orally transmitted materials can produce a high percentage of common vocabulary, but the words found in the same sequence are placed in short phrases of only a few words. These 'same' phrases are scattered throughout the text. Variant versions need not be of the same length and it is quite common to observe shifts in tenses and mood of the verbs. Often synonyms as well as short phrases with similar meaning but different words are substituted. I think it is important to note that their experimental findings support the field research recently conducted by K. Bailey who described the informal oral traditions in modern Arab villages.[32] The findings also are in agreement with the conclusions drawn in the classic works on orality by A. Lord, W. Ong and M. Foley as well as the evidence analysed by J. Dunn in his pioneering paper, 'Jesus and Oral Memory', and the work of his student, Terence Mournet.[33]

---

31. McIver and Carroll (2002).
32. Bailey (1991; 1995).
33. Lord (2nd edn, 2000 [1960]); Ong (1971; 1977; 1982); Foley (1988; 1991; 1995); Dunn (2000); Mournet (2005).

It goes without saying that much more needs to be done in terms of experimental research in *controlled* environments, something which is questionable in McIver's and Carroll's studies. I personally plan to begin conducting such *controlled* experiments within the short term. Until such evidence becomes available, we will remain limited in our discussions of oral multiforms and their differentiation from secondary orality, secondary scribal adaptation and direct literary dependence.

1.4.3.4. *Commonalities between the Thomasine-Synoptic Variants*. If the *Gospel of Thomas* were to show characteristics of orally transmitted materials, what might this mean for the parallels between the *Gospel of Thomas* and the Synoptics? From the studies that have been conducted on orality to date, we would expect, except in the cases of aphorisms which should show very little variation when compared to the Synoptics, that there should be a high percentage of common vocabulary distributed in short phrases of no more than a few words. These phrases should be scattered throughout the sayings. Variants should vary in length and display shifts in tenses and mood of the verbs. Synonyms can be expected.

Is this the case? In order to begin to address this question in the Appendix (Verbal Similarities Between *Thomas* and the Synoptics), I have charted the verbal similarities between *Thomas* and the Synoptics by underlining similar phrases and words across the variants. For the sake of brevity and the fact that we are dealing largely with the comparison of a Coptic text with a Greek text, making absolute verbal agreements difficult to fix, I have chosen to provide the variants in English translation and identify verbal 'similarities' as well as 'agreements.' This allows for the most *inclusive* comparison possible. I have addressed the original language comparisons for individual sayings in the source discussions for each relevant saying in the commentary. So for this, the commentary will need to be consulted.

1.4.3.5. *Thomasine-Synoptic Aphorisms*. In the case of the aphorisms, I find the highest percentage of common vocabulary and sequences of words and phrases between *Thomas*' versions and the Synoptic versions. In most cases, the number of words in common sequence approximates ten to eleven. For instance, L. 4.2–3 is almost an exact parallel to its Synoptic counterparts. The quip, 'Whoever has ears to hear, should listen!' does not deviate substantially from its Synoptic parallels. L. 34 and Matthew 15.14 are nearly identical, 'If a blind person leads a blind person, both will fall into a pit'. L. 26.1–2 parallels nicely Matthew 7.5, 'remove the beam from your eye then you will see clearly to remove the twig from your brother's eye'. None of these aphorisms contains more than fourteen of the same words in sequence, except L. 14.5 which has seventeen common words in sequence, but with a difference in person. What I find significant in this regard is the fact that L. 14.5 is an accretion. Even though orally transmitted aphorisms can yield a higher percentage of commonalities than other orally transmitted materials, could this higher percentage of sequenced words be evidence of literary dependence in this case since the number of words is significantly higher than all other aphorisms located in the Gospel?

1.4.3.6. *Thomasine-Synoptic Parables*. The greatest variation between common versions of the sayings appears in the parables where only a few short phrases and words are the same across the variants while the sequence of the phrases and words, the tenses of verbs, and the details vary substantially. By contrast with the aphorisms which on average had ten to eleven word sequences in common, the parables have two to three word sequences. For example, the parable of the fisherman mentions that a 'net' was cast 'into the sea' and that 'fish' were caught. Beyond this, we do not have verbal agreements, only rough thematic similarities. Moreover, the interpretative angle presented in Matthew 13.49–50 is not explicitly referenced in L. 8. In the Sower parable, we have in common that a 'sower went out', 'birds came', seed 'fell' on a 'path', on 'rock', 'among thorns', and on 'good' earth. The rest of the details vary significantly between L. 9 and its Synoptic parallels. The Mustard Seed parable has in common its subject, a 'mustard seed', although even here the Synoptics call it 'a grain of mustard seed', while *Thomas* only 'a mustard seed'. *Thomas* tells us that the seed is 'smaller than all seeds', while Mark and Matthew say that the seed is the 'smallest of all seeds on earth'. In L. 20, the seed 'puts forth a large branch', while in Mark it is a scrub that 'puts forth large branches'. All agree that 'birds of the sky' or 'air' can 'shelter' or 'nest' in it. What is most noticeable in this parable is the use of synonyms across the versions. The retention of thematic similarities at the cost of verbal agreements appears to be the case with all the other Thomasine parables as well.

1.4.3.7. *An Oral Gospel*. These observations point to the likelihood that most, if not all, of the Thomasine-Synoptic parallels represent orally transmitted material rather than material copied from literary sources. The oral residue becomes even more apparent to me when I observe the commonalities across the Synoptic versions – that is across the Triple Tradition material and Quelle material – and compare them with the commonalities between *Thomas* and the Synoptics. The exact verbal agreement, lengthy sequences of words, and secondary features shared between the Triple Tradition versions and the Quelle versions *far* exceed anything we find in the *Gospel of Thomas*. This observation appears to provide support for the traditional view that *there is a literary connection between the Synoptic Gospels*. But *this does not hold true for Thomas which instead displays the strong features of oral transmission*.

This leads me to think that the Kernel sayings are among our oldest witnesses to the words of Jesus, perhaps even pre-dating Quelle (although this has not been established yet and remains only a possibility requiring future investigation). The variants in the Kernel also suggest to me that Quelle existed in more than one format, that is, Matthew and Luke do not appear to be based on the exact same version (*or* Matthew was a *very* creative user of the document and Luke was not). In fact where the Quelle text varies, the Kernel has a striking number of affinities with Qluke (L. 5.1–2, 14.4, 16.1–2, 16.3, 33.2–3, 39.1–2, 45.1–4, 47.1–2, 61.1, 78.1–3, 89.1–2) while only one with Qmatt (L. 34). It should also be noted that the Kernel contains parallels with the Triple Tradition (L. 9.1–5, 11.1, 20.2–4, 25.1–2, 31.1–2, 35.1–2, 41.1–2, 47.3–4, 47.5, 62.1, 65.1–6, 66, 71, 99.1–3,

100.1–4, 104.1–2), Mark (L. 4.2–3, 21.10), Luke's Special Source (L. 10, 63.1–3, 72.1–3, 79.1–3, 95.1–2), and Matthew's Special Source (L. 8.1–3, 30.1–2, 32, 39.3, 40.1–2, 48, 57.1–2, 62.2, 76.1–2, 90.1–2, 93.1–2, 109.1–3), all of which display features of independent oral transmission rather than literary dependence. These commonalities suggest a pre-Synoptic picture where the sayings of Jesus were being preserved in more fluid conditions than the literary sources we have imagined in the past for the Synoptic authors. To this picture, we should add the Johannine evidence. Material unique to the Johannine tradition is not found in the Kernel, but only in the later accretions (L. 24.1, 38.2, 52.1–2, 61.2–5), suggesting contact with these traditions occurred at a later time among Syrian Christians familiar with *Thomas*.

If the Thomasine-Synoptic parallels derive from the oral sphere as the evidence appears to me to indicate, can we determine if the sayings are examples of 'original' independent multiforms or secondary orality? Are they examples of pre-Synoptic performance variants or have they been influenced by the orator's memory of the Synoptic tradition? At present, the only possibility for making this distinction that comes to my mind is whether or not we can detect features in the Thomasine variant that represent secondary development of the traditional material *and* which we find also in the Synoptic variant. That is, are there present interpretative clauses or details that appear to be secondary to the traditional saying upon examination of all the variants? Do these secondary developments occur both in the Thomasine variant and a Synoptic variant? If so, then it is possible to argue that the Thomasine saying has been influenced by the orator's memory of the Synoptic variant – that the *Gospel of Thomas* preserved an old independent multiform which was altered during a later performance to fit the memory of an orator who knows the Synoptic tradition.

Finally, can we distinguish those sayings that have been affected by scribal memory when they have been adapted, during the translation process, to the scribe's memory of the Synoptic tradition? I think that these situations might be detected when we see cases where the Thomasine variant and the variant in the Coptic New Testament agree on the same word or phrase *against* the Greek New Testament. Although I realize that this is a very minimal criterion, it appears to me to be the logical place to start such an enquiry.

I hope it is quickly recognized that there is no simple or single answer to the dependency question. It is a question that requires a multi-level investigation for each logion and 'the' answer will point to more complexities – to possibilities rather than certainties. To provide a framework for future discussion of these tough issues, I have written in the commentary on each logion a short section that gives an overview of the source discussion for that particular saying. I attempt here to point out the major issues that have been discussed for the saying, as well as my own opinion on the matter. My goal is not to be definitive, but to build a platform that I hope will sustain future thoughts and discussions about these issues – that we will turn to re-examine the assumptions passed on to us by the pioneers in the field, and have the courage to write a new story when the echo of a new story is heard.

Chapter 2

THE KERNEL *GOSPEL OF THOMAS*

2.1. *Speech One: Eschatological Urgency*

(2)   [1](([Jesus said,] 'Whoever seeks should not cease [seeking until] he finds. [2]And when he finds, [he will be amazed. [3]And] when he is [amazed,] he will be a king. [4]And [once he is a king,] he will rest.'))

(4.2-3)   [2'](For many who are first will be last, [3]((and the last will be first))'.

(5)   [1]Jesus said, 'Understand what is in front of you, and what is hidden from you will be revealed to you. [2]For there is nothing hidden that will not be manifested.'

(6.2-3)   [2]Jesus said, 'Do not tell lies [3]and what you hate, do not do.'

(8)   [1]And he said, 'The human being is like a wise fisherman who cast his net into the sea. He drew it up from the sea full of small fish. [2]From among them he found a fine large fish. [3]The wise fisherman cast all of the small fish back into the sea and chose the large fish without difficulty. [4]Whoever has ears to hear should listen!'

(9)   [1]Jesus said, 'Look! The sower went out. He filled his hand (with seeds). He cast (them). [2]Some fell on the road. The birds came and gathered them up. [3]Others fell on the rock and did not take root in the earth or put forth ears. [4]And others fell among thorns. They choked the seeds and worms ate them. [5]And others fell on the good earth, and it produced good fruit. It yielded sixty per measure and a hundred and twenty per measure.'

(10)   Jesus said, 'I have cast fire upon the world. And look! I am guarding it until it blazes.'

(11.1)   [1]Jesus said, 'This heaven will pass away, and the one above it will pass away.'

(14.4)   [4]'When you enter any district and walk around the countryside, if they take you in, whatever they serve you, eat! The people among them who are sick, heal!'

(15)   Jesus said, 'When you see the one who was not born of woman, fall on your face and worship him. That one is your Father.'

(16.1-3) [1]Jesus said, 'Perhaps people think it is peace that I have come to cast upon the world. [2]And they do not know it is division that I have come to cast upon the earth – fire, sword, war! [3]For there will be five (people) in a house. There will be three (people) against two, and two against three, father against son, and son against father.'

2.2. *Speech Two: Eschatological Challenges*

(17)   Jesus said, 'I will give you what no eye has seen, what no ear has heard, what no hand has touched, and (what) has not arisen in the human mind.'

(20.2-4)   He said to them, [2]'(The Kingdom) is like a mustard seed, [2]smaller than all seeds. [4]But when it falls on cultivated soil, it puts forth a large branch and becomes a shelter for birds of the sky.'

(21.5)   [5]'If the owner of a house knows that a thief is coming, he will keep watch before he arrives. He will not allow him to break into his house, part of his estate, to steal his furnishings.'

(21.10)   [10]'When the grain ripened, he came quickly with his sickle in his hand. He harvested it.'

(21.11)   [11]Whoever has hears to hear should listen!'

(23.1)   [1]Jesus said, 'I will select you, one from a thousand, and two from ten thousand.'

(24.2)   [2]He said to them, 'Whoever has ears should listen!'

(24.3)   [3]'There is light inside a person of light. And it lights up the whole world. If it does not shine, it is dark.'

(25)   [1]Jesus said, 'Love your brother like your soul. [2]Watch over him like the pupil of your eye.'

(26)   [1]Jesus said, 'The twig in your brother's eye, you see. But the beam in your eye, you do not see! [2]When you remove the beam from your eye ((then you will see clearly to remove the twig in your brother's eye)).'

(30)   [1][Jesus said,] '((Where there are [three people])), [[God is there]]. [2]Where there is one alone [I say] that I am with him.'

(31)   [1]Jesus said, 'A prophet is not received hospitably in his (own) village. [2]A doctor does not heal the people who know him.'

(32)   Jesus said, 'A city built on a high mountain and fortified cannot fall nor be hidden.'

(33)   [1]Jesus said, 'What you ((hear)) in your ears, preach from your rooftops. [2]For no one lights a lamp and puts it under a bushel basket, nor puts it in a hidden place. [3]Rather the person sets it on a lampstand so that everyone who enters and leaves will see its light.'

(34)   Jesus said, 'If a blind person leads a blind person, both will fall into a pit.'

(35)   [1]Jesus said, 'It is not possible for someone to enter the strong man's house and take it forcibly without binding his hands. [2]Then the person will loot his house.'

(36)   [1](([Jesus said, 'Do not be anxious] from morning [until evening and] from evening [until] morning, neither [about] your [food] and what [you will] eat, [nor] about [your clothing] and what you [will] wear. [2][You are far] better than the [lilies] which [neither] card nor [spin]. [3]As for you, when you have no garment, what [will you put on]? Who might add to your stature? He will give you your garment)).

2.3. *Speech Three: Exclusive Commitment to Jesus*

(38.1) [1]Jesus said, 'The words that I am speaking to you, often you have longed to hear them. And you have no other person from whom to hear them.'

(39) [1]Jesus said, 'The Pharisees and the scribes have taken the keys of knowledge. They have hidden them. [2]Neither have they entered nor have they permitted those people who want to enter (to do so). [3]You, however, be as prudent as serpents and as guileless as doves.'

(40) [1]Jesus said, 'A grapevine has been planted apart from the Father's (planting). [2]Since it is not strong, it will be plucked up by its roots, and it will perish.'

(41) [1]Jesus said, 'Whoever has something in his hand will be given more. [2]And whoever has nothing, even the little that this person has will be taken away.'

(42) Jesus said, 'Be passers-by.'

(44.2-3) [2]'Whoever blasphemes against the Son will be forgiven. [3]But whoever blasphemes against the Holy Spirit will not be forgiven, neither on earth nor in heaven.'

(45) [1]Jesus said, 'Grapes are not harvested from thorn trees, nor are figs picked from thistles, for they do not produce fruit. [2]A good person brings forth good from his treasury. [3]A bad person brings forth evil from his wicked treasury in his heart, and he speaks evil. [4]For from the excessiveness of the heart, he brings forth evil.'

(46) [1]Jesus said, 'From Adam to John the Baptist, no one among those born of women is more exalted than John the Baptist that the person's gaze should not be deferent. [2] Yet I have said, "Whoever from among you will become little, he will be more exalted than John."'

(47) [1]Jesus said, 'It is impossible for a person to mount two horses and to bend two bows. [2]Also it is impossible for a servant to serve two masters, or he will honour the one and insult the other. [3]No one drinks aged wine and immediately wants to drink unaged wine. [4]Also, unaged wine is not put into old wineskins so that they may burst. Nor is aged wine put into a new wineskin so that it may spoil. [5]An old patch is not sewn onto a new garment because a tear would result.'

(48) Jesus said, 'If two people make peace with each other in the same house, they will say to the mountain, "Go forth!" and it will move.'

(54) Jesus said, 'Blessed are the poor, for the Kingdom of Heaven is yours.'

(55) [1]Jesus said, 'The person who does not hate his father and mother cannot become a disciple of mine. [2]And the person who does not hate his brothers and sisters and carry his cross as I do will not be worthy of me.'

(57) [1]Jesus said, 'The Kingdom of the Father is like a person who had [good] seed. [2]His enemy came at night. He added darnel to the good seed. [3]The person did not let them pull out the darnel. He explained to them, "In case you go to pull out the darnel, but pull out the wheat with it. [4]For on the day of the harvest, the darnel will be discernible, and will be pulled up and burned."'

(58)   Jesus said, 'Blessed is the person who has suffered. He has found life.'

(61.1) Jesus said, 'Two people will rest on a couch. One will die. One will live.'

2.4. *Speech Four: Selection of the Worthy Few*

(62)   [1]Jesus said, 'I tell my mysteries to [those people who are worthy of my] mysteries.'

[2]'Do not let your left hand know what your right hand is going to do.'

(63)   [1]Jesus said, 'There was a wealthy man who had many assets. [2]He said, "I will use my assets to sow, harvest, plant and fill my granaries with produce, so that I will not need anything." [3]These were the things he was thinking in his heart. But that very night, he died.'

[4]'Whoever has ears should listen!'

(64.1-11) [1]Jesus said, 'A man had guests. When he had prepared the dinner, he sent his servant to invite the guests.
[2]He went to the first person. He said to him, "My master invites you."
[3]He said, "I have some payments for some merchants. They are coming to me this evening. I must go and give them instructions. I decline the dinner."
[4]He went to another person. He said to him, "My master has invited you."
[5]He said to him, "I have purchased a house and they have requested me for the day. I will not have time."
[6]He went to another person. He said to him, "My master invites you."
[7]He said to him, "My friend is going to be wed and I am the person who will be preparing the meal. I will not be able to come. I decline the dinner."
[8]He went to another person. He said to him, "My master invites you."
[9]He said to him, "I have purchased a villa. Since I am going to collect the rent, I will not be able to come. I decline."
[10]The servant left. He said to his master, "The people whom you invited to the dinner have declined."
[11]The master said to his servant, "Go outside on the streets. The people you find, bring them to dine."'

(65)   [1]He said, 'A creditor owned a vineyard. He leased it to some farmers so that they would work it and he would collect the produce from them.
[2]He sent his servant so that the farmers would give him the produce of the vineyard. [3]They seized his servant. They beat him, a little more and they would have killed him.
The servant returned and he told his master.
[4]The master said, "Perhaps [[they]] did not recognize [[him.]]."
[5]He sent another servant. The farmers beat that one too.
[6]Then the master sent his son. He said, "Perhaps they will be ashamed in front of my son."
[7]Those farmers, since they knew that he was the heir of the vineyard, seized him and killed him.'

[8]'Whoever has ears should listen!'

(66)   Jesus said, 'Show me the stone that the builders rejected. It is the cornerstone.'

(68.1) ¹Jesus said, 'Blessed are you when you are hated and persecuted.'

(69.2) ²'Blessed are those who are hungry, for whosoever desires (it), his belly will be filled.'

(71) Jesus said, 'I will destroy [this] temple, and no one will build it [...].'

(72) ¹A man said to him, 'Tell my brothers that they must share with me my father's possessions.'
²He said to him, 'Mister, who has made me an executor?'
³He turned to his disciples and said to them, 'Surely I am not an executor, am I?'

(73) Jesus said, 'Indeed the harvest is plentiful but the workers are few. So ask the Lord to send out workers to the harvest.'

(74) He said, 'Lord, many people are around the [[well]], but no one is in the [[well]].'

(76) ¹Jesus said, 'The Kingdom of the Father is like a merchant who had some merchandise. He found a pearl. ²That merchant was wise. He sold the merchandise. Then he purchased for himself this single pearl. ³You too, seek his imperishable and enduring treasure where neither moth draws near to eat nor worm destroys.'

(78) ¹Jesus said, 'Why did you come out into the desert? To see a reed shaken by the wind ²and to see a man dressed in soft garments? ³[Behold, your] kings and your prominent men are dressed in soft garments, but they will not be able to understand the truth.'

(79) ¹A woman in the crowd said to him, 'Blessed is the womb that bore you and the breasts that nourished you.'
²He said to [her], 'Blessed are the people who have heard the word of the Father and have truly kept it. ³For there will be days when you will say, "Blessed is the womb that has not conceived and the breasts that have not given milk."'

(81) ¹Jesus said, 'Whoever has grown wealthy, that person should become a king. ²But whoever possesses power, let that person disown (his power).'

(82) ¹Jesus said, 'Whoever is near me, is near the fire. ²But whoever is far away from me, is far away from the Kingdom.'

(86) ¹Jesus said, '[The foxes have] their dens and the birds have their nests, ²but the human being does not have a place to lay down his head and rest.'

(89) ¹Jesus said, 'Why do you wash the cup's exterior? ²Do you not understand that He who created the interior is also He who created the exterior?'

(90) ¹Jesus said, 'Come to me, for my yoke is mild and my lordship is gentle. ²And you will find rest for yourselves.'

(91.2) He said to them, ²'You examine the appearance of the sky and the earth, but, he who is in your midst, you do not understand. Nor this critical time! You do not understand how to examine it.'

2.5. *Speech Five: The Imminent Kingdom of God*

(92)   ¹Jesus said, 'Seek and you will find. ²However, the questions you asked me
previously but which I did not address then, now I want to address, yet you
do not seek (answers).'

(93)   ¹'Do not give what is holy to dogs, or they might toss them on the manure
pile. ²Do not toss the pearls [to] pigs, or they might [break] [[them]].'

(94)   ¹Jesus [said], 'Whoever seeks will find. ²[Whoever knocks], it will be
opened for him.'

(95)   ¹[Jesus said], 'If you have money, do not give it at interest. ²Rather, give
[it] to someone from whom you will not get it (back).'

(96)   ¹Jesus said, 'The Kingdom of the Father is like a woman. ²She took a little
yeast. She buried it in dough. She made the dough into large bread loaves.

³Whoever has ears should listen!'

(97)   ¹Jesus said, 'The Kingdom of the [Father] is like a woman carrying a [jar]
filled with meal. ²While she was walking [on the] road still a long way out,
the handle of the jar broke. Behind her, the meal leaked out onto the road.
³She did not realize it. She had not noticed a problem. ⁴When she arrived at
her house, she put the jar down and found it empty.'

(98)   ¹Jesus said, 'The Kingdom of the Father is like someone who wished to kill
a prominent man. ²While at home, he drew out his knife. He stabbed it into
the wall to test whether his hand would be strong (enough). ³Then he
murdered the prominent man.'

(99)   ¹The disciples said to him, 'Your brothers and your mother are standing
outside.'
²He said to them, 'Those here who do the will of my father, they are my
brothers and my mother. ³They are the people who will enter the Kingdom
of my Father.'

(100.1-3) ¹They showed Jesus a gold coin and said to him, 'Caesar's men extort
taxes from us.'
²He said to them, 'Give to Caesar, what is Caesar's. ³Give to God what is
God's.'

(102)   Jesus said, 'Woe to the Pharisees because they are like a dog sleeping in the
cattle trough. For the dog neither eats nor [lets] the cattle eat.'

(103)   Jesus said, 'Blessed is the man who knows where the thieves are going to
enter, so that [he] may arise, gather at his estate, and arm himself.'

(104)   ¹They said to Jesus, 'Come. Today, let's pray and fast!'
²Jesus said, 'What sin have I committed? Or in what way have I been
defeated? Rather, when the bridegroom leaves the bridal chamber, then
they should fast and pray.'

(107)   ¹Jesus said, 'The Kingdom is like a shepherd who had a hundred sheep.
²One of them, the largest, strayed. He left the ninety-nine. He sought that
one until he found it. ³After he had laboured, he said to the sheep, "I love
you more than the ninety-nine."'

(109)   [1]Jesus said, 'The Kingdom is like a man who had in his field a [hidden treasure], but he did not know about it. [2]And [after] he died, he left it to his [son]. The son [did] not know (about the treasure). He took that field and sold [it]. [3]And the buyer went and ploughed. He [found] the treasure. He started to give money at interest to whomever he wished.'

(111.1) [1]Jesus said, 'The heavens and the earth will roll up in your presence.'

Chapter 3

THE COMPLETE GOSPEL OF THOMAS

(Kernel Text in regular type; *Accretions in italics*)

(Incipit) *((These are the [secret] words that the Living Jesus spoke and that [Judas] Thomas [wrote down.]))*

(1)   *And he said, 'Whoever finds the meaning of these words will not die.'*

(2)   ¹*(([Jesus said,] 'Whoever seeks should not cease [seeking until] he finds. ²And when he finds, [he will be amazed. ³And] when he is [amazed,] he will be a king. ⁴And [once he is a king,] he will rest.))'*

(3)   *(Jesus said, 'If ((your <<leaders>> [say to you, "Look!] the Kingdom is in heaven", then the birds of heaven [will arrive first before you. ²If they say,] "It is under the earth," then the fish of the sea [will enter it, arriving first] before you. ³But the Kingdom [of Heaven] is inside of you and [outside.] ⁴[Whoever] knows [himself] will find it. ⁵[And when you] know yourselves, [you will understand that you are the children] of the [Living] Father. [But if] you will not know yourselves, [you are impoverished] and you are poverty.))'*

(4)   ¹Jesus said, '*The old man will not hesitate to ask a little child seven days old about the place of life, and he will live.* ²For many who are first will be last, ³*((the last will be first,))* ⁴*and they will become single people.'*

(5)   ¹Jesus said, 'Understand what is in front of you, and what is hidden from you will be revealed to you. ²For there is nothing hidden that will not be manifested.'

(6)   ¹*(([His disciples] questioned [him] and said, 'How should we fast? [How should we pray?] How [should we give alms?] What [diet] should we observe?'))* ²Jesus said, 'Do not tell lies ³and what you hate, do not do. ⁴*(([For everything, when faced] with truth, is brought [to light. ⁵For there is nothing] hidden [that will not be manifested.]))'*

(7)   ¹*Jesus said, 'Blessed is the lion that the person will eat, and the lion becomes man. ²And cursed is the person whom the lion eats, [[and the man becomes a lion]].'*

(8)   ¹And he said, 'The human being is like a wise fisherman who cast his net into the sea. He drew it up from the sea full of small fish. ²From among them he found a fine large fish. ³The wise fisherman cast all of the small fish back into the sea and chose the large fish without difficulty. ⁴Whoever has ears to hear should listen!'

(9) ¹Jesus said, 'Look! The sower went out. He filled his hand (with seeds). He cast (them). ²Some fell on the road. The birds came and gathered them up. ³Others fell on the rock and did not take root in the earth or put forth ears. ⁴And others fell among thorns. They choked the seeds and worms ate them. ⁵And others fell on the good earth, and it produced good fruit. It yielded sixty per measure and a hundred and twenty per measure.'

(10) Jesus said, 'I have cast fire upon the world. And look! I am guarding it until it blazes.'

(11) ¹Jesus said, 'This heaven will pass away, and the one above it will pass away. *²And the dead are not alive, and the living will not die. ³In the days when you ate what is dead, you made it something living. When you are in the light, what will you become? ⁴On the day when you were one, you became two. When you are two, what will you become?'*

(12) *¹The disciples said to Jesus, 'We know that you are going to leave us. Who will be our leader?'*
²Jesus said to them, 'No matter where you came from, you should go to James the Righteous One, for whose sake heaven and earth exist.'

(13) *¹Jesus said to his disciples, 'Speculate about me. Tell me, who am I like?'*
²Simon Peter said to him, 'You are like a righteous angel.'
³Matthew said to him, 'You are like a sage, a temperate person.'
⁴Thomas said to him, 'Master, my mouth cannot attempt at all to say whom you are like.'
⁵Jesus said, 'I am not your master. After you drank, you became intoxicated from the bubbling fount which I had measured out.'
⁶And he took him and retreated. He told him three words.
⁷Then, when Thomas returned to his friends, they asked him, 'What did Jesus say to you?'
⁸Thomas said to them, 'If I tell you one of the words which he told me, you will pick up stones and throw them at me. Then fire will come out of the stones and burn you up.'

(14) *¹Jesus said to them, 'If you fast, you give birth in yourselves to sin. ²And if you pray, you will be condemned. ³And if you give alms, you will harm yourselves.'*

⁴'When you enter any district and walk around the countryside, if they take you in, whatever they serve you, eat! The people among them who are sick, heal! *⁵For what goes into your mouth will not make you unclean, rather what comes out of your mouth. It is this which will make you unclean!'*

(15) Jesus said, 'When you see the one who was not born of woman, fall on your face and worship him. That one is your Father.'

(16) ¹Jesus said, 'Perhaps people think it is peace that I have come to cast upon the world. ²And they do not know it is division that I have come to cast upon the earth – fire, sword, war! ³For there will be five people in a house. There will be three people against two, and two against three, father against son, and son against father. *⁴And they will stand as celibate people.'*

(17) Jesus said, 'I will give you what no eye has seen, what no ear has heard, what no hand has touched, and (what) has not arisen in the human mind.'

(18) *¹The disciples said to Jesus, 'Tell us, how will our end come about?'*
²Jesus said, 'Have you discovered the beginning that you seek the end?
Because where the beginning is, the end will be also. ³Whoever will stand
in the beginning is blessed. This person will know the end, yet will not die.'

(19) *¹Jesus said, 'Whoever existed before being born is blessed. ²If you become*
my disciples and listen to my teachings, these stones will support you. ³For
you, there are five trees in Paradise. They do not change, summer and
winter, and their leaves do not fall. Whoever knows them will not die.'

(20) *¹The disciples said to Jesus, 'Tell us, what is the Kingdom of Heaven like?'*
²He said to them, 'It is like a mustard seed, ²smaller than all seeds. ⁴But
when it falls on cultivated soil, it puts forth a large branch and becomes a
shelter for birds of the sky.'

(21) *¹Mary said to Jesus, 'Who are your disciples like?'*
²He said, 'They are like little children sojourning in a field that is not
theirs. ³When the owners of the field come, they will say, "Leave our field!"
⁴In front of them, they strip naked in order to abandon it, returning their
field to them.'
⁵*'For this reason I say*, if the owner of a house knows that a thief is
coming, he will keep watch before he arrives. He will not allow him to
break into his house, part of his estate, to steal his furnishings. *⁶You, then,*
keep watch against the world. ⁷Arm yourselves with great strength so that
the robbers do not find a way to come to you, ⁸because the possessions you
are looking after, they will find. ⁹There ought to be a wise person among
you!'

¹⁰'When the grain ripened, he came quickly with his sickle in his hand. He
harvested it. ¹¹Whoever has hears to hear should listen!'

(22) *¹Jesus saw little babies nursing. ²He said to his disciples, 'These little ones*
nursing are like those who enter the Kingdom.'
³They said to him, 'Will we enter the Kingdom as little babies?'
⁴Jesus said to them, 'When you make the two one, and when you make the
inside like the outside, and the outside like the inside, and the above like the
below. ⁵And when you make the male and the female into a single being,
with the result that the male is not male nor the female female. ⁶When you
make eyes in place of an eye, and a hand in place of a hand, and a foot in
place of a foot, and an image in place of an image, ⁷then you will enter [the
Kingdom.]'

(23) ¹Jesus said, 'I will select you, one from a thousand, and two from ten
thousand. *²And they will stand as single people.'*

(24) *¹His disciples said, 'Teach us about the place where you are, because we*
must seek it.'
²He said to them, 'Whoever has ears should listen! ³There is light inside a
person of light. And it lights up the whole world. If it does not shine, it is
dark.'

(25) ¹Jesus said, 'Love your brother like your soul. ²Watch over him like the
pupil of your eye.'

(26) ¹Jesus said, 'The twig in your brother's eye, you see. But the beam in your
eye, you do not see! ²When you remove the beam from your eye ((then you
will see clearly to remove the twig in your brother's eye)).'

(27)   *[1]((Jesus said)), 'If you do not fast from the world, you will not find the Kingdom. [2]If you do not observe the Sabbath day as a Sabbath, you will not see the Father.'*

(28)   *[1]Jesus said, 'I stood in the midst of the world and I appeared to them in flesh. [2]I found all of them drunk. I found none of them thirsty. [3]And my soul suffered in pain for human beings because they are blind in their hearts and they do not see. For they, empty, came into the world. And they, empty, seek to leave the world. [4]For the moment, they are drunk. When they shake off their wine, then they will repent.'*

(29)   *[1]Jesus said, 'If the flesh existed for the sake of the Spirit, it would be a miracle. [2]If the Spirit (existed) for the sake of the body, it would be a miracle of miracles! [3]Nevertheless, I marvel at how this great wealth settled in this poverty.'*

(30)   [1][Jesus said,] '((Where there are [three people], [[God is there]]. [2]And where there is one alone, [I say] that I am with him. *[3]Lift the stone and you will find me there. [4]Split the piece of wood and I am there.))'*

(31)   [1]Jesus said, 'A prophet is not received hospitably in his (own) village. [2]A doctor does not heal the people who know him.'

(32)   Jesus said, 'A city built on a high mountain and fortified cannot fall nor be hidden.'

(33)   [1]Jesus said, 'What you ((hear)) in your ears, preach from your rooftops. [2]For no one lights a lamp and puts it under a bushel basket, nor puts it in a hidden place. [3]Rather the person sets it on a lampstand so that everyone who enters and leaves will see its light.'

(34)   Jesus said, 'If a blind person leads a blind person, both will fall into a pit.'

(35)   [1]Jesus said, 'It is not possible for someone to enter the strong man's house and take it forcibly without binding his hands. [2]Then the person will loot his house.'

(36)   [1](([Jesus said, 'Do not be anxious] from morning [until evening and] from evening [until] morning, neither [about] your [food] and what [you will] eat, [nor] about [your clothing] and what you [will] wear. [2][You are far] better than the [lilies] which [neither] card nor [spin]. [3]As for you, when you have no garment, what [will you put on]? Who might add to your stature? He will give you your garment.'))

(37)   *[1]His disciples said, 'When will you appear to us? When will we see you?' [2]Jesus said, 'When you strip naked without shame, take your garments, put them under your feet like little children, and trample on them. [3]Then [you will see] the Son of the Living One and you will not be afraid.'*

(38)   [1]Jesus said, 'The words that I am speaking to you, often you have longed to hear them. And you have no other person from whom to hear them. *[2]There will be days when you will seek me, (but) will not find me.'*

(39)   [1]Jesus said, 'The Pharisees and the scribes have taken the keys of knowledge. They have hidden them. [2]Neither have they entered nor have they permitted those people who want to enter (to do so). [3]You, however, be as prudent as serpents and as guileless as doves.'

(40)   ¹Jesus said, 'A grapevine has been planted apart from the Father's (planting). ²Since it is not strong, it will be plucked up by its roots, and it will perish.'

(41)   ¹Jesus said, 'Whoever has something in his hand will be given more. ²And whoever has nothing, even the little that this person has will be taken away.'

(42)   Jesus said, 'Be passers-by.'

(43)   *¹His disciples said to him, 'Who are you to say these things to us?'* *²'From what I say to you, you do not know who I am. ³Rather, you are like the Jews, for they love the tree (but) hate its fruit, or they love the fruit (but) hate the tree.'*

(44)   ¹Jesus said, *'Whoever blasphemes against the Father will be forgiven, ²and* whoever blasphemes against the Son will be forgiven. ³But whoever blasphemes against the Holy Spirit will not be forgiven, neither on earth nor in heaven.'

(45)   ¹Jesus said, 'Grapes are not harvested from thorn trees, nor are figs picked from thistles, for they do not produce fruit. ²A good person brings forth good from his treasury. ³A bad person brings forth evil from his wicked treasury in his heart, and he speaks evil. ⁴For from the excessiveness of the heart, he brings forth evil.'

(46)   ¹Jesus said, 'From Adam to John the Baptist, no one among those born of women is more exalted than John the Baptist that the person's gaze should not be deferent. ² Yet I have said, "Whoever from among you will become a child, *this person will know the Kingdom* and he will be more exalted than John."'

(47)   ¹Jesus said, 'It is impossible for a person to mount two horses and to bend two bows. ²Also it is impossible for a servant to serve two masters, or he will honour the one and insult the other. ³No one drinks aged wine and immediately wants to drink unaged wine. ⁴Also, unaged wine is not put into old wineskins so that they may burst. Nor is aged wine put into a new wineskin so that it may spoil. ⁵An old patch is not sewn onto a new garment because a tear would result.'

(48)   Jesus said, 'If two people make peace with each other in the same house, they will say to the mountain, "Go forth!" and it will move.'

(49)   *¹Jesus said, 'Blessed are the celibate people, the chosen ones, because you will find the Kingdom. ²For you are from it. You will return there again.'*

(50)   *¹Jesus said, 'If they say to you, "Where did you come from?", say to them, "We came from the light" – the place where the light came into being on its own accord and established [itself] and became manifest through their image. ²If they say to you, "Is it you?", say "We are its children, and we are the chosen people of the living Father." ³If they ask you, "What is the sign of your Father in you?", say to them, "It is movement and rest."'*

(51)   *¹His disciples said to him, 'When will the dead rest, and when will the new world come?'* *²He said to them, 'What you look for has come, but you have not perceived it.'*

(52)   ¹*His disciples said to him, 'Twenty-four prophets have spoken in Israel, and all of them have spoken about you.'*
²*He said to them, 'You have left out the Living One who is in your presence and you have spoken about the dead.'*

(53)   ¹*His disciples said to him, 'Is circumcision advantageous or not?'*
²*He said to them, 'If it were advantageous, the father (of the children) would conceive them in their mother already circumcised. ³Rather circumcision in the spirit is true (circumcision). This person has procured all of the advantage.'*

(54)   Jesus said, 'Blessed are the poor, for the Kingdom of Heaven is yours.'

(55)   ¹Jesus said, 'Whoever does not hate his father and mother cannot become a disciple of mine. ²And whoever does not hate his brothers and sisters and carry his cross as I do will not be worthy of me.'

(56)   ¹*Jesus said, 'Whoever has come to know the world has found a corpse. ²The world does not deserve the person who found (that the world is) a corpse.'*
Alternative Translation
¹*'Whoever has come to know the world <<has mastered the body>>. ²The world does not deserve the person who <<has mastered the body>>.'*

(57)   ¹Jesus said, 'The Kingdom of the Father is like a man who had [good] seed. ²His enemy came at night. He added darnel to the good seed. ³The man did not let them pull out the darnel. He explained to them, "In case you go to pull out the darnel, but pull out the wheat with it. ⁴For on the day of the harvest, the darnel will be discernible, and will be pulled up and burned."'

(58)   Jesus said, 'Whoever has suffered is blessed. He has found life.'

(59)   *Jesus said, 'Gaze upon the Living One while you are alive, in case you die and (then) seek to see him, and you will not be able to see (him).'*

(60)   ¹*A Samaritan was carrying a lamb as he travelled to Judea. ²He said to his disciples, 'That man is <<binding>> the lamb.'*
³*They said to him, '(He is binding the lamb) so that he may slaughter it and eat it.'*
⁴*He said to them, 'While it is alive, he will not eat it. Rather, (he will eat the lamb) after he has slaughtered it and it is carcass.'*
⁵*They said, 'He is not permitted to do it any other way.'*
⁶*He said to them, 'Moreover, so that you will not become a carcass and be eaten, seek for yourselves a place within rest!'*

(61)   ¹Jesus said, 'Two people will rest on a couch. One will die. One will live.'

²*Salome said, 'Who are you, sir? That is, from [[whom]]? You have reclined on my couch and eaten at my table.'*
³*Jesus said to her, 'I am he who comes from the one who is an equal. I was given some who belong to my Father.'*
⁴*'I am your disciple.'*
⁵*'Therefore I say, when a person becomes [[equal]] (with me), he will be filled with light. But if he becomes separated (from me), he will be filled with darkness.'*

(62)   ¹Jesus said, 'I tell my mysteries to [those people who are worthy of my] mysteries.'

²'Do not let your left hand know what your right hand is going to do.'

(63)   ¹Jesus said, 'There was a wealthy man who had many assets. ²He said, "I will use my assets to sow, harvest, plant and fill my granaries with produce, so that I will not need anything." ³These were the things he was thinking in his heart. But that very night, he died.'

⁴'Whoever has ears should listen!'

(64)   ¹Jesus said, 'A man had guests. When he had prepared the dinner, he sent his servant to invite the guests.
²He went to the first person. He said to him, "My master invites you."
³He said, "I have some payments for some merchants. They are coming to me this evening. I must go and give them instructions. I decline the dinner."
⁴He went to another person. He said to him, "My master has invited you."
⁵He said to him, "I have purchased a house and they have requested me for the day. I will not have time."
⁶He went to another person. He said to him, "My master invites you."
⁷He said to him, "My friend is going to be wed and I am the person who will be preparing the meal. I will not be able to come. I decline the dinner."
⁸He went to another person. He said to him, "My master invites you."
⁹He said to him, "I have purchased a villa. Since I am going to collect the rent, I will not be able to come. I decline."
¹⁰The servant left. He said to his master, "The people whom you invited to the dinner have declined."
¹¹The master said to his servant, "Go outside on the streets. The people you find, bring them to dine."'

¹²*'Buyers and merchants [will] not enter the places of my Father.'*

(65)   ¹He said, 'A creditor owned a vineyard. He leased it to some farmers so that they would work it and he would collect the produce from them.
²He sent his servant so that the farmers would give him the produce of the vineyard. ³They seized his servant. They beat him, a little more and they would have killed him.
The servant returned and he told his master.
⁴The master said, "Perhaps [[they]] did not recognize [[him.]]."
⁵He sent another servant. The farmers beat that one too.
⁶Then the master sent his son. He said, "Perhaps they will be ashamed in front of my son."
⁷Those farmers, since they knew that he was the heir of the vineyard, seized him and killed him.'

⁸'Whoever has ears should listen!'

(66)   Jesus said, 'Show me the stone that the builders rejected. It is the cornerstone.'

(67)   *Jesus said, 'Whoever knows everything, but needs (to know) himself, is in need of everything.'*

(68)   ¹Jesus said, 'Blessed are you when you are hated and persecuted.'

²*'[[A place will be found, where you will not be persecuted]].'*

(69)   ¹*'Blessed are those who have been persecuted in their hearts. They are the people who truly have known the Father.'*

[2]'Blessed are those who are hungry, for whosoever desires (it), his belly will be filled.'

(70)   [1]Jesus said, 'When you acquire within you that certain thing, what is within you will save you. [2]If you do not have it within you, what you do not have within you will kill you.'

(71)   Jesus said, 'I will destroy [this] temple, and no one will build it […].'

(72)   [1]A man said to him, 'Tell my brothers that they must share with me my father's possessions.'
[2]He said to him, 'Mister, who has made me an executor?'
[3]He turned to his disciples and said to them, 'Surely I am not an executor, am I?'

(73)   Jesus said, 'Indeed the harvest is plentiful but the workers are few. So ask the Lord to send out workers to the harvest.'

(74)   He said, 'Lord, many people are around the [[well]], but no one is in the [[well]].'

(75)   *Jesus said, 'Many people are standing at the door, but those who are celibate are the people who will enter the bridal chamber.'*

(76)   [1]Jesus said, 'The Kingdom of the Father is like a merchant who had some merchandise. He found a pearl. [2]That merchant was wise. He sold the merchandise. Then he purchased for himself this single pearl. [3]You too, seek His imperishable and enduring treasure where neither moth draws near to eat nor worm destroys.'

(77)   *[1]Jesus said, 'I am the light which is above all things. I am everything. From me, everything came forth, and up to me, everything reached.'*

(78)   [1]Jesus said, 'Why did you come out into the desert? To see a reed shaken by the wind [2]and to see a man dressed in soft garments [like your] kings and your prominent men? [3]They are dressed in soft garments, but they will not be able to understand the truth.'

(79)   [1]A woman in the crowd said to him, 'Blessed is the womb that bore you and the breasts that nourished you.'
[2]He said to [her], 'Blessed are the people who have heard the word of the Father and have truly kept it. [3]For there will be days when you will say, "Blessed is the womb that has not conceived and the breasts that have not given milk."'

(80)   *[1]Jesus said, 'Whoever has come to know the world has found the corpse. [2]The world does not deserve the person who has found (that the world is) the corpse.'*
Alternative Translation
[1]'Whoever has come to know the world <<has mastered the body>>. [2]The world does not deserve the person who <<has mastered the body>>.'

(81)   [1]Jesus said, 'Whoever has grown wealthy, that person should become a king. [2]But whoever possesses power, let that person disown (his power).'

(82)   [1]Jesus said, 'Whoever is near me, is near the fire. [2]But whoever is far away from me, is far away from the Kingdom.'

(83)   *¹Jesus said, 'The images are visible to people, but the light in them is concealed in the image of the Father's light. ²The light will be revealed, but his image is concealed by his light.'*

(84)   *¹Jesus said, 'When you see the likeness of yourselves, you are delighted. ²But when you see the images of yourselves which came into being before you – they neither die nor are visible – how much you will suffer!'*

(85)   *¹Jesus said, 'Adam came into being out of a great power and great wealth. But he was not deserving of you. ²For, had he been deserving, [he would] not [have] died.'*

(86)   ¹Jesus said, '[The foxes have] their dens and the birds have their nests, ²but the human being does not have a place to lay down his head and rest.'

(87)   *¹Jesus said, 'Miserable is the body crucified by a body. ²Miserable is the soul crucified by these together.'*

(88)   *¹Jesus said, 'The angels and the prophets will come to you. They will give to you what is yours, ²and, in turn, you will give them what you have. You will say to yourselves, "When will they come and receive what is theirs?"'*

(89)   ¹Jesus said, 'Why do you wash the cup's exterior? ²Do you not understand that He who created the interior is also He who created the exterior?'

(90)   ¹Jesus said, 'Come to me, for my yoke is mild and my lordship is gentle. ²And you will find rest for yourselves.'

(91)   *¹They said to him, 'Tell us so that we may believe in you! Who are you?'* ²He said to them, 'You examine the appearance of the sky and the earth, but, he who is in your midst, you do not understand. Nor this critical time! you do not understand how to examine it.'

(92)   ¹Jesus said, 'Seek and you will find. ²However, the questions you asked me previously but which I did not address then, now I want to address, yet you do not seek (answers).'

(93)   ¹'Do not give what is holy to dogs, or they might toss them on the manure pile. ²Do not toss the pearls [to] pigs, or they might make [break] [[them]].'

(94.)   ¹Jesus [said], 'Whoever seeks will find. ²[Whoever knocks], it will be opened for him.'

(95)   ¹[Jesus said], 'If you have money, do not give it at interest. ²Rather, give [it] to someone from whom you will not get it (back).'

(96)   ¹Jesus said, 'The Kingdom of the Father is like a woman. ²She took a little yeast. She buried it in dough. She made the dough into large bread loaves.'

³'Whoever has ears should listen!'

(97)   ¹Jesus said, 'The Kingdom of the [Father] is like a woman carrying a [jar] filled with meal. ²While she was walking [on the] road still a long way out, the handle of the jar broke. Behind her, the meal leaked out onto the road. ³She did not realize it. She had not noticed a problem. ⁴When she arrived at her house, she put the jar down and found it empty.'

(98)   ¹Jesus said, 'The Kingdom of the Father is like someone who wished to kill a prominent man. ²While at home, he drew out his knife. He stabbed it into

the wall to test whether his hand would be strong (enough). ³Then he murdered the prominent man.'

(99)   ¹The disciples said to him, 'Your brothers and your mother are standing outside.'
²He said to them, 'Those here who do the will of my Father, they are my brothers and my mother. ³They are the people who will enter the Kingdom of my Father.'

(100)   ¹They showed Jesus a gold coin and said to him, 'Caesar's men extort taxes from us.'
²He said to them, ' Give to Caesar, what is Caesar's. ³Give to God what is God's. *⁴And what is mine, give me.'*

(101)   *¹ 'Whoever does not hate his [father] and his mother in the same manner as I do, he cannot be a [disciple] of mine. ²Also whoever does [not] love his [father and] his mother in the same manner as I do, he cannot be a [disciple] of mine. ³For my [birth] mother [gave death], while my true [mother] gave life to me.'*

(102)   Jesus said, 'Woe to the Pharisees because they are like a dog sleeping in the cattle trough. For the dog neither eats nor [lets] the cattle eat.'

(103)   Jesus said, 'Blessed is the man who knows where the thieves are going to enter, so that [he] may arise, gather at his estate, and arm himself.'

(104)   ¹They said to Jesus, 'Come. Today, let's pray and fast!'
²Jesus said, 'What sin have I committed? Or in what way have I been defeated? Rather, when the bridegroom leaves the bridal chamber, then they should fast and pray.'

(105)   *Jesus said, 'Whoever is aquainted with (one's) father and mother will be called, "the child of a prostitute".'*

(106)   *¹Jesus said, 'When you make the two one, you will become children of Man. ²And when you say, "Mountain, go forth!" it will move.'*

(107)   ¹Jesus said, 'The Kingdom is like a shepherd who had a hundred sheep. ²One of them, the largest, strayed. He left the ninety-nine. He sought that one until he found it. ³After he had laboured, he said to the sheep, "I love you more than the ninety-nine."'

(108)   *¹Jesus said, 'Whoever drinks from my mouth will become as I am. ²I myself will become that person, ³and what is hidden will be revealed to him.'*

(109)   ¹Jesus said, 'The Kingdom is like a man who had in his field a [hidden treasure], but he did not know about it. ²And [after] he died, he left it to his [son]. The son [did] not know (about the treasure). He took that field and sold [it]. ³And the buyer went and ploughed. He [found] the treasure. He started to give money at interest to whomever he wished.'

(110)   *Jesus said, 'Whoever has found the world and become wealthy, he should disown the world.'*

(111)   ¹Jesus said, 'The heavens and the earth will roll up in your presence. *²And whoever is alive because of the Living One will not see death. ³Does not Jesus say, "The world does not deserve the person who has found himself"?'*

(112)   *¹Jesus said, 'Alas to the flesh crucified by the soul! ²Alas to the soul
          crucified by the flesh!'*

(113)   *¹His disciples said to him, 'When will the Kingdom come?'
          ²'It will not come by waiting. ³It will not be said, "Look! Here it is!" or
          "Look! There it is!" ⁴Rather, the Kingdom of the Father is spread out over
          the earth, but people do not see it.'*

(114)   *¹Simon Peter said to them, 'Mary should leave us because women do not
          deserve life.'
          ²Jesus said, 'Look, in order to make her male, I myself will <<guide>>
          her, so that she too may become a living spirit – male, resembling you. For
          every woman who will make herself male will enter the Kingdom of
          Heaven.'*

Part II

COMMENTARY ON THE *GOSPEL OF THOMAS*

P.Oxy. 654.1–5

οἴτοι οι {οι} λόγοι οι [ἀπόκρυφοι οὓς ἐλα΄]λησεν Ἰη(σοῦ)ς ο ζῶν κ [αὶ ἔγραψεν Ἰούδα ο] καὶ Θωμᾶ

These are the [secret] words that the Living Jesus spoke and that [Judas] Thomas [wrote down].

NHC II 2.32.10–12

ⲚⲀⲈⲒⲚⲈ Ⲛ̄ϢⲀⲬⲈ ⲈⲐⲎⲦ ⲈⲚⲦⲀ Ⲓ̅Ⲥ̅ ⲈⲦⲞⲚⲊ ⲬⲞⲞⲨ ⲀⲨⲰ ⲀϤⲤⲊⲀⲒ̈ⲤⲞⲨ Ⲛ̄ϬⲒ ⲆⲒⲆⲨⲘⲞⲤ Ⲓ̈ⲞⲨⲆⲀⲤ ⲐⲰⲘⲀⲤ

These are the secret words that the Living Jesus spoke and that Didymos Judas Thomas wrote down.

ATTRIBUTION
Accretion.

TEXT AND TRANSLATION ISSUES
The Greek is given priority since the Coptic appears to be later, further identifying Judas Thomas (Ἰούδα ο] καὶ Θωμᾶ) as 'Didymos', the Greek translation of the Aramaic 'Twin', תאמא.

H.-Ch. Puech, followed by H. Koester, notes early in the discussion of the Gospel that the identity of Didymos Judas Thomas is linked with the Syrian Thomas tradition where the apostle Thomas has the unique appellation 'Judas Thomas'. The *Book of Thomas the Contender* is said to be the writing of Matthaias as it was spoken to 'Judas Thomas (ⲒⲞⲨⲆⲀⲤ ⲐⲰⲘⲀⲤ)' (138.2).

A.F.J. Klijn points out that the Greek *Acts of Thomas* introduce him as 'Judas Thomas who is also Didymos (ἰούδα θῶμας τῷ καὶ δίδυμῳ)', while generally the Syriac reads 'Judas Thomas the Apostle'. In the oldest extant Syriac version of the *Acts*, however, the principle character is simply called 'Judas'. When Eusebius quotes the text of the Abgar Edessian legend, he uses 'Judas Thomas (Ἰούδας ο καὶ θωμᾶς), but in his own summary, he only writes 'Thomas (θωμᾶς)' (1.13.4; 2.1.6). In all these instances, however, in the Syriac translation of Eusebius, 'Judas Thomas' is supplied. In the *Doctrine of Addai*, the apostle is known as 'Judas Thomas'. Significantly, according to the Syrian tradition, the apostle in John 14.22 is known as 'Judas Thomas' or 'Thomas' in the Curetonian Syriac version of John 14.22, 'Judas, not Iscariot' reads 'Judas Thomas' while Codex Syrus Sinaiticus reads simply, 'Thomas'.

What these traditions suggest is that in addition to Judas Iscariot, there was a disciple of Jesus whose actual name was 'Judas'. At some point in time, perhaps to differentiate him from Judas Iscariot, Judas received the nickname 'the Twin': the Aramaic 'תאמא (twin)' has been transliterated into Greek letters as 'θωμᾶ(ς)'. Thus the Syrian Thomas tradition preserves the early Aramaic name of their hero 'Judas' along with the honorific title the 'Twin'. 'Δίδυμος (twin)' is a Greek rendition of the Aramaic 'תאמא (twin)'. It appears to have been added when the Syrian traditions went into translation for audiences unfamiliar with Aramaic. Instead of simply translating the Aramaic, the scribes appended the Greek probably because, by the late first century, 'Thomas' was understood to be the name of the disciple rather than his title. Thus other traditions such as those found in Matthew, Mark, Luke and John remember this apostle as simply 'Thomas'.

R. Uro believes that, because the Twin reference is only found in the Incipit of the Gospel, it cannot be compared to its more extensive use in the *Acts of Thomas*, as Puech, Koester and Klijn have done. Such a claim does not take into account that references to this title do not occur outside of Syrian literature as far as I am aware. From the perspective of *Traditiongeschichte*, this means that the title was known to the Syrian audience and was a trigger for a larger story familiar to them. This story can be reasonably reconstructed from the extant Syrian literature, especially since the collective references to the Twin agree hermeneutically. Uro has referred to *Thomas the Contender* 138.4–21, that it suggests a disjuncture in the tradition's portrayal of Thomas. But this is not a practical interpretation of the text. Thomas is not 'ignorant' here. Rather he is the special disciple, the true Twin and companion, through whom Jesus is revealing knowledge of liberation – that people must examine themselves and learn who they are and how they will come to be. In this manner, it supports the presentation of this disciple in other Syrian texts.

INTERPRETATIVE COMMENT

Coherence to vocabulary characteristic of the accretions is indicated in the title given Jesus, 'Living'. This accretion accrued in the Gospel by 120 CE following the death of the eyewitnesses when the Syrian Christian community was preserving the memories of its leaders.

It is notable that, also in the *Acts of Thomas*, Jesus is given the title 'Living One'. In chapter 136, he is called 'Son of the Living God'. In fact, G. Quispel notes that this technical term is frequently found in Syrian writings and indicates that Jesus has eternal life at his disposal and gives it to others. 'Living' means 'life-giving'. M. Lelyveld attributes this prominent theme to a redactor, perhaps the scribe Thomas. This theme was used to frame the Gospel in her opinion (Incipit, L. 1 and 114), and comes from the prophetic, not sapiential tradition.

The Incipit identifies the genre of literature as a collection of Jesus' sayings, his logia or words (λόγοι or N̄ϣⲁⲭⲉ). M. Meyer notes the frequency of references to Jesus' logia in early Christian literature, occurring in the Synoptic Gospels, Acts, the *Didache, 1 Clement* and Papias. J. Robinson discusses Q and *Thomas* as examples of these λόγοι collections of religious wisdom from the ancient world. He thinks that these collections developed in a trajectory 'from Jewish wisdom literature through Gnosticism, where the esoteric nature of such collections lead to the supplementary designation of them as "secret sayings".' Unlike Robison, M. Lelyveld compares the opening to collections of oracles of the Prophets which were structured using 'λέγω' and with proverbial sayings (Deut. 1.1; Prov. 1.1; 25.1; Eccl. 1.1; Bar. 1.1).

Although Robinson's proposal represents a possible progression of traditions, in my opinion, it does not represent the only or natural one. Although the *Gospel of Philip* and *Pistis Sophia* may support his argument, in the case of the *Gospel of Thomas*, the *Dialogue of the Savior* and *Thomas the Contender*, we find sayings of Jesus that have been developed into speeches honouring encratic Christian ideals, not Gnostic. The *Teachings of Silvanus* is a developed collection of Jesus' words too, but it develops them in a manner more representative of the 'orthodox' teachings of Christianity in Alexandria such as we find in the *Sentences of Sextus*, Clement of Alexandria, Origen and even Athanasius.

Thomas' characterization of Jesus' words as 'secret' appears to me to be developing a theme common in early Christianity, that Jesus' teachings were not entirely exoteric.

Several logia in *Thomas* identify Jesus' teaching as 'secret' or 'hidden'. These words of Jesus signal the revelatory nature of the text (cf. L. 5, 6, 17, 38, 62 and 92). This esoteric aspect of logia traditions appears to have been well-known in early Christianity. As M. Meyer points out, in Luke 9.44–45, Jesus commands his disciples to listen to 'these words' (τοὺς λόγους τούτους) although 'this word' (ῥῆμα τοῦτο) was 'hidden from them'. Or in Mark 4.10–11, Jesus is said to speak enigmatically 'in parables' to outsiders while disclosing to the disciples 'the mystery of the Kingdom of God'. I might add that Paul too is familiar with this tradition, mentioning on more than one occasion that he has been entrusted with 'the mysteries of God' (1 Cor. 4.1), imparting 'a secret and hidden wisdom of God' that 'no eye has seen, nor ear heard, nor the heart of man conceived' (1 Cor. 2.7). He claims direct revelation from God which he wishes to impart 'in words' (ἐν λόγοις) to those people who possess the Spirit (1 Cor. 2.10–13).

These fragments of information tell us that Christians early on were careful to guard certain teachings of Jesus from the uninitiated, a concept that continued well into second-century Christianity. The opening lines of *Thomas* allude to this concern, perhaps signalling that the complete Gospel is intended for the initiated, those Christians who have been baptized and anointed, filled with the Spirit.

SELECT BIBLIOGRAPHY
Klijn (1970); Koester (1971: 127–28); Lelyveld (1987: 5, 134–35); Meyer (1990: 163–66); Puech (1963); Quispel (1975c: 180); Robinson (1971); Uro (2003: 10–15).

Logion 1

And he said, 'Whoever finds the meaning of these words will not die.'

P.Oxy. 654.3–5

καὶ εἶπεν [ὃς ἂν τὴν ερμηνεί]αν τῶν λόγων τούτ[ων εὕρη θανάτου] οὐ μὴ γεύσηται

And he said, '[Whoever finds] the meaning of these words will not [die].'

NHC II 2.32.12–14

ⲁⲩⲱ ⲡⲉⲭⲁϥ ⲭⲉ ⲡⲉⲧⲁϩⲉ ⲉⲑⲉⲣⲙⲏⲛⲉⲓⲁ ⲛ̅ⲛⲉⲉⲓϣⲁⲭⲉ ϥⲛⲁⲭⲓ ϯⲡⲉ ⲁⲛ
ⲙ̅ⲡⲙⲟⲩ

And he said, 'Whoever finds the meaning of these words will not die.'

ATTRIBUTION
Accretion.

TEXT AND TRANSLATION ISSUES
The reconstruction of the Greek appears very firm since the number of letters matches perfectly the available space in the broken area of the manuscript and agrees with the Coptic. The scribe marked the end of the saying with a coronis sign. Beneath the first two letters of line 5 (οὐ), the scribe also struck a paragraphing line. Both marks appear to me to have been used as oration aids, visually distinguishing one saying from the next.

I have rendered ЄΡΜΗΝЄΙλ (hermeneia), 'meaning'. It implies the active interpretation of the text in order to explain the complex meaning of the simple words. J. Kloppenborg has connected this interpretative process to the mode of instruction that was common in the ancient Near East, the Hellenistic gnomologium or chriae collection. These rhetorical collections of words were attributed to particular speakers and their oration involved hermeneutics in order to garner the rich and deeper meaning of the words. For instance, Iambichus observes regarding Pythagoras, 'He was also accustomed to reveal a boundless and complex meaning to his pupils in a symbolic manner through very short utterances, just as Pythian (Apollo) and nature itself indicate an infinite and abstruse mass of ideas and results through handy sayings or seeds small in size.'

The clause ϥΝλΧΙ †ΠЄ λΝ ΜΠΜΟΥ (cf. θανάτου οὐ μὴ γεύσηται) literally reads, 'he will not taste death'. It is an idiomatic statement as B. Fordyce Miller has noted and which I translate here and throughout the gospel, 'will not die'. As J. Behm records, the expression 'to taste death' is commonly found in Semitic languages, meaning 'to die' (i.e. Gn. r. 9 on 1.31; Gn. r. 21 on 3.22; Tg. J. I Dt. 32,1; bJoma, 78b; Midr. Qoh. 12,5). A. Guillaumont notes this idiom in his research as well.

INTERPRETATIVE COMMENT

Coherence to characteristic accretive vocabulary is indicated in the clause, ϥΝλΧΙ †ΠЄ λΝ ΜΠΜΟΥ. This accretion accrued in the Gospel between 60 and 120 CE as a soteriological response to the delay of the Eschaton. This saying was strategically placed here to serve as a new introduction to the old Gospel. Through this saying all the rest of the sayings were now meant to be heard, read and understood. The inclusion of this saying helped to shift the soteriology of the Gospel from an apocalyptic scenario to the later community's development of a utopian consciousness within the boundaries of the Church.

Thus the revised Gospel stressed that these sayings of Jesus were to be understood through a *new* hermeneutic, one that replaced the old. If the believer understood the message of Jesus through this new hermeneutic it would result in redemption for that person. It must be recognized, however, that L. 1 does not provide for the believer this new hermeneutic. Rather, the new hermeneutic would have been controlled by the community, probably provided by the orator during performances of the Gospel's speeches. By studying the accretions as commentary, it is possible to recover this new hermeneutic as I have outlined in the companion monograph, *Recovering*.

SOURCE DISCUSSION

W. Schrage postulates that L. 1 is dependent on John 8.52, even though he admits that the Johannine expression, εἰς τὸν αἰῶνα, is secondary. J. Robinson and S.J. Patterson observe that L. 1 is reminiscent of John 8.52, but M. Meyer does not find any compelling evidence to suggest that *Thomas* is literarily dependent upon John in this instance. G. Quispel actually attributes this saying to the hand of the author of the Gospel.

LITERATURE PARALLELS

John 8.51–52

> 'Truly, truly, I say to you, if any one keeps my word, he will never see death.' The Jews said to him, 'Now we know that you have a demon. Abraham died, as did the prophets; and you say, "If any one keeps my word, he will never taste death"'.

Cf. Mark 9.1; Matt. 16.28; Luke 9.27; Heb. 2.9; Sirach 39.1–3

Agreements in Syrian Gospels, Western Text and Diatessaron

John 8.52 in D b c d ff² 1 S Tᴺᴸ
– never

John 8.52 in S Tᴺᴸ
will not taste << will not see

Select Bibliography
Attridge (1989: 113); Behm (1964); Guillaumont (1981: 191); Kloppenborg (1987: 291–327); Meyer (1990: 166–67); Miller (1967: 53–54); Patterson (1990: 107); Quispel (1981: 265); Robinson (1971: 80).

Logion 2.1–4

¹(([Jesus said,] 'Whoever seeks should not cease [seeking until] he finds. ²And when he finds, [he will be amazed. ³And] when he is [amazed,] he will be a king. ⁴And [once he is a king,] he will rest.'))

P.Oxy. 654.5–9

¹[λέγει Ἰη(σοῦς)] μὴ παυσάσθω ο ζη [τῶν τοῦ ζητεῖν ἕως ἄν] εὕρῃ ²καὶ ὅταν εὕρῃ [θαμβηθήσεται ³καὶ θαμ]βηθεὶς βασιλεύσῃ ⁴κα[ὶ βασιλεύσας ἀναπα]ήσεται

[Jesus said,] 'Whoever seeks should not cease [seeking until] he finds. And when he finds, [he will be amazed. And] when he is [amazed,] he will be a king. And [once he is a king,] he will rest.'

NHC II 2.32.14–19

¹ⲡⲉⲭⲉ ⲓ̅ⲥ̅ ⲙⲛ̅ⲧⲣⲉϥⲗⲟ ⲛ̅ϭⲓ ⲡⲉⲧϣⲓⲛⲉ ⲉϥϣⲓⲛⲉ ϣⲁⲛⲧⲉϥϭⲓⲛⲉ ²ⲁⲩⲱ ϩⲟⲧⲁⲛ ⲉϥϣⲁⲛϭⲓⲛⲉ ϥⲛⲁϣⲧⲣ̅ⲧⲣ̅ ³ⲁⲩⲱ ⲉϥϣⲁⲛϣⲧⲟⲣⲧⲣ̅ ϥⲛⲁⲣ̅ ϣⲡⲏⲣⲉ ⁴ⲁⲩⲱ ϥⲛⲁⲣ̅ⲣ̅ⲣⲟ ⲉϫⲙ̅ ⲡⲧⲏⲣϥ

Jesus said, 'Whoever seeks should not cease seeking until he finds. And when he finds, he will be troubled. And when he is troubled, he will be amazed, and he will be a king ruling over everything.'

Attribution
Kernel saying.

Text and Translation Issues
The final lacunae in the Greek version must have read κα[ὶ βασιλεύσας ἀναπα]ήσεται, rather than [...ἐπαναπα]ήσεται as H. Attridge has reconstructed it. The available space cannot accommodate the prefix ἐπ- even though Clement of Alexandria preserves a version of this saying with the prefix in *Strom.* 5.14.96. It should be noted that Clement also knows of another version of this saying in *Strom.* 2.9.45 which has the shorter ἀναπαήσεται.

A coronis is found following ἀναπαήσεται in the Greek version. The coronis takes up approximately three letter spaces. Immediately below ήσεται on line 9, the scribe struck a paragraphing line, functioning as an orator's aid.

The Coptic papyrus is blank at the beginning of line 18 for approximately two inches between ϥⲛⲁⲣ̅ and ϣⲡⲏⲣⲉ. It appears that the scribe intentionally avoided writing across this area because one layer of the papyrus is effaced. The horizontal papyrus is missing. We know that the papyrus was eroded in this way before the scribe copied the Gospel because the letter ρ (3rd letter, 17 line) has its tail copied over the effaced area.

The older Greek version of L. 2.4 reads, 'once he is a king, he will rest', while the Coptic reads, 'he will be amazed, and he will be a king ruling over everything'. It is most likely that the Coptic version represents a later modification of the Kernel saying since our earliest external witnesses record versions of the saying very close to the Greek Oxy. fragment. Moreover, the ideology in the Greek version is internally consistent with L. 90, another Kernel saying that speaks of the culmination of the spiritual journey in terms of 'rest'. This theme appears to belong to the old Jerusalem traditions since we also find references to it in the *Pseudo-Clementine* corpus (2.22). Later accretions in the Thomasine Gospel, accretions that emphasize the spiritual journey as an *interior or ascent journey* culminating in 'rest' were added to the Gospel to develop this older 'rest' theme (L. 51, 60).

INTERPRETATIVE COMMENT

S. Davies compares L. 2 to other introductions in Wisdom literature (Sir. 51.13–14; Wis. Sol. 1.1–2; 6.12–14) which encourage people to seek wisdom so that upon death they can be at peace. M. Meyer has noted broader parallels in contemporaneous Greco-Roman, Jewish and Christian literature which show that the religious quest for God's wisdom was a matter of concern for people of antiquity. Sirach 6.27–31 urges the reader to seek God's wisdom and, in so doing, progress through a series of developmental stages eventually leading to rest. In Wisdom of Solomon 6.12–20, this religious quest ends in the Kingdom. Matthew 7.7–8 and Luke 11.9–10 urge followers of Jesus to 'seek and find'. Parallels in the *Gospel of the Hebrews*, the *Dialogue of the Savior*, *Thomas the Contender*, and the *Acts of Thomas* contain similar references.

L. 2.3 may be a reference to the old idea from Jerusalem that the flesh had to be ruled by the will of God rather than the passions and desires of the body (James 1.14–15, 27; 3.23; 4.1; 1 Peter 2.11; 4.1–2; 2 Peter 1.4–6; 2.10). This might, indeed, be the meaning of Paul's statement in 1 Corinthians 4.8 where he criticizes the Corinthians for believing that they have 'become kings' since he immediately launches into a tirade against the immorality among the Corinthians (5.1ff.). This became a very popular interpretation of the kingship metaphor in Syrian literature. The *Pseudo-Clementine Recognitions*, in fact, appear to know this interpretation well, stating that the believer must 'become lord of his passions' in order to enter the Kingdom (5.8). The same understanding of the saying is mentioned in *Thomas the Contender*, 'for when you leave the pains and passions of the body, you will receive rest from the Good One, and you will rule with the king' (145.12–16). In fact, the metaphor associating kingship with ruling over one's passions becomes quite developed in the later monastic literature as we find, for instance, in Pseudo-Macarius. It is quite conceivable that the later encratic community associated with the Gospel saw in this old saying support for their extreme ascetic practices. Their goal was to achieve rest by overcoming their bodies of pleasure, becoming 'lords' over their passions.

SOURCE DISCUSSION

G. Quispel is of the opinion that this logion is a quotation from the *Gospel of the Hebrews* or some other Aramaic Jewish-Christian Gospel. Contrary to this, E. Bammel argues that the citation in the *Apocryphon of James* was the basis for the Coptic *Thomas* which led to the development of the citation found in the Greek *Thomas* and the *Gospel of the Hebrews* because he finds the Coptic version in *Thomas* to be less Gnostic than the Greek. Not only is Bammel incorrect regarding his characterization of the Greek version as more 'gnosticizing' than the Coptic, but he also fails to demonstrate that literary dependence along the route he suggests could even have been possible. Patterson argues that it is unlikely that L.4.1 derives from Luke 11.10–13 or Matthew 7.8–11.

LITERATURE PARALLELS

Gospel of the Hebrews *4a (Clem. Alex.* Strom. *2.9.45)*
'One who has marvelled will rule, and one who has ruled will rest.'

Gospel of the Hebrews *4b (Clem. Alex.* Strom. *5.14.96)*
'One who seeks will not stop seeking until he finds. When he finds, he will be astonished, and having been astonished, he will rule. And when he has ruled, he will rest.'

2 Clement *5.5*
'Our stay in this world of the flesh is slight and short, but Christ's promise is great and wonderful, and means rest in the coming Kingdom and in eternal life.'

Thomas the Contender *140.41–141.2*
'Blessed is the wise person who has sought truth and when it has been found, has rested upon it forever, and has not been afraid of those who wish to trouble the wise person.'

Thomas the Contender *145.12–16*
'For when you leave the pains and passions of the body, you will receive rest from the Good One, and you will rule with the king, you united with him and he united with you, from now on, forever and ever.'

2 Apocalypse of James *56.2–6*
'For your (James') sake they will be told [these things], and will come to rest. For your sake they will reign [and will] become kings. For [your] sake they will have pity on whomever they pity.'

Pseudo-Clementine Recognitions *5.8*
'For it is his duty to examine with just judgement the things which we say, and to understand that we speak the words of truth, that, knowing how things are, and directing his life in good actions, he may be found a partaker of the Kingdom of Heaven, subjecting to himself the desires of the flesh, and becoming lord of them, that so at length he himself also may become the pleasant possession of the Ruler of all.'

Pseudo-Clementine Recognitions *2.22*
'Understand that the way is this course of life. The travellers are those who do good works. The gate is the True Prophet, of whom we speak. The city is the Kingdom in which dwells the Almighty Father, whom only those can see who are of pure heart. Let us not, then, think the labour of this journey hard, because at the end of it there shall be rest.'

Acts of Thomas *136*
'Everyone who is worthy takes and finds rest. And when he has found rest, he becomes a king.'

Pseudo-Macarius, Hom. *15.35*
'For his [God's] chosen ones are anointed with the sanctifying oil and are raised up in great dignity to be kings.'

Pseudo-Macarius, Hom. *27.4*
'Acknowledge your nobility, that you are chosen to a kingly dignity... For such Christians co-reign with the heavenly King in the heavenly Church.'

Cf. *Wis. Sol.* 6.12, *Dial. Sav.* 20

SELECT BIBLIOGRAPHY
Bammel (1969); Davies (1983: 38–39); Klijn (1992: 47–51); Meyer (1990: 167–69); Patterson (1993: 19); Quispel (1975c: 3).

Logion 3.1–3

¹Jesus said, 'If ((your <<leaders>> [say to you, "Look!] the Kingdom is in heaven," then the birds of heaven [will arrive first before you. ²If they say,] "It is under the earth," then the fish of the sea [will enter it, arriving first] before you. ³But the Kingdom [of Heaven] is inside of you and [outside.]))'

P.Oxy. 654.9–16

¹Λέγει Ἰ [η(σοῦ)ς ... ἐὰν] οι ἔλκοντες ημᾶς [εἴπωσιν υμῖν ἰδοὺ] η βασιλεία ἐν οὐρα[νῷ υμᾶς φθήσεται] τὰ πετεινὰ τοῦ οὐρ[ανοῦ ²ἐὰν δ εἴπωσιν ο]τι υπὸ τὴν γήν ἐστ[ιν εἰσελεύσονται] οι ἰχθύες τῆς θαλά[σσης προφθάσαν]τες υμᾶς ³καὶ η βασ[ιλεία τῶν οὐρανῶν] ἐντὸς υμῶν [ἐσ]τι [κἀκτός]

Jesus said [..., 'If] your <<leaders>> [say to you, "Look!] the Kingdom is in heaven," then the birds of heaven [will arrive first before you. If they say,] "It is under the earth," then the fish of the sea [will enter it, arriving first] before you. But the Kingdom [of Heaven] is inside of you and [outside.]'

NHC II 2.32.19–25

¹ΠΕΧΕ ⲒⲤ ϫⲉ ⲉⲨϢⲀⲬⲞⲞⲤ ⲚⲎⲦⲚ̅ Ⲛ̅ϬⲒ ⲚⲈⲦⲤⲰⲔ ϨⲎⲦⲦⲎⲨⲦⲚ̅ ϫⲉ ⲈⲒⲤϨⲎⲎⲦⲈ ⲈⲦⲘⲚ̅ⲦⲈⲢⲞ ϨⲚ̅ ⲦⲠⲈ ⲈⲈⲒⲈ Ⲛ̅ϨⲀⲖⲎⲦ ⲚⲀⲢ̅ϢⲞⲢⲠ ⲈⲢⲰⲦⲚ̅ Ⲛ̅ⲦⲈ ⲦⲠⲈ ²ⲈⲨϢⲀⲚⲬⲞⲞⲤ ⲚⲎⲦⲚ̅ ϫⲉ Ⲥ̅ϨⲚ̅ ⲐⲀⲖⲀⲤⲤⲀ ⲈⲈⲒⲈ Ⲛ̅ⲦⲂⲦ ⲚⲀⲢ̅ϢⲞⲢⲠ ⲈⲢⲰⲦⲚ̅ ³ⲀⲖⲖⲀ ⲦⲘⲚ̅ⲦⲈⲢⲞ Ⲥ̅ⲘⲠⲈⲦⲚ̅ϨⲞⲨⲚ ⲀⲨⲰ Ⲥ̅ⲘⲠⲈⲦⲚ̅ⲂⲀⲖ

Jesus said, 'If your <<leaders>> say to you, "Look! the Kingdom is in heaven," then the birds of heaven will arrive first before you. If they say to you, "It is in the sea," then the fish of the sea will arrive first before you. Rather the Kingdom is inside of you and outside of you.'

ATTRIBUTION
Accretion.

TEXT AND TRANSLATION ISSUES
In L. 3.1, the missing part of line 9 of the Greek manuscript (following Λέγει Ἰ) has room for up to 14 spaces. This indicates that the Greek text does not agree with the Coptic as H. Attridge's reconstruction of only 6 spaces has it (Λέγει Ἰ [η(σοῦ)ς ἐὰν]. How the Greek text varied is uncertain. Any reconstruction would be purely conjecture since there is no parallel in the Coptic to aid us. But it is certain that the Greek contained at least another word of five to eight letters, like αὐτοῖς.

I have taken the Greek to be primary since the Coptic appears to reflect a more advanced stage in the literary transmission of the Gospel as D. Mueller has argued. The close parallel between the Greek 'under the earth' and Job 12.78 suggests that the clause was original to the saying. Its omission by the Coptic translator served to streamline the saying.

L. 3.1 literally reads, 'If those who draw you…' G. Garitte traces the strange expression to a Greek scribe translating from our Coptic manuscript since Garitte understands ϹⲰⲔ ϨⲎⲦ⸌ as an idiomatic expression meaning 'to conduct' or 'lead'. The Greek manuscript (which has ἕλκοντες) he thinks was translated from the Coptic, rendering ϹⲰⲔ ϨⲎⲦ⸌ woodenly rather than idiomatically. There is a much simpler explanation in my opinion. A. Guillaumont explains this strange expression by pointing out that the Aramaic נגד means both 'to draw' and 'to lead'. The translator erred in his rendering of the Aramaic meaning into Greek. Clearly the meaning is 'to lead'. This explanation suggests a Semitic substratum. My translation relies on this explanation. It should be noted that the Syriac ܢܓܕ also has this dual meaning.

I have reconstructed the Greek in the lacunae of L. 3.3, η βασ[ιλεία τῶν οὐρανῶν] instead of η βασ[ιλεία τοῦ θεοῦ] because the 15 spaces fills the lacunae (14 to 17 spaces) more faithfully than the shorter τοῦ θεοῦ, 12 spaces. It is preferred too because 'Kingdom of God' as a title appears nowhere in the Gospel except the Greek fragment of L. 27. The *Manichaean Psalm* and Hippolytus' allusion to L. 3 have 'Kingdom of Heaven' as well. This reconstruction is in agreement with O. Hofius and D. Mueller while against J. Fitzmyer and H. Attridge.

INTERPRETATIVE COMMENT
Coherence to a theme characteristic of the accretions is indicated by the emphasis on the fully present Kingdom. This accretion accrued in the Gospel between 60 and 100 CE as a response to the delay of the Eschaton, a response which also was recorded in the Gospel of Luke during this same historical period. It accrued in the beginning of the Thomasine Gospel to serve as the new 'thesis' of the Gospel, orienting the hearer or reader to the new hermeneutic mentioned in the preceding saying. Its accretive doublet, L. 113 completed the reframing of the Gospel, restating this thesis at the conclusion of the text. By doing this, the apocalyptic dimension of the Gospel has shifted so that the mystical dominates the hermeneutic. The Kingdom is not understood as an eschatological event, but a mystical one, the present experience of God. The community appears to have conceived of its Church and encratic praxis as the actualization of the Kingdom as the accretions thoughout the Gospel suggest.

SOURCE DISCUSSION
H. von Schürmann, R. McL. Wilson, R. Grant and D.N. Freedman, and B. Gärtner think that L. 3 (and L. 113) relies on Luke 17.20–21. J.-E. Ménard believes the saying is a Gnostic interpretation of Luke 17.20–21 with reference to sapiential traditions from Deuteronomy 30.11–14 and Romans 10.6–8, while S. Davies believes it to be a sophianic interpretation. According to T.F. Glasson, this saying is dependent on Deuteronomy 30.11–14 and Luke 17.20–21. *Thomas* ridicules the idea that the Kingdom is something afar off, expounding Luke's meaning by reference to this Old Testament passage just as Tertullian has done too (*Adv. Marcionem* 4.35). W. Schrage says that dependence on Luke for L. 3 cannot be proven, but L. 113 proves the dependence for both logia because *Thomas* introduces the logion with the same editorial question that introduces the saying in Luke, 'When will the Kingdom come?'

J. Sieber argues that the question 'When will the Kingdom come?' is an independent logion found also in *2 Clement* 12.2. He notes that Luke does not allow for the question but uses indirect discourse with the Pharisees as the petitioners, while *Thomas* in L. 113

includes the direct question with the disciples as the enquirers. Although both sayings contain secondary developments, Luke was not the source for either logion according to Sieber.

In my opinion, the introduction of the saying in L. 113, 'When will the Kingdom come?' may be an example of secondary orality, that L. 113 has been influenced by the orator's memory of Luke 17.20–21. This may also be the case with L. 3.1–3, although it cannot be proven.

LITERATURE PARALLELS

Luke 17.20–21
> 'The Kingdom of God is not coming with signs to be observed; nor will they say, "Lo, here it is!" or "There!" for behold, the Kingdom of God is within you.'

2 Clement *12.2*
> 'For when someone asked the Lord when his Kingdom was going to come, he said, "When the two shall be one, and the outside like the inside, and the male with the female, neither male nor female."'

Tertullian, Adv. marcionem *4.35*
> 'This [Deuteronomy 30.11–13] means, neither in this place nor that place is the Kingdom of God; for, look! it is within you'.

Pseudo-Macarius, Berthold (1973: vol. 2, p. 43)
> 'As the Lord said, "The Kingdom of God is spread out upon the earth, and men do not see it." And again, "The Kingdom of God is within us."'

Pseudo-Macarius, Klosterman and Berthold (1961: 161)
> 'The Saviour said to us that the Kingdom of Heaven is not here or there, but it is within us.'

Pseudo-Macarius, Great Letter, *Maloney (1992: 266)*
> 'What Kingdom is said to be within us unless that joy that comes through the Spirit from above and is infused into our souls?'

Manichaean Psalm Book *160.20–21*
> 'The Kingdom of Heaven, look, it is inside us. Look, it is outside us. If we believe in it, we shall live in it forever.'

Hippolytus, Ref. *5.7*
> '(The Naassene) says (that a happy nature) is the Kingdom of Heaven to be sought for within a man.'

Cf. Deut. 30.11–14; Rom. 10.6–8; *1 Bar.* 3.29–30

SELECT BIBLIOGRAPHY
Attridge (1989); Baker (1964: 114); Davies (1983: 41–46); Fitzmyer (1971); Garitte (1960a: 161; 1960b: 335–37); Gärtner (1961: 213); Glasson (1976/1977: 151–52); Grant with Freedman (1960: 120–22); Guillaumont (1960: 325–27; 1981: 194); Hofius (1960: 31); Ménard (1970: 137–40); Mueller (1973: 267–68, 271–76); Schrage (1964a: 30–32, 199–200); Schürmann (1963: 248–49); Sieber (1966: 223–25); Wilson (1960a: 82).

Logion 3.4

⁴'(([Whoever] knows [himself] will find it.))'

P.Oxy. 654.16–17

> [ὃς ἂν εαυτὸν] γνῷ ταύτην ευρή[σει]
>
> ['Whoever] knows [himself] will find it.'

ATTRIBUTION
Accretion.

TEXT AND TRANSLATION ISSUES
The Coptic does not have, 'whoever knows himself will find it'. This Greek accretion likely was part of the Gospel before the Coptic translation was made. D. Mueller sees L. 3.4 as original to the Gospel, noting that the context clearly demands it. In my opinion, the saying complements other accretions in the Gospel including L. 67, 'Whoever knows everything, but needs (to know) himself, is in need of everything.' It is also notable that the Coptic Gospel seems to hold a memory of this saying in L. 111.3 'Does not Jesus say, "The world does not deserve the person who has found himself."' The unique structure of the phrase 'Does not Jesus say?' may have been an internal reference at the end of the Gospel to the beginning of the Gospel where Jesus taught that the person who knows himself will find the Kingdom.

  If this is the case, the Coptic version would represent an accidental truncation that happened while the text was still being copied in Greek, the *anablepsis* error perhaps occurring with the initial Greek 'O' of OΣ and OTE. This would mean that the entire clause, [ὃς ἂν εαυτὸν] γνῷ ταύτην ευρή[σει καὶ], would have dropped out of the manuscript *including the connecting* καὶ, *which is also not present in the Coptic.*

INTERPRETATIVE COMMENT
Accrual is dated to the late first century between 80 and 120 CE when the Hermetic traditions were used by the community to provide the final reinterpretation of their gospel traditions, a reinterpretation that offered further explanation of the delayed Eschaton. Both L. 3.4 and 111.3 appear to have been appended to the beginning and the end of the Gospel as a Hermetic frame reinterpreting the older Gospel.

LITERATURE PARALLELS
See L. 67 and 111.3

Dialogue of the Saviour *30*
> '[Everyone] who has known, has seen [it (the place of life)…'

SELECT BIBLIOGRAPHY
Mueller (1973: 268).

Logion 3.5

⁵(([And when you] know yourselves, [you will understand that you are the children] of the [Living] Father. [But if] you will not know yourselves, [you are impoverished] and you are poverty.))'

P.Oxy. 654.17–21

⁵[καὶ ὅτε ὑμεῖς] εαυτοὺς γνώσεσθαι [εἴσεσθε ὅτι υἱοί] ἐστε ὑμεῖς τοῦ πατρὸς τοῦ [ζῶντος εἰ δὲ μή] γνώσ<εσ>θε εαυτοὺς ἐν [τῇ πτωχείᾳ ἐστὲ] καὶ ὑμεῖς ἐστε η πτ[ωχεία]

'[And when you] know yourselves, you [will understand that you are the children] of the [Living] Father. [But if] you will not know yourselves, [you are impoverished] and you are poverty.'

NHC II 32.25–33.5

⁵ϨΟΤΑΝ ΕΤΕΤΝϢΑΝϹΟΥϢΝ ΤΗΥΤΝ ΤΟΤΕ ϹΕΝΑϹΟΥϢ(Ν) ΤΗΝΕ ΑΥϢ ΤΕΤΝΑΕΙΜΕ ϪΕ ΝΤϢΤΝ ΠΕ ΝϢΗΡΕ ΜΠΕΙϢΤ ΕΤΟΝϨ ΕϢϢΠΕ ΔΕ ΤΕΤΝΑϹΟΥϢΝ ΤΗΥΤΝ ΑΝ ΕΕΙΕ ΤΕΤΝϢΟΟΠ ϨΝ ΟΥΜΝΤϨΗΚΕ ΑΥϢ ΝΤϢΤΝ ΠΕ ΤΜΝΤϨΗΚΕ

'When you know yourselves, then you will become known and you will understand that you are the children of the Living Father. But if you will not know yourselves, you are impoverished and you are poverty.'

ATTRIBUTION
Accretion.

TEXT AND TRANSLATION ISSUES
In L. 3.5, the Greek does not have 'then you will become known and'. This accretion, found only in the Coptic version of L. 3.5, breaks the parallelism of the saying and inserts a unique idea into the saying – that is, 'being known'. It appears to me to have been added very late to the Gospel as a further comment on the theme of self-knowledge, perhaps even as late as the scribal translation into Coptic. O. Hofius, R. Grant and D.N. Freedman, and D. Mueller point out that this passage is awkward and must be regarded as a secondary addition probably representing a Coptic marginal note that inadvertently slipped into the text. Thus, I do not include it in my translation, but rely on the Greek.

'Children of the Living Father' literally reads, 'sons of the Living Father'.

INTERPRETATIVE COMMENT
Vocabulary characteristic of the accretions is present in this logion, particularly the Hermetic emphasis on self-knowledge, and the Jewish Christian attribution for God, 'Living'. This saying accrued in the Gospel in the late first century between 80 and 120 CE, to shift the emphasis of the Gospel from eschatological to mystical. The saying would have been particularly relevant to the Thomasine community once the Gentiles had come to dominate the community and welded the voice of Jesus with Hermes.

SOURCE DISCUSSION
G. Quispel traces this saying to a Hermetic anthology.

LITERATURE PARALLELS

Thomas the Contender *138.15–18*

> 'So while you accompany me, although you are uncomprehending, you have (in fact) already come to know, and you will be called, "the one who knows himself". For he who has not known himself has known nothing, but he who has known himself has at the same time already achieved knowledge about the depth of everything.'

Teachings of Silvanus *117.3–5*

> 'If you do not know [yourself], you will not be able to know all of these [God, Christ, the Spirit, the angels, the thrones, the lordships, and the Great Mind.]'

Cf. 1 Corinthians 8.2–3; 13.12; Galatians 4.8–9; *Gospel of Truth* 19.32–33; Pseudo-Macarius, *Hom.* 18.2–3, 28.1

SELECT BIBLIOGRAPHY

Grant with Freedman (1960: 70); Hofius (1960: 31); Mueller (1973: 268); Quispel (1981: 265).

Logion 4.1

[1]Jesus said, 'The old man will not hesitate to ask a little child seven days old about the place of life, and he will live.'

P.Oxy. 654.21–25

[1][λέγει Ἰη(σοῦ)ς] οὐκ ἀποκνήσει ἄνθ[ρωπος παλαιὸς ἡμε]ρῶν ἐπερωτῆσε πα[ιδίον ἑπτὰ ἡμε]ρῶν περὶ τοῦ τόπου τῆ[ς ζωῆς καὶ ζή]σετε

[Jesus said,] 'The [old man] will not hesitate to ask [a little child seven days old] about the place [of life, and] he will [live.]'

NHC II 2.33.5–9

[1]ⲡⲉϫⲉ ⲓ̄ⲥ̄ ϥⲛⲁϫⲛⲁⲩ ⲁⲛ ⲛ̄ϭⲓ ⲡⲣⲱⲙⲉ ⲛ̄ϩ̄ⲗ̄ⲗⲟ ϩ̄ⲛ ⲛⲉϥϩⲟⲟⲩ ⲉⲭⲛⲉ ⲟⲩⲕⲟⲩⲉⲓ ⲛ̄ϣⲏⲣⲉ ϣⲏⲙ ⲉϥϩ̄ⲛ ⲥⲁϣϥ̄ ⲛ̄ϩⲟⲟⲩ ⲉⲧⲃⲉ ⲡⲧⲟⲡⲟⲥ ⲙ̄ⲡⲱⲛϩ ⲁⲩⲱ ϥⲛⲁⲱⲛϩ

Jesus said, 'The old man will not hesitate to ask a little child seven days old about the place of life, and he will live.'

ATTRIBUTION

Accretion.

TEXT AND TRANSLATION ISSUES

As reconstructed, the Greek and Coptic agree.

INTERPRETATIVE COMMENT

This saying coheres to a theme characteristic of the accretions, that is, speculation about the primordial Adam. The believer has become the perfect 'child' by returning to the pre-lapsarian condition of the human being on the seventh day of creation (Genesis 2.2–3).

Such a person has knowledge about the 'place of life'. This knowledge can be used to aid in the redemption of others and centres around the 'childlike' state achieved through encratic performance. The saying accrued between 80 and 120 CE in order to reframe the eschatological Kernel with an encratic and mystical hermeneutic. For more discussion of the meaning of 'child' in the Gospel, see L. 22.1–7.

SOURCE DISCUSSION
G. Quispel thinks that this saying comes from the encratic *Gospel of the Egyptians.*

LITERATURE PARALLELS

Hippolytus, Refutation of All Heresies *5.7*
  'One who seeks will find me in children from seven years, for there, hidden in the fourteenth age, I am revealed.'

Manichaean Psalm Book 192.2–3
  'To the old people with grey hair the little children give instruction; those six years old give instructions to those sixty years old.'

Cf. Matthew 11.25; Luke 10.21; Infancy Gospel of Thomas 7.3

SELECT BIBLIOGRAPHY
Quispel (1981: 265).

Logion 4.2–3

[2] 'For many who are first will be last, [3] ((the last will be first)),'

P.Oxy. 654.25–26

ὅτι πολλοὶ ἔσονται π[ρῶτοι ἔσχατοι] οἱ ἔσχατοι πρῶτοι

'For many who are first [will be last,] the last will be first,'

NHC II 2.33.9

ϪⲈ ⲞⲨⲚ ϨⲀϨ ⲚϢⲞⲢⲡ ⲚⲀⲢ̄ ϨⲀⲈ

'For many who are first will be last,'

ATTRIBUTION
Kernel saying.

TEXT AND TRANSLATION ISSUES
The Coptic does not have 'the last will be first'. The simplest explanation for this is accidental error in the Coptic manuscript due to scribal error, either accidental or deliberate.

  I have reconstructed the lacunae in line 25, π[ρῶτοι ἔσχατοι] instead of π[ρῶτοι ἔσχατοι καὶ] as H. Attridge has reconstructed it. There is only room for 12 letters. So the 15 letters proposed by Attridge looks to me to be implausible.

  In line 25, OTI is written above the line between ΣΕΤΕ and ΠΟΛΛΟΙ.

INTERPRETATIVE COMMENT

In the Kernel Gospel, this saying appears to have functioned rhetorically in the opening call to the first speech about eschatological urgency. The hearer is told in L. 2.1 that he or she must seek the truth, and is promised in L. 2.2–4 an amazing journey that will ultimately lead to 'rest'. In L. 4.2–3, the hearer seems to be taught that, contrary to the wisdom of this world, those who think they already know the truth do not, while those who think they are ignorant will be the ones to gain knowledge: 'for many who are first will be last, (((the last will be first)))'.

Once L. 4.1 and 4.4 accrued, the meaning of the saying would have shifted. In the complete Gospel, L. 4.2–3 would have referred specifically to those honoured celibates in the community who had been restored as 'little children' in the garden of Eden. The traditional hierarchy – adult over child – had been replaced with a new hierarchy – child over adult. This childlike state was characterized by encratic performance, particularly the rejection of marriage and sexual behaviour.

SOURCE DISCUSSION

W. Schrage says that the change from δέ to ⲭⲉ cannot be attributed to scribal error since it is also found in the P. Oxy. fragment (ὅτι), and makes good sense. Although he thinks that L.4.2 depends on Coptic versions of Matthew 19.30 and Mark 10.31, he concludes that L. 4.2(–3) may represent an independent variant. M. Fieger disagrees, claiming that L. 4.2–3 is dependent on Matthew and Mark. The Thomasine author, he says, altered the δέ to ⲭⲉ for theological purposes, although the apocalyptic colour of the Synoptic source is retained.

LITERATURE PARALLELS

Matthew 20.16 (Qmatt)
    'So the last will be first, and the first will be last.'

Luke 13.30 (Qluke)
    'Indeed, some are last who will be first, and some are first who will be last.'

Mark 10.31
    'But many who are first will be last, and the last will be first.'

Matthew 19.30
    'But many who are first will be last, and the last will be first.'

Cf. *Epistle of Barnabas* 6.13

SELECT BIBLIOGRAPHY
Fieger (1991: 29–30); Schrage (1964a: 32–33).

Logion 4.4

⁴'and they will become single people.'

P.Oxy. 654.26–27

    καὶ [εἰς γενήσου]σιν

    'and [they will become single people].'

NHC II 2.33.10

ⲁⲩⲱ ⲛ̅ⲥⲉϣⲱⲡⲉ ⲟⲩⲁ ⲟⲩⲱⲧ

'and they will become single people.'

ATTRIBUTION
Accretion.

TEXT AND TRANSLATION ISSUES
The reconstruction of the Greek is difficult given the 10 to 12 spaces available to complete the lacunae. M. Marcovich's suggestion, [εἰς ἓν καταντήσου]σιν, has been followed by H. Attridge even though it requires 15 letters to complete the lacunae. Marcovich cites Ephesians 4.13, John 17.11, 21, 22 and 23 as parallels to this expression in order to give his reconstruction credibility. But none of these passages provides a complete parallel to L. 4.4. Ephesians uses the verb as a reference to unity but does not have εἰς ἓν, while John uses the expression εἰς ἓν with a completely different verb. Given these facts, I think it best to look at other options. I favour O. Hofius' reconstruction, [εἰς γενήσου]σιν. It not only fits the available space, but it also agrees with the Coptic. Forms of ⲟⲩⲁ ⲡⲟⲩⲱⲧ were used commonly to translate εἰς, rendering the notion 'single one' or 'single person' (Crum, 494a) while ϣⲱⲡⲉ translated γίγνομαι (Crum, 577b).

INTERPRETATIVE COMMENT
Accrual took place in the late first century between 80 and 120 CE when the community was developing an encratic praxis in order to gain the rewards of Paradise while still living on earth. This interpretative clause contains vocabulary characteristic of the accretions, the expression ⲟⲩⲁ ⲟⲩⲱⲧ. It theologically points to the single or unmarried person who has regained the lost condition of Adam, the androgynous primordial Anthropos. The person has returned to paradise as a child, no longer harrassed by sexual differentiation and eros. A. Guillaumont and A.F.J. Klijn followed by F.-E. Morard think that ⲟⲩⲁ ⲟⲩⲱⲧ and ⲙⲟⲛⲁⲭⲟⲥ are equivalent expressions. See L. 16.4 for further discussion.

The attachment of this interpretative clause to L. 4.2–3 served to reinterpret the old Kernel saying. In so doing, celibacy was promoted as the hierarchical ideal rather than marriage. Typically the married person was considered blessed in society. But this community was suggesting that it was the perpetual virgin that was blessed, the one who had returned to the childlike state of the prelapsarian Adam.

LITERATURE PARALLELS
See L. 16, 22, 23, 48 and 106

SELECT BIBLIOGRAPHY
Guillaumont (1981: 202–203); Hofius (1960: 32–34); Kee (1963); Marcovich (1969: 60–61); Morard (1973: 362–77; 1975).

Logion 5.1–2

[1]Jesus said, 'Understand what is in front of you, and what is hidden from you will be revealed to you. [2]For there is nothing hidden that will not be manifested.'

P.Oxy. 654.27–31

¹λέγει Ἰη(σοῦ)ς [γνῶθι τὸ ὂν ἔμπροσ]θεν τῆς ὄψεώς σου καὶ [τὸ κεκαλυμμένον] ἀπό
σου ἀποκαλυφ<θ>ήσετ[αί σοι ²οὐ γάρ ἐσ]τιν κρυπτὸν ὃ οὐ φανε[ρὸν γενήσεται] καὶ
θεθαμμένον ὃ ο[ὐκ ἐγερθήσεται]

Jesus said, '[Understand what is in] front of you, and [what is hidden] from you will be
revealed [to you. For there is nothing] hidden that will not be manifested, nor buried that
[will not be raised.]'

NHC II 2.33.10–14

ⲠⲈⲬⲈ ⲓⲥ ⲤⲞⲨⲰⲚ ⲠⲈⲦⲘ̅ⲠⲘ̅ⲦⲞ Ⲙ̅ⲠⲈⲔϨⲞ ⲈⲂⲞⲖ ⲀⲨⲰ ⲠⲈⲐⲎⲠ ⲈⲢⲞⲔ
ϤⲚⲀϬⲰⲖⲠ ⲈⲂⲞⲖ ⲚⲀⲔ Ⲙ̅Ⲛ̅ ⲖⲀⲀⲨ ⲄⲀⲢ ⲈϤϨⲎⲠ ⲈϤⲚⲀⲞⲨⲰⲚϨ ⲈⲂⲞⲖ
ⲀⲚ

Jesus said, 'Understand what is in front of you, and what is hidden from you will be
revealed to you. ²For there is nothing hidden that will not be manifested.'

ATTRIBUTION
Kernel saying.

TEXT AND TRANSLATION ISSUES
'Understand what is in front of you', literally reads, 'understand what is in front of your
face'.

The Greek witnesses an accretion in L. 5.2 not found in the Coptic, 'nor buried that
[will not be resurrected]'. The saying is a well-known one from Egyptian burial practices.
There is an inscription cited by J. Fitzmyer found on a burial shroud from the fifth or sixth
century that reads: 'Jesus says, "There is nothing buried which will not be resurrected."'
Since the content does not cohere with other *Thomas* logia and the saying is known in
Egypt, it is probable that the Greek represents a late accretion brought into the text by a
scribe. A saying that once referred to the acquisition of truth from Jesus has become in the
Greek text a confession for the empty tomb and the future resurrection of the believer.

INTERPRETATIVE COMMENT
This saying is one of two admonitions leading off the first speech in the Kernel Gospel,
calling hearers to seek the truth. Jesus promises to reveal what has previously been hidden
because 'there is nothing hidden that will not be manifested'.

In the complete Gospel, this accretive admonition is repeated in L. 6.4–5. The saying
signalled that new previously secret sayings of Jesus as well as a new hermeneutic were
being taught. So careful attention was to be paid to the new words and the interpretation
provided.

SOURCE DISCUSSION
Based on a comparison with Coptic New Testament parallels, W. Schrage says that L. 5.2
and 6.4 are dependent on Luke since they agree with Luke 8.17, Luke's revision of Mark
4.22. J. Sieber says that this is not the case since L. 5.2 and 6.4 are not the same saying in
the Greek papyrus although the Coptic translations are similar. So L. 6.4 at least cannot be
dependent on Luke 8.17 since its Greek text is quite divergent from Luke. C. Tuckett says
that, because L. 5.2 agrees with Luke's redaction of Mark (ὃ οὐ for Mark's μή ἵνα),
Thomas appears to know Luke's finished Gospel. Since we have the Greek from the Oxy-
ryhnchus fragment, Tuckett is fairly certain here. Because Sieber does not see Luke 8.17

as an example of Lukan redaction of Mark, but due to one of Luke's sources, he does not think that dependence is certain. In his conclusion he allows for the possibility that Luke was the source because it is *possible* that Luke 8.17 is an editorial revision of Mark 4.22.

I question the limited scope of the agreement in this case, something H. McArthur questioned even though he feels strongly that *Thomas* is dependent on the Synoptics. Is this phrase enough to *prove* Lukan dependence especially when the rest of L. 5.2 is wildly divergent from Luke 8.17, particularly the final clause of the passage which is not known in the Thomasine parallel? It is equally plausible in my mind that Luke and *Thomas* represent versions of the saying which independently were developed in similar directions as for this clause, but, in different directions as for the details, as is common in oral performance. That these types of conjunctions were flexible is proven by the parallel in L. 6.5 which instead of οὐ ἐστιν...ὃ οὐ reads οὐδὲν ἐστιν...ὃ οὐ.

LITERATURE PARALLELS

Matthew 10.26 (Qmatt)
'For nothing is covered that will not be revealed, or hidden that will not be known.'

Luke 12.2 (Qluke)
'Nothing is covered up that will not be revealed, or hidden that will not be known.'

Mark 4.22
'For there is nothing hidden except to be revealed; nor is anything secret, except to come to light.'

Luke 8.17
'For nothing is hidden that will not be revealed, nor is anything secret that will not become known and come to light.'

Pseudo-Clementine Recognitions *3.13*
'For if you had been willing to hear, that saying would have been exemplified in you, of him who said that "there is nothing hidden which shall not be known, nor covered which shall not be disclosed".'

Manichaean Kephalaia *65*
'Know what is in front of your face, and then what is hidden from you will be revealed to you.'

SELECT BIBLIOGRAPHY
Fitzmyer (1971: 383); McArthur (1959/1960: 287); Schrage (1964a: 34–37); Sieber (1966: 107–10, 262); Tuckett (1988: 145–46).

Logion 6.1

[1](([His disciples] questioned [him] and said, 'How should we fast? [How should we pray?] How [should we give alms?] What [diet] should we observe?))'

P.Oxy. 654.32–36

[1][ἐ]ετάζουσιν αὐτὸν ο[ι μαθηταὶ αὐτοῦ καὶ λέ]γουσιν πῶς νηστεύ[σομεν καὶ πῶς προσευ ὁμ]εθα καὶ πῶς [ἐλεημοσύνην ποιήσομεν κα]ὶ τί παρατηρήσ[ομεν περὶ τῶν βρωμάτων]

[His disciples] questioned [him] and said, 'How should we fast? [How should we pray?] [How should we give alms?] What [diet] should we observe?'

NHC II 2.33.14–17

¹ⲁⲩϫⲛⲟⲩϥ ⲛ̄ϭⲓ ⲛⲉϥⲙⲁⲑⲏⲧⲏⲥ ⲡⲉϫⲁⲩ ⲛⲁϥ ϫⲉ ⲕⲟⲩⲱϣ
ⲉⲧⲣⲛ̄ⲣ̄ⲛⲏⲥⲧⲉⲩⲉ ⲁⲩⲱ ⲉϣ ⲧⲉ ⲑⲉ ⲉⲛⲁϣⲗⲏⲗ ⲉⲛⲁ† ⲉⲗⲉⲏⲙⲟⲥⲩⲛⲏ
ⲁⲩⲱ ⲉⲛⲁⲣ̄ⲡⲁⲣⲁⲧⲏⲣⲉⲓ ⲉⲟⲩ ⲛ̄ϭⲓ ⲟⲩⲱⲙ

His disciples questioned him and said to him, 'Do you want us to fast? How should we pray and give alms? And what diet should we observe?'

ATTRIBUTION
Accretion.

TEXT AND TRANSLATION ISSUES
The structure of the questions differs substantially in the Greek and the Coptic. The questions have a more parallel structure in the Greek than in the Coptic. The Greek reads, 'How should we fast? How should we pray? How should we give alms? What diet should we observe?' The Coptic reads, 'Do you want us to fast? How should we pray and give alms? And what diet should we observe?' The Coptic questions appear to have been revised to reflect the practices of later Christians who no longer wished to continue obligatory fasting practices. For these reasons, I consider the Greek questions older and prefer them in my translation.

INTERPRETATIVE COMMENT
This accretion represents questions that the later Thomasine community had regarding the traditional Jewish practices considered customary by the earlier community. They accrued in the Gospel between 60 and 100 CE. The response to these questions in found in L. 14.1–3. For additional comment, refer to L. 14.1–3.

SOURCE DISCUSSION
R. Grant sees L. 6.1 and L. 14.1–3 as dependent upon Matthew 6.1–8. He notes the reverse order of items and suggests the confusion of Naassene exegesis as the culprit. J. Sieber notes correctly that mere reference to three practices is not enough evidence to marshal dependence, especially when the material appears in L. 6.1 in an interrogative form rather than a statement as we find in Matthew. He also notes that the material follows a different sequence from Matthew with other sayings not in Matthew clustering around the material.

LITERATURE PARALLELS

Liber Graduum 20.10
'And he showed them how they should fast and how they should pray and how they should overcome death and how they should destroy sin and that they should teach others as the Lord had taught them.'

Cf. *Liber Graduum* 20.9; L. 14.1–3

SELECT BIBLIOGRAPHY
Grant (1959: 176); Sieber (1966: 50–52).

Logion 6.2–3

²Jesus said, 'Do not tell lies ³and what you hate, do not do.'

P.Oxy. 654.36–37

²λέγει Ἰη(σοῦ)ς [μὴ ψεύδεσθε ³καὶ ὅτι μισ]εῖται μὴ ποιεῖ[τε]

Jesus said, ['Do not tell lies and what] you hate, do not do.'

NHC II 2.33.18–19

²ⲡⲉⲭⲉ ⲓ̅ⲥ̅ ⲭⲉ ⲙ̅ⲡⲣ̅ ⲭⲉ ϭⲟⲗ ³ⲁⲩⲱ ⲡⲉⲧⲉⲧⲙ̅ⲙⲟⲥⲧⲉ ⲙ̅ⲙⲟϥ ⲙ̅ⲡⲣ̅ⲁⲁϥ

Jesus said, 'Do not tell lies and what you hate, do not do.'

ATTRIBUTION
Kernel saying.

TEXT AND TRANSLATION ISSUES
As reconstructed, the Greek agrees with the Coptic.

The negative form of the 'golden rule' (Matthew 7.12) is found in Syriac literature frequently (Ephrem; Aphraates; Philoxenus; the *Didascalia*; and the *Liber Graduum*). This has led R. Connolly to conclude that the Diatessaron contained the negative form of the 'golden rule'. It should also be noted that the Western Text manuscript D contains a negative form of the 'golden rule' in Acts 15.20 and 29 according to B. Metzger.

INTERPRETATIVE COMMENT
This saying appears to have formed the ethical foundation of the words of Jesus in the Kernel Gospel. In the first speech, urgent preparation for God's Judgement is connected to this commandment. In the complete Gospel, this set of commandments serves to answer the disciples' questions about religious practices found in L. 6.1. For further discussion, see L. 6.4–5 and 14.1–3.

SOURCE DISCUSSION
G. Quispel thinks that this saying came from the *Gospel of the Nazarenes* or another Jewish Christian Gospel.

LITERATURE PARALLELS

James 3.14
   'Do not boast and be false to the truth.'

Colossians 3.9
   'Do not lie to one another, seeing that you have put off the old nature with its practices.'

Ephesians 4.25
   'Therefore, putting away falsehood, let every one speak the truth with his neighbour, for we are members one of another.'

Matthew 7.12
> 'In everything, do to others as you would have them do to you.'

Tobit 4.15
> 'Do to no one what you hate.'

Didache *1.2*
> 'Whatever you wish not to be done to you, do not to another.'

Pseudo-Clementine Recognitions *8.56*
> 'For almost the whole rule of our actions is summed up in this, that what we are unwilling to suffer we should not do to others.'

Pseudo-Clementine Homilies *2.6*
> '...he ought not to wrong another, through his not wishing himself to be wronged.'

Epistula Apostolorum *18*
> 'What you do not want done to you, that do to no one else.'

Liber Graduum *15.16*
> 'Love the Lord your God with all your heart and other people as yourself, and do not do to your neighbour what is hateful to you, and as you want people to do to you, so also do to them.'

Liber Graduum *148.4–5, 176.10–11, 376.2–4, and 653.26–56.1*
> 'What you hate, do not do to your neighbour.'

Aphraates, Hom. *23*
> 'Whatsoever is hateful to you, do not do to your neighbor.'

Philoxemus, Dis. *9*
> 'Whatsoever is hateful to you, do not do to your neighbour.'

Ephrem, Comm. Paul, *p. 9*
> 'Whatsoever is hateful to you, do not do to your neighbour.'

b. Shabb. *31a*
> 'When he went before Hillel, he said to him, "What is hateful to you, do not to your neighbour: that is the whole Torah, while the rest is the commentary thereof. Go and learn it."'

Sentences of Sextus *179*
> 'Do not do the things you do not want to happen to you.'

Ahmad ibn Hanbal, al-Zuhd, *p. 99 (no. 332)*
> 'And that which you do not wish done to you, do not do it to others.'

Agreements in Syrian Gospels, Western Text and Diatessaron
Matthew 7.12 in Aphr Phil Ephrem Didasc LibGrad
> Negative form

Acts 15.20 and 29 in D
> Negative form

SELECT BIBLIOGRAPHY
Baker (1965/1966: 51); Connolly (1934); Metzger (1975: 430); Quispel (1981: 265).

> ## *Logion 6.4–5*
>
> [4]((([For everything, when faced] with truth, is brought [to light. [5]For there is nothing] hidden [that will not be manifested.])))'

P.Oxy. 654.37–40

[4][ὅτι πάντα ἐνώπιον τ]ῆς ἀληθ[ε]ίας ἀν[αφαίνεται [5]οὐδὲν γάρ ἐστι]ν ἀ[π]οκεκρ [υμμένον ὃ οὐ φανερὸν ἔσται]

'[For everything, when faced] with truth, is brought [to light. [5]For there is nothing] hidden [that will not be manifested.]'

NHC II 2.33.20–23

[4]ⲬⲈ ⲤⲈⲄⲞⲖⲠ ⲦⲎⲢⲞⲨ ⲈⲂⲞⲖ ⲘⲠⲈⲘⲦⲞ ⲈⲂⲞⲖ ⲚⲦⲠⲈ [5]ⲘⲚ ⲖⲀⲀⲨ ⲄⲀⲢ ⲈϤⲈⲎⲠ ⲈϤⲚⲀⲞⲨⲰⲚϨ ⲈⲂⲞⲖ ⲀⲚ ⲀⲨⲰ ⲘⲚ ⲖⲀⲀⲨ ⲈϤⲈⲞⲂⲤ ⲈⲨⲚⲀϬⲰ ⲞⲨⲈϢⲚ ϬⲞⲖⲠϤ

'For everything, in the face of heaven, is uncovered. For there is nothing hidden that will not be manifested, and there is nothing covered that will not be revealed.'

ATTRIBUTION
Accretion.

TEXT AND TRANSLATION ISSUES
L. 6.4 in Greek reads 'the face of truth' while the Coptic has 'the face of heaven'. The Greek should probably be considered earlier since the error seems to have occurred in the transmission of the Coptic text where ⲘⲈ or 'truth' became ⲠⲈ or 'heaven'.

In L. 6.4, ⲀⲚ is inserted above the line between ⲈⲂⲞⲖ and ⲀⲨⲰ.

The Coptic witnesses an additional phrase not present in the Greek version, 'and there is nothing covered that will not be revealed' (L. 6.6). This is best attributed to a scribe who wished to align the saying to his knowledge of the biblical tradition. So I understand it to be a late accretion paralleling the version of the saying from the Synoptic Gospels and probably dependent on them (Matthew 10.26 and Luke 12.2). For this reason, I prefer the Greek in my translation.

INTERPRETATIVE COMMENT
L. 6.5 is a restatement of L. 5. This repeated saying probably was not part of the Kernel Gospel. It appears to have accrued in the text sometime between 80 and 120 CE to try to make sense of L. 6.1–3 which is a problematic series of sayings since the answer to the questions posed in L. 6.1 does not appear until 14.1–3. It may be that the order of the sayings was compromised early in the transmission of the Gospel since both the Greek and the Coptic agree. It is difficult to determine whether this corruption was accidental or deliberate. I imagine that it is the result of a leaf that was reversed in the process of copying or the result of someone shifting either L. 6.1 or L. 14.1–3 to an alternative place in the Gospel in the course of performance (see L. 14.1–3). The separation of the questions from the answer caused interpretative problems since L. 6.2–3 was not naturally a good answer to the questions in L. 6.1. So a version of L. 5 was repeated following L. 6.3. This shifted the meaning from the negative 'golden rule', 'do not do what you hate to

have done to you', to 'do not do anything you hate to do' because your hatred for it will be revealed at some time and show you to be a hypocrite.

SOURCE DISCUSSION
W. Schrage thinks that L. 6.5 is dependent on Luke 8.17 because it is in agreement with the Lukan version of Mark 4.22. Although this may be the case in the Coptic, J. Sieber notes that it is not the case in the Greek. L. 6.5 does not agree word-for-word with Luke 8.17 according to the Greek fragment.

L. 6.6, present only in the Coptic version, Schrage says is dependent upon Quelle or Mark 4.22, particularly the reference to the second person singular. Given the fact that the Greek papyrus does not contain this phrase, it is quite plausible that it is a late scribal addition dependent on the scribe's memory of the saying in Matthew 10.26 and Luke 12.2.

LITERATURE PARALLELS
See L. 5.

SELECT BIBLIOGRAPHY
Schrage (1964a: 34–37); Sieber (1966: 107–10).

Logion 7.1–2

[1]Jesus said, 'Blessed is the lion that the person will eat, and the lion becomes man. [2]And cursed is the person whom the lion eats, [[and the man becomes a lion]].'

P.Oxy. 654.40–42

[1][- - - μα]κάρι[ός] ἐστιν [ο λέων ὃν ἄνθρωπος ἐσθίει καὶ ο λέ]ων ἔστα[ι ἄνθρωπος [2]καὶ ἀνάθεμα ο ἄνθρωπος] ὃν [λέγων ἐσθίει *et cetera*]

NHC II 2.33.24–29

[1]ⲡⲉϫⲉ ⲓⲥ ⲟⲩⲙⲁⲕⲁⲣⲓⲟⲥ ⲡⲉ ⲡⲙⲟⲩⲉⲓ ⲡⲁⲉⲓ ⲉⲧⲉ ⲡⲣⲱⲙⲉ ⲛⲁⲟⲩⲟⲙϥ
ⲁⲩⲱ ⲛ̄ⲧⲉ ⲡⲙⲟⲩⲉⲓ ϣⲱⲡⲉ ⲣ̄ⲣⲱⲙⲉ [2]ⲁⲩⲱ ϥⲃⲏⲧ ⲛ̄ϭⲓ ⲡⲣⲱⲙⲉ ⲡⲁⲉⲓ
ⲉⲧⲉ ⲡⲙⲟⲩⲉⲓ ⲛⲁⲟⲩⲟⲙϥ ⲁⲩⲱ [[ⲡⲣⲱⲙⲉ ⲛⲁϣⲱⲡⲉ ⲙ̄ⲙⲟⲩⲉⲓ]]

Jesus said, 'Blessed is the lion that the person will eat, and the lion becomes man. And cursed is the person whom the lion eats, [[and the man becomes a lion]].'

ATTRIBUTION
Accretion.

TEXT AND TRANSLATION ISSUES
'Person' literally reads, 'man'.

The final phrase in Coptic, 'and cursed is the human being whom the lion eats, and the lion becomes human' (ⲡⲙⲟⲩⲉⲓ ⲛⲁϣⲱⲡⲉ ⲣ̄ⲣⲱⲙⲉ) appears corrupted. It should probably be amended, 'and the human being becomes a lion' (ⲡⲣⲱⲙⲉ ⲛⲁϣⲱⲡⲉ ⲙ̄ⲙⲟⲩⲉⲓ) which recovers the lost structure and sense of the saying. So I follow A. Guillaumont's emendation here.

INTERPRETATIVE COMMENT

The content of this logion coheres with the emphasis in the accretions on the need to control the bodily passions in order to transform one's soul into the image of God, the primordial 'Man' or Anthropos. For this reason I have retained the masculine reference to 'man' since this would have been important to the original hermeneutic. According to H.M. Jackson's study, the logion states, in metaphorical terms, that the believer has transformed him- or herself from a state of bestiality when the passions controlled the soul to a state of 'manliness' when reason ruled the soul. The image is commonly found in Hellenistic literature.

The saying accrued in the Gospel between 80 and 120 CE when the text was being adapted, incorporating a new hermeneutic which emphasized the individual's need for self-control in order to restore his or her image to its original beauty, that of the Anthropos. The lesson would have been particularly important to the later encratic and largely Gentile population of the Thomasine community.

SOURCE DISCUSSION

G. Quispel attributes the source of this saying to a Hermetic anthology.

LITERATURE PARALLELS

Sayings of the Desert Fathers, *Poimen 178*
> 'Again, he (Poimen) said, "David, when he fought the lion, held him by the throat and straightaway dispatched him. And if we too hold ourselves by the throat and by the belly, with the help of God we shall be victorious over the invisible lion."'

Manichaean Psalm *257*
> 'This lion that is within me, I have strangled him. I have turned him out of my soul, him who ever defiles me.'

Manichaean Psalm *284*
> 'The skins of the lion which clothes my limbs, I have stripped them off.'

Cf. Plato, *Republic* 436A–441C; 588B–589B

SELECT BIBLIOGRAPHY

Guillaumont *et al.* (1959: 4); Jackson (1985: 175–213); Quispel (1981: 265).

Logion 8.1–3

[1]And he said, 'The human being is like a wise fisherman who cast his net into the sea. He drew it up from the sea full of small fish. [2]From among them he found a fine large fish. [3]The wise fisherman cast all of the small fish back into the sea and chose the large fish without difficulty.'

NHC II 2.33.28–34.3

[1]ⲁⲩⲱ ⲡⲉϫⲁϥ ϫⲉ ⲉⲡⲣⲱⲙⲉ ⲧⲛ̄ⲧⲱⲛ ⲁⲩⲟⲩⲱϩⲉ ⲣ̄ⲣⲙⲛ̄ϩⲏⲧ ⲡⲁⲉⲓ
ⲛ̄ⲧⲁϩⲛⲟⲩϫⲉ ⲛ̄ⲧⲉϥⲁⲃⲱ ⲉⲑⲁⲗⲁⲥⲥⲁ ⲁϥⲥⲱⲕ ⲙ̄ⲙⲟⲥ ⲉϩⲣⲁⲓ̈ ϩⲛ̄
ⲑⲁⲗⲁⲥⲥⲁ ⲉⲥⲙⲉϩ ⲛ̄ⲧⲃⲧ ⲛ̄ⲕⲟⲩⲉⲓ [2]ⲛ̄ϩⲣⲁⲓ̈ ⲛ̄ϩⲏⲧⲟⲩ ⲁϥϩⲉ ⲁⲩⲛⲟϭ
ⲛ̄ⲧⲃ̄ⲧ ⲉⲛⲁⲛⲟⲩϥ [3]ⲛ̄ϭⲓ ⲡⲟⲩⲱϫⲉ ⲣ̄ⲣⲙⲛ̄ϩⲏⲧ ⲁϥⲛⲟⲩϫⲉ ⲛ̄ⲛⲕⲟⲩⲉⲓ
ⲧⲏⲣⲟⲩ ⲛ̄ⲧⲃ̄ⲧ ⲉⲃⲟⲗ ⲉⲡⲓⲧⲛ ⲉⲑⲁⲗⲁⲥⲥⲁ ⲁϥⲥⲱⲧⲡ ⲙ̄ⲡⲛⲟϭ ⲛ̄ⲧⲃ̄ⲧ
ⲭⲱⲣⲓⲥ ϩⲓⲥⲉ

ATTRIBUTION
Kernel saying.

TEXT AND TRANSLATION ISSUES
G. Quispel sees a Semitic substratum beneath ⲤⲰⲦⲠ, 'to choose', and the parallel in Matthew 13.48, συλλέγειν, 'to collect'. He finds that the Aramaic ܓܒܐ is ambivalent and can express either 'to choose' or 'to collect'. A. Guillaumont traces this ambiguity to the Syriac ܓܒܐ which has both meanings. T. Baarda, in fact, argues that only the Syriac has this ambiguity. The Aramaic ܓܒܐ, he says, is restricted to the meaning 'to collect'. So Tatian, he concludes, is not referring to an independent tradition connected with *Thomas* as Quispel argues, but has simply translated Matthew's συνέλε αν into Syriac using this ambivalent term.

INTERPRETATIVE COMMENT
A number of scholars including T. Baarda have seen the reference to 'the human being' as redactional since Matthew has 'Kingdom of Heaven'. However, in L. 8 we have a parable about the fisherman while in Matthew the parable is about the net. So the corresponding 'human being' and 'Kingdom' make sense within each version, making the versions appear to be independent oral versions of the story rather than the result of literary redaction. R. Cameron has noted that other Thomasine parables introduce individuals as the subject of comparison (L. 9; 21.1; 57; 63.1; 64.1; 65.1; 76.1; 96.1; 97; 98; 107; 109). So the reference to the fisherman may be traditional, he thinks, not redactional. He defines the parable as a typical sapiential parable, emphasizing the individual's journey to discover wisdom.

The parable, however, does not say that the object of the person's pursuit is 'wisdom'. Rather, the fisherman is noted to be wise because of the decision he makes in the story, casting back the small fish and exclusively keeping the large. So in the context of the Kernel Gospel, this parable probably signalled the important decision that each person who follows Jesus has to make. They must give exclusive allegiance to him as God's Prophet. As the accretions accumulated, the expression ⲠⲢⲰⲘⲈ may well have been understood to refer to the Anthropos, Jesus, who selects the one worthy disciple from the many, an interpretation G. Quispel has suggested.

SOURCE DISCUSSION
W. Schrage, B. Gärtner, R. McL. Wilson, R. Kasser, and E. Haenchen find L. 8 to be a Gnostic redaction of Matthew 13.47–50, a redaction which so altered the material that any Matthean redactional traits no longer persist.

After making a thorough examination of this saying in several sources, T. Baarda concludes that we have two different forms of the parable in *Thomas* and Matthew. *Thomas* might have been dependent on Matthew, but we cannot prove this with certainty. J. Sieber states that the case for dependency is very weak since neither Matthew's editorial trace, παλίν, nor the arrangement of parables from Matthew 13 can be detected in *Thomas*. The striking differences between L. 8 and Matthew 13.47–50 strengthen the case for independence in his mind. In fact, C.-H. Hunzinger views L. 8 as an independent tradition which was a twin parable *in form* to Matthew's parable of the pearl merchant and L. 76. In fact, form critics like J.D. Crossan, S. Davies and H. Koester have assessed the parallel structure and simple meaning of the parable to be a more original version of Matthew 13.47–48, lacking the allegorical interpretation and the secondary recasting of the parable after the pattern of the Parable of the Weeds as Matthew has done.

G. Quispel argues that the parallel found in Philoxenus witnesses to the Diatessaronic text of Matthew 13.47–50 and indirectly witnesses the independence of the Gospel tradition in *Thomas*. He thinks that the source for this saying was the *Gospel of the Nazarenes* or another Jewish Christian Gospel. T. Baarda has written a rebuttal, arguing that there is strong agreement between Philoxenus and the Peshitta so that the view that Philoxenus used the Diatessaron cannot be sustained. However, we should note that there is also Clement of Alexandria who seems aware of a similar variant. According to M. Mees, Clement knew a good Egyptian text related to the Vaticanus and the Sinaiticus and P. Bodmer 75. He also knew a Jewish Christian tradition current in Alexandria. Quispel thinks this to be the same tradition as reflected in Tatian. T. Baarda's response that Clement does not *have* to be dependent on a Jewish-Christian extra-canonical source for his version of the parable is not convincing in my opinion because it does not explain the agreements between Clement and L. 8. Clement could have created the parable, redacting Matthew, I suppose. But then how do we explain the parable turning up also in *Thomas*? A much simpler hypothesis from a tradition critic's standpoint is that L. 8 and Clement are familiar with a version of the parable circulating independent of the Synoptics.

Baarda has studied the version of the parable preserved in the *Heliand* in response to Quispel's use of it as further evidence for a Diatessaronic reading comparable to L. 8. Baarda concludes that the author of the Heliand did not have a Diatessaronic text before him of the type that Quispel suggests in his reconstruction.

Most recently, J. Liebenberg has concluded that the differences in performance elements and focus of the two parables means that L. 8 cannot be dependent on the Matthean performance of the parable. The versions must represent 'two completely different performances of a popular theme in antiquity'.

LITERATURE PARALLELS

Matthew 13.47–50
> [47]'Again, the kingdom of heaven is like a net that was thrown into the sea and caught fish of every kind. [48]When it was full, they drew it ashore, sat down, and put the good into baskets but threw out the bad. [49]So it will be at the end of the age. [50]The angels will come out and separate the evil from the righteous and throw them into the furnace of fire, where there will be weeping and gnashing of teeth.'

Clement of Alexandria, Strom. *6.11.95*
> 'For the present I do not comment on the parable in the gospel which says, "The Kingdom of Heaven is like a man who threw a drag-net into the sea and from the great number of fish caught makes a selection of the better ones."'

Clement of Alexandria, Strom. *1.1.16*
> 'For there is the one pearl among the small pearls, and the good fish in the large catch of fish.'

Pseudo-Macarius, Hom. *15.52*
> 'As many kinds of fish fall into a net and the least useful ones immediately are tossed back into the sea, so also the net of grace is spread over all men and seeks tranquillity. But men do not surrender and for this reason they are thrown back again into the same depths of darkness.'

Philoxenos, Hom. *1.9*
> 'Then one will see the fisherman cast his net into the sea of the world and fill it with fish, small and great...at that time he will draw his net and bring it up to the shore of the sea, as he said it, and he will choose the good fish and put them in his vessels...and he

will throw away the wicked ones into utter darkness, where there will be wailing and gnashing of teeth.'

Aesop's Fable, Babrius 4
'A fisherman drew in a net that he had just cast, and it happened to be full of a variety of fish. The small one among the fish fled to the bottom and slipped out of the porous mesh, but the large one was caught and was laid stretched out in the boat. A way to be safe and clear of trouble is to be small, but seldom will you see a person large in reputation who escapes danger.'

AGREEMENTS IN SYRIAN GOSPELS, WESTERN TEXT AND DIATESSARON

Matthew 13.47–48 in Aphr
fisherman << net

Matthew 13.47–48 in Clem T^{EC}
who cast his net into the sea

Matthew 13.47–48 in T^P
full of...*fish*

Matthew 13.47–48 in T^V
large (and) good << good

Matthew 13.47–48 in a b S C T^{NL}
+ fish

Matthew 13.47–48 in d e k Clem Philox Chrys lat S C P T^P T^{EC} T^A T^T $T^{NL}T^L$
chose << collected

Matthew 13.47–48 in T^A
+ fish[3]

SELECT BIBLIOGRAPHY
Baarda (1992; 1994a; 1994b); Bauer (1962: 283–84); Cameron (1986: 25–26); Crossan (1973: 34); Davies (1983: 9); Gärtner (1961: 233–34); Guillaumont (1981: 197–98); Haenchen (1961: 48); Hunzinger (1960: 217–20); Kasser (1961: 40); Koester (1990: 104); Liebenberg (2001: 275); Mees (1970); Morrice (1985); Nagel (1969b); Quispel (1967a: 112; 1971b; 1974b; 1975c); Schrage (1964a: 37); Sieber (1966: 187–89); Wilson (1960a: 40).

Logion 8.4

[4]'Whoever has ears to hear should listen!'

NHC II 2.34.2–3

ⲡⲉⲧⲉ ⲟⲩⲛ̄ ⲙⲁⲁϫⲉ ⲙ̄ⲙⲟϥ ⲉⲥⲱⲧⲙ̄ ⲙⲁⲣⲉϥⲥⲱⲧⲙ̄

ATTRIBUTION
Kernel saying.

INTERPRETATIVE COMMENT
This saying is an admonition to an audience to listen carefully to the orator's speech and draw from it meaning. It is a common heuristic device in early Christian circles repeatedly

used by preachers as a saying prompting reflection on the part of the audience and pause on the part of the speaker, giving him or her time to consider the continuation of the performance.

SOURCE DISCUSSION

This form of the saying is most similar to the one used by Luke and Mark, 'Whoever has ears to hear, let him hear' (although see Matthew 11.15). W. Schrage does not think it possible to argue for *Thomas*' dependence on the Synoptics based on this logion. J. Sieber argues that *Thomas*' free use of the phrase means that he might be using a tradition or source independent of the Synoptics.

LITERATURE PARALLELS

Matthew 11.15; Mark 4.9; Luke 8.8; 14.35
'He who has ears to hear, let him hear.'

Matthew 13.9, 43
'He who has ears, let him hear.'

Mark 4.23; Revelation 13.9
'If anyone has ears to hear, let him hear.'

Revelation 2.7, 11, 17; 3.6; 3.13; 3.22
'He who has an ear, let him hear what the Spirit says to the churches.'

L. 21.5
'Whoever has ears to hear should listen!'

L. 24.2; 63.2; 65.2; 96.2
'Whoever has ears should listen!'

SELECT BIBLIOGRAPHY
Schrage (1964a: 42); Sieber (1966: 177–78).

Logion 9.1–5

[1]Jesus said, 'Look! The sower went out. He filled his hand (with seeds). He cast (them). [2]Some fell on the road. The birds came and gathered them up. [3]Others fell on the rock and did not take root in the earth or put forth ears. [4]And others fell among thorns. They choked the seeds and worms ate them. [5]And others fell on the good earth, and it produced good fruit. It yielded sixty per measure and a hundred and twenty per measure.'

NHC II 2.34.3–13

[1]ⲡⲉϫⲉ ⲓ̄ⲥ̄ ϫⲉ ⲉⲓⲥϩⲏⲏⲧⲉ ⲁϥⲉⲓ ⲉⲃⲟⲗ ⲛ̄ϭⲓ ⲡⲉⲧⲥⲓⲧⲉ ⲁϥⲙⲉϩ ⲧⲟⲟⲧϥ̄ ⲁϥⲛⲟⲩϫⲉ [2]ⲁϩⲟⲉⲓⲛⲉ ⲙⲉⲛ ϩⲉ ⲉϫⲛ̄ ⲧⲉϩⲓⲏ ⲁⲩⲉⲓ ⲛ̄ϭⲓ ⲛ̄ϩⲁⲗⲁⲧⲉ ⲁⲩⲕⲁⲧϥⲟⲩ [3]ϩⲛ̄ⲕⲟⲟⲩⲉ ⲁⲩϩⲉ ⲉϫⲛ̄ ⲧⲡⲉⲧⲣⲁ ⲁⲩⲱ ⲙ̄ⲡⲟⲩϫⲉ ⲛⲟⲩⲛⲉ ⲉⲡⲉⲥⲏⲧ ⲉⲡⲕⲁϩ ⲁⲩⲱ ⲙ̄ⲡⲟⲩⲧⲉⲩⲉ ϩⲙⲥ̄ ⲉϩⲣⲁⲓ̈ ⲉⲧⲡⲉ [4]ⲁⲩⲱ ϩⲛ̄ⲕⲟⲟⲩⲉ ⲁⲩϩⲉ ⲉϫⲛ̄ ⲛ̄ϣⲟⲛ(ⲛ)ⲧⲉ ⲁⲩⲱϭⲧ ⲙ̄ⲡⲉϭⲣⲟϭ ⲁⲩⲱ ⲁⲡϥ̄ⲛ̄ⲧ ⲟⲩⲟⲙⲟⲩ [5]ⲁⲩⲱ ⲁϩⲛ̄ⲕⲟⲟⲩⲉ ϩⲉ ⲉϫⲛ̄ ⲡⲕⲁϩ ⲉⲧⲛⲁⲛⲟⲩϥ ⲁⲩⲱ ⲁϥϯ ⲕⲁⲣⲡⲟⲥ ⲉϩⲣⲁⲓ̈ ⲉⲧⲡⲉ ⲉⲛⲁⲛⲟⲩϥ ⲁϥⲉⲓ ⲛ̄ⲥⲉ ⲉⲥⲟⲧⲉ ⲁⲩⲱ ϣⲉϫⲟⲩⲱⲧ ⲉⲥⲟⲧⲉ

ATTRIBUTION
Kernel saying.

TEXT AND TRANSLATION ISSUES
L. 9.1 lacks 'to sow'. The same omission is found in some Synoptic manuscripts (D Mark 4.3 and A Luke 8.5), in the Bohairic translation of Mark, and some Bohairic manuscripts of Luke. But, because *1 Clement* has the same omission, *Thomas* probably does not represent a defective Western text or Coptic translation.

L. 9.1 does not have 'as he sowed' as all Synoptic manuscripts include. But this phrase is also lacking in Justin Martyr, Aphraates, the Pepysian Harmony and the Heliand.

L. 9.1 includes a phrase not found in the Synoptics, 'He filled his hand (with seeds). He cast (them).' The fourth-century Syrian father Aphraates reads similarly, perhaps indicating knowledge of the Thomasine version. This version appears to have been popular in the east since two Muslim sources also reference this phrase. To 'fill one's hand' is a Semitic expression (Lev. 9.17; Ps. 129.7). *1 Clement* records similarly 'cast seeds' rather than 'sowed'. He may be a witness to this eastern variant of the Sower parable as well. N. Perrin suggests that the expression is an aural mistake, a scribe hearing the verb ܙܐܥ (zaʾer), 'to take a handful', rather than ܙܪܥ (zarʿe), 'seeds'. Although this is a clever solution, if it were correct, the Coptic would not be missing also the verb 'to sow'.

L. 9.2 has 'on the road' while the Synoptics have παρά. Some late manuscripts of the Synoptics read, ἐπί, and a couple of Latin translations and Diatessaronic witnesses read *super*. G. Quispel notes this variant in the Heliand 2388–2403, 'Some seed fell on top of the hard stone. It had no earth to grow and no root to take hold...Some seed fell *on* the hard road...the birds *gathered* it up.' The Syriac version of the *Pseudo-Clementines Recognitions* reads 'on (עַל) the road'. A. Guillaumont notes that 'by' or 'along' appears to be a Greek mistranslation of the Aramaic עַל which means both 'by' or 'on'. The Thomasine version, even in the Coptic, retains an allusion to the earlier Semitism with the word ⲉⲄⲚ. J. Horman does not think a reversion to Aramaic is necessary to explain ⲉⲄⲚ because he feels that παρά τήν ὁδόν in the Synoptics is a difficult expression and only 'invites' correction in the manner indicated by *Thomas*. The problem with this argument is that this reading occurs in other Syrian texts so *Thomas* cannot be an isolated case of correction.

L. 9.2 has 'gathered them up'. No Synoptic manuscript has this, but similar readings are found in Aphraates, Syˢ Matthew 13.4 (and the birds came and gathered it), the Armenian translation of Ephrem's commentary on the Diatessaron ('they gathered it'), Ps.-Ephrem's anti-Marcionite exposition on the Gospels ('and the birds picked it up'), and the Heliand ('the birds picked it up'). Clearly, this reading derives from a Semitic provenance. A. Guillaumont suggests that a Semitic substratum is supported by the fact that the Syriac word ܠܩܛ can mean both 'to gather' and 'to peck' as a bird would pick up a seed with its mouth.

L. 9.3 literally reads, 'did not take root down into the earth nor send ear up to heaven'. Nothing similar is found in the Synoptic manuscript tradition, except Syˢ Matthew 13.6 which reads, 'and because it had not sent a root down into the earth, it withered' and Sahidic Mark which has ⲘⲠⲞⲨϪⲈ ⲠⲞⲨⲚⲈ. G. Quispel notes a simliar variant in the Heliand 2391–2392. Only L. 9.3 has the parallelism characteristic of Semitic poetry.

L. 9.4 reads that 'the worms ate the seed'. This is peculiar in the variants.

L. 9 lacks the allegorical interpretation found in the Synoptics. It is noteworthy that the *Pseudo-Clementine Recognitions* also is unaware of the Synoptic allegory and instead provides an independent tradition of interpretation: 'These are the things which the good teacher spoke in a parable, when he would point out the different attitudes, which are not like each other.'

INTERPRETATIVE COMMENT

In the Kernel Gospel, the logion is part of the rhetoric of a speech about eschatological urgency. The hearers are presented with an analogy, they should be like the seed that fell on good soil and produced good fruit rather than the seed that the birds gathered, or fell on rock or among thorns and did not survive. Their decision is critical since Jesus, they are told in the next saying, is already casting God's Judgement upon the world (L. 10). Their decision to listen to the words of Jesus, sowing them in their hearts, will yield good fruit by the time of Judgement.

R. Cameron's suggestion that the parable is used here only as an analogy for instruction without eschatological implications is based on several parallels from Hellenistic literature (Antiphon, *fragment* 60; Hippocrates, *Law* 3; Seneca, *Epistle* 38.2; Quintilian, *Education of the Orator* 5.11.24; Plutarch, *Education of Children* 2B). But his interpretation does not take into account that the association of the parable with L. 10 illicits an eschatological hermeneutic, suggesting an interpretation much closer to the Synoptics than Hellenistic literature. The eschatological interpretation of this parable appears to have been standard in eastern Christian circles and is remembered also in the *Pseudo-Clementine Homilies* 11.2.1–3: 'Inasmuch as, by long-continued neglect on your part, to your own injury, your mind has caused to sprout many hurtful conceptions about religion, and you have become like land fallow by the carelessness of the husbandman, you need a long time for your purification, that your mind, receiving like good seed the true word that is imparted to you, may not choke it with evil cares, and render it unfruitful with respect to works that are able to save you. Wherefore it behoves those who are careful of their own salvation to hear more constantly, that their sins which have been long multiplying may, in the short time that remains, be matched with constant care for their purification. Since, therefore, no one knows the time of his end, hasten to pluck out the many thorns of your hearts; but not by little and little, for then you cannot be purified, for you have been long fallow.'

As the accretions accumulated, the analogy would have taken on more ascetic, even encratic, overtones. The person who controls his or her passions as suggested in L. 7 would be compared with the seed that fell on good soil and produced good fruit in this parable. Those who had overcome the temptations of the body, putting aside marriage and worldly ventures, would produce manifold fruit by the time of Judgement.

SOURCE DISCUSSION

W. Schrage's analysis suggests that L. 9 is a combination of all three Synoptic accounts. He notes several minor agreements but none which convinces him of dependence. However, he points out that Sahidic Mark 4.6 agrees with L. 9, rendering ⲘⲠⲞⲨⲬⲈ ⲚⲞⲨⲚⲈ or μὴ βάλλειν ρὶζαν for μὴ ἔχειν. Because of this, he argues for dependence. C. Tuckett attempts to revive this argument but offers no further insight. J. Horman has made a detailed analysis of this parable, comparing it to the Coptic and Greek New Testament versions. He shows that *Thomas*' version is very close to the Synoptics in Coptic and, he surmises, to the Greek as well. Because of this strong agreement, he finds it difficult to attribute the parable to an independent translation from Aramaic. He notes that L. 9 wildly diverges from Matthew 13.5–6//Mark 4.5–6 at the same point that Luke's text does too (8.6). But he demonstrates that Luke's version is not related to the Thomasine since Luke is heavily indebted to Mark here while *Thomas* is not. This leads him to conclude that *Thomas* and Mark independently relied on the same source, especially since arguments for a 'Gnostic' redaction of Mark or Matthew's versions remain unconvincing to him. What Horman fails to explain, however, is the fact that the Thomasine differences can be tracked in the Syrian literature. These similarities certainly point to a Syrian milieu for *Thomas*, but they are also strong indicators for a divergent independent sayings tradition. In fact, G. Quispel goes so far as to conclude that this saying comes from a Jewish Christian Gospel independent of the Synoptic tradition.

J. Sieber thinks that the agreement noted by Schrage (Sahidic Mark 4.6 renders ⲘⲠⲞⲨϪⲈ ⲚⲞⲨⲚⲈ or μὴ βάλλειν ῥίζαν for μὴ ἔχειν) might suggest that *Thomas'* Coptic translation was influenced by the Sahidic versions of the New Testament, but that it cannot tell us anything about his sources. Sieber sees the many Thomasine pecularities which have parallels in Syrian literature to be evidence for extensive changes that occurred during a long period of oral transmission. H. Koester and S. Patterson too remark that nothing indicates the use of a written source or even points to the narrator's attempt to comment on the Synoptic texts. There is no evidence of redactional elements present in L. 9 or deliberate avoidance of such elements. J. Liebenberg concludes from his comparative parabolic analysis that although *Thomas* shares all the elements with Mark, this version differs exactly in the part of the parable where 'the likelihood for Markan "intervention" was the greatest'. He finds no evidence that *Thomas* is dependent on a written copy of Mark, or the other Synoptic accounts.

In my opinion, since there is no dogmatic reason for *Thomas* to change the Synoptic source in the manner seen in L. 9 nor is there a way to derive *Thomas'* additions and omissions from the extant Synoptic manuscripts. L. 9 represents an eastern Semitic version of this parable independent from the Synoptics. This version appears to have been known by other Syrian texts. The agreement with Coptic Mark, however, suggests the possibility of secondary scribal adaptation.

LITERATURE PARALLELS

Mark 4.3–8

[3] 'Listen! A sower went out to sow. [4] And as he sowed, some seed fell along the path, and the birds came and devoured it. [5] Other seed fell on rocky ground, where it had not much soil, and immediately it sprang up, since it had no depth of soil. [6] And when the sun rose it was scorched, and since it had no root it withered away. [7] Other seed fell among thorns and the thorns grew up and choked it, and it yielded no grain. [8] And other seeds fell into good soil and brought forth grain, growing up and increasing and yielding thirtyfold and sixtyfold and a hundredfold.'

Matthew 13.3–8

[3] 'A sower went out to sow. [4] And as he sowed, some seeds fell along the path, and the birds came and devoured them. [5] Other seeds fell on rocky ground, where they had not much soil, and immediately they sprang up, since they had no depth of soil, [6] but when the sun rose they were scorched. And since they had no root, they withered away. [7] Other seeds fell upon thorns, and the thorns grew up and choked them. [8] Other seeds fell on good soil and brought forth grain, some a hundredfold, some sixty, some thirty.'

Luke 8.5–8

[5] 'A sower went out to sow his seed. And as he sowed, some fell along the path, and was trodden under foot, and the birds of the air devoured it. [6] And some fell on the rock, and as it grew up, it withered away because it had no moisture. [7] And some fell among

thorns, and the thorns grew with it and choked it. [8]And some fell into good soil and grew, and yielded a hundredfold.'

1 Clement *24.5*

'The sower went out and cast seeds on the ground. Those which fall on the dry barren ground perish. Then the magnificence of the providence of the Lord raises them up from dissolution, and many develop from the one and bear fruit.'

Justin Martyr, Dialogue with Trypho *125.1*

'A sower went forth to sow the seed. And some fell by the wayside, and some among thorns, and some on stony ground, and some on good ground.'

Pseudo-Clementine Recognitions *(Syriac) 3.14*

'But because it is necessary for a farmer, sowing because of the good quality of land, that only a little of his word is lost, which falls as seed – on the stone, on the road, on the uncultivated land of the thorns. These are the things which the good teacher spoke in a parable, when he would point out the different attitudes, which are not like each other.'

Aphraates, Demonstrations *14.46*

'And the sower filled his hand and threw on his land. One part fell among the thorns, another on the rocks, and another the birds gathered.'

Al-Muhasibi, attributed to Jesus

'The sower went out with his seed and filled his hand and sowed. Part of it fell on the road and soon the birds came. They collected it.'

Kitab Bilankar wa Budasf, attributed to Jesus

'The sower went out with his good seed to sow. When he had filled his hand with it and had strewn the seed, some of it fell on the border of the road, where the birds soon picked it up.'

Cf. Mark 4.13–30; Matthew 13.18–23; Luke 8.11–15; *Pseudo-Clementine Homilies* 11.2.1–3

AGREEMENTS IN SYRIAN GOSPELS, WESTERN TEXT AND DIATESSARON

Matthew 13.3–9//Mark 4.3–9//Luke 8.5–8 in Jst 027 d e (Luke) 7e 28 33 1241 vg. D (Mark) T^{EC} T^A T^T Zach Heliand Pseudo-Clem Rec geo
on the road << along the road

Matthew 13.3–9//Mark 4.3–9//Luke 8.5–8 in S (Matthew) Aphr T^{EC} Heliand
they gathered << they devoured

Matthew 13.3–9//Mark 4.3–9//Luke 8.5–8 in D (Mark) bo (Mark and Luke)
– to sow

Matthew 13.3–9//Mark 4.3–9//Luke 8.5–8 in S C (Matthew) Aphr T^{NL}
+ and did not strike root

Matthew 13.3–9//Mark 4.3–9//Luke 8.5–8 in C (Matthew)
+ in the earth

SELECT BIBLIOGRAPHY
Cameron (1986: 20–24); Guillaumont (1981: 198–99); Horman (1979); Koester (1983: 195–97); Liebenberg (2001: 414); Perrin (2002: 43); Quispel (1958: 183–84; 1962: 146–47; 1981: 265); Patterson (1993: 23); Schrage (1964a: 42–48); Sieber (1966: 157–60); Tuckett (1988: 155).

Logion 10

Jesus said, 'I have cast fire upon the world. And look! I am guarding it until it blazes.'

NHC II 2.34.14–16

ⲡⲉⲝⲉ ⲓ̅ⲥ̅ ⲝⲉ ⲁⲉⲓⲛⲟⲩⲝⲉ ⲛ̅ⲟⲩⲕⲱϩ̅ⲧ ⲉⲝⲛ̅ ⲡⲕⲟⲥⲙⲟⲥ ⲁⲩⲱ
ⲉⲓⲥϩⲏⲏⲧⲉ ϯⲁⲣⲉϩ ⲉⲣⲟϥ ϣⲁⲛⲧⲉϥⲝⲉⲣⲟ

ATTRIBUTION
Kernel saying.

INTERPRETATIVE COMMENT

L. 10 is part of a rhetorical speech about the urgency of the Eschaton and the need to prepare oneself for Judgement. The hearers are admonished to listen to Jesus' words (L. 8.4) because each person has a critical decision to make, to abide by Jesus' words since he is already casting God's Judgement upon the world (L. 10).

In the complete Gospel, the hermeneutic shifted, de-emphasizing the eschatological nature of the logion and turning to a more personal understanding. With the accrual of L. 7, the emphasis in this section of the speech would have shifted to the individual believer overcoming his or her passions. So L. 10 may have taken on the type of hermeneutic that we find in the *Pseudo-Clementine Recognitions* 6.4 which also reinterprets this saying in a personal sense. Jesus is understood to be kindling within the person the fire of righteous indignation, to destroy the lusts of the soul. This same hermeneutic is developed by the later Syriac Father, Pseudo-Macarius (*Hom.* 25.9–10) who further states that the fire renders the mind so pure that it readies the person for mystical experiences.

SOURCE DISCUSSION

W. Schrage and J. Sieber agree that it is impossible to prove dependence of L. 10 on Luke 12.49 because no Lukan editorial traits can be determined. This is against H. von Schürmann who identifies Luke 12.49 as Quelle material with Lukan redactional traces. G. Quispel thinks that this saying comes from the *Gospel of the Nazarenes* or another Jewish Christian Gospel.

LITERATURE PARALLELS

Luke 12.49 (L or Qluke)
'I came to cast fire upon the earth. And would that it were already kindled!'

Pseudo-Clementine Recognitions 6.4
'Is not the fire of most righteous indignation kindled within you for all these things now that the light of truth has shone upon you? And does not the flame of anger which is pleasing to God rise within you, that every sprout may be brought up and destroyed from the root, if haply any shoot of evil concupiscence has budded within you? ... Humans might kindle the fire of salutary anger against the ignorance that had deceived them. On this account, he said, "I have come to send fire on the earth. And how I wish that it were kindled!"'

Pistis Sophia 3.116
'Now concerning the discourse on forgiveness of sins, you spoke to us once in a parable, saying, "I have come to cast fire upon the earth", and also, "What will I except that it burns?"'

Pistis Sophia *4.141*

> 'Furthermore the Spirit draws all souls together and takes them to the place of the light. Because of this, I have said to you, "I have come to cast fire upon the earth." That is, I have come to purify the sins of the whole world with fire.'

Cf. Matthew 10.34 (Qmatt); Luke 12.51 (Qluke); *Pseudo-Clementine Homilies* 11.3; Pseudo-Macarius, *Hom.* 25.9–10.

AGREEMENTS IN SYRIAN GOSPELS, WESTERN TEXT AND DIATESSARON

Luke 12.49 in T^{NL}

> I have cast << I came to cast

Luke 12.49 in S C P T^{NL} T^V Zach sa

> blazes << were kindled

SELECT BIBLIOGRAPHY

Quispel (1981: 265); Schrage (1964a: 49–51); Schürmann (1963: 244–45); Sieber (1966: 114–15).

Logion 11.1

[1]Jesus said, 'This heaven will pass away, and the one above it will pass away.'

NHC II 2.34.16–18

ⲡⲉϫⲉ ⲓ̄ⲥ̄ ϫⲉ ⲧⲉⲉⲓⲡⲉ ⲛⲁⲣ̄ⲡⲁⲣⲁⲅⲉ ⲁⲩⲱ ⲧⲉⲧⲛ̄ⲧⲡⲉ ⲙ̄ⲙⲟⲥ
ⲛⲁⲣ̄ⲡⲁⲣⲁⲅⲉ

ATTRIBUTION
Kernel saying.

INTERPRETATIVE COMMENT

M. Lelyveld notes the importance of this logion as a reminder of the apocalyptic nature of the *Gospel of Thomas*, although she takes L. 11.2 as part of this saying rather than an interpretation of it as I do. According to Lelyveld, L. 11 mentions the passing of the actual cosmos at the end of time and the division of humanity into two parties, those who will live and those who will die. She compares this to L. 61. L. 11.3–4 she finds to be an obscure explication of Genesis 2 when Adam was alone, before being divided into two sexes.

In my opinion in the Kernel Gospel, this logion is an eschatological reminder that the end of the world is yet to arrive. Jesus has already cast God's Judgement upon the world (L. 10) and soon the heavens will pass away (L. 11.1). This expectation was common among contemporary Jews and Christians.

The accretions that accumulated later serve to reinterpret this saying, blunting the eschatological nature of the Kernel logion (11.2–4). No longer interpreted in cosmological terms, the logion becomes a salute to personal transformation into a 'living being' through a return to the prelapsarian Adam, the primal One, perhaps through baptism, unction and the eucharist. This utopian condition was understood to be androgynous. In practicality, this meant to the later Thomasine Christians, a celibate state. It was through celibacy that they thought they were bringing the world to an end. Similar accretive theology and vocabulary is attached to L. 111.1, the doublet to L. 11.1.

SOURCE DISCUSSION
G. Quispel attributes this saying to the *Gospel of the Egyptians* or some other encratic source.

LITERATURE PARALLELS

Mark 13.31; Matthew 24.35; Luke 21.33
> 'Heaven and earth will pass away, but my words will not pass away.'

Matthew 5.18 (Qmatt)
> 'For truly I say to you, till heaven and earth pass away, not an iota, not a dot, will pass from the law until all is accomplished.'

Luke 16.17 (Qluke)
> 'But it is easier for heaven and earth to pass away, than for one dot of the law to become void.'

Isaiah 51.6
> 'Lift up your eyes to the heavens, and look at the earth beneath; for the heavens will vanish like smoke, the earth will wear out like a garment, and they who dwell in it will die like gnats.'

See L. 111.1

SELECT BIBLIOGRAPHY
Lelyveld (1987: 19–20, 55–68); Quispel (1981: 265).

Logion 11.2–4

[2]'And the dead are not alive, and the living will not die. [3]In the days when you ate what is dead, you made it something living. When you are in the light, what will you become? [4]On the day when you were one, you became two. When you are two, what will you become?'

NHC II 2.34.18–25

> [2]ⲀⲨⲰ ⲚⲈⲦⲘⲞⲞⲨⲦ ⲤⲈⲞⲚⲌ ⲀⲚ ⲀⲨⲰ ⲚⲈⲦⲞⲚⲌ ⲤⲈⲚⲀⲘⲞⲨ ⲀⲚ [3]ⲚⲌⲞⲞⲨ ⲚⲈⲦⲈⲦⲚ̄ⲞⲨⲰⲘ ⲘⲠⲈⲦⲘⲞⲞⲨⲦ ⲚⲈⲦⲈⲦⲚ̄ⲈⲒⲢⲈ ⲘⲘⲞϤ ⲘⲠⲈⲦⲞⲚⲌ ⲌⲞⲦⲀⲚ ⲈⲦⲈⲦⲚ̄ϢⲀⲚϢⲰⲠⲈ ⲌⲘ̄ ⲠⲞⲨⲞⲈⲒⲚ ⲞⲨ ⲠⲈⲦⲈⲦⲚⲀⲀϤ [4]ⲌⲘ̄ ⲪⲞⲞⲨ ⲈⲦⲈⲚ̄Ⲟ Ⲛ̄ⲞⲨⲀ ⲀⲦⲈⲦⲚ̄ⲈⲒⲢⲈ ⲘⲠⲤⲚⲀⲨ ⲌⲞⲦⲀⲚ ⲆⲈ ⲈⲦⲈⲦⲚ̄ϢⲀϢⲰⲠⲈ Ⲛ̄ⲤⲚⲀⲨ ⲞⲨ ⲠⲈ ⲈⲦⲈⲦⲚ̄ⲚⲀⲀϤ

ATTRIBUTION
Accretion.

INTERPRETATIVE COMMENT
The saying contains language characteristic of the accretions, particularly the terminology centred around **ⲞⲚⲌ**, and the single state becoming a dual one. The content reflects

retrospection about the Genesis story and would have been particularly meaningful to the encratic constituency of the later Thomasine community. So accrual is judged between 80 and 120 CE.

Hippolytus reports a similar version of L. 11.3 as a teaching of the Naasenes: 'They say indeed, "If you ate dead things and made them living, what will you do if you eat living things?"' (*Ref.* 5.8.32). Could this be a saying from the version of the *Gospel of Thomas* that Hippolytus knows and reports when he quotes the Naasene version of L. 4.1 from the 'gospel according to Thomas' (*Ref.* 5.7.20)? It appears to me that Hippolytus' version of the saying has been less manipulated and may, in fact, represent an earlier version of L. 11.3 than the Coptic translation.

In any case, the referential horizon of the saying appears to evoke the hearer's or reader's knowledge of early Christian initiatory rituals and the eucharist. If this is the case, then L. 11.3 alludes to a Christian teaching purporting that, although one might think that ordinary eating sustains life, it is nothing in comparison to eating the living body of Jesus (Hippolytus) or receiving the purifying 'light' of baptism and unction (*Thomas*). It is noteworthy that Christian traditions about the eucharist suggest that it was understood to be the mechanism which restored the believer to the image of God, the 'Perfect Man' as I have described in 'The True Mysteries'. So L. 11.2–3 appears to be a comment on the Christian life. To be among the 'living' who 'will not die', one must be baptized and anointed, purified by the light which is received from these sacraments. Then the initiate has the opportunity, probably by eating the eucharistic elements, to begin the restorative process, becoming the image of God.

L. 11.4 is a contrary appeal. It references the moment when sin arose: the division of the sexes and the loss of the primal androgynous Image (Genesis 1.26–27 and 2.22). If the hearer or reader rejects Christian initiation, the situation is dire. The person will remain divided and is asked, 'What will you become?' Of course, the answer is obvious. The person will not be able to be restored to the primal androgynous state so he or she will be counted among 'the dead who are not alive'. The preferable situation is one in which the person returns to the prelapsarian condition of singleness which, in practical terms, meant celibacy.

SOURCE DISCUSSION

G. Quispel traces this saying to a possible encratic source like the *Gospel of the Egyptians.*

LITERATURE PARALLELS

Hippolytus, Ref. *5.8.32*

> 'They say indeed, "If you ate dead things and made them living, what will you do if you eat living things?"'

Dialogue of the Saviour *56–57*

> '[Matthew] said, "Tell me, Lord, how the dead die [and] how the living live." The [Lord] said, "[You have] asked me about a saying [...] which eye has not seen, [nor] have I heard it except from you. But I say to you that when what invigorates a man is removed, he will be called 'dead'. And when what is alive leaves what is dead, what is alive will be called upon."'

Acts of Thomas *147*

> 'The dead I have not brought to life and the living I have not put to death.'

Gospel of Philip *73.20–27, 74.1–12*

> 'This world is a corpse-eater. All the things eaten in it themselves die also. Truth is a life-eater. Therefore no one nourished by [truth] will die. It was from that place that Jesus came and brought food. To those who so desired he gave [life, that] they might not die…in the place where I will eat all things is the tree of knowledge. That one killed Adam, but here the tree of knowledge made men alive. The law was the tree. It has power to give the knowledge of good and evil. It neither removed him from evil, nor did it set him in the good, but it created death for those who ate of it. For when he said, "Eat this, do not eat that", it became the beginning of death.'

Pseudo-Macarius, Hom. *15.10*

> 'All things will become light. All are immersed in light and fire and are indeed changed…'

SELECT BIBLIOGRAPHY
DeConick (2001: 231–45); Quispel (1981: 265).

Logion 12.1–2

¹The disciples said to Jesus, 'We know that you are going to leave us. Who will be our leader?'

²Jesus said to them, 'No matter where you came from, you should go to James the Righteous One, for whose sake heaven and earth exist.'

NHC II 2.34.25–30

¹ΠΕϪΕ ⲘⲘⲀⲐⲎⲦⲎⲤ ⲚⲒⲤ ϪⲈ ⲦⲚⲤⲞⲞⲨⲚ ϪⲈ ⲔⲚⲀⲂⲰⲔ ⲚⲦⲞⲞⲦⲚ ⲚⲒⲘ ⲠⲈ ⲈⲦⲚⲀⲢ ⲚⲞϬ Ⲉ2ⲢⲀⲒ̈ ⲈϪⲰⲚ

²ⲠⲈϪⲈ ⲒⲤ ⲚⲀⲨ ϪⲈ ⲠⲘⲀ ⲚⲦⲀⲦⲈⲦⲚⲈⲒ ⲘⲘⲀⲨ ⲈⲦⲈⲦⲚⲀⲂⲰⲔ ⲰⲀ Ⲓ̈ⲀⲔⲰⲂⲞⲤ ⲠⲆⲒⲔⲀⲒⲞⲤ ⲠⲀⲈⲒ ⲚⲦⲀ ⲦⲠⲈ ⲘⲚ ⲠⲔⲀ2 ⲰⲰⲠⲈ ⲈⲦⲂⲎⲦϥ̄

ATTRIBUTION
Accretion.

TEXT AND TRANSLATION ISSUES
L. 12.1 literally reads, 'Who will be great over us?' A. Guillaumont notes that this is different from the comparative structure found both in the Greek and Syriac Synoptic accounts, 'the greatest'. He traces this difference to an Aramaic substratum.

The title 'Righteous One' is fascinating since it was not only given to James but appears to be one of the oldest titles given to Jesus whose holiness and righteousness were believed to sustain life. This is alluded to in Acts where Jesus is called the 'Holy and Righteous One' (τὸν ἅγιον καὶ δίκαιον), the 'beginning' or 'founder of life' (τὸν ἀρχηγὸν τῆς ζωῆς) (3.14–15; cf. Acts 7.52; 22.14).

Of course, the teaching that, in order for this world to continue to exist, there must always be a certain number of *tsaddik* or righteous men is Jewish (30 righteous men (*Gen. Rabba* xcviii, 9, p. 1260; cf. `*Avoda Zara* ii, 1, p. 40b), 36 righteous men (*b. Sukka* 45b; *b. Sanhedrin* 97b), or 45 righteous men (*b. Hullin* 92a). According to the Tannaim, even the existence of one righteous man 'is equivalent to the entire world' (*Mekhilta de-R. Ishmael*, Shira, i, p. 118; cf. *Gen. Rabba*, xxx, 1, p. 270), a teaching developed from

Proverbs 10.25 ('The righteous is the foundation of the world') and found also in *2 Baruch* 14.19 ('The world was created for the righteous'). Rabbi Hiyya bar Abba said according to Rabbi Johanan: 'The world exists even for the sake of one righteous person, as it is said, "And the righteous is the foundation of the world"' (*b. Yoma* 38b). Furthermore, according to these rabbis, 'No righteous man departs from this world until another righteous man like him is created, as it is said, "The sun also rises and the sun goes down" – ere the sun of Eli set, the sun of Samuel the Ramathite had arisen' (*b. Yoma* 38b; cf. *b. Qiddushin* 72b).

Not only can the world exist because of the merit of one righteous man succeeding the other, but there is also a tradition that the righteous aided God in the work of creation (*Gen. Rabba* 8.5; *Ruth R.* 2.3) and that the world was created for the sake of the righteous (*Sifre Deut.* 47). These ideas are largely developed in late mystical texts which incorporate the *tsaddik* in the Sefiroth. He is described as the image of the perfect human being as well as the cosmic potency and foundation: 'The Holy One, blessed be He, has one righteous man in his world, and he is very precious to him, because he maintains the whole world and he is its foundation' (*Bahir*). In fact, creation actually occurs through the *tsaddik*, as is found in the *Bahir*: 'Every language of creation is performed through it.'

These traditions go a long way to explain that the title and its attributes were passed on to Jesus' brother James when he took over the leadership of the Jerusalem community. Logion 12.2 is not alone in this attestation (Eusebius, *Eccl. Hist.* 2.23; Epiphanes, *Panarion* 78.7.7; 78.14.1–6; *Gos. Hebrews* 7; *1 Apocalypse of James* 31.30; 32.1–3; 32.12; 43.19– 21; *2 Apocalypse of James* 44.13–14; 49.9; 59.22; 60.12–13; 61.14). Hegesippus records that James was known as the 'Righteous One' who continually prayed in the Temple for the forgiveness of the people. He was called the 'Oblias', a term which Hegesippus translates to mean 'Fortification of the People'. He states that this was for the fulfilment of a prophetic text. It is very likely that he had in mind Proverbs 10.25: 'the righteous is the foundation of the world'. Furthermore, it appears that James' prayers as a *tsaddik* were believed to have been successful in stemming God's judgement since it was not until immediately after his martyrdom that, Hegesippus says, Vespasian began to attack the Jews (Eusebius, *Eccl. Hist.* 2.23). The destruction of the Temple was soon to follow. This event was clearly interpreted by the Christian Jews to be the judgement of God meted upon Israel (Eusebius, *Eccl. Hist.* 3.5; 3.7; Origen, *Contra. Celsus* 1.47; Origen, *Comm. Matthew* 10.17).

INTERPRETATIVE COMMENT

The dialogue format indicates development of discourses from older traditional material. The question is retrospective although early in the Christian experience, predating James' death. This logion may represent the earliest accretions in the Gospel, dating from 40 to 60 CE. The question was legitimate in the early Christian experience, especially since the Christian Jews developed several factions within only a few years after Jesus' death. This logion, counter the Synoptic tradition where Jesus grants Peter the keys of leadership, entitles James, Jesus' brother. It appears that the community, even in its latest stage which recognized the authority of Judas Thomas, remained connected with the Jerusalem church and looked to Jesus' family for leadership. The primacy of James connects the Thomasine community to the teachings and traditions of the Jerusalem Church and Aramaic Christianity in the East.

R. Uro thinks that the combination of L. 11 and 12 points to the temporary leadership of James, a leadership that 'will pass away' when the follower has 'found himself' and has become superior to the world and its leaders (L. 111). The message of *Thomas*, he says, is one of rejection of the world, its leaders and their localization in any church. It seems to me that two issues have been confused in this interpretation. Certainly the later Thomasine community has withdrawn from the world, rejecting material possessions and marital practices. But this does not in any way suggest that they did not have leaders. The text tells us that, indeed, they did. Jesus in L. 12 personally commissions James to lead them no matter their geographical location. And in L. 13, Judas Thomas is similarly honoured. The connection with L. 11 does not suggest the temporary nature of James' authority, but its permanence. As initiates enter the community and commit to an encratic lifestyle, the world passes away. But the authority of James over their church remains because Jesus commissioned him personally to be their leader and the community members can depend on that heritage. The combination of sayings would have given members a sense of assurance that their commitment to this renunciatory lifestyle was worthy and in accordance with the teachings of Jesus and dependent upon the authority of James, Jesus' brother.

SOURCE DISCUSSION

G. Quispel suggests that this logion comes from a Jewish Christian Gospel independent of the Synoptic tradition since, in the Jewish Christian Gospel traditions, James was the primate of Christianity and Jesus appeared to him first after the resurrection.

R. Grant and D.N. Freedman argue that this logion is based on John 14.5 and Mark 9.34, 10.43 and their parallels. But the parallelism between this logion and these Synoptic passages is so remote that even W. Schrage who is a strong advocate for Synoptic dependence says that the question must be left open in this case. R. Uro thinks that dependency on the Synoptic pericopes is hardly possible given the fact that the Synoptic stories teach a general lesson about humble leadership by referring to slaves and children, while *Thomas'* logion is about the designation of James with a special position. Uro feels that it is more likely that this logion represents a tradition which belongs to the same category as Jesus' words of commission in Matthew 16.17–18 and John 21.15–19.

LITERATURE PARALLELS

Mark 9.34

> 'But they silent, for on the way they had argued with one another who was the greatest.'

Luke 9.46

> 'An argument arose among them as to which one of them was the greatest.'

2 Apocalypse of James *55.24–25, 56.2–6*

> 'You are he whom the heavens bless... For your sake they will be told [these things], and will come to rest. For your sake they will reign [and will] become kings. For [your] sake they will have pity on whomever they pity.'

Epistula Apostolorum *17*

> 'Then we said to him, "Will you really leave us until your coming? Where will we find a teacher?"'

Pseudo-Clementine Recognitions *1.43*

> 'But while they often made such requests to us, and we sought for a fitting opportunity, a week of years was completed from the passion of the Lord, the Church of the Lord which was constituted in Jerusalem was most plentifully multiplied and grew, being governed with most righteous ordinances by James, who was ordained bishop in it by the Lord.'

Clement of Alexandria, Hypotyposes*, in Eusebius,* Hist. eccl. *2.1.3*
> 'Peter, James, and John, after the ascension of the Saviour, did not claim pre-eminence because the Saviour had specially honoured them, but chose James the Righteous as Bishop of Jerusalem.'

Hegesippus in Eusebius, Hist. eccl. *2.23.4*
> 'Control of the Church passed to the apostles, together with the Lord's brother James, whom everyone from the Lord's time till our own has called the Righteous.'

Epiphanius, Pan. *78,7.7–8*
> 'His firstborn was James, surnamed "Oblias", meaning "wall", and also surnamed "Righteous", who was a Nazarite, which means a holy man. He was the first to receive the bishop's chair, the first to whom the Lord entrusted his throne upon the earth.'

AGREEMENTS IN SYRIAN GOSPELS, WESTERN TEXT AND DIATESSARON

Luke 9.48 and parallels in e ff[1] S C (Matthew 18.1) e q P (Luke 9.48) S (Mark 9.37) D d T[EC] T[A] T[L] arm geo
> shall be great << is great

SELECT BIBLIOGRAPHY
Ginzberg (1947: 65–68); Grant with Freedman (1960: 124–25); Guillaumont (1981: 192); Painter (1999); Quispel (1975c: 3); Schrage (1964a: 51); Urbach (1987: 483–511); Uro (2003: 80–105).

Logion 13.1–8

[1]Jesus said to his disciples, 'Speculate about me. Tell me, who am I like?'

[2]Simon Peter said to him, 'You are like a righteous angel.'

[3]Matthew said to him, 'You are like a sage, a temperate person.'

[4]Thomas said to him, 'Master, my mouth cannot attempt to say whom you are like.'

[5]Jesus said, 'I am not your master. After you drank, you became intoxicated from the bubbling fount which I had measured out.'

[6]And he took him and retreated. He told him three words.

[7]Then when Thomas returned to his friends, they asked him, 'What did Jesus say to you?'

[8]Thomas said to them, 'If I tell you one of the words which he told me, you will pick up stones and throw them at me. Then fire will come out of the stones and burn you up.'

NHC II 2.34.30–35.14

[1]ⲡⲉⲝⲉ ⲓ̅ⲥ̅ ⲛ̅ⲛⲉϥⲙⲁⲑⲏⲧⲏⲥ ⲝⲉ ⲧⲛ̅ⲧⲱⲛⲧ ⲛ̅ⲧⲉⲧⲛ̅ⲝⲟⲟⲥ ⲛⲁⲉⲓ ⲝⲉ ⲉⲉⲓⲛⲉ ⲛ̅ⲛⲓⲙ

[2]ⲡⲉⲝⲁϥ ⲛⲁϥ ⲛ̅ϭⲓ ⲥⲓⲙⲱⲛ ⲡⲉⲧⲣⲟⲥ ⲝⲉ ⲉⲕⲉⲓⲛⲉ ⲛ̅ⲟⲩⲁⲅⲅⲉⲗⲟⲥ ⲛ̅ⲇⲓⲕⲁⲓⲟⲥ

[3]ⲡⲉⲝⲁϥ ⲛⲁϥ ⲛ̅ϭⲓ ⲙⲁⲑⲑⲁⲓⲟⲥ ⲝⲉ ⲉⲕⲉⲓⲛⲉ ⲛ̅ⲟⲩⲣⲱⲙⲉ ⲙ̅ⲫⲓⲗⲟⲥⲟⲫⲟⲥ ⲛ̅ⲣⲙ̅ⲛ̅ϩⲏⲧ

⁴ⲡⲉⲭⲁ ⲛⲁ ⲛ̄ϭⲓ ⲑⲱⲙⲁⲥ ϫⲉ ⲡⲥⲁ ϩⲟⲗⲱⲥ ⲧⲁⲧⲁⲡⲣⲟ
ⲛⲁϣ[[ϣ]]ⲁⲡ ⲁⲛ ⲉⲧⲣⲁϫⲟⲟⲥ ϫⲉ ⲉⲕⲉⲓⲛⲉ ⲛ̄ⲛⲓⲙ

⁵ⲡⲉϫⲉ ⲓⲏ̄ⲥ ϫⲉ ⲁⲛⲟⲕ ⲡⲉⲕⲥⲁ ⲁⲛ ⲉⲡⲉⲓ ⲁⲕⲥⲱ ⲁⲕϯϩⲉ ⲉⲃⲟⲗ ϩⲛ̄
ⲧⲡⲏⲅⲏ ⲉⲧⲃ̄ⲣ̄ⲃⲣⲉ ⲧⲁⲓⲉ ⲁⲛⲟⲕ ⲛ̄ⲧⲁⲉⲓϣⲓⲧ̄ⲥ

⁶ⲁⲩⲱ ⲁϥϫⲓⲧ̄ ⲁϥⲁⲛⲁⲭⲱⲣⲉⲓ ⲁϥϫⲱ ⲛⲁ ⲛ̄ϣⲟⲙⲧ ⲛ̄ϣⲁϫⲉ

⁷ⲛ̄ⲧⲁⲣⲉ ⲑⲱⲙⲁⲥ ⲇⲉ ⲉⲓ ϣⲁ ⲛⲉϥϣⲃⲉⲉⲣ ⲁⲩϫⲛⲟⲩ ϫⲉ ⲛ̄ⲧⲁ ⲓ̄ⲥ̄
ϫⲟⲟⲥ ϫⲉ ⲟⲩ ⲛⲁⲕ

⁸ⲡⲉϫⲁ ⲛⲁⲩ ⲛ̄ϭⲓ ⲑⲱⲙⲁⲥ ϫⲉ ⲉⲓϣⲁⲛϫⲱ ⲛⲏⲧⲛ̄ ⲟⲩⲁ ϩⲛ̄ ⲛ̄ϣⲁϫⲉ
ⲛ̄ⲧⲁϥϫⲟⲟⲩ ⲛⲁⲉⲓ ⲧⲉⲧⲛⲁϥⲓ ⲱⲛⲉ ⲛ̄ⲧⲉⲧⲛ̄ⲛⲟⲩϫⲉ ⲉⲣⲟⲉⲓ ⲁⲩⲱ ⲛ̄ⲧⲉ
ⲟⲩⲕⲱϩⲧ ⲉⲓ ⲉⲃⲟⲗ ϩⲛ̄ ⲛ̄ⲱⲛⲉ ⲛ̄<ϥ>ⲣⲱ<ⲕϩ> ⲙ̄ⲙⲱⲧⲛ̄

ATTRIBUTION
Accretion.

TEXT AND TRANSLATION ISSUES
In L. 13.3, ⲡⲙⲛ̄ϩⲏⲧ likely translates σώφρων, meaning a person who has mastery of his or
her mind and body – someone who has control over his or her passions, is moderate,
chaste, sober, and temperate. In the ancient world, this attribute was understood to be the
mark of the sage.

   W. Clarysse has offered an alternative reading of L. 13.5. He suggests that ϣⲓⲧ//
should be read as the status pronominalis of ϣⲓⲧⲉ, 'to dig'. Thus the phrase should be
rendered, 'the bubbling well which I myself dug'. He sees L. 13.5 as a 'free rendering' of
John 4.14. E. Saunders has argued that L. 13.5 suggests that John 7.38 should be
understood as a reference to Christ rather than the believer as the embodiment of the New
Jerusalem from whom 'flow rivers of living water'.

   L. 13.8, ⲛ̄<ϥ>ⲣⲱ<ⲕϩ> has been emended from the manuscript, ⲛⲥⲣⲱϩⲕ, which must
represent a scribal error, inverting the last two letters of the word and attributing an
incorrect pronoun to the antecedent ⲕⲱϩⲧ. A. Guillaumont explains this scribal error as a
distracted translator working with a Semitic original since 'fire' is feminine in Hebrew,
Aramaic and Syriac.

INTERPRETATIVE COMMENT
Development is noted in the dialogue format. The dialogue is retrospective, concerned
with christological issues, particularly developing christological understandings of the
community. In this case, the later Thomasine community develops its earlier opinions
about Jesus, that he was to be compared to God's angel of righteous judgement (L. 13.2)
and to a sage, a person who had achieved mastery of his or her mind and body (L. 13.3).
Based on the feeding texts in Baruch 3.10–14 and 24.21, S. Davies thinks that the
Christology here is Sophiology. But this does not take into account L. 13.6–8 which holds
the key to the later Thomasine Christology in my opinion. According to the view of the
later Thomasine community expressed in L. 13.6–8, Jesus also had been given the inef-
fable unpronounceable divine Name, Yahweh. He was, in fact, Yahweh Manifest. Given its
prominence in this logion, it appears that this christological understanding was believed to
have superseded the other two, although not necessarily replacing them. In fact, this later
Christology represents a development of the earlier angelomorphic Christology. Jesus was
not only God's great angel who bore his Name, but he, by virtue of the possession of the
Name was Yahweh Manifest on earth.

This interpretation of L. 13.6–8 is based on the fact that the penalty for blasphemy in Judaism was stoning (Lev. 24.16; *Sanh.* 7.5). The 'three words' mentioned in L. 13.6 must be a reference to the unutterable and unpronounceable Name of God, the *Shem hamme-phorash.* Jesus has been identified with the divine Name of God found in Exodus 3.14, 'I AM WHO I AM (אהיה אשר אהיה)'. It is notable that Thomas tells his friends that if he says 'one' of these words, he would be stoned. This suggests that אהיה was the primary word that explicated the Tetragrammaton and was understood to be its equivalent as Fossum has intimated and C. Gieschen has discussed. R. Hayward has made a strong case that the *Memra* represents God's אהיה, his name for himself. This name not only signifies God's existence, but his merciful presence with his people. According to Hayward, God says, אהיה, 'I am here!' and יהיה, 'He is there!' is the response of the people. Hayward's discussion complements P. Vermes' observations and is carried on in S. McDonough's book, *YHWH at Patmos.*

It is quite significant that the *Acts of Thomas* not only alludes to L. 13 in chapter 47, but also knows the Name tradition. In chapter 133, it is stated that the Name given to Jesus is 'the exalted Name that is hidden from all'. Moreover, when Judas Thomas is asked by Mazdai, 'What is his [Jesus'] name?' Judas replies, 'You are not able to hear his true Name now at this time, but the name that is given to him is Jesus the Messiah' (ch. 163.)

This Christology is quite cogent with that expressed in the Gospel of John, especially 10.30–39, so accrual is best attributed to a time between 60 and 100 CE, a time when the Johannine community was making similar associations and claims. In John, when Jesus declares, 'I and the Father are one' (10.30), the Jews pick up rocks to stone Jesus (10.31). They tell Jesus that 'we stone you for blasphemy, because you, being a man, make yourself God' (10.34). Thus Jesus in the Gospel of John is expressing unity with God the Father by laying claim to the possession of the divine Name (cf. 17.11). Stoning was the consequence of such claims.

The mention of fire in L. 13.8 references the fact that Thomas, by drinking from Jesus' bubbling fount, has been transformed into Jesus' equal, has drawn near to the fire and survived (cf. 108 and 82). Why will the disciples be burned by fire from the rocks? As C. Morray-Jones has intimated in his article, the gravest of dangers awaits the unprepared person who attempts to encounter God – death by fiery annihilation rather than transformation into a being of light or fire (Philo, *Quaest. Ex.* 2.27–28; 2.40; 2.44; *Mig.* 166; *3 Enoch* 15; *Hekhalot Rabbati* 3.4; *Midrash Gedullah Mosheh* section 2). There is even a story told by the rabbis that the *ḥashmal* (living creatures speaking fire) which surround the enthroned Yahweh sent forth fire and burned up a child who had been reading in his teacher's house the Book of Ezekiel (*Hagigah* 13a–13b).

SOURCE DISCUSSION
G. Quispel attributes this saying to the *Gospel of the Egyptians*. I. Dunderberg wonders if L. 13 might be dependent on John 6.66–71, John's alternative to Peter's confession in the Synoptics. His investigation, however, leads him to conclude that the common elements are too vague to prove literary dependence.

LITERATURE PARALLELS

Mark 8.27–29
> [27]'And Jesus went on with his disciples, to the villages of Caesarea Philippi. And on the way he asked his disciples, "Who do men say that I am?" [28]And they told him, "John the Baptist. And others say, Elijah. And others, one of the prophets." [29]And he asked them, "But who do you say that I am?" Peter answered him, "You are the Christ."'

Matthew 16.13–16

[13]"Now when Jesus came into the district of Caesarea Philippi, he asked his disciples, "Who do men say that the Son of Man is?" [14]And they said, "Some say John the Baptist, others say Elijah, and others Jeremiah or one of the prophets." [15]He said to them, "But who do you say that I am?" [16]Simon Peter replied, "You are the Christ, the Son of the Living God."'

Luke 9.18–20

[18]"Now it happened that as he was praying alone the disciples were with him. And he asked them, "Who do the people say that I am?" [19]And they answered, "John the Baptist. But others say, Elijah. And others, that one of the old prophets has risen." [20]And he said to them, "But who do you say that I am?" And Peter answered, "The Christ of God."'

Matthew 23.8

'But you are not to be called, "Rabbi", for you have one teacher, and you are all brethren.'

John 4.10–14

[10]"Jesus answered her, "If you knew the gift of God, and who it is that is saying to you, 'Give me a drink', you would have asked him, and he would have given you living water." [11]The woman said to him, "Sir, you have nothing to draw with, and the well is deep. Where do you get that living water? [12]Are you greater than our father Jacob, who gave us the well, and drank from it himself, and his sons, and his cattle?" [13]Jesus said to her, "Every one who drinks of this water will thirst again, [14]but whoever drinks of the water that I shall give him will never thirst. The water that I shall give him will become in him a spring of water welling up to eternal life."'

John 6.67–68

[67]"Jesus said to the twelve, "Do you also wish to go away?" [68]Simon Peter answered him, "Lord, to whom shall we go? You have the words of eternal life…"'

John 7.37–38

[37]"On the last day of the feast, the great day, Jesus stood up and proclaimed, "If any one thirst, let him come to me and drink. [38]He who believes in me, as the scripture has said, 'Out of his heart shall flow rivers of living water.'"'

John 15.15

'No longer do I call you servants, for the servant does not know what his master is doing. But I have called you friends, for all that I have heard from my Father I have made known to you.'

Acts of Thomas *47*

'Jesus, the Hidden Mystery that is revealed to us. You are the one who has revealed many mysteries to us. You called me apart from all my fellows and told me three words with which I am inflamed, and I am unable to speak them to others.'

Odes of Solomon *11.6–7*

'And speaking waters touched my lips
From the fountain of the Lord generously.
And so I drank and became intoxicated,
From the living water that does not die.'

Cf. *Gos. Naz.* 14, Hippolytus, *Ref.* 5.8.5

SELECT BIBLIOGRAPHY

Clarysse (1994: 1–9); Davies (1983: 91–94); DeConick (1996: 111–15); Dunderberg (1998b: 67–70); Fossum (1985a: 115–16); Gieschen (1998; 2003); Guillaumont (1981:

196); Hayward (1981); McDonough (1999: 58–122); Morray-Jones (1992); Quispel (1981: 265); Saunders (1963: 47–48); Vermes (1973).

Logion 14.1–3

[1]Jesus said to them, 'If you fast, you will give birth in yourselves to sin. [2]And if you pray, you will be condemned. [3]And if you give alms, you will harm yourselves.'

NHC II 2.35.14–20

[1]ⲡⲉϫⲉ ⲓ̅ⲥ̅ ⲛⲁⲩ ϫⲉ ⲉⲧⲉⲧⲛ̅ϣⲁⲛⲣ̅ⲛⲏⲥⲧⲉⲩⲉ ⲧⲉⲧⲛⲁϫⲡⲟ ⲛⲏⲧⲛ̅
ⲛ̅ⲛⲟⲩⲛⲟⲃⲉ [2]ⲁⲩⲱ ⲉⲧⲉⲧⲛ̅ϣⲁ(ⲛ)ϣⲗⲏⲗ ⲥⲉⲛⲁⲣ̅ⲕⲁⲧⲁⲕⲣⲓⲛⲉ ⲙ̅ⲙⲱⲧⲛ̅
[3]ⲁⲩⲱ ⲉⲧⲉⲧⲛ̅ϣⲱⲁⲛϯ ⲉⲗⲉⲏⲙⲟⲥⲩⲛⲏ ⲉⲧⲉⲧⲛⲁⲉⲓⲣⲉ ⲛ̅ⲟⲩⲕⲁⲕⲟⲛ
ⲛ̅ⲛⲉⲧⲙ̅ⲡ̅ⲛ̅ⲁ̅

ATTRIBUTION
Accretion.

TEXT AND TRANSLATION ISSUES
A. Guillaumont finds the expression ⲛ̅ⲛⲉⲧⲙ̅ⲡ̅ⲛ̅ⲁ̅ in L. 14.3 to be a Semitism, 'your spirits' meaning 'yourselves'. He notes that the use of the word 'soul' reflexively is most common in Semitic languages generally, while 'spirit' is more peculiar to Syriac. So I have translated this idiomatic phrase, 'will harm yourselves'.

It appears that at some point in the transmission of this text, L. 6.1 and 14.1–3 became separated. This was noted by scholars as early as 1960 when S. Giverson proposed that the Coptic *Thomas* was not the 'original form' of *Thomas*. G. Quispel thinks that the final redactor was responsible for this separation and created a new answer to the questions out of L. 5. S. Davies attributes the separation to a technical problem in the transmission of the manuscript due to a tired scribe who mistakenly copied the wrong answer from L. 5. He caught his mistake, however, and copied the original answer before L. 15. In a private conversation with me and a few other scholars at the 1995 Annual Meeting of the Society of Biblical Literature in Philadelphia, B. Pearson said that he thinks the cause of the separation was due to an accidental flip in a manuscript page of the codex. L. 6.1 would have appeared at the bottom of a page while L. 14.1–3 at the top of the next page. At some point in the transmission of the manuscript, these leaves were incorrectly placed so that L. 14.1–3 no longer followed L. 6.1. When it was recopied, the sequence of sayings was disturbed.

My study of oral transmission has led me to another *possibility*. Originally when the accretion accrued in the Gospel, it probably did so as a unit, L. 6.1 was followed immediately by L. 14.1–3. During some later oral reperformance, the orator may have paused after the questions were posed, continued with L. 6.2, and then returned to the saying he just recited, L. 5. He may have done this in order to emphasize the point he was trying to make in his reperformance of Jesus' speech, that Jesus' concerns were ethical not ritual. The orator then proceeded with a sequence of Jesus' sayings, holding the answer, L. 14.1–3, until later when he recited L. 14.4 and 14.5, where he underscored his point a second time, especially emphasizing that Jesus was not concerned about Jewish food laws. In this sequencing, he may have been presenting the argument that the missionaries should not be concerned about observing the Jewish diet when in the field converting Gentiles because Jesus was more interested in a person's ethical practice than anything else.

INTERPRETATIVE COMMENT

Development of Form is indicated by the question and answer unit format of this saying. This is the answer to the questions posed to Jesus by the disciples in L. 6.1. This accretion accrued in the Gospel between 60 and 100 CE in order to accommodate a growing number of Gentiles within the community. In fact, the questions found in L. 6.1 appear to be echoes of the voices of the Gentile converts, 'How should we fast? How should we pray? How should we give alms? What diet should we observe?' From the response in this logion, it appears that this new constituency shifted the interests of the community away from Jewish practices toward a Christianity with its own developing praxis. I do not think that the attitude expressed in this logion meant that religious practices were abandoned altogether by the Thomasine Christians or that they were considered spiritually harmful. Rather, as I have discussed in more detail in the companion volume, *Recovering*, it appears that the language in L. 14.1–3 was understood to be rhetorical rather than literal, perhaps criticizing obligatory practices once customary to the community. The later community appears to have replaced its earlier obligatory practices with a renunciatory lifestyle, fasting from the world (L. 27.1). This position seems to me to be more rigorous not more lenient as some scholars have suggested. A. Marjanen discusses additional scholarly interpretations of this logion in his article.

SOURCE DISCUSSION

G. Quispel attributes this logion to the hand of the author of the Gospel.

LITERATURE PARALLELS

Matthew 6.1–6

[1]'Beware of practising your piety before men in order to be seen by them; for then you will have no reward from your Father who is in heaven. [2]Thus, when you give alms, sound no trumpet before you, as the hypocrites do in the synagogues and in the streets, that they may be praised by men. Truly I say to you, they have received their reward. [3]But when you give alms, do not let your left hand know what your right hand is doing, [4]so that your alms may be in secret; and your Father who sees in secret will reward you. [5]And when you pray, you must not be like the hypocrites; for they love to stand and pray in the synagogues and at the street corners, that they may be seen by men. Truly I say to you, they have received their reward. [6]And when you pray, go into your room and shut the door and pray to your Father who is in secret; and your Father who sees in secret will reward you.'

Abu al-Qasim ibn 'Asakir, Sirat al-Sayyid al-Masih, *p. 172 (no. 196)*

Jesus used to say, 'He who prays and fasts but does not abandon sin is inscribed in the Kingdom of God as a liar.'

Cf. *Didache* 8; 15.4; Hipp., *Ref.* 5.9.4

SELECT BIBLIOGRAPHY

Davies (1983: 153); Giverson (1960); Guillaumont (1958: 117); Marjanen (1998); Quispel (1967a: 35–36; 1981: 265).

Logion 14.4

⁴·When you enter any district and walk around the countryside, if they take you in, whatever they serve you, eat! The people among them who are sick, heal!'

NHC II 2.35.20–24

⁴ⲁⲩⲱ ⲉⲧⲉⲧⲛ̄ϣⲁⲛⲃⲱⲕ ⲉ2ⲟⲩⲛ ⲉⲕⲁ2 ⲛⲓⲙ ⲁⲩⲱ ⲛ̄ⲧⲉⲧⲙ̄ⲙⲟⲟϣⲉ 2ⲛ̄
ⲛ̄ⲭⲱⲣⲁ ⲉⲩϣⲁⲣⲡⲁⲣⲁⲇⲉⲭⲉ ⲙ̄ⲙⲱⲧⲛ̄ ⲡⲉⲧⲟⲩⲛⲁⲕⲁⲁ4 2ⲁⲣⲱⲧⲛ̄
ⲟⲩⲟⲙ4̄ ⲛⲉⲧϣⲱⲛⲉ ⲛ̄2ⲏⲧⲟⲩ ⲉⲣⲓⲑⲉⲣⲁⲡⲉⲩⲉ ⲙ̄ⲙⲟⲟⲩ

ATTRIBUTION
Kernel saying.

INTERPRETATIVE COMMENT
Early on, when the community was missionizing mainly the Jews, this saying may have had nothing to do with abandoning Jewish dietary practices. It probably was understood as an injunction for the Christian Jewish missionary to expect support from those Jews whom he was healing and converting. Later, however, when the community began to actively missionize the Gentiles and accommodate them within their community, this Kernel saying became sandwiched between L. 14.1–3 and 14.5. Its interpretation shifted so that it now was an injunction from Jesus, lifting the Jewish dietary restrictions altogether and refocusing the discussion on ethical practices.

This interpretation appears to coincide with S. Patterson's opinion that L 14.4 is 'simply good advice for homeless vagabonds such as those who promulgated the early sayings tradition'. But once it became associated with L. 14.5, the saying is no longer intended simply to address the question of how a preacher was to obtain food. The question now is whether the preacher must seek only kosher food, 'a question that arises only when Jews have crossed over the social boundaries that separate them from Gentiles'. Patterson notes that Paul uses the same tradition to settle the question put forward by the Corinthian community (1 Cor. 10.27).

SOURCE DISCUSSION
R. Grant and D.N. Freedman, B. Gärtner, and R. McL. Wilson think that this saying is dependent on the Synoptics because the phrase 'heal the sick' is out of place in *Thomas'* context. In their estimation, this signals a Lukan source.

W. Schrage says that Luke represents Q's reading here. Thus he looks elsewhere to argue for dependence. Examining Sahidic Luke, he finds agreement between Luke and L. 14.4 with the reading 'among them' rather than 'heal…in it'. J. Sieber states that this does not provide proof for dependence at the level of the Greek *Vorlage*.

P. Sellew has made a case for Luke 10.8–9 belonging to a pre-Quelle tradition which was in turn used in both Q and *Thomas* since *Thomas'* emphasis on 'lands and regions' is 'rurally evocative' when compared to Q's 'city'. Sellew considers the eating and healing commands to have already connected in the tradition, thus explaining the odd repetition in Luke 10.8. Because he does not consider the wording 'lands and regions' to signal rural districts, R. Uro is not convinced by Sellew. So he regards Luke 10.8–9 as a secondary composition that originated out of a literary redaction of the mission instructions. Thus he views 14.4 as potentially echoing secondary orality based on Luke.

Even though Uro states that L. 14.4 does not come from a presynoptic 'free' tradition of Jesus' sayings, unfortunately he does not lay out convincing reasons for this opinion. Thus, I find Sellew's position much preferred, at least for the origin of the Kernel saying. It is possible that the Kernel saying was secondarily adapted to the Lukan version *at a later date*, an opinion which Uro also suggests.

LITERATURE PARALLELS

Matthew 10.8 (Qmatt)
'Heal the sick, raise the dead, cleanse the leper, cast out demons.'

Luke 10.8–9 (Qluke)
[8]'Whenever you enter a town and they receive you, eat what is set before you. [9]Heal the sick in it and say to them, "The Kingdom of God has come near to you."'

1 Cor. 10.27
'If one of the unbelievers invites you to dinner and you are disposed to go, eat whatever is set before you without raising any question on the ground of conscience.'

SELECT BIBLIOGRAPHY
Gärtner (1961: 35–36); Grant (1959: 176); Grant with Freedman (1960: 133); Patterson (1991: 32–33); Schrage (1964a: 52–54); Sellew (1985: 131–33); Sieber (1966: 209); Uro (1998b: 26–32); Wilson (1960a: 70–71).

Logion 14.5

[5]'For what goes into your mouth will not make you unclean, rather what comes out of your mouth. It is this which will make you unclean!'

NHC II 2.35.24–27

[5]ⲡⲉⲧⲛⲁⲃⲱⲕ ⲅⲁⲣ ⲉϩⲟⲩⲛ ϩⲛ̄ ⲧⲉⲧⲛ̄ⲧⲁⲡⲣⲟ ϥⲛⲁϫⲱϩⲙ̄ ⲑⲩⲧⲛ̄ ⲁⲛ ⲁⲗⲗⲁ ⲡⲉⲧⲛ̄ⲛⲏⲩ ⲉⲃⲟⲗ ϩⲛ̄ ⲧⲉⲧⲛ̄ⲧⲁⲡⲣⲟ ⲛ̄ⲧⲟϥ ⲡⲉⲧⲛⲁϫⲁϩⲙ̄ ⲑⲩⲧⲛ̄

ATTRIBUTION
Accretion.

INTERPRETATIVE COMMENT
Secondary development of the sayings tradition is indicated because this saying's intent is to explain an ideology and activity reflecting post-50 CE Christianity. It presupposes an early Christian decision to use Jesus' words to nullify the Jewish dietary regulations for missionaries staying in Gentile households. It probably accrued in the Gospel in between 60 and 100 CE in order to alleviate the problem that had begun to face Christian Jewish missionaries in the field – the Gentile table. Accommodation of the new Gentile constituency is prominent.

SOURCE DISCUSSION
Dependence on Matthew 15.11 is demonstrated, according to W. Schrage, because of the common references to 'mouth' and the Greek attributive participle in the first part of the

logion. Markan dependence is signalled by Mark's participle phrase, τὰ κοινοῦντα rather than Matthew's κοινοῦ.

J. Sieber notes that these agreements do not establish *Thomas'* dependence on the Synoptics because they are not editorial but represent another version of the material in Matthew's special source. This seems to be in line with J.D. Crossan's opinion that Mark 7.15, Matthew 15.11, and L. 14.5 all represent independent versions of the saying. Sieber also points out that L. 14.5 has 'will not defile you', a more original form than the Synoptic version, 'will not defile a man'. The third person object, Sieber thinks, is needed because the saying is placed in a clearly secondary situation.

R. Uro, however, points out that a standard redaction-critical reading results in the position that Matthew 15.11 is a reformulation of Mark 7.15. This means that L. 14.5 echoes Matthew's redaction in 15.11 since it is almost identical to Matthew apart from the different personal pronoun. Uro thinks that Matthew may have been quoted from memory or that the use of the tradition has been influenced by prior readings of Matthew's Gospel. He says it may be that Matthew's saying was cited independently, detached from its original context and that this reperformance was taken into the Thomasine Gospel.

Given the fact that this saying is an accretion, Uro's description of this saying in terms of secondary orality is particularly noteworthy I think, although I would make the argument based on characteristics of orally transmitted material rather than the traditional appeal to redaction criticism. My own comparative study of L. 14.5 and Matthew 15.11 has shown a very high percentage of common words in sequence. When compared with the average 10 or 11 shared word sequence between the Thomasine-Synoptic aphorisms, in L. 14.5 we find 17. This may indicate that we are seeing here secondary orality if not literary dependence (see Chapter 1.4.3.3–7).

LITERATURE PARALLELS

Mark 7.15
'There is nothing outside a man which by going into him can defile him. But the things which come out of a man are what defile him.'

Mark 7.18–23
[18]'Do you not see that whatever goes into a man from outside cannot defile him, [19]since it enters, not his heart, but his stomach, and so passes on?' (Thus he declared all foods clean.) [20]And he said, 'What comes out of a man is what defiles a man. [21]For from within, out of the heart of man, come evil thoughts, fornication, theft, murder, adultery, [22]coveting, wickedness, deceit, licentiousness, envy, slander, pride, foolishness. [23]All these evil things come from within, and they defile man.'

Matthew 15.11
'Not what goes into the mouth defiles a man, but what comes out of the mouth, this defiles him.'

Matthew 15.17–20
[17]'Do you not see that whatever goes into the mouth passes into the stomach, and so passes on? [18]But what comes out of the mouth proceeds from the heart, and this defiles a man. [19]For out of the heart come evil thoughts, murder, adultery, fornication, theft, false witness, slander. [20]These are what defile a man; but to eat with unwashed hands does not defile a man.'

Cf. Acts 10.14; 11.8.

SELECT BIBLIOGRAPHY
Crossan (1983: 250–55); Schrage (1964a: 55); Sieber (1966: 192–93); Uro (1998b: 23–26).

Logion 15

Jesus said, 'When you see the one who was not born of woman, fall on your face and worship him. That one is your Father.'

NHC II 2.35.27–31

ΠΕΧΕ ΙC ΧΕ ϨΟΤΑΝ ΕΤΕΤΝ̄ϢΑΝΝΑΥ ΕΠΕΤΕ Μ̄ΠΟΥΧΠΟϤ ΕΒΟΛ
ϨΝ̄ ΤϹϨΙΜΕ ΠΕϨΤ ΤΗΥΤΝ̄ ΕΧΜ̄ ΠΕΤΝ̄ϨΟ Ν̄ΤΕΤΝ̄ΟΥΩϢΤ ΝΑϤ.
ΠΕΤΜ̄ΜΑΥ ΠΕ ΠΕΤΝ̄ΕΙΩΤ

ATTRIBUTION
Kernel saying.

TEXT AND TRANSLATION ISSUES
The expression 'not born of woman' is the antonym of the Semitic phrase 'one born of woman' which describes the condition of humanity, its mortality and generation through sexual intercourse (Job 14.1; 15.14; *Sukkah* 52a; *Ma'ayan ha-Hokmah* 60–61; *Pesik. R.* 20,98a; 25,128a; *Megillah* 13b; *3 Enoch* 5.2). The antonym describes the condition of God, referencing his immortality and self-generation (cf. L. 50).

INTERPRETATIVE COMMENT
In the Kernel Gospel, this saying may have been read as instructions for the etiquette for the Day of Judgement (Rev. 4.10; 5.14; 7.11). The interpretative meaning probably shifted to the etiquette for mystical visions once the hermeneutical emphasis of the Gospel shifted away from the eschatological (*1 Enoch* 14.24; *2 Enoch* 22.4).

SOURCE DISCUSSION
G. Quispel attributes this saying to the author of the Gospel.

LITERATURE PARALLELS

Revelation 4.10
> 'The twenty-four elders fall down before him who is seated on the throne and worship him who lives for ever and ever.'

Revelation 5.14
> 'And the elders fell down and worshipped.'

Revelation 7.11
> 'And all the angels stood round the throne and round the elders and the four living creatures, and they fell on their faces before the throne and worshipped God.'

1 Enoch *14.24*
> 'Until then I was prostrate on my face, covered and trembling.'

2 Enoch *22.4*
> 'And I fell down flat and worshipped the Lord'.

Cf. Hipp., *Ref.* 8.13.3

SELECT BIBLIOGRAPHY
DeConick (1996: 99–100); Quispel (1981: 265).

Logion 16.1–2

[1]Jesus said, 'Perhaps people think it is peace that I have come to cast upon the world.

[2]And they do not know it is division that I have come to cast upon the earth – fire, sword, war!'

NHC II 2.35.31–36

[1]ⲡⲉⲭⲉ ⲓ̄ⲥ̄ ⲭⲉ ⲧⲁⲭⲁ ⲉⲩⲙⲉⲉⲩⲉ ⲛ̄ϭⲓ ⲣ̄ⲣⲱⲙⲉ ⲭⲉ ⲛ̄ⲧⲁⲉⲓⲉⲓ ⲉⲛⲟⲩⲭⲉ
ⲛ̄ⲟⲩⲉⲓⲣⲏⲛⲏ ⲉⲭⲙ̄ ⲡⲕⲟⲥⲙⲟⲥ [2]ⲁⲩⲱ ⲥⲉⲥⲟⲟⲩⲛ ⲁⲛ ⲭⲉ ⲛ̄ⲧⲁⲉⲓⲉⲓ
ⲁⲛⲟⲩⲭⲉ ⲛ̄ϩⲛ̄ⲡⲱⲣⲭ ⲉ.ⲭⲛ̄ ⲡⲕⲁϩ ⲟⲩⲕⲱϩⲧ ⲟⲩⲥⲏϥⲉ ⲟⲩⲡⲟⲗⲉⲙⲟⲥ

ATTRIBUTION
Kernel saying.

INTERPRETATIVE COMMENT
This saying in the Kernel is apocalyptic in nature. It is the final logion in the first speech, underscoring the nearness of God's Judgement and Jesus' role in it as God's great angel of Judgement as I have described in the companion volume, *Recovering.* In apocalyptic texts, fire plays a dominant role in God's retributive and punitive actions of Judgement in the last days. In Jewish traditions, it was thought that God or his angel(s) would be responsible for pouring the fire of Judgement onto the earth (Isa. 66; Mal.; *Sib. Or.* 3.689–90; 4.171–81; *1 Enoch* 102.1; *Apoc. Elijah* 5.22–24; *4 Ezra* 13.1–11). This fiery Judgement was anticipated by the first Christians (1 Cor. 3.13–15; 2 Pet. 3.7–14; Rev. 8.5).

In the complete Gospel, with the accrual of L. 16.4 and the delay of the Eschaton, this originally apocalyptic saying came under scrutiny and a new hermeneutic. Now the 'division' (L. 16.1–2) and family separation (L. 16.3) spoken of in the Kernel is understood to refer to the choice of the believer to leave his or her family and become part of a Christian community which preferred celibacy to marriage. The 'fire, sword, war' that was cast upon the earth is recast in psychological terms as it was in the *Pseudo-Clementines*, as the interior battle with the passions, the demons that thwart the advancement of the soul.

SOURCE DISCUSSION
W. von Schürmann traces this logion back to Luke, particularly because of the word 'division' which he considers redactional. W. Schrage argues that L. 16.1–2 is a welding of Matthew 10.34–36 and Luke 12.51–53. Lukan agreements include 'think', and 'division'. Matthean agreements include 'to cast', 'sword' and the repetition of the phrase, 'I have come'.

J. Sieber questions Schrage's analysis of the redactionary elements ascribed to Luke, particularly the word, 'division'. He thinks that Matthew might be the one who has altered Quelle with 'sword' instead of 'division'. Rather Sieber attributes the *Thomas* variant to 'the lateness of the oral tradition on which Thomas is based' since it has secondarily expanded the saying with the addition 'fire, sword, war!' This appears to be similar to H. Koester's view that 'fire, sword, war' is an independent expansion of the original wording in Q, 'sword', which is preserved in Matthew 10.14. Patterson argues that 'sword' and 'cast' were in Matthew's version of Q. Sieber also points out that *Thomas* introduces the logion very differently from the Synoptics, a variant which he thinks is likely the more original introduction to the saying because it is 'an expression of prophetic self-consciousness'.

C. Tuckett disagrees with Sieber and restates that the use of διαμερισμός in Luke 12.51 agrees with *Thomas'* ⲡⲱⲣϫ which is used in Sahidic Luke. This he documents as secondary to Matthew's μάχαιρα. K. Snodgrass points out that διαμερισμός is a *hapax legomenon*, occurring in Luke six times and Acts twice. Outside of this, it only occurs three times, and these times are in the Passion narratives as a word drawn from Psalm 22.19.

G. Quispel thinks that *Thomas* is preserving an independent tradition probably based on a Jewish Christian Gospel. He suggests that allusions to the logion in the *Pseudo-Clementines*, especially *Recognitions* (Syriac) 2.26.6 which reads 'I have not come to cast peace upon the earth but *war*', is an indication that L. 16.1–2 comes from the same Jewish Christian source. *Recognitions* is closer to *Thomas* than Matthew with the phrase, 'war'. Since the words 'war' and 'sword' are variant translations of the Aramaic חרבא, Quispel explains the variant readings in the *Pseudo-Clementines* that have both 'war' (*Rec.* Syriac 2.26.6) and 'sword' (*Rec.* 2.26.6; 2.28.2; 2.32.3; 6.4.6) as translation variants of an earlier Aramaic tradition. *Thomas* is also familiar with this Aramaic tradition.

In my opinion, it is reasonable to argue that L. 16 represents an independent tradition which was also known to Quelle Luke, especially when we realize that the longest sequence of common words between L. 16.1–2 and Luke's version is only four, 'I have come to'. In other words, L. 16 may be evidence that Matthew and Luke had their own versions of Quelle with variant readings, that διαμερισμός was present in Luke's version of Quelle. If, however, one considers διαμερισμός a secondary development rather than an example of a multiform variant, then it is possible that the word came into the logion by way of secondary orality as the passage was reperformed in the oral environment and adapted to the memory of the Lukan version.

LITERATURE PARALLELS

Matthew 10.34 (Qmatt)
> 'Do not think that I have come to bring peace on earth. I have not come to bring peace, but a sword.'

Luke 12.51 (Qluke)
> 'Do you think that I have come to give peace on earth? No, I tell you, but rather division.'

1 Thess. 5.3
> 'When people say, "There is peace and security", then sudden destruction will come upon them as travail comes upon a woman with child, and there will be no escape.'

4 Ezra 16.21
> 'Behold, provisions will be so cheap upon earth that men will imagine that peace is assured them, for then the calamities shall spring up on the earth – sword, famine, and great confusion.'

Pseudo-Clementine Recognitions *(Syriac) 2.26*
> 'I have not come to send peace on earth, but war.'

Pseudo-Clementine Recognitions *2.26, 2.28, 6.4*
> 'I have not come to send peace on earth, but a sword.'

Pseudo-Clementine Recognitions *2.32*

'Elsewhere you say that he said that he would send a sword.'

Pseudo-Clementine Homilies *11.19*

'Whence the Prophet of Truth, knowing that the world was in much error, and seeing it ranged on the side of evil, did not choose that there should be peace to it while it stood in error. So that till the end he sets himself against all those who are in concord with wickedness, setting truth over against error, sending as it were fire upon those who are sober, namely wrath against the seducer, which is likened to a sword, and by holding forth the word he destroys ignorance by knowledge, cutting, as it were, separating the living from the dead. Therefore, while wickedness is being conquered by lawful knowledge, war has taken hold of all.'

Cf. Ezek. 13.11; 14.21; Jer. 14.12; 21.7; Isa. 13.10; 34.4; *1 Enoch* 90.13–20; 91.12–17; 93; *Jubilees* 23.13; *4 Ezra* 5.1; *2 Baruch* 25; Mark 13.13, 20 and parallels; Rev. 6; 8–9; 16; 20.

AGREEMENTS IN SYRIAN GOSPELS, WESTERN TEXT AND DIATESSARON
Luke 12.51//Matthew 10.34 in 1093 1424 Mcion b q l r^l S P sa Aphr Ephr (Luke) T^A T^P T^V
throw << give (Luke), bring (Matthew)

Luke 12.51//Matthew 10.34 in 033 213 e b ff^2 g l (Luke) T^L T^{NL} T^{HD} Zach
+ they do not know

Luke 12.51//Matthew 10.34 in T^V
+ I have come[2]

Luke 12.51//Matthew 10.34 in T^V T^A T^P
+ to throw[2]

Luke 12.51//Matthew 10.34 in T^{NL} Rec C
+ upon the earth

Luke 12.51//Matthew 10.34 in P Rec T^P Ar
+ war

Matthew 10.34 in C
divisions, sword

SELECT BIBLIOGRAPHY
Koester (1990: 94); Patterson (1993: 26); Quispel (1958/1959: 279); Schrage (1964a: 57–61); Schürmann (1963: 245); Sieber (1966: 115–17); Snodgrass (1989: 31 n. 30); Tuckett (1988: 146–47).

Logion 16.3

[3]'For there will be five people in a house. There will be three people against two, and two against three, father against son, and son against father.'

NHC II 2.35.36–36.4

³ογⲛ̄ †ογ ⲅⲁⲣ ⲛⲁϣⲱ[ⲡⲉ] ⲍ̄ⲛ ογⲏⲉⲓ ογⲛ̄ ϣⲟⲙⲧ ⲛⲁϣⲱⲡⲉ ⲉⲝⲛ̄
ⲥⲛⲁ ⲁγⲱ ⲥⲛⲁ ⲉⲝⲛ̄ ϣⲟⲙⲧ ⲡⲉⲓⲱⲧ ⲉⲝⲙ̄ ⲡϣⲏⲣⲉ ⲁγⲱ ⲡϣⲏⲣⲉ
ⲉⲝⲙ̄ ⲡⲉⲓⲱⲧ

ATTRIBUTION
Kernel saying.

TEXT AND TRANSLATION ISSUES
A. Guillaumont notes that L. 16.3, against Luke 12.52, preserves Semitic syntax in its phrasing, 'there will be five people in a house, three will be against two and two against three...' Here, we have two clauses juxtaposed instead of the first clause subordinated as a conditional clause. Guillaumont explains that Luke's Greek text is not satisfactory in its syntax. The translator did not understand the Semitic syntax and wrongly introduced διαμεμερίσμένοι in the first clause. In this case, he feels that *Thomas'* version helps us to understand the Aramaic substratum of the Synoptic Gospels.

INTERPRETATIVE COMMENT
This logion appears to have circulated together with L. 16.1–2 since it is already found attached in Quelle. In the Kernel, the saying was apocalyptic, echoing the common expectation that the end time would be chaotic and families would be in disarray (Micah 7.6; *1 Enoch* 56.7; *Jubilees* 23.16, 19).

The new hermeneutic applied in the later Thomasine Gospel once L. 16.4 accrued indicates a thorough revision of this apocalyptic expectation. The family division was believed to reflect the voluntary dissolution of the nuclear family necessary for the Christian who was committed to Jesus' words and encratic practice.

SOURCE DISCUSSION
W. Schrage sees L. 16.3 as dependent especially upon Luke 12.52–53 even though *Thomas* does not include the phrase ἀπὸ τὸ νῦν. J. Sieber counters by stating that the omission of this Lukan phrase argues for *Thomas'* independence. Further he says that Luke is developed from Micah 7.6 so the relationships described in Luke cannot be assigned to his editorial hand. If this were the case though, Sieber's argument does not work since Luke would be the one modifying Quelle based on his remembrance of Micah. Thus C. Tuckett concludes that it is redactional and L. 16.3 presupposes Luke. He states that the explicit numerical division of 3.2 and 2.3, and the reciprocal pairing of son against father and father against son agrees with Luke against Matthew. Tuckett cites evidence that Luke's wording is redactional because Matthew's wording is closer to Micah 7.6 and Luke, he thinks, has expanded the material secondarily by adding a reference to the hostility of the older generation to the younger. But does Luke's version represent Lukan redaction? If Matthew and Luke had the same version of Quelle which Tuckett presupposes, than it is just as tenable to argue that Matthew redacted Quelle, not Luke, in order to align the Quelle saying with Micah.

In my opinion, however, these arguments for Synoptic dependence do not account for the differences in the versions, including the differences in syntax noted above. L. 16.3 is substantively shorter than Luke or Matthew in the list of relatives. Moreover, *Thomas'* clause, 'For there will be five people in a house' does not contain the reference to 'one house' nor 'divided' as we find in Luke. The similarities are equally arresting. Although *Thomas* has two phrases in common with Luke – 'three against two, and two against three' and 'father against son, and son against father' – Luke breaks them up with additional material – 'they will be divided' – while *Thomas* presents them sequentially. This is evidence for oral variation rather than literary dependence. I think that these differences as well as the similarities can easily be explained if Luke and *Thomas* represent pre-synoptic oral variants of the saying. In fact, *Thomas*' version may lend weight to the hypothesis that Matthew and Luke had different versions of Quelle, in which case each variant echoes the rhetorician's memory of Micah as well as his or her memory of this saying of Jesus. This conclusion finds additional support from Guillaumont's earlier notation that *Thomas*' version appears to represent an Aramaic substratum which may also have been behind Luke 12.52.

LITERATURE PARALLELS

Matthew 10.35–36 (Qmatt)
'For I have come to set a man against his father, and a daughter against her mother, and a daughter-in-law against her mother-in-law. A man's foes will be those of his own household.'

Luke 12.52–53 (Qluke)
'For henceforth in one house there will be five divided, three against two and two against three. They will be divided, father against son and son against father, mother against daughter and daughter against her mother, mother-in-law against daughter-in-law and daughter-in-law against her mother-in-law.'

Pseudo-Clementine Recognitions *2.28*
'And henceforth you shall see father separated from son, son from father, husband from wife and wife from husband, mother from daughter and daughter from mother, brother from brother, father-in-law from daughter-in-law, friend from friend.'

Pseudo-Clementine Recognitions *2.29*
'He proclaims the war of the word and of confutation, and says that 'henceforth you shall see son separated from father, and husband from wife, and daughter from mother, and brother from brother, and daughter-in-law from mother-in-law, and a man's foes shall be they of his own house.'

Pseudo-Clementine Recognitions *2.32*
'And elsewhere you say, that he said that he would send a sword, that he might separate those who are in one house, so that son shall be divided from father, daughter from mother, brother from brother; so that if there be five in one house, three shall be divided against two, and two against three.'

Pseudo-Clementine Recognitions *6.4*
'For it is necessary that, for the sake of salvation, the son, for example, who has received the word of truth, be separated from his unbelieving parents; or again, that the father be separated from his son, or the daughter from her mother. And in this manner the battle of knowledge and ignorance, of truth and error, arises between believing and unbelieving kinsmen and relatives.'

Pseudo-Clementine Homilies *11.19*
'For the submissive son is, for the sake of salvation, separated from the unbelieving father, or the father from the son, or the mother from the daughter, or the daughter from the mother, and relatives from relatives, and friends from associates.'

Micah 7.6
'For the son treats the father with contempt, the daughter rises up against her mother, the daughter-in-law against her mother-in-law. A man's enemies are the men of his own house.'

4 Ezra *5.9*
'All friends shall conquer one another.'

4 Ezra *6.24*
'At that time, friends shall make war on friends like enemies.'

1 Enoch *56.7*

> 'And they shall begin to fight among themselves, and (by) their own right hands they
> shall prevail against themselves. A man shall not recognize his brother, nor a son his
> mother, until there shall be a (significant) number of corpses from among them.'

Cf. *Jub.* 23.16, 19.

AGREEMENTS IN SYRIAN GOSPELS, WESTERN TEXT AND DIATESSARON

Luke *12.52–53 in* 1012
   – henceforth

Luke *12.52–53 in* c D d ff² vg M~T T*^{NL}* T*^A* T*^T* S C Ps.-Clem.
   – divided

Luke *12.52–53 in* S T*^{NL}* Pist. Soph.
   – they will be divided

SELECT BIBLIOGRAPHY
Guillaumont (1958: 118–20); Schrage (1964a: 57); Sieber (1966: 116–17); Tuckett (1991:
356–57).

Logion 16.4

⁴'And they will stand as celibate people.'

NHC II 2.36.5

   ⁴ⲁⲩⲱ ⲥⲉⲛⲁⲱϨⲉ ⲉⲣⲁⲧⲟⲩ ⲉⲩⲟ ⲙⲙⲟⲛⲁⲭⲟⲥ

ATTRIBUTION
Accretion.

TEXT AND TRANSLATION ISSUES
ⲙⲟⲛⲁⲭⲟⲥ is not known in Greek sources prior to the fourth century. But A. Guillaumont,
M. Harl, F.-E. Morard and G. Quispel all note that its Syriac complement ܪܚܝ is used
commonly from the earliest sources of the Syrian Church to reference ascetics who lived
their lives as celibates. The use of monachos in the *Gospel of Thomas* is a precursor to that
which developed in monastic circles in the fourth and fifth centuries, when it came to
mean, as D. Brakke explains, not only the monk's celibacy embraced by his pursuit of
single-hearted devotion to God, but also his personal combat with many demons to regain
his lost unity with his divine identity. Thus I have translated ⲙⲟⲛⲁⲭⲟⲥ, 'celibate person',
in order to bring across this meaning, but to distinguish it from the similar phrase, ⲟⲩⲁ
ⲟⲩⲱⲧ, 'single person', used in other logia and which A.F.J. Klijn shows to be an equivalent expression. R. Uro has tried to make the case that this word is to be associated only
with an anti-familial posture, not celibacy, but he does not offer an alternative explanation
for this word's clear linguistic heritage with reference to singleness and celibacy as found
throughout Syrian literature.

   According to J. Fossum, the 'standing' state is a metaphor that was commonly used by
Jews and Christians to characterize the way in which angels worshipped before the seated

and enthroned God (*1 Enoch* 39.12–13; 40.1; 47.3; 68.2; *2 Enoch* 21.1; *Test. Abr.* 7–8; *Samaritan Lit.* 27.18). The righteous who took their place in heaven were also known by this title (*Asc. Isa.* 9.9–10; *2 Enoch* 22.10; *Memar Marqa* 4.12). M. Williams discusses this metaphor at length.

INTERPRETATIVE COMMENT
Development of the sayings tradition is indicated because this saying is an interpretative clause with vocabulary characteristic of the accretions, **MONAXOC** and **ⲱ2ⲉ ⲉⲣⲁⲧ⸗**. It accrued in the Gospel to reinterpret the previous eschatological sayings in response to the delayed Eschaton between 80 and 120 CE.

This clause is encratic, suggesting that a new hermeneutic was applied to the previous eschatological sayings by a new constituency – Christians with encratic tendencies. The accrual of this clause shifted the meaning of this unit of apocalyptic sayings from a warning to people about the impending Judgement and the dissolution of their families to an injunction from Jesus to abandon their families for the holy life of the single celibate believer. **MONAXOC** comes to mean 'monk' or 'virgin' in later Christian literature. Here it is used in its earlier sense to mean 'single person' or 'bachelor' as M. Harl and F.-E. Morard have shown in their studies. We should note that this use and interpretation of **MONAXOC** is entirely compatible with its use and interpretation in the *Liber Graduum*. According to the studies of A. Baker, the author of the *Liber Graduum* does not advocate a physical withdrawal for the *monachos* as we find in Egyptian monastic literature, but that he or she should leave father and mother, abstain from sexual intercourse, and live a life of virginity (737.9ff.)!

LITERATURE PARALLELS
Cf. L. 4.3, 22, 23, 48, and 106

SELECT BIBLIOGRAPHY
Baker (1965a: 292–94); Brakke (2006: 3–22); Fossum (1985a: 55–58, 120–24, 139–41); Guillaumont (1981: 202–203); Harl (1960: 464–74); Morard (1973; 1980); Quispel (1965); Uro (1998a: 140–62); Williams (1985).

Logion 17

Jesus said, 'I will give you what no eye has seen, what no ear has heard, what no hand has touched, and (what) has not arisen in the human mind.'

NHC II 2.36.5–9

ⲡⲉⲭⲉ ⲓ̅ⲥ̅ ⲭⲉ †ⲛⲁ† ⲛⲏⲧⲛ̅ ⲙ̅ⲡⲉⲧⲉ ⲙ̅ⲡⲉⲃⲁⲗ ⲛⲁⲩ ⲉⲣⲟϥ ⲁⲩⲱ
ⲡⲉⲧⲉ ⲙ̅ⲡⲉ ⲙⲁⲁⲭⲉ ⲥⲟⲧⲙⲉϥ ⲁⲩⲱ ⲡⲉⲧⲉ ⲙ̅ⲡⲉ6ⲓⲭ 6ⲙ̅6ⲱⲙϥ ⲁⲩⲱ
ⲙ̅ⲡⲉϥⲉⲓ ⲉ2ⲣⲁ̈ⲓ 2ⲓ ⲫⲏⲧ ⲣ̅ⲣⲱⲙⲉ

ATTRIBUTION
Kernel saying.

INTERPRETATIVE COMMENT

In the Kernel Gospel, this logion opens the second speech. It calls the hearer to listen to the secret revelation that the orator will give in Jesus' stead. In S. Davies' opinion, the Gospel is referring here to the Spirit of Wisdom which he compares with Paul's application in 1 Corinthians 2.7–10.

SOURCE DISCUSSION

G. Quispel traces this saying to a Jewish-Christian Gospel source, probably the *Gospel of the Nazarenes*.

It has been suggested by P. Prigent that a version of this saying came from the liturgy of the synagogue. The closest liturgical parallel appears to be that mentioned by E. Saunders, 1QS 11.5–8, a Qumran hymn. But Saunders argues for a different *Sitz im Leben* for this logion. It represents the activity of Christian prophets within the community who developed selected Old Testament passages believed to be prophetic of Jesus.

C. Hedrick says that the opinion that L. 17 derived from 1 Corinthians is highly unlikely since *Thomas* reflects no clear awareness of 1 Corinthians and would not have selected one saying out of Paul's letters and placed it on the lips of Jesus. He thinks that *Thomas* derived the logion either from non-Christian tradition or from a stock of Christian tradition that had already associated it with Jesus. Hedrick prefers the latter possibility.

LITERATURE PARALLELS

1 Cor. 2.9–10

[9]'But as it is written, "What no eye has seen, nor ear heard, nor the heart of man conceived, what God has prepared for those who love him", [10]God has revealed to us through the Spirit.'

Dialogue of the Saviour 57

'The Lord said, "[You have] asked me for a word [about that] which eye has not seen, nor have I heard about it, except from you."'

1 Clement 34.8

'Ten thousand times ten thousand stood before him, says Scripture, and thousands did him service, crying, Holy, holy, holy is the Lord of hosts; all creation is full of his glory. In the same way ought we ourselves, gathered together in a conscious unity, to cry to him as it were with a single voice, if we are to obtain a share of his glorious great promises – for it says that no eye has seen, nor ear has heard, no mortal heart has dreamed of the things God has in store for those who wait patiently for him.'

2 Clement 11.7

'If, then, we have done what is right in God's eyes, we shall enter his Kingdom and receive the promises which ear has not heard or eye seen, or which man's heart has not entertained.'

Martyrdom of Peter 10

'Therefore, you also brethren, having taken refuge with him and having learned that in him alone you exist, will obtain those things of which he says to you – what eye has not seen or ear heard, nor did they enter the heart of man.'

Acts of Peter 39

'To him, brethren, you also take refuge and learn that your existence is in him alone, and you shall then obtain that of which he said to you, "Eye has not seen, nor ear heard, neither has it entered into the heart of man."'

Acts of Thomas *36*

> 'But we speak of God and our Lord Jesus, and of the angels and the guardian spirits and the saints, and of the new world; and of the incorruptible food of the tree of life, and of the draught (of the water) of life; of what eye has not seen nor ear heard nor has entered into the heart of man (to conceive), – what God has prepared from of old for those who love him.'

Pseudo-Clementine Recognitions *1.44*

> 'For as no one can see without eyes, nor hear without ears, nor smell without nostrils, nor taste without tongue, nor handle anything without hands, so it is impossible, without the True Prophet, to know what is pleasing to God.'

Pseudo-Philo, Liber antiquitatum biblicarum *26, 13*

> 'And then I will take those and many others better than they are from where eye has not seen nor ear heard and it has not entered into the heart of man, until the like should come to pass in the world.'

Pseudo-Titus Epistle

> 'Great and honourable is the divine promise which the Lord has made with his own mouth to them that are holy and pure. He will bestow upon them what eyes have not seen nor ears heard, nor has it entered the human heart. And from eternity to eternity there will be a race incomparable and incomprehensible.'

Prayer of the Apostle Paul *1,A,26–35*

> 'Grant what no angel eye has [seen] and no archon ear (has) heard and what has not entered into the human heart which came to be angelic and (modelled) after the image of the psychic God when it was formed in the beginning, since I have faith and hope.'

Apostolic Constitutions *7.32*

> '"Then shall the wicked go away into everlasting punishment, but the righteous shall go into life eternal", to inherit those things "which eye has not seen, nor ear heard, nor have entered into the heart of man, such things as God has prepared for those who love him".'

Turfan Manichaean Fragment, M 789

> '…that I may redeem you from death and annihilation, I will give you what you have not seen with the eye nor heard with the ears nor grasped with the hand.'

Isaiah 64.4

> 'From of old no one has heard or perceived by the ear, no eye has seen a God besides you, who works for those who wait for him.'

SELECT BIBLIOGRAPHY
Davies (1983: 89–90); Hedrick (1989/1990: 46); Prigent (1958: 428); Saunders (1963: 49–55).

Logion 18.1–3

[1]The disciples said to Jesus, 'Tell us, how will our end come about?'

[2]Jesus said, 'Have you discovered the beginning that you seek the end? Because where the beginning is, the end will be also. [3]Whoever will stand in the beginning is blessed. This person will know the end, yet will not die.'

NHC II 2.36.9–17

¹ⲡⲉⲝⲉ ⲙⲙⲁⲑⲏⲧⲏⲥ ⲛⲓⲥ̄ ⲝⲉ ⲝⲟⲟⲥ ⲉⲣⲟⲛ ⲝⲉ ⲧⲛ̄ⲅⲁⲏ ⲉⲥⲛⲁϣⲱⲡⲉ ⲛⲁϣ ⲛ̄ⲅⲉ

²ⲡⲉⲝⲉ ⲓⲥ̄ ⲁⲧⲉⲧⲛ̄ϭⲱⲗⲡ ⲅⲁⲣ ⲉⲃⲟⲗ ⲛ̄ⲧⲁⲣⲭⲏ ⲝⲉⲕⲁⲁⲥ ⲉⲧⲉⲧⲛⲁϣⲓⲛⲉ ⲛ̄ⲥⲁ ⲑⲁⲅⲏ ⲝⲉ ⲅⲙ̄ ⲡⲙⲁ ⲉⲧⲉ ⲧⲁⲣⲭⲏ ⲙⲙⲁⲩ ⲉⲑⲁⲅⲏ ⲛⲁϣⲱⲡⲉ ⲙⲙⲁⲩ ³ⲟⲩⲙⲁⲕⲁⲣⲓⲟⲥ ⲡⲉⲧⲛⲁⲱⲅⲉ ⲉⲣⲁⲧϥ ⲅⲛ̄ ⲧⲁⲣⲭⲏ ⲁⲩⲱ ϥⲛⲁⲥⲟⲩⲱⲛ ⲑⲁⲅⲏ ⲁⲩⲱ ϥⲛⲁⲝⲓ ϯⲡⲉ ⲁⲛ ⲙⲙⲟⲩ

ATTRIBUTION
Accretion.

TEXT AND TRANSLATION ISSUES
In L. 18.3, the manuscript reads ⲡⲉⲧⲛⲁⲅⲱⲅⲉ. The scribe, however, has crossed out the first ⲅ. I have deleted the extra letter since it was a recognized error on the part of the scribe.

See L. 1 for discussion of the phrase, 'will not taste death', and its rendering in my translation, 'will not die'.

INTERPRETATIVE COMMENT
Secondary development of traditional material is signalled because this saying is part of a dialogue created to answer a question posed by the community. Moreover, the logion contains vocabulary characteristic of the accretions, ⲛⲁⲝⲓ ϯⲡⲉ ⲁⲛ ⲙⲙⲟⲩ. The community wants Jesus to explain what the End will be like, a question that grew out of the eschatological crisis experienced by this community. Thus the saying accrued in the Gospel in response to the delayed Eschaton between 60 and 100 CE. It possibly accumulated following the Kernel saying, L. 17, because it developed further Jesus' statement that he is going to tell the hearer or reader what has never occurred previously to the human mind.

In Jewish Christian literature, the New World ushered in by the Eschaton frequently was described in analogous terms with creation (Isa. 65.17; 66.22; *Jub.* 1.29; *1 Enoch* 91.16–17; *4 Ezra* 7.30–31; 2 Pet. 3.12–13; Rev. 21.1, 5), as a restitution of creation (*Test. Levi* 18.10–11; *Jub.* 23.26–28; *1 Enoch* 90.37–38; Rom. 3.24; 5.2; 8.19–21; Col. 1.15–20; Rev. 20.13; 21.4), as a transformation of creation (Isa. 26.1–3; 60.19–20; Dan. 12.3; *1 Enoch* 45.4–5; *2 Bar.* 51; Rev. 21.13), as an identification with creation (*1 Enoch* 24–25; Rev. 2.7; 21.1, 14, 17, 19), as the reservation of particular aspects of creation (*4 Ezra* 6.49–50; *2 Bar.* 29.4), as the pre-existence of certain aspects of creation that will appear at the End (*4 Ezra* 4.36–37; 7.70; Rev. 17.8; 21.2). Sometimes Eden will appear at the End in an earthly manifestation (*Test. Levi* 18.10–11) while other writings believe it to be heavenly (*1 Enoch* 61.12; 70.3–4; *2 Enoch* 8.1–3; *2 Bar.* 4.3; 51.11; *4 Ezra* 6.26; 7.28, 36–38; 13.52; 14.9, 49). Behind these images is the tradition that God would restore the creation and fix what had gone wrong, bringing to perfection what he had already created.

This accretion puns these traditions, using common eschatological imagery for mystical purposes. As M. Lelyveld states, understanding the End now implicitly means understanding the primordial condition. In other words, the End is understood to be a return to Paradise which can be achieved by the disciples when they 'stand' in Eden, an expression indicating that they have ascended to Paradise, are like Adam before he sinned and are the angels worshipping before God's throne (see L. 16.4). It is implied by this dialogue that the community previously has misunderstood the End to refer to the eschatological renewal of creation through cosmic endings, rather than the mystical renewal of creation and the original Adam through encratic practice and personal transformation.

Although this accretion is not distinctively Hermetic, it would have taken on additional meaning for community members familiar with Hermetism since the Hermetics taught that the goal of each human was to return his or her soul its heavenly origin as J.-P. Mahé has described. Thus, they thought that, at death, 'all things go back again to the place whence they have come down' (*Excerpt of Stobaeus* 26.12; *cf. Asc.* 11; *C.H.* 1.21; 13.18–19) or 'the human being rushes up through the cosmic framework' to the abode from which he or she came (*C.H.* 1.25). This experience could be mystically achieved through initiation such as is recorded in the *Discourse on the Eighth and the Ninth.* This association with Hermetic themes was already noted by B. Fordyce Miller in her 1967 article exegeting this saying.

A. Baker notes that the *Liber Graduum* states that the human being is now connected with sin 'because he tasted death from the beginning' (856.5–6). The reference, of course, is to Adam who sinned and therefore died. Similarly 729.15–16 has an interpolation into Genesis 2.17, 'in the day you transgress my word, you will taste death'. This appears to represent the same tradition found in L. 18.

SOURCE DISCUSSION
G. Quispel attributes this saying to the hand of the author of the Gospel.

LITERATURE PARALLELS

Matthew 24.3
'As he sat on the Mount of Olives, the disciples came to him privately, saying, "Tell us, when will this be, and what will be the sign of your coming and of the close of the age?"'

Mark 13.3–4
[3]'And as he sat on the Mount of Olives opposite the Temple, Peter and James and John and Andrew asked him privately, [4]"Tell us, when will this be, and what will be the sign when these things are all to be accomplished?"'

Luke 21.7
'And they asked him, "Teacher, when will this be, and what will be the sign when this is about to take place?"'

Origen, On First Principles *1.6.2*
'Seeing, then, that such is the end, when all enemies will be subdued to Christ, when death – the last enemy – shall be destroyed, and when the kingdom shall be delivered up to God the Father by Christ to whom all things are subject. Let us, I say, from such an end as this, contemplate the beginnings of things. For the end is always like the beginning.'

Koh. R. *2 (78a)*
'At the end of a thing does its beginning appear.'

Epis. Barn. *6.13*
'I will make the last things as the first.'

4 Ezra *7.30–31*
'And the world shall be turned back to primeval silence for seven days, as it was at the first beginnings.'

SELECT BIBLIOGRAPHY
Baker (1965/1966: 52–53); Lelyveld (1987: 33–43); Mahé (1998); Miller (1967); Quispel (1981: 265).

> ## *Logion 19.1–3*
>
> ¹Jesus said, 'Whoever existed before being born is blessed. ²If you become my disciples and listen to my teachings, these stones will support you. ³For you, there are five trees in Paradise. They do not change, summer and winter, and their leaves do not fall. Whoever knows them will not die.'

NHC II 2.36.17–25

¹ΠΕΧΕ ĪC ΧΕ ΟΥΜΑΚΑΡΙΟC ΠΕΝΤΑ2ϢϢΠΕ 2Α ΤΕ2Η ΕΜΠΑ-
ΤΕϤϢϢΠΕ ²ΕΤΕΤ̄ΝϢΑΝϢϢΠΕ ΝΑΕΙ Μ̄ΜΑΘΗΤΗC Ν̄ΤΕΤ̄ΝCϢΤΜ̄
ΑΝΑϢΑΧΕ ΝΕΕΙϢΝΕ ΝΑΡ̄ΔΙΑΚΟΝΕΙ ΝΗΤ̄Ν ³ΟΥΝ̄ΤΗΤ̄Ν ΓΑΡ Μ̄ΜΑΥ
Ν̄†ΟΥ Ν̄ϢΗΝ 2Μ̄ ΠΑΡΑΔΙCΟC ΕCΕΚΙΜ ΑΝ Ν̄ϢϢΜ Μ̄ΠΡϢ ΑΥϢ ΜΑΡΕ
ΝΟΥϬϢΒΕ 2Ε ΕΒΟΛ ΠΕΤΝΑCΟΥϢΝΟΥ ϤΝΑΧΙ †ΠΕ ΑΝ Μ̄ΜΟΥ

ATTRIBUTION
Accretion.

Text and Translation Issues

P. Nagel thinks that L. 19 alludes to the Tree of Life in Eden, not 'five trees' as the Coptic preserves. He attributes this to a translation error where 'five' was mistaken for 'middle', a transliteration of חמשה (five) for ἥμισυ (middle). Because the idea that there were 'five' trees in Paradise is unprecedented in Jewish literature, and the Tree of Life is found in the 'middle' of the Garden, it would appear that Nagel's appeal to translation error from Aramaic to Greek might be correct. But is this idea unprecedented? According to *3 Baruch* 4.7 (Slavonic), God commanded the angels to plant five trees in Eden: the olive, the apple, the nut, the melon, and the vine. This appears to be a variation of the rabbinic tradition that discussed what type of tree the Tree of Knowledge was. Was it wheat, vine, olive, citrus, or fig? The rabbinic references are collected by Billerbeck and Ginzberg. Philo also knows of five trees in Eden which he lists as the virtues, 'life, immortality, knowledge, apprehension, understanding of the conception of good and evil' (φυτὰ ζωῆς, ἀθανασίας, εἰδήσεως, καταλήψεως, συνέσεως καλοῦ καὶ πονηροῦ φαντασίας) (*De Plantatione* 36). This tradition appears to have been familiar and crops up in Manichaeism as discussed by I. Culianu, although it may have been introduced into Manichaeism by way of the *Gospel of Thomas* rather than an independent Jewish tradition. At any rate, I am not convinced that Nagel is correct in this case, especially since his theory would also mean that the plural 'trees' and their consistent plural reference throughout the logion would be mistaken as well.

M. Lelyveld reminds us that the arbour in Eden is common in apocalyptic literature as well as references to the life-giving properties of the trees. She understands the reference to 'five' in L. 19.3 to refer to the five parts of Nous. Although she does not mention it, this concept must be connected to the ancient understanding of the formation of the soul as it descends into the body and gains various aspects (see Interpretative Comment below).

See L. 1 for discussion of the phrase, 'will not taste death', and its rendering in my translation, 'will not die'.

INTERPRETATIVE COMMENT

Development is indicated because this saying contains vocabulary characteristic of the accretions, ΝΑΧΙ †ΠΕ ΑΝ Μ̄ΜΟΥ. It accrued following L. 18 to explain further the notion of a mystical return to the beginning, to the state of being before birth. It belongs to those accretions that developed the story of the recovery of the original Image through mystical transformation. As such, it represents a response to the delayed Eschaton and accrued in the Gospel between 80 and 120 CE. As M. Lelyveld states, the Eschaton has been realized.

The imagery in this unit evokes the Jewish-Hermetic story of ascent to Paradise and the transformation of the soul into its primal condition, here through the cultivation of the five trees of virtue as I have described in *Seek To See Him* and the companion volume to this monograph, *Recovering*. This idea is connected with the ancient religious notion that a specific number of vices and virtues form the human being. These aspects of the soul are acquired when the soul descends into its human vessel. In life, the soul is supposed to cultivate the virtues and eradicate the vices through virtuous living and study. This restores the soul to its lofty state of godliness and makes it possible for the soul to ascend back to its heavenly origin. R. Reitzenstein and G. Mussies outline these lists of vices and virtues, finding that they are based on two numerical systems, the twelve divisions of the Zodiac and the five planetary spheres and the five elements. This idea appears to have been long-lived, emerging in the later writings of the Syrian Father, Pseudo-Macarius (*Hom.* 37.8–9). According to L. 19, a person overcomes death because he or she has experienced a transformation into his or her original Image which existed before birth by cultivating the five trees of virtue (cf. L. 84). This person is a disciple of Jesus. He or she has listened to his teachings and abided by them. The person who feasts on the trees in Paradise has no need for normal food because he or she regained the primordial condition and eats from the trees as God had originally intended, a theme popular in apocalyptic literature as detailed by B. Otzen.

Moreover, L. 19 indicates that such a person can even be sustained by a diet of stones! This is probably a reference to the ancient idea that the person who has returned to the virtuous state of Adam, experiences an actual transformation of the physical body as discussed by D. Jacquat and C. Thommassett, and T. Shaw. Because the body was no longer fuelled by indulging the passions, gluttony on the top of the list, it was believed that the body of the virtuous person had returned to its primal condition of equilibrium, needing little to no food to support its survival. This idea became very prominent in monastic circles as I have outlined in 'The Great Mystery of Marriage' (cf. Athan., *Life of Ant.* 14; Chrysostom, *Hom. 13 in Tim. 5;* Tert., *De Ieiunio* 5).

SOURCE DISCUSSION

G. Quispel thinks that this saying came from the *Gospel of the Egyptians* or some other encratic source while H. Koester finds a strong association with the Johannine tradition (John 8.31–32). But Koester thinks that the Gospel has preserved the more original form of the saying, emphasizing the power of Jesus' words rather than 'abiding in' Jesus as John has it.

LITERATURE PARALLELS

John 8.31–32

31'If you continue in my word, you are truly my disciples, 32and you will know the truth, and the truth will make you free.'

Gospel of Philip *64.10–12*

'Blessed is the person who exists before being born. For he who exists has been and will be.'

Irenaeus, Epideixis *43*

'And again he [Jesus] says, "Blessed is the person who existed before becoming human."'

Lactantius, Divine Institutes *4.8*

> 'For we especially testify that he [Christ] was born twice, first in spirit and afterwards in the flesh. Whence it is thus said in Jeremiah, "Before I formed you in the womb, I knew you." And also in the same work, "Blessed is the person who existed before being born", which happened to no one else except Christ.'

Pseudo-Macarius, Hom. *37.8*

> '"Five words" refers to the whole complex of virtues that build up the total person in various ways. For just as he who speaks in the Lord through five words comprehends all wisdom, so he who obeys the Lord builds up all piety by means of the five virtues. For they are five and embrace all the others. First is prayer, then temperance, almsgiving, poverty, long-suffering.'

Manichaean Psalm-Book *161.17–18*

> 'For there are [five] trees in Paradise...in summer and winter.'

Cf. Jer. 1.5; Ezek. 47.12; Philo, *Leg. All.* 1.97–98; Philo, *De conf. ling.* 61; Philo, *De mig. Abr.* 36–37; Philo, *De plant.* 36; Philo, *Quest. Gen.* 1.6; 1.9; 1.56; Philo, *De. agric.* 8–19; *3 Baruch* 4.7; *Pistis Sophia* 1.1; *Books of Jeu* 100; *Manichaean Psalm-Book* 161.15–29; *Kephalia* 1.30.20–23; 1.48.15; 1.121.7–8; *C.H.* 13.7–10; *Physiologus* 34.18–20; *Odes Sol.* 11.16–19.

Select Bibliography
Culianu (1992: 161–88); DeConick (1996: 80–86; 2003: 312–15); Jacquart and Thommasset (1988: 48–86); Koester (1990: 115–16); Lelyveld (1987: 44–49); Mussies (1981); Nagel (1969a: 382); Otzen (1993); Reitzenstein (1978: 47–51, 209–12, 338–51); Shaw (1998: 27–28: 161–219).

Logion 20.1

¹The disciples said to Jesus, 'Tell us, what is the Kingdom of Heaven like?'

NHC II 2.36.26–27

¹ⲡⲉⲭⲉ ⲙ̄ⲙⲁⲑⲏⲧⲏⲥ ⲛ̄ⲓ̄ⲥ̄ ⲭⲉ ⲭⲟⲟⲥ ⲉⲣⲟⲛ ⲭⲉ ⲧⲙ̄ⲛ̄ⲧⲉⲣⲟ ⲛ̄ⲙ̄ⲡⲏⲩⲉ ⲉⲥⲧⲛ̄ⲧⲱⲛ ⲉⲛⲓⲙ

Attribution
Accretion.

Interpretative Comment
Development is obvious by the rhetorical introduction to the mustard seed parable, a question posed by the disciples similar in style to that found in the accretion, L. 18.1. It was probably added to the Kernel parable, L. 20.2–4, sometime between 60 and 100 CE. Since the parable itself does not appear to reflect later Christian interests, there is no reason to think that it was not already present in the Kernel. The introductory clause, however, raises concerns about the community's expectations of the Kingdom. For this reason, I find it likely that L. 20.1 accrued in the Gospel in order to explain the non-event. Thus the community reasoned, 'Did not Jesus say that it was like a mustard seed, not a cosmic event?' In this way they offered a new hermeneutic for an originally eschatological parable

that spoke about the imminent cultivation of God's Kingdom which would be like a mustard seed sown on tilled soil, quickly maturing into a 'large branch'.

Logion 20.2–4

[2]He said to them, 'It is like a mustard seed, [2]smaller than all seeds. [4]But when it falls on cultivated soil, it puts forth a large branch and becomes a shelter for birds of the sky.'

NHC II 2.36.27–33

[2]ⲡⲉⲝⲁϥ ⲛⲁⲩ ⲝⲉ ⲉⲥⲧⲛ̅ⲧⲱⲛ ⲁⲩⲃⲁ̅ⲃⲓⲗⲉ ⲛ̅ϣⲁ̅ⲧⲁⲙ [3][[ⲥ]]ⲥⲟⲃ̅ⲕ
ⲡⲁⲣⲁ ⲛ̅ϭⲣⲟϭ ⲧⲏⲣⲟⲩ [4]ϩⲟⲧⲁⲛ ⲇⲉ ⲉⲥϣⲁ(ⲛ)ϩⲉ ⲉⲝⲙ̅ ⲡⲕⲁϩ ⲉⲧⲟⲩⲣ̅
ϩⲱⲃ ⲉⲣⲟϥ ϣⲁϥⲧⲉⲩⲟ ⲉⲃⲟⲗ ⲛ̅ⲛⲟⲩⲛⲟϭ ⲛ̅ⲧⲁⲣ ⲛ̅ϥϣⲱⲡⲉ ⲛ̅ⲥⲕⲉⲡⲏ
ⲛ̅ϩⲁⲗⲁⲧⲉ ⲛ̅ⲧⲡⲉ

ATTRIBUTION
Kernel saying.

Text and Translation Issues

In L. 20.4, the manuscript reads ⲉⲥϣⲁϩⲉ. The ⲛ must be supplied to make sense of the word.

INTERPRETATIVE COMMENT
The Kernel saying would not have been introduced by the disciples' question (L. 20.1). The rhetorical character of the second speech which discusses the eschatological challenges of discipleship used this parable as rationale, that the time is ripe for Jesus' revelation since the Kingdom of God is already breaking into the world. Like a tiny seed, it will soon mature into a large plant. This parable is followed by a series of analogies underscoring that the disciple must be ready for the coming of God's Kingdom and the chaos that is expected to come along with it (L. 21.5), and that the Judgement is as near as the sickle which is in hand ready to reap the ripened grain (L. 21.9–10).

In the complete Gospel, the accretions serve to shift the hermeneutic. The introduction of the question (L. 20.1) shows concern over the delayed Eschaton. Jesus' response would have been heard as a confirmation that the community had misunderstood the issue. 'Didn't Jesus say', the community reasoned, 'that the coming of the Kingdom was like a mustard seed, not a cosmic event? It is not something to anticipate in the future, but has already been established in our midst.'

SOURCE DISCUSSION
L. Cerfaux observes that L. 20 is significantly closer to Mark than to the form of the parable in Matthew or Luke. W. Schrage points out parallels between L. 20 and the Synoptics. Because of the agreement between L. 20 and Matthew over the phrase 'Kingdom of Heaven', he feels that dependence on Matthew is at least proven. The other minor agreements Schrage says do not prove dependence.

J. Sieber argues that the 'Kingdom of Heaven' is not an exclusively Matthean phrase. It is, in fact, a preferred Thomasine phrase and may suggest a Jewish heritage. Because Sieber does not consider it an editorial trait, he says that dependence on Matthew cannot be sustained. Sieber notes many secondary developments in the logion though: the disciple's introductory question (L. 20.1), the brevity, the rearrangement of elements to make for a better flow, and the phrase 'a large branch'. He traces these changes to the oral development of the saying.

C. Tuckett attempts to make the case that some of the agreements between L. 10 and Mark are identified as Markan redactions, particularly the phrase 'smaller than all the seeds' which he says was a proverbial tradition in Palestine that Mark added to explain the significance of the mustard seed for Gentile readers. Also, Mark's phrase, 'producing a great branch', is secondary to Quelle's, 'becoming a tree', he says, even though current opinion is the opposite since mustard seeds do not produce trees. But, these types of arguments are difficult to maintain because we do not have Mark's sources. It is equally possible that Mark's source contained these phrases. H. Koester, in fact, notes that Mark and *Thomas* use the appropriate term 'vegetable', and they correctly describe the birds as nesting under the branches. What both hold in common, he thinks, are original features of the parable.

Because of this, I think it better to conclude that L. 20 and Mark were familiar with a pre-synoptic version of the Mustard Seed parable which was different from the versions found in Quelle Matthew or Quelle Luke. The differences in the versions, even at this early stage, were due to the oral performance field.

LITERATURE PARALLELS

Mark 4.30–32
> [30]'And he said to them, "With what can we compare the Kingdom of God, or what parable shall we use for it? [31]It is like a grain of mustard seed which, when sown upon the ground, is the smallest of all the seeds on earth. [32]Yet when it is sown, it grows up and becomes the greatest of all shrubs, and puts forth large branches, so that the birds of the air can make nests in the shade."'

Matthew 13.31–32 (Qmatt)
> [31]'The Kingdom of Heaven is like a grain of mustard seed which a man took and sowed in his field. [32]It is the smallest of all seeds, but when it has grown it is the greatest of shrubs and becomes a tree, so that the birds of the air come and make nests in its branches.'

Luke 13.18–19 (Qluke)
> [18]'What is the Kingdom of God like? And to what shall I compare it? [19]It is like a grain of mustard seed which a man took and sowed in his garden. And it grew and became a tree, and the birds of the air made nests in its branches.'

Cf. Ezekiel 17.22–23; Daniel 4.20–21

AGREEMENTS IN SYRIAN GOSPELS, WESTERN TEXT AND DIATESSARON

Matthew 13.31–32//Mark 4.30–32//Luke 13.18–19 in T^P T^{EC}
> mustard seed + smaller than all seeds

Matthew 13.31–32//Mark 4.30–32//Luke 13.18–19 in aur c f q P (Matthew) e f g h bo (Luke) geo (B) sa aeth (Matthew)
> a great branch << a tree

SELECT BIBLIOGRAPHY
Cerfaux and Garitte (1957: 311); Koester (1990: 109); Schrage (1964a: 61–66); Sieber (1966: 173–75); Tuckett (1988: 148–53).

> ### *Logion 21.1–4*
>
> [1]Mary said to Jesus, 'Who are your disciples like?'
>
> [2]He said, 'They are like little children sojourning in a field that is not theirs. [3]When the owners of the field come, they will say, "Leave our field!" [4]In front of them, they strip naked in order to abandon it, returning their field to them.'

NHC II 2.36.33–37.7

[1]ⲠⲈⲬⲈ ⲘⲀⲢⲒϨⲀⲘ ⲚⲒⲤ ⲬⲈ ⲈⲚⲈⲔⲘⲀⲐⲎⲦⲎⲤ ⲈⲒⲚⲈ Ⲛ̄ⲚⲒⲘ
[2]ⲠⲈⲬⲀϥ ⲬⲈ ⲈⲨⲈⲒⲚⲈ Ⲛ̄Ⲛ̄ϢⲎⲢⲈ ϢⲎⲘ ⲈⲨϬ|ⲈⲀⲒⲦ ⲀⲨⲤⲰϢⲈ
ⲈⲦⲰⲞⲨ ⲀⲚ ⲦⲈ [3]ϨⲞⲦⲀⲚ ⲈⲨϢⲀⲈⲒ Ⲛ̄ϬⲒ Ⲛ̄ⲬⲞⲈⲒⲤ Ⲛ̄ⲦⲤⲰϢⲈ
ⲤⲈⲚⲀⲬⲞⲞⲤ ⲬⲈ ⲔⲈ ⲦⲚ̄ⲤⲰϢⲈ ⲈⲂⲞⲖ ⲚⲀⲚ [4]Ⲛ̄ⲦⲞⲞⲨ ⲤⲈⲔⲀⲔⲀϨⲎⲨ
Ⲙ̄ⲠⲞⲨⲘ̄ⲦⲞ ⲈⲂⲞⲖ ⲈⲦⲢⲞⲨⲔⲀⲀⲤ ⲈⲂⲞⲖ ⲚⲀⲨ Ⲛ̄ⲤⲈ†ⲦⲞⲨⲤⲰϢⲈ ⲚⲀⲨ

ATTRIBUTION
Accretion.

TEXT AND TRANSLATION ISSUES
N. Perrin notes that the Coptic word-choice, 'to strip naked', stems from a translation error since in Syriac the standard word meaning 'to disrobe', ܦܫܛ, also means 'to renounce'. So it is possible that the original sense of the logion was, 'In their presence, they will give up rights to the field in order to let them have their field back.'

INTERPRETATIVE COMMENT
Development is indicated since this unit is introduced by a question posed by a disciple, forming a short dialogue about discipleship. The encratic response indicates that a new constituency has developed within the community, a constituency with severe ascetic tendencies. The accretion accrued in the Gospel between 80 and 120 CE. It may have entered the text at this point as part of a rhetorical series of questions posed to Jesus following the promise of L. 17, that Jesus would reveal to his disciples what had been previously unknown. The series advances from explanations about the End (L. 18–19) to the Kingdom (L. 20) and finally to discipleship (L. 21–22).

The question raised by the community asks for a redefinition of discipleship. It is part of a series of questions presented by a community in the process of recasting its expectations: 'How will our end take place?' (L. 18); 'What is the Kingdom of Heaven like?' (L. 20a); 'Who are your disciples like?' (L. 21a); 'Shall we, as children, enter the kingdom?' (L. 22). The response to the question is encratic, highlighting the ideal disciple as someone who is like a 'child' temporarily sojourning in this world. This child abandons this world to the ruling demons when he or she strips naked, a metaphor for renouncing the body (cf. L. 37). R. Uro provides a more Stoic interpretation, suggesting that this logion encouraged a 'moderate or internalized detachment' rather than an extreme asceticism. But his reading does not take into consideration that the sequence of logia in this cluster works to apply an encratic hermeneutic to this accretive parable, a hermeneutic that Jesus provides in L. 21.6 and 7, that they are supposed to 'keep watch against the world' and 'arm themselves' so that the demons cannot enter their souls and steal the precious possessions that they have been gathering. This is not the language of Stoicism, but the language of the apocalyptic internalized, where the battleground of the angels and demons is the human soul rather than the cosmos.

SOURCE DISCUSSION
This 'parable' is not so much a metaphor as it is an allegory. As such, it is not characteristic of the earliest Jesus traditions as W. Stoker has pointed out. It appears to me to have developed later within the field of oral performance and reflects encratic ideology retrospective of our earliest Christian texts.

SELECT BIBLIOGRAPHY
Perrin (2002: 43–44); Stoker (1988: 103–104); Uro (2003: 65–70).

Logion 21.5

[5]For this reason I say, 'If the owner of a house knows that a thief is coming, he will keep watch before he arrives. He will not allow him to break into his house, part of his estate, to steal his furnishings.'

NHC II 2.37.7–10

Ⲇⲓⲁ ⲧⲟⲩⲧⲟ ϯⲭⲱ ⲙⲙⲟⲥ ⲭⲉ ⲉϥϣⲁⲉⲓⲙⲉ ⲛ̄ϭⲓ ⲡⲭⲉⲥ⳪ⲛ̄ⲏⲉⲓ ⲭⲉ
ϥⲛⲏⲩ ⲛ̄ϭⲓ ⲡⲣⲉϥⲭⲓⲟⲩⲉ ϥⲛⲁⲣⲟⲉⲓⲥ ⲉⲙⲡⲁⲧⲉϥⲉⲓ ⲛ̄ϥⲧⲙ̄ⲕⲁⲁϥ ⲉϣⲟⲭⲧ
ⲉϩⲟⲩⲛ ⲉⲡⲉϥⲏⲉⲓ ⲛ̄ⲧⲉ ⲧⲉϥⲙⲛ̄ⲧⲉⲣⲟ ⲉⲧⲣⲉϥϥⲓ ⲛ̄ⲛⲉϥⲥⲕⲉⲩⲟⲥ

ATTRIBUTION
Kernel saying.

TEXT AND TRANSLATION ISSUES
H. Quecke and A. Guillaumont trace the odd expression with the double possessive article, literally, 'his house of his kingdom', to a mistranslation of a Syriac proleptic genitive suffix. Since it could also be explained as a Coptic explicative genitive, there is no reason to turn to the Syriac solution. So I have understood and translated it as a Coptic explicative genitive. Thus, 'his house, part of his estate'.

INTERPRETATIVE COMMENT
This saying is part of a rhetorical cluster in the Kernel Gospel, teaching people that the Eschaton is near and that preparations should be made for it and the following Judgement. The Kingdom has already been sown like a mustard seed and is reaching maturity as a plant (L. 20.2–4). Readiness and watchfulness are required (L. 21.5). Once the grain is ripened, the harvest will come (L. 21.10).

Once the accretive materials surrounded this text, the hermeneutic was reshaped so that the parable becomes an encratic story about being on guard against 'the world' and its 'robbers', the demons who might enter your soul and steal the precious possessions it harbours (21.6–8). Such is the teaching of Pseudo-Macarius in reference to this parable (*Hom.* 3.4). This understanding of the parable is similar to that discussed by T. Zoeckler and R. Uro while contrary to the opinion held by J. Leipoldt and H.M. Schnecke, H.C. Kee and J. Ménard, that the robbers are the Archons which appear in Gnostic mythologies.

SOURCE DISCUSSION

W. Schrage, R. Kasser, R. Grant and D.N. Freedman, and B. Gärtner are of the opinion that the Synoptics served as the source for L. 21.5 and its parallel L. 103. H. von Schürmann points specifically to Luke 12.35 and 37. W. Schrage outlines the details suggesting that 'there I say to you' comes from Luke 12.44 and 12.37. The notion of watching is from Matthew 24.43. The parable of the Strong Man in Mark 3.27 and its parallels is the source for the 'goods' motif.

J. Sieber argues that none of these are editorial traits of any of the Synoptic authors so dependence cannot be proven. The synthesis of the variety of elements in *Thomas* suggests to Sieber an oral source rather than a written one. Interestingly, H. Koester notes that L. 21.5 contains a complete version of the parable while QLuke 12.39–40 has been shortened in order to add a reference to the coming of the Son of Man. So the purpose of the coming of the thief only remains in *Thomas,* signalling that we have preserved in L. 21.5 a more original form of the parable.

In my opinion, the parable displays all the characteristics of orally transmitted material, having a few words and phrases in common with the Synoptic versions but no sequences beyond four words. There is no evidence of secondary orality. So I find that this parable is probably an independent multiform developed within the field of oral performance.

LITERATURE PARALLELS

Matthew 24.43 (Qmatt)
> 'But know this, that if the householder had known in what part of the night the thief was coming, he would have watched and would not have let his house be broken into.'

Luke 12.39 (Qluke)
> 'But know this, that if the householder had known at what hour the thief was coming, he would not have left his house to be broken into.'

L. 103
> Jesus said, 'Blessed is the man who knows where the thieves are going to enter, so that [he] may arise, gather at his estate, and arm himself.'

Revelation 3.3
> 'If you will not awake, I will come like a thief, and you will not know at what hour I will come upon you.'

Revelation 16.15
> 'Lo, I am coming like a thief! Blessed is he who is awake, keeping his garments that he may not go naked and be seen exposed!'

1 Thessalonians 5.2
> [2]'For you yourselves know well that the day of the Lord will come like a thief in the night.'

2 Peter 3.10
> 'But the day of the Lord will come like a thief, and then the heavens will pass away with a loud noise, and the elements will be dissolved with fire, and the earth and the works that are upon it will be burned up.'

Didache *16.1*
> 'Be watchful over your life. Never let your lamps go out or your loins be ungirt, but keep yourselves always in readiness, for you can never be sure the hour when our Lord may be coming.'

Pseudo-Macarius, Hom. *3.4*

> 'There are not just three categories of sin against which one must guard oneself, but the number is legion... Are you not obligated to war against these in your inner thoughts? If a robber invades your house, are you not at once greatly distressed? He does not allow you to be freed from anxious worries. You begin to fight back against him. You exchange blows. So ought also the soul to strike back, to resist, to strike blow for blow.'

AGREEMENTS IN SYRIAN GOSPELS, WESTERN TEXT AND DIATESSARON

Matthew 24.43//Luke 12.39 in T^{NL.}
+ therefore I say

Matthew 24.43//Luke 12.39 in T^{V}
that << in what part of the night

Matthew 24.43//Luke 12.39 in Pal T^{P}
watch << be ready

SELECT BIBLIOGRAPHY

Gärtner (1961: 176–83); Grant with Freedman (1960: 141–42); Guillaumont (1981: 195); Kasser (1961: 58); Kee (1963: 311); Koester (1990: 98); Leipoldt and Schenke (1960: 14 n. 2); Ménard (1975: 111); Quecke (1963); Schürmann (1963: 243–44); Schrage (1964a: 67–69); Sieber (1966: 257–58); Uro (2003: 65–67); Zoeckler (1999: 208).

Logion 21.6–8

[6]'You, then, keep watch against the world. [7]Arm yourselves with great strength so that the robbers do not find a way to come to you, [8]because the possessions you are looking after, they will find.'

NHC II 2.37.11–15

[6]ⲚⲦⲰⲦⲚ ⲆⲈ ⲢⲞⲈⲒⲤ ϨⲀ ⲦⲈϨⲎ ⲘⲠⲔⲞⲤⲘⲞⲤ [7]ⲘⲞⲨⲢ ⲘⲘⲰⲦⲚ ⲈⲜⲚ
ⲚⲈⲦⲚ̄ϯⲦⲈ ϨⲚ̄Ⲛ ⲞⲨⲚⲞϬ Ⲛ̄ⲆⲨⲚⲀⲘⲒⲤ ϢⲒⲚⲀ ⲬⲈ ⲚⲈⲚⲀϨⲤⲦⲎⲤ ϨⲈ ⲈϨⲒⲎ
ⲈⲈⲒ ϢⲀⲢⲰⲦⲚ̄ [8]ⲈⲠⲈⲒ ⲠⲈⲬⲢⲈⲒⲀ ⲈⲦⲈⲦⲚ̄ϬⲰϢⲦ ⲈⲂⲞⲖ ϨⲎⲦⲤ̄ ⲤⲈⲚⲀϨⲈ
ⲈⲢⲞⲤ

ATTRIBUTION
Accretion.

TEXT AND TRANSLATION ISSUES
The phrase 'because the possessions you are looking after, they will find' might also be translated: 'because the affair you expect will be found'. I chose the former rendering because it is more sensible.

The expression ⲘⲞⲨⲢ ⲘⲘⲰⲦⲚ ⲈⲜⲚ ⲚⲈⲦⲚ̄ϯⲦⲈ literally reads 'strap your loins'. It is an idiomatic expression for arming oneself. Thus my translation, 'arm yourselves'.

INTERPRETATIVE COMMENT
Development is indicated by the presence of an interpretative clause that continues the encratic theme from the accretion L. 21.5, the command to 'keep watch against the world'.

This logion accrued in the Gospel between 80 and 120 CE to reinterpret the old parable, L. 21.5, which had highlighted the preparation needed to endure the chaos of the Last Days. L. 21.6–8 is an interpretative clause that provides new meaning to the old parable. The new hermeneutic applied to the parable is encratic. The householder is supposed to keep watch against the thief, the world itself. To do so, the person must arm him- or herself with great strength so that the robbers, probably understood to be the demons who are loose in the world, do not slip in and wreak havoc in the soul. This hermeneutic is similar to that voiced by Pseudo-Macarius (*Hom.* 3.4; 16.11).

SOURCE DISCUSSION
This appears to be an interpretation of the preceding parable that developed during oral performance.

LITERATURE PARALLELS

Pseudo-Macarius, *Hom.* 3.4
> 'There are not just three categories of sin against which one must guard oneself, but the number is legion... Are you not obligated to war against these in your inner thoughts? If a robber invades your house, are you not at once greatly distressed? He does not allow you to be freed from anxious worries. You begin to fight back against him. You exchange blows. So ought also the soul to strike back, to resist, to strike blow for blow.'

Pseudo-Macarius, *Hom.* 16.11
> 'For thieves are attacking. Just like a person who has suffered many muggings by robbers and undergone dangers, and then escapes with great difficulty, who then later comes into great wealth and good fortune and fears no more dread of loss because of his abundance of wealth, so too spiritual persons, who before passed through many temptations and dangerous places and then were filled with grace and heaped up good things, are no longer afraid of those who seek to rob them since their wealth is so great. Still they are not without fear – fear, I say, not of those who quake before evil spirits, but fear and concern as to how they may best use the spiritual gifts entrusted to them.'

Logion 21.9

⁹'There ought to be a wise person among you!'

NHC II 2.37.15–17

⁹ⲘⲀⲢⲉϥϣⲱⲡⲉ ϨⲚ ⲦⲉⲦⲚ̅ⲘⲎⲦⲉ Ⲛ̅Ϭⲓ ⲞⲨⲢⲱⲘⲉ Ⲛ̅ⲉⲡⲓⲤⲦⲎⲘⲱⲚ

ATTRIBUTION
Accretion.

INTERPRETATIVE COMMENT
This phrase is an interpretative clause used to amonish the hearer or reader that the old parable (L. 21.5) has been reinterpreted and should be understood through this new hermeneutic (L. 21.6–8).

Logion 21.10

[10]'When the grain ripened, he came quickly with his sickle in his hand. He harvested it.'

NHC II 2.37.17–18

[10]ⲚⲦⲀⲢⲈⲠⲔⲀⲢⲠⲞⲤ ⲠⲰⲢ ⲀϤⲈⲒ ⲢⲚⲚ ⲞⲨⲂⲈⲠⲎ ⲈⲠⲈϤⲀⲤⲢ ⲢⲚ ⲠⲈϤϬⲒⲬ
ⲀϤⲢⲀⲤϤ

ATTRIBUTION
Kernel saying.

INTERPRETATIVE COMMENT
In the Kernel Gospel, this saying is part of a sequence of logia teaching about the eschatological nature of the times. The emphasis would have been on the fact that the events of the End were already in process and that soon the harvest or Judgement would occur. The disciple must be prepared and ready for this final day. In the complete Gospel, the accretions would have served to reinterpret the cosmological battle as the internal war of the soul against the demons and the responsibility of the believer to be on guard against the world and its temptations. L. 21.10 reminded the hearer or reader that he or she would be judged on the basis of his or her success or failure in this arena.

LITERATURE PARALLELS

Mark 4.29
'When the grain is ripe, at once he puts in the sickle, because the harvest has come.'

Revelation 14.15–16
[15]'And another angel came out of the temple, calling with a loud voice to him who sat upon the cloud, "Put in your sickle, and reap, for the hour to reap has come, for the harvest of the earth is fully ripe." [16]So he who sat upon the cloud swung his sickle on the earth, and the earth was reaped.'

Joel 3.13
'Put in the sickle, for the harvest is ripe.'

AGREEMENTS IN SYRIAN GOSPELS, WESTERN TEXT AND DIATESSARON

Mark 4.29 in P T^A *T*^{NL} *geo (A) boh*
when the grain ripened << is produced

Mark 4.29 in T^{NL}
+ reaped it

Logion 21.11

[11]'Whoever has hears to hear should listen!'

NHC II 2.37.18–19

[11]ⲠⲈⲦⲈ ⲞⲨⲚ ⲘⲀⲀⲬⲈ ⲘⲘⲞϤ ⲈⲤⲰⲦⲘ ⲘⲀⲢⲈϤⲤⲰⲦⲘ

ATTRIBUTION
Kernel saying.

INTERPRETATIVE COMMENT
See L. 8.4.

LITERATURE PARALLELS
See L. 8.4.

Logion 22.1–7

[1]Jesus saw little babies nursing. [2]He said to his disciples, 'These little ones nursing are like those who enter the Kingdom.'

[3]They said to him, 'Will we enter the Kingdom as little babies?'

[4]Jesus said to them, 'When you make the two one, and when you make the inside like the outside, and the outside like the inside, and the above like the below. [5]And when you make the male and the female into a single being, with the result that the male is not male nor the female female. [6]When you make eyes in place of an eye, and a hand in place of a hand, and a foot in place of a foot, and an image in place of an image, [7]then you will enter [the Kingdom.]'

NHC II 2.37.20–35

[1]ⲁⲓⲥ ⲛⲁⲩ ⲁϩⲛ̄ⲕⲟⲩⲉⲓ ⲉⲩϫⲓ ⲉⲣⲱⲧⲉ [2]ⲡⲉⲭⲁϥ ⲛ̄ⲛⲉϥⲙⲁⲑⲏⲧⲏⲥ ϫⲉ
ⲛⲉⲉⲓⲕⲟⲩⲉⲓ ⲉⲧϫⲓ ⲉⲣⲱⲧⲉ ⲉⲩⲧⲛ̄ⲧⲱⲛ ⲁⲛⲉⲧⲃⲏⲕ ⲉϩⲟⲩⲛ ⲁⲧⲙⲛ̄ⲧⲉⲣⲟ
[3]ⲡⲉϫⲁⲩ ⲛⲁϥ ϫⲉ ⲉⲉⲓⲉⲛⲟ ⲛ̄ⲕⲟⲩⲉⲓ ⲧⲛ̄ⲛⲁⲃⲱⲕ ⲉϩⲟⲩⲛ ⲉⲧⲙⲛ̄ⲧⲉⲣⲟ
[4]ⲡⲉϫⲉ ⲓⲏⲥ ⲛⲁⲩ ϫⲉ ϩⲟⲧⲁⲛ ⲉⲧⲉⲧⲛ̄ϣⲁⲡ̄ ⲡⲥⲛⲁⲩ ⲟⲩⲁ ⲁⲩⲱ
ⲉⲧⲉⲧⲛ̄ϣⲁⲡ̄ ⲡⲥⲁ ⲛϩⲟⲩⲛ ⲛ̄ⲑⲉ ⲙ̄ⲡⲥⲁ ⲛⲃⲟⲗ ⲁⲩⲱ ⲡⲥⲁ ⲛⲃⲟⲗ ⲛ̄ⲑⲉ
ⲙ̄ⲡⲥⲁ ⲛϩⲟⲩⲛ ⲁⲩⲱ ⲡⲥⲁ (ⲛ)ⲧⲡⲉ ⲛ̄ⲑⲉ ⲙ̄ⲡⲥⲁ ⲙⲡⲓⲧⲛ̄ [5]ⲁⲩⲱ ϣⲓⲛⲁ
ⲉⲧⲉⲧⲛⲁⲉⲓⲣⲉ ⲙ̄ⲫⲟⲟⲩⲧ ⲙⲛ̄ ⲧⲥϩⲓⲙⲉ ⲙ̄ⲡⲓⲟⲩⲁ ⲟⲩⲱⲧ ϫⲉⲕⲁⲁⲥ ⲛⲉ
ⲫⲟⲟⲩⲧ ⲣ̄ ϩⲟⲟⲩⲧ ⲛ̄ⲧⲉ ⲧⲥϩⲓⲙⲉ ⲣ̄ ⲥϩⲓⲙⲉ [6]ϩⲟⲧⲁⲛ ⲉⲧⲉⲧⲛ̄ϣⲁⲉⲓⲣⲉ
ⲛ̄ϩⲛⲃⲁⲗ ⲉⲡⲙⲁ ⲛ̄ⲟⲩⲃⲁⲗ ⲁⲩⲱ ⲟⲩϭⲓϫ ⲉⲡⲙⲁ ⲛ̄ⲛⲟⲩϭⲓϫ ⲁⲩⲱ
ⲟⲩⲉⲣⲏⲧⲉ ⲉⲡⲙⲁ ⲛ̄ⲟⲩⲉⲣⲏⲧⲉ ⲟⲩϩⲓⲕⲱⲛ ⲉⲡⲙⲁ ⲛ̄ⲟⲩϩⲓⲕⲱ(ⲛ) [7]ⲧⲟⲧⲉ
ⲧⲉⲧⲛⲁⲃⲱⲕ ⲉϩⲟⲩⲛ |ⲉⲧⲙⲛ̄ⲧⲉⲣ|ⲟ

ATTRIBUTION
Accretion.

TEXT AND TRANSLATION ISSUES
In L. 22.4, ⲛ must be supplied before the manuscript reading, ⲧⲡⲉ.
   In L. 22.6, the manuscript reads, ⲛⲟⲩϩⲓⲕⲱ. ⲛ must be supplied at the end of the word.

INTERPRETATIVE COMMENT
Development is indicated by the dialogue format. The response is encratic and accrued in the Gospel between 80 and 120 CE in response to the delay of the Eschaton. The dialogue shows signs that the community is questioning its understanding of the Kingdom and its 'entrance' requirements. The resolution favours a personal transformation through encratic

behaviour, particularly celibacy, rather than a cosmic one. The person is admonished to become a 'little one', which is understood to be the androgynous primal Adam as discussed by W. Meeks, A.F.J. Klijn, M. Meyer, D.R. MacDonald and E. Castelli. Noteworthy is A. Baker's observation that the understanding of 'child' in the *Liber Graduum* is similar to this: 'unless you are converted and become as little children, you will not be as you were before you sinned' (341.21–24). In fact, the prelapsarian Adam and Eve are described as naked nursing babies (341.2–3) who were not ashamed just as nursing babies are not ashamed (341.4–5). Thus we must become as these little infants (341.20–21). The image of the prelapsarian couple as children in Eden, innocent of sexuality, is common in patristic writings as discussed by E. Peterson. In practical terms, this was a call to encratic performance as R. Valantasis recently argues and G. Quispel long ago pointed out.

This transformation involves restoring one's self to its original Image, refashioning every aspect from the eye to the foot to the hand. This, in fact, is the resurrected body created in the present moment rather than at the end of time. In many ways it may be most similar to Paul's view of the progressive glorification of the person into the Image (2 Cor. 3.18), although he is quite clear that the full realization of this transformation cannot take place until the Eschaton itself (1 Cor. 15.35–36).

For further discussion of celibacy in the Gospel, see L. 16.4.

SOURCE DISCUSSION
T. Baarda's comparative analysis leads him to the conclusion that *2 Clement, Thomas* and the *Gospel of the Egyptians* offer us three different developments of one and the same saying. He presents this case against G. Quispel who thinks that the source of *Thomas'* saying *was* the *Gospel of the Egyptians*. T. Callan's study supports Baarda's position that these three sources represent independent streams of early Christian tradition. Further, he tries to make the case that the agreement between the three witnesses favours the conclusion that it is an 'authentic saying of Jesus'.

LITERATURE PARALLELS

Galatians 3.27–28
> [27]'For as many of you as were baptized into Christ have put on Christ. [28]There is neither Jew nor Greek, there is neither slave nor free, there is neither male nor female; for you are all one in Christ Jesus.'

2 Clement *12.2*
> 'For when the Lord himself was asked by someone when his Kingdom would come, he said, "When the two will be one, and the outside as the inside, and the male with the female neither male nor female."'

Gospel of the Egyptians *(Clement of Alexandria,* Strom. *3.13.92)*
> 'When Salome asked when the things would be known that she asked about, the Lord said, "When you have trampled on the garment of shame and when the two become one and the male with the female is neither male nor female."'

Gospel of Philip *67.30–34*
> 'He [said], "I came to make [the things below] like the things [above and the things] outside like the things [inside. I came to unite] them in the place."'

Gospel of Philip *70.9–17*
> 'If the woman had not separated from the man, she would not die with the man. His separation became the beginning of death. There Christ came to correct the separation

which was from the beginning and to unite the two again and to give life to those who died in the separation and to unite them.'

Gospel of Philip *68.22–26*

'When Eve was still in Adam, death did not exist. When she was separated from him, death came into being. If he enters again and attains his former self, death will be no more.'

Hippolytus, Ref. *5.7.14–15*

'For the man is androgynous, he says. Therefore, according to this conception of theirs, the intercourse of woman with man is shown, in conformity with such teaching, to be an altogether wicked and forbidden matter. For, he says, Attis has been castrated. That is, he has passed over from the earthly parts of the creation below to the eternal substance above, where, he says, there is neither male nor female, but a new creature, a new man, which is androgynous.'

Pseudo-Macarius, Hom. *2.2*

'When, indeed, the Apostle says, "Put off the old man" (Eph. 4.22), he refers to the entire man, having new eyes in place of the old, ears replacing ears, hands for hands, feet for feet.'

Pseudo-Macarius, Hom. *2.4*

'All who have put off the old and earthly man and from whom Jesus has removed the clothing of the Kingdom of Darkness have put on the new and heavenly man, Jesus Christ, so that once again the eyes are joined to new eyes, ears to ears, head to head, to be completely pure and bearing the heavenly Image.'

Pseudo-Macarius, Hom. *34.2*

'In that place there is "neither male nor female, slave nor free" (Gal. 3.28), for all are being transformed into a divine nature, being made noble and gods and children of God.'

Liber Graduum *341.21–24*

'Unless you are converted and become as little children, you will not be as you were before you sinned.'

Acts of Peter *38*

'Concerning these things, the Lord said in a mystery, "Unless you make the things on the right as those on the left and the things on the left as those on the right and the things above as those below and the things behind as those before, you will not recognize the Kingdom."'

Acts of Philip *140 (34)*

'For the Lord said to me, "Unless you make the things below into the things above and the things on the left into the things on the right, you will not enter my Kingdom."'

Acts of Thomas *147*

'The inside I [Thomas] have made outside and the outside <inside>, and all your fullness has been fulfilled in me. I have not turned back to the things behind, but have gone forward to the things before, so that I might not become a reproach.'

Acts of Thomas *147, Syriac*

'The internal I have made external, and the external internal. Let your will be fulfilled in all my members. I have not turned back, and I have not stretched forward. Let me not be a wonder and a sign.'

Liber Graduum *792.17–22*

  'If two of you gather together (Matthew 18.19), which two are the interior man and the exterior man which unite in observance of precepts.'

Liber Graduum *253.23–25*

  'For the inside man is not different from the outside, nor the outside from the inside.'

Testament of the Lord *1.28*

  'He, being the Christ, who was crucified, by whom the [things] that were on the left hand were [placed] on the right hand, and those which were beneath [were] as those which [were] above, and those which [were] behind as those which [were] before, when he rose from the dead, and trod down Sheol, and by death slew death…'

Mark 10.14–15

  [14]'When Jesus saw it he was indignant, and said to them, "Let the children come to me, do not hinder them, for to such belongs the Kingdom of God. [15]Truly I say to you, whoever does not receive the Kingdom of God like a child will not enter it."'

Matthew 19.14

  'Jesus said, "Let the children come to me, and do not hinder them; for to such belongs the Kingdom of Heaven."'

Matthew 18.3

  'Truly I say to you, unless you turn and become like children, you will never enter the Kingdom of Heaven.'

Luke 18.16

  'But Jesus called them to him, saying, "Let the children come to me, and do not hinder them; for to such belongs the Kingdom of God. Truly, I say to you, whoever does not receive the Kingdom of God like a child will not enter it."'

Acts of Thomas *129*

  'Would that the days passed swiftly over me, my mother, and that all the hours were one, that I might go forth from this world, and go see that Beautiful One of whom I have heard tell, that Living One and Giver of Life to those who believe in him, where there is neither night nor day, and no darkness, but light, and neither good nor bad; nor rich nor poor, nor male nor female, nor slaves nor free, nor any who are proud and uplifted over those who are humble.'

Acts of Peter *38*

  'Concerning this the Lord says in a mystery, "Unless you make what is on the right hand as what is on the left and what is on the left hand as what is on the right and what is above as what is below and what is behind as what is before, you will not recognize the Kingdom."'

Cf. *Liber Graduum* 540.23–541.2; *Acts of Archelaus* 24.2

Select Bibliography

Baarda (1983b); Baker (1965/1966: 53); Callan (1990); Castelli (1991); DeConick (1996: 17–21); Klijn (1962); MacDonald (1987); Meeks (1974); Meyer (1985); Peterson (1959: 195); Quispel (1965; 1967a: 7, 89–109); Valantasis (1999).

Logion 23.1

¹Jesus said, 'I will select you, one from a thousand, and two from ten thousand.'

NHC II 2.38.1–2

¹ⲡⲉⲝⲉ ⲓ̅ⲥ̅ ⲝⲉ ⲧ̇ⲛⲁⲥⲉ|ⲧ|ⲡ ⲧⲏⲛⲉ ⲟⲩⲁ ⲉⲃⲟⲗ ϩ̅ⲛ ϣⲟ ⲁⲩⲱ ⲥⲛⲁⲩ ⲉⲃⲟⲗ ϩ̅ⲛ ⲧⲃⲁ

ATTRIBUTION
Kernel saying.

INTERPRETATIVE COMMENT
In the Kernel Gospel, this logion immediately followed L. 21.9–11, reminding the hearer that the Judgement was as near as the sickle which is in the hand and ready to reap the ripened grain. Jesus promises in L. 23.1 that he himself will be the Judge, choosing 'you, one from a thousand, and two from ten thousand'. The eschatological selection of the few believers is a common expectation in apocalyptic literature (*4 Ezra* 7.45–61; *1 Enoch* 1, 51, 93; Luke 17.34–35; Matthew 24.40–41). The accrual of the interpretative clause L. 23.2, however, shifted the meaning of the saying to Jesus' selection of the unmarried virgins who are already like the angels standing next to God's throne.

SOURCE DISCUSSION
G. Quispel attributes this logion to a Jewish Christian Gospel, probably the *Gospel of the Nazarenes.*

LITERATURE PARALLELS

Matthew 22.14
'For many are called, but few are chosen.'

Irenaeus, Adv. haer. *1.24.6*
'However, the multitude cannot understand these things, but one out of a thousand and two out of ten thousand.'

Epiphanius, Pan. *24.5.4*
'And he (Basilides) says that it is necessary not to reveal to anyone at all the things that concern the Father and his mystery and to keep (these things) in silence among themselves, but to reveal (them) to one in a thousand and to two in ten thousand, and he charged his disciples, saying, "Know all things, but let no one (else) know."'

Pistis Sophia *3.134*
'The Savior answered and said to Mary, "I say to you, they will find one in a thousand and two in ten thousand to complete the mystery of the first mystery."'

Mandaean Prayers, *90*
'He chose one out of a thousand, and from two thousand, he chose two.'

Cf. Deut. 32.30; Eccl. 7.28

SELECT BIBLIOGRAPHY
Quispel (1981: 265).

Logion 23.2

²'And they will stand as single people.'

NHC II 2.38.2–3

²ⲁⲩⲱ ⲥⲉⲛⲁⲱ︤ⲣ︤ⲉ ⲉⲣⲁⲧⲟⲩ ⲉⲩⲟ ⲟⲩⲁ ⲟⲩⲱⲧ

ATTRIBUTION
Accretion.

TEXT AND TRANSLATION ISSUES
A.F.J. Klijn has shown that the expression ⲟⲩⲁ ⲟⲩⲱⲧ is equivalent to μονάχος. For a fuller discussion of this issue, see L. 16.4.

INTERPRETATIVE COMMENT
Development is indicated by the presence of an interpretative clause with vocabulary characteristic of the accretions, ⲱ︤ⲣ︤ⲉ ⲉⲣⲁⲧ⸗ and ⲟⲩⲁ ⲟⲩⲱⲧ. The change of person from second plural to third plural is additional evidence that this is a clause added to an earlier Kernel saying in order to reinterpret it. The saying being reinterpreted is an eschatological saying about the selection of faithful at Judgement. Its reinterpretation forces an encratic hermeneutic onto the old saying. The saying accrued in the collection between 80 and 120 CE

The new encratic hermeneutic suggests that Jesus has already selected his faithful from the masses of unbelievers. They are the celibate people who are like the angels, the ones who 'stand' in God's presence. For further discussion, see L. 4.3 and 16.4.

LITERATURE PARALLELS
See L. 16.4.

Logion 24.1

¹His disciples said, 'Teach us about the place where you are, because we must seek it.'

NHC II 2.38.3–6

¹ⲡⲉⲭⲉ ⲛⲉ︤ϥⲙⲁⲑⲏⲧⲏⲥ ϫⲉ ⲙⲁⲧⲥⲉⲃⲟⲛ ⲉⲡⲧⲟⲡⲟⲥ ⲉⲧⲕ︤ⲙⲙⲁⲩ ⲉⲡⲉⲓ
ⲧⲁⲛⲁⲅⲕⲏ ⲉⲣⲟⲛ ⲧⲉ ⲉⲧⲣⲛ︤ⲱⲓⲛⲉ ⲛ︤ⲥⲱ︤ϥ

ATTRIBUTION
Accretion.

Interpretative Comment
Development is indicated by the dialogue format. This accretion is retrospective and responsive, enquiring about where Jesus has gone. It accrued in the Gospel to provide a mystical reinterpretation of the Kernel saying, L. 24.2–3, between 60 and 100 CE. Because this

introductory clause does not form a tight verbal unit with the following saying, L. 24.2–3, it appears that L. 24.2–3 was already present in the Kernel while L. 24.1 is a later appendage.

This dialogue, then, did not accrue in the Gospel as a complete unit. Rather the introductory clause was appended to an older saying in order to provide new teaching about mysticism. This question, posed by the disciples, represents the eschatological concerns of the community. They are asking to be shown where Jesus lives because they believe that they must seek this 'place' in order to be saved. This introductory clause serves to append the language of mystical journey to the 'place' where Jesus resides with an older Kernel saying about the interior 'man of light', the soul. So the accretive clause reorients the traditional meaning of the Kernel saying. According to the accretive hermeneutic, the disciple is understood to be a person who can seek Jesus by turning inward to his or her soul, a soul that has been transformed into the very reflection of Jesus, the Anthropos, the heavenly Man of Light.

As I have argued in *Voice of the Mystics*, the Johannine community may be involved in a polemic against the Thomasine position, arguing that it is not possible for anyone to ascend to the place where Jesus has gone. Only when Jesus returns, will the ascent to the place he has prepared occur.

SOURCE DISCUSSION
G. Quispel attributes this saying to the author of the Gospel.

LITERATURE PARALLELS

John 7.33–34
 [33]'I will be with you a little longer. And then I go to him who sent me. [34]You will seek me and you will not find me. Where I am you can not come.'

John 8.21
 'I go away, and you will seek me and die in your sin. Where I am going, you can not come.'

John 13.33
 'Little children, yet a little while I am with you. You will seek me. And as I said to the Jews so now I say to you, "Where I am going you can not come."'

John 13.36–37
 [36]'Simon Peter said to him, "Lord, where are you going?" [37]Jesus answered, "Where I am going you can not follow me now. But you will follow afterward."'

John 14.3–5
 [3]'"And when I go and prepare a place for you, I will come again and will take you to myself, that where I am you may be also. [4]And you know the way where I am going". [5]Thomas said to him, "Lord, we do not know where you are going. How can we know the way?"'

Apocryphon of James *2.23–25*
 'I shall go to the place from which I have come. If you desire to come with me, come.'

Cf. *Dialogue of the Saviour* 27–28; 34

SELECT BIBLIOGRAPHY
DeConick (2001a: 34–42, 68–85); Quispel (1981: 265).

Logion 24.2

²He said to them, 'Whoever has ears should listen!'

NHC II 2.38.6–7

²ⲡⲉⲭⲁϥ ⲛⲁⲩ ϫⲉ ⲡⲉⲧⲉⲩⲛ̄ ⲙⲁⲁϫⲉ ⲙ̄ⲙⲟϥ ⲙⲁⲣⲉϥ ⲥⲱⲧⲙ̄

ATTRIBUTION
Kernel saying.

INTERPRETATIVE COMMENT
This saying is an admonition to an audience to listen carefully to the orator's speech and draw from it meaning. It is a common heuristic device in early Christianity which preachers used repeatedly in order to prompt reflection and to provide pause, giving the preacher time to consider the continuation of the performance.

SOURCE DISCUSSION
The form of this saying is most similar to the one used by Matthew, 'Whoever has ears, let him hear' (although see Matthew 11.15). W. Schrage does not think it possible to argue for *Thomas'* dependence on the Synoptics based on this saying. J. Sieber goes a step further, concluding that *Thomas'* free use of the phrase suggests that he is referring to an independent tradition or source.

LITERATURE PARALLELS
See L. 8.4

SELECT BIBLIOGRAPHY
Schrage (1964a: 42); Sieber (1966: 177–78).

Logion 24.3

³'There is light inside a person of light. And it lights up the whole world. If it does not shine, it is dark.'

P.Oxy. 655 (Fragment d)

[…]ν […φ]ωτεινῷ […κο]σμῷ […]η […ἐ]στιν

NHC II 2.38.7–10

³ⲟⲩⲛ̄ ⲟⲩⲟⲉⲓⲛ ϣⲟⲟⲡ ⲙ̄ⲫⲟⲩⲛ ⲛ̄ⲛⲟⲩⲣⲙ̄ⲟⲩⲟⲉⲓⲛ ⲁⲩⲱ ϥⲣ̄ ⲟⲩⲟⲉⲓⲛ
ⲉⲡⲕⲟⲥⲙⲟⲥ ⲧⲏⲣϥ ⲉϥⲧⲙ̄ⲣ̄ ⲟⲩⲟⲉⲓⲛ ⲟⲩⲕⲁⲕⲉ ⲡⲉ

ATTRIBUTION
Kernel saying.

TEXT AND TRANSLATION ISSUES

E. Saunders argues that this logion can help us understand Luke 11.36 and its problematic manuscript tradition. In his opinion, the apodosis of the Lukan saying must represent an error in translation. Behind the Greek is the Aramaic word 'whole' (*kolla* or כֹּלָּא) which was mistakenly read as an adjective rather than a noun. The true sense of the Lukan passage, Saunders thinks, would be: 'If your whole (*kolla*) body is full of light, all (*kolla*) will be light, just as the lamp lights you with its brightness.'

INTERPRETATIVE COMMENT

The Kernel saying suggested that a person should shine forth his or her light in order to bring the world out of its darkness. Once the introductory clause accrued, the saying took on a new hermeneutic. The ecstatic journey about which the disciples have spoken in L. 24.1 is connected to an internal experience in L. 24.3. The disciple is literally called a 'man of light', a person whose soul has regained its original luminous form. Because the transformed soul is a reflection of Jesus, the heavenly Man of Light, the disciple can turn inward now and encounter Jesus within him- or herself. Only then will it be possible for this person to radiate this light externally, bringing further transformation to the world.

SOURCE DISCUSSION

R. Grant and D.N. Freedman view L. 24.3 as a Gnostic paraphrase of Matthew 6.22–23 and Luke 11.34–36. J. Sieber, however, correctly notes that there is no editorial evidence to support the argument for Synoptic dependence here.

LITERATURE PARALLELS

Matthew 6.22–23 (Qmatt)

[22]'The eye is the lamp of the body. So, if your eye is sound, your whole body will be full of light. [23]But if your eye is not sound, your whole body will be full of darkness. If then the light in you is darkness, how great is the darkness!'

Luke 11.34–35 (Qluke)

[34]'Your eye is the lamp of your body. When your eye is sound, your whole body is full of light. But when it is not sound, your body is full of darkness. [35]Therefore, be careful lest the light in you be darkness.'

John 11.9–10

[9]'If any one walks in the day, he does not stumble, because he sees the light of this world. [10]But if any one walks in the night, he stumbles, because the light is not in him.'

Matthew 5.14–16

[14]'You are the light of the world. A city set on a hill can not be hid. [15]Nor do men light a lamp and put it under a bushel, but on a stand, and it gives light to all in the house. [16]Let your light so shine before men, that they may see your good works and give glory to your Father who is in heaven.'

Dialogue of the Saviour *8*

'The Saviour [said], "The lamp [of the body] is the mind. As long as [the things inside] you are set in order, that is, [...] your bodies are [luminous]. As long as your hearts are [dark], the luminosity you anticipate [...]..."'

Dialogue of the Saviour *14*

'If one does not [...] darkness, he will be able to see [...]. So I tell you [...] light is the darkness [...] stand in [...] not see the light [...]'

Dialogue of the Saviour *34*

'If one does not stand in the darkness, he will not be able to see the light.'

Gospel of the Saviour *97.20–22*

'You are the lamp that illuminates the world.'

John 8.12

'I am the light of the world. He who follows me will not walk in darkness, but will have the light of life.'

John 9.4–5

[4]'We must work the works of him who sent me, while it is day. Night comes, when no one can work. [5]As long as I am in the world, I am the light of the world.'

John 12.35–36

[35]'The light is with you a little longer. Walk while you have the light, lest the darkness overtake you. He who walks in the darkness does not know where he goes. [36]While you have the light, believe in the light, that you may become sons of light.'

Pseudo-Macarius, Hom. *33.4*

'When you gaze on a light, look into your soul to see whether you have found the true and good light... For there is another man within, beyond the sensible one.'

SELECT BIBLIOGRAPHY

Grant with Freedman (1960: 145–46); Saunders (1963: 55–58); Sieber (1966: 62).

Logion 25.1–2

[1]Jesus said, 'Love your brother like your soul. [2]Watch over him like the pupil of your eye.'

NHC II 2.38.10–12

[1]ⲡⲉⲭⲉ ⲓ̅ⲥ̅ ϫⲉ ⲙⲉⲣⲉⲡⲉⲕⲥⲟⲛ ⲛ̅ⲑⲉ ⲛ̅ⲧⲉⲕⲯⲩⲭⲏ [2]ⲉⲣⲓⲧⲏⲣⲉⲓ ⲙ̅ⲙⲟϥ
ⲛ̅ⲑⲉ ⲛ̅ⲧⲉⲗⲟⲩ ⲙ̅ⲡⲉⲕⲃⲁⲗ

ATTRIBUTION

Kernel saying.

TEXT AND TRANSLATION ISSUES

G. Garitte, A. Guillaumont and G. Quispel maintain that the phrase, 'as you own soul' (ⲛ̅ⲑⲉ ⲛ̅ⲧⲉⲕⲯⲩⲭⲏ), is a Hebraism meaning 'as yourself'. It is a reflexive use of נֶפֶשׁ (Gen. 27.19, 31; Isa. 43.4). K.H. Kuhn states that this does not have to point to an Aramaic substratum but may be nothing more than a Biblicism. I have retained the idiom in my translation only to signal a difference with the Synoptic parallels. Syriac versions of the New Testament and the Peshitta of Leviticus 19.18 read 'as your soul' while the LXX and Hebrew read 'as yourself'. In my view, the saying points to an Aramaic substratum where 'your soul' was the idiom meaning 'yourself'. The Greek translator of *Thomas* rendered it literally, 'your soul', while the tradition known to the Greek Synoptics rendered it less literally, 'yourself'. The Syriac New Testament versions and the Peshitta retained the Semitism.

L. 25.1 has 'your brother' rather than 'your neighbour' as found in the New Testament. *Liber Graduum* 396.8, when commenting on John 15.12, similarly has 'place your soul for your brothers' rather than 'his friends' as found in John.

INTERPRETATIVE COMMENT

L. 25 is part of the rhetoric in which Jesus discusses the eschatological challenges of discipleship in the second speech. In this cluster, he is particularly interested in teaching ethics. He expects the hearer to follow him as a 'person of light' who will light up the whole world (L. 24.3). He admonishes hearers to love and watch over their brothers like their own souls (L. 25). He wants them to remove the beam in their own eyes before worrying about the twig in their brother's eye (L. 26).

SOURCE DISCUSSION

There is no evidence, according to W. Schrage or J. Sieber, to support the position that this logion is based on the Synoptic texts (there appears to be a misprint in line 14, page 249 of Sieber's dissertation: 'evidence' should read 'no evidence'). M. Fieger thinks that L. 25.2 shows aquaintance with Jewish literature (cf. Deut. 32.10; Ps. 117.8; Sir. 17.22) and that L. 25.1 may owe itself to the love commandment in the Synoptics. He does not think, however, that this can be established with certainty because the second element of the Synoptic saying is missing in *Thomas*, the command to love God.

G. Quispel thinks that a saying of Jesus not commanding to love God, but to love your neighbour or brother more than your soul was current in free oral tradition since both the *Didache* and *Thomas* reference it, and the Gospel of John appears to be familiar with it. He traces the saying to Jewish Christian circles from Palestine, migrating to Mesopotamia at an early date. He does not think that L. 25 came from the *Gospel of the Hebrews*, however, because Origen references 'you shall love your neighbor as yourself' not 'love your brother as your soul'. So he says that L. 25 may have come from the *Gospel of the Nazarenes*.

I find L. 25 to be a fine example of an independent saying traditional to the oral field. It cannot be effectively argued that it is based on Old Syriac Gospels because a similar form of the saying found in the *Didache* was already circulating in Western Syria in the first century.

LITERATURE PARALLELS

Mark 12.31
    'The second is this, "Love your neighbour as yourself."'

Matthew 19.19
    'Honour your father and your mother, and You shall love your neighbour as yourself.'

Matthew 22.39
    'And a second is like it, You shall love your neighbour as yourself.'

Luke 10.27
    '...and your neighbour as yourself.'

Romans 13.9
    'The commandments...are summed up in this sentence, "You shall love your neighbour as yourself."'

Galatians 5.14

'For the whole law is fulfilled in one word, "You shall love your neighbour as yourself."'

James 2.8

'If you really fulfil the royal law according to the scripture, "You shall love your neighbour as yourself", you do well.'

Didache *1*

'The Way of Life is this: You shall love first the Lord your Creator, and secondly, your neighbour as yourself; and you shall do nothing to anyone that you would not wish to be done to yourself.'

Epistle of Barnabas *19.5, 9*

'Cherish no ill-natured designs upon your neighbour… Love your neighbour more than yourself.'

Leviticus 19.18

'…you shall love your neighbour as yourself.'

Gospel of the Hebrews *5 (Jerome,* Commentary on Ephesians *3)*

'And never rejoice except when you look upon your brother with love.'

1 John 2.10

'Only the man who loves his brother dwells in light. There is nothing to make him stumble.'

John 13.34–35

[34]'I give you a new commandment: love one another. As I have loved you, so you are to love one another. [35]By this all men will know that you are my disciples, if you have love for one another.'

John 15.12

'This is my commandment: love one another, as I have loved you.'

CD 6.20

'For each to love his brother like himself.'

Test. Sim. *4.7*

'And you, children, each of you, love his brothers with a good heart.'

Test. Gad *6.1*

'Now, my children, each of you love his brother.'

Test. Zeb. *8.5*

'Whomever you see, do not harbour resentment, my children. Love one another, and do not calculate the wrong done by each to his brothers.'

Didache *2*

'You are to have no malicious designs on a neighbour. You are to cherish not feelings of hatred for anybody. Some you are to reprove, some to pray for, and some again to love more than your own soul.'

Pseudo-Clementine Ep. Clem. *8.5*

'But I know that you will do these things if you fix love into your minds.'

Pseudo-Clementine Homilies *12.32*

'But having devoted himself to love his neighbour as himself, he is not afraid of poverty, but becomes poor by sharing his possessions with those who have none. But neither does he punish the sinner. For he who loves his neighbour as himself, as he knows that when he has sinned he does not wish to be punished, so neither does he punish those who sin. And as he wishes to be praised, and blessed, and honoured, and to have all his sins forgiven, thus he does to his neighbour, loving him as himself. In one word, what he wishes for himself, he wishes also for his neighbour.'

Pseudo-Clementine Recognitions *2.29*
'He mourned over those who lived in riches and luxury, who bestowed nothing upon the poor, proving that they must render an account, because they did not pity their neighbours, even when they were in poverty, whom they ought to love as themselves.'

Liber Graduum *16.4*
'For he (Jesus) said to you, "Love your brother more than your soul."'

Liber Graduum *22.7*
'Love the son of your flesh as your soul.'

Test. Sim. *4.5–6*
'Guard yourselves therefore, my children, from all jealousy and envy. Live in integrity of your heart, so that God might give you grace and glory and blessing upon your heads, just as you have observed in Joseph. In all his days, he did not reproach us for this deed, but he loved us as his own soul.'

Test. Ben. *4.3*
'He loves those who wrong him as he loves his own soul.'

Deut. 32.10
'He encircled him, he cared for him, he kept him as the apple of his eye.'

Ps. 17.8
'Keep me as the apple of the eye. Hide me in the shadow of your wings.'

Sirach 17.22
'A man's almsgiving is a signet with him (the Lord), and he will keep a person's kindness as the apple of his eye.'

Epistle of Barnabas *19.9b*
'Love as the apple of your eye everyone who speaks the word of the Lord to you.'

AGREEMENTS IN SYRIAN GOSPELS, WESTERN TEXT AND DIATESSARON

Matthew 22.39//Luke 10.27//Mark 12.31 in S C T^{NL} T^v T^{EC} T^P T^{HD}
love << you shall love

Matthew 22.39//Luke 10.27//Mark 12.31 in T^{NL} T^V T^P Heliand
your brother << your neighbour

Matthew 22.39//Luke 10.27//Mark 12.31 in S C P T^P T^T Aphr
as your soul << as yourself

SELECT BIBLIOGRAPHY
Fieger (1991: 104–105); Garitte (1957: 65–66); Guillaumont (1958: 117–18); Kuhn (1960: 322–23); Quispel (1975b: 169–79); Schrage (1964a: 70–71); Sieber (1966: 249).

Logion 26.1–2

[1]Jesus said, 'The twig in your brother's eye, you see. But the beam in your eye, you do not see! [2]When you remove the beam from your eye ((then you will see clearly to remove the twig in your brother's eye)).'

P.Oxy. 1.1–4

[2]...καὶ τότε διαβλέψεις ἐκβαλεῖν τὸ κάρφος τὸ ἐν τῷ ὀφθαλμῷ τοῦ ἀδελφοῦ σου

'...and then you will see clearly to remove the twig in your brother's eye'.

NHC II 2.38.12–17

[1]ΠΕΧΕ ΙC ΧΕ ΠΧΗ ΕΤ2Μ ΠΒΑΛ ΜΠΕΚCΟΝ ΚΝΑΥ ΕΡΟϤ ΠCΟΕΙ ΔΕ
ΕΤ2Μ ΠΕΚΒΑΛ ΚΝΑΥ ΑΝ ΕΡΟϤ [2]2ΟΤΑΝ ΕΚϢΑΝΝΟΥΧΕ ΜΠCΟΕΙ
ΕΒΟΛ 2Μ ΠΕΚΒΑΛ ΤΟΤΕ ΚΝΑΝΑΥ ΕΒΟΛ ΕΝΟΥΧΕ ΜΠΧΗ ΕΒΟΛ
2Μ ΠΒΑΛ ΜΠΕΚCΟΝ

Jesus said, 'The twig in your brother's eye, you see. But the beam in your eye, you do not see! When you remove the beam from your eye then you will see clearly to remove the twig from your brother's eye.'

ATTRIBUTION
Kernel saying.

TEXT AND TRANSLATION ISSUES
The fragment of Greek agrees with the Coptic, except with the addition of καὶ and the preposition 'in' instead of 'from' as the Coptic renders it.

INTERPRETATIVE COMMENT
The teaching in the Kernel speech centres on the challenging ethics required of the disciple as the Judgement approaches. They are told to love their brothers as their souls and to worry about the beam in their own eyes before removing the twig from their brother's eye. These charges appear to be central ethical guidelines given by Jesus to the community.

SOURCE DISCUSSION
W. Schrage thinks that L. 26.1–2 is a conflation of Matthew 7.3–5 and Luke 6.41–42 because 'the beam' in *Thomas* is placed before the prepositional phrases 'in your eye' and 'from your eye' just as τήν is placed in Luke. 'Your eye' agrees with Matthew's σῷ, the position of 'to cast out' with ἐκβαλεῖν in Matthew, and 'from your eye' with Matthew. Patterson notes that these latter two elements derive from Q, not Matthew.

J. Sieber attributes the word order of 'the beam' with Coptic grammar. He notes that P.Oxy. 1 has 'in' rather than 'from your eye' which agrees with Luke, not Matthew. He asks, 'Did Thomas' *Vorlage* read ἐκ or ἐν?' He cites the only editorial trait, Luke's ἀδελφέ, as missing from *Thomas* and thus concludes that the variant is the result of oral transmission rather than literary development. This opinion appears to be supported by the fact that the saying also reflects the characteristics of orally transmitted materials, common words and phrases with varying sequences and inflections.

It appears to me that the older variant preposition is represented in the Greek 'in', since it provides the most difficult reading in my opinion. If this is the case, then the Coptic variation can be explained in terms of secondary scribal adaptation to Matthew's version.

LITERATURE PARALLELS

Matthew 7.3–5 (Qmatt)
[3]'Why do you see the speck that is in your brother's eye, but do not notice the log that is in your own eye? [4]Or how can you say to your brother, "Let me take the speck out of

your eye", when there is a log in your own eye? ⁵You hypocrite, first take the log out of your own eye, and then you will see clearly to take the speck out of your brother's eye'.

Luke 6.41–42 (Qluke)
⁴¹'Why do you see the speck that is in your brother's eye, but do not notice the log that is in your own eye? ⁴²Or how can you say to your brother, "Brother, let me take out the speck that is in your eye", when you yourself do not see the log that is in your own eye? You hypocrite, first take the log out of your own eye, and then you will see clearly to take out the speck that is in your brother's eye.'

b. 'Arakin *16b*
'It was taught: Rabbi Tarfon said, "I wonder whether there is anyone of this generation who accepts reproof? For if one says to him, 'Remove the chip from between your eyes', he would say to him, 'Remove the beam from between your eyes.'"'

AGREEMENTS IN SYRIAN GOSPELS, WESTERN TEXT AND DIATESSARON

Matthew 7.3–5//Luke 6.41–42 in c e Pal Tᵀ Tⱽ Tᴺᴸ Tᴾ geo (A) sa
see² << notice

SELECT BIBLIOGRAPHY
Patterson (1993: 30); Schrage (1964a: 71–74); Sieber (1966: 72–74).

Logion 27.1

¹((Jesus said)), 'If you do not fast from the world, you will not find the Kingdom.'

P.Oxy. 1.4–8

¹Λέγει Ι(ησοῦς) ἐὰν μὴ νηστεύσηται τὸν κοσμον, οὐ μὴ εὕρηται τὴν βασιλείαν τοῦ θ(εο)ῦ

Jesus said, 'If you do not fast from the world, you will not find the Kingdom of God.'

NHC II 2.38.17–19

¹ⲈⲦⲈ<ⲦⲚ̅>ⲦⲘ̅ⲢⲚⲎⲤⲦⲈⲨⲈ ⲈⲠⲔⲞⲤⲘⲞⲤ ⲦⲈⲦⲚⲀϨⲈ ⲀⲚ ⲈⲦⲘⲚ̅ⲦⲈⲢⲞ

'If you do not fast from the world, you will not find the Kingdom.'

ATTRIBUTION
Accretion.

TEXT AND TRANSLATION ISSUES
In L. 27.1, the Greek manuscript contains the traditional introductory clause, 'Jesus said', while the Coptic does not. I have given priority to the earlier Greek manuscript, especially since this introductory clause is consistent with the manner in which the majority of logia are introduced in the Gospel.

Also in L. 27.1, the Greek has Kingdom 'of God' while the Coptic does not. It is difficult to judge whether 'of God' is an addition. Internally, however, 'Kingdom' is found elsewhere in *Thomas* while 'Kingdom of God' is not, so I consider 'of God' to be a scribal addition in the Greek.

A. Guillaumont and A. Baker separately have shown that the Syriac preposition *l* may be responsible for both the accusative (Greek) and dative (Coptic) translations of 'to fast from the world' since ܠ may signify either a direct or indirect object. Furthermore, Guillaumont and Baker demonstrate that, in the Syriac tradition, this phrase is quite common and signals severe ascetic behaviour.

INTERPRETATIVE COMMENT

Development is indicated by the presence of a theme characteristic of the accretions, disdain for the world. The saying is responsive to the delay of the Eschaton, refocusing the Kingdom expectation on the personal performance of abstinence from this world rather than cosmic endings. Its accrual can be traced to a time between 80 and 120 CE.

As I have discussed in *Seek to See Him*, this saying associates encratic behaviour with entrance to the Kingdom and visionary experience. Its purpose was to highlight the encratic lifestyle as a preparation for visionary experience when the person would enter the Kingdom and worship before the Father. The connection with Sabbath observation in L. 27.2 is very noteworthy since there was a Jewish tradition that proper Sabbath observation included celibacy (*Jub.* 50.8–9). G. Anderson has suggested that the basis for this practice can be traced to similarities between the creation of the Sabbath in Genesis 2.1–3 and the creation of the tabernacle in Exodus 39.32, 43 and 40.9, 33–34. Since sexual activity was forbidden in the Temple, it was also prohibited on the Sabbath. The tradition of Sabbath celibacy was even popular among the Samaritans because they thought intercourse caused Levitical impurity (Lev. 15.18). Strict Jews, like the *Hasîdîm* said that one had to remain celibate from the preceding Wednesday (*b. Nid.* 38ab). This *baraita*, according to L. Finkelstein, may reflect an early ascetic branch of Judaism that was sexually abstinent for three days prior to the Sabbath so as to be in a clean state for the holy day when they came into God's presence. Exodus 19.10 and 15 were the source of this three-day calculation.

This nexus of traditions in this accretion provides astounding evidence that the Thomasite Christians were living celibate lives in order to be in a permanent state of readiness for mystical experiences. It may be that certain encratic performances were particularly important for them on the Sabbath, the holy day when they worshipped as a community in God's presence.

SOURCE DISCUSSION

G. Quispel traces this saying to a Jewish Christian Gospel like the *Gospel of the Nazarenes.*

LITERATURE PARALLELS

Clement of Alexandria, Eclogae proph. *14.1*
> 'In the literal sense, fasting is abstinence from food…however, in the spiritual sense it is clear that, as life comes from food for each of us and the lack of food is a symbol of death, so it is necessary that we fast from worldly things, in order that we might die to the world and after this, having partaken of divine nourishment, live to God.'

Clement of Alexandria, Strom. *3.15.99*
> 'But blessed are those who have made themselves eunuchs, (free) from all sin, for the sake of the Kingdom of Heaven. These are the people who fast from the world.'

Acts of Paul and Thecla *5*
> 'Blessed are those who renounce this world, for they will be pleasing to God.'

Liber Graduum *89.22–25*
> 'Brother, blessed are the holy and pure, for they see the Lord Jesus and are not ashamed in his presence, and they are free from all evil and fast from the world and its delights.'

Liber Graduum *373.18–19; 373.23–24; 828.13*
> 'fasting from the world'

Pseudo-Macarius, Hom. *4.16*
> 'Let us renounce all love for the world.'

Pseudo-Macarius, Hom. *19.1*
> 'The person who wishes to come to the Lord and to be deemed worthy of eternal life…ought to begin first by believing firmly in the Lord and giving himself completely to the words of his commands and renouncing the world in all things.'

Muhyi al-Din ibn 'Arabi, al-Futuhat al-Makkiyya *4.663*
> 'Fast from the world and break your fast with death.'

Abu Bakr ibn Abi al-Dunya, Kitab Dhamm al-Dunya, *in* Mawsu`at Rasa'il *2.170 (no. 415)*
> 'Hate the world and God will love you.'

SELECT BIBLIOGRAPHY

Anderson (1989: 129–30); Baker (1965a: 291–94); DeConick(1996: 126–43); Finkelstein (1932: 529–30); Guillaumont (1962); Quispel (1981: 265).

Logion 27.2

²'If you do not observe the Sabbath day as a Sabbath, you will not see the Father.'

P.Oxy. 1.4–11

²[κα]ὶ ἐὰν μὴ σαββατίσητε τὸ [σ]άββατον, οὐκ ὄψ[εσ]θε τὸ(ν) π(ατέ)ρα

'If you do not observe the Sabbath day as a Sabbath, you will not see the Father.'

NHC II 2.38.19–20

²ⲉⲧⲉⲧⲛ̄ⲧⲙ̄ⲉⲓⲣⲉ ⲙ̄ⲡⲥⲁⲙⲃⲁⲧⲟⲛ ⲛ̄ⲥⲁⲃⲃⲁⲧⲟⲛ ⲛ̄ⲧⲉⲧⲛⲁⲛⲁⲩ ⲁⲛ ⲉⲡⲉⲕⲱⲧ

'If you do not observe the Sabbath day as a Sabbath, you will not see the Father.'

ATTRIBUTION
Accretion.

TEXT AND TRANSLATION ISSUES
The phrase to 'observe the Sabbath as a Sabbath' in the Greek fragment is the same expression employed in this regard in the Septuagint version of Leviticus 23.32 (σαββατιεῖτε τὰ σάββατα) and 2 Chronicles 36.21 (τὰ σάββατα σαββατίσαι). In the case of Leviticus, the expression translates the Hebrew תשבתו שבתכם. So this accretion may be seen as a witness to a Semitism meaning, 'to observe the Sabbath day as a Sabbath'.

P. Brown has proposed that the final clause should be translated, 'if you keep not the (entire) week as Sabbath'. He bases this argument on the employment of **ⲤⲀⲂⲂⲀⲦⲞⲨ** in Mark 16.9 where it translates 'on the first day of the week (πρώτη σαββάτου)'. Mark 16.9, however, is not the best parallel to this accretion which uses **Ⲛ̄ⲤⲀⲂⲂⲀⲦⲞⲚ** in conjunction with the verbal construction **ⲈⲦⲈⲦⲚ̄ⲦⲘ̄ⲈⲒⲢⲈ Ⲙ̄ⲠⲤⲀⲘⲂⲀⲦⲞⲚ**. This construction exactly parallels Leviticus 23.32 and 2 Chronicles 36.21 where the meaning clearly delineates observation of the Sabbath day.

INTERPRETATIVE COMMENT

The saying is responsive to a population shift within the community, maintaining Sabbath observation when it appears to have been challenged by new Gentile converts. Its accrual can be traced to sometime between 60 and 100 CE.

T. Baarda is of the mind that the use of 'Sabbath' as a parallel to the 'world' is to be associated with the Gnostic understanding of the 'Sabbath' as the Demiurge and the world as the created cosmos of the Demiurge. This means, in his estimation, that 'fasting' and 'sabbatizing' denote the rejectionary Gnostic attitude towards the world as the realm of matter and the creator god as the ruler. He bases this position on his presupposition that 'sabbatizing' and 'fasting' are synonyms, a presupposition which, in my opinion, has no foundation in the ancient literature. Rather, as mentioned above, the expression 'to sabbatize the Sabbath' is most likely echoing a Semitism meaning 'to observe the Sabbath as a Sabbath'. Baarda's position that the logion is an allegorical reference to the Demiurge can only be maintained through forcing the reading of the logion. His endeavour is eisegetical rather than exegetical, dismissive of a straightforward historical reading of the text.

For a discussion of the connection between visionary experience and Sabbath observation, see L. 27.1.

SOURCE DISCUSSION

G. Quispel attributes this saying to a Jewish Christian Gospel, probably the *Gospel of the Nazarenes*.

SELECT BIBLIOGRAPHY

Baarda (1988); Brown (1992: 193); Quispel (1981: 265).

Logion 28.1–4

[1]Jesus said, 'I stood in the midst of the world and I appeared to them in flesh. [2]I found all of them drunk. I found none of them thirsty. [3]And my soul suffered in pain for human beings because they are blind in their hearts and they do not see. For they, empty, came into the world. And they, empty, seek to leave the world. [4]For the moment, they are drunk. When they shake off their wine, then they will repent.'

P.Oxy. 1.11–21

[1]λέγει [Ἰ (ησοῦς) ἔστην ἐν] μέσῳ τοῦ κόσμου καὶ ἐν σαρκὶ ὤφθην αὐτοῖς [2]καὶ εὗρον πάντας μεθύοντας καὶ οὐδένα εὗρον δειψῶ(ν)τα ἐν αὐτοῖς [3]καὶ πονεῖ ἡ ψυχή μου ἐπὶ τοῖς υιοῖς τῶν ἀν(θρώπ)ων ὅτι τυφλοί εἰσιν τῇ καρ[δί] α αὐτῶ[ν κ≥αὶ οὐ] βλε[...]

[Jesus] said, '[I stood in] the midst of the world and I appeared to them in flesh. And I found all of them drunk. And I found none of them thirsty. And my soul suffered greatly for human beings because they are blind in their hearts [and they do not see…]'

NHC II 2.38.20–31

¹ΠΕΧΕ ⲓⲥ ΧΕ ⲀΕΙⲰⳚΕ ΕⲢⲀⲦ ⳚⲚ ⲦⲘⲎⲦⲈ ⲘⲠⲔⲞⲤⲘⲞⲤ ⲀⲨⲰ
ⲀΕΙⲞⲨⲰⲚⳚ ⲈⲂⲞⲖ ⲚⲀⲨ ⳚⲚ ⲤⲀⲢⳢ ²ⲀΕΙⳚⲈ ⲈⲢⲞⲞⲨ ⲦⲎⲢⲞⲨ ⲈⲨⲦⲀⳚⲈ
ⲘⲠΙⳚⲈ ⲈⲖⲀⲀⲨ Ⲛ̄ⳚⲎⲦⲞⲨ ⲈϥⲞⲂⲈ ³ⲀⲨⲰ ⲀⲦⲀⲮⲨⲬⲎ † ⲦⲔⲀⲤ ⲈⲬⲚ̄
Ⲛ̄ϢⲎⲢⲈ Ⲛ̄ⲢⲢⲰⲘⲈ ΧⲈ ⳚⲚ̄Ⲃ̄ⲖⲈⲈⲨⲈ ⲚⲈ ⳚⲘ̄ ⲠⲞⲨⳚⲎⲦ ⲀⲨⲰ ⲤⲈⲚⲀⲨ
ⲈⲂⲞⲖ ⲀⲚ ΧⲈ Ⲛ̄ⲦⲀⲨ ⲈⲒ ⲈⲠⲔⲞⲤⲘⲞⲤ ⲈⲨϢⲞⲨⲈⲒⲦ ⲈⲨϢⲒⲚⲈ ⲞⲚ
ⲈⲦⲢⲞⲨⲈⲒ ⲈⲂⲞⲖ ⳚⲘ̄ ⲠⲔⲞⲤⲘⲞⲤ ⲈⲨϢⲞⲨⲈⲒⲦ ⁴ⲠⲖⲎⲚ ⲦⲈⲚⲞⲨ ⲤⲈⲦⲞⳚⲈ
ⳚⲞⲦⲀⲚ ⲈⲨϢⲀⲚⲚⲈⳚ ⲠⲞⲨⲎⲢⲠ ⲦⲞⲦⲈ ⲤⲈⲚⲀⲢ̄ⲘⲈⲦⲀⲚⲞⲈⲒ

Jesus said, 'I stood in the midst of the world and I appeared to them in flesh. I found all of them drunk. I found none of them thirsty. And my soul suffered in pain for human beings because they are blind in their hearts and they do not see. For they, empty, came into the world. And they, empty, seek to leave the world. For the moment, they are drunk. When they shake off their wine, then they will repent.'

ATTRIBUTION
Accretion.

TEXT AND TRANSLATION ISSUES
In L. 28.1 of the Greek, the manuscript reads σαρκει, where the ε is crossed out.

Literally the Greek and Coptic read, 'the sons of men'. I have rendered 'sons of men', 'human beings', which was the meaning of this Semitic idiom.

†-ⲦⲔⲀⲤ, 'to give or have pain', and πονέω, 'to suffer greatly, to be afflicted or distressed', seems to be an allusion to Jesus' crucifixion (cf. Mark 14.34; Matt. 26.38; John 12.27). The idea that the human soul suffers crucifixion is a theme also found in L. 87 and 112.

INTERPRETATIVE COMMENT
Development is indicated in the retrospective christological assertions, reflecting material that would have been anachronistic to the Kernel. The content and language is akin to Hermetic traditions, particularly the idea that humans live in a condition of drunkenness, in need of sobriety and revelation. In this case, Jesus is the revealer rather than Hermes. It appears that christological speculations about Jesus similar to those found in the Gospel of John, particularly the Prologue, have been welded with notions associated with Hermetic initiations: the individual must be awakened, his or her consciousness stirred from drunkenness by Jesus-Hermes. Then the person will be able to turn away from the world and its passions, crucifying the body as Jesus had done. This accretion should be dated to 80–120 CE.

SOURCE DISCUSSION
G. Quispel traces this saying to a Jewish Christian Gospel like the *Gospel of the Nazarenes*.

I. Dunderberg thinks that L. 28 is related to the Gospel of John because the theme of Jesus' incarnation is mentioned along with the theme of human ignorance. He notes agreements between P.Oxy. 1.11–12 and John in regard to the verb ἵστημι and the expression ἐν μέσῳ. After some discussion of more tentative 'agreements', Dunderberg wisely concludes that L. 28 does not betray direct contact with the Johannine literature. But he does not find S. Davies' suggestion that the Gospel had its origins in the Johannine community convincing since it does not account for terminological variations or the different uses that the texts make of Wisdom literature. He finally states that L. 28 echoes a relatively late phase of early Christianity as does John 1.14.

Since agreements between L. 28 and John 1.14 are more thematic than verbal, I suggest reliance on a tradition common to John and *Thomas* rather than direct literary dependence, or even secondary orality. That these texts were connected as far as their traditional background, I have discussed fully in my book *Voices of the Mystics*.

LITERATURE PARALLELS

John 1.14
  'And the Logos became flesh and dwelt among us, full of grace and truth.'

John 1.10–11
  'He was in the world, and the world was made through him, yet the world knew him not. He came to his own home, and his own people received him not.'

1 Timothy 3.16
  'He was manifested in the flesh.'

Cf. *C.H.* 1.27; *Prayer of Thanksgiving* 64.8–15

SELECT BIBLIOGRAPHY
DeConick (2001a); Dunderberg (1998a: 46–49).

Logion 29.1–3

[1]Jesus said, 'If the flesh existed for the sake of the Spirit, it would be a miracle. [2]If the Spirit (existed) for the sake of the body, it would be a miracle of miracles! [3]Nevertheless, I marvel at how this great wealth settled in this poverty.'

P.Oxy. 1.22

[...]ὴν πτωχεία(ν)

NHC II 2.38.31–39.2

[1]ⲡⲉϫⲉ ⲓ̅ⲥ̅ ⲉϣϫⲉ ⲛ̅ⲧⲁ ⲧⲥⲁⲣⲝ ϣⲱⲡⲉ ⲉⲧⲃⲉ ⲡⲛ̅ⲁ̅ ⲟⲩϣⲡⲏⲣⲉ ⲧⲉ [2]ⲉϣϫⲉ ⲡⲛ̅ⲁ̅ ⲇⲉ ⲉⲧⲃⲉ ⲡⲥⲱⲙⲁ ⲟⲩϣⲡⲏⲣⲉ ⲛ̅ϣⲡⲏⲣⲉ ⲡⲉ [3]ⲁⲗⲗⲁ ⲁⲛⲟⲕ ϯⲣ̅ ϣⲡⲏⲣⲉ ⲙ̅ⲡⲁⲉⲓ ϫⲉ ⲡⲱ|ⲥ| ⲁⲧ|ⲉⲉ|ⲓ̣ⲛⲟϭ ⲙ̅ⲙⲛ̅ⲧⲣⲙ̅ⲙⲁⲟ ⲁⲥⲟⲩⲱϩ ϩⲛ̅ ⲧⲉⲉⲓⲙⲛ̅ⲧϩⲏⲕⲉ

ATTRIBUTION
Accretion.

TEXT AND TRANSLATION ISSUES
In the Greek fragment, ε is written above the line between χ and ι.

The phrases, 'it would be a miracle' and 'it would be a miracle of miracles', literally read 'it is a miracle' and 'it is a miracle of miracles'. I have rendered them in this way to highlight the conditional nature of the 'if' clauses: even though the flesh did not come into existence for the sake of the Spirit nor did the Spirit come into existence for the sake of the body, nevertheless the Spirit has taken up residence within the flesh.

INTERPRETATIVE COMMENT

This accretion coheres to themes and vocabulary unique to other accretions, particularly its disdain for the body and the phrases 'great wealth' (ΝΟϬ ΜΜΝΤΡΜΜΑΟ) and 'poverty' (ΤΕΕΙΜΝΤϨΗΚΕ) (cf. L. 3, 85). It would have been particularly meaningful to the encratic constituency of Christians who were responsible for reshaping much of the Gospel. This accretion accrued between 80 and 120 CE.

This saying represents an anthropology common among early Christians. The human being consisted of body and soul. The soul of the pious person struggled against the flesh. To aid the person in this struggle, the Christians believed that God or Christ's Spirit would indwell them. This Spirit strengthened the soul particularly in its struggle against the passions, helping the person maintain a righteous life. It also acted as a guardian spirit, keeping demonic spirits who might corrupt the soul at bay. Christians believed that this Spirit indwelled them during the initiation ceremony when they were baptized and anointed (cf. 1 Cor. 12.13; 2 Cor. 1.22). This indwelling was believed to be a true wonder since the flesh and the Spirit were opposed to each other. The flesh was interested in corrupting the soul with its desires, while the Spirit was interested in strengthening the soul to resist these desires (cf. Galatians 5.17; Romans 7–8). R. Uro correctly notes that it is not the simple indwelling of the Spirit in the body that saves a person. According to *Thomas* it is a *process* by which the Spirit helps to transform the soul according to the original Image. I think that it is this Spirit which Jesus refers to in this accretion. This accretion, in fact, may provide some evidence that baptism and anointing was practised among the Thomasine Christians.

SOURCE DISCUSSION

G. Quispel attributes this saying to the hand of the author of the Gospel.

LITERATURE PARALLELS

Cf. Galatians 5.17; Romans 8.9–11

SELECT BIBLIOGRAPHY

Quispel (1981: 265); Uro (2003: 64–65).

Logion 30.1–2

[1][Jesus said,] '((Where there are [three people,] [[God is there]]. [2]And where there is one alone, [I say] that I am with him.))'

P.Oxy. 1.23–30

[1][λέγ]ει [I(ηο̣ῦ)ς ὅπ]ου ἐὰν ὦσιν [τρ]ε[ις] ε[ἰσ]ι̣ν θεοὶ [2]καὶ [ὅπ]ο̣[υ] ἐ[ὰν] ἐστιν μόνος [λέ]γ̣ω ἐγὼ εἰμι μετ᾿ αὐτ[οῦ]

[Jesus said], 'Where there are [three], gods are there. And where there is one alone, [I say] that I am with him.'

NHC II 2.39.4–6

> ¹ⲡⲉⲭⲉ ⲓ̅ⲥ̅ ⲭⲉ ⲡⲙⲁ ⲉⲩⲛ̅ ϣⲟⲙⲧ ⲛ̅ⲛⲟⲩⲧⲉ ⲙ̅ⲙⲁⲩ ϩⲛ̅ⲛⲟⲩⲧⲉ ⲛⲉ
> ²ⲡⲙⲁ ⲉⲩⲛ̅ ⲥⲛⲁⲩ ϩ ⲟⲩⲁ ⲁⲛⲟⲕ ϯϣⲟⲟⲡ ⲛⲙⲙⲁϥ

Jesus said, 'Where there are three gods, they are gods. Where there is two or one, I am with him.'

ATTRIBUTION
Kernel saying.

TEXT AND TRANSLATION ISSUES
In the standard critical edition of the Greek fragments of the *Gospel of Thomas* by Harold Attridge, he offers the reading, Ε[ΙΣΙ]Ν̲ Α̲ΘΕΟΙ. He states that the first letter to the left of the Θ appears to be one that consisted 'of a line sloping from the upper left to the lower right portions of the letter space'. He also sees below and to the left of this line the bare trace of a curved stroke. He imagines that this curved stroke could have continued on a diagonal upwards, until it intersected the sloping line. Thus he concludes that this letter is Α. This opinion is in conformity with B. Grenfell and A. Hunt's statement that this letter could be Α, Χ, or Λ, although Α was preferred.

To the immediate left of this letter, Attridge describes a vertical stroke consistent with Η, Ι, Ν, Π, Γ, Τ and Ψ. Attridge favours Ν. Scholars have agreed, including Attridge, that the letter space to the left of this letter has room for two letters. Attridge's reconstruction, however, shows three letters, although two of them are iotas. Thus, Attridge's reconstruction of the last segment of line 24 follows F. Blass which Grenfell and Hunt accepted: Ε[ΙΣΙ]Ν̲ Α̲ΘΕΟΙ.

But Blass and Grenfell and Hunt did not have the Coptic in front of them to aid in their reconstruction. If they had, they would have been concerned that their reconstruction disparages the Greek and Coptic texts since the Coptic reads, ϩⲛ̅ⲛⲟⲩⲧⲉ ⲛⲉ. Why did Attridge, who had the Coptic, render the Greek in such a way that would perpetuate opposite and contentious readings in these manuscripts? The reason for continuing this disparate reconstruction appears to be because the Coptic is nonsense, 'Where there are three gods, they are gods.' Clearly the Coptic is a corrupted text. Attridge's reconstruction of the Greek makes a case for corruption at the level of Coptic translation where the A-privative was accidentally lost. The problem with this line of reasoning is that the Greek reconstruction is not any more sensible than the Coptic, 'Where there are three, they are without gods.'

My journey to the aspiring (and inspiring) towers of Oxford and the grand Bodleian has made this reconstruction doubtful in my mind, if not impossible. The manuscript in the area in question is eroded, leaving only traces of partial letters. The Θ is clear. In the letter space left of the Θ are traces of ink in a distinct pattern. Visible traces move from the top left corner diagonally to the lower right corner. There is a dot of ink in the lower left corner and what appears to be a trace in the upper right corner. When the ink traces are connected, the only letters they could be according to the hand of the scribe are Χ or Ν. To the left of this letter, in the centre of the letter space is a strong vertical stroke that fills almost half of the vertical space. Because the stroke appears centred in the space with no trace of a horizontal cross stroke, the letter must be either Τ or Ι. What about the letter space to the left of this letter? The manuscript is extremely eroded and fragile here, but the space is indicative of two letters, not three as Attridge's reconstruction has it.

What reconstruction does this leave us with? Only one, and one consistent with the Coptic, Ε[ΙΣ]ΙΝ̲ ΘΕΟΙ. This suggests that the Greek read, 'Where there are three, they are gods.' Like the Coptic, it is nonsense. Even the Coptic scribe was confused by it, since he tries to make some sense by interpreting 'three' as a specific reference to the 'gods'. So he adds ⲚⲚⲞⲨⲦⲈ after ϢⲞⲘⲦ.

But this certainly was not the meaning of the Greek. How do we explain the Greek? Quite easily. It appears that the Greek translation ΘΕΟΙ was a mistranslation of a Semitic plural form of 'Elohim'. The saying must have been, 'Where there are three (people), Elohim is there.' Such a saying has full parallels in Jewish literature and belongs to this historical context (cf. *Mekilta, Bahodesh* 11; *Pirke Aboth* 3.2, 6–7; *b. Berkakoth* 6a). The Greek translator was sloppy since he mistook Elohim, the Hebrew name for God, for ΘΕΟΙ.

A. Guillaumont proposed this as an explanation for the Coptic manuscript almost fifty years ago in 1958. But it appears not to have been taken seriously given the accepted reconstruction of line 24, even though Guillaumont, J. Fitzmyer and T. Akagi each envisioned the same reconstruction I have set forth here upon my physical examination of the original leaf. My re-examination of the Greek papyrus lends further credibility to Guillaumont's old insight. It offers a simple solution to a perplexing logion, to its difficult interpretative as well as textual history. Put simply, the Greek reconstruction of the critical reading of the *Gospel of Thomas* P. Oxy. 1.24 should be emended, Ε[ΙΣ]ΙΝ ΘΕΟΙ.

This analysis of L. 30 is strong evidence that the Gospel was composed in a Semitic dialect, and then translated into Greek and Coptic.

INTERPRETATIVE COMMENT

This logion is steeped in Jewish traditions of exegesis as A. Guillaumont has shown (cf. *Mekilta, Bahodesh* 11; *Pirke Aboth* 3.2; *b. Berkakoth* 6a). For instance, in *Pirke Aboth* 3.6–7, Rabbi Halaphta takes Psalm 82.1, 'Elohim stands in the congregation of El', to mean that when as many as ten people study the Torah, the *Shekhinah* is among them. He goes on to say that the *Shekhinah* is also present when three or two or even one studies the Law. L. 30 would have been understood by Christian Jews to mean that Jesus is the *Shekhinah*, the presence of God that rested upon them whenever they gathered together and studied as well as whenever they were alone.

SOURCE DISCUSSION

G. Quispel attributes this saying to a Jewish Christian Gospel like the *Nazarenes*.

On the basis of Coptic similarities between Sahidic Matthew and L. 30, W. Schrage argues for dependence. J. Sieber states that the Coptic agreements tell us nothing about dependence at the level of the Greek *Vorlage*.

In my opinion, this saying is evidence that the Kernel Gospel was composed in Aramaic. So any agreements at the level of the Coptic translation cannot be used to argue for Synoptic dependence. Agreements may be indicative of scribal tendencies to harmonize the text at the level of Coptic translation, selecting Coptic words that echoed the scribe's memories of the Coptic New Testament passages.

LITERATURE PARALLELS

Matthew 18.20

    'For where two or three are gathered in my name, I am there among them.'

Ephrem, Commentary on the Diatessaron *14.24*

    'And as Christ has taken care of his flock in all necessities, so he has consoled it in the sadness of solitude when he said, "where one is, there am I", lest all who are in solitude be sad. For he himself is our joy and he is with us. And "where two are I am", because his grace overshadows us. And "when we are three", as we come together in the church, this is the perfected body, the image of Christ.'

Pirke Aboth *3.6*

'R. Halafta ben Dosa of Kefar Hanania said: If ten men sit together and occupy themselves in the Law, the Shekhinah rests among them, for it is written, "God stands in the congregation of God." And whence [do we learn this] even of five? Because it is written, "And has founded his group upon the earth." And whence even three? Because it is written, "Then they that feared the Lord spoke one with another; and the Lord hearkened and heard." And whence even of one? Because it is written, "In every place where I record my name I will come to you and I will bless you."'

Al-Raghib al-Isfahani, Muhadarat al-Udaba' *2.402*

'Jesus said, "O God, who is the most honourable of men?" God replied, "He who when alone knows that I am with him, and so respects my majesty that he would not want me to witness his sins."'

Cf. *Mekilta, Bahodesh* 11; *b. Berakoth* 6a

AGREEMENTS IN SYRIAN GOSPELS, WESTERN TEXT AND DIATESSARON
Matthew 18.20 in omnes exc aur d f l q vg S C P T^{EC} T^P T^V T^T

I am + ego

SELECT BIBLIOGRAPHY
Akagi (1965); Attridge (1979: 155–56; 1989: 96–128; Blass (1897: 498–500); Englezakis (1978: 262–72); Fitzmyer (1971: 398); Grenfell and Hunt (1897: 13); Guillaumont (1958: 114–16); Marcovich (1969); Quispel (1981: 265); Roberts (1970: 91–92); Schrage (1964a: 74–75); Sieber (1966: 203).

Logion 30.3–4

³'((Lift the stone and you will find me there. ⁴Split the piece of wood and I am there.))'

P.Oxy. 1.27–30

ἔγει[ρ]ον τὸν λίθο(ν) κ[ά]κεῖ [ευ]ρήσεις με σχίσον τὸ ὕλον κἀγὼ ἐκεῖ εἰμι

'Lift the stone and you will find me there. Split the piece of wood and I am there.'

NHC II 2.46.22–28

ΠⲰϨ ⲚⲚⲞⲨϢⲈ ⲀⲚⲞⲔ ϮⲘ̄ⲘⲀⲨ ϤⲒ Ⲙ̄ⲠⲰⲚⲈ ⲈϨⲢⲀⲒ̈ ⲀⲨⲰ ⲦⲈⲦⲚⲀϨⲈ ⲈⲢⲞⲈⲒ Ⲙ̄ⲘⲀⲨ

'Split a piece of wood. I am there. Lift up the stone, and you will find me there.'

ATTRIBUTION
Accretion.

TEXT AND TRANSLATION ISSUES
My reconstruction is based on the primacy of P. Oxy. 1.27 where the stone–wood saying is combined with L. 30.1–2. In the Coptic text, another version of the stone–wood saying

is combined with L. 77.1. It may be impossible to determine which sequence is oldest although Kuhn has suggested that the two distinct verbs ⲡⲱϩ are repeated as a Coptic linking word which suggests to him that the movement of L. 77.2–3 here is secondary. The Coptic arrangement does seem secondary to me, reflecting a Christological interest, that Jesus' presence and power is extended universally on the 'wood' or cross (see L. 77). Whatever the original sequence, the movement of the logia would have occurred at the level of the accretions so it would not have affected the sequence of the Kernel.

A.F. Walls has argued that the combination of the sayings in the P. Oxy. fragment reflects liturgical interests since ἐγείρειν is a word used of the raising of temples (John 2.19–21; Josephus, *Ant.* 15.391 and 20.228) and σχίζειν is used for the preparation of the wood of sacrifice (Gen. 22.3; 1 Kgs 6.14 LXX). This combination of logia is a call to worship Jesus, preparing the altar and sacrifice. Walls argues that this preparation would not have been understood in a literal sense but as the spiritual sacrifice of the believer commonly discussed in early Christian literature.

INTERPRETATIVE COMMENT
It appears to have accrued in the Gospel as an interpretative clause further elaborating the point in L. 30.1–2 that Jesus' presence can be found on earth. Not only can he be found in the gathering of believers, but also in the world itself.

SOURCE DISCUSSION
This may be an example of a Hellenistic aphorism such as we find alluded to in Lucian's *Hermotimus*.

LITERATURE PARALLELS

Lucian, Hermotimus *81*
> 'God is not in heaven but permeates all things, such as wood and stone and living beings, even the least significant.'

Cf. Pseudo-Macarius, *Hom.* 12.12, 16.5.

SELECT BIBLIOGRAPHY
Kuhn (1960: 317–19); Walls (1962).

Logion 31.1–2

[1]Jesus said, 'A prophet is not received hospitably in his (own) village. [2]A doctor does not heal the people who know him.'

P.Oxy. 1.30–35

> [1]λέγει Ἰ(ησοῦ)ς οὐκ ἔστιν δεκτὸς προφήτ[ης ἐν τη] π(ατ)ρίδι αὐτ[ο]ῦ [2][οὐ]δὲ ἰατρὸς ποιεῖ θεραπείας εἰς τοὺς [γε]ινώ[σ]κοντας αὐτό(ν)

Jesus said, 'A prophet is not received hospitably in his village. Nor does a doctor heal the people who know him.'

NHC II 2.39.5–7

¹ⲡⲉⲝⲉ ⲓ̅ⲥ̅ ⲙ̅ⲛ̅ ⲡⲣⲟⲫⲏⲧⲏⲥ ϣⲏⲡ ϩ̅ⲙ̅ ⲡⲉϥϯⲙⲉ ²ⲙⲁⲣⲉ ⲥⲟⲉⲓⲛ
ⲣ̅ⲑⲉⲣⲁⲡⲉⲩⲉ ⲛ̅ⲛⲉⲧⲥⲟⲟⲩⲛ ⲙ̅ⲙⲟϥ

Jesus said, 'A prophet is not received hospitably in his village. A doctor does not heal
the people who know him.'

ATTRIBUTION
Kernel saying.

TEXT AND TRANSLATION ISSUES
The expression ποιεῖ θεραπείας in the Greek papyrus has been discussed by G. Garitte.
He sees the Greek construction as strange, citing P. Cersoy who noted that the Greek is
unsatisfactory. So G. Garitte explains it as a Greek translator working from our Coptic text
ⲣ̅-ⲑⲉⲣⲁⲡⲉⲩⲉ, suggesting that the Greek papyrus is a translation of the Coptic. A.
Guillaumont responded to Garitte's theory, noting that the Greek expression is not unknown in other Greek sources. He quotes Plato, τὰς τῶν καμνόντων θεραπείας ποιεῖσθαι,
as evidence (*Plt.* 298e).

INTERPRETATIVE COMMENT
This logion is part of the second speech in the Kernel Gospel in which the challenges of
discipleship are discussed. Not only does this saying speak to the character of the early
Christology of the community which viewed Jesus as a rejected prophet, it also serves as a
warning for his followers that they can expect to be treated as he was. Like all prophets,
they will be rejected, like a physician, they cannot heal people they know. The Rejected
Prophet Christology is early, having its roots in the traditions from Jerusalem as I have
discussed in the companion volume, *Recovering*.

SOURCE DISCUSSION
W. Schrage argues that L. 31.1 supports the Lukan reading δεκτός and ϣⲏⲡ which he considers redactional on the part of Luke, as does H. von Schürmann. *Thomas* also omits εἰ μή
and two καὶ ἐν phrases which Luke also omits from Mark. Further *Thomas* agrees with
Mark and Matthew, reading οὐκ ἔστιν, against Luke. This proves, he says, that *Thomas*
depended upon Mark 6.5 and Luke 4.24. K. Snodgrass thinks that δεκτός is almost certainly
a Lukan redactionary element influenced by the use of the same word in the quotation of
Isaiah 61.2 in Luke 4.19. The word, he says, is a *hapax legomenon*, appearing nowhere
else in the Gospels.

J. Sieber, however, argues that Mark 6.5 is a secondary development of the saying which
was a 'widely circulated saying of Jesus'. Further, he traces the Lukan reading δεκτός to
his dependence on Isaiah in verses 18–19, suggesting that Luke was familiar with a version of the saying such as we find in *Thomas*. Luke preferred this version of the saying over
Mark's because it agrees with Isaiah. Sieber admits in his conclusion, however, that δεκτός
and ϣⲏⲡ may be one of the cases where we can see dependence on Luke. If dependence
on Luke is argued on this basis, I think that it must be done on the level of secondary
orality rather than direct literary dependence given the fact that the saying displays
characteristics of orally transmitted materials.

In my opinion, L. 31 represents a version of the saying that is pre-Markan. This was
first suggested by E. Wendling in 1908 when discussing P.Oxy. 1, and was confirmed by

the form-critical analysis of R. Bultmann in 1921 decades prior to the discovery of the *Gospel of Thomas*. This remains the view of H. Koester and S. Patterson as well.

I am not convinced by H. Schürmann or K. Snodgrass that the second half of the logion developed as a response to the proverb cited in Luke 4.23, 'Physician, heal yourself.' Rather it appears to me that an early independent tradition is responsible for the Thomasine logion and that this tradition may have been known also to Luke who rewrites it in the secondary format found in Luke 4.23.

LITERATURE PARALLELS

Luke 4.23–24
[23]'And he said to them, "Doubtless you will quote to me this proverb, 'Doctor, heal yourself. What we have heard you did in Capernaum, do here also in your own country.'"
[24]And he said, "Truly I say to you, no prophet is received hospitably in his own country."'

Mark 6.4
'A prophet is not without honour, except in his own country, and among his own kin, and in his own house.'

Matthew 13.57
'A prophet is not without honour except in his own country and in his own house.'

John 4.44
'For Jesus himself testified that a prophet has no honour in his own country.'

SELECT BIBLIOGRAPHY
Bultmann (1961: 31–32); Cersoy (1898: 417–18); Garitte (1960a: 160–61; 1960b: 337–39); Guillaumont: (1960: 328–29); Koester (1971: 129–30); Patterson (1993: 31); Schrage (1964a: 75–77); Schürmann (1963: 237–38); Sieber (1966: 23, 262); Snodgrass (1989: 31–32).

Logion 32

Jesus said, 'A city built on a high mountain and fortified cannot fall nor be hidden.'

P.Oxy. 1.36–41

[λ]έγει Ἰ(ησοῦ)ς πόλις οἰκοδομ[ημέ]νη ἐπ' ἄκρον [ὄρ]ους ὑψηλοῦ{ς} καὶ ἐσ[τ] ηριγμένη οὔτε πε[σ]εῖν δύναται οὔτε κρυ[β]ῆναι

Jesus said, 'A city built on a high mountain and fortified cannot fall, nor can it be hidden.'

NHC II 2.39.7–10

ΠΕΧΕ ΙC ΧΕ ΟΥΠΟΛΙC ΕΥΚШΤ ΜΜΟC ϨΙΧΝ ΟΥΤΟΟΥ ΕϤΧΟCΕ ΕCΤΑΧΡΗΥ ΜΝ 6ΟΜ ΝCϨΕ ΟΥΛΕ CΝΑШϨШΠ ΑΝ

Jesus said, 'A city built on a high mountain and fortified cannot fall nor be hidden.'

ATTRIBUTION
Kernel saying.

INTERPRETATIVE COMMENT
This Kernel saying compares the disciples' behaviour as preachers (L. 33.1) with the image of a city built on a high mountain that cannot be sieged successfully or hidden from view. This appears to be a common application of the saying, given its comparable interpretation in the *Pseudo-Clementine Recognitions* 8.4.

SOURCE DISCUSSION
G. Quispel traces this saying to a Jewish Christian Gospel since the wording, 'built', differs from the Synoptic text but is paralleled in the *Pseudo-Clementines*. The source, he thinks, would have been used by both authors.

J. Jeremias, E. Haenchen, W. Schrage, R. Kasser, and R. Grant and D.N. Freedman agree that L. 32 is a combination of Matthew 5.14b and Matthew 7.24–25. J. Sieber notes, however, that L. 32 is not a mixture in the sense of two separate sayings being joined together, but as two words, ᾠκοδόμησεν and ἔπεσεν which appear elsewhere in the New Testament in connection with cities (cf. Rev. 14.8; 16.19; 18.12). Nor can Matthew 7.24–25 explain the rest of the expansion of L. 32: the city is 'fortified' in L. 32 while it is built on rock and sand in Matthew. Moreover, the editorial link 'you are the light…' is missing. So dependence cannot be proven.

LITERATURE PARALLELS

Matthew 5.14
> 'You are the light of the world. A city set on a hill cannot be hidden.'

Pseudo-Clementine Homilies *3.67*
> 'It is necessary that the Church, as a city built upon a hill, have an order approved of God, and good government. In particular, let the bishop, as chief, be heard in the things that he speaks. And let the elders give heed that the things ordered be done…'

Pseudo-Clementine Recognitions *8.4*
> 'Those who speak the word of truth, and who enlighten the souls of men, seem to me to be like the rays of the sun, which, when once they have come forth and appeared to the world, can no longer be concealed or hidden, while they are not so much seen by men, as they afford sight to all. Then it was well said by one to the heralds of the truth, "You are the light of the world, and a city set upon a hill cannot be hid. Neither do men light a candle and put it under a bushel, but upon a lampstand, that it may enlighten all who are in the house." '

Cf. Matthew 7.24–25 (Qmatt); Luke 6.47–48 (Qluke)

SELECT BIBLIOGRAPHY
Grant with Freedman (1960: 150); Haenchen (1961: 11, 38 and n. 11); Jeremias (1948: 13–14); Kasser (1961: 66); Quispel (1957: 190); Schrage (1964a: 78); Sieber (1966: 43–44).

Logion 33.1

[1]Jesus said, 'What you ((hear)) in your ears, preach from your rooftops.'

P.Oxy. 1.41–42

¹λέγει Ἰ(ησοῦ)ς <ὃ> ἀκούεις [ε]ἰς τ≥[ὸ ἓν ω]τίον σ≥ο≥υ [...]

'Jesus said, 'What you hear in one of your ears...'

NHC II 2.39.10–13

¹ⲡⲉϫⲉ ⲓ̅ⲥ̅ ⲡⲉⲧⲕⲛⲁⲥⲱⲧⲙ̅ ⲉⲣⲟϥ ϩⲙ̅ ⲡⲉⲕⲙⲁⲁϫⲉ ϩⲙ̅ ⲡⲕⲉⲙⲁⲁϫⲉ
ⲧⲁϣⲉ ⲟⲉⲓϣ ⲙ̅ⲙⲟϥ ϩⲓϫⲛ̅ ⲛⲉⲧⲛ̅ϫⲉⲛⲉⲡⲱⲣ

Jesus said, 'What you will hear in your ear, in the other ear, preach from your rooftops.'

ATTRIBUTION
Kernel saying.

TEXT AND TRANSLATION ISSUES
In L. 33.1, the Greek has, 'what you hear in one of your ears [...]', while the Coptic has 'what you will hear in your ear, in the other ear'. I am not certain how the final lacunae in the Greek manuscript of L. 33.1 should be filled. So I have left it empty in the Greek transcription. It may well have included the phrase 'the other ear' as J. Ménard has suggested and which would complement the Coptic. It has been commonly accepted that the Coptic of L. 33.1 represents a case of dittography where a scribe mistakenly wrote the phrase twice. But the situation does not seem this simple because the scribe would also have to have inverted ⲉⲕ to ⲕⲉ in the scribing process when writing ϩⲙ̅ ⲡⲉⲕⲙⲁⲁϫⲉ ϩⲙ̅ ⲡⲕⲉⲙⲁⲁϫⲉ. A. Guillaumont argued that the phrase represents a Semitic pattern of repetition in order to get across a sense of the distributive. N. Perrin, however, traces this Semitism to a mistranslation where the Syriac phrase, *tartayhen*, 'both of them', was understood by the translator to be *d-tartayhen*, 'the other'. I have rendered the phrase idiomatically, 'in your ears'.

INTERPRETATIVE COMMENT
In the Kernel Gospel, this logion functions as the major instruction to Jesus' followers. Even though they will be rejected as he was, his followers are to be like a city built on a high mountain (L. 32), preaching from the rooftops the message that Jesus, God's Prophet, taught them orally (L. 33.1).

SOURCE DISCUSSION
W. Schrage thinks that L. 33 is dependent on Matthew's version of Quelle through the source Matthew because *Thomas* and Matthew agree on 'hear' and 'preach' in the imperative form. Also, neither mention Luke's phrase 'in private rooms'.

J. Sieber points out, however, that the one true Matthean editorial trait in Matthew 10.27, Matthew's altercation of Q where he uses the first person in 10.27a, is not found in L. 33.1. The imperative form of the saying, Sieber traces to a time prior to and independent of Matthew.

I consider the imperative form of the saying found in L. 33.1 and Matthew 10.27 to be less developed than the second person version found in Luke, so we are not witnessing Matthean redactional elements in the case of the agreements between L. 33.1 and Matthew. What we have is evidence of pre-Synoptic traditions pointing to an oral field of performance. *Thomas*, Qmatthew, and Qluke represent variants from this field.

Literature Parallels

Matthew 10.27 (Qmatt)
> 'What I tell you in the dark, utter in the light. And what you hear whispered, proclaim upon the housetops.'

Luke 12.3 (Qluke)
> 'Therefore, whatever you have said in the dark shall be heard in the light, and what you have whispered in private rooms shall be proclaimed upon the housetops.'

Agreements in Syrian Gospels, Western Text and Diatessaron

Matthew 10.27///Luke 12.3 in T^{EC} T^T T^V T^{NL} geo(A)
   preach + that
Matthew 10.27///Luke 12.3 in 1 22 118 209
   from *your* housetops

Select Bibliography
Guillaumont (1981: 195, 200); Ménard (1975: 130); Perrin (2002: 44–45); Schrage (1964a: 79–81); Sieber (1966: 110–11).

Logion 33.2–3

[2]'For no one lights a lamp and puts it under a bushel basket, nor puts it in a hidden place. [3]Rather the person sets it on a lampstand so that everyone who enters and leaves will see its light.'

NHC II 2.39.13–18

[2]ⲙⲁⲣⲉ ⲗⲁⲁⲩ ⲅⲁⲣ ϫⲉⲣⲉ ϩⲏⲃⲥ ⲛϥⲕⲁⲁϥ ϩⲁ ⲙⲁⲁϫⲉ ⲟⲩⲇⲉ
ⲙⲁϥⲕⲁⲁϥ ϩⲙ ⲙⲁ ⲉϥϩⲏⲡ [3]ⲁⲗⲗⲁ ⲉϣⲁⲣⲉϥⲕⲁⲁϥ ϩⲓϫⲛ ⲧⲗⲩⲭⲛⲓⲁ
ϫⲉⲕⲁⲁⲥ ⲟⲩⲟⲛ ⲛⲓⲙ ⲉⲧⲃⲏⲕ ⲉϩⲟⲩⲛ ⲁⲩⲱ ⲉⲧⲛⲛⲏⲩ ⲉⲃⲟⲗ ⲉⲩⲛⲁⲛⲁⲩ
ⲁⲡⲉϥⲟⲩⲟⲉⲓⲛ

Attribution
Kernel saying.

Text and Translation Issues
L. 33.3 contains a Semitic expression also seen in Deuteronomy 28.6 and 31.2, 'to come in and to go out', as noted by A. Guillaumont. I have rendered the expression 'to enter and leave'.

Interpretative Comment
This saying continues to elaborate the disciples' purpose as preachers. They are supposed to be like lamps set out on stands. Their message is compared to the light of the lamp that helps people see. Significantly, the *Pseudo-Clementine Recognitions* (8.4) understands this saying to be a command from Jesus to those who preach the truth to teach openly, a hermeneutic very similar to that put forward in the Kernel Gospel (L. 33.1 followed by 33.2–3).

SOURCE DISCUSSION

SOURCE DISCUSSION

W. Schrage, R. Kasser, R. Grant and D.N. Freedman see in L. 33.2–3 a combination of Synoptic phrases. With Luke it agrees on οὐδείς, ἀλλα, τίθημι, and the final ἵνα clause. Also, Luke's κρύπτη, 'in a cellar' was translated in L. 33.2 as 'in a hidden place' ϨΜ ΜΑ ЄϤϨΗΠ. With Matthew, they note that L. 33.2–3 agrees on the phrases 'under a bushel', 'on the lampstand', and ἀλλά. With Mark it agrees on 'under a bushel', 'on the lampstand', and τίθημι. K. Snodgrass also finds agreement between κρύπτη, 'in a cellar', and ϨΜ ΜΑ ЄϤϨΗΠ, 'in a hidden place'. In fact, he insists that it is an editorial trait, remarking that κρύπτη is a *hapax legomenon* occurring in Luke.

J. Sieber says that L. 33.2–3 is closer to Luke than either of the other Synoptics. He notes that the order of the two prepositional phrases is simply reversed in L. 33.2–3 with two additions: 'he places' and 'and leaves'. He attributes these to secondary development, but he does not see the commonalities between the sayings as necessitating an argument for dependence since there are no definitive Lukan editorial traits present. The agreement with οὐδείς, he argues, could come from Q.

G. Quispel has noted a parallel between L. 33.2–3 and the *Liège* Diatessaron. It reads: 'No one when the light is kindled sets or hides it under the grain vessel or under a bed or in a hidden place, but on the candlestand one sets it so that it may give light to all who are in the house.' He traces these similarities to a Judaic-Christian source familiar to *Thomas* and Tatian.

In my opinion, the commonality, κρύπτη/ϨΜ ΜΑ ЄϤϨΗΠ, must be explained as well as the oral characteristics of the logion. When compared to its Synoptic counterparts (including Luke), we note that the versions share common words and phrases, but mixed sequences (cf. 'in a cellar or hidden place'/'under a bushel basket') and additional words ('the person sets it'; 'and leaves') are also present. It is possible that Μ ΜΑ ЄϤϨΗΠ may be an example of secondary orality. But more likely the phrase in L. 33.2–3 and Luke is evidence for different versions of Quelle known to Matthew and Luke, the Lukan version being most similar to the independent tradition found in the Kernel *Thomas*. The phrase appears to me to be a Semitism, deriving from סתר, which means 'a hiding place' (cf. 1 Sam. 19.2). Unlike Sieber, I do not find 'leave' to be a secondary expansion in L. 33, but an early Aramaism which is preserved in *Thomas*' version, 'to come in and go out'.

LITERATURE PARALLELS

Matthew 5.15 (Qmatt)

'Nor do men light a lamp and put it under a bushel basket, but on a stand, and it gives light to all in the house.'

Luke 11.33 (Qluke)

'No one after lighting a lamp puts it in a cellar or under a bushel basket, but on a stand, that those who enter may see the light.'

Mark 4.21

'Is a lamp brought in to be put under a bushel basket, or under a bed, and not on a stand?'

Luke 8.16

'No one after lighting a lamp covers it with a vessel, or puts it under a bed, but puts it on a stand, that those who enter may see the light.'

Pseudo-Clementine Recognitions *8.4.2*

'Those who speak the word of truth, and who enlighten the souls of men, seem to me to be like the rays of the sun, which, when once they have come forth and appeared to the world, can no longer be concealed or hidden, while they are not so much seen by men, as they afford sight to all. Therefore it was well said by one to the heralds of the truth, "You are the light of the world, and a city set upon a hill cannot be hid; neither do men light a candle and put it under a bushel, but upon a candlestick, that it may enlighten all who are in the house."'

Pseudo-Macarius, Homilies *11.3*
'But how can anyone discover them, discern and lead them out of one's own fire? Here the soul has need of a divine lamp, namely, the Holy Spirit, who puts in order and beautifies the darkened house. The soul needs the shining Sun of justice which illumines and shines upon the heart.'

Cf. Clement of Alexandria, *Strom.* 6.15.124

AGREEMENTS IN SYRIAN GOSPELS, WESTERN TEXT AND DIATESSARON

Matthew 5.15//Mark 4.21//Luke 8.16//Luke 11.33 in S C (Matthew) T^{NL} T^P Heliand Aphr Clem
no one (=Luke)

Matthew 5.15//Mark 4.21//Luke 8.16//Luke 11.33 in P^{45} 1 118 209 C (Luke) T^L T^T T^{NL} T^V Heliand arm bo
in a hidden place << in a cellar (Luke 11)

Matthew 5.15//Mark 4.21//Luke 8.16//Luke 11.33 in C T^L T^{NL} T^T Aphr
bushel...hidden place << hidden place...bushel

Matthew 5.15//Mark 4.21//Luke 8.16//Luke 11.33 in rr^1 (Luke 11) S C (Matthew; Luke) T^P T^{NL} T^V Heliand Zach Aphr
but + he puts (=Luke 8)

Matthew 5.15//Mark 4.21//Luke 8.16//Luke 11.33 in a (Luke 11) S C P (Luke 8) T^P Aphr
+ all (=Matthew)

Matthew 5.15//Mark 4.21//Luke 8.16//Luke 11.33 in 039 (Luke 8) L 0124 1200 (Luke 11)
+ go *out*

Matthew 5.15//Mark 4.21//Luke 8.16//Luke 11.33 in S C P Pal (Luke) Aphr
its light << the light

SELECT BIBLIOGRAPHY
Grant with Freedman (1960: 150–51); Kasser (1961: 66–67); Quispel (1969: 328–29; 1962: 142–44); Schrage (1964a: 81–85); Sieber (1966: 45–47); Snodgrass (1989: 33).

Logion 34

Jesus said, 'If a blind person leads a blind person, both will fall into a pit.'

NHC II 2.39.18–20

ΠΕΧΕ ΙC ΧΕ ΟΥΒⲀⲀⲈ ⲈⳤϢⲀⲚⲤⲰⲔ ⳘⲎⲦϤ Ⲛ̄ⲚⲞⲨⲂⲀ̄ⲀⲈ ϢⲀⳘⲈ
ⳘⲠⲈⳤⲚⲀⳙ ⲈⲠⲈⳤⲎⲦ ⲈⳙⳘⲈⲒⲦ

ATTRIBUTION
Kernel saying.

INTERPRETATIVE COMMENT
In the rhetorical pattern of the Kernel's second speech, this saying functions as a statement from the opposite. The followers of Jesus are supposed to be like a city built on a high mountain, preaching from the rooftops (L. 32, 33.1) or a lamp set on a lampstand rather than hiding under a bushel basket (L. 33.2–3). They are not to be like blind people leading blind people (L. 34).

SOURCE DISCUSSION
W. Schrage says that the agreement between L. 34 and Matthew 15.14 with respect to the conditional form of the logion proves Matthean dependence. J. Sieber feels that the conditional form of the saying is not something that can be attributed to Matthew's hand, so dependence is not proven.

LITERATURE PARALLELS

Matthew 15.14 (Qmatt)
'And if a blind man leads a blind man, both will fall into a pit.'

Luke 6.39 (Qluke)
'Can a blind man lead a blind man? Will they not both fall into a pit?'

Ep. Apost. *47*
'For a blind man who leads a blind man, both will fall into a ditch.'

Pseudo-Clementine Ep. Petr. *3*
'Thus they may keep the faith, and everywhere deliver the rule of truth, explaining all things after our tradition; lest being themselves dragged down by ignorance, being drawn into error by conjectures after their mind, they bring others into the like pit of destruction.'

SELECT BIBLIOGRAPHY
Schrage (1964a: 85); Sieber (1966: 194–95).

Logion 35.1–2

[1]Jesus said, 'It is not possible for someone to enter the strong man's house and take it forcibly without binding his hands. [2]Then the person will loot his house.'

NHC II 2.39.20–24

[1]ⲡⲉϫⲉ ⲓ̄ⲥ̄ ⲙ̄ⲛ̄ ϭⲟⲙ ⲛ̄ⲧⲉ ⲟⲩⲁ ⲃⲱⲕ ⲉϩⲟⲩⲛ ⲉⲡⲏⲉⲓ ⲙ̄ⲡϫⲱⲱⲣⲉ ⲛ̄ϥϫⲓⲧϥ ⲛ̄ϫⲛⲁϩ ⲉⲓ ⲙⲏⲧⲓ ⲛ̄ϥⲙⲟⲩⲣ ⲛ̄ⲛⲉϥϭⲓϫ [2]ⲧⲟⲧⲉ ϥⲛⲁⲡⲱⲱⲛⲉ ⲉⲃⲟⲗ ⲙ̄ⲡⲉϥⲏⲉⲓ

ATTRIBUTION
Kernel saying.

INTERPRETATIVE COMMENT

The followers of Jesus are instructed in the second speech of the Kernel Gospel regarding the challenges of discipleship in face of the coming Eschaton. They are told that they must preach from the rooftops (L. 33.1) and not be like blind people leading the blind (L. 34). Using the analogy of the Strong Man, Jesus gives them practical advice: when faced with an opponent, they should bind him first and then take him on (L. 35). In the complete Gospel, the accretive hermeneutic may have shifted the understanding of this logion to the interior battle of the human soul where the person is instructed to bind the demons, the passions, that suffer the soul from liberty. This appears to be the hermeneutic known to Clement of Alexandria when he refers to this parable (*Exc. Theo.* 52.1).

SOURCE DISCUSSION

W. Schrage shows that *Thomas'* version of this saying is very close to Mark. Because we cannot identify editorial changes, it is not possible to argue for literary dependence on Mark. So Schrage works to compare Sahidic Matthew and finds some agreements. Both L. 35 and Matthew 12.29 translate εἰ μὴ as ⲈⲒⲘⲎⲦⲈ and omit καί before τότε. One Sahidic manuscript agrees with L. 35, omitting πρῶτον/ⲚⲰⲞⲢⲠ. J. Sieber says that these agreements do not prove dependence at the level of the Greek *Vorlage*, but may suggest that *Thomas'* Coptic translation is related in some way to Sahidic Matthew. So it may be that the Coptic agreements are the result of secondary scribal adaptation.

LITERATURE PARALLELS

Mark 3.27

'But no one can enter a strong man's house and plunder his goods, unless he first binds the strong man. Then indeed he may plunder his house.'

Matthew 12.29

'Or how can one enter a strong man's house and plunder his goods, unless he first binds the strong man?'

Luke 11.21–22

[21]'When a strong man, fully armed, guards his own palace, his goods are in peace. [22]But when one stronger than he assails him and overcomes him, he takes away his armour in which he trusted, and divides his spoil.'

Clement of Alexandria, Exc. Theo. 52.1

'And the Savior exhorts us to bind it (the body) and to seize its possessions as those of a strong man who is making war against the heavenly soul.'

Pseudo-Clementine Recognitions 2.60

'You represent him as weak enough. For if, as you say, he is more powerful than all, it can never be believed the weaker wrenched the spoils from the stronger.'

SELECT BIBLIOGRAPHY

Schrage (1964a: 89); Sieber (1966: 142–43).

Logion 36.1–3

[1]([[Jesus said, 'Do not be anxious] from morning [until evening and] from evening [until] morning, neither [about] your [food] and what [you will] eat, [nor] about [your clothing] and what you [will] wear. [2][You are far] better than the [lilies] which [neither] card nor [spin]. [3]As for you, when you have no garment, what [will you put on]? Who might add to your stature? He will give you your garment.'))

P.Oxy. 655, col. i.1–17

[1][λέγει Ἰ(ησοῦ)ς μὴ μεριμνᾶτε ἀ]πὸ πρωὶ [ἕως ὀψὲ μήτ]ε [ἀ]φ᾽ ἑσπ[έρας ἕως πρ]ωὶ μήτε [τῇ τροφῇ ὑμω]ν [τ]ί φ[άγητε μήτε τ]ῇ στ[ολῇ ὑμῶν τ]ί ἐνδ[ύσησθε πολ]λῷ κρ[ε]ί[σσονές ἐστε τ]ῶν [κρί]νων ἅτι[να ο]ὐ ξα[ί]νει οὐ[δ]ὲ ν[ήθε]ι [3][μηδ]ὲν [ἔχο]ντ[ες ἔνδυ]μα τ[ί] ἐν[δύεσθε κ]αὶ ὑμεῖς τίς ἂν πρ[οσ]θ<εί>η ἐ πὶ τὴν εἰλικίαν ὑμῶν αὐτὸ[ς δ]ώσ[ε]ι ὑμεῖν τὸ ἔνδυμα ὑμῶν

Jesus said, 'Do not be anxious] from morning [until evening and] from evening [until] morning, neither [about] your [food] and what [you will] eat, [nor] about [your clothing] and what you [will] wear. [You are far] better than the [lilies] which [neither] card nor [spin]. As for you, when you have no garment, what [will you put on]? Who might add to your stature? He will give you your garment.'

NHC II 2.39.24–27

[1]ΠΕΧΕ ⲓ̄ⲥ̄ ⲘⲚ̄ϥⲒ ⲢⲞⲞⲨ Ⲱ ⲬⲒ(Ν) ϨⲦⲞⲞⲨⲈ ϢⲀ ⲢⲞⲨϨⲈ ⲀⲨⲰ ⲬⲒⲚ ϨⲒⲢⲞⲨϨⲈ ϢⲀ ⲦⲞⲞⲨⲈ ⲬⲈ ⲞⲨ ⲠⲈ<Ⲧ>ⲈⲦⲚⲀⲦⲀⲀϥ ϨⲒⲰⲦ ⲐⲨⲦⲚ̄

Jesus said, 'Do not be anxious from morning until evening and from evening until morning about what you will wear.'

ATTRIBUTION
Kernel saying.

TEXT AND TRANSLATION ISSUES

The Greek manuscript is eroded extensively and very fragmentary. This reconstruction relies on restorations made by Grenfell and Hunt particularly in the first eight lines. Grenfell and Hunt's reconstruction of lines 11.8–10 (τῶν [κρί]νων ἅτι[να α]ὐξά[ν]ει) has been challenged by R. Merkelbach because it is 'intolerable Greek'. He suggests a better reading which I rely on above ([τ]ῶν [κρί]νῳν ἅτι[να ο]ὐ ξα[ί]νει).

The longer version provided by the Greek appears to be earlier than the Coptic truncation, 'Jesus said, "Do not be anxious from morning until evening and from evening until morning about what you will wear."' The truncation may have been made to ease the difficulty created when L. 37 accrued following it. Once L. 37 accrued in the Gospel, L. 36 appeared contradictory since it suggested that one's garment was a gift from God that one had to put on. In the following accretion, L. 37, the garment is something to be taken off and renounced. So L. 36 was truncated as we find it in the Coptic. In this way, the Coptic reasoning flowed: do not be anxious about what you will wear, because you will have to strip off and renounce your 'garment' in order to see the Son of the Living One.

A. Guillaumont notes that the expression 'from morning until evening and from evening until morning', is a Semitic idiom meaning 'continuously' (cf. Exodus 18.13 and 27.21).

INTERPRETATIVE COMMENT

This logion, in the Kernel, brought the second speech to a close. It underscored the need for the followers of Jesus to rely solely on God for the necessities of life since they laboured for him, preaching from the rooftops the message of the coming Kingdom and Judgement.

Once L. 37 accrued, however, L. 36 became problematic to interpret since there is a disjuncture between the two sayings regarding the very catchword that brought the two sayings together in the first place: garment. In L. 36, the disciple is told that God will give him or her clothing as a gift, while in L. 37 the disciple is told that he or she must strip off the clothing and renounce it in order to see Jesus. As long as the hearer understood the first to mean physical clothing and the second to refer to the body, the logia remained connected in their entirety as we find in the Greek papyrus. But the hermeneutical tension seems to have become too much so that, by the time of the Coptic translation, the old Kernel saying (P.Oxy. version) had been reduced to a few lines introducing L. 37 (Coptic version). All references to God providing clothing had been eliminated from L. 36. Now the believers are told that they should not be concerned about what they wear. Why? Because Jesus said that it is necessary to remove their garments and renounce them in order to return to Paradise and see God's Son.

SOURCE DISCUSSION

G. Quispel notes similarities between Grenfell and Hunt's reconstruction of P.Oxy. 655, τῶν [κρί]νων ἅτι[να α]ὐξά[ν]ει and the Heliand 1680. He also points out agreements between the P.Oxy. fragment and Matthew 6.28 in the Diatessaron. This is evidence he thinks for a Judaeo-Christian source known to *Thomas* and Tatian.

W. Schrage, R. Grant and D.N. Freedman maintain that L. 36, both the Coptic truncation and the P.Oxy. fragment, rely on Matthew and Luke, although neither discusses the agreements or disagreements. J. Sieber in fact points out a host of textual differences between P.Oxy. 655 and the Synoptics which he thinks is best ascribed to the use of a 'different rescension of the saying' than that known in Quelle. In my opinion, the two versions of this saying in *Thomas* when compared with the Synoptic versions provide us with excellent examples of oral multiforms having similarities in a few phrases and words scattered in the logia.

LITERATURE PARALLELS

Matthew 6.25–30 (Qmatt)

[25]'Therefore I tell you, do not be anxious about your life, what you shall eat or what you shall drink, nor about your body, what you shall put on. Is not life more than food and the body more than clothing? [26]Look at the birds of the air – they neither sow nor reap nor gather into barns, and yet your heavenly Father feeds them. Are you not of more value than they? [27]And which of you by being anxious can add one cubit to his span of life? [28]And why are you anxious about clothing? Consider the lilies of the field, how they grow. They neither toil nor spin. [29]Yet I tell you, Solomon in all his glory was not arrayed like one of these. [30]But if God so clothes the grass of the field, which today is alive and tomorrow is thrown into the oven, will he not much more clothe you, O men of little faith?'

Luke 12.22, 27–28 (Qluke)

[22]'Therefore I tell you, do not be anxious about your life, what you shall eat nor about your body, what you shall put on. [23]For life is more than food, and the body more than clothing. [24]Consider the ravens – they neither sow nor reap, they have neither storehouse nor barn, and yet God feeds them. Of how much more value are you than the birds!

²⁵And which of you by being anxious can add a cubit to his span of life? ²⁶If then you are not able to do as small a thing as that, why are you anxious about the rest? ²⁷Consider the lilies, how they grow. They neither toil nor spin. Yet I tell you, even Solomon in all his glory was not arrayed like one of these. ²⁸But if God so clothes the grass which is alive in the field today and tomorrow is thrown into the oven, how much more will he clothe you, O men of little faith.'

AGREEMENTS IN SYRIAN GOSPELS, WESTERN TEXT AND DIATESSARON

Matthew 6.27///Luke 12.22, 27–28 in a b h k (Matthew) D d (Luke) C T^{NL} 1293 Tert. Hil.
- μεριμνῶν

Matthew 6.27///Luke 12.22, 27–28 in aur f q e vg Mcion T^{NL} T^{V} T^{T} P^{45} θ
- οὔτε ὑφαίνει

SELECT BIBLIOGRAPHY

Glasson (1962: 331–32); Grant with Freedman (1960: 152); Guillaumont (1981: 200); Merkelbach (1984: 640); Quispel (1962: 145); Schrage (1964a: 90–91); Sieber (1966: 65–67).

Logion 37.1–3

¹His disciples said, 'When will you appear to us? When will we see you?'

²Jesus said, 'When you strip naked without shame, take your garments, put them under your feet like little children, and trample on them. ³Then [you will see] the Son of the Living One and you will not be afraid.'

P.Oxy. 655 col. i.17–col. ii.1

¹λ[έ]γουσιν αὐτῷ οἱ μαθηταὶ αὐτοῦ πότε ἡμεῖν ἐμφανὴς ἔσει καὶ πότε σε ὀψομεθα λέγει ὅταν ἐκδύσησθε καὶ μὴ αἰσχυνθῆτε[...οὐδὲ φοβη]θ[ήσεσθε]

His disciples said to him, 'When will you appear to us? When will we see you?'
He said, 'When you strip naked and are without shame...'

NHC II 2.39.27–40.2

¹ⲡⲉϫⲉ ⲛⲉϥⲙⲁⲑⲏⲧⲏⲥ ϫⲉ ⲁϣ ⲛ̄ϩⲟⲟⲩ ⲉⲕⲛⲁⲟⲩⲱⲛϩ ⲉⲃⲟⲗ ⲛⲁⲛ ⲁⲩⲱ ⲁϣ ⲛ̄ϩⲟⲟⲩ ⲉⲛⲁⲛⲁⲩ ⲉⲣⲟⲕ
²ⲡⲉϫⲉ ⲓ̅ⲥ̅ ϫⲉ ϩⲟⲧⲁⲛ ⲉⲧⲉⲧⲛ̄ϣⲁⲕⲉⲕ ⲑⲏⲩⲧⲛ̄ ⲉϩⲏⲩ ⲙ̄ⲡⲉⲧⲛ̄ϣⲓⲡⲉ ⲁⲩⲱ ⲛ̄ⲧⲉⲧⲛ̄ϥⲓ ⲛ̄ⲛⲉⲧⲛ̄ϣⲧⲏⲛ ⲛ̄ⲧⲉⲧⲛ̄ⲕⲁⲁⲩ ϩⲁ ⲡⲉⲥⲏⲧ ⲛ̄ⲛⲉⲧⲛ̄ⲟⲩⲉⲣⲏⲧⲉ ⲛ̄ⲑⲉ ⲛ̄ⲛⲓⲕⲟⲩⲉⲓ ⲛ̄ϣⲏⲣⲉ ϣⲏⲙ ⲛ̄ⲧⲉⲧⲛ̄ϫⲟⲡϫⲡ̄ ⲙ̄ⲙⲟⲟⲩ ³ⲧⲟⲧ|ⲉ ⲧⲉⲧⲛⲁⲛⲁ|ⲩ ⲉⲡϣⲏⲣⲉ ⲙ̄ⲡⲉⲧⲟⲛϩ̄ ⲁⲩⲱ ⲧⲉⲧⲛⲁⲣ̄ ϩⲟⲧⲉ ⲁⲛ

His disciples said, 'When will you appear to us? When will we see you?'
Jesus said, 'When you strip naked without shame, take your garments, put them under your feet like little children, and trample on them. Then [you will see] the Son of the Living One and you will not be afraid.'

ATTRIBUTION
Accretion.

In L. 37.2, 'When you strip naked without shame' literally reads in the Greek 'When you strip naked and are not ashamed.' Also, the Greek reads, 'He said', while the Coptic, 'Jesus said'.

G. Riley has suggested an alternative reconstruction of the damaged portion of L. 37.3: 'then you will come' (TOT|ϵTϵT|N|N|HY) instead of 'then you will see'. He defends his reading by saying that it takes into consideration the ink traces and available space he sees on plate 49 of the *Facsimile Edition*, making H a more probable reading than ⲁ near the end of line 34.

M. Meyer, however, has written a rebuttal to this position, noting that in other photographs, including the negatives and the microfilm in the Nag Hammadi Archive housed in the Institute for Antiquity and Christianity at Claremont Graduate University, there is no evidence for the horizontal stroke near the end of line 34 which Riley saw in the *Facsimile Edition*. His re-examination of the original fragments in the Coptic Museum in Old Cairo also showed no trace of such a horizontal ink stroke. He concludes that the line Riley saw 'is not ink at all but rather an unretouched portion of the black background of the photograph'.

I too have examined this line carefully in the original Coptic manuscript. There is no evidence of a horizontal stroke such as we can see in the *Facsimile Edition*. The original looks like this:

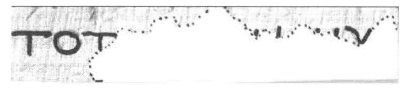

In order to record this finding, I asked the curator to take a photograph of this section of the manuscript. When I returned to the Coptic Museum to pick up the photograph and continue my examination of the papyri, I was shocked to see the same dark horizontal line appear in my photograph that is visible in the *Facsimile*. It immediately occurred to me that the error might be the result of a shadow line cast by the thickness of the papyri and the unique break line on the edge of the manuscript. So I asked for permission to have a second photograph taken with the manuscript leaf turned upside down. When this was done, the dark line disappeared, reproducing more faithfully the original ink marks. So, by accident, I have discovered why the *Facsimile* is in error. The shadow line from the thickness of the papyrus was enough to create a dark line in the *Facsimile* photo. The error was an illusion of photography and light.

I have made a very careful reconstruction of the line based on the original ink marks. NⲀY remains the best reconstruction which I have preferenced in my translation.

Development is noted by the dialogue format. The question is responsive to the Non-Event. The answer reflects encratic and mystical ideologies that developed between 60 and 100 CE. This dialogue accrued in the Gospel at this time.

J.Z. Smith long ago argued that this saying reflects early Christian baptismal practice. He based his argument on comparisons to stripping and trampling imagery in later texts (*Gospel of Philip* 75.21–25; Cyril of Jerusalem, *Mystagogical Catechesis* 2.2; Augustine, *Sermon* 216.10–11). M. Lelyveld is hesitant to accept this baptismal interpretation, preferring to interpret it as an ascetic exegesis of the Genesis story. In an article I co-authored with J. Fossum, we too challenged Smith's 'standard' interpretation, noting that 'stripping' commonly refers to the removal of the physical body in early Jewish and Christian traditions. Trampling on the garments is another common image for bodily renunciation. As Lelyveld has emphasized too, the reference to childlike behaviour reflects the encratic ideal of purity and innocence, the state attributed in early Christian literature to the youth Adam in the Garden before the Fall. For further discussion, see L. 22.

Moreover, we pointed out that the early literature further suggests that the initiatory ritual, anointing, was believed to aid in overcoming the world and its powers, ultimately effecting a vision of God. Thus, if a ritual is being alluded to in this saying, it is anointing which was performed at the time of baptism. The community may have thought it necessary to live as a renunciate before the initiation ceremony when it was believed that the initiate would achieve a mystical vision of the Son of God.

SOURCE DISCUSSION
G. Quispel traces this saying to an encratic source like the *Gospel of the Egyptians.*

LITERATURE PARALLELS

Gospel of the Egyptians, *Clement of Alexandria,* Strom. *3.13.92*
> 'When Salome asked when the things would be known that she had enquired about, the Lord said, "When you have trampled on the garment of shame and when the two have become one and the male with the female is neither male nor female."'

Acts of Thomas *14*
> 'I shall no longer remain covered, since the garment of shame has been taken away from me.'

Dialogue of the Saviour *84–85*
> 'Judas said to Matthew, "We [want] to understand the sort of garments we are to be [clothed] with [when] we depart the decay of the [flesh]." The Lord said, "The rulers and the administrators possess garments granted [only for a time] which do not last. [But] you, as children of truth, not with these transitory garments are you to clothe yourselves. Rather, I say [to] you that you will become [blessed] when you strip [yourselves]!"'

Pseudo-Macarius, Hom. *20.1*
> 'If anyone is naked and lacks the divine and heavenly garment which is the power of the Spirit, as it is said, "If anyone does not have the Spirit of Christ, he does not belong to him" (Rom. 8.9), let him weep and beg the Lord that he may receive from Heaven the spiritual garment. Let him beg that now stripped of any divine energies, he may be clothed, since the man who is not clothed with the garment of the Spirit is covered with great shame of "evil affections" (Rom. 1.26).'

Manichaean Psalm *278.99.27–30*
> 'The vain garment of this flesh I put off (saved and sanctified!).
> I caused the clean feet of my soul to trample confidently upon it.
> The Gods who are clothed with Christ, with them I stood in line.'

Ahmad ibn Hanbal, al-Zuhd, *p. 146 (no. 488)*
> 'O disciples, do not seek the world by destroying yourselves. Seek salvation by abandoning what is in the world. Naked you came into the world and naked you shall depart.'

Cf. *Dialogue of the Saviour* 49–52; Pseudo-Macarius, *Hom.* 20.2–3.

SELECT BIBLIOGRAPHY
DeConick and Fossum (1991: 123–50); Lelyveld (1987: 83–86); Meyer (1998: 413–16); Mirecki (1991); Quispel (1981: 265); Riley (1995b: 179–81); Smith (1966: 217–38).

Logion 38.1

> [1]Jesus said, 'The words that I am speaking to you, often you have longed to hear them. And you have no other person from whom to hear them.'

P.Oxy. 655 col. ii.2–7

λέ[…]ο[…]τ[…]γ[…]κα[…]ν[…]

NHC II 2.40.2–5

[1]ΠΕΧΕ ΙC ΧΕ ϨΑϨ ΝСΟΠ ΑΤΕΤΝ̄ΡΕΠΙΘΥΜΕΙ ЕСШΤΜ̄ ΑΝΕΕΙϢΑΧΕ ΝΑΕΙ ΕϯΧШ Μ̄ΜΟΟΥ ΝΗΤΝ̄ ΑΥШ ΜΝ̄ΤΗΤΝ̄ ΚΕΟΥΑ ЕСΟΤΜΟΥ Ν̄ΤΟΟΤϥ̄

ATTRIBUTION
Kernel saying.

TEXT AND TRANSLATION ISSUES
The Greek is too fragmentary to reconstruct accurately.

INTERPRETATIVE COMMENT
This logion is the introductory call of the orator in the third speech in the Kernel Gospel. It invites the audience to attend to the speech. The theme of the speech unfolds, demanding exclusive commitment to Jesus because he alone can reveal God's words to the attentive follower.

SOURCE DISCUSSION
G. Quispel attributes this saying to a Jewish Christian Gospel, perhaps the *Gospel of the Nazarenes.*

LITERATURE PARALLELS

Matthew 13.17 (Qmatt)
> 'Truly I say to you, many prophets and righteous men longed to see what you see, and did not see it, and to hear what you hear, and did not hear it.'

Luke 10.24 (Qluke)
> 'For I tell you that many prophets and kings desired to see what you see, and did not see it, and to hear what you hear, and did not hear it.'

Irenaeus, Adv. haer. *1.20.2*
> 'Often I have desired to hear one of these words, and I have had no one to tell me...'

Epiphanius, Pan. *34.18*
> 'Often I have desired to hear one of these words, and I have no one to tell me...'

Acts of John *98*
> 'John, there must be one person to hear these things from me, for I need one who is going to hear.'

Manichaean Psalm Book *187.28–29*
> 'I have something to say. I have no one to whom to say it.'

SELECT BIBLIOGRAPHY
Quispel (1981: 265).

Logion 38.2

²'There will be days when you will seek me, (but) will not find me.'

P.Oxy. 655 col. ii.8–11

κα̣[...]η[...]σ[...]

NHC II 2.40.5–7

²ΟῩΝ ̄2Ν̄2ΟΟΥ ΝΑϢϢΠΕ Ν̄ΤΕΤΝ̄ϢΙΝΕ Ν̄CϢΕΙ ΤΕΤΝΑ2Ε ΑΝ ΕΡΟΕΙ

ATTRIBUTION
Accretion.

TEXT AND TRANSLATION ISSUES
The Greek is too fragmentary to reconstruct.

INTERPRETATIVE COMMENT
This accretion represents an interpretative clause that served to recontextualize the Kernel saying, L. 38.1, at a time when the events of the Eschaton had been so delayed as to be questioned by the community. It accrued in the Gospel between 60 and 100 CE as a mitigative response to the Non-Event.

The rationalization of the Non-Event is quite pronounced since the older Kernel saying, L. 38.1, is appended with this startling new observation: 'There will be days when you will seek me and will not find me!' This accretive clause serves to alleviate the disappointment of Jesus' non-appearance, noting that Jesus had predicted this. Further, this accretion has mystical overtones, highlighting the very practical problem that faces all mystics: religious experiences can be sought but not always achieved. In this way, L. 38.2 appeals to L. 37, reminding the hearer that even though Jesus did promise the encratite Christian a vision of himself, this might not happen 'on demand'.

The author of the Gospel of John seems to be engaged in a polemic with this hermeneutic, arguing that mystical journeys to seek Jesus will fail because no one except Jesus can ascend into heaven. I have argued this position at length in my monograph, *Voices of the Mystics.*

SOURCE DISCUSSION

S. Davies thinks that this logion is derived directly from Proverbs 1.28 – 'They will seek me diligently but will not find me' – and 2.28 – 'When they call upon me, I will not answer them. When they search for me, they shall not find me.'

LITERATURE PARALLELS

John 7.34

'You will seek me and you will not find me. Where I am going you cannot come.'

John 7.36

'What does he mean by saying, "You will seek me and you will not find me", and "Where I am going you cannot come"?'

John 8.21

'I go away, and you will seek me and die in your sin. Where I am going, you cannot come.'

Cyprian, Three Books of Testimonies to Quirinus *3.29*

'For a time will come and you will seek me, both you and those who will come after, to hear a word of wisdom and understanding, and you will not find (me).'

Proverbs 1.28

'Then they will call upon me, but I will not answer. They will seek me diligently but will not find me.'

Cf. Proverbs 2.28

AGREEMENTS IN SYRIAN GOSPELS, WESTERN TEXT AND DIATESSARON

John 7.34 in S C P T^{NL} T^V T^T P^{75} B X 565 1–209–872 Sa Bo
    + me²

SELECT BIBLIOGRAPHY

Davies (1983: 37–38, 95); DeConick (2001a).

Logion 39.1–2

¹Jesus said, 'The Pharisees and the scribes have taken the keys of knowledge. They have hidden them. ²Neither have they entered nor have they permitted those people who want to enter (to do so).'

P.Oxy. 655 col. ii.11–19

¹[λέγει Ι(ησοῦ)ς οἱ Φαρισαῖοι καὶ οἱ γραμματεὶς] ἔλ[αβον τὰς κλεῖδας] τῆς [γνώσεως αὐτοὶ ἔ]κρυ[ψαν αὐτάς οὔτε] εἰσῆ[λθον οὔτε τοὺς] εἰσερ[χομένους ἀφῆ]καν [εἰσελθεῖν]

[Jesus said, 'The Pharisees and the scribes] have taken [the keys] of [knowledge. They] have hidden [them. Neither] have they entered [nor have they permitted to enter those people who were about to] come in.'

NHC II 2.40.7–11

¹ⲡⲉⲝⲉ ⲓ̅ⲥ̅ ⲝⲉ ⲙ̅ⲫⲁⲣⲓⲥⲁⲓⲟⲥ ⲙ̅ⲛ ⲛ̅ⲅⲣⲁⲙⲙⲁⲧⲉⲩⲥ ⲁⲩⲭⲓ ⲛ̅ϣⲁϣⲧ

ⲚⲦⲄⲚⲰⲤⲒⲤ ⲀⲨⲢⲞⲠⲞⲨ ²ⲞⲨⲦⲈ ⲘⲠⲞⲨⲂⲰⲔ ⲈⲢⲞⲨⲚ ⲀⲨⲰ ⲚⲈⲦⲞⲨⲰϢ
ⲈⲂⲰⲔ ⲈⲢⲞⲨⲚ ⲘⲠⲞⲨⲔⲀⲀⲨ

ATTRIBUTION
Kernel saying.

TEXT AND TRANSLATION ISSUES
The Greek is very fragmentary. Its reconstruction is tentative, so the Coptic is preferred.
A. Guillaumont posits an Aramaic substratum, קבל, to explain the verbal ambiguity
between *Thomas'* ϫⲓ, 'have taken' or 'received', and Luke's ἤρατε (in Sahidic Luke, ϥⲓ)
'have taken away'. G. Quispel suggests שׁקל as the substratum.

INTERPRETATIVE COMMENT
In the Kernel Gospel, this saying belongs to a cluster of sayings that address the issue of a
disciple's exclusive commitment to Jesus and his teachings. Jesus is presented in this
speech as the prophet to whom God has given his mysteries, the prophet who should be
heard and obeyed. Unlike the Pharisees and scribes who have taken the keys of knowledge
and hidden them, Jesus has been given knowledge of God which he will reveal to those
who are exclusively committed to him. This particular hermeneutic emerges also in the
Pseudo-Clementine Homilies 18.15–16.

SOURCE DISCUSSION
W. Schrage, B. Gärtner, E. Haenchen, R. Kasser, R. Grant and D.N. Freedman understand
Matthew 23.13 and Luke 11.52 to be the source of L. 39.1–2. 'Pharisees and scribes' and
'do not allow' come from Matthew, while 'keys of knowledge' comes from Luke (although
it is singular in Luke!), as does the past tense and the use of the verb 'to hide' which is
found in Luke 11.52. D.C. Tuckett agrees that L. 39.1–2 is close to Luke, having no object
of the verb 'to enter' and 'knowledge'. He says that Luke's version is secondary because it
contains the image 'entering' which presupposes Matthew's reference to the Kingdom, and
calls the keys, 'keys of gnosis' which introduces an alien idea into the saying. K. Snodgrass
expresses similar sentiment. Oddly, Tuckett incorrectly states that Matthew has 'keys of the
Kingdom' when Matthew actually never mentions them, nor is the reference in Luke plural
as he states, but singular, 'key of knowledge'.

J. Sieber does not consider any of these to be editorial traits in Matthew or Luke. He
does admit in his conclusion, however, that the change from 'Kingdom' to 'knowledge'
may be a Lukanism and thus may signal *Thomas'* dependence on Luke in this logion. He
favours the position though that L. 39.1–2 demonstrates to us that there was more than one
strand of tradition and that they were not all dependent on the Synoptics. R. McL. Wilson
also is not certain about the question of dependency, noting the differences between L. 39
and Luke 11.52, especially the plural 'keys' and 'those who wished to enter whom the
opponents did not allow'.

The discussions of the Quelle version of this saying and the redactional activity of
Matthew and Luke is very complex as A.J. Hultgren has reviewed in his article on this saying. He, in fact, argues that Matthew has redacted Quelle, while Luke preserves Quelle more
accurately. Matthew's redactional work is seen in three areas: the address 'Scribes and
Pharisees, hypocrites', the phrase 'Kingdom of Heaven', and the prepositional phrase
'against people'. He notes that it is difficult to entertain the thought that Luke would sub-
stitute 'key of knowledge' for 'Kingdom of God' unless it appeared in his source. L. 39.1–2,

Hultgren thinks to be an independent tradition not only of the Greek Synoptics but also the Syrian canonical tradition since they differ in that *Thomas* lacks a 'woe', a conjunction 'for', and the use of the third person 'they'.

In my opinion, all three variants of this saying appear to have secondary elements, which is what we would expect to see in a rhetorical culture where oral performance was the primary mode of transmission. But the question regarding the secondary nature of Luke's 'key of Gnosis' is the linchpin for those arguing for Thomasine dependence. I think that it is very questionable whether or not this secondary element is the result of Lukan redaction of Quelle since 'gnosis' is not a Lukan idea, only occurring in Luke 1.77 in Zechariah's poem. In my opinion, it is more likely that this element was already present in Luke's version of Quelle or some other pre-Lukan tradition, a point which even Tuckett admits. Moreover, L. 39.1–2 appears to be different enough from Luke to make initial dependence unlikely. The Pharisees and scribes *possess* (λαμβάνω) *and have hidden* the *keys* (plural) according to *Thomas*, while they have *removed* (αἴρω) the *key* (singular) in Luke. *Thomas*' variant must have been known in Syria since the *Pseudo-Clementines* allude to it (*Rec.* 2.30) and the Western tradition reflects it. Tatian agrees with *Thomas* on 'keys of knowledge' (plural) and the verb 'to hide'. The plural 'keys' also is known to Justin Martyr and in Syriac versions of Luke 11.52. 'You have hidden' appears in Codex Bezae and other Western textual witnesses including the Old Latin texts and Syriac versions of the New Testament. G. Quispel stakes the independence of L. 39 on these very observations, arguing that the Thomasine version was taken from a Jewish-Christian Gospel.

I do not think that it is necessary to postulate reliance on a lost written Gospel to explain this situation, especially in a lively rhetorical culture. Our texts are preserving early variants of this saying that developed mainly in the field of oral performance, although Luke and *Thomas* appear to stem from a common remembrance of the saying. This seems to be evidence for the theory that Matthew and Luke had at their disposal different versions of Quelle, Luke having a form closer to the Kernel Gospel than Matthew. H. Koester, in fact, argues on a form-critical basis for the priority of the Thomasine version since it does not contain the secondary reference to 'hypocrites' found in Mattthew, nor 'lawyers' found in Luke.

LITERATURE PARALLELS

Matthew 23.13 (Qmatt)

> 'But woe to you, scribes and Pharisees, hypocrites! because you shut the Kingdom of Heaven against men. For you neither enter yourselves, nor allow those who would enter to go in.'

Luke 11.52 (Qluke)

> 'Woe to you lawyers! for you have taken away the key of knowledge. You did not enter yourselves, and you hindered those who were entering.'

Pseudo-Clementine Recognitions *2.30*

> 'But you have not enquired whose is the time of the Kingdom and whose is the seat of prophecy, although he indicates it is himself, saying, "The scribes and Pharisees sit on Moses' seat. Listen to them in all things that they say to you." He spoke to them as entrusted with the key of the Kingdom, which is knowledge, which alone is able to open the gate of life, through which alone there is entrance to eternal life. Indeed, he says, they hold the key, but they do not permit those who wish to enter.'

Pseudo-Clementine Homilies *3.18*

> ' "The scribes and the Pharisees sit in Moses' seat. All things whatsoever they say to

you, hear them." Hear them, he said, as entrusted with the key of the Kingdom, which is knowledge, which alone can open the gate of life, through which alone is the entrance to eternal life. But truly, he says, they possess the key, but those wishing to enter they do not suffer to do so.'

Pseudo-Clementine Homilies *18.15–16*

'Now the word, "You have concealed", implies that they had once been known to them (the wise). For the key of the Kingdom of Heaven, that is, the knowledge of the secrets, lay with them. And do not say he acted impiously towards the wise in hiding these things from them. Far be such a supposition from us. For he did not act impiously, but since they hid the knowledge of the Kingdom, and neither themselves entered nor allowed those who wished to enter, on account, and justly, inasmuch as they hid the ways from those who wished, were in like manner the secrets hidden from them, in order that they themselves might experience what they had done to others, and with what measure they had measured, an equal measure might be meted out to them. For to him who is worthy to know, is due that which he does not know. But from him who is not worthy, even should he seem to have anything, it is taken away, even if he be wise in other matters. And it is given to the worthy, even should they be babes as far as the times of their discipleship are concerned.'

Justin, Dialogue with Trypho *17.4*

'Woe to you, scribes, for you have the keys and do not enter yourselves, and you hinder those who are entering.'

Muhyi al-Din ibn 'Arabi, Muhadarat al-Abrar *2.30*

'Jesus said to the religious lawyers, "You sit on the road to the afterlife, but you neither walked this road to its end, nor allowed anyone else to pass by. Woe to him who is beguiled by you!" '

AGREEMENTS IN SYRIAN GOSPELS, WESTERN TEXT AND DIATESSARON

Matthew 23.13//Luke 11.52 in 1604 Ps.-Clem. Rec.
+ have received

Luke 11.52 in q S C P T^P T^{EC} T^A arm Bo Aphr. Just.
the keys << the key

Matthew 23.13//Luke 11.52 in D 157 θ Ps.-Clem. *a b c d e q r^2 S C T^{EC} T^A arm geo aeth*
have hidden << have taken away

Matthew 23.13//Luke 11.52 in 1093 Ps.-Clem. *S C T^P T^T T^V Mt(H)*
+ wished

Matthew 23.13//Luke 11.52 in Ps.-Clem. *S C T^A Mt(H) Aphr*
they did not let – who were entering

SELECT BIBLIOGRAPHY

Gärtner (1961: 36–37); Grant with Freedman (1960: 154); Guillaumont (1981: 199); Haenchen (1961: 53; 1961/1962: 326–27); Hultgren (1991: 165–182); Kasser (1961: 105); Koester (1990: 92); Quispel (1957: 3–4, 13); Schrage (1964a: 91–94); Sieber (1966: 252, 262); Snodgrass (1989: 33); Tuckett (1991: 354).

Logion 39.3

³'You, however, be as prudent as serpents and as guileless as doves.'

P. Oxy. 655 col. ii.19–23

³ὑμεῖς] δὲ γεί[νεσθε φρόνι]μοι ὡ[ς ὄφεις καὶ ἀ]κέραι[οι ὡς περιστε]ρ[αί]

'[You], however, [be as prudent] as [serpents and] as guileless [as doves].'

NHC II 2.40.11–13

³ⲚⲦⲰⲦⲚ ⲆⲈ ⲰⲰⲠⲈ ⲘⲫⲢⲞⲚⲒⲘⲞⲤ ⲚⲐⲈ ⲚⲚϨⲞϤ ⲀⲨⲰ ⲚⲀⲔⲈⲢⲀⲒⲞⲤ
ⲚⲐⲈ ⲚⲚϬⲢⲞⲘⲠⲈ

'You, however, be as prudent as serpents and as guileless as doves.'

ATTRIBUTION
Kernel saying.

TEXT AND TRANSLATION ISSUES
The Greek reconstruction is heavily dependent on the Coptic fragment.

INTERPRETATIVE COMMENT
In the Kernel Gospel, this saying functioned to interpret the preceding warning against listening to the Pharisees. The hearer needs to be prudent and guileless in this regard.

SOURCE DISCUSSION
G. Quispel thinks that the source for this saying is a Jewish Christian Gospel.

LITERATURE PARALLELS
Matthew 10.16
> 'Behold, I send you out as sheep in the midst of wolves. So be wise as serpents and innocent as doves.'

Ignatius, Polycarp 2.2
> 'Be wise as a serpent in all things and innocent as the dove forever.'

Gospel of the Nazarenes 7
> The Jewish Gospel: (wise) more than serpents.

Cant. R. *2.14*
> 'R. Johanan said, "The Holy One, blessed be He, said, 'I call Israel a dove, as it is written, And Ephraim is become like a silly dove, without understanding (Hos. 7.11). To Me they are like a dove, but to the nations they are like various kinds of beasts...'"'

Cant. R. *2.14*
> 'R. Judah said in the name of R. Simon, "With Me they are innocent like doves, but with the nations they are cunning like serpents."'

SELECT BIBLIOGRAPHY
Quispel (1981: 265).

Logion 40.1–2

[1]Jesus said, 'A grapevine has been planted apart from the Father's (planting). [2]Since it is not strong, it will be plucked up by its roots, and it will perish.'

NHC II 2.40.13–16

[1]ΠΕΧΕ Ι̅Ϲ̅ ΟΥΒΕΝΕΛΟΟΛΕ ΑΥΤΟϬϹ Μ̅ΠϹΑ ΝΒΟΛ Μ̅ΠΕΙѠΤ [2]ΑΥѠ ΕϹΤΑΧΡΗΥ ΑΝ ϹΕΝΑΠΟΡΚϹ̅ ϨΑ ΤΕϹΝΟΥΝΕ Ν̅ϹΤΑΚΟ

ATTRIBUTION
Kernel saying.

INTERPRETATIVE COMMENT
Speech three in the Kernel Gospel focuses on the theme that *only* Jesus reveals the truth so the hearer must listen to him and serve him exclusively (L. 38.1). Jesus insists that the Pharisees should not be heeded because they have no intention to reveal the truth (L. 39.1–2). Hearers should be wiser than they (L. 39.3). The rationale is contained in L. 40.1–2. Because the Pharisees are like a grapevine that is not of the Father's planting, they will be yanked out by their roots.

SOURCE DISCUSSION
W. Schrage holds for some connection with Matthew 15.13, although there is not enough evidence to prove dependence. Since the only editorial trait in Matthew 15.13, Matthew's choice of context, is missing, J. Sieber states that L. 40 shows no evidence for dependence.

G. Quispel thinks that L. 40 evidences an independent tradition. He bases this opinion on an examination of the parallels in Syrian tradition which preserve 'Father' as L. 40 has it rather than 'my Father' as Matthew. He traces the discrepancy to a Semitic substratum where אבא can be translated 'Father' or 'my Father' as is done in the Mishnah and the Targum.

LITERATURE PARALLELS

Matthew 15.13
'Every plant which my heavenly Father has not planted will be rooted up.'

John 15.5–6
'I am the vine, you are the branches. He who abides in me, and I in him, he it is that bears much fruit, for apart from me you can do nothing. If a man does not abide in me, he is cast forth as a branch and withers. And the branches are gathered, thrown into the fire and burned'.

Gospel of Philip *85.29–31*
'[Every] plant [that] my Father who is in heaven [has not] planted [will be] plucked up.'

Ignatius, Trall. *11.1*
'Flee, therefore, from the wicked offshoots that produce deadly fruit, which if anyone eats he will die. For these are not the planting of the Father.'

Ignatius, Phil. *3.1*
'Keep away from evil plants that Jesus Christ does not cultivate, because they are not the planting of the Father.'

Pseudo-Clementine Homilies *3.52*

> 'Since, then, while the heaven and the earth shall stand, sacrifices have passed away, and
> kingdoms, and prophecies among those who are born of woman, and such like, as not
> being ordinances of God; hence therefore he says, "Every plant which the heavenly
> Father has not planted shall be rooted up." '

Cf. Isaiah 5.1–7; Ezekiel 19.10–14; L. 57; Matthew 13.24–30; *Thom. Cont.* 144.19–36.

AGREEMENTS IN SYRIAN GOSPELS, WESTERN TEXT AND DIATESSARON

Matthew 15.13 in Ephr T^{EC}
    has been planted << has planted

Matthew 15.13 in Ps.-Clem. *ff² S Didymus*
    the father << my father

Matthew 15.13 in T^{EC} T^{NL} geo(OT)
    + by its roots

SELECT BIBLIOGRAPHY

Quispel (1958: 188–89); Schrage (1964a: 95); Sieber (1966: 193–94).

Logion 41.1–2

¹Jesus said, 'Whoever has something in his hand will be given more. ²And whoever has
nothing, even the little that this person has will be taken away.'

NHC II 2.40.16–18

¹ΠΕΧΕ ΙC ΧΕ ΠΕΤΕΥΝΤΑ϶ ϨΝ ΤΕ϶ϬΙΧ CΕΝΑϯ ΝΑ϶ ²ΑΥШ ΠΕΤΕ
ΜΝΤΑ϶ ΠΚΕШΗΜ ΕΤΟΥΝΤΑ϶ CΕΝΑ϶ΙΤϥ ΝΤΟΟΤϥ

ATTRIBUTION
Kernel saying.

TEXT AND TRANSLATION ISSUES
N. Perrin explains the difference between *Thomas*' expression 'little (ШΗΜ) he has' and
the Synoptics' use of the indefinite relative pronoun, 'what he has', with a reference to an
intermediary Syriac expression בצר ד which is found in Syriac Matthew 13.12 and Mark
4.25. The meaning is either 'that which' as an attributive relative clause, or 'a little of X'
as an indefinite substantive with the genitive.

INTERPRETATIVE COMMENT
The meaning of this logion in its rhetorical context in the Kernel appears to be twofold: that
the Pharisees have nothing to offer the hearer and will be deprived even of that; and that
the worthy believer will be taught more than he or she now knows. The *Pseudo-Clementine
Homilies* appear to be familiar with this application of the saying, also suggesting that it
applies to the unworthy who will be deprived of what they appear to possess even though
they might be wise in some matters.

SOURCE DISCUSSION

W. Schrage notes that L. 41 has 'in his hand' and 'little' which are not found in the Synoptics. Also *Thomas* omits the two times γάρ occurs. He finds no evidence of Matthew, Luke or Quelle and cannot argue for dependence on Mark because he can only posit parallels and not redactional activity.

J. Sieber agrees with Schrage but pushes the conclusion further, stating that the absence of agreements with Matthew or Luke as well as the absence of editorial traits means that *Thomas* did not use the Synoptic Gospels as his sources.

LITERATURE PARALLELS

Mark 4.25

'For to him who has will more be given. And from him who has not, even what he has will be taken away.'

Matthew 13.12

'For to him who has will more be given, and he will have abundance. But from him who has not, even what he has will be taken away.'

Luke 8.18

'For to him who has will more be given, and from him who has not, even what he thinks that he has will be taken away.'

Matthew 25.29 (Qmatt)

'For to every one who has will more be given, and he will have abundance. But from him who has not, even what he has will be taken away.'

Luke 19.26 (Qluke)

'I tell you, that to every one who has will more be given. But from him who has not, even what he has will be taken away.'

Pseudo-Clementine Homilies *18.16*

'For to him who is worthy to know, is due that which he does not know. But from him who is not worthy, even should he seem to have any thing, it is taken away, even if he be wise in other matters; and it is given to the worthy, even should they be babes as far as the time of their discipleship is concerned.'

Cf. *Apocalypse of Peter* 83.26–84.6.

SELECT BIBLIOGRAPHY

Perrin (2002: 45); Schrage (1964a: 96–98); Sieber (1966: 164–65).

Logion 42

Jesus said, 'Be passers-by.'

NHC II 2.40.19

ⲡⲉϫⲉ ⲓ̅ⲥ̅ ϫⲉ ϣⲱⲡⲉ ⲉⲧⲉⲧⲛ̅ⲣ̅ⲡⲁⲣⲁⲅⲉ

ATTRIBUTION

Kernel saying.

TEXT AND TRANSLATION ISSUES

INTERPRETATIVE COMMENT
Various scholars have explained this saying in different ways: Gnostic exhortation to 'come into being as you pass away' (J. Leipoldt, W. Schoedel, B. Gärtner, R.M. Grant and D.N. Freedman); 'Be passers-by' from ἔστε παρερχόμενοι (R. Kasser); 'Be Hebrews', from γίνεσθε περαταί and עברי (T. Baarda); admonition to become a wanderer, from γίνεσθε παράγοντες and עבר (J. Jeremias, G. Quispel); 'Become itinerants', from γίνεσθε παρεχόμενοι (S. Patterson); 'Be transient(s)' (Dewey); and P. Sellew (funerary epigraphy).

I propose another possibility which allows for a shift in hermeneutics from the early Kernel to the later accretions. In the Kernel, from its context among sayings about the exclusivity of Jesus' teaching, L. 42 seems to indicate that the worthy disciple is supposed to 'pass by (ⲣ̅-ⲡⲁⲣⲁⲅⲉ)' the teachings of the Pharisees and all others. This hermeneutic parallels a passage in the *Pseudo-Clementines* where a person is told that he or she ought to 'pass by (παρέρχομαι)' all teachings other than those of Jesus and 'commit himself to the Prophet of the truth alone' (*Hom.* 2.9). Thus it is conceivable that the Coptic translation ⲣ̅-ⲡⲁⲣⲁⲅⲉ was rendering the Greek phrase, ἔστε παρερχόμενοι. It is also quite possible that this expression translated the Hebrew עבר as several scholars have suggested. However, it did not originally evoke the image of a traveller or wanderer, but the notion to pass by or turn away from someone or something such as we find in Psalm 119.37: 'Turn my eyes away from looking at vanities: and give me life in your ways' (cf. 2 Sam. 12.13; 1 Kgs 15.12; Eccl. 11.10). In this particular case, Jesus was instructing them to pass by the teachings of the Pharisees and other teachers, to listen exclusively to his words. In the later Gospel when the accretions had accumulated, the meaning of this saying may have shifted to a more encratic hermeneutic: to pass by the world.

SOURCE DISCUSSION
G. Quispel attributes this saying to a Jewish Christian Gospel source.

LITERATURE PARALLELS

Pseudo-Clementines, Homilies *2.9*
> 'Whence a person ought to pass by all else, and commit himself to the Prophet of truth alone.'

'Abdallah ibn Qutayba, 'Uyun *2.328*
> 'The world is a bridge. Cross this bridge but do not build upon it.'

SELECT BIBLIOGRAPHY
Baarda (1983a); Dewey (1994); Gärtner (1961: 243–45); Grant with Freedman (1960: 147); Jeremias (1948: 107–10, esp. nn. 240 and 251); Kasser (1961: 71); Leipoldt (1958: 488); Patterson (1993: 130–31); Quispel (1967a: 20–22; 1974a: 197; 1981: 265); Sellew (2006).

Logion 43.1–3

[1]His disciples said to him, 'Who are you to say these things to us?'
[2]'From what I say to you, you do not know who I am. [3]Rather, you are like the Jews, for they love the tree (but) hate its fruit, or they love the fruit (but) hate the tree.'

NHC II 2.40.21–26

¹ⲡⲉⲭⲁⲩ ⲛⲁϥ ⲛ̄ϭⲓ ⲛⲉϥⲙⲁⲑⲏⲧⲏⲥ ⲭⲉ ⲛ̄ⲧⲁⲕ ⲛⲓⲙ ⲉⲕⲭⲱ ⲛ̄ⲛⲁⲓ̈ ⲛⲁⲛ
²ϩⲛ̄ ⲛⲉⲧ̇ⲭⲱ ⲙ̄ⲙⲟⲟⲩ ⲛⲏⲧⲛ̄ ⲛ̄ⲧⲉⲧⲛ̄ⲉⲓⲙⲉ ⲁⲛ ⲭⲉ ⲁⲛⲟⲕ ⲛⲓⲙ ³ⲁⲗⲗⲁ
ⲛ̄ⲧⲱⲧⲛ̄ ⲁⲧⲉⲧⲛ̄ϣⲱⲡⲉ ⲛ̄ⲑⲉ ⲛ̄ⲛⲓ̈ⲟⲩⲇⲁⲓⲟⲥ ⲭⲉ ⲥⲉⲙⲉ ⲙ̄ⲡϣⲏⲛ
ⲥⲉⲙⲟⲥⲧⲉ ⲙ̄ⲡⲉϥⲕⲁⲣⲡⲟⲥ ⲁⲩⲱ ⲥⲉⲙⲉ ⲙ̄ⲡⲕⲁⲣⲡⲟⲥ ⲥⲉⲙⲟⲥⲧⲉ
ⲙ̄ⲡϣⲏⲛ

ATTRIBUTION
Accretion.

TEXT AND TRANSLATION ISSUES
A. Guillaumont solves the problem of the Coptic ⲁⲩⲱ in L. 43.3 which can only be translated 'or' to make sense of the passage, 'for they love the tree (but) hate its fruit, or (ⲁⲩⲱ) they love the fruit (but) hate the tree'. The solution falls to the Aramaic ⲓ as the conjunction, 'and' as well as 'either…or'. But it should be noted that the same is true of the Syriac conjunction ⲁ. The Greek translator misunderstood this second usage and opted incorrectly for the first. See L. 78 where this same problem is detected.

INTERPRETATIVE COMMENT
Development is indicated by the dialogue format. The christological concern expressed as well as the negative presentation of the 'Jews' as 'Other' suggest a date for this accretion between 60 and 100 CE, probably nearer the end of the century than sooner. The content reflects the shifting constituency of the community as it became dominated by Gentile converts.

This dialogue probably accrued in this particular speech to expand the tight rhetorical argument: Jesus speaks with authority and insists that his disciples exclusively follow him, not the Pharisees or the Scribes. The disciples are supposed to pass by their teachings. The disciples ask him who he thinks he is to criticize the Pharisees who possess the keys of knowledge. He replies that, because they have not understood his words, they are like the 'Jews' who cannot make up their minds whether to love the tree or its fruit. This is the voice of a community which is in the process of separating itself from its Jewish roots.

SOURCE DISCUSSION
T. Baarda suggests that L. 42 and 43 together are dependent on John 8.30–48. Because he thinks that L. 42 should read, 'Hebrews', this raises the question of Jesus' authority and his response that they have become like the Jews. This suggestion, however, relies solely on his idiosyncratic interpretation of the meaning of L. 42. The only verbal agreements between the passage in question and L. 43 is the question, 'Who are you?' – hardly enough to demonstrate dependence.

I. Dunderberg's opinion is more sensible – that literary affinities are not found. In my opinion, the negative view towards the Jews is a common feature in later Christianity and turns up in this accretive logion as well as the Gospel of John.

LITERATURE PARALLELS

John 14.9
'Jesus said to him, "Have I been with you so long, and yet you do not know me, Philip?"'

Abu Hamid al-Ghazadi, Ihya' 'Ulum al-Din *1.38*

> 'Jesus said, "How many trees there are but not all bear fruit! How many fruits there are but not all are good to eat! How many sciences there are but not all are useful!" '

Cf. Luke 6.43–44 (Qluke); Matthew 7.17–18 (Qmatt); Matthew 7.16a, 20; Matthew 12.33 (Qmatt).

SELECT BIBLIOGRAPHY
Baarda (1983a: 196–97); Dunderberg (1998a: 61–62); Guillaumont (1981: 193).

Logion 44.1–3

[1]Jesus said, 'Whoever blasphemes against the Father will be forgiven, [2]and whoever blasphemes against the Son will be forgiven. [3]But whoever blasphemes against the Holy Spirit will not be forgiven, neither on earth nor in heaven.'

NHC II 2.40.26–31

> [1]ΠΕΧΕ ΙC ΧΕ ΠΕΤΑΧΕ ΟΥΑ ΑΠΕΙШΤ CΕΝΑΚШ ΕΒΟΛ ΝΑϥ [2]ΑΥШ
> ΠΕΤΑΧΕ ΟΥΑ ΕΠШΗΡΕ CΕΝΑΚШ ΕΒΟΛ ΝΑϥ [3]ΠΕΤΑΧΕ ΟΥΑ ΔΕ
> ΑΠΠΝΑ ΕΤΟΥΑΑΒ CΕΝΑΚШ ΑΝ ΕΒΟΛ ΝΑϥ ΟΥΤΕ ϨΜ ΠΚΑϨ ΟΥΤΕ
> ϨΝ ΤΠΕ

ATTRIBUTION
Kernel saying with accretive interpretation.

TEXT AND TRANSLATION ISSUES
In L. 44.3, the phrase 'in heaven' is a well-known Semitism meaning 'by God' as noted by G. Quispel.

INTERPRETATIVE COMMENT
The Kernel saying appears to have been adapted at a later time (80–120 CE) to incorporate the triadic formula: Father, Son and Holy Spirit. So the form of the earlier Kernel saying has been lost. The Kernel saying may have been similar to its Synoptic parallels, admonishing people that blaspheming against a human being or 'son of man' could be forgiven, but blaspheming against a prophet like Jesus who was filled with God's Holy Spirit could not. Such a saying would have made rhetorical sense in this particular sequence of logia where Jesus is demanding exclusivity as God's prophet. Once Jesus became identified with the Son of Man in Christian tradition, the interpretation of the saying must have become exceedingly difficult. So the saying became corrupted as it was transmitted: in Mark the difficult segment of the saying was discarded while in *Thomas* it was recast with a triadic formula.

The Rabbis held that blasphemy was a capital offence and included speaking imprudently about the Torah (*S. Nu.* 112 on 15.30), idolatry (*S. Nu.* 112 on 15.31), and misuse of the Divine Name Yahweh (*b. Pes.* 93b). The earliest Christians use the concept 'blasphemy' to refer to offence spoken against the Law (Acts 6.11–14; Titus 2.5) or the improper use of God's Name (Rev. 13.6; 16.9; 1 Tim. 6.1). There is also a tradition that a person can commit blasphemy against a heavenly being or power (Philo, *Conf. Ling.* 154; *Som.* II, 131; Rev. 13.6; Jude 8).

From these traditions, it appears that it was believed to be blasphemous to speak against a prophet filled with God's Spirit since the Spirit was concerned with the realm of revelation. The prophet was the voice of God. 2 Peter 1.20–21 helps us here: 'First of all you must understand this, that no prophecy of scripture is a matter of one's interpretation, because no prophecy ever came by the impulse of man, but holy men moved by the Holy Spirit spoke from God.' Luke relates that Jesus is blasphemed against because of his prophecies (Luke 22.64–65). In some manuscripts of 1 Peter 4.14, blasphemy is also related to the Spirit which possesses holy people. The *Didache* preserves this old interpretation of the saying of Jesus: 'While a prophet is making ecstatic utterances, you must not test or examine him. For "every sin will be forgiven", but this sin "will not be forgiven"' (11.7).

SOURCE DISCUSSION

G. Quispel points out a parallel with the Tuscan Diatessaron version of Matthew 12.32: 'He who shall speak a word *against the Father*, it shall be forgiven him; and he who shall speak a word *against the Son*, it shall be forgiven him; but he who shall blaspheme against the Holy Spirit, to him it shall not be forgiven, neither in this world nor in the other.' This parallel suggests to Quispel an independent source common to Tatian and *Thomas.*

W. Schrage thinks that L. 44 is dependent upon the Synoptics, particularly Matthew and Luke since he does not see any affinities with Mark other than those found in Matthew and Luke. J. Sieber, however, says that the logion translates a Greek sentence similar to Mark 3.29, ὃς δέ ἂν βλασφήμῃ, 'whoever blasphemes'. So Sieber thinks that L. 44 shares similarities with Mark and Quelle. Any specifically Matthean or Lukan editorial traits are absent. L. 44 represents a third version of the saying. What about Q's misrepresentation of the Son of Man? Sieber sees this as a natural error arising among Greek-speaking Christians. The inclusion of the Trinitarian formula, he traces along the same course. Once the saying (which had originally spoken about the unforgiveable sin against the spirit of the prophet) was understood to be referring to the Son and the Spirit, it was 'natural' to expand the saying and include the Father. The saying Sieber thinks derives from a late stage in oral tradition.

H. Koester thinks that Q, like Mark, originally spoke about blasphemy against the Holy Spirit, uttered by a 'son of man', a human being. This clause came to be titular later and referenced Jesus. L. 44 he thinks is based on a saying close to the Markan version and was elaborated independently.

In my opinion, clearly the form that this logion takes has been secondarily developed and elaborated in the oral field apart from its Synoptic counterparts. It is difficult to discuss dependency because it is difficult to recover the 'original' Kernel saying. It appears, however, that the commonalities at this early level of transmission included a string of ten words in sequence, the average number of word sequences between the Thomasine–Synoptic parallel aphorisms – 'whoever blasphemes against the Holy Spirit will not be forgiven'. Since there are no features of secondary orality, this suggests to me that the Kernel L. 44 is an old multiform developed independently in the field of oral performance.

LITERATURE PARALLELS

Mark 3.28–30

[28]"Truly, I say to you, all sins will be forgiven the sons of men, and whatever blasphemies they utter. [29]But whoever blasphemes against the Holy Spirit never has forgiveness, but is guilty of an eternal sin"—[30]for they had said, "He has an unclean spirit."'

Matthew 12.31–32 (Qmatt)

[31]'Therefore I tell you, every sin and blasphemy will be forgiven men, but the blasphemy against the Spirit will not be forgiven. [32]And whoever says a word against the son of man will be forgiven; but whoever speaks against the Holy Spirit will not be forgiven, either in this age or in the age to come.'

Luke 12.10 (Qluke)

'And everyone who speaks a word against the son of man will be forgiven. But he who blasphemes against the Holy Spirit will not be forgiven.'

Pseudo-Clementine Homilies *3.6*

'Such is the nature of the one and only God who made the world and who created us, and who has given us all things, that as long as any one is within the limit of piety, and does not blaspheme his Holy Spirit, through his love towards him he brings his soul to himself by reason of his love towards it.'

Damascus Document *5.11–12*

'They desecrate the Holy Spirit, blaspheming with their tongue and opening their mouths against the laws of the divine covenant.'

AGREEMENTS IN SYRIAN GOSPELS, WESTERN TEXT AND DIATESSARON

Mark 3.29//Matthew 12.32//Luke 12.10 in T^T

+whoever blasphemes against the Father

Mark 3.29//Matthew 12.32//Luke 12.10 in T^T

the Son – of Man

SELECT BIBLIOGRAPHY

Koester (1990: 92–93); Quispel (1967b: 470; 1969: 328–29); Schrage (1964a: 98–100); Sieber (1966: 146–48).

Logion 45.1–4

[1]Jesus said, 'Grapes are not harvested from thorn trees, nor are figs picked from thistles, for they do not produce fruit. [2]A good person brings forth good from his treasury. [3]A bad person brings forth evil from his wicked treasury in his heart, and he speaks evil. [4]For from the excessiveness of the heart, he brings forth evil.'

NHC II 2.40.31–41.6

[1]ⲡⲉϫⲉ ⲓ̅ⲥ̅ ⲙⲁⲩϫⲉⲗⲉ ⲉⲗⲟⲟⲗⲉ ⲉⲃⲟⲗ ϩⲛ̄ ϣⲟⲛⲧⲉ ⲟⲩⲧⲉ ⲙⲁⲩⲕⲱⲧϥ ⲕⲛ̄ⲧⲉ ⲉⲃⲟⲗ ϩⲛ̄ ⲥⲣ̄ϭⲁⲙⲟⲩⲗ ⲙⲁⲩϯ ⲕⲁⲣⲡⲟⲥ ⲅⲁⲣ [2]ⲟⲩⲁⲅⲁⲑⲟⲥ ⲣ̄ⲣⲱⲙⲉ ϣⲁϥⲉⲓⲛⲉ ⲛ̄ ⲟⲩⲁⲅⲁⲑⲟⲛ ⲉⲃⲟⲗ ϩⲓⲙ̄ ⲡⲉϥⲉϩⲟ [3]ⲟⲩⲕⲁⲕⲟⲥ ⲣ̄ⲣⲱⲙⲉ ϣⲁϥⲉⲓⲛⲉ ⲛ̄ϩⲛ̄ⲡⲟⲛⲏⲣⲟⲛ ⲉⲃⲟⲗ ϩⲙ̄ ⲡⲉϥⲉϩⲟ ⲉⲑⲟⲟⲩ ⲉⲧϩⲛ̄ ⲡⲉϥϩⲏⲧ ⲁⲩⲱ ⲛ̄ϥϫⲱ ⲛ̄ϩⲛ̄ⲡⲟⲛⲏⲣⲟⲛ [4]ⲉⲃⲟⲗ ⲅⲁⲣ ϩⲙ̄ ⲫⲟⲩⲟ ⲙ̄ⲫⲏⲧ ϣⲁϥⲉⲓⲛⲉ ⲉⲃⲟⲗ ⲛ̄ϩⲛ̄ⲡⲟⲛⲏⲣⲟⲛ

ATTRIBUTION

Kernel saying.

TEXT AND TRANSLATION ISSUES

A. Guillaumont notes that the expression 'which is in your heart' is a Semitic expression also found in the Syriac versions of Matthew 12.35 and Luke 6.45.

INTERPRETATIVE COMMENT

In the Kernel Gospel, this saying was part of the rhetoric arguing for Jesus' exclusivity as God's prophet. The Pharisees are particularly singled out as authorities who should not be heeded L. 39. L. 45 provides part of that rationale. The truth cannot be harvested from the Pharisees because they have evil in their hearts. In the complete Gospel, the encratic accretions may have lent a more personal hermeneutic to this logion, shifting the meaning to the believer's own internal condition. A worthy disciple would be characterized as someone who had control over his passions and a clean heart.

SOURCE DISCUSSION

G. Quispel notes similarities between Luke 4.44–45 in the Diatessaron and the Heliand 1755. These parallels signal in his mind a common source for L. 45 and Tatian.

W. Schrage thinks that L. 45 is dependent on Luke 6.44–45 because both combine two sayings into one while Matthew has them in separate spots in his Gospel. L. 45.2–4 agrees with Luke's order as well as the addition 'which is in his heart' and the γάρ clause. He also sees ΟΥΤΕ in L. 45.1 as dependent on Luke while the order of the grapes and figs, as well as the word 'thistles', he sees as coming from Matthew. L. 45.2–4 also contains, in Schrage's opinion, references to Matthew: the additions of 'man' and 'treasure'; the omission of 'of heart'. J. Sieber points out that *Thomas*' order and verbal agreements in L. 45.1–2 might show dependence on Quelle but not necessarily on Luke or Matthew.

H.-W. Bartsch argues that the Thomasine additions 'for they give no fruit' and 'and speaks evil things' signals secondary development which must mean that *Thomas* is developing Synoptic material here. J. Sieber traces this development to another source, oral transmission. He notes in his conclusion, however, that this secondary development could represent a reworking of Luke.

In my opinion, the correlations between L. 45 and the Synoptics suggest that L. 45 is an early oral multiform independent of the Synoptics. The common words and phrases do not necessarily appear in the same sequence, and word equivalents are used. There is no sign of secondary orality – that is, no sign of secondary development in the Synoptic sayings showing up in the Thomasine. The affinities with Qluke against Qmatt suggest that *Thomas* and Luke must have known a common version of this saying.

LITERATURE PARALLELS

Luke 6.44–45 (Qluke)

'For figs are not gathered from thorns, nor are grapes picked from a bramble bush. The good man out of the good treasure of his heart produces good, and the evil man out of his evil treasure produces evil. For out of the abundance of the heart his mouth speaks.'

Matthew 7.16 (Qmatt)

'Are grapes gathered from thorns, or figs from thistles?'

Matthew 12.34–35 (Qmatt)

'You brood of vipers! how can you speak good, when you are evil? For out of the abundance of the heart the mouth speaks. The good man out of his good treasure brings forth good, and the evil man out of his evil treasure brings forth evil.'

James 3.12
> 'Can a fig tree, my brethren, yield olives, or a grapevine figs?'

Ignatius, Ephesians *14*
> 'All that makes for a soul's perfection follows in their train, for nobody who professes faith will commit sin, and nobody who possesses love can feel hatred. As the tree is known by its fruits, so they who claim to belong to Christ are known by their actions.'

Pseudo-Clementine Homilies *19.7.1*
> 'For thus said our Teacher who always spoke the Truth, "Out of the abundance of the heart the mouth speaks."'

Aphrahat, Demon. *14.48*
> 'One does not gather grapes from thorns, nor figs from thistles, for a good tree produces good fruit and a bad tree produces bad fruit. A good tree cannot yield bad fruit, and a bad tree cannot yield good fruit. A good man brings forth and speaks good things from the good treasures which are in his heart, and an evil man brings forth and speaks evil things from the abundance of his heart, for the lips speak from the abundance of the heart.'

Aphrahat, Demon. *9.11*
> 'Remember what our Saviour says. "The good tree produces good fruit, and the bad tree produces bad fruit. The bad tree cannot produce good fruit, and the good tree cannot produce bad fruit, for the tree is known by its fruit. So the good man produces and speaks good things from the good treasures which are in his heart, and the evil man produces and speaks evil things from the evil treasures which are in his heart. For the lips speak from the abundance of the heart."'

Apocalypse of Peter *76.4–8*
> 'For they do not gather figs from thorns nor from thorn trees, if they are wise, nor grapes from thorns.'

Sirach 27.6
> 'Its fruit discloses the cultivation of the tree. So the expression of a thought discloses the cultivation of a man's mind.'

AGREEMENTS IN SYRIAN GOSPELS, WESTERN TEXT AND DIATESSARON

Matthew 7.16//Luke 6.44 in a C (Matthew) T^A T^{NL} Aphr
> nor (Luke) << or (Matthew)

Matthew 12.35//Luke 6.45 in 485 b (Matthew) i t (Luke)
> + for

Matthew 12.35//Luke 6.45 in D (Matthew)
> a good man << the good man

Matthew 12.35//Luke 6.45 in ff² D Sa Bo
> out of his treasure << out of the treasure

Matthew 12.35//Luke 6.45 in L 33 P (Luke) Pal (Matthew) S C T^A T^P T^{NL} T^V Heliand Sa Aphr
> + *which is in* his heart

Matthew 12.35//Luke 6.45 in Aphr
> + and speaks evil things

Matthew 12.34//Luke 6.45 in k S (Matthew)
> brings forth << speaks

Matthew 12.34//Luke 6.45 in e (Luke) ff¹ (Matthew) D d
    + evil things

SELECT BIBLIOGRAPHY
Bartsch (1959/1960: 253–55); Guillaumont (1981: 197); Quispel (1962: 145–46); Schrage (1964a: 100–106); Sieber (1966: 87–90, 262).

Logion 46.1–2

¹Jesus said, 'From Adam to John the Baptist, no one among those born of women is more exalted than John the Baptist that the person's gaze should not be deferent. ² Yet I have said, "Whoever from among you will become a child, this person will know the Kingdom and he will be more exalted than John."'

NHC II 2.41.6–12

¹ⲡⲉⲭⲉ ⲓ̅ⲥ̅ ⲭⲉ ⲭⲓⲛ ⲁⲇⲁⲙ ϣⲁ ⲓ̈ⲱ̧ⲁ(ⲛ)ⲛⲏⲥ ⲡⲃⲁⲡⲧⲓⲥⲧⲏⲥ ϩⲛ̅ ⲛ̅ⲭⲡⲟ
ⲛ̅ⲛ̧ⲓⲟⲙⲉ ⲙⲛ̅ ⲡⲉⲧⲭⲟⲥⲉ ⲁ ⲓ̈ⲱ̧ⲁⲛⲛⲏⲥ ⲡⲃⲁⲡⲧⲓⲥⲧⲏⲥ ϣⲓⲛⲁ ⲭⲉ
ⲛⲟⲩⲱϭⲡ ⲛ̅ϭⲓ ⲛⲉϥⲃⲁⲗ ²ⲁⲉⲓⲭⲟⲟⲥ ⲇⲉ ⲭⲉ ⲡⲉⲧⲛⲁϣⲱⲡⲉ ϩⲛ̅
ⲧⲏⲩⲧⲛ̅ ⲉϥⲟ ⲛ̅ⲕⲟⲩⲉⲓ ϥⲛⲁⲥⲟⲩⲱⲛ ⲧⲙⲛ̅ⲧⲉⲣⲟ ⲁⲩⲱ ϥⲛⲁⲭⲓⲥⲉ ⲁ
ⲓ̈ⲱ̧ⲁⲛⲛⲏⲥ

ATTRIBUTION
Kernel saying with accretive clause.

TEXT AND TRANSLATION ISSUES
'That the person's gaze should not be deferent', literally reads, 'that the person's eyes should not break'. This translation attempts to make sensible a difficult passage, by rendering it idiomatically. The gaze of a subordinate should be one in which his or her eyes do not stare, but look away with deference and respect.

INTERPRETATIVE COMMENT
Although this saying appears to have been part of the Kernel Gospel, it contains an accretive interpretative clause, 'this person will know the Kingdom'. This vocabulary represents vocabulary characteristic of the accretions.

    The shift to understanding ⲕⲟⲩⲉⲓ as a reference to 'a child' rather than a simple diminutive may also represent a later adaption in the Kernel of an earlier form of the tradition which has been preserved in Matthew and Luke. This adaptation would have occurred as the later encratic constituency developed within the Thomasine community. For these reasons, it is impossible to recover the 'original' Kernel saying entirely. According to G. Quispel, Macarius was aware of the version of the saying as it appears in the *Gospel of Thomas* since he has μικρός // ⲕⲟⲩⲉⲓ instead of μικρότερος as we find in Matthew and Luke. Both *Thomas* and Macarius say that only the 'little one' or 'child' is greater than John whereas Matthew and Luke say the 'least' in the Kingdom are greater than John. D. Baker notes that, in fact, Macarius assumes that this 'little one', this 'child', is a virgin soul who is wedded to Christ (*Hom.* 28.6). There was an old tradition that John the Baptist was a virgin. This was understood to be the reason for John's superiority (cf. *Pseudo-Clementines, De Virginitate* (Diekamp, *Patres Apostolici*, pp. 9–10; Lefort, *Pères Apostoliques*, CSCO 136,

p. 33); *Bücher der Einsetzung der Erzengel Michael und Gabriel* (Detlef and Mueller, CSCO 32, pp. 35–36)). This tradition, of course, fits well the encratic hermeneutic of the later Thomasine community and may well have represented the community's interpretation of this saying. If so, the hermeneutic would have assumed John's superiority and given deference to him due to his virginity while also challenging community members to take up virginity themselves, to become children. Only in this capacity would they be able to be greater than John and come to 'know' the Kingdom.

SOURCE DISCUSSION

B. Gärtner, R. Grant and D.N. Freedman, and W. Schrage think that L. 46 is dependent upon Matthew and Luke due to similarity of the sayings. Schrage points to some particulars such as the full name, 'John the Baptist' instead of 'John' as we find in Luke. J. Sieber does not think that the difference of name can be solidly attributed to Matthew's hand.

My own examination of this saying against its parallels suggests that it has several secondary developments as the result of oral transmission, particularly the understanding of the diminutive 'little' as 'becoming a child', and the inclusion of 'knowledge' of the Kingdom as an entrance requirement. Perhaps even the idiom of deference is secondary. The former two accretive clauses I attribute to development at a time when the community became encratic (see *Interpretative Comment*). Because of these late developments, it is difficult to reconstruct the version of the saying as it may have existed in the Kernel. But even upon removing these secondary phrases – 'From Adam to John the Baptist, no one among those born of women is more exalted than John the Baptist that the person's gaze should not be deferent. Whoever from among you will become little, he will be more exalted than John' – the patterns of variation favour multiform orality rather than literary dependence.

LITERATURE PARALLELS

Matthew 11.11 (Qmatt)

'Truly I say to you, among those born of women there has risen no one greater than John the Baptist. Yet he who is least in the Kingdom of Heaven is greater than he.'

Luke 7.28 (Qluke)

'I tell you, among those born of women none is greater than John. Yet he who is least in the Kingdom of God is greater than he.'

Pseudo-Clementine Recognitions *1.60*

'And behold, one of the disciples of John asserted that John was the Christ, and not Jesus, inasmuch as Jesus himself declared that John was greater than all men and all prophets. "If then", he said, "he be greater than all, he must be held greater than Moses, and than Jesus himself. But if he be the greatest of all, then he must be the Christ." To this Simon the Canaanite answering, asserted that John was indeed greater than all the prophets, and all who are born of women, yet that he is not greater than the Son of Man. Accordingly Jesus is also the Christ, whereas John is only a prophet: and there is as much difference between him and Jesus, as between the forerunner and him whose forerunner he is, or as between him who gives the law and him who keeps the law.'

Pseudo-Macarius, Hom. *28.6*

'Indeed, "among those born of women, there is no greater than John the Baptist." For he is the fulfilment of all the prophets… "But he who is least in the Kingdom of Heaven, is greater than he." – those who have been born from above, of God, namely, the Apostles… This is the little one who is greater than John the Baptist.'

Ahmad ibn Hanbal, al-Zuhd, pp. 98–99 (no. 330)
'Whoever has learned, acted, and acquired knowledge, he is the one who is called great in the Kingdom of Heaven.'

Cf. *Pseudo-Clementine Homilies* 2.17, 3.23, 3.52.

AGREEMENTS IN SYRIAN GOSPELS, WESTERN TEXT AND DIATESSARON

Matthew 11.11//Luke 7.28 in D
+ I have said

Matthew 11.11//Luke 7.28 in S C P Pal T^d Aphr Mac
as a child << least

SELECT BIBLIOGRAPHY
Gärtner (1961: 223–29); Grant with Freedman (1960: 158–59); Schrage (1964a: 107–108); Sieber (1966: 129–31).

Logion 47.1–2

[1]Jesus said, 'It is impossible for a person to mount two horses and to bend two bows.
[2]Also it is impossible for a servant to serve two masters, or he will honour the one and insult the other.'

NHC II 2.41.12–17

[1]ⲡⲉϫⲉ ⲓ̅ⲥ̅ ϫⲉ ⲙⲛ̅ ϭⲟⲙ ⲛ̅ⲧⲉ ⲟⲩⲣⲱⲙⲉ ⲧⲉⲗⲟ ⲁ²ⲧⲟ ⲥⲛⲁⲩ ⲛ̅ϥϫⲱⲗⲕ
ⲙ̅ⲡⲓⲧⲉ ⲥⲛ̅ⲧⲉ [2]ⲁⲩⲱ ⲙⲛ̅ ϭⲟⲙ ⲛ̅ⲧⲉ ⲟⲩ²ⲙ̅ϩⲁ̅ⲗ̅ ⲱ̅ⲙ̅ⲱⲉ ϫⲟⲉⲓⲥ ⲥⲛⲁⲩ
ⲏ ϥⲛⲁⲣ̅ⲧⲓⲙⲁ ⲙ̅ⲡⲟⲩⲁ ⲁⲩⲱ ⲡⲕⲉⲟⲩⲁ ϥⲛⲁⲣ̅²ⲩⲃⲣⲓⲍⲉ ⲙ̅ⲙⲟϥ

ATTRIBUTION
Kernel saying.

INTERPRETATIVE COMMENT
This saying continues elaborating the theme of the Kernel speech that exclusive commitment to Jesus and his teaching is necessary in order to enter the Kingdom.

SOURCE DISCUSSION
W. Schrage argues for dependence on Luke based on the agreement οἰκέτης. J. Sieber admits that this might be an example of a Lukan editorial trait, but does not wish to concede dependence based on one word. H. Koester says that it cannot be determined with certainty that οἰκέτης is a Lukanism, although Koester does state that it is possible that Luke is responsible for οἰκέτης. He argues for an early independent form because L. 47.1–2 shows no sign of the unnecessary duplication 'hate the one and love the other' nor the secondary application of the proverb that one cannot serve God and mammon. Patterson points out that ϩⲙ̅ϩⲁⲗ is more likely translated δοῦλος than οἰκέτης.

In my opinion, the Kernel saying was likely independent since there is no parallel for L. 47.1 and L. 47.2 has striking differences when compared with Luke 16.13, differences perhaps produced in the field of oral performance. The Thomasine version has phrases similar to the Synoptic ('to serve two masters'; 'insult the other'). But additional material is found in the Synoptic versions (cf. 'for either he will hate the one and love the other'). It may be that L. 47.2 is evidence for a common source for Qluke and *Thomas*, a source which manifests independently in Luke and L. 47.2. In this case, we are witnessing in Luke and Matthew different versions of Quelle, and L. 47.2 appears closer to Luke's Quelle than Matthew's. If, however, Luke is responsible for οἰκέτης, not his source, then it may have entered the Gospel when it was translated as secondary scribal adaptation.

LITERATURE PARALLELS

Matthew 6.24 (Qmatt)
> 'No one can serve two masters. For either he will hate the one and love the other, or he will be devoted to the one and despise the other.'

Luke 16.13 (Qluke)
> 'No servant can serve two masters. For either he will hate the one and love the other, or he will be devoted to the one and despise the other.'

2 Clement *6.1*
> 'And the master says, "No servant can serve two masters."'

AGREEMENTS IN SYRIAN GOSPELS, WESTERN TEXT AND DIATESSARON

Matthew 6.24//Luke 16.13 in 1241 (Matthew) L 037 21 T^A
> + servant

Matthew 6.24//Luke 16.13 in Mcion
> – for either he will...love the other

Matthew 6.24//Luke 16.13 in P T^P T^A T^{EC}
> he will honour << he will be devoted

Matthew 6.24//Luke 16.13 in Mcion
> insult << despise

SELECT BIBLIOGRAPHY
Koester (1957: 75; 1990: 90); Patterson (1993: 41); Schrage (1964a: 109–11); Sieber (1966: 102).

Logion 47.3–4

[3] 'No one drinks aged wine and immediately wants to drink unaged wine. [4] Also, unaged wine is not put into old wineskins so that they may burst. Nor is aged wine put into a new wineskin so that it may spoil.'

NHC II 2.41.17–22

> [3] ⲘⲀⲣⲈ ⲣⲰⲘⲈ ⲤⲈ ⲡ̄ⲡⲀⲤ ⲀⲨⲰ Ⲛ̄ⲧⲈⲨⲚⲞⲨ Ⲛ̄ϤⲈⲡⲓⲐⲨⲘⲈⲓ ⲀⲤⲰ ⲎⲢⲡ̄
> Ⲃ̄ⲂⲢ̄ⲢⲈ [4] ⲀⲨⲰ ⲘⲀⲨⲚⲞⲨⳖ ⲎⲢⲡ̄ Ⲃ̄ⲂⲢ̄ⲢⲈ ⲈⲀⲤⲔⲞⲤ Ⲛ̄ⲀⲤ ⳖⲈⲔⲀⲀⲤ
> Ⲛ̄ⲚⲞⲨⲡⲦⲰⳞ ⲀⲨⲰ ⲘⲀⲨⲚⲈⳖ ⲎⲢⲡ̄ Ⲛ̄ⲀⲤ ⲈⲀⲤⲔⲞⲤ Ⲃ̄ⲂⲢ̄ⲢⲈ ⳞⲒⲚⲀ ⳖⲈ
> ⲚⲈϤⲦⲈⲔⲀϤ

ATTRIBUTION
Kernel saying.

INTERPRETATIVE COMMENT
In a Kernel speech, this proverb is used to elaborate the theme of exclusive commitment to
Jesus and his teachings.

SOURCE DISCUSSION
Because L. 47.3 is similar to Luke's addition in 5.39, W. Schrage says that *Thomas* is
dependent on Luke. That *Thomas* knows the Lukan saying also is discussed by H. von
Schürmann who thinks it was harmonized with Mark 12.21–22. Schrage acknowledges,
however, that this verse could have been a secular mashal known to Luke and *Thomas*
independently. He also points to Sahidic Luke which agrees with this logion's translation
of the word 'wine'. As for L. 47.4, Schrage argues for Matthean dependence since *Thomas*
is closer to that version than Mark or Luke.

J. Sieber states that it is possible that L. 47.3 may have already been welded to the wine
saying in the oral sphere. The Coptic commonalities he thinks do not help us understand
the source of the saying in *Thomas' Vorlage*. Further, he sees no Matthean redactional
material and notes that *Thomas'* sequence of sayings gives no indication that he knew the
Synoptic sequence. He also notes that *Thomas* uses ἵνα μή while the Synoptics use εἰ δὲ
μή. He cannot see why this change would have been made deliberately.

The Synoptics have phrases not found in *Thomas* (cf. 'the wine is lost, and so are the
skins'; 'new wine is for fresh skins') and significant differences in the sequence of the
words and phrases including inversions of parts of the saying. In my opinion, all of this
points to a process of oral transmission that was originally independent of the Synoptics.

LITERATURE PARALLELS

Mark 2.22
> 'And no one puts new wine into old wineskins. If he does, the wine will burst the skins,
> and the wine is lost, and so are the skins. But new wine is for fresh skins.'

Matthew 9.17
> 'Neither is new wine put into old wineskins. If it is, the skins burst, and the wine is
> spilled, and the skins are destroyed. But new wine is put into fresh wineskins, and so
> both are preserved.'

Luke 5.37–39
> [37]'And no one puts new wine into old wineskins. If he does, the new wine will burst the
> skins and it will be spilled, and the skins will be destroyed. [38]But new wine must be put
> into fresh wineskins. [39]And no one after drinking old wine desires new. For he says,
> "The old is good."'

AGREEMENTS IN SYRIAN GOSPELS, WESTERN TEXT AND DIATESSARON

Luke 5.39 in P[4] ℵ[C] B 579 892
> – and

Matthew 6.24//Luke 5.39 in P T[P] T[A]
> drinks << after drinking

Luke 5.39 in P T^P T^A
   old + wine

Luke 5.39 in P T^P T^A
   + and

Luke 5.39 in aur f q C Θ 33 892 Koine vg P T^A T^L T^T
   + immediately

Luke 5.39 in T^P T^PEP
   new + wine

SELECT BIBLIOGRAPHY
Nagel (1960); Schrage (1964a: 112–16); Schürmann (1963: 238–40); Sieber (1966: 98–102).

Logion 47.5

⁵'An old patch is not sewn onto a new garment because a tear would result.'

NHC II 2.41.22–23

⁵ⲘⲀⲨⲬⲀ̄Ⲟ́ ⲧⲟⲉⲓⲥ ⲛ̄Ⲁⲥ Ⲁ(Ⲱ)Ⲧ(Ⲏ)Ⲛ ⲛ̄(Ⲱ)Ⲁⲉⲓ ⲉⲡⲉⲓ ⲟⲨⲛ ⲟⲨⲡⲱⲢ
ⲛⲀ(Ⲱ)(Ⲱ)ⲡⲉ

ATTRIBUTION
Kernel saying.

INTERPRETATIVE COMMENT
This saying is an example that further elaborates the theme of one of the Kernel's speeches
– that the disciple must be exclusively commited to Jesus and his teachings.

SOURCE DISCUSSION
See L. 47.3–4

LITERATURE PARALLELS

Mark 2.21
   'No one sews a piece of unshrunk cloth on an old garment. If he does, the patch tears
   away from it, the new from the old, and a worse tear is made.'

Matthew 9.16
   'And no one puts a piece of unshrunk cloth on an old garment, for the patch tears away
   from the garment, and a worse tear is made.'

Luke 5.36
   'He told them a parable also, "No one tears a piece from a new garment and puts it upon
   an old garment. If he does, he will tear the new, and the piece from the new will not
   match the old."'

Mark 2.21// Matthew 9.16// Luke 5.36 in Mcion T^P
> they << no one

Mark 2.21// Matthew 9.16// Luke 5.36 in T^P
> an old patch on a new garment

Logion 48

Jesus said, 'If two people make peace with each other in the same house, they will say to the mountain, "Go forth!" and it will move.'

NHC II 2.41.24–27

ⲡⲉϫⲉ ⲓ̅ⲥ̅ ϫⲉ ⲉⲣϣⲁ ⲥⲛⲁⲩ ⲣ̅ ⲉⲓⲣⲏⲛⲏ ⲙⲛ̅ ⲛⲟⲩⲉⲣⲏⲩ ϩⲙ̅ ⲡⲉⲓⲏⲉⲓ
ⲟⲩⲱⲧ ⲥⲉⲛⲁϫⲟⲟⲥ ⲙ̅ⲡⲧⲁⲩ ϫⲉ ⲡⲱⲱⲛⲉ ⲉⲃⲟⲗ ⲁⲩⲱ ϥⲛⲁⲡⲱⲱⲛⲉ

ATTRIBUTION
Kernel saying.

TEXT AND TRANSLATION ISSUES
'The same house' literally reads, 'this one house'.

A. Guillaumont sees an Aramaic influence in this logion. He says that *Thomas*', 'if two people make peace with each other', and Matthew's, 'if two of you agree on earth', represent independent translations of an Aramaic substratum which contained the word שׁלם meaning both 'to make peace' and 'to agree'. N. Perrin thinks the same is true of the Syriac ܐܟ which stands in the Syriac version of Matthew 18.19. The Syriac ܐܟ, however, does not have this dual meaning. The root means 'equal, alike, same, sufficient, worthy, agree' (Payne Smith, 561–62). So Syriac Matthew reflects a very good translation of the Greek, 'become agreed' or 'like-minded'. The Coptic ⲣ̅ ⲉⲓⲣⲏⲛⲏ cannot be explained as a translation of the Syriac Matthew or ܐܟ if this word occurred in the Diatessaron.

INTERPRETATIVE COMMENT
In the third Kernel speech, Jesus admonishes the hearers to choose to serve him alone. Rationales and analogies from the proverbial tradition are provided (L. 47). Promises are given in L. 48. Serving Jesus means that the disciple is a peacemaker whose words will have tremendous power, even moving mountains.

SOURCE DISCUSSION
W. Schrage and R. Grant think that this logion results from the author combining Matthew 18.19 and 17.20. Schrage tries to make this firm by pointing out that both Sahidic Matthew and L. 48 and L. 106 translate μεταβαίνειν with ⲡⲱⲱⲛⲉ rather than ⲡⲱⲱⲛⲉ ⲉⲃⲟⲗ.

J. Sieber says that this is not evidence to prove dependency at the level of the Greek texts. Further the combination of sayings found in *Thomas* matches the *Didascalia* which suggests to Sieber that *Thomas* and the *Didascalia* represent a separate tradition. This position appears to be supported by the published work of form critics. J.D. Crossan argues that the original core of the logion is preserved in the single-stich aphorism from the Latin

Didascalia which becomes a double-stich saying in the Syriac. He thinks that it represents an independent version of the saying, not a conflation of Matthew 18.19 and 21.21 as Achelis and Flemming, the editors of the German edition, conclude, because it more adequately explains the performance in L. 48 (and L. 106) which continues the original single-stich. C.W. Hedrick is of a different opinion, stating that although *Thomas* presents an independent version of the saying, the Syriac *Didascalia* has combined two independent sayings from the sources used by the Synoptic writers and reflects a different oral performance of the traditional saying. The Latin version is derived from the Syriac, representing a condensation harmonizing it with Mark 11.23//Matthew 21.21. Thus he finds at least three independent versions of the saying: Matthew 21.21 (derived from Mark 11.22–23); Matthew 17.20//Luke 17.6 (derived from either Q, M and Q, or M and L); L. 48 and 106.

LITERATURE PARALLELS

Matthew 17.20 (Qmatt)
> 'For truly, I say to you, if you have faith as a grain of mustard seed, you will say to this mountain, "Move from here to there", and it will move. And nothing will be impossible to you.'

Luke 17.6 (Qluke)
> 'And the Lord said, "If you had faith as a grain of mustard seed, you could say to this sycamine tree, 'Be rooted up, and be planted in the sea', and it would obey you."'

Matthew 18.19
> 'Again, I say to you, if two of you agree on earth about anything they ask, it will be done for them by my Father in heaven.'

Mark 11.23
> 'Truly, I say to you, whoever says to this mountain, "Be taken up and cast into the sea", and does not doubt in his heart, but believes that what he says will come to pass, it will be done for him.'

Matthew 21.21
> 'Truly I say to you, if you have faith and never doubt, you will not only do what has been done to the fig tree, but even if you say to this mountain, "Be taken up and cast into the sea", it will be done.'

1 Corinthians 13.2
> 'And if I have prophetic powers and understand all the mysteries and all knowledge, and if I have all faith, so as to remove mountains, but have not love, I am nothing.'

L. 106
> [1]Jesus said, 'When you make the two one, you will become children of Man. [2]And when you say, "Mountain, go forth!" it will move.'

Didascalia *(Latin) 15*
> 'If two shall agree together and shall say to this mountain, take and cast yourself into the sea, it will happen.'

Didascalia *(Syriac) 15*
> 'If two shall agree together, and shall ask concerning anything whatsoever, it shall be given them. And if they say to a mountain that it be removed and fall into the sea, it shall be done.'

Pseudo-Clementine Homilies *11.16*
> 'For the Jew believes God and keeps the law, by which faith he removes also other sufferings, though like mountains and heavy.'

Pseudo-Clementine Recognitions *5.2*

> 'For thus the true Prophet promised us, saying, "Verily I say to you, that if you have faith as a grain of mustard seed, you shall say to this mountain, Remove hence, and it shall remove." '

Pseudo-Clementine Recognitions *5.34*

> 'He is the true worshipper of God who not only is himself free from passions, but also sets others free from them. Though they be heavy that they are like mountains, he removes them by means of faith with which he believes in God. Yea, by faith he truly removes mountains with their trees, if it be necessary.'

Aphraates, Homilies

> 'The disciples said to Jesus, "Increase our faith." He said to them, "If you have faith, a mountain will give way before you." And he said to them, "Do not doubt lest you be swallowed up in the world, as Simon, since he doubted and began to sink in the sea." '

AGREEMENTS IN SYRIAN GOSPELS, WESTERN TEXT AND DIATESSARON

Matthew 17.20 in e S Aphr T^{EC} geo(OT)
– from here

Matthew 17.20 in 33 517 713 1424 g^2 l S C P Aphr T^{EC} T^A T^L T^T T^V Mt(Heb) aeth
– to there

Matthew 18.19 in a h ff^1 T^P T^{NL} 33 sa Mac
if two make peace – of you

SELECT BIBLIOGRAPHY
Crossan (1983: 295–302); Grant (1959: 178); Guillaumont (1981: 199–200); Hedrick (1990); Schrage (1964a: 116); Sieber (1966: 202–03).

Logion 49.1–2

[1]Jesus said, 'Blessed are the celibate people, the chosen ones, because you will find the Kingdom. [2]For you are from it. You will return there again.'

NHC II 2.41.27–30

> [1]ΠΕΧΕ ΙC ΧΕ ϨΕΝΜΑΚΑΡΙΟC ΝΕ ΝΜΟΝΑΧΟC ΑΥⲰ ΕΤCΟΤΠ ΧΕ ΤΕΤΝΑϨΕ ΑΤΜΝ̄ΤΕΡΟ [2]ΧΕ Ν̄ΤⲰΤΝ̄ ϨΝ̄ΕΒΟΛ Ν̄ϨΗΤC̄ ΠΑΛΙΝ ΕΤΕΤΝΑΒⲰΚ ΕΜΑΥ

ATTRIBUTION
Accretion.

INTERPRETATIVE COMMENT
Development is indicated by the characteristic vocabulary, **MONAXOC**, found in other accretions. The accretion comes from the years between 80 and 120 CE and is indicative of the theology of an encratic constituency. In this case, those who are unmarried and celibate are the elect of God who are from the Kingdom and will return to it. See L. 16.4 for further discussion of this term.

SOURCE DISCUSSION
G. Quispel attributes this saying to the creative pen of the author of the Gospel.

LITERATURE PARALLELS

Dialogue of the Saviour *I*

'But when I came, I opened the path and I taught them about the passage which they will traverse, the chosen, the single people, [who have known the Father, having believed] the truth and [all] the praises while you offered praise.'

SELECT BIBLIOGRAPHY
Quispel (1981: 265).

Logion 50.1–3

[1]Jesus said, 'If they say to you, "Where did you come from?", say to them, 'We came from the light', – the place where the light came into being on its own accord and established [itself] and became manifest through their image. [2]If they say to you, "Is it you?", say "We are its children, and we are the chosen people of the living Father". [3]If they ask you, "What is the sign of your Father in you?", say to them, "It is movement and rest"'.

NHC II 2.41.30–42.7

[1]ΠΕΧΕ Ι͞C ΧΕ ΕΥϢΑΝΧΟΟC ΝΗΤ͞Ν ΧΕ Ν͞ΤΑΤΕΤΝ͞ϢϢΠΕ ΕΒΟΛ
ΤⲰΝ ΧΟΟC ΝΑΥ ΧΕ Ν͞ΤΑΝΕΙ ΕΒΟΛ Ϩ͞Μ ΠΟΥΟΕΙΝ ΠΜΑ ΕΝΤΑ
ΠΟΥΟΕΙΝ ϢⲰΠΕ [Μ͞ΜΑ]Υ ΕΒΟΛ ϨΙΤΟΟΤ϶ ΟΥΑΑΤ϶ ΑϤⲰϨΙΕ ΕΡΑΤϤ
ΑΙΥⲰ ΑϤΟΥⲰΝ[Ϩ] ΕΙΒ[Ο]Λ Ϩ͞Ν ΤΟΥϨΙΚⲰΝ [2]ΕΥϢΑΧΟΟC ΝΗΤ͞Ν ΧΕ
Ν͞ΤⲰΤ͞Ν ΠΕ ΧΟΟC ΧΕ ΑΝΟΝ ΝΕϤϢΗΡΕ ΑΥⲰ ΑΝΟΝ Ν͞CⲰΤΠ
Μ͞ΠΕΙⲰΤ ΕΤΟΝϨ [3]ΕΥϢΑΝΧΝΕ ΤΗΥΤ͞Ν ΧΕ ΟΥ ΠΕ ΠΜΑΕΙΝ
Μ͞ΠΕΤΝ͞ΕΙⲰΤ ΕΤϨ͞Ν ΤΗΥΤ͞Ν ΧΟΟC ΕΡΟΟΥ ΧΕ ΟΥΚΙΜ ΠΕ Μ͞Ν
ΟΥΑΝΑΠΑΥCΪC

ATTRIBUTION
Accretion.

INTERPRETATIVE COMMENT
Development is indicated by the presence of vocabulary characteristic of the accretions, particularly the phrase, Μ͞ΠΕΙⲰΤ ΕΤΟΝϨ. This saying accrued in the Gospel between 60 and 100 CE as a result of the apocalyptic shift that occurred in the communal memory, a response to the Non-Event. The shift resulted in an emphasis on the mystical aspect of the apocalyptic rather than the eschatological. Also present are Hermetic concepts welded with old Jewish traditions, suggesting a shift in the constituency of the group.

As I have discussed in detail in a previous monograph, the contextual possibilities for L. 50 include a catechismal paradigm, a community dispute, the interrogation of the soul at death, and the interrogation of the soul during a mystical ascent. Since another accretion, L. 59, demands a mystical journey to God, a journey before death, in order to achieve immortality, it is arguable that the hermeneutic assumed by the community for understanding L. 50 was also such a mystical frame. This hermeneutic would have developed out of a very prominent set of traditions from early Jewish and Christian mysticism found in a variety of apocalyptic and Hekhalot literature listed in this logion's *LITERATURE PARALLELS*. These traditions concerning soul interrogation were known and developed independently by certain Gnostic communities at a time later than the *Thomas* materials as the parallel to *1 Apocalypse of James* and other Gnostic texts demonstrate.

The answers provided in this saying weave together old Jewish ideas and Hermetic traditions. Concepts such as the Hermetic notion of the self-generated God have joined with Jewish and Hermetic beliefs about the pre-existent Light, the great Anthropos. The expository clause that the Light is manifested into the creation of humans through 'their' image is a reference to Genesis 1.26 and to the Jewish teaching that the human being was created in the Image of the Anthropos through an angelic interface. The Thomasine Christians believed themselves to be God's chosen, not by adoption as the Jews, but because of their natural origin as children of God, 'sons of the light'. The coupling of 'movement' and 'rest' is to be associated with the Hermetic concept, the Unmoved Mover. So, the Thomasine Christians were saying here that the sign that should allow them access to heaven is the knowledge that they participate in the very nature of God, both the movement of the universe and its state of rest. This participation in God's nature is a present experience, not a future eschatological hope.

SOURCE DISCUSSION
G. Quispel attributes this saying to a Hermetic anthology.

LITERATURE PARALLELS

1 Apocalypse James *32.28–34.20*
> 'The Lord [said] to [him, "James], behold, I shall reveal to you your redemption. When [you] are seized, and you undergo these sufferings, a multitude will arm themselves against you that <they> might seize you. And in particular three of them will seize you – they who sit (there) as toll collectors. Not only will they demand toll, but they also take away souls by theft. When you come into their power, one of them who is their guard will say to you, 'Who are you or where are you from?' You are to say to him, 'I am a son, and I am from the Father.' He will say to you, 'What sort of son are you, and to what father do you belong?' You are to say to him, 'I am from the Pre-existent Father, and a son in the Pre-existent One.' [When he says] to you, […], you are to [say to him,…] in the […] that I might […of] alien things?' You are to say to him, 'They are not entirely alien, but they are from Acamoth, who is the female. And these she produced as she brought down the race from the Pre-existent One. So then they are not alien, but they are ours. They are indeed ours because she who is mistress of them is from the Pre-existent One. At the same time they are alien because the Pre-existent One did not have intercourse with her, when she produced them.' When he also says to you, 'Where will you go?' you are to say to him, 'To the place from which I have come, there shall I return.' And if you say these things, you will escape their attacks."'

Apocalypse of Paul *22.24–23.26*
> 'The old man spoke, saying to [me], "Where are you going Paul, O blessed one and the one who was set apart from his mother's womb?"… And I replied, saying to the old man, "I am going to the place from which I came." And the old man responded to me, "Where are you from?" But I replied saying, "I am going down to the world of the dead in order to lead captive the captivity that was led captive in the captivity of Babylon."

The old man replied to me, saying, "How will you be able to get away from me?..."
[The] Spirit spoke, saying, "Give him [the] sign that you have, and [he will] open for
you." And then I gave [him] the sign.'

Cf. Philo, *De Cherubim* 114; *Aboth* 3.1; *Derekh Eres Rabba* 3; *Aboth de-R. Nathan* 2.32;
Excerpts of Theodotus 78.2; *Silvanus* 4.92.10–11; *Acts of Thomas* 15; *Asc. Isa.* 10.28–29;
3 Enoch 2, 4 and 5; *Apoc. Abr.* 13.6; *Bavli Hagigah* 15b; *Bavli Shabbat* 88b–89a; *Shemot
Rabba* 42.4; *Pesikta Rabbati* 96b–98a; *Gedullat Mosheh* 273; *Hekhalot Fragments* lines
28–38; *History of the Rechabites* 5.1–2; *Apoc. Abr.* 17–18; *Hekhalot Rabbati* 1.1, 2.5–5.3,
16.4–25.6; *Hekhalot Zutt.* 413–415; *Bavli Hagigah* 14b; *Ma'aseh Merkavah* 9, 11, 15;
Gospel of Mary 15.14, 16.14–15; Origen, *c. Cels.* 6.30, 7.40; *Pistis Sophia*; 1 and 2 *Books
of Jeu*; *Untitled Gnostic Treatise.*

SELECT BIBLIOGRAPHY
DeConick (1996: 43–96); Quispel (1981: 265).

Logion 51.1–2

[1]'His disciples said to him, 'When will the dead rest, and when will the new world come?'

[2]'He said to them, 'What you look for has come, but you have not perceived it.'

NHC II 2.42.7–12

[1]ⲡⲉⲭⲁⲩ ⲛⲁϥ ⲛ̄ϭⲓ ⲛⲉϥⲙⲁⲑⲏⲧⲏⲥ ⲭⲉ ⲁⲱ ⲛ̄ϩⲟⲟⲩ ⲉⲧⲁⲛⲁⲡⲁⲩⲥⲓⲥ
ⲛ̄ⲛⲉⲧⲙⲟⲟⲩⲧ ⲛⲁⲱϣⲱⲡⲉ ⲁⲩⲱ ⲁⲱ ⲛ̄ϩⲟⲟⲩ ⲉⲡⲕⲟⲥⲙⲟⲥ ⲃ̄ⲃⲣ̄ⲣⲉ ⲛⲏⲩ
[2]ⲡⲉⲭⲁϥ ⲛⲁⲩ ⲭⲉ ⲧⲏ ⲉⲧⲉⲧⲛ̄ϭⲱϣⲧ ⲉⲃⲟⲗ ϩⲏⲧⲥ̄ ⲁϭⲉⲓ ⲁⲗⲗⲁ
ⲛ̄ⲧⲱⲧⲛ̄ ⲧⲉⲧⲛ̄ⲥⲟⲟⲩⲛ ⲁⲛ ⲙ̄ⲙⲟⲥ

ATTRIBUTION
Accretion.

TEXT AND TRANSLATION ISSUES
'When will the dead rest' literally reads, 'When will the rest of the dead take place?' The
former translation is offered to compensate for the clumsiness of the literal.

INTERPRETATIVE COMMENT
Secondary development is indicated by the dialogue format of the saying. The question
and answer suggest responsiveness to the problem of the delayed Eschaton. Accrual in the
Gospel took place between 60 and 100 CE.

The reference to the 'rest of the dead' is a comment on the post-mortem state of the
journeying soul in Hermetic tradition when it is reincorporated into God who exists at 'rest'
(*C.H.* 9.10; 13.20; *Disc.* 60.1–61.18; *C.H.* 2.6; 2.12; 6.1; *Asc.* 7, 32). Thus, this saying picks
up the Hermetic theme of 'rest' from the previous logion. This concept, however, has been
recontextualized within traditional Jewish eschatological expectations, particularly the
advent of the new world. Such expectations were held by an earlier constituency within
the Thomasine community, but these have been replaced with a new expectation, a new
explanatory schema, in face of their experience of disconfirmation when the Kingdom did
not come.

This saying probably serves as a corrective to an earlier belief shared by the community in the 'resurrection of the dead'. Hence the awkward substitution the 'rest of the dead'. As the Thomasine community incorporated more and more Hermetic philosophy into their belief system, it seems that they shifted away from the traditional Jewish belief in a resurrected body to the immortalization of the soul or somehow had fused the two tensive expectations together. It is noteworthy that the difference between 'rest' and 'resurrection' in Coptic is only three letters: ⲀⲚⲀⲠⲀⲨⲤⲓⲤ and ⲀⲚⲀⲤⲧⲀⲤⲓⲤ. So it is quite possible in my mind that the earliest form of the question in the Gospel was, 'When will the resurrection of the dead take place?' The community may have understood Jesus' response – 'It has already happened!' – in terms of the re-creation of the Edenic glorified body through encratic performance and mystical encounters with God. But in the early second century, the phrase in this saying seems to have shifted to, 'When will the rest of the dead take place?' This shift took place at a time when more Hellenized notions of the afterlife began to be appropriated in the face of continued pressure of the unfulfilled events of the Eschaton – the resurrection of the dead being one of the unfulfilled promises. This shift from 'resurrection' to 'rest' allowed for the *immediate* 'rest' of the soul following an individual's death. Thus Jesus' response – 'It has already happened!' – becomes more intelligible.

At any rate, the community has collapsed their apocalyptic expectations. The Kingdom, the new world, was not to be understood anymore to be a future event. Rather it was something that the Thomasine Christians had realized within the parameters of their community by recreating Eden and the utopian body of Adam through encratic performance and mystical journeys.

Apocalyptic collapse was not unknown to other Christian communities, the most documented example being the community responsible for the Gospel of John. In this schema, the expectations of the Eschaton were believed to have already happened, including Jesus' *parousia* and Judgement (3.13, 17–21; 6.62; 16.28). The person who believes in Jesus, was said to already have eternal life (1.12; 5.24; 11.26).

SOURCE DISCUSSION

H. von Schürmann finds L. 51.1–2 dependent on Luke 17.20–21 even though the so-called 'agreements' are little more than thematic while G. Quispel thinks that the author of the Gospel created this saying.

LITERATURE PARALLELS

2 Timothy 2.17–18
> [17]'Among them are Hymenaeus and Philetus [18]who have swerved from the truth by holding that the resurrection is past already.'

Pseudo-Macarius, Hom. *6.7*
> 'Do you, therefore, see how the beginning of Judgement appeared? A new world appeared there. Authority to sit and judge, even in this world, was given to them, the Apostles. And it is granted them also to sit and pass judgement at the coming of the Lord in the resurrection of the dead. Nevertheless, it is also done here, by the same Holy Spirit sitting on the thrones in their minds.'

Pseudo-Macarius, Hom. *36.1*
> 'The resurrection of the souls of the dead takes place even now in the time of death. But the resurrection of the bodies will take place in that day.'

Treatise on the Resurrection *49.9–25*

> 'Therefore, do not think in part, O Rheginos, nor live in conformity with this flesh for
> the sake of unanimity, but flee from the divisions and fetters, and already you have the
> resurrection. For if he who will die knows about himself that he will die – even if he
> spends many years in this life, he is brought to this – why not consider yourself as risen
> and (already) brought to this?'

Cf. John 3.17–18.

SELECT BIBLIOGRAPHY
Quispel (1981: 265); Schürmann (1963: 249–50).

Logion 52.1–2

¹His disciples said to him, 'Twenty-four prophets have spoken in Israel, and all of them
have spoken about you.'

²He said to them, 'You have left out the Living One who is in your presence and you
have spoken about the dead.'

NHC II 2.42.12–18

¹ⲡⲉⲭⲁⲩ ⲛⲁϥ ⲛ̅ϭⲓ ⲛⲉϥⲙⲁⲑⲏⲧⲏⲥ ⲭⲉ ⲭⲟⲩⲧⲁϥⲧⲉ ⲙ̅ⲡⲣⲟⲫⲏⲧⲏⲥ
ⲁⲩϣⲁⲭⲉ ϩ̅ⲙ ⲡⲓⲥⲣⲁⲏⲗ ⲁⲩⲱ ⲁⲩϣⲁⲭⲉ ⲧⲏⲣⲟⲩ ϩⲣⲁⲓ ⲛ̅ϩⲏⲧⲕ
²ⲡⲉⲭⲁϥ ⲛⲁⲩ ⲭⲉ ⲁⲧⲉⲧⲛ̅ⲕⲱ ⲙ̅ⲡⲉⲧⲟⲛϩ ⲙ̅ⲡⲉⲧⲛ̅ⲙ̅ⲧⲟ ⲉⲃⲟⲗ ⲁⲩⲱ
ⲁⲧⲉⲧⲛ̅ϣⲁⲭⲉ ϩⲁ ⲛⲉⲧⲙⲟⲟⲩⲧ

ATTRIBUTION
Accretion.

INTERPRETATIVE COMMENT
This saying is a constructed dialogue, indicating secondary development. It also contains
vocabulary, ⲡⲉⲧⲟⲛϩ, characteristic of the accretions. It belongs to an early Christian
discussion about the relevance of the Hebrew prophets to Jesus, a discussion that seems to
have been quite old, beginning with the Jerusalem Church (cf. Acts 2.22–36; 3.18–26;
4.11; 7.37) and Paul (cf. 1 Cor. 15.3–4), and carrying through the literature of the late first
and early second centuries (cf. Matthew 1.22–23; 2.5–6; 2.17–18, etc.; Luke 24.27; 24.44;
Acts 26.22; 28.23; *Barn.* 6.9–10; *Papyrus Egerton 2*). M. Lelyveld views this logion as a
reinterpretation of older christological beliefs.

   In my opinion, since this saying is providing some kind of corrective to the earlier
Thomasine Christology that Jesus was the final Prophet in a line of prophets of Israel who
foretold his advent and mission, accrual most likely took place sometime between 60 and
100 CE. The community has modified its old Prophet Christology by presenting here its
new understanding of Jesus as the 'Living God', the true God in contrast to 'dead' prophets
whom the Jews rely on for their religious 'life'. This seems to be a pun on the old tradition
from Second Temple Judaism that a proselyte must set aside worship of idols, 'dead'
gods, and exclusively worship Yahweh, the 'Living One'.

   This saying, however, does not have to suggest that the Thomasine Christians have come
to the point of completely denying the relevance of the Hebrew scriptures for Christianity,
such as we find in the second century with Marcion. There is a tradition in the *Pseudo-*

Clementine Recognitions 1.59 that suggests an alternative. As the Ebionites of the early second century began defining themselves over and against the Jews, they recorded the tradition that Jesus was not to be believed because the Jewish prophets foretold his advent and mission. Rather it was the 'presence and coming of Christ' that showed the prophets to be truly prophets 'for testimony must be borne by the superior to his inferiors, not by the inferiors to their superior'. This may, in fact, be a better interpretative foil for L. 52. The disciples are rebuked for thinking that the prophets bore witness to Jesus, when, in fact, Jesus, the Living God, is the one whose testimony must be heard and heeded. This tradition may be located in a nascent form in John 5.36–40.

SOURCE DISCUSSION
G. Quispel attributes this saying to the author of the Gospel.

LITERATURE PARALLELS

John 5.39–40
> [39]'You search the scriptures, because you think that in them you have eternal life. Yet it is they that bear witness to me. [40]But you refuse to come to me that you may have life.'

Pseudo-Clementine Recognitions *1.59*
> 'After him James the son of Alphaeus gave an address to the people, with the view of showing that we are not to believe on Jesus on the ground that the prophets foretold concerning him, but rather that we are to believe the prophets because the Christ bears testimony to them. For it is the presence and coming of Christ that show that they are truly prophets. For testimony must be borne by the superior to his inferiors, not by the inferiors to their superior.'

Acts of Thomas *170*
> 'You did not believe in the Living One. Will you believe in one who is dead?'

P. Egerton 2.1
> 'Master Jesus, we know that you have come from God, for what you do bears testimony to you, (testimony) that goes beyond that of all the prophets.'

Augustine, C. adv. leg. et proph. *2.4.14*
> 'But he said, when the apostles asked how the Jewish prophets were to be regarded, who were thought to have proclaimed his coming beforehand, our Lord, disturbed that they still held this conception, answered, "You have forsaken the Living One who is before you and speak about the dead."'

Cf. 2 Esdras 14.45.

SELECT BIBLIOGRAPHY
Lelyveld (1987: 77–83); Quispel (1981: 265).

Logion 53.1–3

[1]His disciples said to him, 'Is circumcision advantageous or not?'

[2]He said to them, 'If it were advantageous, the father (of the children) would conceive them in their mother already circumcised. [3]Rather circumcision in the spirit is true (circumcision). This person has procured all of the advantage.'

NHC II,2.42.18–23

¹ⲡⲉⲭⲁⲩ ⲛⲁϥ ⲛ̄ϭⲓ ⲛⲉϥⲙⲁⲑⲏⲧⲏⲥ ⲭⲉ ⲡⲥⲃ̄ⲃⲉ ⲣ̄ⲱⲫⲉⲗⲉⲓ ⲏ ⲙ̄ⲙⲟⲛ
²ⲡⲉⲭⲁϥ ⲛⲁⲩ ⲭⲉ ⲛⲉϥⲣ̄ⲱⲫⲉⲗⲉⲓ ⲛⲉ ⲡⲟⲩⲉⲓⲱⲧ ⲛⲁⲭⲡⲟⲟⲩ ⲉⲃⲟⲗ ⲍ̄ⲛ̄
ⲧⲟⲩⲙⲁⲁⲩ ⲉⲩⲥⲃ̄ⲃⲏⲩ ³ⲁⲗⲗⲁ ⲡⲥⲃ̄ⲃⲉ ⲙ̄ⲙⲉ ⲍ̄ⲙ ⲡⲛ̄ⲁ ⲁϥϭⲛ̄ ⲍⲏⲩ ⲧⲏⲣϥ̄

ATTRIBUTION
Accretion.

TEXT AND TRANSLATION ISSUES
'The father (of the children)', literally reads, 'their father'.

INTERPRETATIVE COMMENT
Development is indicated by the dialogue format. The dialogue is responsive to the situation that developed in post-50 CE Christianity when Gentile converts questioned the legitimacy of physical circumcision. The response suggests a constituency shift within the Thomasine community, advocating a circumcision of the spirit for Gentile converts rather than physical circumcision. The accretion resonates with the early Christian tradition that the convert had to be circumcised by the Holy Spirit rather than physically. But it also reflects an anti-Jewish argument that is found developed in texts much later than Paul. Thus, it is more likely that this saying accrued in the Gospel in the years between 60 and 100 CE than earlier.

SOURCE DISCUSSION
G. Quispel attributes this saying to the author's own hand.

LITERATURE PARALLELS

Romans 3.1
'Then what advantage has the Jew? Or what is the value of circumcision?'

Romans 2.28–29
²⁸'For he is not a real Jew who is one outwardly, nor is true circumcision something external and physical. ²⁹He is a Jew who is one inwardly, and real circumcision is a matter of the heart, spiritual and not literal. His praise is not from men but from God.'

Philippians 3.3
'For we are the true circumcision, who worship God in spirit, and glory in Christ Jesus, and put no confidence in the flesh.'

Colossians 2.11
'In him also you were circumcised with a circumcision made without hands, by putting off the body of flesh in the circumcision of Christ.'

Justin Martyr, Dialogue with Trypho *19.3*
'For if circumcision were necessary, God would not have made Adam uncircumcised.'

Tanhuma B 7 (18a)
'The ruler Rufus said to him, "If God is so pleased with circumcision, why does the child not come out of the womb circumcised?" R. Akiva answered him, "Why then does it come out with the umbilical cord attached? Doesn't the mother have to cut that off too? And why is the child not born circumcised? Because God has give the commandments in order to lead Israel to obedience through them."'

Odes of Solomon *11.1–3*

'My heart was pruned and its flower appeared,
Then grace sprang up from in it,
And it produced fruits for the Lord.
For the Most High circumcised me by his Holy Spirit,
Then he uncovered my inward being towards him,
And filled me with his love.
And his circumcising became my salvation,
And I ran in the way, in his peace,
In the way of truth.'

Deuteronomy 10.16

'Circumcise therefore the foreskin of your heart, and be no longer stubborn.'

Jeremiah 4.4

'Circumcise yourselves to the Lord, remove the foreskin of your hearts, O men of Judah
and inhabitants of Jerusalem; lest my wrath go forth like fire, and burn with none to
quench it, because of the evil of your doings.'

Cf. 1 Cor. 7.18–19; Gal. 5.6; Gal. 6.15; *Epistle of Barnabas* 9.1–5; Justin Martyr, *Dialogue
with Trypho* 113.7; Epiphanius, *Panarion* 33.5.11, quoting the *Letter to Flora* by Ptolemy

SELECT BIBLIOGRAPHY
Bauer (1962: 284–85); Quispel (1981: 265).

Logion 54

Jesus said, 'Blessed are the poor, for the Kingdom of Heaven is yours.'

NHC II 2.42.23–24

ΠΕϪΕ ΙC ϪΕ ϨⲚΜΑΚΑΡΙΟC ΝΕ ΝϨⲎΚΕ ϪΕ ΤⲰΤⲚ ΤΕ ΤΜⲚ̄ΤΕΡΟ
ΝⲘ̄ΠΗΥΕ

ATTRIBUTION
Kernel saying.

INTERPRETATIVE COMMENT
This saying, contextually within the Kernel Gospel speech, appealed to the complete
commitment of the disciple to Jesus and his mission. His or her interests were not to be
divided with money or possessions. Thus the disciple was told that Jesus blessed the poor
and promised them the Kingdom.

SOURCE DISCUSSION
W. Schrage sees dependence on Luke because both L. 54 and Luke use the second person
while Matthew uses the third person. The Matthean trait 'Kingdom of Heaven' shows up
in L. 54, which he ascribes to dependence on Matthew.

J. Sieber does not see the attribution of person as an editorial trait peculiar enough to
warrant dependence. He further argues that nowhere does *Thomas* use 'Kingdom of God'
so the phrase 'Kingdom of Heaven' is natural to the author, not redactional. It should be

pointed out, however, that the P. Oxy. fragment for L. 27 does use 'Kingdom of God', a detail that Sieber seems unaware of. He suggests that the author may have used 'Heaven' instead of 'God' because he could have learned the phrase from any Jewish Christian source. He points out that L. 54 is missing Matthew's 'in spirit' which he considers rightly a better example of a Matthean redactional element.

G. Quispel traces the variant 'in Heaven' to a Jewish Christian Gospel which both *Thomas* and the *Pseudo Clementines* relied on since *Recognitions* 2.28 also references the variant, blessing the poor who will obtain the Kingdom of Heaven. The parallel clearly understands the reference to 'the poor' to refer to the economically impoverished, rather than the Matthean reference to 'spiritual' poverty. This similar hermeneutic is significant in my opinion, reflecting common knowledge of an independent tradition. Clearly we are not faced here with secondary orality but instead with primary multiform orality.

LITERATURE PARALLELS

Matthew 5.3 (Qmatt)
'Blessed are the poor in spirit, for theirs is the Kingdom of Heaven.'

Luke 6.20b (Qluke)
'Blessed are the poor, for yours is the Kingdom of God.'

James 2.5
'Listen, my beloved brethren. Has not God chosen those who are poor in the world to be rich in faith and heirs of the Kingdom which he has promised to those who love him?'

Polycarp, Phil. 2.3
'Blessed are the poor and those who are persecuted for righteousness' sake, for theirs is the Kingdom of God.'

Pseudo-Clementine Homilies *15.10*
'But our teacher pronounced the faithful poor blessed.'

Pseudo-Clementine Recognitions *1.61*
'The Caiaphas attempted to impugn the doctrine of Jesus, saying that he spoke vain things, for he said that the poor are blessed.'

Pseudo-Clementine Recognitions *2.28*
'At the beginning of his preaching, as wishing to invite and lead all to salvation, and induce them to bear patiently labours and trials, he blessed the poor, and promised that they should obtain the Kingdom of Heaven for their endurance of poverty, in order that under the influence of such a hope they might bear with equanimity the weight of poverty, despising covetousness, for covetousness is one, and the greatest, of most pernicious sins.'

AGREEMENTS IN SYRIAN GOSPELS, WESTERN TEXT AND DIATESSARON

Matthew 5.3//Luke 6.20 in 118 157 517 1424 Mcion c f S Pal T^d bo Ps.-Clem.
of Heaven << of God

SELECT BIBLIOGRAPHY
Quispel (1957: 4); Schrage (1964a: 118–19); Sieber (1966: 30–32).

Logion 55.1–2

[1]Jesus said, 'Whoever does not hate his father and mother cannot become a disciple of mine. [2]And whoever does not hate his brothers and sisters and carry his cross as I do will not be worthy of me.'

NHC II,2.42.25–29

[1]ⲡⲉⲭⲉ ⲓ̅ⲥ̅ ϫⲉ ⲡⲉⲧⲁⲙⲉⲥⲧⲉ ⲡⲉϥⲉⲓⲱⲧ ⲁⲛ ⲙⲛ̅ ⲧⲉϥⲙⲁⲁⲩ ϥⲛⲁϣⲡ̅
ⲙⲁⲑⲏⲧⲏⲥ ⲁⲛ ⲛⲁⲉⲓ [2]ⲁⲩⲱ ⲛ̅ϥⲙⲉⲥⲧⲉ ⲛⲉϥⲥⲛⲏⲩ ⲙⲛ̅ ⲛⲉϥⲥⲱⲛⲉ ⲛ̅ϥϥⲉⲓ
ⲙ̅ⲡⲉϥⲥⲧⲟⲥ ⲛ̅ⲧⲁϩⲉ ϥⲛⲁϣⲱⲡⲉ ⲁⲛ ⲉϥⲟ ⲛ̅ⲁⲝⲓⲟⲥ ⲛⲁⲉⲓ

ATTRIBUTION
Kernel saying.

TEXT AND TRANSLATION ISSUES
A. Guillaumont and G. Quispel point to two Semitisms in L. 55: ⲣ̅ ⲙⲁⲑⲏⲧⲏⲥ ⲛⲁⲉⲓ and the repetition of the possessive pronoun in ⲡⲉϥⲉⲓⲱⲧ...ⲧⲉϥⲙⲁⲁⲩ...ⲛⲉϥⲥⲛⲏⲩ... ⲛⲉϥⲥⲱⲙⲉ. K.H. Kuhn wonders if these are Semitisms at all since they also appear in the Sahidic version of Luke 14.26. In his defence against Kuhn, Guillaumont points out that the fact that the Coptic does not negate L. 55.2 as it does 55.1 is a misconstrual of Semitic grammar. When a negative particle modifies the first verb in the string, it also modifies those following in the sentence. Guillaumont is convinced that the grammar behind the Coptic is Semitic.

INTERPRETATIVE COMMENT
The general opinion expressed by the majority of scholars, that *Thomas* is not interested in Jesus' death, is without merit. The presence of this saying in the Kernel Gospel suggests that even the earliest Thomasine community knew of Jesus' crucifixion and believed its imitation necessary for their salvation. This imitative death was hermeneutically understood in this early period to involve severing one's connection with one's biological family. It should be noted that the *Liber Graduum* emphasizes taking up the cross in *imitation* of Jesus as we find it in *Thomas* but not in the Synoptics.

Once the Gospel had incorporated the accretive sayings, L. 87 and 112, the crucifixion of Jesus and its imitation took on new meaning for the members of the later Thomasine community. It came to be understood by them in terms reflexive of Alexandrian Christianity. It was the ultimate model of the soul conquering the passions and the miserable state of embodiment, a theme taken up later by Pseudo-Macarius (*Great Letter*, Maloney: 258–59). Thus, we find the accrual of L. 56 immediately following. In the same way that Jesus did, the believer was supposed to bring his or her body and its appetites under the control of their awakened souls. This was the new meaning of 'carrying the cross'. See L. 87 and 112 for further discussion.

SOURCE DISCUSSION
The combination of L. 55.1 and 55.2 is found also in Matthew 10.37–38 and Luke 14.26–27, suggesting that the sequence was already established in Quelle. W. Schrage, however, sees L. 55 as dependent upon Matthew, which is signalled by the inclusion of the phrase 'worthy of me'. Lukan dependence is marked by the agreement, 'be my disciple'. C. Tuckett

points also to these phrases and argues that Matthew's phrase 'worthy of me' is 'almost universally agreed' to be redactional since Matthew is fond of using ἄξιος (cf. Matthew 10.11, 13). He also mentions the list of relatives which is longer in Luke, including brothers and sisters. This Lukan list is redactional and is paralleled in L. 55.

J. Sieber does not consider either of these phrases to be editorial so he assigns the mixture of phrases to a very late stage in the oral tradition, 'a stage in which several versions of the saying had been blended together into an oral conflation'. Sieber argues similarly with regard to the agreement between the relatives list in Luke and *Thomas*. I might add the observation that the phrase 'brothers and sisters' does not even occur in the same saying in *Thomas* as it does in Luke! In Luke, the phrase is part of the saying about hating one's family in order to be a disciple. In *Thomas*, the phrase is part of the saying about carrying the cross in order to be worthy.

K. Snodgrass argues for Lukan dependence because the phrase οὐ δύναται εἶναί μου μαθητής is a Lukan expression occurring three times in Luke 14.25–33. The problem with this argument is that the phrase could just as easily have been part of Luke's source in this cluster of sayings, perhaps repeated by Luke in v. 33 to draw this speech to a conclusion.

Because I am less certain than Schrage, Tuckett and Snodgrass about 'the' text of Quelle and the alleged redactions made by either Matthew or Luke, I do not conclude a certain Matthean redactional trait with ἄξιος, nor do I find that 'brothers and sisters' must rely on Luke. The version of Quelle in Matthew's hand does not appear to me to be the same version as was known to Luke. So I find it more likely that we are seeing various pre-Synoptic recensions of this saying. The variations were the result of the oral performance field.

LITERATURE PARALLELS

Matthew 10.37–38 (Qmatt)
[37]'He who loves father or mother more than me is not worthy of me. And he who loves son or daughter more than me is not worthy of me. [38]And he who does not take his cross and follow me is not worthy of me.'

Luke 14.26–27 (Qluke)
[26]'If anyone comes to me and does not hate his own father and mother and wife and children and brothers and sisters, yes, and even his own life, he can not be my disciple. [27]Whoever does not bear his own cross and come after me, can not be my disciple.'

Mark 8.34
'If any man would come after me, let him deny himself and take up his cross and follow me.'

Matthew 16.24
'If any man would come after me, let him deny himself and take up his cross and follow me.'

Luke 9.23
'If any man would come after me, let him deny himself and take up his cross daily and follow me.'

L. 101
[1]'Whoever does not hate his [father] and his mother in the same manner as I do, he cannot be a [disciple] of mine. [2]Also whoever does [not] love his [father and] his mother in the same manner as I do, he cannot be a [disciple] of mine. [3]For my [birth] mother [gave death], while my true [mother] gave life to me.'

Liber Graduum *3.5*

> 'If one will not renounce all that he has and take up his cross and follow me and imitate me, he is not worthy of me.'

Liber Graduum *20.15*

> 'He who does not take up his cross and walk in my footsteps and in my manner is not worthy of me.'

Liber Graduum *29.12–13*

> 'I will make an example to my disciples that they do as I.'

Liber Graduum *30.26*

> 'And if you wish to attain this great portion and perfection and imitate me and be gloried with me, leave everything and take up your cross and follow me. And if you do not, you are not worthy of me.'

Untitled Gnostic Text from Codex Brucianus, *c. 15*

> 'The one who leaves father and mother and brother and sister and wife and child and possessions and takes his cross and follows me will receive promises I promised him.'

Manichaean Psalm-Book *175.25–30*

> 'I left father and mother and brother and sister.
> I became a stranger because of your Name.
> I took up my cross. I followed you.
> I left the things of the body for the things of the Spirit.
> I despised the glory of the world because of your glory which does not pass away.'

Cf. Pseudo-Macarius, *Hom.* 9.10, 25.4.

AGREEMENTS IN SYRIAN GOSPELS, WESTERN TEXT AND DIATESSARON

Matthew 10.38//Luke 14.26–27 in S C P T^P T^A Clem
> whoever << if any one

Matthew 10.38//Luke 14.26–27 in D d S C P T^A T^L T^{NL} T^V sa bo
> *his* mother << mother

Matthew 10.38//Luke 14.26–27 in C P T^A
> to me << my

Matthew 10.38//Luke 14.26–27 in S C P T^A T^{NL}
> *his* brothers << brothers

Matthew 10.38//Luke 14.26–27 in S C P T^A T^{NL}
> *his* sisters << sisters

Matthew 10.38//Luke 14.26–27 in S C P T^P T^A
> order – father–mother–brothers–sisters

Matthew 10.38//Luke 14.26–27 in T^P
> Will not be worthy of me << cannot be my disciple

SELECT BIBLIOGRAPHY
Guillaumont (1981: 192–93); Kuhn (1960: 322); Quispel (1958/1959: 287); Schrage (1964a: 120–21); Sieber (1966: 120–22); Snodgrass (1989: 34–35); Tuckett (1988: 148–49).

Logion 56.1–2

¹Jesus said, 'Whoever has come to know the world has found a corpse. ²The world does not deserve the person who has found (that the world is) a corpse.'

Alternative Translation
'Whoever has come to know the world <<has mastered the body>>. The world does not deserve the person who <<has mastered the body>>.'

NHC II 2.42.29–32

¹ⲡⲉⲭⲉ ⲓⲥ ⲭⲉ ⲡⲉⲧⲁϩⲥⲟⲩⲱⲛ ⲡⲕⲟⲥⲙⲟⲥ ⲁϥϩⲉ ⲉⲩⲡⲧⲱⲙⲁ ²ⲁⲩⲱ
ⲡⲉⲛⲧⲁϩϩⲉⲉ ⲁⲡⲧⲱⲙⲁ ⲡⲕⲟⲥⲙⲟⲥ ⲙⲡϣⲁ ⲙⲙⲟϥ ⲁⲛ

ATTRIBUTION
Accretion.

TEXT AND TRANSLATION ISSUES
I think that the Coptic form of this saying represents a corruption. The Coptic literally reads, 'has found a corpse'. In my opinion, the Coptic is nonsense. I agree with A. Guillaumont that the corrupt translation of this saying supposes an Aramaic or Syriac substratum which makes meaning where otherwise there is none. In this saying, we find ⲡⲧⲱⲙⲁ instead of ⲥⲱⲙⲁ which is found in the doublet L. 80. Guillaumont notes that these represent different translations of the same Aramaic term, ⲡⲅⲣⲁ, or Syriac term, ܦܓܪܐ, meaning 'corpse' or 'body'. K.H. Kuhn explains these variants as the consequence of the graphic similarity in the Coptic language between ⲥⲱⲙⲁ and ⲡⲧⲱⲙⲁ. Although this latter option is possible, the former is better since it also explains the content of the saying which makes no sense, in my opinion, translated 'Whoever has come to know the world has found a corpse. The world does not deserve the person who has found a corpse'. Clearly the intent points to a Semitic substratum where it meant 'body'. Further, Guillaumont suggests that the expression 'has found the corpse' relies on a mistranslation of the word מצא or ܐܫܟܚ, meaning either 'to find' or 'to master'.

Certainly this makes for a more sensible text than the Coptic transcription, both internally and externally, marking the encratic nature of this accretion where mastery of the body was so much the catechism. My scholarly instincts tell me that this saying originally read either in Aramaic or Syriac, 'Whoever has come to know the world has mastered the body. The world does not deserve the person who has mastered the body.' When it was translated into Greek, bad word choice was made by the scribe, corrupting the saying so that it no longer makes sense. I refrained from putting this reconstruction directly into my translation of the Gospel only because the Coptic would not be faithfully represented, but I have presented it as an alternative translation.

The expression, 'the world does not deserve the person who…' is Semitic as M. Meyer pointed out to me in a personal correspondence (cf. *Mekilta de-Rabbi Ishmael*, Pisha 5; Heb. 11.37–38).

INTERPRETATIVE COMMENT
This saying contains vocabulary and themes characteristic of the accretions, particularly the phrase ⲡⲕⲟⲥⲙⲟⲥ ⲙⲡϣⲁ ⲙⲙⲟϥ ⲁⲛ and ⲥⲟⲩⲱⲛ which describes a salvific state. The saying has affinities with encratic ideology, particularly the description of the mastery

of the body, while at the same time, with the Hermetic theme that knowledge liberates. Accrual can be estimated to the latter part of the first century, 80–120 CE.

SOURCE DISCUSSION
G. Quispel attributes this saying to a Hermetic anthology.

LITERATURE PARALLELS
See L. 80.

SELECT BIBLIOGRAPHY
Guillaumont (1958: 117; 1981: 194); Kuhn (1960: 318–19); Quispel (1981: 265).

Logion 57.1–4

[1]Jesus said, 'The Kingdom of the Father is like a man who had [good] seed. [2]His enemy came at night. He added darnel to the good seed. [3]The man did not let them pull out the darnel. He explained to them, "In case you go to pull out the darnel, but pull out the wheat with it. [4]For on the day of the harvest, the darnel will be discernible, and will be pulled up and burned."'

NHC II,2.42.32–43.7

[1]ⲡⲉϪⲉ ⲓⲥ Ϫⲉ ⲧⲙⲛ̄ⲧⲉⲣⲟ ⲙ̄ⲡⲉⲓⲱⲧ ⲉⲥⲧⲛ̄ⲧⲱ(ⲛ) ⲁⲩⲣⲱⲙⲉ ⲉⲩⲛ̄ⲧⲁϥ
ⲙⲙⲁⲩ ⲛ̄ⲛⲟⲩϬⲣⲟϬ [ⲉⲛⲁⲛⲟⲩ]ϥ [2]ⲁⲡⲉϥϪⲁϪⲉ ⲉⲓ ⲛ̄ⲧⲟⲩϢⲏ ⲁϥⲥⲓⲧⲉ
ⲛ̄ⲟⲩⲍⲓⲍⲁⲛⲓ[ⲟ]ⲛ ⲉ[Ϫⲓ]ⲛ̄ ⲡⲉϬⲣⲟ|Ϭ ⲉ|ⲧⲛⲁⲛⲟⲩϥ [3]ⲙ̄ⲡⲉ ⲡⲣⲱⲙⲉ ⲕⲟⲟⲩ
ⲉϨⲱⲗⲉ ⲙ̄ⲡⲍⲓⲍⲁⲛⲓⲟⲛ ⲡⲉϪⲁϥ ⲛⲁⲩ Ϫⲉ ⲙⲏⲡⲱⲥ ⲛ̄ⲧⲉⲧⲛ̄ⲃⲱⲕ Ϫⲉ
ⲉⲛⲁϨⲱⲗⲉ ⲙ̄ⲡⲍⲓⲍⲁⲛⲓⲟ(ⲛ) ⲛ̄ⲧⲉⲧⲛ̄Ϩⲱⲗⲉ ⲙ̄ⲡⲥⲟⲩⲟ ⲛⲙ̄ⲙⲁϥ [4]Ϩⲙ̄
ⲫⲟⲟⲩ ⲅⲁⲣ ⲙ̄ⲡⲱϨⲥ̄ ⲛ̄ⲍⲓⲍⲁⲛⲓⲟⲛ ⲛⲁⲟⲩⲱⲛϨ ⲉⲃⲟⲗ ⲥⲉϨⲟⲗⲟⲩ
ⲛ̄ⲥⲉⲣⲟⲕϨⲟⲩ

ATTRIBUTION
Kernel saying.

INTERPRETATIVE COMMENT
In the Kernel speech, this saying was meant to remind the hearer that his or her decision to follow Jesus exclusively is critical because he or she will be held accountable. There will be a Judgement, a harvest. The hearer should not make a wrong decision and, like a weed, be pulled up on the last day and burned.

This reading of the parable in the context of the Kernel Gospel is cogent with J. Lieben-berg's mapping of the metaphorical meaning of the parable. He says that the parable has a conventional meaning based on certain well-known metaphors such as God is a father, God is a King, people are plants, God is the gardener of good seeds, divine punishment is burning by fire, divine destruction is uprooting, Judgement is harvest, and so on. He deter-mines that the parable served to warn those people who did not manage to find the King-dom that they would be identified and punished in the end. The parable stressed that the wicked had not yet been identified for punishment, highlighting the Gospel's repeated message to seek the Kingdom.

SOURCE DISCUSSION

G. Quispel notes verbal similarities between this logion and the Diatessaron manuscript tradition which suggests to him a common source for Tatian and *Thomas*.

W. Schrage makes an interesting observation about L. 57, that it is a condensation of the parable. He thinks it presupposes Matthew 13.24–30 because L. 57.3–4 assumes knowledge of the question of the labourers found in Matthew 13.27. He also points out that ⲚⲀⲨ does not have an antecedent in L. 57.3.

J. Sieber agrees with Schrage that *Thomas*' parable is not more original than Matthew's, but he does not trace its form to a condensation of Matthew 13.24–30. In this he agrees with R. McL. Wilson who traces the developments to *Thomas*' access to the same tradition but at a later date than Matthew. Sieber goes as far as arguing that L. 57 is evidence for an independent written version of the parable, one recorded at a date later than the Synoptic version of the parable.

H. Koester takes an opposite stance on the abbreviation of the parable. He views this parable to be form-critically prior to Matthew's version, because it is shorter and gives no reference to Matthew's allegorical interpretation.

J. Liebenberg appears to me to express the most nuanced opinion on this matter. He finds nothing in L. 57 which necessitates knowledge of Matthew 13.24–30 in order for the parable to be understood. L. 57 is only perceived by us to be missing an element because we know Matthew's version. Liebenberg provides an interpretation of the parable that is intelligible on its own, needing no knowledge of Matthew's version in order to understand it (see above). The conventional metaphors which both versions use, he says, overlap. Knowledge of these metaphors makes it possible to understand L. 57 without Matthew, even though Liebenberg finds the mapping to be more 'elliptical' than its Matthean counterpart. So he allows for the possibility of dependence through secondary orality, but not direct literary dependence.

In my opinion, this logion displays the characteristics of an orally transmitted parable. Its commonalities with Matthew's version amount to a few 'signal' words like 'good seed', 'enemy came', 'pull out the wheat', 'harvest', and 'burned'. Although the general message of the parable is maintained across the versions, the details and presentations are strikingly different. On the one hand, *Thomas*' version appears to me to have been abridged during years of oral performance since the appearance of 'them' in L. 57.3 is unforeseen. Matthew's version, on the other hand, appears to me to have been expanded during its transmission so that it contains secondary elements as well, particularly the long dialogue between the servants and the owner in 13.27–28 and the proverbial statement in 13.30. This leads me to think that both versions of the parable represent later developments of an earlier form no longer extant.

LITERATURE PARALLELS

Matthew 13.24–30

[24]'The Kingdom of Heaven may be compared to a man who sowed good seed in his field. [25]But while men where sleeping, his enemy came and sowed weeds among the wheat, and went away. [26]So when the plants came up and bore grain, then the weeds appeared also. [27]And the servants of the householder came and said to him, "Sir, did you not sow good seed in your field? How then has it weeds?" [28]He said to them, "An enemy has done this." The servants said to him, "Then do you want us to go and gather them?" [29]But he said, "No, lest in gathering the weeds you root up the wheat along with them. [30]Let both grow until harvest. And at harvest time I will tell the reapers, 'Gather the weeds first and bind them in bundles to be burned, but gather the wheat into my barn.'"'

Pseudo-Clementine Homilies *19.2*

'And elsewhere he said, "He who sowed the bad seed is the devil."'

Epiphanius, recording Manichaean version of this parable, Pan. *66.65.1*

'Mani seizes upon a similar passage where the Saviour says, "The Kingdom of Heaven is like the head of a household who sowed good seed <in> his field. But while the men were sleeping, an enemy came and sowed weeds…"'

AGREEMENTS IN SYRIAN GOSPELS, WESTERN TEXT AND DIATESSARON

Matthew 13.24–30 in 1604 *Man S C P T^P T^V T^{NL}*

is like << may be compared

Matthew 13.24–30 in T^{NL}

by night << while men were sleeping

Matthew 13.24–30 in T^{NL}

sleeping

Matthew 13.24–30 in D e k q S C P T^P T^A T^L T^{NL} Iren sa bo

sowed << ἐπέσπειρεν

Matthew 13.24–30 in TitB T^P T^T T^{NL}

the seed << the wheat

Matthew 13.24–30 in TitB T^{NL}

the *good* seed, + good

Matthew 13.24–30 in D W Σ N 33 Man a b c d f h k E Q R S C P T^A T^{NL} Heliand sa geo

He said + to them

Matthew 13.24–30 in P T^A geo

– No

Matthew 13.24–30 in Man

μηπως << μηποτε

Matthew 13.24–30 in Man S C T^P T^A T^V T^{NL} Heliand arm bo geo

pull up[1] << gather

Matthew 13.24–30 in D e S C T^L geo

the wheat with it << the wheat along with them

Matthew 13.24–30 in S C T^P T^A Heliand Aphr

pull[3] << gather

SELECT BIBLIOGRAPHY

Koester (1990: 103); Liebenberg (2001: 212–22); Quispel (1968); Schrage (1964a: 124–26); Sieber (1966: 168–69); Wilson (1960a: 91).

Logion 58

Jesus said, 'Whoever has suffered is blessed. He has found life.'

NHC II 2.43.7–9

ⲡⲉϫⲉ ⲓ̅ⲥ̅ ϫⲉ ⲟⲩⲙⲁⲕⲁⲣⲓⲟⲥ ⲡⲉ ⲡⲣⲱⲙⲉ ⲛ̅ⲧⲁϩϩⲓⲥⲉ ⲁϥϩⲉ ⲁⲡⲱⲛϩ

ATTRIBUTION
Kernel saying.

TEXT AND TRANSLATION ISSUES
Alternative translations for 'has suffered' are, 'has toiled' or 'is wearied'. 'Has suffered' is favoured because it reflects a tradition with parallels in other Christian literature (i.e. 1 Peter 3.14a; 4.13–14; James 1.12; *2 Clement* 19.3). It also is consistent internally with other sayings that invoke the state of suffering as 'blessed' or necessary for salvation (i.e. L. 55, 68 and 69).

INTERPRETATIVE COMMENT
M. Lelyveld traces this logion to the experience of persecution suffered by the community. In my opinion, the situation is more complex. The saying in the Kernel Gospel may have signalled physical persecution since the accretion, L. 68.2, tells us that the community eventually relocated to a place where they could live more peacefully. But in the complete Gospel, this logion came to reference the internal struggle of the soul against the body and its passions, the internal persecution of the demons. The saying would have come to mean that those who suffered in this battle while conquering the body (L. 56) in imitation of Jesus (L. 55) were blessed. They had found life.

SOURCE DISCUSSION
G. Quispel compares L. 58 to Proverbs 8.34–35, *Berakh.* 61b, James 1.12 and 1 Peter 3.14. He suggests that its style and content reflects Palestinian origin.

LITERATURE PARALLELS

1 Peter 3.14a
> 'But even if you do suffer for righteousness' sake, you will be blessed.'

1 Peter 4.13–14
> [13]'But rejoice in so far as you share Christ's sufferings, that you may also rejoice and be glad when his glory is revealed. [14]If you are reproached for the name of Christ, you are blessed, because the spirit of glory and of God rests upon you.'

James 1.12
> 'Blessed is the man who endures trial, for when he has stood the test he will receive the crown of life which God has promised to those who love him.'

2 Clement *19.3*
> 'Blessed are those who obey these commands. Though they suffer evil in this world for a short time, they will gather the immortal fruit of the resurrection.'

Liber Graduum *853.14*
> 'Labour while you are in this world so that you may live forever.'

Acts of Philip *29*
> 'Blessed is the good workman.'

SELECT BIBLIOGRAPHY
Lelyveld (1987: 69–76); Quispel (1957: 14).

Logion 59

Jesus said, 'Gaze upon the Living One while you are alive, in case you die and (then) seek to see him, and you will not be able to see (him).'

NHC II 2.43.9–12

ⲡⲉⲝⲉ ⲓⲥ ⲝⲉ ϭⲱϣⲧ ⲛ̄ⲥⲁ ⲡⲉⲧⲟⲛϩ ϩⲱⲥ ⲉⲧⲉⲧⲛ̄ⲟⲛϩ ϩⲓⲛⲁ ⲝⲉ
ⲛⲉⲧⲙ̄ⲙⲟⲩ ⲁⲩⲱ ⲛ̄ⲧⲉⲧⲛ̄ϣⲓⲛⲉ ⲉⲛⲁⲩ ⲉⲣⲟϥ ⲁⲩⲱ ⲧⲉⲧⲛⲁϣϭⲙ̄ ϭⲟⲙ
ⲁⲛ ⲉⲛⲁⲩ

ATTRIBUTION
Accretion.

INTERPRETATIVE COMMENT
Vocabulary characteristic of the accretions is found in this saying, particularly the reference to ⲡⲉⲧⲟⲛϩ. The saying reflects a shift in theology to the view that pre-mortem mystical experiences of God are necessary for salvation, rather than post-mortem or eschatological. The shift appears to be part of the mystical response made by the Thomasine Christians to the delayed Eschaton, a response noted in many other accretions, dating the accrual to the years between 60 and 100 CE.

As I have discussed in *Voices of the Mystics*, the Johannine Gospel appears to be in direct dialogue with the traditions expressed in this accretion, building a theology in contradiction to the mystical ideas recorded in this saying. John stresses that Jesus, because he existed pre-temporally with the Father in heaven, is the only person who has ever seen God (1.18; 5.37; 6.46). Since the historical presence of Jesus has brought God's Form or Glory, his Kavod, to earth, those who saw Jesus while he was alive actually saw the Father's Glory and received life eternal because of this vision (1.14; 2.11; 6.30–40; 11.40; 12.23, 28; 13.32; 14.7, 9, 19; 17.1, 4–5, 20–26). Thus there is no rebirth apart from Jesus (3.3–13) nor can any one ascend into heaven and enter the Kingdom of God unless through Jesus (3.13). Because the deity has been manifested historically, there is no need for ascension to heaven in order to view God and be transformed. The mystical experience has been brought to earth through the incarnation of Jesus.

This situation, however, made the historical absence of Jesus particularly problematic. Instead of opening the door of heaven to Christian mystics journeying to God's throne to gaze upon the Kavod as we find in the Thomasine tradition, John keeps the door to heaven locked (7.33–34; 8.21; 13.33, 36; 14.3). To resolve the dilemma, John introduces the notion of the Paraclete, a spirit from God which journeys to earth, a spirit which functions as God's presence within the Christian community. Although visions of this spirit are not possible, its presence will be known to the community in the form of divine love shared (14.22–23). As such, the Paraclete mediates God to the community. Proleptic visionary ascents are not necessary because the Paraclete has come down to earth in Jesus' absence. To this schema, John adds the concept that faith actually replaces visionary experiences in terms of transforming the believer (20.29). It is especially the case in John that the faithful can encounter Jesus' spirit through the sacraments even though he is no longer alive (3.5–8, 13, 15; 4.10–14; 6.35–63).

SOURCE DISCUSSION
G. Quispel attributes this saying to the author's hand.

LITERATURE PARALLELS

Pseudo-Macarius, Hom. *30.4*
    'If anyone does not continually gaze at him, overlooking all else, the Lord will not paint
    his image with his own light. It is necessary that we gaze on him, believing and loving
    him, casting aside all else and attending to him so that he may paint his own heavenly
    image and send it into our souls. And thus carrying Christ, we may receive eternal life
    and even here, filled with confidence, we may be at rest.'

SELECT BIBLIOGRAPHY
DeConick (1996: 123–25; 2001a); Quispel (1981: 265).

Logion 60.1–5

¹A Samaritan was carrying a lamb as he travelled to Judea. ²He said to his disciples,
'That man is <<binding>> the lamb.'

³They said to him, '(He is binding the lamb) so that he may slaughter it and eat it.'

⁴He said to them, 'While it is alive, he will not eat it. Rather, (he will eat the lamb) after
he has slaughtered it and it is carcass.'

⁵They said, 'He is not permitted to do it any other way.'

NHC II 2.43.12–20

¹ⲀⲨⲤⲀⲘⲀⲢⲈⲒⲦⲎⲤ ⲈϤϤⲒ ⲚⲚⲞⲨ2ⲒⲈⲒⲂ ⲈϤⲂⲎⲔ Ⲉ2ⲞⲨⲚ ⲈϮⲞⲨⲆⲀⲒⲀ
²ⲠⲈⲬⲀϤ ⲚⲚⲈϤⲘⲀⲐⲎⲦⲎⲤ ⲬⲈ ⲠⲎ ⲘⲠⲔ.ⲦⲈ ⲘⲠⲈ2ⲒⲈⲒⲂ
³ⲠⲈⲬⲀⲨ ⲚⲀϤ ⲬⲈⲔⲀⲀⲤ ⲈϤⲚⲀⲘⲞⲞⲨⲦϤ ⲚϤⲞⲨⲞⲘϤ
⁴ⲠⲈⲬⲀϤ ⲚⲀⲨ 2.Ⲥ ⲈϤⲞⲚ2 ϤⲚⲀⲞⲨⲞⲘϤ ⲀⲚ ⲀⲖⲖⲀ ⲈϤ.ⲀⲘⲞⲞⲨⲦϤ
ⲚϤ.ⲦⲠⲈ ⲚⲞⲨⲠⲦ.ⲘⲀ
⁵ⲠⲈⲬⲀⲨ ⲬⲈ ⲚⲔⲈⲤⲘⲞⲦ ϤⲚⲀ.ⲀⲤ ⲀⲚ

ATTRIBUTION
Accretion.

TEXT AND TRANSLATION ISSUES
I do not emend the text, adding before ⲀⲨⲤⲀⲘⲀⲢⲈⲒⲦⲎⲤ, as B. Layton, <ⲀⲨⲚⲀⲨ>, or as
Bethge, <ⲀϤⲚⲀⲨ>. Rather, I prefer to understand, as P. Nagel does, ⲀⲨⲤⲀⲘⲀⲢⲈⲒⲦⲎⲤ
ⲈϤϤⲒ, to be an attempt to translate an Aramaic predicate participal construction.
    The odd expression in Coptic, ⲠⲎ ⲘⲠⲔ.ⲦⲈ ⲘⲠⲈ2ⲒⲈⲒⲂ (literally, 'That man is around
the lamb' or 'That man surrounds the lamb') must be corrupt. It can be explained as a mis-
translation of the Syriac ܢ܂ which can mean both 'to surround' and 'to bind' (Payne
Smith, 226–27).

INTERPRETATIVE COMMENT
This dialogue represents a development of an earlier saying of Jesus, perhaps a now lost
parable. The dialogue itself is not particularly well-constructed from the saying, but sense
can be made of the situation. The content of the dialogue suggests an early Christian discussion about eating meat that has been slaughtered. The judgement of Jesus is that before
preparing the meat to eat, even a Samaritan must slaughter the animal properly, making

sure that the lifeblood has been drained from the animal, that it is a carcass. This position on slaughter is quite similar to that held by the Jerusalem Church and received by the Antiochean Church in western Syria (Acts 15.19–20, 29; contra. Paul, 1 Cor. 8.8–13; 10.25–29) and may represent the Thomasine community's judgement on the issue when Gentiles were first joining their group and posing this as a question. So it likely accrued in the Gospel between 60 and 70 CE although it could have been as late as 100. It probably accrued at a time before L. 59 became part of the text. So it originally followed L. 58, accruing on the basis of the catchword ⲱⲚ2 and ⲟⲚ2 in each saying. The meaning of this dialogue shifted with the accrual of L. 60.6 (see L. 60.6).

SOURCE DISCUSSION
G. Quispel thinks that the author of the Gospel is responsible for the creation of this saying.

LITERATURE PARALLELS
Cf. Acts 15.19–20, 29; 1 Cor. 8.8–13; 10.25–29.

SELECT BIBLIOGRAPHY
Bethge (1997: 534); Layton (1989: 74); Nagel (1969a: 379–80); Quispel (1981: 265).

Logion 60.6

⁶He said to them, 'Moreover, so that you shall not become a carcass and be eaten, seek for yourselves a place within rest!'

NHC II 2.43.20–23

⁶ⲡⲉⲭⲁϥ ⲚⲀⲨ ⲭⲉ ⲚⲧⲱⲧⲚ̄ 2ⲱⲧⲦⲎⲨⲦⲚ̄ ⲰⲒⲚⲉ Ⲛ̄ⲤⲀ ⲞⲨⲦⲞⲡⲞⲤ ⲚⲎⲦⲚ̄
ⲉ2ⲞⲨⲚ ⲉⲨⲀⲚⲀⲡⲀⲨⲤⲒⲤ ⲭⲉⲔⲀⲀⲤ Ⲛ̄ⲚⲉⲦⲦⲚ̄ⲰⲰⲡⲉ Ⲙ̄ⲡⲦⲱⲘⲀ
Ⲛ̄ⲤⲉⲞⲨⲰⲚ ⲦⲎⲨⲦⲚ̄

ATTRIBUTION
Accretion.

INTERPRETATIVE COMMENT
This saying is an interpretative logion added to an older dialogue about rules for slaughtering meat properly. Vocabulary characteristic of the accretions is present, ⲰⲒⲚⲉ Ⲛ̄ⲤⲀ ⲞⲨⲦⲞⲡⲞⲤ ⲚⲎⲦⲚ̄ ⲉ2ⲞⲨⲚ ⲉⲨⲀⲚⲀⲡⲀⲨⲤⲒⲤ. The saying accrued in the Gospel between 60 and 100 CE, probably in the latter years of this range.

This accretion works to reinterpret the older dialogue, shifting the emphasis of the dialogue from a discussion about the proper way to slaughter meat to a discussion about soteriology. This reinterpretation probably took place at a time when the discussion of slaughtering meat was no longer a question for the community. How does a person avoid death and the cruel fate of being eaten by worms? By seeking the place of rest. Thus, this accretion speaks of the same Hermetic tradition evidenced also in L. 50 and 51.

SOURCE DISCUSSION
The content of this saying may reflect a development of the type of Jesus tradition found in Matthew 6.19–20. If this were the case, we would be witnessing a fine example of

secondary orality where memories of a saying from the Synoptic tradition were reshaped drastically to serve new purposes.

LITERATURE PARALLELS

Matthew 6.19–20

[19]'Do not lay up for yourselves treasures on earth, where moth and worm eat and where thieves break in and steal, [20]but lay up for yourselves treasures in heaven, where neither moth nor worm eats and where thieves do not break in and steal.'

Logion 61.1

Jesus said, 'Two people will rest on a couch. One will die. One will live.'

NHC II 2.43.23–25

ⲡⲉϫⲉ ⲓ̅ⲥ̅ ⲟⲩⲛ̅ ⲥⲛⲁⲩ ⲛⲁⲙ̅ⲧⲟⲛ ⲙ̅ⲙⲁⲩ ϩⲓ ⲟⲩϭⲗⲟϭ ⲡⲟⲩⲁ ⲛⲁⲙⲟⲩ
ⲡⲟⲩⲁ ⲛⲁⲱⲛϩ

ATTRIBUTION
Kernel saying.

TEXT AND TRANSLATION ISSUES
A. Guillaumont attributes the construction ⲡⲟⲩⲁ...ⲡⲟⲩⲁ to a literal translation of an Aramaic (הד...והד) or Hebrew (אהד...ואהד) phrase. K. Grobel's comments have strengthened this position. He notes that ὁ εἷς...ὁ εἷς is unknown in New Testament Greek, and that ⲡⲟⲩⲁ...ⲡⲟⲩⲁ defies Coptic idiom which requires ⲡⲉⲕⲟⲩⲁ as the second element. So he also traces the grammar to the Hebrew idiom. Furthermore, he notes that in the LXX, most translators treated this Semitism as Luke did ὁ εἷς...ὁ ἕτερος, except in one case which parallels our situation, τὴν μίαν...τὴν μίαν (1 Kings 12.29). C.W. Hedrick, however, notes one case where the Coptic translator of the Sahidic New Testament employs an expression similar to L. 61.1 when rendering Luke 17.34, ὁ εἷς...ὁ ἕτερος.

INTERPRETATIVE COMMENT
This saying closes the third speech in the Kernel Gospel, reminding the hearers that at the End, only the few who make the right choices and commit to Jesus and his teachings will receive the final reward, immortal. All others will die.

SOURCE DISCUSSION
R. Grant and D.N. Freedman, B. Gärtner, and R. Kasser say that L. 61.1 is based on Luke 17.34. W. Schrage is less sure because of the lace of editorial evidence. Comparisons with Sahidic Luke, however, reveal an agreement: ⲟⲩⲁ is repeated twice. M. Fieger explains the differences from Luke to be due to the author's spontaneous citation of the Synoptic text.

J. Sieber agrees that editorial traces are missing and suggests oral tradition is the source for the saying, not Luke, because the logion has been secondarily developed with the substitutions of 'live' and 'die' and with the different order of their appearance in *Thomas*. I am uncertain if 'live' and 'die' are secondary developments or examples of early multiform variation. In either case, the logion when compared with the Synoptic versions displays characteristics of oral transmission and shows no signs of secondary orality.

LITERATURE PARALLELS

Matthew 24.40–41 (Qmatt)
[40]'Then two men will be in the field. One is taken and one is left. [41]Two women will be grinding at the mill. One is taken and one is left.'

Luke 17.34–35 (Qluke)
[34]'I tell you, in that night there will be two in one bed. One will be taken and the other left. [35]There will be two women grinding together. One will be taken and the other left.'

AGREEMENTS IN SYRIAN GOSPELS, WESTERN TEXT AND DIATESSARON

Luke 17.34 in T^L T^T T^{NL}
– I tell you

Luke 17.34 in T^L T^T T^{NL}
– in that night

Luke 17.34 in T^P T^{NL}
will rest << will be

Luke 17.34 in c d l D S C T^L sa
the one…the one << the one …the other

SELECT BIBLIOGRAPHY
Fieger (1991: 178); Gärtner (1961: 170–71); Grant with Freedman (1960: 167); Grobel (1962: 370); Guillaumont (1981: 190–91); Hedrick (1994a: 245); Kasser (1961: 86); Schrage: 1964a: 126–28); Sieber (1966: 228–29).

Logion 61.2–5

[2]Salome said, 'Who are you, sir? That is, from [[whom]]? You have reclined on my couch and eaten at my table.'

[3]Jesus said to her, 'I am he who comes from the one who is an equal. I was given some who belong to my Father.'

[4]'I am your disciple.'

[5]'Therefore I say, when a person becomes [[equal]] (with me), he will be filled with light. But if he becomes separated (from me), he will be filled with darkness.'

NHC II 2.43.25–34

²ⲡⲉⲭⲉ ⲥⲁⲗⲱⲙⲏ ⲛ̅ⲧⲁⲕ ⲛⲓⲙ ⲡⲣⲱⲙⲉ ϩⲱⲥ ⲉⲃⲟⲗ ϩⲛ̅ ⲟⲩⲁ ⲁⲕⲧⲉⲗⲟ
ⲉⲝⲙ̅ ⲡⲁⲃⲗⲟϭ ⲁⲩⲱ ⲁⲕⲟⲩⲱⲙ ⲉⲃⲟⲗ ϩⲛ̅ ⲧⲁⲧⲣⲁⲡⲉⲍⲁ
³ⲡⲉⲭⲉ ⲓ̅ⲥ̅ ⲛⲁⲥ ⲭⲉ ⲁⲛⲟⲕ ⲡⲉ ⲡⲉⲧϣⲟⲟⲡ ⲉⲃⲟⲗ ϩⲙ̅ ⲡⲉⲧϣⲏϣ
ⲁⲩⲧ̅ ⲛⲁⲉⲓ ⲉⲃⲟⲗ ϩⲛ̅ ⲛⲁ ⲡⲁⲉⲓⲱⲧ
⁴ⲁⲛⲟⲕ ⲧⲉⲕⲙⲁⲑⲏⲧⲏⲥ
⁵ⲉⲧⲃⲉ ⲡⲁⲉⲓ ⳨ ⲭⲱ ⲙ̅ⲙⲟⲥ ⲭⲉ ϩⲟⲧⲁⲛ ⲉϥϣⲁϣⲱⲡⲉ ⲉϥϣⲏ<ϣ>
ϥⲛⲁⲙⲟⲩϩ ⲟⲩⲟⲉⲓⲛ ϩⲟⲧⲁⲛ ⲇⲉ ⲉϥϣⲁⲛϣⲱⲡⲉ ⲉϥⲡⲏϣ ϥⲛⲁⲙⲟⲩϩ
ⲛ̅ⲕⲁⲕⲉ

ATTRIBUTION
Accretion.

TEXT AND TRANSLATION ISSUES
The Coptic manuscript has ϣΗϥ in line 32. So it has been emended to ϣΗϣ to retain the parallelism and sense of the dialogue begun in line 30.

My reading follows A. Guillamont's observation that the expression ⳞⲰⲤ ⲈⲂⲞⲖ ⳞⲚ ⲞⲨⲀ probably was a mistranslation of ὡς ἐκ τίνος, 'as from whom'. The translator rendered into Coptic instead ὡς ἐκ τινός, 'as from somebody'. This makes better sense of the dialogue and the grammar than H. Attridge's attempt to render the meaning, 'as if you are from someone special', or Bethge's understanding that the Greek ὡς ξένος, 'as a stranger', was mistranslated as ὡς ἐξ ἑνός, 'as from someone'. This latter explanation is particularly problematic since the rendering does not make sense within the dialogue itself. I. Dunderberg prefers the translation, 'as though from the One', based on his exegesis of *Exc. Theo.* 36.1. Since the expression 'One' as a Name of God is not found anywhere else in the Gospel, this translation is not preferable either. N. Perrin has offered another possibility, that the Syriac phrase ܚܕ is responsible since it means literally 'from one' but also 'suddenly'. So the meaning of L. 61.2 would be, 'Who are you, sir, that you have suddenly reclined on my couch and eaten at my table.' But this rendering makes even less sense to me given the context.

Clearly the dialogue is a christological inquest, serving to explain Jesus' origins and connection with the Father as well as his relationship with his disciples. After finishing supper (in the proper Greek posture where the guests recline on couches around the table), Salome poses the christological question of the Thomasine comunity: Who is Jesus? So I think it is best to understand the ⳞⲰⲤ in this clause as an adverb of manner, indicating 'that' or 'for instance' to further limit the question at hand. Specifically, Salome asks, 'From whom does Jesus come?'

INTERPRETATIVE COMMENT
Development is indicated by the dialogue format. The content represents retrospective thinking about Christology with parallels in Johannine traditions. So a date between 80 and 120 CE is appropriate for the accrual of this dialogue.

In this, the Thomasine dialogue shares the tradition also found in the Gospel of John and Philippians, that Jesus comes from the Father and that the Father and Jesus are equal (cf. John 5.18b; 10.29–30, 38b; Phil. 2.6). Furthermore, the dialogue has in common the theme found highlighted in chapter 17 of John that God gave the disciples to Jesus and they are one with him and the Father, sharing in their equality. Thus my rendering of ⲚⲀ ⲠⲀⲈⲒⲰⲦ reads 'some who belong to my Father' rather than, as past translations, 'some things which belong to my Father'. The point of the dialogue is that Jesus is one with the Father, he comes from the Father, and he was given the disciples by the Father. The disciples share in this relationship of equals, being filled with light.

These ideas about the equality of God and Jesus are grounded in the early Christian understanding of Jesus as the one who bears God's unutterable Name, having his Form or Glory, his illuminous Kavod. Those who come into Jesus' presence have come into God's presence and are transformed in the process. Both *Thomas*, in this saying, and John, in 11.9–10, use the imagery of light to indicate this theme. The imagery in *Thomas* is part of the Jewish-Hermetic story which was adapted in many of the accretions to tell *Thomas'* story about the recreation of the luminous image of God within each person through their mystical experience of God's presence.

SOURCE DISCUSSION

W. Schrage has compared L. 61.3 to Matthew 11.27 and Luke 10.22. According to J. Sieber, since the texts are identical for Matthew and Luke, it is impossible to conclude literary dependence on either of them.

J. Sell discusses this logion as a variant associated with the tradition found in John 5.18–23 and John 3.35, 10.29 and 13.3. Surprisingly, Sell does not make the connection between John 17 and L. 61.3 as I do, and so he struggles to explain the phrase NA ΠΑΕΙШΤ trying to associate it with John 5.19–23. He states that meaning can be made of this 'seemingly enigmatic dialogue' if we are knowledgable of these Johannine materials. In fact, he sees this as an example of the development of *Thomas* where direct knowledge of John is shown.

I do not find direct literary dependence to be the case because the 'parallels' are less verbal quotations than they are thematic allusions. I. Dunderberg is of the same opinion. Rather, here I think we uncover another example of the interdependence of the Thomasine and Johannine traditions, each text developing similar traditions in their own direction as I have argued in *Voices of the Mystics.*

LITERATURE PARALLELS

Matthew 11.27a; Luke 10.22a
'All things have been delivered to me by my Father.'

John 3.35
'the Father loves the Son, and has given all things into his hand'.

John 5.18b
'but he also called God his own Father, making himself equal with God'.

John 6.37
'All that the Father gives me will come to me; and he who comes to me, I will not cast out.'

John 10.29–30
'My Father, who has given them to me, is greater than all, and no one is able to snatch them out of the Father's hand. I and the Father are one.'

John 10.38b
'the Father is in me and I am in the Father'.

John 13.3a
'Jesus, knowing that the Father had given all things into his hands'

John 14.20
'In that day you will know that I am in the Father, and you in me, and I in you.'

John 17.8–9
'For I have given them words which you gave me, and they have received them and know in truth that I came from you; and they have believed that you sent me. I am praying for them; I am not praying for the world but for those whom you have given to me, for they are mine.'

John 17.21–24
'that they may all be one; even as you, Father, are in me, and I in you, that they also may be in us, so that the world may believe that you sent me. The glory which have given me I have given to them, that they may be one even as we are one, I in them and you in me, that they may become perfectly one, so that the world may know that you sent me and

loved me. Father, I desire that they also, whom you have given me, may be with me where I am, to behold my glory which you gave me in your love for me before the foundation of the world.'

Gospel of the Nazarenes *23*

'I choose for myself the most worthy. The most worthy are those whom my Father in heaven has given me.'

Phil. 2.6

'who, though he was in the form of God, did not count equality with God a thing to be grasped'

Apocryphon of James *4.39–5.9*

'But if you are oppressed by Satan and are persecuted and you do his (the Father's) will, I [say] that he will love you and will make you equal with me and will consider that you have become [beloved] through his providence according to your free choice. Will you not cease, then, being lovers of the flesh and being afraid of sufferings?'

Acts of Thomas *70*

'You [Jesus] are divided without being separated, and are one though divided. And everything subsists in you and is subject to you, because everything is yours.'

Matthew 6.22–23a

'The eye is the lamp of the body. So, if your eye is sound, your whole body will be full of light; but if your eye is not sound, your whole body will be full of darkness.'

Luke 11.34

'Your eye is the lamp of your body; when your eye is sound, your whole body is full of light; but when it is not sound your body is full of darkness.'

John 11.9–10

'If any one walks in the day, he does not stumble, because he sees the light of this world. But if any one walks in the night, he stumbles, because the light is not in him.'

SELECT BIBLIOGRAPHY

Attridge (1981: 30–32); Bethge (1997: 534); DeConick (2001a); Dunderberg (1998a: 49–52); Guillaumont *et al.* (1959: 35); Schrage (1964a: 128); Sell (1980); Sieber (1966: 134–35).

Logion 62.1

[1]Jesus said, 'I tell my mysteries to [those people who are worthy of my] mysteries'.

NHC II 2.43.34–44.1

[1]ⲡ|ⲉ|ⲭⲉ ⲓ̅ⲥ̅ ⲭⲉ ⲉⲓ̈ⲭⲱ ⲛ̅ⲛⲁⲙⲩⲥⲧⲏⲣⲓⲟⲛ ⲛ̅ⲛ|ⲉⲧⲙ̅ⲡ|ϣⲁ|ⲛ̅ⲛⲁ| ⲙⲩⲥⲧⲏⲣⲓⲟⲛ

ATTRIBUTION
Kernel saying.

INTERPRETATIVE COMMENT
This logion served as the opening call to the fourth speech in the Kernel Gospel, emphasizing that Jesus reveals his mysteries to a select number of people who are worthy.

This theme appears to have been popular in eastern Christianity in particular. For instance, the theme is quite consistent throughout the *Pseudo-Clementine* corpus and may indicate an old tradition from the Jerusalem Church which emerges also in Luke 9.44–45, Mark 4.10–11, and 1 Corinthians 2.7, 2.10–13, and 4.1 (see Incipit). Jesus explains the 'mysteries' to the disciples because the truth has been hidden from the impious (*Hom.* 19.20). Teachers are warned to be very cautious when setting forth the truth in a mixed crowd because, 'if he set forth pure truth to those who do not desire to obtain salvation, he does injury to him by whom he has been sent' (*Rec.* 3.1). Jesus 'knows hidden things' (*Hom.* 3.13), and 'enables some to find easily what they seek, while to others he renders even that obscure which is before their eyes'. This preserves the truth for the righteous, the worthy people whose minds 'will fill up secretly' with understanding (*Rec.* 2.25; *Hom.* 18.8).

The theme that the Prophet Jesus has esoteric revelation for the worthy appears to be a development of a Jewish tradition about God's prophets. In *4 Ezra* 14.5, the Lord reveals to the Prophet Moses 'many wondrous things, and showed him secrets of the times and declared to him the end of times'. He tells Moses that some things he can make public while others he must only relate 'in secret to the wise' (14.26; cf. 14.45–46). The Qumranites are known to have developed this tradition in their own way. They thought that the Mosaic Torah was the 'manifest' teaching while their own laws were the 'hidden' teaching.

SOURCE DISCUSSION

M. Fieger traces L. 62.1 to the author's spontaneous citation of Mark 4.11 and its parallels. H. Koester, however, views this reference to the parables as 'secrets' as confirmation of an older tradition known also to Mark, that Jesus' teaching in parables conveyed 'secrets'. So L. 62.1 could rely on pre-Synoptic tradition. This appears most plausible to me given the broad spread of references to this idea (see above.) In fact, G. Quispel even has argued for the Palestinian origin of this saying, tracing it to a Jewish Christian Gospel.

LITERATURE PARALLELS

Mark 4.11
> 'To you has been given the secret of the Kingdom of God, but for those outside everything is in parables.'

Matthew 13.11
> 'To you it has been given to know the secrets of the Kingdom of Heaven, but to them it has not been given.'

Luke 8.10
> 'To you it has been given to know the secrets of the Kingdom of God, but for others they are in parables, so that seeing they may not see, and hearing they may not understand.'

Gospel of the Nazarenes *23*
> 'I choose for myself the most worthy. The most worthy are those whom my Father in heaven has given me.'

Clement of Alexandria, Strom. *5.10*
> 'It is for only a few to understand these things. For it is not in the way of envy that he says the Lord announced in some Gospel, "My mystery is for me, and for the sons of my house…"'.

Ps.-Clementine Homilies, *19.20.1*
> 'And Peter said, "We remember that our Lord and Teacher commanded us and said, 'Keep the mysteries for me and the sons of my house.' Therefore he also explained the mysteries of the Kingdom of Heaven privately to his disciples."'

John Chrysostom, In Epist. I ad Cor. Hom. *7*
  'And therefore elsewhere, "My mystery is for me and for those who are mine."'

Theodoret, In Psal. *65.16 and 67.14*
  'And, my mysteries are for me, and for those who are mine.'

John of Damascus, De sacra parallelis *9.1*
  'The mystery is for me and for those who are mine.'

LXX (var.) to Isaiah 24.16
  'My mystery is for me and for those who are mine.'

Apocryphon of John *7.29–30*
  'For they will tell this Name to those who are worthy of it.'

SELECT BIBLIOGRAPHY
Fieger (1991: 181); Koester (1990: 100–01); Quispel (1981: 265).

Logion 62.2

²'Do not let your left hand know what your right hand is going to do.'

NHC II 2.44.1–2

² ⲡⲉⲓⲧⲓⲉ ⲧⲉⲕⲟⲩⲛⲁⲙ ⲛⲁⲁϥ ⲙ̄ⲛ̄ⲧⲣⲉ ⲧⲉⲕϩⲃⲟⲩⲣ ⲉⲓⲙⲉ ϫⲉ ⲉⲥⲣ ⲟⲩ

ATTRIBUTION
Kernel saying.

INTERPRETATIVE COMMENT
This particular saying follows Jesus' promise to reveal his mysteries to the worthy. He compares this situation to an old adage that a person generally does not let his left hand know what his right hand is doing. It is striking that the *Pseudo-Clementines* know this hermeneutic and sequence of logia. Embedded in a discussion about preaching to an audience that potentially contains both worthy and unworthy company, is the explanatory note, 'Since God, who is just, judges the mind of each one, he would not have wished this [truth] to be given through the left hand to those on the right hand.' Thus, those present and listening must all be known to the Son and worthy of the revelation. The Son is 'alone appointed to give the revelation to those to whom he wishes to give it' (*Hom.* 18.3). The striking hermeneutical similarities between the logia cluster L. 62.1 and 62.2 and the *Pseudo-Clementine Homily* 18.3 is strong evidence, in my opinion, that some form of the Kernel Gospel was a source for part of the *Pseudo-Clementines*. It should not go unnoticed that Matthew 6.3 uses a version of this saying to address a completely different topic – almsgiving, not preaching to the worthy as we find in both *Thomas* and *Homily* 18.

SOURCE DISCUSSION
W. Schrage compares this logion to Sahidic Matthew and concludes that it is dependent, even though he notes some striking differences: L. 62.2 twice uses the τί clause and the future tense in the first of these clauses.

J. Sieber traces the saying to oral tradition rather than Matthew since the saying does not appear in any sequence familiar to Matthew. Further he cannot find Matthean editorial traits in the logion. Given the different hermeneutical application in L. 62.2 and Matthew 6.3 (see above), I find literary dependence highly unlikely and agree with Sieber in regard to its independence.

LITERATURE PARALLELS

Matthew 6.3
> 'But when you give alms, do not let your left hand know what your right hand is doing.'

'Abdallah ibn al-Mubarak, al-Zuhd, *pp. 48–49 (no. 150)*
> 'If he gives with the right hand, let him hide this from his left hand.'

Ahmad ibn Hanbal, al-Zuhd, *p. 94 (no. 307)*
> 'Jesus used to say, "If any of you gives alms with the right hand, let him hide this from his left."'

SELECT BIBLIOGRAPHY
Schrage (1964a: 130); Sieber (1966: 53–54).

Logion 63.1–3

[1]Jesus said, 'There was a wealthy man who had many assets. [2]He said, "I will use my assets to sow, harvest, plant and fill my granaries with produce, so that I will not need anything." [3]These were the things he was thinking in his heart. But that very night, he died.'

NHC II 2.44.2–9

[1]ⲡⲉϫⲉ ⲓ̅ⲥ̅ ϫⲉ ⲛⲉⲩⲛ̅ ⲟⲩⲣⲱⲙⲉ ⲙ̅ⲡⲗⲟⲩⲥⲓⲟⲥ ⲉⲩⲛ̅ⲧⲁϥ ⲙ̅ⲙⲁⲩ ⲛ̅ϩⲁϩ ⲛ̅ⲭⲣⲏⲙⲁ [2]ⲡⲉϫⲁϥ ϫⲉ ϯⲛⲁⲣ̅ⲭⲣⲱ ⲛ̅ⲛⲁⲭⲣⲏⲙⲁ ϫⲉⲕⲁⲁⲥ ⲉⲉⲓⲛⲁϫⲟ ⲛ̅ⲧⲁⲱⲥϩ ⲛ̅ⲧⲁⲧⲱ6ⲉ ⲛ̅ⲧⲁⲙⲟⲩϩ ⲛ̅ⲛⲁⲉϩⲱⲣ ⲛ̅ⲕⲁⲣⲡⲟⲥ ϣⲓⲛⲁ ϫⲉ ⲛⲓⲡ̅ 6ⲣⲱϩ ⲁ̅ⲗⲁⲁⲩ [3]ⲛⲁⲉⲓ ⲛⲉⲛⲉϥⲙⲉⲉⲩⲉ ⲉⲣⲟⲟⲩ ϩ̅ⲙ ⲡⲉϥϩⲏⲧ ⲁⲩⲱ ϩⲛ̅ ⲧⲟⲩϣⲏ ⲉⲧⲙ̅ⲙⲁⲩ ⲁϥⲙⲟⲩ

ATTRIBUTION
Kernel saying.

TEXT AND TRANSLATION ISSUES
In L. 63.2, ⲛ̅ⲧⲁⲱⲥϩ actually reads in the manuscript ⲛ̅ⲧⲁⲱϩⲥϩ. The scribe has crossed out the first ϩ.

INTERPRETATIVE COMMENT
This story is used rhetorically in the Kernel speech as a statement of the opposite. Jesus explains the characteristics of those not worthy of his teaching. He tells the hearer that they do not want to be like the foolish man who worked so hard for his own personal material gain while neglecting his true spiritual needs. The story serves as an example of the kind of lifestyle and mindset that Jesus does not consider beneficial to the soul.

SOURCE DISCUSSION

R. Grant and D.N. Freedman, H. von Schürmann, and E. Haenchen think that L. 63.1–2 is a condensation of Luke 12.16–21 even though there are striking differences between the parables. These differences have led W. Schrage to say that they cannot be explained as the programme of a Gnostic author. But M. Fieger explains the differences as evidence of the spontaneous adaption of Luke.

J. Sieber notes that the Lukan sequence of material is separated in *Thomas* (L. 63 and 36). The secondary developments in L. 63 look to be developments of another text entirely. Sieber identifies these developments as the use of ἵνα in L. 63.2 and the lack of ἀναπαύω which Sieber thinks would be very hard to explain as a Gnostic redaction of Luke. H. Koester approaches the logion as more original in formulation than the versions available in Matthew, Luke or Q since L. 63 lacks Luke's conclusion and moralizing discourse.

In my opinion, the verbal agreements, common phrasing and sequencing are so minor ('rich man'; 'night') that an argument for literary dependence is impossible to maintain. Rather the parable yields signs of oral transmission with no indication of secondary orality or scribal adaptation. Here is a fine example of an independent oral multiform.

LITERATURE PARALLELS

Luke 12.16–21 (Qluke or L)

> [16]'The land of a rich man brought forth plentifully. [17]And he thought to himself, "What shall I do, for I have nowhere to store my crops?" [18]And he said, "I will do this. I will pull down my barns, and build larger ones. And there I will store my grain and my goods. [19]And I will say to my soul, 'Soul, you have ample goods laid up for many years. Take your ease, eat, drink, be merry.'" [20]But God said to him, "Fool! This night your soul is required of you. And the things you have prepared, whose will they be?" [21]So is he who lays up treasure for himself, and is not rich toward God.'

Pseudo-Clementine Recognitions *10.45*

> 'Nor let the rich man delay his conversion by reason of worldly care, while he thinks how he may dispose the abundance of his fruits. Nor say within himself, "What shall I do? Where shall I bestow my fruits?" Nor say to his soul, "You have much goods laid up for many years. Feast and rejoice." For it shall be said to him, "You fool! This night your soul shall be taken from you, and whose shall those things be which you have provided?" Therefore let every age, every sex, every condition, haste to repentance, that they may obtain eternal life.'

AGREEMENTS IN SYRIAN GOSPELS, WESTERN TEXT AND DIATESSARON

Luke 12.16–20 in S C P T[P] T[A] T[T] T[NL]
There was a rich man

Luke 12.16–20 in b e q ff[2] i l m
who had much money

Luke 12.16–20 in e m b q ff[2] i l m
much money

Luke 12.16–20 in C T[A] T[NL] Aphr Ephr
he thought *in his heart* << I say to my soul

Luke 12.16–20 in H U
+ whoever has ears let him hear

Luke 12.16–20 in a b d D
– So is he who lays up treasure for himself, and is not rich toward God.

SELECT BIBLIOGRAPHY
Fieger (1991: 183); Grant with Freedman (1960: 169); Haenchen (1961/1962: 175); Koester (1990: 97–98); Schürmann (1963: 242–43); Schrage (1964a: 131–33); Sieber (1966: 217).

Logion 63.4

⁴'Whoever has ears should listen!'

NHC II 2.44.9–10

⁴ⲡⲉⲧⲉⲩ̄ⲙ ⲙⲁϫⲉ ̄ⲙⲙⲟϥ ⲙⲁⲣⲉϥⲥⲱⲧ̄ⲙ

ATTRIBUTION
Kernel saying.

See L. 8.4.

Logion 64.1–11

¹Jesus said, 'A man had guests. When he had prepared the dinner, he sent his servant to invite the guests.

²He went to the first person. He said to him, "My master invites you."

³He said, "I have some payments for some merchants. They are coming to me this evening. I must go and give them instructions. I decline the dinner."

⁴He went to another person. He said to him, "My master has invited you."

⁵He said to him, "I have purchased a house and they have requested me for the day. I will not have time."

⁶He went to another person. He said to him, "My master invites you."

⁷He said to him, "My friend is going to be wed and I am the person who will be preparing the meal. I will not be able to come. I decline the dinner."

⁸He went to another person. He said to him, "My master invites you."

⁹He said to him, "I have purchased a villa. Since I am going to collect the rent, I will not be able to come. I decline."

¹⁰The servant left. He said to his master, "The people whom you invited to the dinner have declined."

¹¹The master said to his servant, "Go outside on the streets. The people you find, bring them to dine."'

NHC II 2.44.10–34

¹ⲡⲉⲝⲉ ⲓ̅ⲥ̅ ⲝⲉ ⲟⲩⲣⲱⲙⲉ ⲛⲉⲩⲛ̅ⲧⲁϥ ϩⲛ̅ϣⲙ̅ⲙⲟ ⲁⲩⲱ ⲛ̅ⲧⲁⲣⲉϥⲥⲟⲃⲧⲉ
ⲙ̅ⲡⲇⲓⲡⲛⲟⲛ ⲁϥⲝⲟⲟⲩ ⲙ̅ⲡⲉϥϩⲙ̅ϩⲁⲗ ϣⲓⲛⲁ ⲉϥⲛⲁⲧⲱϩⲙ̅ ⲛ̅ⲛ̅ϣⲙ̅ⲙⲟⲉⲓ
²ⲁϥⲃⲱⲕ ⲙ̅ⲡϣⲟⲣⲡ̅ ⲡⲉⲝⲁϥ ⲛⲁϥ ⲝⲉ ⲡⲁϫⲟⲉⲓⲥ ⲧⲱϩⲙ̅ ⲙⲙⲟⲕ
³ⲡⲉⲝⲁϥ ⲝⲉ ⲟⲩⲛ̅ⲧⲁⲉⲓ ϩⲛ̅ϩⲟⲙⲧ ⲁϩⲉⲛⲉⲙⲡⲟⲣⲟⲥ ⲥⲉⲛⲛⲏⲩ ϣⲁⲣⲟⲉⲓ
ⲉⲣⲟⲩϩⲉ †ⲛⲁⲃⲱⲕ ⲛ̅ⲧⲁⲟⲩⲉϩ ⲥⲁϩⲛⲉ ⲛⲁⲩ †ⲡ̅ⲣ̅ⲡⲁⲣⲁⲓⲧⲉⲓ ⲙ̅ⲡⲇⲓⲡⲛⲟⲛ
⁴ⲁϥⲃⲱⲕ ϣⲁ ⲕⲉⲟⲩⲁ ⲡⲉⲝⲁϥ ⲛⲁϥ ⲝⲉ ⲁⲡⲁⲝⲟⲉⲓⲥ ⲧⲱϩⲙ̅ ⲙⲙⲟⲕ
⁵ⲡⲉⲝⲁϥ ⲛⲁϥ ⲝⲉ ⲁⲉⲓⲧⲟⲟⲩ ⲟⲩⲏⲉⲓ ⲁⲩⲱ ⲥⲉⲣ̅ⲁⲓⲧⲉⲓ ⲙ̅ⲙⲟⲉⲓ
ⲛ̅ⲟⲩϩⲏⲙⲉⲣⲁ †ⲛⲁⲥⲣ̅ϥⲉ ⲁ(ⲛ)
⁶ⲁϥⲉⲓ ϣⲁ ⲕⲉⲟⲩⲁ ⲡⲉⲝⲁϥ ⲛⲁϥ ⲝⲉ ⲡⲁⲝⲟⲉⲓⲥ ⲧⲱϩⲙ̅ ⲙⲙⲟⲕ
⁷ⲡⲉⲝⲁϥ ⲛⲁϥ ⲝⲉ ⲡⲁϣⲃⲏⲣ ⲛⲁⲣ̅ϣⲉⲗⲉⲉⲧ ⲁⲩⲱ ⲁⲛⲟⲕ ⲉⲧⲛⲁⲣ̅
ⲇⲓⲡⲛⲟⲛ †ⲛⲁϣⲓ ⲁⲛ †ⲡ̅ⲣ̅ⲡⲁⲣⲁⲓⲧⲉⲓ ⲙ̅ⲡⲇⲓⲡⲛⲟⲛ
⁸ⲁϥⲃⲱⲕ ϣⲁ ⲕⲉⲟⲩⲁ ⲡⲉⲝⲁϥ ⲛⲁϥ ⲝⲉ ⲡⲁⲝⲟⲉⲓⲥ ⲧⲱϩⲙ ⲙⲙⲟⲕ
⁹ⲡⲉⲝⲁϥ ⲛⲁϥ ⲝⲉ ⲁⲉⲓⲧⲟⲟⲩ ⲛ̅ⲟⲩⲕⲱⲙⲏ ⲉⲉⲓⲃⲏⲕ ⲁⲝⲓ ⲛ̅ϣⲱⲙ †ⲛⲁϣⲓ
ⲁⲛ †ⲡ̅ⲣ̅ⲡⲁⲣⲁⲓⲧⲉⲓ
¹⁰ⲁϥⲉⲓ ⲛ̅ϭⲓ ⲡϩⲙ̅ϩⲁⲗ ⲁϥⲝⲟⲟⲥ ⲁⲡⲉϥⲝⲟⲉⲓⲥ ⲝⲉ ⲛⲉⲛⲧⲁⲕⲧⲁϩⲙⲟⲩ
ⲁⲡⲇⲓⲡⲛⲟⲛ ⲁⲩⲡⲁⲣⲁⲓⲧⲉⲓ
¹¹ⲡⲉⲝⲉ ⲡⲝⲟⲉⲓⲥ ⲙ̅ⲡⲉϥϩⲙ̅ϩⲁⲗ ⲝⲉ ⲃⲱⲕ ⲉⲡⲥⲁ ⲛⲃⲟⲗ ⲁⲛϩⲓⲟⲟⲩⲉ
ⲛⲉⲧⲕ̅ⲛⲁϩⲉ ⲉⲣⲟⲟⲩ ⲉⲛⲓⲟⲩ ⲝⲉⲕⲁⲁⲥ ⲉⲩⲛⲁⲣ̅ⲇⲓⲡⲛⲉⲓ

ATTRIBUTION
Kernel saying.

TEXT AND TRANSLATION ISSUES
Since Luke 14.18 has ἀγρός, A. Guillaumont notes that ⲕⲱⲙⲏ might be traced to the Syriac ⲣⲇⲓⲟ, which means both field and village. This explanation is not necessary since ⲕⲱⲙⲏ can mean farm or country villa, which ἀγρός can also mean.

In L. 64.6, there is an erased word under ⲡⲁⲝⲟⲉⲓⲥ. It looks like the scribe started to copy the next line with ϣⲃⲏⲣ following ⲡⲁ. He caught the mistake, erased the incorrect word, and wrote over it ⲝⲟⲉⲓⲥ.

Areas of L. 64.11 are eroded with tiny lacunae.

INTERPRETATIVE COMMENT
This parable continued the theme that Jesus only teaches his mysteries to the worthy, by comparing this situation to the situation of a wealthy man who invited many people to a special banquet. Each person he invited gave excuses for not being able to attend his supper because they had other (more important) obligations. One of the points of this story within the context of the Kernel speech is that the hearer should not respond to Jesus' invitation like these foolish people whose obligations keep them from the Messianic banquet table. Another point appears to be that everyone is invited and must make their own crucial decision.

SOURCE DISCUSSION
Thomas' logion has no editorial relationship with Matthew 22.2–10. Also *Thomas* does not have the only Lukan editorial trace in the parable, the reference to the Gentile mission. So W. Schrage says that dependence cannot be determined. J. Sieber agrees. According to H. Koester, Matthew and Luke relied on and edited written sources in very different ways, Matthew substituting an allegory while Luke preserved the original dimension of the narrative. Luke expanded the original conclusion with 14.21–22 which appears in neither

Matthew nor *Thomas*. L. 64.1–11 shows no Lukan or Matthean redactional pecularities or changes including the allegorical and secondary features found in the Synoptic versions.

The parable appears to me to display the characteristics of orally transmitted materials and offers us an early alternative version of this famous parable.

LITERATURE PARALLELS

Matthew 22.2–10 (Qmatt)

> [2]'The Kingdom of heaven may be compared to a king who gave a marriage feast for his son, [3]and sent his servants to call those who were invited to the marriage feast. But they would not come. [4]Again he sent other servants, saying "Tell those who are invited, Behold, I have made ready my dinner, my oxen and my fat calves killed, and everything is ready. Come to the marriage feast." [5]But they made light of it and went off, one to his farm, another to his business, [6]while the rest seized the servants, treated them shamefully, and killed them. [7]The king was angry, and he sent troops and destroyed those murderers and burned their city. [8]Then he said to his servants, "The wedding is ready, but those invited were not worthy. [9]Go therefore to the thoroughfares, and invite to the marriage feast as many as you find." [10]And those servants went out into the streets and gathered all whom they found, both bad and good. So the wedding hall was filled with guests.'

Luke 14.16–24 (Qluke)

> [16]'A man once gave a great banquet, and invited many. [17]And at the time for the banquet he sent his servant to say to those who had been invited, "Come! For all is now ready." [18]But they all alike began to make excuses. The first said to him, "I have bought a field, and I must go out and see it. I pray you, have me excused." [19]And another said, "I have bought five yoke of oxen, and I go to examine them. I pray you, have me excused." [20]And another said, "I have married a wife, and therefore I cannot come." [21]So the servant came and reported this to his master. Then the householder in anger said to his servant, "Go out quickly to the streets and lanes of the city, and bring in the poor and maimed and blind and lame." [22]And the servant said, "Sir what you commanded has been done, and still there is room." [23]And the master said to the servant, "Go out to the highways and hedges, and compel people to come in, that my house may be filled. [24]For I tell you, none of those men who were invited shall taste my banquet."'

Pseudo-Clementine Homilies *8.22*

> 'However, the King of the impious, striving to bring over to his own counsel the King of the pious, and not being able, ceased his efforts, undertaking to persecute him [Jesus] for the remainder of his life. But you, being ignorant of the foreordained law, are under his power through evil deeds. Wherefore you are polluted in body and soul, and in the present life you are tyrannized over by sufferings and demons, but in that which is to come you shall have your souls to be punished. And this not you alone suffer through ignorance, but also some of our nation, who by evil deeds having been brought under the power of the Prince of Wickedness, like persons invited to a supper by a father celebrating the marriage of his son, have not obeyed. But instead of those who through pre-occupation disobeyed, the Father celebrating the marriage of his Son, has ordered us, through the Prophet of Truth, to come into the partings of the ways, that is, to you, and to invest you with the clean wedding-garment, which is baptism, which is for the remission of the sins done by you, and to bring the good to the supper of God by repentance, although at first they were left out of the banquet.'

Pseudo-Clementine Homilies *15.3*

> 'What is it then that prevents you from coming to our faith? Tell me, that we may begin our discussion with it. For many are the hindrances. The faithful are hindered by occupation with merchandise, or public business, or the cultivation of the soil, or cares, and such like. The unbelievers, of whom you also are one, are hindered by ideas such as that the

gods, which do not exist, really exist, or that all things are subject to genesis or self-action, or that souls are mortal, or that our doctrines are false because there is no providence.'

Pseudo-Clementine Recognitions *4.35*
> 'Meantime he has commanded us to go forth to preach, and to invite you to the supper of the heavenly King, which the Father has prepared for the marriage of his son, and that we should give you wedding garments, that is the grace of baptism. Which whosoever obtains, as a spotless robe with which he is to enter to the supper of the King, ought to beware that it be not in any part of it stained with sin, and so he be rejected as unworthy and reprobate.'

Deuteronomy 20.5–7
> [5]"Then the officers shall speak to the people, saying, "What man is there that has built a new house and has not dedicated it? Let him go back to his house, lest he die in the battle and another man dedicate it. [6]And what man is there that has planted a vineyard and has not enjoyed its fruit? Let him go back to his house, lest he die in the battle and another man enjoy its fruit. [7]And what man is there that has betrothed a wife and has not taken her? Let him go back to his house, lest he die in the battle and another man take her."'

Deuteronomy 24.5
> 'When a man is newly married, he shall not go out with the army or be charged with any business. He shall be free at home one year, to be happy with his wife whom he has taken.'

Cf. *j.Sanh.* 6.23c par. *j. Hagh.* 2.77d; *Midr. Tanh.* B Num VIII, 3 para. 12; *b. Shab.* 153a; *Qoh. R.* 9.8; *Shem. R.* 25.7; *Midr. Teh.* Ps. 23, para. 7

AGREEMENTS IN SYRIAN GOSPELS, WESTERN TEXT AND DIATESSARON

Luke 14.16–24//Matthew 22.1–10 in e Mcion X arm bo
> great dinner – great

Luke 14.16–24//Matthew 22.1–10 in a aur b c e ff² l q rˡ vg S C P Tᴸ Tᵀ Tᴺᴸ
> farm << field

Luke 14.16–24//Matthew 22.1–10 in e S C P Tᴾ Tᴬ Tᴺᴸ sa
> the servant came, he said << when the servant came back he reported

Luke 14.16–24//Matthew 22.1–10 in D
> bring those who you will find << bring in

SELECT BIBLIOGRAPHY
Guillaumont (1981: 198); Koester (1983: 197–98); Schrage (1964a: 134–35); Sieber (1966: 242–43).

Logion 64.12

> [12]'Buyers and merchants [will] not enter the places of my Father.'

NHC II 2.44.34–35

> [12]ⲚⲢⲈϤⲦⲞⲞⲨ ⲘⲚ̄ ⲚⲈϢⲞ|ⲦⲈ ⲤⲈⲚⲀⲂⲰ|Ⲕ ⲀⲚ ⲈϨⲞⲨⲚ ⲈⲚⲦⲞⲠⲞⲤ Ⲙ̄ⲠⲀⲒ̈ⲰⲦ

ATTRIBUTION
Accretion.

INTERPRETATIVE COMMENT
This saying is an interpretative clause which accrued in order to fix meaning to the parable. Since the earliest community upheld voluntary poverty as an ideal, this clause may represent a very old interpretation of the saying. Accrual could have taken place as early as 60 CE.

This clause reflects the ideal of poverty held fast by the early Christians in Jerusalem (Acts 4.32–5.11; Rom. 15.26). This ideal is rooted not only in the teachings of Jesus (Matt. 5.3 and parallels), but also in other Jewish teachings since it was believed that possessions may constitute an occasion for sin (Sirach 26.29–27.2). H. Koester notes that a similar situation is reflected in James 4.13–17 which accepts members of the mercantile profession only under certain conditions. The *Pseudo-Clementine Homily* 15.3 knows that those who are merchants and businessmen are hindered from the faith.

LITERATURE PARALLELS

Sirach 26.29–27.2
[29]'A merchant can hardly keep from wrongdoing and a tradesman will not be declared innocent of sin. [27.1]Many have committed sin for a trifle, and whoever seeks to get rich will avert his eyes. [2]As a stake is driven firmly into a fissure between stones, so sin is wedged in between selling and buying.'

Pseudo-Clementine Homilies *15.3*
'What is it then that prevents you from coming to our faith? Tell me, that we may begin our discussion with it. For many are the hindrances. The faithful are hindered by occupation with merchandise, or public business, or the cultivation of the soil, or cares, and such like. The unbelievers, of whom you also are one, are hindered by ideas such as that the gods, which do not exist, really exist, or that all things are subject to genesis or self-action, or that souls are mortal, or that our doctrines are false because there is no providence.'

SELECT BIBLIOGRAPHY
Koester (1983: 198).

Logion 65.1–7

[1]He said, 'A creditor owned a vineyard. He leased it to some farmers so that they would work it and he would collect the produce from them.

[2]He sent his servant so that the farmers would give him the produce of the vineyard. [3]They seized his servant. They beat him, a little more and they would have killed him.

The servant returned and he told his master.

[4]The master said, "Perhaps [[they]] did not recognize [[him.]]."

[5]He sent another servant. The farmers beat that one too.

[6]Then the master sent his son. He said, "Perhaps they will be ashamed in front of my son."

[7]Those farmers, since they knew that he was the heir of the vineyard, seized him and killed him.

NHC II 2.45.1–15

¹ⲡⲉⲭⲁϥ ϫⲉ ⲟⲩⲣⲱⲙⲉ ⲛ̄ⲭⲣⲏ|ⲥⲧⲏ|ⲥ ⲛⲉⲩⲛ̄|ⲧⲁϥ| ⲛ̄ⲟⲩⲙⲁ ⲛ̄ⲉⲗⲟⲟⲗⲉ
ⲁϥⲧⲁⲁϥ ⲛ̄|ϩ|ⲛ̄ⲟⲩⲟⲉⲓⲉ ϣⲓⲛⲁ ⲉⲩⲛⲁⲣ̄ ϩⲱⲃ ⲉⲣⲟϥ ⲛ̄ϥϫⲓ ⲙ̄ⲡⲉϥⲕⲁⲣⲡⲟⲥ
ⲛ̄ⲧⲟⲟⲧⲟⲩ ²ⲁϥϫⲟⲟⲩ ⲙ̄ⲡⲉϥϩⲙ̄ϩⲁⲗ ϫⲉⲕⲁⲁⲥ ⲉⲛⲟⲩⲟⲉⲓⲉ ⲛⲁϯ ⲛⲁϥ
ⲙ̄ⲡⲕⲁⲣⲡⲟⲥ ⲙ̄ⲡⲙⲁ ⲛ̄ⲉⲗⲟⲟⲗⲉ
³ⲁⲩⲉⲙⲁϩⲧⲉ ⲙ̄ⲡⲉϥϩⲙ̄ϩⲁⲗ ⲁⲩϩⲓⲟⲩⲉ ⲉⲣⲟϥ ⲛⲉ ⲕⲉⲕⲟⲩⲉⲓ ⲡⲉ
ⲛ̄ⲥⲉⲙⲟⲟⲩⲧϥ ⲁⲡϩⲙ̄ϩⲁⲗ ⲃⲱⲕ ⲁϥϫⲟⲟⲥ ⲉⲡⲉϥϫⲟⲉⲓⲥ
⁴ⲡⲉϫⲉ ⲡⲉϥϫⲟⲉⲓⲥ ϫⲉ ⲙⲉϣⲁⲕ ⲙ̄ⲡ|[ⲟⲩ]|ⲥⲟⲩⲱⲛ|[ϥ]|
⁵ⲁϥϫⲟⲟⲩ ⲛ̄ⲕⲉϩⲙ̄ϩⲁⲗ ⲁⲛⲟⲩⲟⲉⲓⲉ ϩⲓⲟⲩⲉ ⲉⲡⲕⲉⲟⲩⲁ
⁶ⲧⲟⲧⲉ ⲁⲡϫⲟⲉⲓⲥ ϫⲟⲟⲩ ⲙ̄ⲡⲉϥϣⲏⲣⲉ ⲡⲉϫⲁϥ ϫⲉ ⲙⲉϣⲁⲕ
ⲥⲉⲛⲁϣⲓⲡⲉ ϩⲏⲧϥ ⲙ̄ⲡⲁϣⲏⲣⲉ
⁷ⲁⲛⲟⲩⲟⲉⲓⲉ ⲉⲧⲙ̄ⲙⲁⲩ ⲉⲡⲉⲓ ⲥⲉⲥⲟⲟⲩⲛ ϫⲉ ⲛ̄ⲧⲟϥ ⲡⲉ
ⲡⲉⲕⲗⲏⲣⲟⲛⲟⲙⲟⲥ ⲙ̄ⲡⲙⲁ ⲛ̄ⲉⲗⲟⲟⲗⲉ ⲁⲩϭⲟⲡϥ ⲁⲩⲙⲟⲟⲩⲧϥ

ATTRIBUTION
Kernel saying.

TEXT AND TRANSLATION ISSUES
In L. 65.1, the lacunae may also be restored, ⲛ̄ⲭⲣⲏ|ⲥⲧⲟ|ⲥ, an 'honest' man.

The text ⲙ̄ⲡⲉϥⲥⲟⲩⲱⲛⲟⲩ, 'he did not recognize them', appears to be corrupt. So my reading follows the emendation ⲙ̄ⲡⲟⲩⲥⲟⲩⲱⲛϥ, 'they did not recognize him'.

INTERPRETATIVE COMMENT
This narrative is used rhetorically in the Kernel Gospel to speak of the most unworthy people of all. They are like the tenant farmers who killed the owner's son. This narrative appears to have been interpreted metaphorically as a reference to those who rejected Jesus' message and killed him, since we find immediately attached to the narrative, a proof text commonly used by the Christians for this purpose (L. 66). The presence of this narrative and its interpretation suggests that, even as early as the Kernel Gospel, the community knew about Jesus' death and taught an interpretation of it comparable to the first Christian Jews in Jerusalem. He was the rejected cornerstone mentioned in the ancient prophecies referencing Psalm 118.22, the 'rejected stone which has become the head of the corner' (Acts 4.11; Mark 12.10–11; Matthew 21.42; Luke 20.17; 1 Peter 2.5–6).

SOURCE DISCUSSION
R. Grant and W. Schrage think that L. 65–66 are based on Matthew 21.33–41, Mark 12.1–12 and Luke 20.9–16. Schrage finds agreements between Matthew and *Thomas* with their use of the possessive with 'servant', a substantive object in the seizing of the first servant, the omission of the third sending of the servant, and the omission of 'beloved' and 'sent him away empty-handed'. J. Sieber states that these are not Matthean editorial traces but 'simply readings of Matthew's text'. He thinks that Matthew and Luke had available to them other versions of this parable than just the Markan, so establishing deliberate redactional activity on either of their parts is difficult. With Mark, Schrage states that *Thomas* agrees because both use a purpose clause in the sending of the first servant. Sieber says that this does not mean that *Thomas* depends on Mark since this cannot be identified as a Markan editorial trait.

J.B. Sheppard's investigation of the parables in the Gospel agreed that *Thomas* did not use Matthew or Mark, but that *Thomas* may have used Luke or the tradition behind Luke. This opinion is shared by many, so the discussion about dependence has centred on Luke.

Even as early as 1959, H. McArthur notes that, although L. 65 and 66 are not in verbatim agreement, there are Lukan editorial revisions of Mark present. First, Luke has eliminated the language of Isaiah 5 which begins Mark's parable. Second, Luke reserves the killing for the son. Third, Luke only quotes Psalm 118.11 while Mark quotes also vv. 22–23. Later Schrage points also to Lukan agreement with δώσουσιν αὐτῷ in Luke 20.10 and ἴσως in Luke 20.13. He feels that these two points are the key evidence for dependence on Luke since they are considered Lukan stylistic and theological improvements. B. Dehandschutter follows this opinion, citing the brevity of the introduction which lacks the reference to Isaiah 5.1, Lukan agreement with a singular 'fruit', the agreement of δώσουσιν in Luke 20.10, the second mission of the servant in Luke 20.11, ἴσως in Luke 20.13, and the termination of the parable in the son's death. K.R. Snodgrass points also to these verbal contacts, arguing that ἴσως is a *hapax legomenon* added to make the owner's action more plausible. That *Thomas* has 'perhaps' cannot be coincidence he says. Furthermore, he states that Syr[S] of Mark 12.6 has added 'perhaps' under the influence of Luke. This shows harmonizing tendencies in Syria and that they may have been at work on *Thomas*' Gospel. He points to the fact that the Syriac texts of Mark and Luke abbreviate the parable to bring them more in line with Matthew's two-fold sending of the servants. Thus he concludes that *Thomas* does not represent the earliest form but a later abbreviated form shaped in the Syrian oral environment of transmission. W.G. Morrice disagrees, suggesting instead that the omission of the second servant in Mark 12.4 in Syr[S] and of the third servant in Luke 20.2 in Syr[C] may be dependent on an independent tradition in Syria which also emerges in *Thomas*.

J. Sieber's opinion is that δώσουσιν αὐτῷ in Luke 20.10 and ἴσως in Luke 20.13 are Lukan readings but not redactional traces. In the first place, δώσουσιν αὐτω is not a Lukan stylistic modification but must be traced to a Lukan source other than Mark because Luke does not regularly use ἵνα with the future indicative. As for ἴσως in Luke 20.13, he does not think as Schrage that it represents a Lukan theological modification because it would only increase God's blame for sending his son, not alleviate it. Further he argues that L. 65 is not dependent on Luke because it contains readings that cannot be explained by the Synoptics or Gnostic exegesis: the master's explanation of the beating of the first servant; τότὲ; ἐπεί; the addition of 'ears' to the saying. Also, the fact that the parable is connected to the same Psalm quote as found in the Synoptics is significant since L. 65–66 do not have the same Synoptic linkage or reference to the Old Testament. This means that the two sayings had been transmitted orally together for a long time. So Sieber concludes that L. 65–66 are independent from the Synoptics. Patterson suggests that the present position of L. 66 may represent a scribal alteration based on knowledge of the Synoptics.

G. Quispel as early as 1957 argued that L. 65 is a prime example of a saying that may 'have preserved the words of Jesus in a form more primitive than that found in the canonical gospels'. He feels that it is a more reasonable hypothesis to argue that it is an independent tradition derived from a Jewish Christian Gospel or the source behind this Gospel. The opinion that the form of this parable is very old is upheld by J.D. Crossan who says that L. 65 probably represents an independent tradition rather than an abbreviation of the Synoptic parable because it preserves the parable as a story instead of an allegory as the Synoptics have it. This opinion is voiced also by H. Koester.

In my opinion, direct literary dependence cannot be demonstrated since we do not find sequences of words or phrases longer than five or six. Comparison with the Synoptic versions suggests that the parable was orally transmitted and may represent an older independent multiform. If one thinks that 'perhaps' is a secondary development of the parable found in both Luke and *Thomas*, then we might be witnessing secondary orality which influenced the performance of the text at a later time.

LITERATURE PARALLELS

Mark 12.1–9

[1]'A man planted a vineyard, and set a hedge around it, and dug a pit for a wine press, and built a tower. He let it out to tenants, and went into another country. [2]When the time came, he sent a servant to the tenants, to get from them some of the fruit of the vineyard. [3]And they took him and beat him, and sent him away empty-handed. [4]Again he sent to them another servant, and they wounded him in the head, and treated him shamefully. [5]And he sent another, and him they killed. And so with many others, some they beat and some they killed. [6]He had still one other, a beloved son. Finally he sent him to them, saying, "They will respect my son." [7]But those tenants said to one another, "This is the heir. Come, let us kill him, and the inheritance will be ours." [8]And they took him and killled him, and cast him out of the vineyard. [9]What will the owner of the vineyard do? He will come and destroy the tenant, and give the vineyard to others.'

Matthew 21.33–41

[33]'There was a householder who planted a vineyard, and set a hedge around it, and dug a wine press in it, and built a tower. He let it out to tenants, and went into another country. [34]When the season of fruit drew near, he sent his servants to the tenants, to get his fruit. [35]And the tenants took his servants and beat one, killed another, and stoned another. [36]Again he sent other servants, more than the first. And they did the same to them. [37]Afterward, he sent his son to them, saying, "They will respect my son." [38]But when the tenants saw the son, they said to themselves, "This is the heir. Come, let us kill him and have his inheritance." [39]And they took him and cast him out of the vineyard, and killed him. [40]When therefore the owner of the vineyard comes, what will he do to those tenants?' [41]They said to him, 'He will put those wretches to a miserable death, and let out the vineyard to other tenants who will give him the fruits in their seasons.'

Luke 20.9–16

[9]'A man planted a vineyard, and let it out to tenants, and went into another country for a long while. [10]When the time came, he sent a servant to the tenants, that they should give him some of the fruit of the vineyard. But the tenants beat him, and sent him away empty-handed. [11]And he sent another servant. Him also they beat and treated shamefully, and sent him away empty-handed. [12]And he sent yet a third. This one they wounded and cast out. [13]Then the owner of the vineyard said, "What shall I do? I will send my beloved son. It may be they will respect him." [14]But when the tenants saw him, they said to themselves, "This is the heir. Let us kill him, that the inheritance may be ours." [15]And they cast him out of the vineyard and killed him. What then will the owner of the vineyard do to them? [16]He will come and destroy those tenants, and give the vineyard to others.'

Cf. Hermas, *Sim.* 5.2

AGREEMENTS IN SYRIAN GOSPELS, WESTERN TEXT AND DIATESSARON

Matthew 21.33–39//Mark 12.1–8//Luke 20.9–15 in d (Mark, Luke) b q (Mark) S C (Matthew) Pal T[A] sa bo geo
    he gave it << let it out

Matthew 21.33–39//Mark 12.1–8//Luke 20.9–15 in T[P] geo(OT) Mt(H)
    + so that they would work it

Matthew 21.33–39//Mark 12.1–8//Luke 20.9–15 in S P (Mark) S C P (Luke) T[A]
    he sent *his* servant << a servant (Mark, Luke)

Matthew 21.33–39//Mark 12.1–8//Luke 20.9–15 in W 033 (Mark) D e (Luke) sa (Mark)
    he sent another servant, – again

Matthew 21.33–39//Mark 12.1–8//Luke 20.9–15 in T^{EC} T^{NL}
then << afterward (finally)

Matthew 21.33–39//Mark 12.1–8//Luke 20.9–15 in 28 Orig e m ff^d (Matthew) D d 544 l vg (Mark) C T^{EC} geo(OT)
the owner sent his son, – to them

Matthew 21.33–39//Mark 12.1–8//Luke 20.9–15 in T^{EC}
knew << saw

Matthew 21.33–39//Mark 12.1–8//Luke 20.9–15 in T^{EC}
heir + of the vineyard

SELECT BIBLIOGRAPHY
Crossan (1971: 451–65); Dehandschutter (1974: 212–16); Grant (1959: 178); Koester (1983: 199); McArthur (1959/1960: 286); Morrice (1986: 106); Patterson (1993: 51); Quispel (1957; 1975c: 186–89); Schrage (1964a: 137–41); Sheppard (1965: 210); Sieber (1966: 234–36); Snodgrass (1974: 142–44; 1989: 21–31).

Logion 65.8

8'Whoever has ears should listen!'

NHC II 2.45.15–16

⁸ΠΕΤΕΥⲘ ⲘⲀⲀⲬⲈ ⲘⲘⲟϥ ⲘⲀⲣⲉϥ ⲤⲰⲦⲘ̄

ATTRIBUTION
Kernel saying.

See L. 8.4.

Logion 66

Jesus said, 'Show me the stone that the builders rejected. It is the cornerstone.'

NHC II 2.45.16–19

ΠⲈⲬⲈ ⲓ̅ⲥ̅ ⲬⲈ ⲘⲀⲦⲤⲈⲂⲟⲈⲓ ⲈⲠⲰⲚⲈ ⲠⲀⲈⲓ ⲚⲦⲀⲨⲤⲦⲟϥ ⲈⲂⲟⲗ ⲚϬⲓ
ⲚⲈⲦⲔⲰⲦ ⲚⲦⲟϥ ⲠⲈ ⲠⲰⲰⲚⲈ ⲚⲔⲰϨ

ATTRIBUTION
Kernel saying.

INTERPRETATIVE COMMENT
Significantly, this prooftext is attached also to the Synoptic versions of the same parable. Although it might be argued that this ordering suggests literary dependence, this does not have to be the case. In fact, it is more likely that this particular prooftext attached itself to

this parable very early in the public orations of Jesus' sayings. K. Snodgrass thinks, in fact, that Psalm 118.22 has always been attached to this parable, serving as the key to understanding the parable. It functioned as the original conclusion to the parable connected by the Semitic wordplay between בֵּן, 'son', and אֶבֶן, 'stone'. In my opinion, this wordplay prooftext seems to have confused Synoptic writers since they do not transmit 'a' known interpretation of it in light of the parable. In fact, it seemed to enjoy its own variety of interpretations as the Synoptic and Thomasine usage demonstrates. In Mark, it is meant to demean the 'multitude' and resulted in their desire to arrest Jesus (12.12). According to Matthew, by this Jesus meant that the Kingdom of God would be taken away from the Jews and given to another nation (21.43). Luke writes engimatically that 'everyone who falls on that stone will be broken into pieces. But when it falls on any one it will crush him' (20.18). In *Thomas* it appears to be understood in line with Acts 4.11, that Jesus, the son, is rejected and killed in a line of prophets, servants of God, who endured similar fates. He is the rejected cornerstone prophesied in the Psalms.

SOURCE DISCUSSION
See L. 65

LITERATURE PARALLELS

Mark 12.10
'Have you not read this scripture: "The very stone which the builders rejected has become the head of the corner"?'

Matthew 21.42
'Jesus said to them, "Have you never read in the scriptures: 'The very stone which the builders rejected has become the headn of the corner'?"'

Luke 20.17
'But he looked at them and said, "What then is this that is written: 'The very stone which the builders rejected has become the head of the corner'?"'

Acts 4.11
'This is the stone which was rejected by you builders, but which has become the head of the corner.'

1 Peter 2.7
'To you therefore who believe, he is precious, but for those who do not believe, "The very stone which the builders rejected has become the head of the corner."'

Barnabas 6.4
'Are we really to pin our hopes to a stone, then? Of course not. What is signified is the enduring strength with which the Lord has endued his human body. "He has set me", he says, "like a solid block of stone." Elsewhere, too, the prophet says, "the stone which the builders rejected has become the cornerstone", adding, "this is the great and wonderful day which the Lord has made."'

Psalm 118.22
'The stone which the builders rejected has become the head of the corner.'

SELECT BIBLIOGRAPHY
Snodgrass (1989: 30–31).

Logion 67

Jesus said, 'Whoever knows everything, but needs (to know) himself, is in need of everything.'

NHC II 2.45.19–20

ΠΕΧΕ ΙC ΧΕ ΠΕΤCΟΟΥΝ ΜΠΤΗΡϤ ΕϤⲢ ϬⲢⲰϨ ΟΥΑΑϤⲢ ϬⲢⲰϨ
ΜΠΜΑ ΤΗⲢϤ

ATTRIBUTION
Accretion.

INTERPRETATIVE COMMENT
The language characteristic of the accretions is present, particularly the emphasis on the redemptive nature of 'knowledge', **COOYN**. Further, the Hermetic theme that knowing the self is superior to all other forms of knowledge is being expressed here as G. Quispel has indicated in his work. Accrual can be dated to the late first century, 80–120 CE.

SOURCE DISCUSSION
G. Quispel traces this saying to a Hermetic anthology.

LITERATURE PARALLELS

Thomas the Contender *138.16–18*
    'For he who has not known himself has not known anything, but he who has known himself has at the same time already achieved knowledge about the depth of everything.'

Definitions of Hermes Trismegistos
    'Whoever knows himself, knows everything.'

Cf. Matthew 16.26; Mark 8.36; Luke 9.25; *2 Clement* 6.2

SELECT BIBLIOGRAPHY
Quispel (1981: 265; 1989: 188–90).

Logion 68.1

Jesus said, 'Blessed are you when you are hated and persecuted.'

NHC II 2.45.21–23

¹ΠΕΧΕ ΙC ΧΕ ΝΤⲰΤΝ ϨΜΜΑΚΑⲢΙΟC ϨΟΤΑ(Ν) ΕΥϢΑΝΜΕCΤΕ
ΤΗΥΤΝ ΝCΕⲢⲆΙⲰΚΕ ΜΜⲰΤΝ

ATTRIBUTION
Kernel saying.

INTERPRETATIVE COMMENT

This Kernel saying occurs in the fourth speech which provides a detailed description of the few people whom Jesus will find worthy to bring into the Kingdom. In this case, he suggests that those who are hated and persecuted are the worthy ones. It may be that the original hermeneutic aligned with that preserved in the *Pseudo-Clementine Homilies* (12.29): if the person maintains his or her goodness in face of persecution and suffering at the hands of unbelievers, eternal life will be the reward.

The presence of this saying may suggest that the early community was experiencing some form of actual persecution, although it is unclear the extent or context. See L. 68.2 and 69.1 for further discussion.

SOURCE DISCUSSION

R. Grant and D.N. Freedman, and B. Gärtner understand L. 68 to be dependent upon Luke 5.22 and Matthew 5.11 although neither offer any explanation. W. Schrage sees L. 68.1 as dependent on Matthew and Luke, pointing out these parallels: μακάριοι...ὅταν, διώκω (Matthew) and μισέω (Luke). C. Tuckett ascribes διώκω to the Matthean hand and so argues for dependency on Matthew, but one wonders how he explains *Thomas'* reference to 'hate' which does not occur in Matthew but only Luke.

J. Sieber argues that neither of the verbs can be assigned to the editorial hands of Matthew or Luke and the lack of true redactional elements like ἕνεκεν favours the opposite conclusion. H. Koester finds this logion to preserve a form of this saying more original than Quelle since it lacks the Lukan phrase, 'and cast out your name as evil on account of the Son of Man'. Rather it retains the reference to persecution which is also shown in the Matthean variant.

Since I am less certain about the text(s) of Quelle that Matthew and Luke used, I find it difficult to positively identify redactional changes on the part of either Matthew or Luke. But, the lack of either 'righteousness' as we find in Matthew, or the phrase 'cast out your name as evil on account of the Son of Man' as we find in Luke is strong evidence against literary dependence in my opinion. Rather, L. 68.1 appears to be a pre-Quelle variant of the saying developed in the field of oral performance.

LITERATURE PARALLELS

Matthew 5.10–11 (Qmatt)
> 'Blessed are those who are persecuted for righteousness sake, for theirs is the kingdom of heaven. Blessed are you when men revile you and persecute you and utter all kinds of evil against you falsely on my account.'

Luke 6.22 (Qluke)
> 'Blessed are you when men hate you, and when they exclude you and revile you, and cast out your name as evil, on account of the Son of Man.'

Matthew 10.22
> 'and you will be hated by all for my name's sake.'

1 Peter 3.14
> 'But even if you do suffer for righteousness' sake, you will be blessed.'

Polycarp, Phil. 2.3
> 'Happy are the poor and they who are persecuted because they are righteous, for theirs is the Kingdom of God.'

Polycarp, Phil. *12.3*
> 'Pray for all God's people. Pray too for our sovereign lords, and for all governors and rulers; for any who ill-use you or dislike you; and for the enemies of the Cross. Thus the fruits of your faith will be plain for all to see, and you will be perfect in him.'

Clement of Alexandria, Strom. *4.6.41*
> 'Blessed are you when men hate you, when they exclude and when they cast out your name as evil on account of the Son of Man.'

Clement of Alexandria, Strom. *4.6.41*
> 'Blessed are those who are persecuted for righteousness, for they will be perfect.'

Clement of Alexandria, Strom. *4.6.41*
> 'Blessed are those who are persecuted for righteousness, for they will be called sons of God.'

Pseudo-Clementine Homilies *11.20*
> 'And therefore the unbelievers, not wishing to hearken to them, make war against them, banishing, persecuting, hating them. But those who suffer these things, pitying those who are ensnared by ignorance, by the teaching of wisdom pray for those who contrive evil against them, having learned that ignorance is the cause of their sin.'

Pseudo-Clementine Homilies *12.29*
> 'This being so, this is the judgement of God, that he who, as by a combat, comes through all misfortune and is found blameless, he is deemed worthy of eternal life; for those who by their own will continue in goodness, are tempted by those who continue in evil by their own will, being persecuted, hated, slandered, plotted against, struck, cheated, accused, tortured, disgraced, – suffering all these things by which it seems reasonable that they should be enraged and stirred up to vengeance.'

AGREEMENTS IN SYRIAN GOSPELS, WESTERN TEXT AND DIATESSARON

Matthew 5.11//Luke 6.22 in S (Matthew)
> hate << revile

Matthew 5.11//Luke 6.22 in g^l (Matthew) S T^A T^L T^{NL} T^T Ps.-Clem. Polyc Did
> you are hated and persecuted + hated

SELECT BIBLIOGRAPHY
Gärtner (1961: 249); Grant with Freedman (1960: 173); Koester (1990: 89); Schrage (1964a: 147); Sieber (1966: 33); Tuckett (1991: 350–51).

Logion 68.2

²'[[A place will be found, where you will not be persecuted]].'

NHC II 2.45.23–24

> ²ⲁⲩⲱ ⲥⲉⲛⲁϨⲉ ⲁⲛ ⲉⲧⲟⲡⲟⲥ Ϩⲙ̄ ⲡⲙⲁ ⲉⲛⲧⲁⲩⲇⲓⲱⲕⲉ ⲙ̄ⲙⲱⲧⲛ̄ Ϩⲣⲁⲓ̈ ⲛ̄Ϩⲏⲧϥ

ATTRIBUTION
Accretion.

TEXT AND TRANSLATION ISSUES

The Coptic literally translates, 'No place will be found there, where you have been persecuted.' Based on Clement's preservation of a variant of this saying ('Blessed are those who are persecuted for my sake, for they will have a place where they will not be persecuted'), the Coptic must be a corruption due to a misplaced negative. So I have read the negative **ⲁⲛ** with the apodosis in agreement with A. Guillaumont, H.-Ch. Puech, G. Quispel, W. Till, Y. 'Abd Al Masih, J. Ménard and E. Haenchen.

INTERPRETATIVE COMMENT

This passage is an interpretative clause, responding to a specific persecution that the community appears to have experienced. It served to give them hope, perhaps bolstering support for a physical relocation of the community. G. Quispel argues that the persecution mentioned here refers to the experience of some Christians in Jerusalem in the 60s who fled east to Pella to avoid the atrocities of the Jewish War. This would suggest a date in the 60s for this accretion. H.M. Schenke, however, thinks it belongs to the context of the Bar Kochba Revolt which would mean a very late date for the accretion, approximately 135 CE.

The date of 135 CE seems to me to be too late because this logion became problematic to the community on an interpretative level. Once the physical persecution ceased, the community turned to reinterpret the logion further by appending L. 69.1. This newest clause moved the discussion of persecution from external sources to the interior person, a hermeneutical shift common to the majority of accretions that accrued between the years 80 and 120 CE. In fact, I tend to place this experience of persecution between 50 and 60 CE, understanding it in connection with the leadership crisis signalled in L. 12. The persecution may have been connected to that mentioned by Paul and recorded in Acts, causing the dispersal of the community to the east. The community chose at that time to retain its connection to the Jerusalem Church and the leadership of James.

SOURCE DISCUSSION

G. Quispel thinks that the source of this saying was a Jewish-Christian Gospel.

LITERATURE PARALLELS

Clement of Alexandria, Strom. *4.6.41*
> 'Blessed are those who are persecuted for my sake, for they will have a place where they will not be persecuted.'

Pseudo-Clementine Recognitions *(Syriac) 1.37*
> 'Those who believed in him (Jesus) were gathered through the wisdom of God for their salvation into a strong place of the land and so kept safe during the war.'

Mani, Unpublished Letter, Böhlig (57, n. 5)
> 'What the Saviour preached: "Blessed are those who are persecuted, for they shall rest in light."'

SELECT BIBLIOGRAPHY

Guillaumont *et al.* (1959: 39); Haenchen (1962: 19–29); Ménard (1975: 68); Quispel (1981: 225–26, 265); Schenke (1994: 9–30).

Logion 69.1

[1]'Blessed are those who have been persecuted in their hearts. They are the people who truly have known the Father.'

NHC II 2.45.24–27

[1]ⲡⲉϫⲉ ⲓ̅ⲥ̅ ϩⲙ̅ⲙⲁⲕⲁⲣⲓⲟⲥ ⲛⲉ ⲛⲁⲉⲓ ⲛ̅ⲧⲁⲩⲇⲓⲱⲕⲉ ⲙ̅ⲙⲟⲟⲩ ϩⲣⲁⲓ̈ ϩⲙ̅
ⲡⲟⲩϩⲏⲧ ⲛⲉⲧⲙ̅ⲙⲁⲩ ⲛⲉⲛⲧⲁϩⲥⲟⲩⲱⲛ ⲡⲉⲓⲱⲧ ϩⲛ̅ ⲟⲩⲙⲉ

ATTRIBUTION
Accretion.

TEXT AND TRANSLATION ISSUES
'Hearts' literally reads 'heart'.

INTERPRETATIVE COMMENT
This saying contains language characteristic of the accretions, particularly the theme that 'knowledge', ⲥⲟⲩⲱⲛ, of the Father is redemptive. This accretion dates to the late first century (60–100 CE), providing the Gospel with a new hermeneutic by which to understand Jesus' old Kernel saying about persecution. Persecution has become an internal experience rather than an external one, suggesting that any persecutions experienced by the community had tapered off by this time. Thus the need for the new hermeneutic.

This accretion has remarkable similarities with Alexandrian traditions as preserved by Clement. 'Persecution within the heart' was probably understood to be the fight of the soul against the pleasures, passions and desires, the true enemy. Once these were overcome, knowledge of the Father was possible.

SOURCE DISCUSSION
W. Schrage understands this saying to demonstrate that *Thomas* knew Matthew since Bultmann had shown Matthew 5.10 to be a Matthean construction. J. Sieber, however, notes that the only parallel between L. 69.1 and Matthew 5.10 are the words 'blessed' and 'persecuted'. Since these same two words appear in L. 68, their derivation from Matthew is questionable. Furthermore, the phrase 'in their heart' is not parallel to Matthew 5.8, 'in heart'. More importantly for Sieber is the absence of a truly Matthean editorial trait, 'for the sake of righteousness', which is in Matthew 5.10 but not L. 69.1

In my opinion, this accretion was built from L. 68.1 as a reinterpretation. This new hermeneutic shifted the persecution from an external experience to an internal one, happening in the heart of each believer.

LITERATURE PARALLELS

Clement of Alexandria, Who is the Rich Man? *25*
> 'There is a persecution which arises from without, from men assailing the faithful, either out of hatred, or envy, or avarice, or through diabolic agency. But the most painful persecution is internal persecution, which proceeds from each man's own soul being vexed by impious lusts, and diverse pleasures, and base hopes, and destructive dreams…
> More grievous and painful is this persecution, which arises from within, which is ever with a man, and which the persecuted cannot escape, for he carries the enemy about everywhere in himself.'

SELECT BIBLIOGRAPHY
Schrage (1964a: 149–51); Sieber (1966: 34–35).

Logion 69.2

[2]'Blessed are those who are hungry, for whosoever desires (it), his belly will be filled.'

NHC II 2.45.27–29

[2]ϩⲙⲙⲁⲕⲁⲣⲓⲟⲥ ⲛⲉⲧϩⲕⲁⲉⲓⲧ ϣⲓⲛⲁ ⲉⲩⲛⲁⲧⲥⲓⲟ ⲛⲑ̄ⲏ ⲙⲡⲉⲧⲟⲩⲱϣ

ATTRIBUTION
Kernel saying.

INTERPRETATIVE COMMENT
This Kernel saying continues to elaborate the type of person worthy to enter the Kingdom. In this case, it is the hungry, like the poor, who Jesus blesses.

SOURCE DISCUSSION
W. Schrage sees L. 69.2 as dependent upon Luke 6.21 and Matthew 5.6. J. Sieber does not agree with Schrage that the parallels represent editorial activity. He points out several missing elements that he does consider redactional: 'thirsting after righteousness' (Matthew), αὐτοί (Matthew), and νῦν (Luke). He notes that Matthew and Luke use ὅτι while L. 69.2 ἵνα. Since both can translate the Aramaic ⲗ, *Thomas* may have preserved a 'genuine translational variant'. This may be evidence for an Aramaic substratum for the Kernel Gospel.

LITERATURE PARALLELS

Matthew 5.6 (Qmatt)
   'Blessed are those who hunger and thirst for righteousness, for they will be filled.'

Luke 6.21 (Qluke)
   'Blessed are you who are hungry now, for you will be filled.'

Pseudo-Clementine Recognitions *1.61*
   'He promised that those who maintain righteousness shall be satisfied with meat and drink.'

Pseudo-Clementine Recognitions *2.28*
   'He promised also that the hungry and the thirsty should be satisfied with the eternal blessings of righteousness, in order that they might bear poverty patiently, and not be led by it to undertake any unrighteous work.'

Mani, Unpublished Letter
   'Blessed are those who hunger and thirst, for they shall be satisfied.'

Abu Nu'aym al-Isbahani, Hilyat al-Awliya' *2.370*
   'Leave yourselves to hunger and thirst, go naked and exhaust yourselves, that your hearts might know God Almighty.'

SELECT BIBLIOGRAPHY
Schrage (1964a: 149–51); Sieber (1966: 35–36).

Logion 70.1–2

[1]Jesus said, 'When you acquire within you that certain thing, what is within you will save you. [2]If you do not have it within you, what you do not have within you will kill you.'

NHC II 2.45.29–33

ⲡⲉⲝⲉ ⲓ̅ⲥ̅ ϩⲟⲧⲁⲛ ⲉⲧⲉⲧⲛ̅ϣⲁⲝⲡⲉ ⲡⲏ ϩⲛ̅ ⲑⲩⲧⲛ̅ ⲡⲁⲓ ⲉⲧⲉⲩⲛ̅ⲧⲏⲧⲛ̅ϥ̅
ϥⲛⲁⲧⲟⲩⲝⲉ ⲑⲩⲧⲛ̅ ⲉϣⲱⲡⲉ ⲙⲛ̅ⲧⲏⲧⲛ̅ ⲡⲏ ϩⲛ̅ |ⲑⲩⲧ|ⲛ̅ ⲡⲁⲉⲓ
ⲉⲧⲉⲙⲛ̅ⲧⲏⲧⲛ̅ϥ̅ ϩⲛ̅ ⲑⲏⲛⲉ ϥ|ⲛⲁⲙ|ⲟⲩⲧ ⲑⲏⲛⲉ

ATTRIBUTION
Accretion.

INTERPRETATIVE COMMENT
Coherence to a theme peculiar to the accretions is seen in this saying, particularly the admiration for the divine Self and its redemptive nature. This logion accrued in the Gospel between 60 and 100 CE when the Thomasine Christians were developing their mystical teachings.

This saying speaks to the early Christian belief that the soul alone cannot achieve immortality for itself. Rather, the Christian must possess the Holy Spirit (here indicated by the demonstrative ⲡⲏ), the 'great wealth' within (L. 29) which aids the soul in its process of transformation. The two unite, strengthening the soul and making it possible for the soul to overcome the temptations of the body. The soul devoid of the spirit will succumb to the desires of the body and will not be able to be transformed.

SOURCE DISCUSSION
G. Quispel attributes this logion to the *Gospel of the Egyptians* or some other encratite source.

LITERATURE PARALLELS

Pseudo-Macarius, Hom. *18.2*
> 'For he who is indigent and poor and a beggar in the world cannot acquire anything. His destitution restrains him. But he who possesses the treasure, as I said, easily acquires whatever possessions he wishes without much effort. The soul that is naked and stripped of the fellowship of the Spirit and lives under the terrible poverty of sin is unable, even if it wished to do so, to produce the fruit of the Spirit of righteousness in truth, unless it becomes a participator of the Spirit.'

'Abdallah ibn Qutayba, 'Uyun *2.370*
> 'A person can bring forth only what is within him.'

SELECT BIBLIOGRAPHY
Quispel (1981: 265).

Logion 71

Jesus said, 'I will destroy [this] temple, and no one will build it [...]'

NHC II 2.45.34–35

ⲡⲉⲝⲉ ⲓ̅ⲥ̅ ⲝⲉ †ⲛⲁϣⲟⲣ|ϣⲣ̅ ⲙ̅ⲡⲉⲉ|.ⲓⲏⲉⲓ ⲁⲩⲱ ⲙ̅ⲛ̅ ⲗⲁⲁⲩ ⲛⲁϣⲕⲟⲧϥ|...|

ATTRIBUTION
Kernel saying.

TEXT AND TRANSLATION ISSUES
The saying is fragmentary, occurring in the last two lines of manuscript p. 45 where the bottom right hand corner is torn. In addition, the top left corner of p. 46 is broken. This makes the reconstruction of the last portion of saying 71 and the last portion of 72 very difficult. It looks like L. 72 began with the first letter and word on the top of p. 46, ⲡⲉⲝⲉ. So this means that the 8 to 9 letters following ⲛⲁϣⲕⲟⲧϥ on the bottom of p. 45 must belong to L. 71.

It is impossible to know exactly how the sentence ended. This makes any interpretation of the saying tentative at best. Any reconstruction favouring 6 letters has to be incorrect since my observation has demonstrated that the line had to contain 8 to 9 letters to the written edge. Thus, the favoured reconstruction, 'again' (ⲛ̅ⲕⲉⲥⲟⲡ), as seen most recently in Bethge's edition, cannot be accurate. A. Guillaumont long ago suggested [ⲁⲛ ⲛⲕⲉⲥⲟ|ⲡ] which makes use of the available space. But I have not been able to observe myself the final ⲡ which he appears to have noticed. There is not enough letter space for any reconstruction containing the words 'three days' (ϣⲟⲙⲛ̅ⲧ ⲛ̅ϩⲟⲟⲩ).

INTERPRETATIVE COMMENT
G. Riley has made an extensive interpretation of L. 71 based on his theory that the Thomasine community has changed the word 'temple' to 'house' in order to indicate the human body as the house of the soul. He further concludes that the saying must be an early witness to 'a Christianity which did not accept physical resurrection' in contradiction to this saying's use by the Johannine community. This thesis develops an old opinion held by B. Gärtner and L. Gaston that the author or editor of the Gospel intends this logion to be a polemic against the concept of bodily resurrection. Riley feels that the different views of Jesus' body echoed in L. 71 and John 2.19–22 indicate that the communities who produced these Gospels were debating, each using the traditional saying in opposing ways as they responded to each other.

But does this saying refer to the body of Jesus? Perhaps metaphorically if read with knowledge of the Johannine hermeneutic. Although I agree with Riley that the Thomasine and Johannine traditions had some connection, I do not see in this saying a reference denying physical resurrection or supporting spiritual resurrection. Riley's interpretation is problematic because it assumes that the author of the Gospel knew the canonical, or at least the Johannine interpretation of this saying and was responding to it. Does this mean that the Gospel has literary connections with the canonical Gospels? The answer is unclear in Riley's presentation.

Several other scholars including E. Haenchen, R. Kasser, J. Leipoldt, J.-É. Ménard, M. Fieger, R. Kuntzmann and R. Valantasis have suggested that 'house' here refers to some aspect of the material world. Most of these interpretations have been made under the assumption that the Gospel is a Gnostic text containing metaphorical allusions to Gnostic truths.

The saying can be read quite literally to refer to the Jewish temple, belonging to a host of variants preserved in other contexts with the same reference point, a fact that R. McL. Wilson, J.D. Crossan and G. Quispel have argued previously. Since we have several variants of this saying in the canonical Gospels and Acts, it is most probable in my opinion that this logion is also about the Temple in Jerusalem. The Coptic ϨⲈⲒ is associated in Greek with σκηνή (temple or house), οἶκος (temple or house of god), οἴκημα (temple, chamber, or chapel), μυχός (the innermost room), and δίαιτα (room) (Crum 66a). Jesus talks about destroying the Jerusalem Temple in all the variants, but only in L. 71 does he state that the Temple will be destroyed unconditionally.

The logion appears to me to be a straightforward reference in the Kernel to the fate of the Temple at the End of time. I. Dunderberg's statement that 'no one will rebuild it' is anti-eschatological and explicable only in a post-Jewish War context does not take into consideration the rich Jewish expectations about the Temple in the New World, one of which was that it would not be rebuilt (cf. *Test. Moses* 5–10; Rev. 21.22).

But we must be very careful here, since we do not know how the saying concluded. A reference to the rebuilding of the Temple may have been part of the logion after all. I see no reason, however, to think that a 'prophetic' saying of this type could not have originated with Jesus himself, given the political and religious climate of the time and the fate of the Temple during turbulent periods. The 'authenticity' of the saying bears out in my mind since Matthew, Mark and John laboured to revise it in light of Jesus' death, suggesting that the saying referred to Jesus' body, its entombment in the earth for three days, and its resurrection on the third day, not the actual destruction of the Temple. The reference to rebuilding the Temple in three days smacks of Christian theological revision of a saying that either embarrassed the Christians or was unpopular. Since the Temple did indeed fall, the account that Jesus predicted its fall certainly would not have been embarrassing, but it very well could have been unpopular. Although the Jews (*Test. Moses* 5–10) and Christians (Rev. 21.22) toyed with the possibility that the Eschaton might bring the destruction of the Temple with no hope of restoration, this idea was not the favoured expectation. It remains even within contemporary apocalyptic hopes of Jews and Christians that the destroyed Temple will be rebuilt! So it may be that *Thomas* is preserving the oldest, harshest (and least popular) remembrance of this saying, that the Temple would be destroyed unconditionally. The antiquity of this tradition may have been known to Luke as well, who refers to the tradition twice but does not quote the saying itself (Luke 21.5–6; Acts 6.14).

It is certainly possible that this saying came to be understood by the later community to prove that the earthly Temple is unnecessary. Instead God was known to be present in the heavenly Temple where the mystic now must journey in order to worship him.

SOURCE DISCUSSION
G. Quispel attributes this saying to a Jewish Christian Gospel.

LITERATURE PARALLELS

Mark 14.58
> 'I will destroy this temple that is made with hands, and in three days I will build another, not made with hands.'

Matthew 26.61

> 'I will destroy this temple that is made with hands, and in three days I will build another, not made with hands.'

Mark 15.29

> 'You who would destroy the temple and build it in three days...'

Matthew 27.40

> 'You who would destroy the temple and build it in three days...'

John 2.19

> 'Destroy this temple, and in three days I will raise it up.'

Acts 6.14

> '"for we have heard him say that this Jesus of Nazareth will destroy this place and will change the customs that Moses handed on to us"'.

Ahmad ibn Hanbal, al-Zuhd, p. 146 (no. 486)

> 'Truly I say to you, God will not leave one stone of this mosque upon another but will destroy it utterly because of the sins of its people. God does nothing with gold, silver, or these stones. More dear to God than all these are the pure in heart. Through them, God builds up the earth, or else destroys it if these hearts are other than pure.'

Cf Luke 21.5–6.

SELECT BIBLIOGRAPHY

Bethge (1997: 537); Crossan (1983: 307–12); Dunderberg (1998a: 56–58); Fieger (1991: 202–203); Gärtner (1961: 158, 172–74); Gaston (1970: 152); Guillaumont *et al.* (1959: 41); Haenchen (1961: 64 and 66); Kasser (1961: 95); Kuntzmann (1993: 28–29); Leipoldt (1967: 69); Ménard (1975: 172–73); Quispel (1981: 265; 1988: 197–99); Riley (1995a: 147–56); Valantasis (1997: 150); Wilson (1960a: 114–15).

Logion 72.1–3

[1]A man said to him, 'Tell my brothers that they must share with me my father's possessions.'

[2]He said to him, 'Mister, who has made me an executor?'

[3]He turned to his disciples and said to them, 'Surely I am not an executor, am I?'

NHC II 2.46.1–6

[1]|ⲡⲉ|ϫⲉ ⲟ|ⲩⲣⲱⲙⲉ| ⲛ|ⲁ|ϥ ϫⲉ ϫⲟⲟⲥ ⲛ̄ⲛⲁⲥⲛⲏⲩ ϣⲓⲛⲁ ⲉⲩⲛ|ⲁⲡ|ⲱϣⲉ ⲛ̄ⲛ̄ϩⲛⲁⲁⲩ ⲙ̄ⲡⲁⲉⲓⲱⲧ ⲛ̄ⲙⲙⲁⲉⲓ
[2]ⲡⲉϫⲁϥ ⲛⲁϥ ϫⲉ ⲱ ⲡⲣⲱⲙⲉ ⲛⲓⲙ ⲡⲉ ⲛ̄ⲧⲁϩⲁⲁⲧ ⲛ̄ⲣⲉϥⲡⲱϣⲉ
[3]ⲁϥⲕⲟⲧϥ̄ ⲁⲛⲉϥⲙⲁⲑⲏⲧⲏⲥ ⲡⲉϫⲁϥ ⲛⲁⲩ ϫⲉ ⲙⲏ ⲉⲉⲓϣⲟⲟⲡ ⲛ̄ⲣⲉϥⲡⲱϣⲉ

ATTRIBUTION
Kernel saying.

TEXT AND TRANSLATION ISSUES

It is possible that the Hebrew חלק or Aramaic פלג, meaning 'to divide', is behind the expression ⲣⲉϥⲡⲱϣⲉ, 'divider', which is an odd expression in Coptic, and also μεριστα which is present in Luke. In fact, the Hebrew expression is used in the sense of dividing inheritance in the Hebrew Bible (Prov. 17.2; Josh. 14.5; 18.2). According to J. Lightfoot, in the Talmudic traditions the μερισται, or 'dividers', were arbitrators who were chosen to oversee the equality of division of property in inheritance settlements. So I have rendered ⲣⲉϥⲡⲱϣⲉ, 'executor', to make clear the contextual meaning of this Coptic phrase. The man is asking Jesus to serve as an executor of his father's estate, to divide and distribute his father's possessions fairly among his sons.

INTERPRETATIVE COMMENT

In the Mishnaic period, חלק came also to mean 'to dissent', and referred to schismatics. This has prompted D. Gershenson and G. Quispel to suggest that the meaning of the Thomasine story is a pun on חלק, that Jesus is not a schismatic. I see no reason to turn to this interpretation since the story very clearly is about a man who feels that his brothers have cheated him out of his father's estate and wishes Jesus to intervene in the role of an executor.

In the Kernel, it appears to have functioned rhetorically in the Fourth Speech, 'The Selection of the Worthy Few', as an example from the opposite. The worthy disciple was not supposed to be like the foolish man who came to Jesus concerned about his inheritance. Instead, if he is to be worthy of Jesus' message, he is supposed to devote himself exclusively to Jesus' mission.

In the complete Gospel, the story functioned similarly as an example from the opposite. With the accrual of L. 75, however, the foolish man's concern for worldly possessions and family would have been underscored since the encratic hermeneutic would have dominated this cluster of sayings. Now Jesus would be understood as an advocate for leaving one's family and becoming a worthy celibate within the Thomasine community, a disciple devoted exclusively to Jesus.

SOURCE DISCUSSION

W. Schrage sees evidence for dependence on Luke 12.13–14 and Gnostic redaction on the part of *Thomas*. This argument is based on the presence of so-called secondary elements in L. 72, such as the phrase 'my father's possessions' which he believes *Thomas* substituted for Luke's 'the family inheritance'. H. von Schürmann argues also for Lukan dependence although he is of the opinion that this pericope belongs to Lukan Quelle. He sees redactional traits present in L. 72.1–3. But J. Sieber points out that L. 72 is lacking what he calls the only true Lukan editorial trait, ἐκ τοῦ ὄχλου. So dependence cannot be proven according to Sieber.

G. Quispel argues for an early Jewish-Christian source largely based on the close parallel found in the Muslim source ʿAbd al-Gabbar. T. Baarda concludes that the Thomasine version represents secondary Gnostic development and is probably dependent on Luke because L. 72.2 uses the unusual vocative ἄνθρωπε (ⲱ ⲡⲣⲱⲙⲉ) which occurs only in Luke (12.14; 5.20; 22.58; 22.60). One of the problems with this reasoning is that it makes ʿAbd al-Gabbar's text, which also omits 'judge or', difficult to explain since it would have had to have been abbreviated independently in Muslim tradition. So Baarda attributes the agreement with *Thomas* as 'odd coincidence', but the best alternative to G. Quispel's Jewish-Christian source hypothesis in his opinion.

K. Snodgrass aligns the evidence differently, suggesting Lukan dependence. However, he is hesitant to make a certain statement in this regard because the pericope comes from Luke's special material. So, he says, it is just as likely that the vocative expression was part of Luke's special source which *Thomas'* Gospel may also have known.

In my opinion, we are witnessing here pre-Synoptic variants that developed in the field of oral performance and eventually became incorporated in our respective texts. This is the solution that explains not only the similarity between Luke and L. 72, but also the difference. It also offers a better explanation for the Muslim remembrance of this story than Baarda's 'odd coincidence'. It is highly likely that the version we find in L. 72 was known in the East independent of Luke's Greek version.

LITERATURE PARALLELS

Luke 12.13–14 (L or Qluke)
   [13]'Someone in the crowd said to him, "Teacher, tell my brother to divide the family inheritance with me." [14]But he said to him, "Friend, who set me to be a judge or arbitrator over you?"'

'Abd al-Gabbar, Tathbit Dala'il Nubuwwat Sayyidina Muhammad, *folia 53a*
   'A man said to him, "Master, let my brother share (with me) my father's wealth." He said, "Who set me over you as divider?"'

Cf. *b. Shabbat* 116b

AGREEMENTS IN SYRIAN GOSPELS, WESTERN TEXT AND DIATESSARON

Luke 12.13–14 in T^V
   – teacher
Luke 12.13–14 in T^{PEP}
   + my father's
Luke 12.13–14 in Sa
   – judge

SELECT BIBLIOGRAPHY
Baarda (1975); Gershenson and Quispel (1958); Lightfoot (1997 reprint: 132); Quispel (1975d: 146–58); Schrage (1964a: 151–52); Schürmann (1963: 243–44); Sieber (1966: 216); Snodgrass (1989: 35).

Logion 73

Jesus said, 'Indeed the harvest is plentiful but the workers are few! So ask the Lord to send out workers to the harvest.'

NHC II 2.46.6–9

ⲡⲉⲝⲉ ⲓ̅ⲥ̅ ⲝⲉ ⲡⲱⲅⲥ ⲙⲉⲛ ⲛⲁϣⲱϥ ⲛ̅ⲉⲣⲅⲁⲧⲏⲥ ⲇⲉ ⲥⲟⲃⲕ ⲥⲟⲡⲥ̅ ⲇⲉ
ⲙ̅ⲡⲝⲟⲉⲓⲥ ϣⲓⲛⲁ ⲉϥⲛⲁⲛⲉⲝ ⲉⲣⲅⲁⲧⲏⲥ ⲉⲃⲟⲗ ⲉⲡⲱⲅ̅ⲥ̅

ATTRIBUTION
Kernel saying.

INTERPRETATIVE COMMENT

L. 73 in the Kernel was part of the Fourth Speech, 'The Selection of the Worthy Few'. It functioned rhetorically as an analogy comparing the worthy disciple to the few hardworking field hands bringing in a large harvest. In the complete Gospel, L. 73 would have taken on an encratic hermeneutic with the accrual of L. 75. The cluster would have pointed toward the celibate who is among the few labourers working for God.

SOURCE DISCUSSION

W. Schrage notes Coptic affinities between L. 73, Matthew 9.37 and Luke 10.2. But, since L. 73 agrees very closely to the Synoptic version and no redactionary elements can be identified, it is impossible, according to J. Sieber, to sustain an argument for dependence at the level of the Greek *Vorlage* by comparing the Coptic Gospel variants with L. 73 as Schrage attempts. Sieber's position appears to me to be the most tenable based on the evidence, and the fact that aphorisms preserve the verbal structure much more faithfully than other forms of speech in oral transmission.

LITERATURE PARALLELS

Matthew 9.37–38 (Qmatt)
> '[37]Then he said to his disciples, "The harvest is plentiful, but the labourers are few. [38]Therefore ask the Lord of the harvest to send out labourers into his harvest."'

Luke 10.2 (Qluke)
> 'He said to them, "The harvest is plentiful, but the labourers are few. Therefore ask the Lord of the harvest to send out labourers into his harvest."'

AGREEMENTS IN SYRIAN GOSPELS, WESTERN TEXT AND DIATESSARON

Luke 10.2 in D S Pal
> – therefore

Matthew 9.37–38//Luke 10.2 in 579 pc
> ἵνα<<ὁπώς

SELECT BIBLIOGRAPHY

Schrage (1964a: 153–54); Sieber (1966: 208–209).

Logion 74

He said, 'Lord, many people are around the [[well]], but no one is in the [[well]].'

NHC II 2.46.9–11

> ΠΕΧΑϤ ΧΕ ΠΧΟΕΙС ΟΥⲚ ϨⲀϨ ⲘⲠΚⲰΤΕ ⲚΤ‖(ⲱ)‖ⲰΤΕ ⲘⲚ ⲀⲀⲀⲨ
> ⲀⲈ ϨⲚ ΤⲰ(ⲱ)‖Τ‖Ⲉ

ATTRIBUTION

Kernel saying.

TEXT AND TRANSLATION ISSUES
Based on Origen's preservation of this saying from a 'Heavenly Dialogue', I agree with A. Guillaumont's emendations. In line 10, TXⲱTE has been emended to TⲩⲱTE and, in line 11, TⲩⲱNE has been emended to TⲩⲱTE. R. Kasser has suggested that XⲱTE is a dialectic peculiarity of ⲩⲱTE.

Note that ⲗⲁⲁⲩ might also be translated 'nothing', and this is the usual translation in other editions of the Gospel. However, I have rendered this expression 'no one' since this parallels Origen's rendering of the same saying. It also makes historical contextual sense, since there existed professionals in the ancient world whose job it was to fetch out water vessels and anything else that had fallen or been thrown into wells, according to the research of H.M. Jackson.

INTERPRETATIVE COMMENT
The meaning of this logion parallels the surrounding logia in the Fourth Speech about the worthy few who are selected by Jesus. The idea repeated in this cluster of logia, both in the Kernel speech and the full Gospel, is that there are many people who flirt with religious devotion, but only a few who act accordingly. In the case of L. 74, it assumes, as H.M. Jackson demonstrates from careful scrutiny of Hellenistic lore, that something has fallen into the well. There are many people who stand around watching, none of whom are willing to take the risk of descending into the well to rescue what has fallen in.

In the complete Gospel, after the accrual of L. 75, an encratic tenor would have resounded. L. 74 would have pointed to the difficulty of commitment to a life of celibacy and the very few who are able to take up the challenge.

SOURCE DISCUSSION
G. Quispel attributes the source of this saying to an encratic Gospel.

LITERATURE PARALLELS

Origen, Contra Celsum *8.15.16*
    'How is it that there are many people around the well, but no one in it?'

SELECT BIBLIOGRAPHY
Guillaumont *et al.* (1959: 4); Jackson (1992); Kasser (1961: 97 n. 2); Quispel (1981: 265).

Logion 75

Jesus said, 'Many people are standing at the door, but those who are celibate are the people who will enter the bridal chamber.'

NHC II 2.46.11–13

ⲠⲈⲬⲈ ⲒⲤ ⲞⲨⲚ ⳨Ⲁ⳨ Ⲁ⳨ⲈⲢⲀⲦⲞⲨ ⳨ⲒⲢⲘ ⲠⲢⲞ Ⲁⲗⲗⲁ ⲘⲘⲞⲚⲀⲬⲞⲤ
ⲚⲈⲦⲚⲀⲂⲱⲔ Ⲉ⳨ⲞⲨⲚ ⲈⲠⲘⲀ ⲚⲩⲈⲗⲈⲈⲦ

ATTRIBUTION
Accretion.

TEXT AND TRANSLATION ISSUES
For discussion of ΜΟΝ&ΧΟC, see L. 16.4.

INTERPRETATIVE COMMENT
Development of characteristic accretive vocabulary is noted in this saying, particularly its use of the phrase ΜΟΝ&ΧΟC, representing the unmarried single state. This state was the ideal for the encratite Christians, suggesting that this saying accrued in the Gospel sometime in the late first century (80–120 CE), once the constituency of the community had become dominantly encratic.

Noteworthy is the parallel in the *Liber Graduum* 5.13.12, especially when it is realized that the 'perfect' is equivalent to the *monachos* in 132.19. In the *Acts of Thomas*, true marriage is understood to be a union with Jesus, so he is called the 'True Husband', and it is in his bridal chamber that the believer is supposed to enter (chs 14; 98; 124; 129). The requirement for marriage to Jesus is that the believer is celibate (chs 12–16). These encratic traditions about the bridal chamber are to be distinguished from the Valentinian which understood the bridal chamber to be an eschatological event where the pneumatic Image marries his or her angelic counterpart and participates in marital relations just as the Aeons in the Pleroma, as I have documented and explained in a set of articles published in *Vigiliae Christianae*.

L. 75 is in line with encratic traditions about the bridal chamber. It was probably understood by the late Thomasine community to be a literal metaphor. Because of their celibacy, the members of the community would be admitted to God's bridal chamber, his Kingdom. This saying may, in fact, imply what the *Acts of Thomas* make explicit, that the believers thought that giving up a human spouse prepared them to unite with Jesus in spiritual matrimony.

SOURCE DISCUSSION
G. Quispel attributes this saying to the hand of the author of the Gospel while H. von Schürmann thinks that it is dependent upon Luke 13.25. But this Lukan verse, in my opinion, is not in any way a parallel of L. 75.

LITERATURE PARALLELS

Matthew 25.10
> 'And while they went to buy it, the bridegroom came, and those who were ready went with him into the wedding banquet. And the door was shut.'

Dialogue of the Saviour *50*
> 'When you rid yourselves of jealousy, then you will clothe yourselves in light and enter the bridal chamber.'

Acts of Thomas *12*
> 'As soon as you preserve yourselves from this filthy intercourse, you become pure temples... You shall be numbered with those who enter into the bridal chamber.'

Liber Graduum *19.36*
> 'Indeed this path of great commandments leads to the house of the Lord and enters into his bridal chamber.'

Liber Graduum *5.13.12*
> The way of the perfect 'leads to the house of the Lord and to his bridal chamber he enters in'.

Pseudo-Macarius, Hom. *4.6*

> 'For behold the five wise virgins, sober and occupying themselves with the host of their nature, receiving oil in the containers of their hearts, which is the gift of the spirit from above, are able to enter with the bridegroom into the heavenly bridal chamber.'

Pseudo-Macarius, Great Letter, *Maloney (1992: 268)*

> '…who, because they did not bring with them the spiritual oil in the containers of their hearts, which is the working of the previously mentioned virtues through the spirit, are called fools and are excluded from the spiritual bridal chamber of the kingdom'.

Gregory of Nyssa, De instituto Christiano *83.9–12*

> 'Wherefore, also scripture called them foolish, their virtue having been quenched before the bridegroom came, and because of this he shut out the wretched ones from the heavenly bridal chamber.'

SELECT BIBLIOGRAPHY

DeConick (2001b; 2003); Quispel (1981: 265); Schürmann (1963: 245–46).

Logion 76.1–2

[1]Jesus said, 'The Kingdom of the Father is like a merchant who had some merchandise. He found a pearl. [2]That merchant was wise. He sold the merchandise. Then he purchased for himself this single pearl.'

NHC II 2.46.13–19

[1]ⲡⲉⲝⲉ ⲓ̅ⲥ̅ ⲝⲉ ⲧⲙⲛ̅ⲧⲉⲣⲟ ⲙ̅ⲡⲉⲓⲱⲧ ⲉⲥⲧⲛ̅ⲧⲱⲛ ⲁ ⲩⲣⲱⲙⲉ ⲛ̅ⲉϣⲱⲱⲧ ⲉⲩⲛ̅ⲧⲁϥ ⲙ̅ⲙⲁⲩ ⲛ̅ⲟⲩⲫⲟⲣⲧⲓⲟⲛ ⲉⲁϥϩⲉ ⲁⲩⲙⲁⲣⲅⲁⲣⲓⲧⲏⲥ [2]ⲡⲉϣⲱⲧ ⲉⲧⲙ̅ⲙⲁⲩ ⲟⲩⲥⲁⲃⲉ ⲡⲉ ⲁϥϯ ⲡⲉⲫⲟⲣⲧⲓⲟⲛ ⲉⲃⲟⲗ ⲁϥⲧⲟⲟⲩ ⲛⲁϥ ⲙ̅ⲡⲓⲙⲁⲣⲅⲁⲣⲓⲧⲏⲥ ⲟⲩⲱⲧ

ATTRIBUTION

Kernel saying.

TEXT AND TRANSLATION ISSUES

A. Guillaumont has suggested that 'he purchased *for himself* this single pearl', is a Semitism such as found in Ruth 4.8. He also finds it in the Syriac version of Matthew 13.46 but not the Peshitta.

INTERPRETATIVE COMMENT

In the Kernel, L. 76.1–2 is a parable set within the rhetorical speech about Jesus' selection of a few disciples from the many. Particularly, Jesus is describing in this cluster the type of person he chooses to be his disciple. This parable functions as an analogy for the listener. The type of person Jesus selects is comparable to the shrewd merchant who sold everything that he had for a single pearl. The parable reverberates the theme that has been developing in this cluster that exclusive commitment to Jesus is necessary to be his disciple. It further develops the theme by emphasizing the unprecedented value of Jesus' message which he wishes to give to the hearer. This rhetorical interpretation of L. 72 developed in the Kernel is very similar to the interpretation provided in the *Pseudo-Clementine Recognitions* 3.62.2

and provides either an example of a shared common hermeneutical tradition or the possibility that some form of the Kernel was a source for the *Recognitions.*

Within the complete Gospel, this parable is sandwiched between L. 75, a call to celibacy, and L. 77, a christological statement about Jesus' origin. These accretions serve to reorient the parable so that the merchant who gives up all else for the pearl would have been understood by the listener to be the celibate who has left behind his or her family and possessions in order to devote him- or herself to Jesus, to receive the treasure he has to give. Why? Because Jesus is the light above all things, from whom everything came forth.

SOURCE DISCUSSION

W. Schrage, R. Grant and D.N. Freedman, B. Gärtner, R. Kasser and B. Dehandschutter all are of the opinion that L. 76.1–2 is a Gnostic revision of Matthew 13.45–46. Unless one is willing, however, to argue that this parable is a Matthean construction rather than from Matthew's special source, parallels cannot be used to prove dependence between the documents as J. Sieber correctly notes.

G. Quispel traces the reference to the 'wise' merchant to a Jewish Christian Gospel familiar also to the author of the *Pseudo-Clementine Recognitions* (3.62.2) while H. Koester thinks that L. 109 has contaminated L. 76.1–2 – the merchant finds the pearl by accident like the man who finds the treasure in the field, so a treasure saying is appended (L. 76.3). Thus Koester thinks that the Thomasine author is aware of the traditional association of the two parables as is also seen in Matthew's source. But, if this were the case, one wonders why the author would not have simply appended L. 109 itself rather than another saying about treasure.

In my opinion, this parable like the others with Synoptic correspondents, shows characteristics typical of orally transmitted material – similarities in key words like 'merchant' and 'pearl', 'bought' and 'sold', but very few words in common sequences. Details unique to the variants are preserved (*Thomas* – 'wise' merchant, bought 'for himself', sold his 'merchandise'; Matthew – 'fine pearls', 'great value', sold 'all that he had'). Since I see no way to maintain an argument for secondary orality, I think this saying is another example of an early multiform variant independent of the Synoptic tradition.

LITERATURE PARALLELS

Matthew 13.45–46 (M)

[45]'Again, the Kingdom of Heaven is like a merchant in search of fine pearls. [46]On finding one pearl of great value, he went and sold all that he had and bought it.'

Pseudo-Clementine Recognitions 3.62

'Who is he that is earnest toward instruction, and that studiously enquires into every particular, except him who loves his own soul to salvation, and renounces all the affairs of this world, that he may have leisure to attend to the word of God only? Such is he whom alone the True Prophet deems wise, even he who sells all that he has and buys the one true pearl, who understands what is the difference between temporal things and eternal, small and great, humans and God.'

AGREEMENTS IN SYRIAN GOSPELS, WESTERN TEXT AND DIATESSARON

Matthew 13.46 in Ps.-Clem. Rec. T^P T^{NL} T^{EC}
  The one pearl << it

Matthew 13.46 in S C sa
  + for himself

Matthew 13.46 in T^{EC}
  + merchandise

Matthew 13.46 in T^{EC} *and* Ps.-Clem. Rec.
  + wise

SELECT BIBLIOGRAPHY
Dehandschutter (1979); Gärtner (1961: 37–39); Grant with Freedman (1960: 177); Guillaumont (1981: 197); Hunzinger (1960: 219–20); Kasser (1961: 98–99); Koester (1990: 103–104); Quispel (1958: 191; 1981: 265); Schippers (1959); Schrage (1964a: 155–59); Sieber (1966: 183–85).

Logion 76.3

[3]'You too, seek his imperishable and enduring treasure where neither moth draws near to eat nor worm destroys'.

NHC II 2.46.19–22

[3]ⲚⲦⲰⲦⲚ ⲌⲰⲦ ⲐⲨⲦⲚ ϢⲒⲚⲈ ⲚⲤⲀ ⲠⲈϤⲈⲌⲞ ⲈⲘⲀϤⲰⲞⲬⲚ ⲈϤⲘⲎⲚ ⲈⲂⲞⲖ ⲠⲘⲀ ⲈⲘⲀⲢⲈ ⲬⲞⲞⲖⲈⲤ Ⲧ2ⲚⲞ Ⲉ2ⲞⲨⲚ ⲈⲘⲀⲨ ⲈⲞⲨⲰⲚ ⲞⲨⲀⲈ ⲘⲀⲢⲈ ϤϤⲚⲦ ⲀⲔⲞ

ATTRIBUTION
Kernel saying.

TEXT AND TRANSLATION ISSUES
The scribe originally wrote ⲠⲈϤ2Ⲟ, 'his face', and then corrected this by adding a super-linear Ⲉ. Thus the transcription, ⲠⲈϤⲈ2Ⲟ, 'his treasure'. A. Guillaumont thinks that the scribe then failed to erase ⲉϤ, so the translation 'the treasure' is preferred by some scholars.

INTERPRETATIVE COMMENT
In the Kernel, this saying serves to interpret the Parable of the Pearl. It reinforces the rhetorical point that has been building in this cluster of sayings, that exclusive commitment to Jesus is necessary. L. 76.3 provides the rationale. The person wants to give up everything for Jesus' sake because the treasure he offers is eternal, a treasure that even the grave cannot destroy.

In the complete Gospel, the encratic accretion preceding this saying would have suggested to the listener that he or she had to give up marriage and family in order to commit exclusively to Jesus. But, in return, Jesus would give him or her a treasure that would endure the grave. The succeeding accretion provides further rationale. Why does Jesus have a treasure that will endure beyond the grave? Because he is the light above all things and from him everything came forth.

SOURCE DISCUSSION
R. Grant and W. Schrage argue that L. 76.3 was added to the Parable of the Pearl because of the catchword 'treasure' which appears in Matthew 13.44, the Parable of the Hidden Treasure which precedes the Pearl parable. J. Sieber points out the weakness of this argument.

Since *Thomas* contains the Parable of the Treasure, if it were relying on Matthew, we could expect L. 76.3 to be placed around L. 109, not separated as it is. The separation of the cluster would have to be explained which Sieber thinks is not possible.

R. McL. Wilson suggests that L. 76.3 is the result of free quotation from the author's memory of the Gospels including John 6.27. K. Snodgrass argues that *Thomas* reflects two rare words in Luke 12.33, ἀνέκλειπτος and θησαυρός. The mention of a worm in L. 76.3 is probably from βρῶσις in Matthew as is ἀφανίζειν, he says. Luke supplied διαφθείρειν. As for these Matthean and Lukan agreements which Schrage also points out, Sieber thinks that they cannot be attributed to the editorial hand of either Synoptic author. The only certain editorial trait, βαλλάντια, according to Sieber, is absent form L. 76.3. Moreover, the beginning of L. 76.3 is entirely different from either Matthew or Luke.

I might add that the differences between the Synoptic versions and *Thomas* is striking. *Thomas* does not mention a thief or thieves, but a moth. Nor does L. 76.3 have a parallel to the Lukan verb ἐγγίζειν. It is much more likely that we are seeing here pre-Synoptic variants created in the field of oral performance.

LITERATURE PARALLELS

Matthew 6.19–20 (Qmatt)
[19]'Do not store up for yourselves treasures on earth, where moth and worm consume and where thieves break in and steal. [20]But store up for yourselves treasures in heaven, where neither moth nor rust consumes and where thieves do not break in and steal.'

Luke 12.33 (Qluke)
'Make purses for yourselves that do not wear out, an unfailing treasure in heaven, where no thief comes near and no moth destroys.'

Ahmad ibn Hanbal, al-Zuhd, *p. 95 (no. 313)*
'Jesus said, "Place your treasures in heaven, for the heart of man is where his treasure is."'

AGREEMENTS IN SYRIAN GOSPELS, WESTERN TEXT AND DIATESSARON

Matthew 6.20//Luke 12.33 in Clem
– heaven

Matthew 6.20//Luke 12.33 in S C T^P
there where << where

Matthew 6.19 in C T^NL
no moth + comes near

Matthew 6.19 in T^P T^N Matt(H)
+ devour

Matthew 6.20 in C T^A T^P T^NL T^V Hel Aphr
the treasure<<the treasures

Matthew 6.20 in the P T^A
worm << rust

SELECT BIBLIOGRAPHY
Grant (1959: 178); Guillaumont *et al.* (1959: 42); Johnson (1997); Schrage (1964a: 159); Sieber (1966: 57–59); Snodgrass (1989: 35–36); Wilson (1960a: 92).

Logion 77

Jesus said, 'I am the light which is above all things. I am everything. From me, everything came forth, and up to me, everything reached.'

NHC II 2.46.22–28

¹ⲡⲉⲭⲉ ⲓ̅ⲥ̅ ⲭⲉ ⲁⲛⲟⲕ ⲡⲉ ⲡⲟⲩⲟⲉⲓⲛ ⲡⲁⲉⲓ ⲉⲧϩⲓϫⲱⲟⲩ ⲧⲏⲣⲟⲩ ⲁⲛⲟⲕ
ⲡⲉ ⲡⲧⲏⲣϥ ⲛ̅ⲧⲁ ⲡⲧⲏⲣϥ ⲉⲓ ⲉⲃⲟⲗ ⲛ̅ϩⲏⲧ ⲁⲩⲱ ⲛ̅ⲧⲁ ⲡⲧⲏⲣϥ ⲡⲱϩ
ϣⲁⲣⲟⲉⲓ

ATTRIBUTION
Accretion.

TEXT AND TRANSLATION ISSUES
ⲡⲧⲏⲣϥ is translated 'everything', since Sahidic 1 Cor. 8.6 and Rom. 11.36 translates τὰ
πάντα with a singular form ⲧⲡⲧⲏⲣϥ. It doubtless refers to the visible world and Jesus'
role in creation.

L. 77 in the Coptic manuscript has appended a saying found combined with L. 30.1–2
in P.Oxy. 1.27–30. I have taken the Greek combination as primary (see L. 30). The Coptic
combination reads: 'Jesus said, "I am the light which is above all things. I am everything.
From me, everything came forth, and up to me, everything reached. Split a piece of wood.
I am there. Lift the stone, and you will find me there."'

The combination of sayings in the Coptic L. 77 may have been created to be a reference
to Jesus' cross since ϣⲉ was especially used in Christian Coptic texts to translate σταυρός
(Crum 546a). 'Wood', along with a 'tree', were common *testimonia* in the patristic literature taken as references to Jesus' cross, as G. Q. Reijners details. Moreover, there was a
tradition that became very popular in the second century that Jesus' extension on the vertical
and horizontal arms of the cross had universal power, separating the passions from the soul
by overcoming the demons or powers that controlled the soul. This universalism of Jesus'
presence and power is described by Irenaeus in terms quite similar to the Coptic L. 77:

> Because he is himself the Word of God Almighty, whose invisible presence is spread
> abroad in us and fills the whole world, he extends his influence in the world through its
> length, breadth, height and depth…and the Son of God has been crucified for all having
> traced the sign of the Cross on all things. For it was right and necessary that he who
> made himself visible, should lead all visible things to participate in his cross. And it is in
> this way that, in a form that can be perceived, his own special influence has had its
> sensible effect on visible things: for it is he that illumines the heights, that is the
> heavens; it is he that penetrates that which is beneath; he that traverses the whole vast
> extent of north and south, summoning to the knowledge of his father those scattered in
> every place. (Iren., *Dem.* 34)

Gregory of Nyssa also is aware of this tradition, stating that the cross is divided into four
branches from the centre, signifying the 'power' and 'providence' which come from Jesus
'who is seen upon it' and which 'penetrate everything'. Developing his thoughts on Ephesians 3.18, he states that the cross signified that 'there is nothing which is not under the
empire of divine power, neither that which is above heaven, nor that which is under the
earth, nor that which extends transversally to the limits of being'. These ideas are also
present in the *Acts of Peter* 38 and the *Acts of John* 98–99. J. Daniélou states that the cross
came to represent the universal providence of Jesus.

INTERPRETATIVE COMMENT

This saying may be one of our earliest references to the fact that the Christians identified Jesus with the heavenly *Anthropos* popular in ancient Jewish lore, a theme discussed in J. Fossum and G. Quispel's publications. As I have discussed in my previous book, one of the roles of this Man of Light was cosmogonic. Creation of the world came out of his light and was infused with his light.

It is quite possible that the interpretative trajectory represented by the Coptic L. 77 with the combination of the 'stone–wood' saying is that of the universal power of Jesus in the event of his cross, the wood (see above), and perhaps even his resurrection, lifting the stone. The combination in the Coptic text would have made this interpretation likely along with the transposition of 'wood' and 'stone' since the crucifixion occurred before the empty tomb and the resurrection.

This saying is retrospective, showing an interest in the development of Christology. Accrual can be dated to a time between 80 and 120 CE when similar teachings about Jesus were developing in the Johannine circles.

SOURCE DISCUSSION

G. Quispel traces this saying to an encratic Gospel source.

LITERATURE PARALLELS

John 1.3–4

> [3]'All things came into being through him, and without him not one thing came into being that has come into being. [4]In him was life, and the life was the light of all people.'

John 1.9

> 'The true light, which enlightens everyone, was coming into the world.'

John 8.12

> 'Again Jesus spoke to them, saying, "I am the light of the world. Whoever follows me will never walk in darkness but will have the light of life."'

John 9.5

> 'As long as I am in the world, I am the light of the world.'

John 12.46

> 'I have come as light into the world, so that everyone who believes in me should not remain in the darkness.'

Romans 11.36

> 'For from him and through him and to him are all things. To him be glory forever. Amen.'

1 Corinthians 8.6

> 'Yet for us there is one God, the Father, from whom are all things and for whom we exist, and one Lord, Jesus Christ, through whom are all things and through whom we exist.'

Ephesians 4.6

> '...one God and Father of everything, who is above everything and through everything and in everything'.

Colossians 1.16

> 'For in him all things in heaven and on earth were created, things visible and invisible, whether thrones or dominions or rulers or powers – all things have been created through him and for him.'

Hebrews 2.10
> 'It was fitting that God, for whom and through whom all things exist, in bringing children to glory, should make the pioneer of their salvation perfect through suffering.'

Acts of Thomas *70*
> 'You [Jesus] are divided without being separated, and are one though divided; and everything subsists in you and is subject to you, because everything is yours.'

Martyrdom of Peter 10
> 'You are everything, and everything is in you. And you are what is, and there is nothing else that is except you alone.'

Pseudo-Macarius, Hom. *12.12*
> 'He is everywhere, both under the earth and above the heavens and also indwelling us. He is everywhere.'

Cf. John 3.19

SELECT BIBLIOGRAPHY

DeConick (1996: 19–20, 65–68); Fossum (1983: 266–67; 1985b: 202–39; 1996: 529–39); Quispel (1980: 6); Reijners (1965).

Logion 78.1–3

[1]Jesus said, 'Why did you come out into the desert? To see a reed shaken by the wind [2]and to see a man dressed in soft garments [like your] kings and your prominent men? [3]They are dressed in soft garments, but they will not be able to understand the truth.'

NHC II 2.46.28–47.3

[1]ⲡⲉⲝⲉ ⲓ̅ⲥ̅ ⲝⲉ ⲉⲧⲃⲉ ⲟⲩ ⲁⲧⲉⲧⲛ̅ⲉⲓ ⲉⲃⲟⲗ ⲉⲧⲥⲱϣⲉ ⲉⲛⲁⲩ ⲉⲩⲕⲁϣ
ⲉϥⲕⲓⲙ ⲉ|ⲃⲟⲗ| ϩⲓⲧⲙ̅ ⲡⲧⲏⲩ [2]ⲁⲩⲱ ⲉⲛⲁⲩ ⲉⲩⲣ|ⲱⲙⲉ ⲉⲩ|ⲛ̅ϣⲧⲏⲛ
ⲉⲩϭⲏⲛ ϩⲓⲱⲱⲃ |ⲛ̅ⲑⲉ ⲛ̅ⲛⲉⲧⲛ̅|ⲣ̅ⲣⲱⲟⲩ ⲙⲛ̅ ⲛⲉⲧⲙ̅ⲙⲉⲅⲓⲥⲧⲁⲛⲟⲥ [3]ⲛⲁⲉⲓ
ⲉⲛ|ⲉϣⲧⲏ̣ⲛ ⲉ|ⲧ|ϭⲏⲛ ϩⲓⲱⲟⲩ ⲁⲩⲱ ⲥⲉⲛ̣|ⲁ|ϣⲥ̅ⲥⲟⲟⲩⲛ ⲧⲙⲉ ⲁⲛ

ATTRIBUTION

Kernel saying. It is possible, however, that the final clause 'but they will not be able to understand the truth', may be an accretion since it does contain language characteristic of the accretions, particularly the phrase 'understand (ⲥⲟⲟⲩⲛ) the truth'. However, there is no attempt in this saying to contextualize this 'knowledge' as soteriological, as is the case in other accretions. Because of this uncertainty, I have left the clause in the Kernel Gospel.

TEXT AND TRANSLATION ISSUES

My reconstruction of the lacunae in line 32 agrees with B. Layton (ⲛ̅ⲑⲉ ⲛ̅ⲛⲉⲧ) rather than A. Guillaumont (ⲉⲓⲥ ⲛⲉⲧⲛ̅) because the first letter in the lacunae has a superlinear stroke.

L. 78.2 '*and* (ⲁⲩⲱ) to see a man' should probably read '*or* to see a man'. The Coptic rendering ⲁⲩⲱ, and the Greek subtext καί, most likely represent a mistranslation of the Aramaic ו which means both 'and' and 'either…or'. This was pointed out by A. Guillaumont. In L. 43, the same problem occurs (see L. 43).

INTERPRETATIVE COMMENT

In the Kernel, this saying begins a series of logia focused on revealing the truth about Jesus to the worthy. The worthy disciple is not like those people who journey to the desert to see great men because Jesus is not like a king of other men. In the complete Gospel, this saying's meaning would have shifted to a more encratic tone, reminding the practitioner that roles of prominence and worldly affairs should be renounced just as Jesus had said. Noteworthy is the accrual of L. 80 immediately following this Kernel cluster (78 and 79), an accrual that serves to reinterpret this cluster in this fashion.

SOURCE DISCUSSION

W. Schrage looks for agreements between Sahidic Luke and L. 78, pointing to the fact that both have a definite article before 'wind' and that both omit 'and in luxury' which can be found in Greek Luke. To account for the differences, H. von Schürmann even conjectures that Luke 7.24–25 has been harmonized with Acts 6.15 in a post-Synoptic source that *Thomas* relied on.

J. Sieber admits some influence on L. 78 from other Coptic translations of the New Testament, but states that the differences from Sahidic Luke, particularly the location of the infinitive 'to see' in the sentence, demonstrate *Thomas'* independence, a point which R. McL. Wilson had argued previously. Sieber also notes that the Baptist sequence found in Matthew and Luke is broken in *Thomas* since L. 46 occurs elsewhere in the Gospel.

The evidence appears to indicate, in my opinion, that we have an old multiform that may have been adapted to the memory of Coptic Luke at the scribal level.

LITERATURE PARALLELS

Matthew 11.7–8 (Qmatt)

> [7]'What did you go out into the wilderness to look at? A reed shaken by the wind? [8]What then did you go out to see? Someone dressed in soft robes? Look, those who wear soft robes are in royal palaces.'

Luke 7.24–25 (Qluke)

> 'What did you go out into the wilderness to look at? A reed shaken by the wind? What then did you go out to see? Someone dressed in soft robes? Look, those who put on fine clothing and live in luxury are in royal palaces.'

AGREEMENTS IN SYRIAN GOSPELS, WESTERN TEXT AND DIATESSARON

Matthew 11.7–8//Luke 7.24–25 in S P Pal T^P T^V
> *to see* a reed

Matthew 11.7–8//Luke 7.24–25 in ℵ 1355 S P Pal T^P
> *to see* a man

SELECT BIBLIOGRAPHY

Guillaumont (1981); Guillaumont *et al.* (1959: 42); Layton (1989: 82); Schrage (1964a: 161–62); Schürmann (1963: 250); Sieber (1966: 128–29); Wilson (1960a: 63–64).

Logion 79.1–3

[1]A woman in the crowd said to him, 'Blessed is the womb that bore you and the breasts that nourished you.'

[2]He said to [her], 'Blessed are the people who have heard the word of the Father and have truly kept it. [3]For there will be days when you will say, "Blessed is the womb that has not conceived and the breasts that have not given milk."'

NHC II 2.47.3–12

[1]ⲡⲉⲝⲉ ⲟⲩⲥϩⲓⲙⲉ| ⲛⲁϥ ϩⲙ̄ ⲡⲙⲏⲱ̣ⲉ ⲝⲉ ⲛⲉⲉⲓⲁⲧ|ⲥ ⲛ̄|ⲑϩⲏ ⲛ̄ⲧⲁϩϥⲓ
ϩⲁⲣⲟⲕ ⲁⲩⲱ ⲛ̄ⲕ̣ⲓ|ⲃ|ⲉ̣ ⲉⲛⲧⲁϩⲥⲁⲛⲟⲩⲱ̣ⲕ
[2]ⲡⲉⲝⲁϥ ⲛⲁ|ⲥ| ⲝⲉ ⲛⲉⲉⲓⲁⲧⲟⲩ ⲛ̄ⲛⲉⲛⲧⲁϩⲥⲱⲧⲙ̄ ⲁⲡⲗⲟⲅⲟⲥ ⲙ̄ⲡⲉⲓⲱⲧ
ⲁⲩⲁⲣⲉϩ ⲉⲣⲟϥ ϩⲛ̄ ⲟⲩⲙⲉ [3]ⲟⲩⲛ̄ ϩⲛ̄ϩⲟⲟⲩ ⲅⲁⲣ ⲛⲁⲱ̣ⲱⲡⲉ ⲛ̄ⲧⲉⲧⲛ̄ⲝⲟⲟⲥ
ⲝⲉ ⲛⲉⲉⲓⲁⲧⲥ̄ ⲛ̄ⲑϩⲏ ⲧⲁⲉⲓ ⲉⲧⲉ ⲙ̄ⲡⲥⲱ ⲁⲩⲱ ⲛ̄ⲕⲓⲃⲉ ⲛⲁⲉⲓ ⲉⲙⲡⲟⲩϯ
ⲉⲣⲱⲧⲉ

ATTRIBUTION
Kernel saying.

TEXT AND TRANSLATION ISSUES
In line 6, the copyist cancelled ϥ in ⲥⲁ‖ϥ‖ⲛⲟⲩⲱ̣ⲕ, thus ⲥⲁⲛⲟⲩⲱ̣ⲕ in my transcription.

A. Guillaumont notes that the turn of phrase, 'the breasts that *nourished* you', is found in *Thomas* while the Greek Luke 11.27 has 'the breasts that *nursed* you'. This he explains by an Aramaic substratum, יניק, which has both senses. He notes that the Syriac versions of Luke are closer to *Thomas,* having the verb ܐܝܢܩ 'the breasts that have *made suck*' or '*given suck*'.

INTERPRETATIVE COMMENT
In the Kernel Gospel, this saying functioned as a warning to people that the worst calamities are yet to come as the world is destroyed. As such it represents a common eschatological expectation expressed in other Jewish and Christian sources.

But with the accrual of L. 80, L. 79 appears to contrast the Kingdom with the world and sexual propagation. B. Fordyce Miller notes that the 'editor' of *Thomas* does not give any contextual interpretation of this logion, and because of this, an ascetic hermeneutic characterizes the passage.

SOURCE DISCUSSION
H. von Schürmann, W. Schrage, B. Gärnter, R. Grant and D.N. Freedman, E. Haenchen, and R. McL. Wilson agree that L. 79 is a welding of Luke 11.27–28 and 23.29. Schrage points out that sense can only be made of the plural 'you will say' in L. 79.3 within the Lukan context. K. Snodgrass picks up this opinion in his work, opting for *possible* dependence based on the phrases ἐκ τοῦ ὄχλου, ἔρξονται, ἡμέραι, and φυλάσσειν which he thinks are all Lukan traits.

The only editorial trace that J. Sieber can see is the combination 'hear and do the word of my Father' which he says may be Lukan. More probably, Sieber thinks, it is due to Luke's special source since Luke did not create this saying. Sieber offers an alternative explanation to Schrage's argument regarding the presence of 'you will say' in L. 79, that

Thomas' source for the saying may have been the same as Luke's or a tradition of another type presented in a similar context. Sieber, however, does concede in his conclusion that this Logion may contain a Lukanism in this case.

In my opinion, although these agreements are worth noting, especially the phrase 'you will say', they do not make the case for dependence because here we are dealing with special Lukan material. It is just as plausible that these phrases were part of Luke's source. If so, then we are seeing here variants that developed independently out of pre-Synoptic traditions. This latter hypothesis actually fits the evidence better given Guillaumont's observation about the Aramaic substratum, רבק and the Syriac parallels.

LITERATURE PARALLELS

Luke 11.27–28 (L or Qluke)
> [27]'While he was saying this, a woman in the crowd raised her voice and said to him, "Blessed is the womb that bore you and the breasts that you sucked!" [28]But he said, "Blessed rather are those who hear the word of God and obey it!"'

John 13.17
> 'If you know these things, you are blessed if you do them.'

James 1.25
> 'But those who look into the perfect law, the law of liberty, and persevere, being not hearers who forget but doers who act – they will be blessed in their doing.'

Luke 23.29 (L)
> 'For the days are surely coming when they will say, "Blessed are the barren, and the wombs that never bore, and the breasts that never gave suck."'

Mark 13.17
> 'Woe to those who are pregnant and to those who are nursing infants in those days!'

Matthew 24.19
> 'Woe to those who are pregnant and to those who are nursing infants in those days!'

Luke 21.23
> 'Woe to those who are pregnant and to those who are nursing infants in those days!'

Ahmad ibn Hanbal, al-Zuhd, p. 143 (no. 470)
> 'She said, "Blessed is the belly that carried you and the breasts from which you fed." Jesus said, "Blessed is he whom God has taught his book and who dies without having become haughty."'

AGREEMENTS IN SYRIAN GOSPELS, WESTERN TEXT AND DIATESSARON

Luke 11.27 in e Mcion S C P Pal T^P T^A T^{EC} Arm Boh Ar
> that nourished you//that gave you suck << that you sucked

Luke 11.27 in r^2 S C P T^A
> – but

Luke 11.27 in a c r^2 S C P T^A T^{NL} T^{PEP} bo aeth
> + to (her)

Luke 11.27 in a a^2 b f ff^2 i q E S C P Pal T^p T^{EC} T^A arm
> – rather

Luke 11.27 in S P T^A
> have heard << hear

Luke 23.29 in D a b d e ff² l r¹ S C Tᴾ Tᴱᶜ Tᴬ Tᴺᴸ Tⱽ Tᴸ P⁷⁵ f¹³
– behold

Luke 23.29 in S C
γάρ<<ὅτι

Luke 23.29 in D a b c d e f ff² l r¹ S C Tᴾ Tᴱᶜ Tᴬ Tᴸ Tⱽ Tᴺᴸ f¹³
will be << are coming

Luke 23.29 in S C P Tᴾ Tᴱᶜ Tᴬ Tᴺᴸ
you will say << they will say

Luke 23.29 in Tᴾ
– the barren and

Luke 23.29 in Tᴺ
conceived << bore

Luke 23.29 in Koine aur f vulg S C P Tᴾ Tᴬ Tᴸ Tⱽ Tᴺᴸ Tᵀ aeth arm sa
have suckled << gave suck

SELECT BIBLIOGRAPHY
Grant with Freedman (1960: 179); Guillaumont (1981: 197 and n. 18); Haenchen (1961: 55); Miller (1967: 56); Schrage (1964a: 165–66); Schürmann (1963: 240–41); Sieber (1966: 211–13, 262); Snodgrass (1989: 36–37); Wilson (1960a: 81).

Logion 80.1–2

¹Jesus said, 'Whoever has come to know the world has found the corpse. ²The world does not deserve the person who has found [that the world is] the corpse.'

Alternative Translation

'Whoever has come to know the world <<has mastered the body>>. The world does not deserve the person who <<has mastered the body>>.'

NHC II 2.47.12–15

¹ⲡⲉⲭⲉ ⲓ̅ⲥ̅ ⲭⲉ ⲡⲉⲛⲧⲁϩⲥⲟⲩⲱⲛ ⲡⲕⲟⲥⲙⲟⲥ ⲁϥϩⲉ ⲉⲡⲥⲱⲙⲁ
²ⲡⲉⲛⲧⲁϩϩⲉ ⲇⲉ ⲉⲡⲥⲱⲙⲁ ⲡⲕⲟⲥⲙⲟⲥ ⲙ̅ⲡϣⲁ ⲙ̅ⲙⲟϥ ⲁⲛ

ATTRIBUTION
Accretion.

TEXT AND TRANSLATION ISSUES
In this saying, we find ⲥⲱⲙⲁ instead of ⲡⲧⲱⲙⲁ which is found in the doublet L. 56. For further discussion, see L. 56.

The clause 'the world does not deserve' is Semitic. See L. 56 for more details.

INTERPRETATIVE COMMENT
This saying contains vocabulary and themes characteristic of the accretions, particularly the phrase ⲡⲕⲟⲥⲙⲟⲥ ⲙ̅ⲡϣⲁ ⲙ̅ⲙⲟϥ ⲁⲛ and ⲥⲟⲩⲱⲛ which describes a salvific state. The saying has affinities with encratic ideology (particularly the description of the mastery

of the body if an Aramaic substratum is assumed as is the case with the doublet L. 56) while at the same time, with the Hermetic theme that knowledge liberates. Accrual can be estimated to the latter part of the first century, 60–100 CE.

SOURCE DISCUSSION
G. Quispel attributes this saying to a Hermetic source.

LITERATURE PARALLELS

L. 56

[1]Jesus said, 'Whoever has come to know the world has found a corpse. [2]The world does not deserve the person who found (that the world is) a corpse.'

Alternative Translation

[1]'Whoever has come to know the world <<has mastered the body>>. [2]The world does not deserve the person who <<has mastered the body>>.'

L. 111

[1]'Jesus said, "The heavens and the earth will roll up in your presence. [2]And whoever is alive because of the Living One will not see death." [3]Does not Jesus say, "The world does not deserve the person who has found himself?"'

SELECT BIBLIOGRAPHY
Quispel (1981: 265).

Logion 81.1–2

[1]Jesus said, 'Whoever has grown wealthy, that person should become a king. [2]But whoever possesses power, let that person disown (his power).'

NHC II 2.47.15–17

[1]ⲡⲉⲭⲉ ⲓ̅ⲥ̅ ⲭⲉ ⲡⲉⲛⲧⲁϩⲣ̅ ⲣ̅ⲙ̅ⲙⲁⲟ ⲙⲁⲣⲉϥⲣ̅ ⲣ̅ⲣⲟ [2]ⲁⲩⲱ ⲡⲉⲧⲉⲩⲛ̅ⲧⲁϥ ⲛ̅ⲟⲩⲇⲩⲛⲁⲙⲓⲥ ⲙⲁⲣⲉϥⲁⲣⲛⲁ

ATTRIBUTION
Kernel saying.

INTERPRETATIVE COMMENT
In the Kernel, this saying is part of a rhetorical speech that progressively reveals the truth about Jesus to the worthy disciple. He is not like the kings and prominent men dressed in soft clothing (L. 78) because he alone is blessed from the womb and is a prophet speaking God's word (L. 79). He admonishes the wealthy to be kings, but warns them that God is not the God of kings and powerful men. Devotion to God demands the opposite, renunciation of power (L. 81). This latter message belongs to eschatological traditions that anticipate a time when the world order and the *status quo* are reversed in terms of procreation, economics, institutions, conventions and empires.

In the complete Gospel, the accretion preceding L. 81 would have provided a new hermeneutic for this saying. Mastery of the body was demanded (L. 80), which included complete renunciation of personal wealth and power (L. 81). In this way, the words of Jesus in L. 81 were heard as support for an encratic praxis.

SOURCE DISCUSSION
G. Quispel thinks that this saying comes from a Jewish Christian Gospel source.

LITERATURE PARALLELS

1 Corinthians 4.8
> 'Already you have all you want! Already you have become wealthy! Quite apart from us you have become kings! Indeed, I wish that you had become kings, so that we might be kings with you!'

L. 110
> Jesus said, 'Whoever has found the world and become wealthy, he should disown the world.'

Dialogue of the Saviour *20*
> 'Let the person [who possesses] power renounce [it and repent].'

Pseudo-Macarius, Hom. *27.5*
> 'Being rich before God, they regard themselves as poor.'

Pseudo-Macarius, Hom. *32.7*
> 'If you wish to be in the world and become rich, every kind of misfortune meets you. You begin to reason with yourself, "Because I have not succeeded in the world, should I leave it, renounce it, and serve God?" After you reach this point, you hear the command saying, "Sell the things you possess."'

Abu Hayyan al-Tawhidi, al-Basa'ir wa'l Dhakha'ir *1.23*
> 'As for kings, leave their world to them and they will leave the other world to you.'

'Abdallah ibn al-Mubarak, al-Zuhd, *p. 96 (n. 284)*
> 'Just as kings have left wisdom to you, so you should leave the world to them.'

'Abdallah ibn Qutayba, 'Uyun al-Akhbar *1.266*
> 'If people appoint you as their heads, be like tails.'

Cf. Pseudo-Macarius, *Hom.* 27.10

SELECT BIBLIOGRAPHY
Quispel (1981: 265).

Logion 82.1–2

[1]Jesus said, 'Whoever is near me, is near the fire. [2]But whoever is far away from me, is far away from the Kingdom.'

NHC II 2.47.17–19

[1]ⲡⲉⲭⲉ ⲓ̅ⲥ̅ ϫⲉ ⲡⲉⲧϨⲏⲛ ⲉⲣⲟⲉⲓ ⲉϥϨⲏⲛ ⲉⲧⲥⲁⲧⲉ [2]ⲁⲩⲱ ⲡⲉⲧⲟⲩⲏⲩ
ⲙ̅ⲙⲟⲉⲓ ϥⲟⲩⲏⲩ ⲛ̅ⲧⲙⲛ̅ⲧⲉⲣⲟ

ATTRIBUTION
Kernel saying.

In the Kernel, this saying continues the rhetorical revelation of Jesus' identity to the worthy disciple. He is not like other leaders, neither king nor prominent man (L. 78). He is God's prophet, blessed from the womb and speaking with God's voice (L. 79). In contrast to worldly kings (L. 81), Jesus dwells in a heavenly Kingdom of fire, and it is here that he will reveal himself to the worthy (L. 82). Thus this Logion echoes the mystical dimension of apocalyptic present in the Kernel. It reveals a theophantic tradition that identifies Jesus with the fire of the heavenly realm, the Kingdom. Believers who draw near to him can trust that they will experience a fiery theophany, while those who remain far away from him will not be able to enter the Kingdom at the end of time.

Once the hermeneutic shifted to an immanent apocalypse rather than imminent, the theophany mentioned in L. 82 becomes an end unto itself, a mystical pre-mortem vision of Jesus. This understanding of L. 82 is explicit in the *Gospel of the Saviour* which records a version of this saying in a fabulous context. John speaks to the resurrected Jesus, begging him to reveal himself to the disciples in a diminished glory so that they will be able to bear the vision and not despair from fear. Jesus prohibits John from touching his glorified body because 'If one is [near] me, he will [burn.] I am the [fire that] blazes; the one who [is near to me, is] near to [the fire]; the one who is far from me is far from life.' The tradition echoed here runs through Jewish apocalpytic and mystical literature, that unprepared humans who touch heavenly beings will be burned and destroyed. In the writings of Pseudo-Ephrem, the mystical meaning of the saying has been developed further, suggesting the transformative effect of encountering Jesus. 'Nearness' is understood to mean 'unity' so that the believer who unites with Jesus becomes like him, a being of fire.

SOURCE DISCUSSION

G. Quispel thinks that a Jewish Christian Gospel was the source of this saying.

LITERATURE PARALLELS

Gospel of the Saviour *107.43–48*
> 'Whoever is near me, is near the fire. Whoever is far away from me, is far away from life.'

Origen, Hom. in Jer. *L.I (III), 3.104–105*
> 'Whoever is near to me, is near the fire. Whoever is far from me, is far from the Kingdom.'

Didymus the Blind, In Ps. *88.8*
> 'Whoever is near me, is near the fire. Whoever is far from me, is far from the Kingdom.'

Pseudo-Ephrem, Exposition of the Gospel *83*
> 'He who joins me, joins with fire. And he who is far from me, is far from life.'

SELECT BIBLIOGRAPHY
Quispel (1981: 265).

Logion 83.1–2

[1]Jesus said, 'The images are visible to people, but the light in them is concealed in the image of the Father's light. [2]The light will be revealed, but his image is concealed by his light.'

NHC II 2.47.19–24

¹ΠΕΧΕ ΙC ΧΕ ΝϨΙΚШΝ CΕΟΥΟΝϨ ΕΒΟΛ ΜΠΡШΜΕ ΑΥШ ΠΟΥΟΕΙΝ
ΕΤΝϨΗΤΟΥ ϥϨΗΠ ϨΝ ΘΙΚШΝ ΜΠΟΥΟΕΙΝ ΜΠΕΙШΤ ²ϥΝΑϬШΛΠ
ΕΒΟΛ ΑΥШ ΤΕϥϨΙΚШΝ ϨΗΠ ΕΒΟΛ ϨΙΤΝ ΠΕϥΟΥΟΕΙΝ

ATTRIBUTION
Accretion.

INTERPRETATIVE COMMENT
This saying develops two themes common to the accretions: speculation about the primor-dial Adam and admiration for the internal light, the divine Self. It accrued in the Gospel between 80 and 120 CE, most likely as a result of dialogue between the Syrian and Alexandrian Christian communities.

This saying reflects speculation about Genesis 1.26–28 where the human being is made in God's image. Thus the saying begins by affirming that human beings are the visible 'images' of God, images which contain a divine element, 'the light' (cf. L. 24). This inter-nal divine light is concealed in the 'image of the Father's light'. This represents a teaching that inside the individual person the divine element of light is contained in some type of internal image, form or body of God. This appears to reflect a Jewish-Christian teaching. According to the *Acts of Thomas* 10 (Syriac), Christ put on the first man. As the first man, Christ was understood to be 'a general soul' (Symmachians in Marius Victorinus, *ep. Ad Gal.* 1.15). In the *Pseudo-Clementine Recognitions* 1.28.4, we are told that God created the human with an 'internal Form (*interna species*)' that is 'older' than the human body itself. This internal Form is none other than the Form or Body of God.

The second half of this saying contrasts the first. Drawing on a well-established Jewish tradition that the image of God, the Kavod, is hidden by a screen of light, the saying explains that God's condition is opposite the human. In fact, his image is not visible but is 'concealed by his light'.

SOURCE DISCUSSION
G. Quispel traces this saying to an encratic Gospel source.

SELECT BIBLIOGRAPHY
DeConick (1996: 100–105, 115–17); Fossum (1983: 267–68); Quispel (1981: 265).

Logion 84.1–2

¹Jesus said, 'When you see the likeness of yourselves, you are delighted. ²But when you see the images of yourselves which came into being before you – they neither die nor are visible – how much you will suffer!'

NHC II 2.47.24–29

¹ΠΕΧΕ ΙC ΝϨΟΟΥ ΕΤΕΤΝΝΑΥ ΕΠΕΤΝΕΙΝΕ ШΑΡΕΤΝΡΑШΕ ²ϨΟΤΑΝ
ΔΕ ΕΤΕΤΝШΑΝΑΥ ΑΝΕΤΝϨΙΚШΝ ΝΤΑϨШШΠΕ ϨΙ ΤΕΤΝΕϨ ΟΥΤΕ
ΜΑΥΜΟΥ ΟΥΤΕ ΜΑΥΟΥШΝϨ ΕΒΟΛ ΤΕΤΝΑϥΙ ϨΑ ΟΥΗΡ

ATTRIBUTION
Accretion.

INTERPRETATIVE COMMENT
This saying develops a theme common to the accretions: speculation about the primordial Adam. It accrued in the Gospel at the same time as L. 83, between 80 and 120 CE. As I have argued at length in my monograph *Seek To See Him*, this saying references Genesis 1.26–28 where the human being is said to have been made in God's image, a discussion common to first-century Jewish and Christian texts. This was interpreted by some to be a divine image of the person, not the human body. The discussion focused on Adam's fall which resulted in a loss of or separation from this eternal heavenly self image. Salvation was understood in terms of the person regaining, in some way, this heavenly eternal self.

Thus, the 'likeness' of the person differs from the 'image'. The likeness represents the human appearance which, when viewed, brings delight to the onlooker. Viewing the heavenly image, however, results in suffering since the person is coming face to face with his or her own perfection. This suffering may be the result of the physical transformation that the ancients believed occurred when the beholder gazed upon the beholden.

SOURCE DISCUSSION
G. Quispel thinks that this saying comes from a Jewish Christian Gospel.

LITERATURE PARALLELS

Pseudo-Macarius, Hom. *7.6–7*
> 'Does one see the soul through revelation and divine light? Just as our eyes see the sun, so also the enlightened see the images of the soul, but few Christians attain this. Does the soul have any form? It has a form and image similar to that of an angel. For as angels have an image and form and as the outer man has his image so also the inner man has an image that is similar both to that of the angel and that of the exterior man.'

Pseudo-Macarius, Hom. *30.3*
> 'For this body is a likeness of the soul and the soul is an image of the Spirit.'

Manichaean Psalm *1.14–17*
> 'He established chambers of life;
> He set up living images in them;
> He set up living images in them that never perish.'

SELECT BIBLIOGRAPHY
DeConick (1996: 157–72); Quispel (1981: 265).

Logion 85.1–2

[1]Jesus said, 'Adam came into being out of a great power and great wealth. But he was not deserving of you. [2]For, had he been deserving, [he would] not [have] died.'

NHC II 2.47.29–34

[1]ⲡⲉⲭⲉ ⲓ̅ⲥ̅ ⲭⲉ ⲛ̅ⲧⲁ ⲁⲇⲁⲙ ϣⲱⲡⲉ ⲉⲃⲟⲗ ϩⲛ̅ⲛ ⲟⲩⲛⲟϭ ⲛ̅ⲇⲩⲛⲁⲙⲓⲥ
ⲙⲛ̅ ⲟⲩⲛⲟϭ ⲙ̅ⲙⲛ̅ⲧⲣⲙ̅ⲙⲁⲟ ⲁⲩⲱ ⲙ̅ⲡⲉϥϣⲱⲡⲉ ⲉϥ[ϥ]ⲙ̅ⲡϣⲁ ⲙ̅ⲙⲱⲧⲛ̅
[2]ⲛⲉⲩⲁϫⲓⲟⲥ ⲅⲁⲣ ⲡⲉ [ⲛⲉϥⲛⲁⲭⲓ †]ⲡ[ⲉ] ⲁⲛ ⲙ̅ⲡⲙⲟⲩ

ATTRIBUTION
Accretion.

TEXT AND TRANSLATION ISSUES
The text literally reads, 'he would not have tasted death'. For the expression, 'to taste death', see L. 1.
   For the Semitic expression, 'does not deserve', see L. 56.

INTERPRETATIVE COMMENT
This saying is part of a sequence of accretions beginning with L. 83 that speculate about Adam's primordial condition and fall. Furthermore, this particular saying contains vocabulary characteristic of the accretions, particularly the phrase that literally reads, 'he would not have tasted death'. Accrual is dated from 80–120 CE.
   The saying follows a sequence of logia that provide a commentary on the Genesis story. The sayings progress by detailing the human condition as it compares to the divine. The human condition is one in which the soul, the internal image of God, exists in a condition which is described as either separated or diminished from its eternal heavenly image. This condition was understood to be the result of Adam's sin. Even though he came into existence out of 'a great power and great wealth', – he was, in fact, the glorious primordial Man – he sinned and experienced death. In this way, Adam is the paradigm, the metaphor for all humans who need to regain the glory of their primordial selves. Once this is accomplished, the believer overcomes death as Adam was unable to do.
   The title 'Great Power' is an alternative for 'Great Glory'. M. Lelyveld discusses these terms as they are applied to Adam in Jewish apocalyptic literature, where he is described as the glorious primordial Man. These epithets were not uncommon references to the Name of God or his Kavod in Jewish apocalyptic and mystical texts, and to the Son in Jewish-Christian documents as J. Fossum has detailed in his various publications. For instance, in the Jewish-Christian writing, the *Teachings of Silvanus,* it is said of Jesus: 'A Great Power and Great Glory has made the universe known' (112.8–10; cf. 106.21–23). The Syriac version of the *Acts of Thomas* addresses Christ as the 'Great Power' (ch. 12). Justin Martyr refers to this tradition when he writes that among the names of the Son is 'Power of God' (*1 Apol.* 33.6) and that God begat as 'Beginning' a 'Power from himself' that is also called the 'Glory of the Lord' and sometimes 'Son' (*Dial.* 61.1). Elchasai, the Jewish-Christian sect leader, appeared as the Prophet-Like-Moses and was designated the 'Hidden Power', the final manifestation of Christ. Simon Magus also appeared as the eschatological Prophet-Like-Moses and was called the 'Great Power', a divine manifestation which superseded his prior incarnation in Jesus.
   Undoubtedly, L. 85 belongs to this referential horizon, when it states that Adam originated from the Great Power and Great Wealth, but that he was not worthy and died. This is a reference to the story of the fall of Adam. The language is indicative of Syrian Christianity. For instance, in the *Liber Graduum*, it is explained that originally Adam subjected everything to himself, 'in the power of the all-sustaining Lord' (604.10–12). Adam was provided for by God as befitted the 'wealth' of his bounty (601.1). After he sinned, however, Adam and Eve became poor 'from the wealth above' (612.21–22). When they left heaven, they left 'the heavenly wealth' too (613.22). This Syrian concept is explained by Pseudo-Marcarius in *Hom.* 12.1–2. He says that Adam lost 'the full heavenly inheritance' which was stored for him within the Image of God. 'A very great wealth and inheritance was prepared for him… Such was the vessel of Adam before his disobedience, like a very

valuable estate. When, however, he entertained evil intentions and thoughts, he lost God. We nevertheless do not say that he was totally lost and was blotted out of existence and died. He died as far as his relationship with God was concerned, but in his nature, however, he still lives.' Similar themes are discussed in *Homily* 15.39.

What is fascinating about L. 85 is its emphasis on the nature of the Thomasine believer who is characterized here as more 'deserving' than Adam. Why? Because the believer has been able to regain the primordial state, perhaps through a vision of his or her heavenly counterpart (L. 84), overcoming 'death' as Adam was unable to do.

SOURCE DISCUSSION
G. Quispel thinks that this saying was created by the author of the Gospel.

LITERATURE PARALLELS

Pseudo-Macarius, Hom. *15.39*
> 'In what way are Christians superior to the first Adam? Indeed, he was immortal and not only was he incorruptible in soul, but also in body. But Christians die and decompose. The real death takes place interiorly in the heart. It lies hidden. The interior man perishes. If anyone, therefore, has passed from death into the hidden life, that one truly lives forever and does not die.'

Cf. *Liber Graduum,* cols. 601.1; 604.10–12; 612.21–22; 613.22

SELECT BIBLIOGRAPHY
Baker (1965/1966: 52); Fossum (1985b: 179–91; 1989a: 368–77; 1989b: 190–93); Lelyveld (1987: 49–54); Quispel (1981: 265).

Logion 86.1–2

[1]Jesus said, '[The foxes have] their dens and the birds have their nests, [2]but the human being does not have a place to lay down his head and rest.'

NHC II 2.47.34–48.4

[1]ⲡⲉⲝⲉ ⲓ̅ⲥ̅ ⲝⲉ [ⲛ̅ⲃⲁϣⲟⲣ ⲟⲩⲛ̅ⲧ]ⲁⲩ ⲛ|ⲟⲩ|ⲃⲏⲃ| ⲁⲩⲱ ⲛ̅ϩⲁⲗⲁⲧⲉ
ⲟⲩⲛ̅ⲧⲁⲩ ⲙ̅ⲙⲁⲩ ⲙ̅|ⲡⲉ|ⲩⲙⲁϩ [2]ⲡϣⲏⲣⲉ ⲇⲉ ⲙ̅ⲡⲣⲱⲙⲉ ⲙⲛ̅ⲧⲁϥ
ⲛ̅|ⲛⲟⲩ|ⲙⲁ ⲉⲣⲓⲕⲉ ⲛ̅ⲧⲉϥⲁⲡⲉ ⲛ̅ϥ̅ⲙⲧⲟⲛ ⲙ̅ⲙⲟ|ϥ

ATTRIBUTION
Kernel saying.

TEXT AND TRANSLATION ISSUES
The phrase, ⲡϣⲏⲣⲉ ⲙ̅ⲡⲣⲱⲙⲉ, is translated 'human being', rendering the Aramaic idiom for 'son of man'.

A. Strobel thinks that the phrase, 'and rest', which does not occur in Matthew or Luke, is due to a double translation of an original Syriac phrase.

We note that the Syrian father Macarius also witnesses this additional phrase, 'and rest'. In fact, this final clause is particularly important to Macarius since the context for the quotation is a homily in which we are told how Jesus will bring our souls to rest at the end of our lives. But, in the meantime, we, like Christ, cannot rest but must labour in imitation of the Lord's life by overcoming our passions.

INTERPRETATIVE COMMENT

What is the meaning of this saying? In the Kernel, the meaning appears to be apocalyptic, that the human being does not belong to this world as the animals do, but to God's Kingdom where he or she ultimately will find rest. One's real home is to be found in the coming New World, not this dying world. Indeed, there may be an allusion here to the itinerant preacher as M. Casey and S. Patterson have argued for this aphorism, or persecution of the group as M. Lelyveld has suggested, but the aphorism seems to me to be inclusive of all human beings, not just referencing a restricted social group.

Once the Thomasine community became encratic, its interpretation of this aphorism shifted. Given its new context as L. 83, 84, 85 and 87 accrued, the saying was probably read as an exhortation to the angelic life in imitation of the Lord, where the believer was expected to leave this world behind and restore him- or herself to the primordial Image, the prelapsarian Adam, the Anthropos or Son of Man.

SOURCE DISCUSSION

W. Schrage attempts to argue for dependence on the Synoptics on the basis of a short list of minor agreements which he compares with the Sahidic New Testament. J. Sieber thinks that the closeness of *Thomas* to Q means that the argument for Synoptic dependence is undermined. A. Strobel's examination of the Syriac textual tradition in comparison to L. 86 has led him to conclude that there was a written Syriac source behind the Gospel that was shared with Tatian.

LITERATURE PARALLELS

Matthew 8.20 (Qmatt)

'And Jesus said to him, "Foxes have holes, and birds of the air have nests; but the human being has nowhere to lay his head."'

Luke 9.58 (Qluke)

'And Jesus said to him, "Foxes have holes, and birds of the air have nests; but the human being has nowhere to lay his head."'

Pseudo-Macarius, Hom., Klosterman and Berthold (1961: 26)

'The human being has nowhere to lay his head and rest.'

AGREEMENTS IN SYRIAN GOSPELS, WESTERN TEXT AND DIATESSARON

Matthew 8.20//Luke 9.58 in T^{EC} T^V T^{PEP}
     + their[1]

Matthew 8.20//Luke 9.58 in T^{NL} T^{PEP}
     – of the air

Matthew 8.20//Luke 9.58 in T^V T^{NL} T^{PEP}
     + their[2]

Matthew 8.20//Luke 9.58 in S C P T^P T^T T^V geo aeth(Matt)
     nest<<nests

Matthew 8.20//Luke 9.58 in b(Luke) S C T^{EC} T^A T^P T^{NL} T^{PEP} sa bo Aphr L Gr
     has no place<<nowhere

Matthew 8.20//Luke 9.58 in T^V T^{NL} T^{PEP}
  + have[2]

Matthew 8.20//Luke 9.58 in a b c g[l] h Cypr (Matt) b c r[l] e aur goth (Luke) S C P Pal T^{EC}
T^P T^{PEP} T^A T^L T^V T^{NL} *sa bo ar per aeth*
  his head<<τὴν κεφαλήν

Matthew 8.20//Luke 9.58 in $T^{NL}$$T^L$ T^{EC} *Mac*
  + and to rest

SELECT BIBLIOGRAPHY
Baker (1964: 219–20); Casey (1985: 9–10, 15); Doran (1991); Lelyveld (1987: 54); Patterson (1993: 133–34); Schrage (1964a: 169–70); Sieber (1966: 93–94); Strobel (1963).

Logion 87.1–2

[1]Jesus said, 'Miserable is the body crucified by a body. [2]Miserable is the soul crucified by these together.'

NHC II 2.48.4–7

[1]ⲡⲉϫⲁϥ ⲛ̄ϭⲓ ⲓ̄ⲥ̄ ϫⲉ ⲟⲩⲧⲁⲗⲁⲓⲡⲱⲣⲟⲛ ⲡ|ⲉ| ⲡⲥⲱⲙⲁ ⲉⲧⲁϣⲉ
ⲛ̄ⲟⲩⲥⲱⲙⲁ [2]ⲁⲩⲱ ⲟⲩⲧ|ⲁ|ⲗⲁⲓⲡⲱⲣⲟⲥ ⲧⲉ ⲧⲯⲩⲭⲏ ⲉⲧⲁϣⲉ ⲛ̄ⲛⲁⲉⲓ
ⲙ̄|ⲡ|ⲥⲛⲁⲩ

ATTRIBUTION
Accretion.

TEXT AND TRANSLATION ISSUES
ⲧⲁⲗⲁⲓⲡⲱⲣⲟⲥ is probably derived from ⲧⲁⲗⲁⲡⲉⲓⲣⲟⲥ, 'suffering, miserable'. Thus my rendering, 'Miserable is the body…'.

The meaning of ⲉⲓϣⲉ is usually lost in translation when it is rendered 'to depend'. In fact, the common translation, 'which depends on the body' and 'which depends on these two', although technically possible does not make good sense particularly when taken along with ⲧⲁⲗⲁⲓⲡⲱⲣⲟⲥ which is derived from ⲧⲁⲗⲁⲡⲉⲓⲣⲟⲥ, indicating an extreme condition of suffering or misery.

There is a better explanation, in my opinion. Since this is the Coptic word that is used to describe Jesus' crucifixion by 'hanging' or 'suspension' (refer to Matt. 20.19 *B*; Mark 15.14 *BF*; Gal. 5.24 *B*; Heb. 6.6 *SB*; Acts 2.23 *SB*; Luke 23.39 *S* which translate σταυρόω as ⲉⲓϣⲉ), I have tried to provide a translation that presents the English reader with this meaning, translating it 'to be crucified'. Thus, the saying identifies the terrible predicament of the human being. The body suffers because of its own nature, while the soul suffers because it is united with the body. The situation that body and soul face is likened to the suffering of crucifixion.

INTERPRETATIVE COMMENT
This saying coheres to one of the themes characteristic of the accretions, namely its disdain for the body. This saying would have held special importance hermeneutically for the Thomasine encratic constituency since encratic Christians saw 'self-control' as a cure for

the predicament of the soul which suffered extremely while embodied, an idea also fostered in Hermetic circles. Accrual can be attributed to a time between 80 and 120 CE.

R. Uro has a helpful summary of Platonic ideas about embodiment as the context for L. 87 and 112, although his discussion regarding the 'interdependence' of body and soul is problematic for the context of this saying. Neither L. 87 nor 112 state that a healthy person who has a balanced interaction between body and soul can be in a state of non-suffering. The point of the logia, in fact, is that *embodiment is a dire situation with suffering resulting for both body and soul.*

This saying shows affinities with early Alexandrian teaching about the soul. Relying on Platonic ideas about embodiment, Clement envisions the plight of the human soul to be akin to the horrific experience of crucifixion, each pleasure and pain literally 'nailing' the soul to the body (*Strom.* 2.20). The human soul is constantly 'tortured and corrected, being in a state of sensation lives, though said to suffer' (*Strom.* 5.14). This understanding is developed theologically in the Syrian tradition as can be seen in the writings of Pseudo-Macarius who tells us that the embodied 'soul enters into an agony' particularly as it struggles against carnal sensations and thoughts that keep us 'occupied with the material world'. But this condition is necessary, he says, because our torturous struggle against the passions imitates Jesus' crucifixion – 'when he came upon earth, suffered and was crucified, so you also suffer with him' (*Hom.* 32.9).

Can the human soul become liberated from this plight? Again, Alexandrian traditions help us here. According to Clement, Jesus' crucifixion and death is the extraordinary example of the moment when perfect passionlessness finally was achieved. This happened because the extraordinarily virtuous man Jesus was able to completely separate the passions from his soul, to crucify his flesh. This, Clement says, is 'what the cross means'. Jesus, by overcoming his passions, struggled with the 'spiritual powers', and conquered these demons who invade the soul and turn it away from virtue to follow the passions (*Strom.* 2.20; cf. *Rich Man* 29). Clement understands the Christian life to be based on imitation of Jesus' crucifixion. He states that the Christian, 'bearing the cross of the Saviour, will follow the Lord's footsteps, as God, having become a holy of holies' (*Strom.* 2.20). We Christians, Clement says, have to 'crucify our own flesh' just as Jesus did his flesh (*Frags.* 1.4; cf. *Strom.* 4.3–4; 4.6; 7.3; 7.12). Our imitation will result in liberation at death because the soul will be freed from the demons which would otherwise continue to hamper its redemption. This interpretative tradition appears to me to have originated in Paul's writings since he states in Galatians 5.24–25, 'Those who belong to Christ have crucified the flesh with its passions and lusts. If we live by the Spirit let us also walk in the Spirit.'

L. 87 and 112 hark to this ideology, the paradoxical state of our existence. The soul while embodied suffers as if the nails of the cross were being driven into it. Yet the body by its own nature suffers too the miseries of crucifixion, especially when the soul works to drive out its passions and control its desires.

The Syrian father Macarius appears to know this saying, although its meaning has changed considerably. In Macarius, the body is said to *rely on itself,* while the soul *relies on itself.* He says that the body, if it relies solely on its own nature for salvation, will be damned. The soul, if it is devoid of the Holy Spirit and trusts its own nature for salvation, will be damned. Macarius represents another shift in the verbal remembrance and, thus, the meaning of this saying.

SOURCE DISCUSSION
G. Quispel thinks this saying comes from a Hermetic source.

LITERATURE PARALLELS

L. 112

Jesus said, 'Alas to the flesh crucified by the soul! Alas to the soul crucified by the flesh!'

Pseudo-Macarius, Hom. *1.11*

'Woe to the body if it were to rely solely on its own nature, because it would by nature disintegrate and die. Woe also to the soul if it finds its whole being in its own nature and trusts solely in its own operations, refusing the participation of the Divine Spirit because it does not have the eternal and divine life as a vital part of itself.'

SELECT BIBLIOGRAPHY

Quispel (1981: 265); Uro (2003: 58–62).

Logion 88.1–2

[1]Jesus said, 'The angels and the prophets will come to you. They will give to you what is yours, [2]and, in turn, you will give them what you have. You will say to yourselves, "When will they come and receive what is theirs?"'

NHC II 2.48.7–12

[1]ⲡⲉϫⲉ ⲓ̅ⲥ̅ ϫⲉ ⲛ̅ⲁⲅⲅⲉⲗⲟⲥ ⲛⲏⲩ ϣⲁⲣⲱⲧⲛ̅ ⲙⲛ̅ ⲛ̅ⲡⲣⲟⲫⲏⲧⲏⲥ ⲁⲩⲱ
ⲥⲉⲛⲁϯ ⲛⲏⲧⲛ̅ ⲛ̅ⲛⲉⲧⲉⲩⲛ̅ⲧⲏⲧⲛ̅ⲥⲉ [2]ⲁⲩⲱ ⲛ̅ⲧⲱⲧⲛ̅ ϩⲱⲧⲧⲏⲩⲧⲛ̅
ⲛⲉⲧⲛ̅ⲧⲟⲧⲧⲏⲛⲉ ⲧⲁⲁⲩ ⲛⲁⲩ ⲛ̅ⲧⲉⲧⲛ̅ϫⲟⲟⲥ ⲛⲏⲧⲛ̅ ϫⲉ ⲁϣ ⲛ̅ϩⲟⲟⲩ
ⲡⲉⲧⲟⲩⲛ̅ⲛⲏⲩ ⲛ̅ⲥⲉϫⲓ ⲡⲉⲧⲉ ⲡⲱⲟⲩ

ATTRIBUTION

Accretion.

TEXT AND TRANSLATION ISSUES

'Angel' was a term occasionally interchangable with 'prophet' (2 Chron. 36.15–16; Isa. 44.26; Hag. 1.12–13; Jer. 23.18–22; *Lev. Rab.* 1.1). Even the title assumed by the prophet 'Malachi' means simply 'my angel' (מלאכי). In Luke, Jesus sends his 'angels' to a Samaritan village to prepare the people to receive him (9.52). The reference seems to be to Jesus' disciples.

INTERPRETATIVE COMMENT

The content of this saying reflects a discussion that occurred in early Christianity in the mid- to late first century as stable Christian communities began to be established. The discussion centres on the relationship between these established Christian communities and itinerant prophets. The expectation that the prophet would be supported by the community he or she taught was probably grounded in Jesus' teaching about discipleship and seems to have been the practice of the Jerusalem mission (Matt. 10.11). Paul, however, challenged this expectation by supporting himself through his own labour. But he received criticism because of it (1 Cor. 9.1–18). The *Didache* 11–13 contains references to the abuse of this system of compensation and generates further rules to protect the communities from fraud. The Thomasine community chose to retain the practice of the Jerusalem church, referring to Jesus' authority on the subject. Accrual likely occurred between 60 and 100 CE.

SOURCE DISCUSSION
G. Quispel thinks that this saying comes from a Jewish Christian Gospel.

LITERATURE PARALLELS

Luke 16.12
> 'And if you have not been faithful in that which is another's, who will give you that which is your own?'

SELECT BIBLIOGRAPHY
Quispel (1981: 265).

Logion 89.1–2

[1]Jesus said, 'Why do you wash the cup's exterior? [2]Do you not understand that He who created the interior is also He who created the exterior?'

NHC II 2.48.13–16

[1]ⲡⲉⲭⲉ ⲓ̅ⲥ̅ ⲭⲉ ⲉⲧⲃⲉ ⲟⲩ ⲧⲉⲧⲛ̅ⲉⲓⲱⲉ ⲙ̅ⲡⲥⲁ ⲛⲃⲟⲗ ⲙ̅ⲡⲡⲟⲧⲏⲣⲓⲟⲛ [2]ⲧⲉⲧⲛ̅ⲡⲛⲟⲉⲓ ⲁⲛ ⲭⲉ ⲡⲉⲛⲧⲁϩⲧⲁⲙⲓⲟ ⲙ̅ⲡⲥⲁ ⲛϩⲟⲩⲛ ⲛ̅ⲧⲟϥ ⲟⲛ ⲡⲉⲛⲧⲁϥⲧⲁⲙⲓⲟ ⲙ̅ⲡⲥⲁ ⲛⲃⲟⲗ

ATTRIBUTION
Kernel saying.

TEXT AND TRANSLATION ISSUES
A. Baker has argued based on comparative analysis of Matthew 23.25 in Syriac New Testament witnesses, Aphraat, the *Liber Graduum* and *Pseudo-Macarius* that the Diatessaronic reading approximated the tradition in *Thomas*, 'to wash', rather than the tradition in the Greek Synoptics, 'to purify'.

INTERPRETATIVE COMMENT
In this saying, Jesus joins the first-century debate over the purity of containers (cf. Matthew 23.25–26; Luke 11.39–40; *Mishnah Kelim* 25.1, 7–8; *Mishnah Berakot* 8.2). According to Jesus, the interior of the cup is contrasted with and valued over the exterior. The interior is in a state of cleanliness because it has been created by God. This is the key to a clean exterior, not the washing of the cup itself. In fact, the status of the interior of the cup determines the overall status of the cup.

What is the Jewish debate in which Jesus and the first Thomasine Christians were involved? According to *Mishnah Kelim*, some Jews believed that a container was divided into three parts – the interior, the exterior, and the handle or grip – and that each part had its *own independent* status of purity (25.7). Nothing is said in this Mishnah regarding the purity or impurity of one part determining the overall purity of the container as Jesus seems to be arguing in his saying. In fact, we are told that if the exterior of the cup is unclean and it is picked up by clean hands on the grip, the hands are not made unclean. Nor does the impure status of the exterior of a cup affect the purity of the interior of the cup and its contents even when one's lips touch both the inside and the outside of the container (25.7).

So why worry about cleaning the exterior of the cup at all? According to E. Sanders, this seems to have been a concern for the Pharisees from the House of Shammai when it came to mixing liquids in a cup. This concern most likely points to their interpretation of the purity laws in Leviticus 11.32–38. What if one's hands had contacted a dead insect? The exterior of the cup would become impure when touched and this impurity could then pass to the interior through splashed liquid (*Tosefta Berakot* 5.26). How could this situation be avoided? By handwashing. Thus, those from the House of Shammai contended that one should 'wash the hands and then mix the cup' (*Mishnah Berakot* 8.2). This means that the Pharisaic school of Shammai taught that, in addition to one's hands, the exterior of the cup could be made clean as well, and should be immersed to remove any contaminants prior to use.

This position was at odds with the school of Hillel which taught that the exterior of the container should *always* be deemed unclean, probably because one could never know for certain if a dead insect had fallen on the cup after it had been immersed (*Tosefta Berakot* 5.26). So one should 'mix the cup and then wash the hands' (*Mishnah Berakot* 8.2). In this way, any impurity which had been conveyed to the hands from the outside of the cup through moisture during the mixing process would be removed from one's hands. The status of the contents inside would be protected since there would be no moisture to convey impurity to the inside of the cup. So, similar to Jesus and his followers, the Pharisees of the school of Hillel would not have been concerned about washing the exterior of the cup.

Having said this, however, it is important to recognize, as A. Saldarini does, that their reasons for this differed. For the Hillelites, the exterior of the cup was always in a state of impurity, so it was necessary to wash one's hand after mixing in order to put a halt to the contamination. Since, for the early Thomasine Christians, the interior of the cup determined the purity standards of the whole cup, handwashing would not have played a role in determining the cleanness of the cup's interior and so probably was not practised by them (cf. Mark 7.1–4). Secondarily, they may have understood this debate as an analogy of an individual's righteousness which they may have based on the person's inward condition rather than on the external. At any rate, in the rhetorical Kernel speech, the question, 'Why do you wash the cup's exterior?' would have been posed to the Thomasine audience, asking the congregants to consider whether they have chosen the leadership of other Jews who wash the cup's exterior or whether they have chosen the leadership of Jesus who demands internal cleanliness and, as the next logion indicates, whose yoke is 'easy' and lordship 'mild'.

SOURCE DISCUSSION

L. 89 is supposed to be a welding of Matthew 13.25–26 and Luke 11.39–40, according to W. Schrage, B. Gärtner, E. Haenchen, R. Grant and D.N. Freedman, and R. Kasser. Schrage points out that Luke 11.40 is secondary in form and this agrees with L. 89.

J. Sieber thinks that Luke does not have to be the source for the form. The similarity in form could just as easily have come from the same or similar sources used by the authors of Luke and *Thomas*. H. Koester has noted that L. 89 preserves a form of this saying that is earlier than Q, having no reference to the Pharisees, and lacking the secondary phrases 'are full of exhortation and wickedness' and 'you fool!'.

The inversion of 'inside…outside' in L. 89 should also be noted, I think, especially since this is the reference found in the Syrian father Pseudo-Macarius. Accounting for this difference between L. 89 and Luke is easier explained as the result of oral performance than literary dependence. In my opinion, the evidence suggests the pre-Synoptic oral field of performance as the source for L. 89 and the saying in Q.

Matthew 23.25–26 (Qmatt)
[25]'Woe to you, scribes and Pharisees, hypocrites! for you cleanse the outside of the cup and of the plate, but inside they are full of extortion and rapacity. [26]You blind Pharisee! first cleanse the inside of the cup and of the plate, that the outside also may be clean.'

Luke 11.39–41 (Qluke)
[39]'Now you Pharisees cleanse the outside of the cup and of the dish, but inside you are full of extortion and wickedness. [40]You fools! Did not He who made the outside make the inside also? [41]But give for alms those things which are within; and behold, everything is clean for you.'

Pseudo-Clementines, Hom. *11.29*
'However, to the hypocrites he said, "Woe to you, Scribes and Pharisees, hypocrites, for you make clean the outside of the cup and the platter, but the inside is full of filth. You blind Pharisee! cleanse first the inside of the cup and the platter, that their outsides may be clean also."'

Pseudo-Clementines, Rec. *6.11.3*
'To some therefore of them – not to all – he said, "Woe to you, Scribes and Pharisees, hypocrites! because you cleanse the outside of the cup and platter, but the inside is full of pollution. O blind Pharisees! first make clean what is within, and what is without shall be clean also."'

Pseudo-Macarius, Great Letter, *Maloney (1992: 264)*
'It seems to me such persons are really similar to those "who clean the outside of the cup and the dish and leave the inside full of all sorts of evil."'

Cf. Mark 7.1–4; *Mishnah Kelim* 25.1, 7–8; *Mishnah Berakot* 8.2; *Tosefta Berakot* 5.26

Luke 11.39 in Mcion
the outside of the cup<<the outside of the cup and plate

Matthew 23.26//Luke 11.40 in Mcion T^P T^A T^T T^V T^{NL} L Gr Mac Aug
wash<<cleanse

Luke 11.40 in Mcion
– and of the dish
Luke 11.40 in C D pc e a c d T^{NL} P^{45} Cypr mss. C Γ
he who made the inside is also he who made the outside<<he who made the outside, makes also the inside

Matthew 23.25–26//Luke 11.39–40 in D a d e ff^2 r^1 S W θ
the outside of the cup<<the outside of the cup and plate

SELECT BIBLIOGRAPHY
Baker (1965b); Gärtner (1961: 36–37); Grant with Freedman (1960: 183–84); Haenchen (1961: 66–67); Haenchen (1961/1962: 326–27); Kasser (1961: 105); Koester (1990: 91–92); Miller (1989); Saldarini (1994: 139–40); Sanders (1990: 39, 203–204); Schrage (1964a: 170–72); Sieber (1966: 252).

Logion 90.1–2

[1]Jesus said, 'Come to me, for my yoke is mild and my lordship is gentle. [2]And you will find rest for yourselves.'

NHC II 2.48.16–20

[1]ⲡⲉⲭⲉ ⲓ̅ⲏ̅ⲥ̅ ⲭⲉ ⲁⲙⲉⲓⲧ̅ⲛ̅ ⲱⲁⲣⲟⲉⲓ ⲭⲉ ⲟⲩⲭⲣⲏⲥⲧⲟⲥ ⲡⲉ ⲡⲁⲛⲁϩⲃ
ⲁⲩⲱ ⲧⲁⲙⲛ̅ⲧ̅ⲭⲟⲉⲓⲥ ⲟⲩⲣⲙ̅ⲣⲁⲱ ⲧⲉ [2]ⲁⲩⲱ ⲧⲉⲧⲛⲁϩⲉ
ⲁⲩⲁⲛⲁ[[ⲡⲁⲩ]]ⲥⲓⲥ ⲛ̅ⲏⲧ̅ⲛ̅

ATTRIBUTION
Kernel saying.

TEXT AND TRANSLATION ISSUES
According to my own study, 'The Yoke Saying in the *Gospel of Thomas* 90', concluded that L. 90 displays Aramaic tendencies, especially preserving 'lordship' rather than 'burden'.

The manuscript has ⲁⲩⲁⲛⲁⲩⲡⲁⲥⲓⲥ. It has been emended ⲁⲩⲁⲛⲁ[[ⲡⲁⲩ]]ⲥⲓⲥ since the manuscript appears to me to contain a spelling error.

INTERPRETATIVE COMMENT
In the Kernel, this saying begins to draw to a conclusion the fourth speech, emphasizing the importance of choosing Jesus' leadership over others like the Pharisees (L. 89). It may have carried the additional meaning as a final call to those who are seeking the truth elsewhere, but not finding it, as the *Pseudo-Clementine Homilies* preserve. Since additional sayings did not accrue around this logion, it is difficult to judge any shift in meaning once *Thomas* became a fuller text. It may be that the 'yoke' was associated with encratic practices that were believed to bring the soul into the blessed state of passionlessness.

SOURCE DISCUSSION
After comparing L. 90 to Matthew 11.28–30, W. Schrage finds no evidence of dependency between the Sahidic texts and *Thomas*. But he still concludes that it is most probable that L. 90 reached *Thomas* through Matthew.

Since we are dealing with special Matthean material, there are no editorial traits in Matthew 11.28–30. So the only way to prove that L. 90 is dependent upon Matthew is to first prove that Matthew created the saying, according to J. Sieber. Since this cannot be done, Sieber considers them to be the same saying transmitted independently in Matthew and *Thomas*.

My own work on this logion concludes similarly. In fact, according to the form-critical study of this saying that I published in 1990, *Thomas*' saying represents an *older* independent version of the yoke saying than is preserved in Matthew.

LITERATURE PARALLELS

Matthew 11.28–30 (M)
[28]'Come to me, all who labour and are heavy laden, and I will give you rest. [29]Take my yoke upon you, and learn from me; for I am gentle and lowly in heart, and you will find rest for your souls. [30]For my yoke is easy, and my burden is light.'

Dialogue of the Saviour *68*
'When you abandon the works which will not be able to follow you, then you will rest.'

Pseudo-Clementines, Rec. *10.51*

> 'And when he has entertained a sure faith concerning him, he will without labour take upon him the yoke of righteousness and piety. And so great sweetness will he perceive in it, that not only will he not find fault with any labour being in it, but will even desire something further to be added or imposed upon him'.

Pseudo-Clementines, Hom. *3.52*

> 'He cried and said, "Come unto me, all who labour", that is, who are seeking the truth, and not finding it.'

Pistis Sophia *2.95*

> 'Everyone who is weary and heavy-laden, come to me and I will give you rest. For my burden is light and my yoke is gentle.'

Cf. *Sirach* 6.19; 6.27–28; 24.19–20; 51.23, 26–27

SELECT BIBLIOGRAPHY
DeConick (1990); Schrage (1964a: 172–73); Sieber (1966: 138–39).

Logion 91.1–2

[1]They said to him, 'Tell us, so that we may believe in you, who are you?'

[2]He said to them, 'You <<examine>> the appearance of the sky and the earth, but, he who is in your midst, you do not understand. Nor this critical time! you do not understand how to <<examine>> it.'

NHC II 2.48.20–25

[1]ⲡⲉⲭⲁⲩ ⲛⲁϥ ⲭⲉ ⲭⲟⲟⲥ ⲉⲣⲟⲛ ⲭⲉ ⲛ̄ⲧⲕ ⲛⲓⲙ ϣⲓⲛⲁ ⲉⲛⲁⲣ̄ⲡⲓⲥⲧⲉⲩⲉ
ⲉⲣⲟⲕ [2]ⲡⲉⲭⲁϥ ⲛⲁⲩ ⲭⲉ ⲧⲉⲧⲛ̄ⲣ̄ⲡⲓⲣⲁⲍⲉ ⲙ̄ⲡ ⲟ ⲛ̄ⲧⲡⲉ ⲙⲛ̄ ⲡⲕⲁϩ
ⲁⲩⲱ ⲡⲉⲧⲛ̄ⲡⲉⲧⲛ̄ⲙⲧⲟ ⲉⲃⲟⲗ ⲙ̄ⲡⲉⲧⲛ̄ⲥⲟⲩⲱⲛϥ ⲁⲩⲱ ⲡⲉⲉⲓⲕⲁⲓⲣⲟⲥ
ⲧⲉⲧⲛ̄ⲥⲟⲟⲩⲛ ⲁⲛ ⲛ̄ⲣ̄ⲡⲓⲣⲁⲍⲉ ⲙ̄ⲙⲟϥ

ATTRIBUTION
Kernel saying, with accretive introductory clause.

TEXT AND TRANSLATION ISSUES
The Coptic expression, ⲣ̄ⲡⲓⲣⲁⲍⲉ, means literally, 'to try' or 'test' a person, a meaning which does not make much sense here. A. Guillaumont has suggested a Semitic substratum based on the fact that Luke 12.56 has δοκιμάξειν which is translated in the Syriac version as the verb ܪܚ. This Syriac word equally means 'to test' or 'to examine'. In the Syriac version of Exodus 20.20 it translates πειράζειν while in 2 Corinthians 8.8, δοκιμάξειν. The Greek translator of *Thomas* appears to have interpreted the verb in the sense of πειράζειν rather than δοκιμάξειν as Luke has it. I have relied on this argument in order to explain the presence of the Coptic phrase and provide a more sensible translation of it.

INTERPRETATIVE COMMENT
My best judgement is that L. 91.1 is accretive since it reflects the same type of christological question found in other accretive dialogues (L. 13, 43 and 61) although the saying itself, L. 91.2, is attributed to the Kernel since it does not contain material reflective of later

Christian thought. It *may* be the case, however, that the entire pericope should be attributed to later accretive materials, especially since there is evidence of a Syriac substratum in L. 91.2 rather than an Aramaic.

SOURCE DISCUSSION

W. Schrage, R. Grant and D.N. Freedman understand L. 91 to be a combination of Matthew 16.3 and Luke 12.56. Schrage says that *Thomas* agrees with Luke's addition τῆς γῆς to τὸ πρόσωπον, and takes πειράζειν from Matthew 16.1.

J. Sieber notes that Matthew identifies the opponents as the Pharisees and Sadducees while L. 91 does not. This suggests a secondary development in Matthew, *not Thomas*. He does not use the Lukanisms, τοῖς ὄχλοις nor ὑποκριταί, a point that H. Koester also notes. Thus Sieber argues for an independent tradition of sayings for the source of L. 91.

In my opinion, this logion exhibits signs of orally transmitted material with select words in common with the Synoptic variants ('the appearance of the sky and the earth'; 'time'), but no long sequences. Performance differences highlight the rest of the logion. The logion appears to me to be an early multiform developed in the field of oral performance. I find no evidence of secondary orality since I do not know for certain if 'the earth' is a Lukan addition to Quelle or a Matthean deletion. Or it may also be the case that we are witnessing different versions of Quelle, L. 91.1–2 showing more affinity with Qluke than Qmatt.

LITERATURE PARALLELS

Matthew 16.1–3 (Qmatt)
> [1]'And the Pharisees and the Sadducees came, and to test him they asked him to show them a sign from heaven. [2]He answered them, "When it is evening, you say, 'It will be fair weather, because the sky is red.' [3]And in the morning, 'It will be stormy today, because the sky is red and threatening.' You understand how to interpret the appearance of the sky, but you cannot interpret the signs of the times."'

Luke 12.54–56 (Qluke)
> [54]'He said to the multitudes, "When you see a cloud rising in the west, you say at once, 'A shower is coming.' And so it happens. [55]And when you see the south wind blowing, you say, 'There will be scorching heat.' And so it happens. [56]You hypocrites! You know how to interpret the appearance of earth and sky, but why do you not know how to interpret the present time?"'

Gospel of the Nazarenes *13*

Jerome, Commentary on Matthew, *on 16.2–3*
> 'What is marked with an asterisk [Matthew 16.2–3] is not found in other manuscripts, also it is not found in the Jewish Gospel.'

AGREEMENTS IN SYRIAN GOSPELS, WESTERN TEXT AND DIATESSARON

Luke 12.56//Matthew 16.3 in Mcion
> – you know

Luke 12.56//Matthew 16.3 in S C
> test<<interpret

Luke 12.56//Matthew 16.3 ℵ[c] *D d P*[75] *L 28 33 157 713 1241 Koine Mcion lat S C T*[A] *sa bo aeth*
> of the sky...of the earth<<of the earth...of the sky

Luke 12.56//Matthew 16.3 in D 1241 1573 *Mcion c d e ff^2 S C T^4*
  – but why

Luke 12.56//Matthew 16.3 in P^{75} ℵ B C L Θ 33 1241 *pc ff^2 1 Mcion T^4 T^P sa bo aeth*
  + *you do...know* (to test)

SELECT BIBLIOGRAPHY
Grant with Freedman (1960: 184–85); Guillaumont (1981: 198); Koester (1990: 94–95);
Schrage (1964a: 175–77); Sieber (1966: 219–22).

Logion 92.1–2

¹Jesus said, 'Seek and you will find. ²However, the questions you asked me previously
but which I did not address then, now I want to address, yet you do not seek (answers).'

NHC II 2.48.25–30

¹ΠΕΧΕ Ι͞C ΧΕ ϢΙΝΕ ΑΥⲱ ΤΕΤΝΑϬΙΝΕ ²ΑⲗⲗΑ ΝΕΤΑΤΕΤⲚⲬΝΟΥΕΙ
ΕΡΟΟΥ Ⲛ͞ΝΙ2ΟΟΥ ΕⲘΠΙΧΟΟΥ ΝΗΤⲚ͞ Ⲙ͞ΦΟΟΥ ΕΤⲘ͞ΜΑΥ ΤΕΝΟΥ
Ε2ΝΑⲓ̈ ΕΧΟΟΥ ΑΥⲱ ΤΕΤⲚϢΙΝΕ ΑΝ Ⲛ͞CⲱΟΥ

ATTRIBUTION
Kernel saying.

TEXT AND TRANSLATION ISSUES
The antecedent, 'answers', is supplied based on the context and the plural reference in the
expression Ⲛ͞CⲱΟΥ.

INTERPRETATIVE COMMENT
In the Kernel Gospel, this saying introduced the fifth speech in which the truth about
God's Kingdom is revealed. This speech begins with an admonition similar to the other
four speeches, a call to the hearer to seek the truth from Jesus even if he or she has not
always done so.

SOURCE DISCUSSION
G. Quispel thinks that this saying comes from an encratic source.

LITERATURE PARALLELS

Matthew 7.7–8 (Qmatt)
  ⁷'Ask, and it will be given you. Seek, and you will find. Knock, and it will be opened to
  you. ⁸For everyone who asks receives, and he who seeks, finds, and to him who knocks
  it will be opened.'

Luke 11.9–10 (Qluke)
  ⁹'And I tell you, Ask, and it will be given you. Seek, and you will find. Knock, and it
  will be opened to you. ¹⁰For everyone who asks receives, and he who seeks finds, and to
  him who knocks it will be opened.'

John 16.4–5

[4]'I did not say these things to you from the beginning, because I was with you. [5]But now I am going to him who sent me, yet none of you asks me, "Where are you going?"'

John 16.23–24

[23]'In that day, you will ask nothing of me. Truly, truly, I say to you, if you ask anything of the Father, he will give it to you in my name. [24]Hitherto you have asked nothing in my name. Ask, and you will receive, that your joy may be full.'

John 16.29–30

[29]'His disciples said, "Ah, now you are speaking plainly, not in any figure! [30]Now we know that you know all things, and need none to question you. By this we believe that you came from God."'

Dialogue of the Saviour *20*

'And [let] him who[…]seek and find and [rejoice.]'

Dialogue of the Saviour *16*

'But I say to [you as for what] you seek after [and you] enquire about, [behold, it is] in you.'

Pseudo-Clementines, Hom. *3.52*

'Wherefore also he cried, and said, "Come unto me, all who labour", that is, who are seeking the truth, and not finding it; and again, "My sheep hear my voice"; and elsewhere, "Seek and find", since the truth does not lie on the surface.'

L. 2

[1]'((Jesus said, "Whoever seeks should not cease seeking until he finds. [2]And when he finds, he will be amazed. [3]And when he is amazed, he will be a king. [4]And once he is a king, he will rest."'

L. 94

[1]'Jesus [said], "Whoever seeks will find. [2][Whoever knocks], it will be opened for him."'

SELECT BIBLIOGRAPHY
Quispel (1981: 265).

Logion 93.1–2

[1]'Do not give what is holy to dogs, or they might toss them on the manure pile. [2]Do not toss the pearls [to] pigs, or they might make [break] [[them]].'

NHC II 2.48.30–33

[1]ⲙⲡⲣ̄ϯ ⲡⲉⲧⲟⲩⲁⲁⲃ ⲛ̄ⲛⲟⲩϩⲟⲟⲣ ϫⲉⲕⲁⲥ ⲛⲟⲩⲛⲟϫⲟⲩ ⲉⲧⲕⲟⲡⲣⲓⲁ
[2]ⲙⲡⲣ̄ⲛⲟⲩϫⲉ ⲛ̄ⲙⲁⲣⲅⲁⲣⲓⲧⲏ|ⲥ ⲛ̄|ⲛⲉϣⲁⲩ ϣⲓⲛⲁ ϫⲉ ⲛⲟⲩⲁⲁ||ⲩ||
ⲛ̄ⲁⲁ|ϫⲧⲉ|

ATTRIBUTION
Kernel saying.

TEXT AND TRANSLATION ISSUES

I do not follow B. Layton's emendation, adding <Jesus said> to the beginning of the saying where it is not in the manuscript.

ⲚⲞⲨⲀⲀϥ has been emended to ⲚⲞⲨⲀⲀ[[Ⲩ]] as is expected grammatically in the sentence.

The final lacunae is difficult to fill. There have been several suggestions although most of them have grammatical problems. J. Leipoldt has offered Ⲛ̄ⲀⲀ[ⲀⲨ], 'bring it [to naught]', or possibly Ⲛ̄ⲀⲀ[ⲔⲈ] or ⲚⲀⲀ[Ⲕ̄Ⲙ̄], 'break them [to pieces]'. B. Layton favours the latter. Although P. de Suarez's reconstruction is contextually favourable ('they might make them muddy', ⲚⲞⲨⲀⲀ[[Ⲩ]] Ⲛ̄ⲀⲀ[ⲬⲦⲈ] and is followed by H.-G. Bethge, I think that ⲚⲀⲀ[Ⲕ̄Ⲙ̄], 'break them', is the best reconstruction because this reading agrees with the one found in *Pseudo-Clementine Recognitions* 3.1.5–6, 'not to throw the pearls of his words before swine and dogs, who, striving against them with arguments and sophisms, roll them in the mud of carnal understanding, and by their barkings and base answers *break* (*rumpō*) and weary the preachers of God's word'.

INTERPRETATIVE COMMENT

L. 93 occurs in the beginning of the fifth speech in the Kernel Gospel. It provides the rationale for Jesus' statement in L. 92, that the hearers should seek the truth because Jesus wants to reveal it now even though Jesus has not always done so. Why? Jesus has not revealed the truth previously because he has had to be careful not to give 'what is holy to the dogs' or toss 'the pearls to the swine'. This precise interpretation of L. 93 is also evident in the *Pseudo-Clementine Recognitions*, applying this logion to the same situation as we find in *Thomas* but not in Matthew 7.6. We discover in the *Recognitions* that 'we ought to be careful, yea, extremely careful, that we cast not our pearls before pigs' when we preach the words of truth to an audience filled with worthy and unworthy people alike (*Rec.* 2.3). The teacher must be very cautious when setting forth the truth in a mixed crowd because 'if he set forth pure truth to those who do not desire to obtain salvation, he does injury to him by whom he has been sent, and from whom he received the commandment not to throw the pearls of his words before pigs and dogs' (*Rec.* 3.1). This interpretation probably would have remained stable in the complete Gospel since there are no accretions to indicate a shift in this hermeneutic. It is noteworthy that this same hermeneutic survives in the Islamic Hadith tradition.

SOURCE DISCUSSION

W. Schrage notes several differences with Greek Matthew and states that nothing conclusive can be said about the origin of L. 93. But, when he compares Sahidic Matthew with *Thomas* he notes that Matthew omits three elements that *Thomas* also omits: the definite article on ⲠⲈⲦⲞⲨⲀⲀⲂ, 'your' and 'before'. This, Schrage suggests, means that L. 93 is dependent on Matthew.

J. Sieber says that the similarities between L. 93 and Sahidic Matthew might show that *Thomas'* Coptic text has been influenced by the Sahidic version of Matthew, but tells us nothing about the relationship between *Thomas'* Vorlage and Greek Matthew. Sieber traces L. 93.2 to secondary development in oral tradition rather than a literary allusion to Luke 14.35 as others have suggested.

I find Sieber's evaluation suitable, especially when one considers the habit of scribes to harmonize versions, selecting particular words when translating in order to bring the text into agreement with New Testament versions with which they were familiar. It is very reasonable to assume that the scribe translating the Greek *Thomas* into Coptic would be influenced by his knowledge of Sahidic Matthew. This would explain why L. 93 does not agree with Greek Matthew while it does in at least three instances with Coptic Matthew. Although L. 93 was originally an independent tradition, developed within the field of oral performance, it appears to have been secondarily harmonized with the Sahidic version of Matthew during the scribal translation process.

LITERATURE PARALLELS

Matthew 7.6 (M)
> 'Do not give dogs what is holy, and do not throw your pearls before swine, lest they trample them under foot and turn to attack you.'

Didache *9.5*
> 'No one is to eat or drink of your eucharist but those who have been baptized in the Name of the Lord. For the Lord's own saying applies here, "Give not that which is holy unto dogs."'

Pseudo-Clementine Recognitions *2.3*
> 'How much more it is proper for us to ascertain who or what sort of man he is to whom the words of immortality are to be committed! For we ought to be careful, yea, extremely careful, that we cast not our pearls before swine.'

Pseudo-Clementine Recognitions *3.1*
> 'What then shall he do who has to address a mixed multitude? Shall he conceal what is true? How then shall he instruct those who are worthy? But if he set forth pure truth to those who do not desire to obtain salvation, he does injury to him by whom he has been sent, and from whom he as received commandment not to throw the pearls of his words before swine and dogs, who, striving against them with arguments and sophisms, roll them in the mud of carnal understanding, and by their barkings and base answers break and weary the preachers of God's word.'

Ahmad ibn Hanbal, al-Zuhd, *p. 144 (no. 477)*
> 'Jesus said to the disciples, "O disciples, do not cast pearls before swine, for the swine can do nothing with them. Do not impart wisdom to one who does not desire it, for wisdom is more precious than pearls and whoever rejects wisdom is worse than a swine."'

Cf. Luke 14.35

AGREEMENTS IN SYRIAN GOSPELS, WESTERN TEXT AND DIATESSARON

Matthew 7.6 in Ps.-Clem. Rec.
> manure pile (mud)

Matthew 7.6 in C Pal T^{EC} T^V Ps.-Clem. Rec. *bo cod 2 Clem Hipp Orig Chrys Basil L Gr*
> the pearls << your pearls

Matthew 7.6 in Tert Ps.-Clem. Rec.
> to the swine << before swine

SELECT BIBLIOGRAPHY
Bethge (1997: 541); Layton (1989: 86); Leipoldt (1967); Schrage (1964a: 179); Sieber (1966: 78–79); Suarez (1974).

Logion 94.1–2

¹Jesus [said], 'Whoever seeks will find. ²[Whoever knocks], it will be opened for him.'

NHC II 2.48.33–34

> ¹|ⲡⲉⲝⲉ| ⲓ̅ⲥ̅ ⲡⲉⲧϣⲓⲛⲉ ϥⲛⲁϭⲓⲛⲉ ²|ⲡⲉⲧⲧⲱϩ̅ⲙ ⲉϩⲟⲩⲛ ⲥⲉⲛⲁⲟⲩⲱⲛ
> ⲛⲁϥ

ATTRIBUTION
Kernel saying.

INTERPRETATIVE COMMENT
In the Kernel and the complete Gospel, this promise follows the statement that Jesus has not always been able to reveal the truth because he has been concerned about giving his message to the unworthy. But now he promises to reveal the truth to those who seek and knock. If the hearer seeks the truth, Jesus will reveal it to him or her. If the hearer knocks on the door, Jesus will let him or her in.

SOURCE DISCUSSION
W. Schrage understands L. 94 to depend on Matthew 7.7–8 although his examples are based on Sahidic translations. J. Sieber argues that these Coptic examples do not demonstrate *Thomas'* use of Greek materials. He traces any similarities in Coptic to independent translation choices.

Because we cannot identify editorial similarities between L. 94 and Matthew or Luke, nor can we identify in L. 94 distinctions in Quelle's version(s), it is not possible to maintain a position of dependence. The similarities between Sahidic Matthew and L. 94 probably do not represent 'independent translation choices' as Sieber suggests. Rather when the scribe was translating the Greek *Thomas* into Coptic, he choose Coptic words which tended to align L. 94 with his memory of the Sahidic version of the New Testament.

LITERATURE PARALLELS

Matthew 7.7–8 (Qmatt)
> ⁷'Ask, and it will be given you. Seek, and you will find. Knock, and it will be opened to you. ⁸For everyone who asks receives, and he who seeks, finds, and to him who knocks it will be opened.'

Luke 11.9–10 (Qluke)
> ⁹'And I tell you, Ask, and it will be given you. Seek, and you will find. Knock, and it will be opened to you. ¹⁰For everyone who asks receives, and he who seeks finds, and to him who knocks it will be opened.'

Cf. L. 2 and 94

AGREEMENTS IN SYRIAN GOSPELS, WESTERN TEXT AND DIATESSARON

Matthew 7.8//Luke 11.10 in d (Luke 11.10) f 1 (Matt 7.8) S C P T^P T^A T^{NL} sa geo Pist. Soph.
    will find << finds

Luke 11.10 in aur f r^1 C P
    + for him

Matthew 7.8 in S C P
  + for him

SELECT BIBLIOGRAPHY
Schrage (1964a: 177–78); Sieber (1966: 82–83).

Logion 95.1–2

[1][Jesus said], 'If you have money, do not give it at interest. [2]Rather, give [it] to someone from whom you will not get it (back).'

NHC II,2.48.35–49.2

[1]|ⲡⲉⲝⲉ ⲓ̅ⲥ̅ ⲝⲉ| ⲉⲩⲱⲡⲉ ⲟⲩⲛ̅ⲧⲏⲧⲛ̅ ϩⲟⲙⲧ ⲙ̅ⲡⲣ̅ϯ ⲉⲧⲙⲏⲥⲉ [2]ⲁⲗⲗⲁ
ϯ |ⲙ̅ⲙⲟϥ| ⲙ̅ⲡⲉⲧ|ⲉ|ⲧⲛⲁⲝⲓⲧⲟⲩ ⲁⲛ ⲛ̅ⲧⲟⲟⲧϥ

ATTRIBUTION
Kernel saying.

INTERPRETATIVE COMMENT
L. 95, in the Kernel, is part of a series of logia that address the promise of truth to those who seek it. Jesus has just explained that the he has not always been able to talk about the truth because he has been speaking to the worthy and unworthy alike. But now he will reveal the truth to those who ask him. He implies in L. 95 that, because the hearer is receiving the truth freely, he must now freely give it to others, by presenting an analogous situation in which a person is told that it is not even good enough to give money at no interest. In fact, a person must give to people who cannot even repay the principal! In the complete Gospel, this ethic would have been particularly meaningful to the encratic Christian and represented to him or her Jesus' endorsement of the rejection of worldly goods.

SOURCE DISCUSSION
C. Tuckett argues that Luke 6.34 is the basis for L. 95.1–2 because it mentions some kind of return of a loan or gift. He expresses the opinion of W.C. van Unnik that this represents redactional development of Q 6.34 by Luke's hand, a critique of the reciprocity ethic. H. Koester, however, views L. 95 as more original in form than Qluke 6.34 since it lacks the secondary addition, 'Even sinners led to sinners…'

The main difficulty with this reasoning is that it is not known if Luke 6.34 was contained in Quelle, L, or represents Luke's own redaction of Q 6.30. It is even possible that it represents an independent saying altogether, a position I favour because the subject found in the variants Luke 6.34, L. 95 and *Didache* 1.5 is too different from Q 6.30 to have any direct relationship. Q 6.30 is about giving money or goods to beggars, while the saying variants in Luke 6.34, L. 95 and *Didache* 1.5 are about giving money, not only without interest, but to someone who cannot even pay back the principal. Luke 6.34 and *Didache* 1.5 appear to represent the positive formulations of this saying, while *Thomas* the negative. It is more reasonable to explain these variants as independent developments within the field of oral performance than developments out of a genealogy of literary dependence.

LITERATURE PARALLELS

Luke 6.34–35 (L or Qluke)
[34]'And if you lend to those from whom you hope to receive, what credit is that to you? Even sinners lend to sinners, to receive as much again. [35]But love your enemies, and do good, and lend, expecting nothing in return. And your reward will be great, and you will be sons of the Most High. For he is kind to the ungrateful and the selfish.'

Didache 1.5
'Give to everyone who asks, without looking for any repayment, for it is the Father's pleasure that we should share his gracious bounty with all people.'

Matthew 5.42 (Qmatt)
'Give to him who begs from you. Do not refuse him who would borrow from you.'

Luke 6.30 (Qluke)
'Give to everyone who begs from you. Of every one who takes away your goods do not ask them again.'

Pseudo-Clementine Homilies 11.32
'If he who is in error lends to those who have, let us give to those who have not.'

Pseudo-Clementine Recognitions 6.13
'If they lend to those who have the means of paying, we should give to those from whom we do not hope to receive anything.'

Liber Graduum 929.18
'He [the just man] lends to the poor and receives what he lent...without interest, but to those who have not he gives the grace of God.'

Exodus 22.25
'If you lend money to any of my people with you who is poor, you shall not be to him as a creditor, and you shall not exact interest from him.'

Leviticus 25.35–37
[35]'And if your brother becomes poor, and cannot maintain himself with you, you shall maintain him. As a stranger and a sojourner, he shall live with you. [36]Take no interest from him nor increase, but fear your God; that your brother may live beside you. [37]You shall not lend him your money at interest, nor give him your food for profit.'

Ahmad ibn Hanbal, al-Zuhd, pp. 144–45 (no. 480)
'If you desire to devote yourselves entirely to God...lend to those who do not repay you.'

Cf. *Liber Graduum* 325.21–22.

AGREEMENTS IN SYRIAN GOSPELS, WESTERN TEXT AND DIATESSARON

Luke 6.35 in T^P
give << you lend

SELECT BIBLIOGRAPHY
Koester (1990: 90); Tuckett (1991: 351–52).

Logion 96.1–2

[1]Jesus said, 'The Kingdom of the Father is like a woman. [2]She took a little yeast. She buried it in dough. She made the dough into large bread loaves.'

NHC II 2.49.2–5

[1]ⲡⲉϫⲉ ⲓ̅ⲥ̅ ϫⲉ ⲧⲙⲛ̅ⲧⲉⲣⲟ ⲙ̅ⲡⲉⲓⲱⲧ ⲉⲥⲧⲛ̅ⲧⲱⲛ ⲁⲩⲥ̅ϩⲓⲙⲉ [2]ⲁⲥϫⲓ ⲛ̅ⲟⲩⲕⲟⲩⲉⲓ ⲛ̅ⲥⲁⲉⲓⲣ [3]ⲁⲥϩⲟⲡϥ ϩⲛ̅ ⲟⲩⲱϣⲧⲉ ⲁⲥⲁⲁϥ ⲛ̅ϩⲛ̅ⲛⲟϭ ⲛ̅ⲛⲟⲉⲓⲕ

ATTRIBUTION
Kernel saying.

TEXT AND TRANSLATION ISSUES
I have rendered ϩⲱⲡ, 'bury or cover', as its cognate in Greek, κρύπτω, allows. This translation makes more sense of the woman's action, putting the yeast into the dough than 'hide' which other translators (including NT translators) have preferred.

I have identifed the antecedent from ⲁⲥⲁⲁϥ with 'the dough' and include this in the translation instead of leaving the ambiguous 'it' as other translators have done. The phrase literally reads, 'She made it into large bread loaves.'

INTERPRETATIVE COMMENT
This logion appears in a sequence of parables and examples that reveal the truth about God's Kingdom. L. 96 is the first of these parables, opening the sequence with the story of a woman baking bread. Jesus compares the inauguration of the Kingdom to the mystery of a woman taking a pinch of leaven and rising large loaves of bread. In the Kernel, the parable may have been read with an eschatological hermeneutic, emphasizing the future inauguration as an event that will happen inevitably but mysteriously. The hermeneutic may have shifted once the Gospel came into its complete form so that God's Kingdom was understood as the present experience of God's mysterious power and reign within the parameters of the encratic community.

SOURCE DISCUSSION
W. Schrage says that it cannot be determined if L. 96 is dependent on Matthew or Luke. He thinks that this parable may be derived from Quelle and refashioned in the *Gospel of Thomas*. He observes that the author of *Thomas* may have been responsible for the omission of the question at the beginning of the parable, an omission which Matthew also witnesses. He notes that sy[C] and a couple of old Latin manuscripts omit the reference to three measures of meal just as *Thomas* does.

J. Sieber thinks that the most convincing argument for an independent tradition here is that this parable is separated from the mustard seed parable which Matthew and Luke cite together and may have been part of the Quelle sequence.

In my opinion, this parable is a prime example of an independent oral variant. When compared with the Synoptic versions, we have only key words in common – 'Kingdom; a woman; yeast; buried'. The rest of the details differ as we would expect with an oral variant. There is no compelling evidence of secondary orality.

LITERATURE PARALLELS

Matthew 13.33 (Qmatt)

'The Kingdom of Heaven is like leaven which a woman took and buried in three measures of floor, until it was all leavened.'

Luke 13.20–21 (Qluke)

[20]'To what shall I compare the Kingdom of God? [21]It is like leaven which a woman took and buried in three measures of flour, until it was all leavened.'

AGREEMENTS IN SYRIAN GOSPELS, WESTERN TEXT AND DIATESSARON

Matthew 13.33//Luke 13.20–21 in T^V T^{PEP}
    a little yeast << yeast

Matthew 13.33//Luke 13.20–21 in a b c ff^2 i l q (Luke) C (Matt) T^{EC} T^V
    – three measures

Matthew 13.33//Luke 13.20–21 in T^V T^{PEP}
    + has made large loaves of it

SELECT BIBLIOGRAPHY

Schrage (1964a: 183–85); Sieber (1966: 175–77).

Logion 96.3

[3]'Whoever has ears should listen!'

NHC II 2.49.6

ΠΕΤΕΥⲘ ΜΑⲀⲬⲈ ⲘⲘⲞϥ ΜΑ|ⲢⲈϥ|ϹⲰΤⲘ

ATTRIBUTION

Kernel saying.

See L. 8.

Logion 97.1–4

[1]Jesus said, 'The Kingdom of the [Father] is like a woman carrying a [jar] filled with meal. [2]While she was walking [on the] road still a long way out, the handle of the jar broke. Behind her, the meal leaked out onto the road. [3]She did not realize it. She had not noticed a problem. [4]When she arrived at her house, she put the jar down and found it empty.'

NHC II 2.49.7–15

[1]ⲠⲈⲬⲈ ⲒϹ ⲬⲈ ΤⲘⲚΤⲈⲢⲞ ⲘⲠⲈ|ⲒⲰΤ Ⲉ|ϹΤⲚΤⲰⲚ ⲀⲨϹ2ⲒΜⲈ Ⲉϥϥ 2Ⲁ ⲞⲨ6Ⲁ|ΜⲈⲈⲒ| ⲈϥΜⲈ2 ⲚⲚⲞⲈⲒΤ [2]ⲈϹΜⲞⲞⲨϢⲈ 2|Ⲓ ΤⲈ|2ⲒⲎ ⲈϹⲞⲨⲎⲞⲨ ⲀⲠⲘⲀⲀⲬⲈ ⲘⲠ6ⲀΜ|ⲈⲈⲒ| ⲞⲨⲰ6Π ⲀⲠⲚⲞⲈⲒΤ ϢⲞⲨⲞ ⲚϹⲰϹ |2|Ⲓ .

ΤΕϨΙΗ ³ΝΕССΟΟΥΝ ΑΝ ΠΕ ΝΕ ΜΠΕСΕΙΜΕ ΕϨΙСΕ ⁴ΝΤΑΡΕСΠⲰϨ
ΕϨΟΥΝ ΕΠΕСΗΕΙ ΑСΚΑ ΠϬⲀΜΕΕΙ ΑΠΕСΗΤ ΑСϨΕ ΕΡΟϥ ΕϥⲰΟΥΕΙΤ

ATTRIBUTION
Kernel saying.

TEXT AND TRANSLATION ISSUES
Guillaumont refers to several Semitisms in L. 97. For instance, he explains the difficult
Coptic expression ϨΙ ΤΕϨΙΗ ΕСΟΥΗΟΥ, literally 'on the road being distant', as corresponding exactly to the Hebrew expression בדרך רחקה (cf. Num. 9.10) which is also
preserved in the Peshitta (ܪ̈ܘܚܩܐ ܒܐܘܪܚܐ). Also, 'she did not realize it' may rest on
either ידע or ראה, in Aramaic חזא, which can mean either 'to comprehend' or 'to realize', 'to see' or 'to know'. The 'problem', ϨΙСΕ, probably corresponds to the Aramaic
בישא which is equivalent to the Syriac (ܒܝܫ) in Sirach 29.12.

INTERPRETATIVE COMMENT
This logion appears in a sequence of Kingdom parables that reveal the truth about its
inauguration. In the Kernel, the parable would have had an eschatological interpretation,
stressing that the future inauguration would be unexpected and astonishing like the reac-
tion of the woman who returns home with a jar of meal, only to find it empty because the
handle had broken off on the way. In the complete Gospel, the parable would have told the
story of expectations dashed, that the Kingdom had not come as people had expected.

SOURCE DISCUSSION
There is no Synoptic parallel for L. 97. Because the parallel exhibits Synoptic-like characteristics and does not contain elements which form-critics would view as redactional or
late, Montefoire, Jeremias, Higgins and Koester have viewed this parable as an authentic
parable of Jesus. It appears to have belonged to the Kernel Gospel, drawn from the oral
memory of the first Christians. G. Quispel argues that its style and content reflects a Palestinian milieu and origin isolated from Pauline theology. Thus he thinks the parable was
derived from a Jewish Christian Gospel.

SELECT BIBLIOGRAPHY
Guillaumont (1981: 201); Higgins (1960: 304); Jeremias (1963: 175 n. 12); Koester (1968:
220 n. 56); Merkelbach (1985); Montefoire (1960/1961: 242); Quispel (1957: 15); Scott
(1987: 77–80).

Logion 98.1–3

¹Jesus said, 'The Kingdom of the Father is like someone who wished to kill a prominent
man. ²While at home, he drew out his knife. He stabbed it into the wall to test whether
his hand would be strong (enough). ³Then he murdered the prominent man.'

NHC II 2.49.15–20

¹ΠΕΧΕ Ι̅С̅ ΤΜΝ̅ΤΕΡΟ ΜΠΕΙⲰΤ ΕСΤΝ̅ΤⲰΝ ΕΥΡⲰΜΕ ΕϥΟΥⲰϢ
ΕΜΟΥΤ ΟΥΡⲰΜΕ Μ̅ΜΕΓΙСΤΑΝΟС ²ΑϥϢⲰⲀΜ Ν̅ΤСΗϥΕ ϨΜ̅ ΠΕϥΗΕΙ

ⲀϤϪⲞⲦⲄ ⲚⲦϪⲞ <u>ϪⲈ</u>ⲔⲀⲀⲤ ⲈϤⲚⲀⲈⲒⲘⲈ ϪⲈ ⲦⲈϤϬⲒϪ ⲚⲀⲦⲰⲔ ⲈⲌⲞⲨⲚ
³ⲦⲞⲦⲈ ⲀϤⲌⲰⲦⲂ̄ ⲘⲠⲘⲈⲄⲒⲤⲦⲀⲚⲞⲤ

ATTRIBUTION
Kernel saying.

TEXT AND TRANSLATION ISSUES
G. Garitte and A. Guillaumont explain the phrase ⲀϤϪⲞⲦⲄ̄ ⲚⲦϪⲞ as a proleptic use of
the pronoun common to Aramaic syntax. The Peshitta of Matthew 26.24 is cited as a case
in point.

INTERPRETATIVE COMMENT
In the Kernel Gospel, this parable is an analogy in which the Kingdom is compared to an
assassin who prepares himself before killing his target. The point of the parable is that it is
necessary to prepare oneself for the inauguration of God's Kingdom. In the complete
Gospel, the encratic hermeneutic may have stressed the importance of testing one's
strength against the obstacles of desire.

SOURCE DISCUSSION
There is no Synoptic parallel for L. 98, although stylistically the parable is similar to
Synoptic parables. It does not contain secondary expansions or modifications from a form-
critical perspective. The imagery of violence is not uncommon to Jesus' sayings (cf. Mark
3.27 and parallels). The story may reflect the political intrigue of Galilee at the time of Jesus
as J. Jeremias has indicated. L.H. Hunzinger argues extensively for its authenticity and his
opinion appears to have become standard as noted by S. Davies and W. Stoker. This saying,
drawn from the oral field of early Christian performance, was part of the Kernel Gospel.

SELECT BIBLIOGRAPHY
Davies (1983: 9); Garitte (1957: 66); Guillaumont (1981: 196); Hunzinger (1960: 211–17);
Jeremias (1963: 196–97); Stoker (1988: 101–102).

Logion 99.1–3

¹The disciples said to him, 'Your brothers and your mother are standing outside.'

²He said to them, 'Those here who do the will of my father, they are my brothers and
my mother. ³They are the people who will enter the Kingdom of my Father.'

NHC II 2.49.21–26

¹ⲠⲈϪⲈ ⲘⲘⲀⲐⲎⲦⲎⲤ ⲚⲀϤ ϪⲈ ⲚⲈⲔⲤⲚⲎⲨ ⲘⲚ̄ ⲦⲈⲔⲘⲀⲀⲨ ⲤⲈⲀⲌⲈⲢⲀⲦⲞⲨ
ⲌⲒ ⲠⲤⲀ ⲚⲂⲞⲗ ²ⲠⲈϪⲀϤ ⲚⲀⲨ ϪⲈ ⲚⲈⲦⲚ̄ⲚⲈⲈⲒⲘⲀ ⲈⲦⲢⲈ ⲘⲠⲞⲨⲰϢ
ⲘⲠⲀⲈⲒⲰⲦ ⲚⲀⲈⲒⲚⲈ ⲚⲀⲤⲚⲎⲨ ⲘⲚ̄ ⲦⲀⲘⲀⲀⲨ ³Ⲛ̄ⲦⲞⲞⲨ ⲠⲈ ⲈⲦⲚⲀⲂⲰⲔ
ⲈⲌⲞⲨⲚ ⲈⲦⲘⲚ̄ⲦⲈⲢⲞ ⲘⲠⲀⲈⲒⲰⲦ

ATTRIBUTION
Kernel saying.

INTERPRETATIVE COMMENT

L. 99 is part of a sequence of sayings in which Jesus reveals the truth about God's Kingdom. Here he identifies those people who do the will of God with those who will enter the Kingdom and form a family that will replace their human families. To this end, it is noteworthy that L. 99 differs from its parallels in that it has the additional phrase, 'They are the people who will enter the Kingdom of my Father', an early development that connects the saying into the sequence of Kingdom parables which make up the heart of the fifth speech in the Kernel. In the complete Gospel, the stress on abandoning home and family in order to take up the encratic praxis would have been emphasized.

SOURCE DISCUSSION

W. Schrage thinks that dependence on Luke hinges on the fact that L. 99 and Luke 8.19–21 agree in the way that Luke combines two sentences into one from his source Mark 3.34–35. Both also omit the question posed in Mark 3.33. Dependence on Matthew is demonstrated, according to Schrage, based on the agreement between Matthew 12.50 and L. 99.2 since both have 'the will of my Father' whereas Mark has 'the will of God' and Luke, nothing. However, he notes that the saying with similar agreements is also found in the *Gospel of the Ebionites* and *2 Clement.* So he concludes that L. 99 might come from an ancient Gospel harmony like the *Gospel of the Nazarenes.* This agrees with the opinion of G. Quispel who suggested a Jewish Christian Gospel source for this saying as early as 1957. J. Sieber also thinks that this logion may indicate that *Thomas* had contact with some type of written source independent of the Synoptics. H. Koester notes that L. 99 lacks Mark's elaborate introductory setting for the discourse as well as Mark's restatement of the rhetorical question. Except for L. 99.3 which Koester considers secondary, *Thomas'* version corresponds to the saying's more original form.

I see no compelling reason to argue for a written source especially since we do not have anything extant. L. 99 could easily represent an orally derived variant from the East. This, in fact, would better explain the verbal differences as well as the agreements with the Synoptic parallels.

LITERATURE PARALLELS

Mark 3.31–35

[31]'And his mother and his brothers came; and standing outside they sent to him and called him. [32]And a crowd was sitting about him; and they said to him, "Your mother and your brothers are outside, asking for you." [33]And he replied, "Who are are my mother and my brothers?" [34]And looking around on those who sat about him, he said, "Here are my mother and my brothers! [35]Whoever does the will of God is my brother, and sister, and mother."'

Matthew 12.46–50

[46]'While he was still speaking to the people, behold, his mother and his brothers stood outside, asking to speak to him. [48]But he replied to the man who told him, "Who is my mother, and who are my brothers?" [49]And stretching out his hand toward his disciples, he said, "Here are my mother and my brothers! [50]For whoever does the will of my Father in heaven is my brother, and sister, and mother."'

Luke 8.19–21

[19]'Then his mother and his brothers came to him, but they could not reach him for the crowd. [20]And he was told, "Your mother and your brothers are standing outside, desiring to see you." [21]But he said to them, "My mother and my brothers are those who hear the word of God and do it."'

Gospel of the Ebionites *5 (Epiphanius,* Haer. *30.14–15)*

> 'Moreover, they deny that he was a man, evidently on the ground of the word which the Saviour spoke when it was reported to him, "Behold, your mother and your brothers are standing outside", namely, "Who is my mother and who are my brothers?" And he stretched forth his hand towards his disciples and said, "There are my brothers and mother and sisters, who do the will of my Father."'

2 Clement *9.11*

> 'For the Lord said, "My brothers are these who do the will of my Father."'

Clement, Eclogae propheticae *20.3*

> 'The Lord said, "For my brothers and fellow heirs are those who do the will of my Father."'

AGREEMENTS IN SYRIAN GOSPELS, WESTERN TEXT AND DIATESSARON

Luke 8.19 in Mcion
– his mother...for the crowd

Luke 8.21 in b Gos. Ebion.
my brothers and mother << my mother and brothers

Matthew 12.46 in Gos. Ebion.
– asking to speak to him

Matthew 12.46 in Gos. Ebion. 2Clem. Cl k
My father, – in heaven

SELECT BIBLIOGRAPHY
Koester (1990: 110); Quispel (1957: 190); Schrage (1964a: 185–89); Sieber (1966: 151–52); Smith (1990: 80–84).

Logion 100.1–4

¹They showed Jesus a gold coin and said to him, 'Caesar's men extort taxes from us.'

²He said to them, 'Give to Caesar, what is Caesar's. ³Give to God what is God's. ⁴And what is mine, give me.'

NHC II 2.49.27–31

> ¹ⲀⲨⲦⲤⲈⲂⲈ ⲓ̅ⲥ̅ ⲀⲨⲚⲞⲨⲂ ⲀⲨⲱ ⲠⲈⲬⲀⲨ ⲚⲀϤ ϪⲈ ⲚⲈⲦⲎⲠ ⲀⲔⲀⲒⲤⲀⲢ ⲤⲈϢⲒⲦⲈ Ⲙ̅ⲘⲞⲚ Ⲛ̅Ⲛ̅ϢⲰⲘ
> ²ⲠⲈⲬⲀϤ ⲚⲀⲨ ϪⲈ † ⲚⲀ ⲔⲀⲒⲤⲀⲢ Ⲛ̅ⲔⲀⲒⲤⲀⲢ ³† ⲚⲀ ⲠⲚⲞⲨⲦⲈ Ⲙ̅ⲠⲚⲞⲨⲦⲈ ⁴ⲀⲨⲱ ⲠⲈⲦⲈ ⲠⲰⲈⲒ ⲠⲈ ⲘⲀⲦⲚ̅Ⲛ̅ⲀⲈⲒϤ

ATTRIBUTION
Kernel saying with accretive clause.

TEXT AND TRANSLATION ISSUES
J. Guey has suggested that the Coptic, 'a piece of gold', is a mistranslation of ⲓⲗ.ⲧ which can refer either to the Roman *denarius* or to a piece of gold or silver.

INTERPRETATIVE COMMENT

L. 100.4 appears to be an accretive clause concerned with christological issues, elevating the stature of Jesus to God.

Payment of taxes to foreign pagan rulers was a disputed issue for some Jews beginning around 6 CE at the time of Quirinius' census when Judas the Galilean first put forward the idea that it was sinful to pay tribute to a Gentile ruler (Josephus, *Jewish Antiquities* 18.4). Judas may have been the founder of the Zealot party, the fourth 'philosophy', since Josephus connects Judas and the revolt in 6 CE with policies that eventually led to the Zealot uprising which started the Jewish War. If this is the case, according to Bruce, then one of the distinguishing features of the Zealot party may have been their belief that it was impious to pay imperial taxes.

This idea might have been popular with those Jews who resented Rome's dominion, especially if they were apocalyptically minded, understanding Rome's authority to be illegitimate because it was grounded in the temporary dominion of the forces of evil. They, in fact, may have expected Jesus to rule on this in favour of the Zealot's position. But he does not. In a clever legal response, Jesus tells the Jews and his followers that they should, 'give to Caesar what is Caesar's' and 'give to God what is God's'. Jesus remarks that, since it is self-evident that the coin belongs to Caesar (maybe because it bears his image as is elaborated in the Synoptic versions of this story; Matt. 22.15–22; Mark 12.13–19; Luke 20.20–26), it should be given back to him. Thus, Jesus seems to align himself with the prophetic injunctions to serve the rulers of Israel even during periods of foreign domination since their domination was a punishment for Israel's sinfulness (cf. Ezek. 21.25–27; Jer. 27.4–7; Mal. 1.8; 1QpHab ix.2–4; Ps. Sol. 17.5–7).

From the context in the Kernel, this logion reminds the hearer that God's reign is not like Caesar's and his earthly kingdom, Rome. God does not demand money or taxes of his subjects. Rather, God demands the commitment of one's life to the mission of spreading the news about the immanent Kingdom and how to prepare for his Judgement. Further, his commitment and obedience to God is not compromised by paying Caesar taxes. In the complete Gospel, the accretive clause, 'and what is mine, give to me', is a christological statement, reflecting the community's devotion to Jesus and the commitment of their lives to his cause. Accrual of the final clause is estimated between 80 and 120 CE.

SOURCE DISCUSSION

B. Gärtner, R. Kasser, R. Grant and D.N. Freedman see L. 100 as an abbreviated form of the Synoptic saying. W. Schrage argues for dependency based on agreements between the opening words in L. 100 and the Synoptics. Lukan dependence is signalled by the agreement φόρος.

J. Sieber states that these agreements are parallels only, that they do not represent editorial traces. The phrase 'what is mine give me' is a secondary addition, but this tells us nothing about Synoptic dependence. Thus there is no evidence to support an argument for dependence. He says that *Thomas*' reference to a gold coin is quite different from the Synoptic reference to a silver coin. This may suggest another tradition of the saying or a different milieu for the development of the saying. Given J. Guey's explanation of the coin, Sieber appears to be correct. The saying looks to be a variant developed within the Syrian tradition. H. Koester notes the lack of narrative in L. 100 when compared with Mark 12. He thinks that the Gospel preserves the basis of Mark's developed apophthegm except for the last phrase, L. 100.4 which is a 'later expansion'.

G. Quispel thinks that this saying is a strong indicator of the independent tradition of saying preserved in Tatian's *Diatessaron* and the *Gospel of Thomas*. He points out variants of this saying in the *Diatessaron Haarense*, the *Tuscan Diatessaron*, the Armenian version of Ephrem's *Commentary on the Diatessaron*, and the *Persian Diatessaron*, which agree with L. 100, '*give* the things of God to God'. He notes that no Western text contains this variant, although the Bohairic version of the New Testament has it. Because the age of the Bohairic witness is unknown, he argues that it cannot be used to prove that the Sahidic *Thomas* was influenced by it. He states, 'The numerous parallels between the *Gospel of Thomas* and Tatian's *Diatessaron* make it methodologically preferable to assume that the Coptic translation of "Thomas" preserved the primitive version of its Edessene author.'

LITERATURE PARALLELS

Mark 12.13–17

[13]'And they sent to him some of the Pharisees and some of the Herodians, to entrap him in his talk. [14]And they came and said to him, "Teacher, we know that you are true, and care for no man; for you do not regard the position of men, but truly teach the way of God. Is it lawful to pay taxes to Caesar, or not? [15]Should we pay them, or should we not?" But knowing their hypocrisy, he said to them, "Why put me to the test? Bring me a coin, and let me look at it." [16]And they brought one. And he said to them, "Whose likeness and inscription is this?" They said to him, "Caesar's." [17]Jesus said to them, "Render to Caesar the things that are Caesar's, and to God the things that are God's." And they were amazed at him.'

Matthew 22.15–22

[15]'Then the Pharisees went and took counsel how to entangle him in his talk. [16]And they sent their disciples to him, along with the Herodians, saying, "Teacher, we know that you are true, and teach the way of God truthfully, and care for no man; for you do not regard the position of men. [17]Tell us, then, what you think. Is it lawful to pay taxes to Caesar, or not?" [18]But Jesus, aware of their malice, said, "Why put me to the test, you hypocrites? [19]Show me the money for the tax." And they brought him a coin. [20]And Jesus said to them, "Whose likeness and inscription is this?" [21]They said, "Caesar's." Then he said to them, "Render therefore to Caesar the things that are Caesar's, and to God the things that are God's." [22]When they heard it, they marvelled; and they left him and went away.'

Luke 20.20–26

[20]'So they watched him, and sent spies, who pretended to be sincere, that they might take hold of what he said, so as to deliver him up to the authority and jurisdiction of the governor. [21]They asked him, "Teacher, we know that you speak and teach rightly, and show no partiality, but truly teach the way of God. [22]Is it lawful for us to give tribute to Caesar, or not?" [23]But he perceived their craftiness, and said to them, [24]"Show me a coin. Whose likeness and inscription has it?" They said, "Caesar's." [25]He said to them, "Then render to Caesar the things that are Caesar's, and to God the things that are God's." [26]And they were not able to catch him by what he said; but marvelling at his answer they were silent.'

Papyrus Egerton 2, *fragment 2 recto, lines 43–59*

'...came to him to tempt him, saying, "Teacher Jesus, we know that you have come from God, for the things which you bear witness beyond all the prophets. Tell us then, is it lawful to render to kings what pertains to their rule? Shall we render it to them or not?" But Jesus, knowing their mind, said to them with indignation, "Why do you call me teacher with your mouth, when you do not do what I say? Well did Isaiah prophesy of you when he said, 'This people honours me with its lips, but their heart is far from me; in vain do they worship me, (teaching as doctrines merely human) commandments.'"'

Justin, Apology *1.17.2*

'For at that time some people came to him and asked him if it is necessary to pay tribute to Caesar. And he answered, "Tell me, whose image does the coin have?' And they said, "Caesar's." And again he answered them, "Therefore give the things of Caesar to Caesar and things of God to God."'

Pistis Sophia *3.113*

'Now concerning these words you once said to us, when a stater was brought to you and you saw that it was of silver and copper you asked, "Whose image is this?" They said, "It is the king's." But when you saw that is was silver mixed with copper, you said, "Give, therefore, what is the king's to the king, and what is God's to God."'

Sentences of Sextus *20*

'Give precisely the things of the world to the world and the things of God to God.'

AGREEMENTS IN SYRIAN GOSPELS, WESTERN TEXT AND DIATESSARON

Luke 20.24 in ℵ *C L* 33 1241 fam 1 21 157 1604 *c e S C* T^{nl} T^{PEP} T^{l} *arm*
they showed

Mark 12.17///Matthew 22.17///Luke 20.25 in T^{p} T^{EC} T^{T}
+ give[2]

SELECT BIBLIOGRAPHY

Arai (1994); Bruce (1984: 256–62); Cuvillier (1992/1993); Gärtner (1961: 32–33); Grant with Freedman (1960: 189); Guey (1960: 478–79); Kasser (1961: 111); Koester (1990: 112); Quispel (1971b: 34–35); Sieber (1966: 245–46).

Logion 101.1–3

[1]'Whoever does not hate his [father] and his mother in the same manner as I do, he cannot be a [disciple] of mine. [2]Also whoever does [not] love his [father and] his mother in the same manner as I do, he cannot be a [disciple] of mine. [3]For my [birth] mother [gave death], while my true [mother] gave life to me.'

NHC II 2.49.32–50.1

[1]ⲡⲉⲧⲁⲙⲉⲥⲧⲉ ⲡⲉϥⲉⲓⲱⲧ ⲁⲛ ⲙⲛ̄ ⲧⲉϥⲙⲁⲁⲩ ⲛ̄ⲧⲁϩⲉ ϥⲛⲁϣ̄ⲡ
ⲙ̄ⲁⲑⲏⲧⲏⲥ ⲛⲁⲉⲓ ⲁⲛ] [2]ⲁⲩⲱ ⲡⲉⲧⲁⲙ̄ⲣ̄ⲣⲉ ⲡⲉϥⲉⲓⲱⲧ ⲁⲛ ⲙⲛ̄]
ⲧⲉϥⲙⲁⲁⲩ ⲛ̄ⲧⲁϩⲉ ϥⲛⲁϣ̄ⲡ ⲙ̄ⲁⲑⲏⲧⲏⲥ ⲛⲁⲉⲓ ⲁⲛ [3]ⲧⲁⲙⲁⲁⲩ ⲅⲁⲣ
ⲛ̄ⲧⲁⲥ|ⲭⲡⲟⲓ †ⲭⲱⲕ ⲉⲃ|ⲟⲗ |ⲧⲁⲙⲁⲁⲩ| ⲇⲉ ⲙ̄ⲙⲉ ⲁⲥ† ⲛⲁⲉⲓ ⲙ̄ⲡⲱⲛϩ

ATTRIBUTION
Accretion.

TEXT AND TRANSLATION ISSUES

For L. 101.3, I offer a possibility for completing the lacunae (9 or 10 letter spaces) which occurs on the last line at the bottom of p. 49 and the first two letters at the top of p. 50: ⲛ̄ⲧⲁⲥ|ⲭⲡⲟⲓ †ⲭⲱⲕ ⲉⲃ|ⲟⲗ: 'who begot me gave death'. This construction not only fits the lacunae, but also provides contextual sense and offers a complementary parallel to the final clause. So I prefer it over Layton's reconstruction which does not fill the space (ⲚⲦⲀϤⲓϮ ⲚⲀⲈⲒ Ⲙ|ⲂⲞⲖ: 'who gave me falsehood'). Bethge's suggestions are equally problematic. ⲚⲦⲀϤ|ⲜⲠⲞⲒ ⲀⳠⲂⲞⲖⲦ ⲈⲂ|ⲞⲖ, 'who has given birth to me, has destroyed me', exceeds the space limitations, while ⲚⲦⲀϤⲓϮ ⲚⲀⲈⲒ ⲘⲠ6|ⲞⲖ, 'who has deceived me', is too short.

INTERPRETATIVE COMMENT
This saying is a doublet of L. 55, showing secondary development particularly in the final clause where it displays retrospective christological thinking about Jesus. Unlike L. 55, this later version of the saying has been interpreted through an encratic lens. The saying would have had special meaning for an encratic community which hated the world and its perpetuation while loving the heavenly world. They would have supported 'hating' their biological origins while 'loving' their spiritual. This accretion belongs to a time between 80 and 120 CE.

The final clause develops the early Jewish Christian tradition that the Holy Spirit was Jesus' mother, as found in the *Gospel of the Hebrews* 3 ('Even so did my mother, the Holy Spirit, take me by one of my hairs and carry me away on the great mountain Tabor', Origen, *Commentary on John* 2.12.87, on John 1.3) and the *Apocryphon of James* 5.20 ('Make yourselves like the son of the Holy Spirit').

SOURCE DISCUSSION
G. Quispel attributes the saying to an encratic source, but I think that L. 101 is simply an encratic reformulation of L. 55 made by a teacher in the later Thomasine community.

LITERATURE PARALLELS
See L. 55.

SELECT BIBLIOGRAPHY
Bethge (1997: 543); Layton (1989: 88–89); Quispel (1981: 265).

Logion 102

Jesus said, 'Woe to the Pharisees because they are like a dog sleeping in the cattle trough. For the dog neither eats nor [lets] the cattle eat.'

NHC II 2.50.2–5

ⲠⲈⲜⲈ ⲒⲤ |ⲜⲈ ⲞⲒ|ⲨⲞⲈⲒ ⲚⲀⲨ Ⲙ̄ⲪⲀⲢⲒⳞⲀⲒⲞⳞ ⲜⲈ ⲈⲨⲈⲒⲚⲈ |Ⲛ̄Ⲛ|ⲞⲨⲞⲨⳘⲞⲢ
ⲈϤⲚ̄ⲔⲞⲦⲔ ⳘⲒⲜⲚ̄ ⲠⲞⲨⲞⲚⲈϤ Ⲛ̄|ⳘⲚ̄Ⲛ|ⲈⳘⲞⲞⲨ ⲜⲈ ⲞⲨⲦⲈ ϤⲞⲨⳘⲘ ⲀⲚ
ⲞⲨⲦⲈ ϤⲔ|Ⳙ Ⲁ|Ⲛ Ⲛ̄ⲚⲈⳘⲞⲞⲨ ⲈⲞⲨⳘⲘ

ATTRIBUTION
Kernel saying.

TEXT AND TRANSLATION ISSUES
I have rendered the antecedent for ϤⲞⲨⳘⲘ as 'the dog eats' rather than the literal, 'it eats'.

'Woe to the Pharisees', reads literally, 'Woe to them, the Pharisees'. A. Guillaumont traces this to Aramaic syntax which uses determinative suffixes, since the Coptic would normally read ⲞⲨⲞⲈⲒ ⲚⲘ̄ⲪⲀⲢⲒⲤⲀⲒⲞⲤ (cf. Sahidic Matthew 18.7).

INTERPRETATIVE COMMENT

In the Kernel, the saying develops Jesus' revelation about the truth of God's Kingdom. After sharing a few parables about the Kingdom, Jesus tells the hearer that the Kingdom of God will replace one's human family, that it is unlike Caesar's Kingdom, demanding commitment to God rather than extorting taxes from its citizens, that it is not found with the Pharisees who are like dogs sleeping in the cattle trough, neither eating nor letting the cattle eat.

SOURCE DISCUSSION

R. Grant and D.N. Freedman noted that L. 102 is proverbial known as early as the second century from the Greek satirist Lucian (*Timon* 14; *Adv. Indoctum* 30) and told as a folk fable of Aesop (228). Because of its widespread proverbial nature, Grant and Freedman say that 'its presence in these literary or semi-literary sources does not mean that it was unknown outside of them. Thomas could have picked it up anywhere.' The study made by J.F. Priest confirms this opinion and stresses that 'the presence of the saying in contemporary pagan and Jewish/Christian sources reminds us of the cultural interpenetrations of the late Hellenistic world'. R. McL. Wilson, in fact, thinks that Jesus himself may have used this popular proverb since 'the originality lies not in the saying, but in its application, in the rapier-like thrust of the attack'.

In my opinion, the presence of this logion in *Thomas* is a fine example of the use of proverbial folk wisdom gathered from the oral field to develop an argument in a rhetorical speech.

LITERATURE PARALLELS

Lucian, Timon *14*

'They thought it to be sufficient enjoyment not only not to enjoy (riches) themselves, but also to share the enjoyment with no one, just as the dog in the manger which neither ate the barley nor allowed the hungry horse to eat.'

Lucian, Adv. indoctum *30*

'Therefore you could lend the books to someone who wants them, since you can not use them yourself. However, you never lent a book to anyone, but you act like the dog lying in the manger who neither eats the barley herself, nor allows the horse which can eat to eat.'

Straton, Gr. Anth. *12*

'A certain eunuch has good looking servant boys – for what use? – and he does them abominable injury. Truly, like the dog in the manger with the roses, and stupid by barking, he neither gives the good thing to himself nor to anyone else.'

Aesop's Fables *228*

'A dog, lying in the manger, neither ate of the barley herself nor allowed the horse who could eat to eat.'

Aesop's Fables *702*

'A mean dog was lying in a trough filled with hay. When the cattle came to eat, it would not let them but bared its teeth in a threatening manner. Then the cattle said to it, "It is not fair that you begrudge us the natural appetite that you do not have. For it is not your nature to eat hay, and yet you prevent us from eating it."'

Cf. Matthew 23.13 (Qmatt); Luke 11.52 (Qluke); L. 39

SELECT BIBLIOGRAPHY
Grant with Freedman (1960: 190); Guillaumont (1981: 194); Priest (1985); Wilson (1960a: 76–77).

Logion 103

Jesus said, 'Blessed is the man who knows where the thieves are going to enter, so that [he] may arise, gather at his estate, and arm himself.'

NHC II 2.50.5–10

ΠΕΧΕ ΙC ΧΕ ΟΥΜΑΙΚΑΙΡΙΟC ΠΕ ΠΡШΜΕ ΠΑΕΙ ΕΤCΟΟΥΙΙΝΙΙ ΧΕ
ϨΙΝ ΑШΙ ΜΜΕΡΟC ΕΝΛΗCΤΗC ΝΗΥ ΕϨΟΥΙΙΝΙΙ ШΙΝΑ ΙΕϤΙΝΑΤШΟΥΝ
ΝϤCШΟΥϨ ΝΤΕϤΜΝΤΕΙΡΟΙ ΝϤΜΟΥΡ ΜΜΟϤ ΕΧΝ ΤΕϤϮΠΕ ϨΙΑΙ
ΤΕϨΗ ΕΜΠΑΤΟΥΕΙ ΕϨΟΥΝ

ATTRIBUTION
Kernel saying.

TEXT AND TRANSLATION ISSUES
The expression ΝϤΜΟΥΡ ΜΜΟϤ ΕΧΝ ΤΕϤϮΠΕ literally reads 'strap his loins'. It is an idiomatic expression for arming oneself. Thus my translation, 'arm himself'.

INTERPRETATIVE COMMENT
The rhetorical speech about God's Kingdom is continued with L. 103. In the Kernel, the interpretation would have emphasized the eschatological dimension of the saying, that the believer, like the estate owner mustering himself against the thieves, must be prepared for the inauguration of God's Kingdom which could happen at any moment. In the complete Gospel, like its parallel L. 21.5, the saying was probably reinterpreted as a reference to the internal battle of the soul against the demons, the desires of the body. The person should be on guard at all times against temptation which is like a thief stealing into one's estate.

SOURCE DISCUSSION
G. Quispel traces this saying's origin to a Jewish Christian Gospel.

LITERATURE PARALLELS
See L. 21.5

SELECT BIBLIOGRAPHY
Quispel (1981: 265).

Logion 104.1–2

[1]They said to Jesus, 'Come. Today, let's pray and fast!'

[2]Jesus said, 'What sin have I committed? Or in what way have I been defeated? Rather, when the bridegroom leaves the bridal chamber, then they should fast and pray.'

NHC II 2.50.10–16

¹ⲡⲉⲭⲁⲩ ⲛ̄[ⲓⲥ̄] ϫⲉ ⲁⲙⲟⲩ ⲛ̄ⲧⲛ̄ϣⲗⲏⲗ ⲙ̄ⲡⲟⲟⲩ ⲁⲩⲱ ⲛ̄ⲧⲛ̄ⲣ̄ⲛⲏⲥⲧⲉⲩⲉ
²ⲡⲉϫⲉ ⲓⲥ̄ ϫⲉ ⲟⲩ ⲅⲁⲣ ⲡⲉ ⲡⲛⲟⲃⲉ ⲛ̄ⲧⲁⲉⲓⲁⲁϥ ⲏ ⲛ̄ⲧⲁⲩϫⲣⲟ ⲉⲣⲟⲉⲓ
ϩⲛ̄ ⲟⲩ ³ⲁⲗⲗⲁ ϩⲟⲧⲁⲛ ⲉⲣϣⲁⲛ ⲡⲛⲩⲙⲫⲓⲟⲥ ⲉⲓ ⲉⲃⲟⲗ ϩⲙ̄ ⲡⲛⲩⲙⲫⲱⲛ
ⲧⲟⲧⲉ ⲙⲁⲣⲟⲩⲛⲏⲥⲧⲉⲩⲉ ⲁⲩⲱ ⲙⲁⲣⲟⲩϣⲗⲏⲗ

ATTRIBUTION
Kernel saying.

TEXT AND TRANSLATION ISSUES
The parallelism in Jesus' question in L. 104, 'What sin have I committed? Or how have I
been conquered?' has been explained by A. Guillaumont as a reference to an Aramaic substratum, ⳉ11, or a Syriac substratum, ‎سмⲭ, which can mean both 'to be conquered' or 'to
sin'.

INTERPRETATIVE COMMENT
Logion 104 represents a discussion over a point of legal interpretation, in this case, the
practice of fasting. Fasting among Jews was practised in this period to atone for sins either
communally on the Day of Atonement (Lev. 16.29, 31; 23.27, 32; Num. 29.7) or individu-
ally (*Ps. Sol.* 3.8), to mourn (Judith 8.1–6; cf. Zech. 7.3, 5), to offer contrition (1 Sam. 7.6)
or to purge the soul of the demonic influences that battle within the person particularly in
regard to the passions (*Apoc. Elijah* 1.15–22). Thus, when asked by other Jews to join a
particular fast that appears to have fallen on someone's wedding day, Jesus first asks them
what purpose the fast has. In his mind, there seem to be two legitimate purposes for fasting
– atonement and battling one's passions – since he asks two pointed questions, 'What sin
have I committed?' and 'In what way have I been defeated?' Although we do not know
the particulars regarding this fast, it seems from the continuation of Jesus' response, that
Jesus is telling these Jews that he had no personal reason to fast on that day.

In addition, Jesus indicates that their timing for the fast was inappropriate. He states that
fasting should not occur on someone's wedding day: 'But when the bridegroom comes out
of the bridal chamber, then let them fast and pray.' This, too, is a reference to Jewish custom
since weddings were celebrated with marriage feasts lasting about seven days (Gen. 29.27;
Judges 14.12, 17; *Jos. Asen.* 21.6–7; cf. Tobias 8.20, 10.7, 12.1; Josephus, *Ant.* 5.289–294).
Rabbinic law, in fact, exempts the groom and whoever directly participates in the wedding
celebration from several religious commandments (*m. Ber.* 2.5–8; *t. Ber.* 1.3, 2.10; *j. Ber.*
1.6, 3b; *b. Ber.* 16a; *j. Suk.* 2.5, 52a; *b. Suk.* 25a–b).

Although we do not know the particulars of the fasting practices of the Thomasine
Christians from this saying, it is probable that fasting would have been a favourable practice within the early community. The presence of this story in the Kernel suggests that the
early Thomasine Christians may have practised fasting in order to atone for sins or battle
their inner demons. It also may be possible that the early Thomasine Christians identified
Jesus with the bridegroom in this logion. In this case, the early Thomasine Christians
would have understood this saying as a *promotion* for fasting in the absence of Jesus, the
bridegroom. This interpretation is quite plausible given the fact that this seems to be the
way in which the saying was understood in its Synoptic variations (Mark 2.18–20; Matt.
9.14–15; Luke 5.33–35). The practice of obligatory fasting in the early Thomasine community fits with the practices of other early Christians, some of whom set aside Wednesdays
and Fridays for this purpose (i.e. *Didache* 8.1). Moreover, according to Matthew, Jesus

commanded his followers to fast in a manner which would distinguish them from other Jews: instead of putting on a dismal face so that others would know that they were fasting, Jesus' followers should instead anoint their heads and wash their faces so that they would not bring attention to themselves (6.16–18).

This obligatory practice, however, is criticized by the later Thomasine Christians as the accretions suggest, particularly L. 6, 14 and 27. The combination of these logia with 104 suggests that the language in L. 14.1–3 largely is rhetorical, offering sincere criticism of the earlier obligatory practices of the community. The later community wished to make central to their Christian practices, a lifestyle of renunciation which replaced the older obligatory fasts (L. 27). Rather than participating in regular community fasts, they wished to fast from the entire world on a routine basis (L. 27)! Furthermore, they wanted to establish as central to this lifestyle the 'golden rule', 'Do not do what you hate', and a second ethic, 'Do not lie' (L. 6.2). They believed these ethics to be of more importance than the kosher diet, obligatory fasting, prayer, or almsgiving (6.1–2). They felt that this lifestyle of 'fasting from the world' (L. 27) helped them to conquer their inner demonic passions and atone for their sins (L. 104).

Source Discussion

R. Grant and D.N. Freedman think that L. 104 is dependent on the Synoptics. The discrepancies are explained by them as retrospective on the part of *Thomas* who is considering the theological problems associated with the sinlessness of Jesus. W. Schrage says that L. 104 alludes to Mark 2.19–20. He notes, however, that both Luke and *Thomas* add references to prayer. He assumes that *Thomas* presupposes the Synoptic scene.

J. Sieber says that *Thomas*' scene differs from the Synoptics, referencing Jesus' opponents rather than the disciples. The addition of prayer, Sieber concedes in his conclusion, may be Lukan since we are analysing triple tradition, and thus evidence for dependence in this case. K. Snodgrass also thinks that Luke may have had a redactional interest in prayer although the evidence is not 'air tight' in his estimation. But H. Koester says that form-critically L. 104 lacks the narrative framework found in the Markan setting and the extended Markan apophthegm. So its form should be considered primary even though L. 104.2a is a secondary expansion. G. Quispel points out an interesting parallel with the *Gospel of the Nazarenes* (see below) which he argues demonstrates *Thomas*' use of an independent source.

I am interested in explaining the differences as well as the agreements between L. 104 and Luke 5.33–35. L. 104 appears to me to be very different from Luke, having a completely different introductory clause and mentioning the bridegroom leaving the bridal chamber rather than being taken away from the disciples. In fact, *Thomas*' version appears to me to be primary by comparison with Luke's since L. 104 retains the local wedding imagery, while Luke 5.35 clearly has modified retrospectively the tradition to refer to Jesus' death. In addition, Luke 5.35 does not mention prayer, only fasting, while L. 104.2 references both prayer and fasting. One possible explanation is that we have in *Thomas* an independent variant that was modified later during an oral performance, bringing it in line with the orator's memory of Luke's variant. The problem with this explanation is that it does not fully explain how or why the reference to prayer would turn up in L. 104.2 when it is not in Luke 5.35. Another possibility is that L. 104 is an example of a pre-Synoptic independent variant which may also have been known to Luke and used by the Lukan author to modify the Markan variant.

LITERATURE PARALLELS

Mark 2.18–20

> [18]'Now John's disciples and the Pharisees were fasting. And people came and said to him, "Why do John's disciples and the disciples of the Pharisees fast, but your disciples do not fast?" [19]And Jesus said to them, "Can the wedding guests fast while the bridegroom is with them? As long as they have the bridegroom with them they can not fast. [20]The days will come, when the bridegroom is taken away from them, and then they will fast in that day."'

Matthew 9.14–15

> [14]'Then the disciples of John came to him saying, "Why do we and the Pharisees fast, but your disciples do not fast?" [15]And Jesus said to them, "Can the wedding guests mourn as long as the bridegroom is with them? The days will come, when the bridegroom is taken away from them, and then they will fast."'

Luke 5.33–35

> [33]'And they said to him, "The disciples of John fast often and offer prayers, and so do the disciples of the Pharisees, but yours eat and drink." [34]And Jesus said to them, "Can you make wedding guests fast while the bridegroom is with them? [35]The days will come, when the bridegroom is taken away from them, and then they will fast in those days."'

Gospel of the Nazarenes *2, Jerome,* Adversus Pelagianos *3.2*

> 'Behold, the mother of the Lord and his brothers said to him, "John the Baptist baptizes for the remission of sins, let us go and be baptized by him." But he said to them, "How have I sinned that I should go and be baptized by him? Unless what I have said is ignorance."'

AGREEMENTS IN SYRIAN GOSPELS, WESTERN TEXT AND DIATESSARON

Mark 2.20//Matthew 9.15//Luke 5.35 in 472 (Matt) T^V arab vel

> leaves << is taken away

SELECT BIBLIOGRAPHY

Guillaumont (1981: 194); Koester (1990: 109–110); Lowy (1958); Quispel (1957: 4); Satlow (2001: 162–81).

Logion 105

Jesus said, 'Whoever is acquainted with one's father and mother will be called, "the child of a prostitute."'

NHC II 2.50.16–18

ΠΕΧΕ ⲒⲤ ΧΕ ΠΕΤΝⲀⲤΟΥⲰΝ ΠΕΙⲰⲦ ⲘⲚ ΤΜⲀⲀΥ ⲤΕΝⲀΜΟΥΤΕ ΕΡΟϤ ΧΕ ΠϢΗΡΕ ⲘΠΟΡΝΗ

ATTRIBUTION
Accretion.

TEXT AND TRANSLATION ISSUES
I have understood the definite articles preceding 'father' and 'mother' to be signalling a

specific 'father' and 'mother', namely the subject's Father and Mother. Thus, my rendering, 'one's'.

INTERPRETATIVE COMMENT

This saying polemizes against marriage, understanding it to be an institution of prostitution. This opinion also is held by the Alexandrian encratic Christians described by Clement of Alexandria. They appear to have said that even the virgin bride who engaged in marital sex was a prostitute (*Strom.* 3.18.108).

The saying in its present form reinforces the position already garnered in L. 55 and 101, that the Christian should separate himself or herself from his or her biological parents. If the person remains attached to his or her parents, he or she is a child of a prostitute rather than a child of Man as the next logion indicates (see L. 106).

This logion appears to have accrued in the Gospel sometime between 80 and 120 CE, attaching itself to L. 104 in order to reinterpret the wedding reference so that the hearer would understand Jesus to be speaking against marriage rather than supporting it.

SOURCE DISCUSSION

G. Quispel attributes this saying to the hand of the author himself.

LITERATURE PARALLELS

Clement of Alexandria, Strom. *3.18.108*

> 'And to show that he [Paul] does not regard marriage as fornication he goes on, "Do you not know that he who is joined to a harlot is one body with her?" Or who will assert that before she is married a virgin is a prostitute?'

Gospel of Philip *52.21–25*

> 'When we were Hebrews, we were orphans and had only our mother, but when we became Christians we had both father and mother.'

SELECT BIBLIOGRAPHY

Quispel (1981: 265).

Logion 106.1–2

[1]Jesus said, 'When you make the two one, you will become children of Man. [2]And when you say, "Mountain, go forth!" it will move.'

NHC II 2.50.18–22

> [1]ⲡⲉϫⲉ ⲓ̅ⲥ̅ ϫⲉ ⳿ⲍ̅ⲟⲧⲁⲛ ⲉⲧⲉⲧⲛ̅ⲱ̣ⲁⲣ̅ ⲡⲥⲛⲁⲩ ⲟⲩⲁ ⲧⲉⲧⲛⲁϣⲱⲡⲉ
> ⲛ̅ϣⲏⲣⲉ ⲙ̅ⲡⲣⲱⲙⲉ [2]ⲁⲩⲱ ⲉⲧⲉⲧⲛ̅ϣⲁⲛϫⲟⲟⲥ ϫⲉ ⲡⲧⲟⲟⲩ ⲡⲱⲱⲛⲉ
> ⲉⲃⲟⲗ ϥⲛⲁⲡⲱⲱⲛⲉ

ATTRIBUTION

Accretion.

TEXT AND TRANSLATION ISSUES

L. 106.1, 'children of Man', literally reads, 'sons of Man'.

INTERPRETATIVE COMMENT

This saying contains vocabulary characteristic of the accretions, particularly its emphasis on the 'two becoming one'. This expression was favoured by the encratic constituency of the later Thomasine community dating this accretion to the years between 80 and 120 CE.

Like L. 22, this saying advocates a personal transformation through an encratic lifestyle which was believed to restore the pristine androgynous state of Adam. The encratic lifestyle restores the believer to his or her original state – an image that reflected the primal Anthropos or 'Man' as the saying states. Thus they became 'children of Man' rather than 'children of a prostitute' as indicated by the previous logion. Noteworthy is the similar usage of the phrase 'children of Man' (literally, 'sons of Man') in the *Liber Graduum* and its interpretation: that the believer is transformed into 'a new creature in Christ' (581.3–4).

SOURCE DISCUSSION

Although G. Quispel thinks that this saying comes from an encratic Gospel, in my opinion, this saying is a prime example of modification at the hands of a teacher in the community of an earlier Kernel saying in order to reflect the beliefs of a later constituency. In this case, L. 48, a Kernel saying, has been repeated and adapted to reflect later encratic theology. The 'two' people 'making peace' with each other in 'one' house are now 'the two being made one'. When this is accomplished, their primal Image is restored. They become 'like God' as mentioned in Genesis, possessing the power to 'move mountains'.

LITERATURE PARALLELS

Liber Graduum *581,3–4*
> '[Jeremiah 31.17] that is, become children of Man, they become a new creature in Christ.'

Liber Graduum *589.13*
> 'So then, pray that they become children of Man.'

Liber Graduum *737.24*
> 'I wish that they become all children of Man.'

See L. 22, 48

SELECT BIBLIOGRAPHY
Klijn (1962).

Logion 107.1–3

[1]Jesus said, 'The Kingdom is like a shepherd who had a hundred sheep. [2]One of them, the largest, strayed. He left the ninety-nine. He sought that one until he found it. [3]After he had laboured, he said to the sheep, "I love you more than the ninety-nine."'

NHC II 2.50.22–27

[1]ⲡⲉⲝⲉ ⲓⲥ ⲝⲉ ⲧⲙⲛ̄ⲧⲉⲣⲟ ⲉⲥⲧⲛ̄ⲧⲱ(ⲛ) ⲉⲩⲣⲱⲙⲉ ⲛ̄ϣⲱⲥ ⲉⲩⲛ̄ⲧⲁϥ
ⲙ̄ⲙⲁⲩ ⲛ̄ϣⲉ ⲛ̄ⲉⲥⲟⲟⲩ [2]ⲁⲟⲩⲁ ⲛ̄ϩⲏⲧⲟⲩ ⲥⲱⲣⲙ ⲉⲡⲛⲟϭ ⲡⲉ ⲁϥⲕⲱ
ⲙ̄ⲡⲥⲧⲉⲯⲓⲧ ⲁϥϣⲓⲛⲉ ⲛ̄ⲥⲁ ⲡⲓⲟⲩⲁ ϣⲁⲛⲧⲉϥϩⲉ ⲉⲣⲟϥ [3]ⲛ̄ⲧⲁⲣⲉϥϩⲓⲥⲉ
ⲡⲉⲝⲁϥ ⲙ̄ⲡⲉⲥⲟⲟⲩ ⲝⲉ ϯⲟⲩⲟϣⲕ ⲡⲁⲣⲁ ⲡⲥⲧⲉⲯⲓⲧ

ATTRIBUTION
Kernel saying.

TEXT AND TRANSLATION ISSUES
Guillaumont explains the phrase ⲧⲟⲩⲟⲱⲕ by a Semitic substratum, particularly the verb צבה which can mean both 'to wish' or 'to delight in'. The Semitic verb can translate into the Greek εὐδοκεῖν which he supposes to be the Greek intermediary between the Aramaic and the Coptic. This theory helps to explain why the Synoptics employ forms of the Greek χαίρειν, while *Thomas* has ⲟⲩⲱϣ.

107.3 reads ⲥⲟⲩⲟⲩ with the final ⲩ above the line. Clearly a mistake has been made, so I have emended the reading to ⲥⲟⲟⲩ.

INTERPRETATIVE COMMENT
In the Kernel, this logion is part of the speech revealing the truth about God's Kingdom. It is to be compared to a wedding, a time of celebration rather than a time of fasting and prayer (L. 104). It is compared to the joyous story about recovering a sheep that had strayed from the flock (L. 107). Especially given the apocalyptic hermeneutic of the early Thomasine community, elements of the parable probably evoked memories of Ezekiel 34.11–16, the eschatological ingathering of the scattered sheep, the tribes of Israel.

SOURCE DISCUSSION
Most early commentators (K. Beyschlag, L. Cerfaux, R. Grant and D.N. Freedman, J.-É. Ménard, H. Montefiore, F. Schnider, W. Schrage) regard L. 107 as dependent upon the Synoptic recensions and modified into an esoteric Gnostic saying. W. Schrage says that L. 107 is a combination of Matthew 18.12–14 and Luke 15.3–7, sharing with Matthew the statement format of the saying and the reference to seeking the sheep, and with Luke the ἔχων and ἕως phrase. Sahidic Luke also includes the reference to seeking, an inclusion due to scribal harmonization with Matthew. J. Sieber argues that the Coptic agreements with L. 107 pointed out by Schrage cannot be used to argue dependence at the Greek level. He also notes the absence of editorial traits of either Matthew or Luke. Thus he argues for an independent tradition here.

W.L. Petersen's form-critical study agrees, showing that L. 107 has not been redacted by a Gnostic. Rather, it preserves a tradition independent of the Synoptics and in a form older than the Synoptics, a less complex form steeped in Jewish imagery. L. 107 lacks the contextualization present in the Synoptics and the infusion with allegorical overtones. He notes that *Thomas* alone has retained the eschatological nature of the parable as a reference to Ezekiel 34.16 where God reveals to Ezekiel that he must 'prophesy against the shepherds of Israel', so that God can seek out his sheep, judge them, and give them rest in the pastures. H. Koester also notes the lack of the secondary applications found in Matthew 18.14 and Luke 16.7.

The oral texture of the saying predominates. Careful attention to the Thomasine-Synoptic commonalities – 'a hundred sheep', 'strayed', 'until he found it', 'the ninety-nine' – shows that the bones of the parable are similar, but the performance details are strikingly different. There appears to be no evidence for secondary orality, so I think this parable is another example of an independent multiform developed in the field of oral performance.

LITERATURE PARALLELS

Matthew 18.12–13 (Qmatt)

[12]'What do you think? If a man has a hundred sheep, and one of them has gone astray, does he not leave the ninety-nine on the mountains and go in search of the one that went astray? [13]And if he finds it, truly, I say to you, he rejoices over it more than over the ninety-nine that never went astray.'

Luke 15.4–7 (Qluke)

[4]'What man of you, having a hundred sheep, if he has lost one of them, does not leave the ninety-nine in the wilderness, and go after the one which is lost, until he finds it? [5]And when he has found it, he lays it on his shoulders, rejoicing. [6]And when he comes home, he calls together his friends and his neighbours, saying to them, "Rejoice with me, for I have found my sheep which was lost." [7]Just so, I tell you, there will be more joy in heaven over one sinner who repents than over ninety-nine righteous people who need no repentance.'

Gospel of Truth 31.35–32.10

'He is the shepherd who left behind the ninety-nine sheep which were not lost. He went searching for the one which had gone astray. He rejoiced when he found it, for ninety-nine is a number that is in the left hand which holds it. But when the one is found, the entire number passes to the right (hand).'

Cf. Ezekiel 34.15–16

AGREEMENTS IN SYRIAN GOSPELS, WESTERN TEXT AND DIATESSARON

Matthew 18.12//Luke 15.4 in T^P

the one<<the one that went astray

SELECT BIBLIOGRAPHY

Beyschlag (1974: 131); Cerfaux and Garitte (1957: 323); Grant with Freedman (1960: 181); Guillaumont (1958: 120); Koester (1990: 99); Ménard (1975: 205); Montefiore (1960/1961: 234); Peterson (1981); Schnider (1977); Schrage (1964a: 194–96); Sieber (1966: 205–206).

Logion 108.1–3

[1]Jesus said, 'Whoever drinks from my mouth will become as I am. [2]I myself will become that person, [3]and what is hidden will be revealed to him.'

NHC II 2.50.28–30

[1]ⲡⲉⲝⲉ ⲓⲥ ⲝⲉ ⲡⲉⲧⲁⲥⲱ ⲉⲃⲟⲗ ϩⲛ̄ ⲧⲁⲧⲁⲡⲣⲟ ϥⲛⲁϣⲱⲡⲉ ⲛ̄ⲧⲁϩⲉ
[2]ⲁⲛⲟⲕ ϩⲱ ϯⲛⲁϣⲱⲡⲉ ⲉⲛⲧⲟϥ ⲡⲉ [3]ⲁⲩⲱ ⲛⲉⲑⲏⲡ ⲛⲁⲟⲩⲱⲛϩ ⲉⲣⲟϥ

ATTRIBUTION

Accretion.

INTERPRETATIVE COMMENT

The Christology assumed by this saying belongs to later Christianity so as to be anachronistic to the early Kernel. This is one of three sayings in *Thomas* which use consumption imagery to explain mystical transformation, describing the result as a condition in which the person has become 'like' or 'equal' with Jesus (cf. L. 13, 61). L. 108 explicitly states that the believer who drinks from Jesus' mouth becomes Jesus! The metaphor of drink and its association with mystical transformation is known in Jewish literature (cf. Philo, *Leg. all.* 1.82–84; *1 Enoch* 48.1–2; *4 Ezra* 14.38–41; *4 Ezra* 1.47; *2 Baruch* 59.7; *Memar Marqa* 2.1). L. 107, in fact, may allude to eucharistic ideology and the mystical transformative properties of the elements common in later eastern Christianity. Accrual can be dated from 80 to 120 CE.

SOURCE DISCUSSION
G. Quispel thinks that the author of the Gospel created this saying.

SELECT BIBLIOGRAPHY
DeConick (1996: 105–15); Quispel (1981: 265).

Logion 109.1–3

[1]Jesus said, 'The Kingdom is like a man who had in his field a [hidden treasure], but he did not know about it. [2]And [after] he died, he left it to his [son]. The son [did] not know (about the treasure). He took that field and sold [it]. [3]And the buyer went and ploughed. He [found] the treasure. He started to give money at interest to whomever he wished.'

NHC II 2.50.31–51.3

[1]ⲡⲉⲝⲉ ⲓ̅ⲥ̅ ⲝⲉ ⲧⲙⲛ̅ⲧⲉⲣⲟ ⲉⲥⲧⲛ̅ⲧⲱⲛ ⲉⲩⲣⲱⲙⲉ ⲉⲩⲛ̅ⲧⲁϥ ⲙ̅ⲙⲁⲩ ⲉⲥ̅
ⲧⲉϥⲥⲱϣⲉ ⲛ̅ⲛⲟⲩⲉϩⲟ ⲉϥϩⲏ|ⲡ ⲉϥ|ⲟ ⲛ̅ⲁⲧⲥⲟⲟⲩⲛ ⲉⲣⲟϥ [2]ⲁⲩⲱ
ⲙ̅|ⲙⲛ̅ⲛⲥⲁ ⲧ|ⲣⲉϥⲙⲟⲩ ⲁϥⲕⲁⲁϥ ⲙ̅ⲡⲉϥ|ϣⲏⲣⲉ ⲛⲉ|ⲡϣⲏⲣⲉ ⲥⲟⲟⲩⲛ ⲁⲛ
ⲁϥϫⲓ ⲧⲥⲱϣⲉ ⲉⲧⲙ̅ⲙⲁⲩ ⲁϥⲧⲁⲁ|ⲥ ⲉⲃⲟⲗ [3]ⲁⲩⲱ ⲡ|ⲉⲛ|ⲧⲁϩⲧⲟⲟⲩⲥ
ⲁϥⲉⲓ ⲉϥⲥⲕⲁⲉⲓ ⲁ|ϥϩⲉ| ⲁⲡⲉϩⲟ ⲁϥⲁⲣⲭⲉⲓ ⲛ̅ϯ ϩⲟⲙⲧ ⲉⲧⲙⲏⲥⲉ
ⲛ̅|ⲛⲉⲧ|ϥⲟⲩⲟϣⲟⲩ

ATTRIBUTION
Kernel saying.

TEXT AND TRANSLATION ISSUES
C. Hedrick thinks that ⲙ̅ⲡⲉ fits the lacunae better than B. Layton's reconstruction, ⲛⲉ. But the Imperfect requires ⲁⲛ which we have in our text. So I prefer Layton's recon-struction. Also, C. Hedrick completes the lacunae ⲙ̅|ⲡⲁⲧϥⲙⲟⲩ ⲡ|ⲡⲉϥⲙⲟⲩ instead of ⲙ̅|ⲙⲛ̅ⲛⲥⲁ ⲧ|ⲣⲉϥⲙⲟⲩ which Layton uses because Hedrick finds Layton's restoration one or two letters short for the lacunae. But my reexamination of the hole and measurements of the letters confirms that the space could have been filled with the six letters restored as Layton has done. The space has enough room for six letters, seven at the upper limit. The eight proposed by Hedrick could not have fitted the space unless the lacunae also contained a scribal correction above the line.

There appears to be a Semitic idiom in L. 109.3 as pointed out by C. Hedrick, 'to go and plough', rather than a periphrastic construction, 'went ploughing' as B. Layton has rendered it, or as a circumstantial in a dependent clause, 'he went while ploughing', as A. Guillau-mont and J. Ménard have understood it.

A similar Semitic idiom appears in L. 109.2, 'He took that field and sold [it].' As Hedrick notes, the expression, 'take X and do Y with X' is a common idiom in Hebrew scriptures as well as the New Testament.

INTERPRETATIVE COMMENT

In the Kernel, L. 109 is part of a rhetorical speech explaining the nature of the Kingdom of God. It is compared to the joyous celebration of a wedding or the recovery of a sheep that had strayed from the flock. The Kingdom is compared to the surprise and elation that a farmer feels when finding a hidden treasure in a field and being able to loan money to other people. In the complete Gospel, the accretions, especially L. 110, would have forced a new hermeneutic upon this parable so that the treasure would not have been understood in materialistic terms but spiritual, that the world and materialism must be rejected. Once this 'treasure' is 'found', the person has gained access to God's Kingdom.

SOURCE DISCUSSION

L. Cervaux was the first to suggest that the author of *Thomas* welded together elements from Matthew 13.44, the rabbinic parable of Rabbi Simeon ben Yohai, and *Aesop's Fable* 98, creating a Gnostic secondary text. This position was maintained in the early literature on *Thomas* (cf. H. Montefiore, R. McL. Wilson, and R. Grant and D.N. Freedman, B. Gärtner, R. Kasser, W. Schrage, *et al.*). B. Dehandschutter explains dependence on Matthew as a Gnostic *interpretation* of the Matthean parable.

Since we cannot determine any Matthean editorial traits, J. Sieber says that the parallels between L. 109 and Matthew cannot tell us anything about the issue of dependence. More recently, Scott takes both versions of the parables to be different performances of one 'originating structure'. C. Hedrick has argued that *Thomas'* version of the parable fits the ministry and teaching of Jesus, having nothing to do with Gnosticism, and claims that this version could have originated from Jesus himself. He finds *Thomas'* version form-critically to be closer to the 'originating structure' than Matthew's.

In my opinion, there is nothing Gnostic about L. 109 except scholars' *eisegesis*. The parable fits quite well within first-century Jewish traditions. It represents a variation of the Treasure Parable as it was developed in the field of oral performance by early preachers. If the parable is to be attributed to Jesus, he himself was drawing on a Jewish folk tale familiar to him. *Thomas* indeed may be preserving a version of the story very close to the oral folk tale, while Matthew may have a version that has undergone more substantial development as Hedrick argues.

LITERATURE PARALLELS

Matthew 13.44

'The Kingdom of Heaven is like a treasure hidden in a field, which a man found and covered up. Then in his joy he goes and sells all that he has and buys that field.'

Mekilta de-Rabbi Ishmael, Beshallah *2*

'R. Simon the son of Yohai, giving a parable says, "To what can this be compared? To a man to whom there had fallen as an inheritance a residence in a far off country which he sold for a trifle. The buyer, however, went and discovered in it hidden treasures and stores of silver and gold, of precious stones and pearls. The seller, seeing this, began to choke with grief."'

Midrash Rabba, Songs of Songs *4.12.1*

'R. Simeon b. Yohai taught, "[The Egyptians were] like a man who inherited a piece of ground used as a manure pile. Being an indolent man, he went and sold it for a trifling sum. The purchaser began working and digging it up, and he found a treasure there, out of which he built himself a fine palace, and he began going about in public followed by a retinue of servants – all out of the treasure he found in it. When the seller saw it he was ready to choke, and he exclaimed, 'Alas, what have I thrown away?' ' '

Philo, The Unchangeableness of God *20.91*
> 'But often we experience things, of which we beforehand have not even dreamed, such as the story of the farmer who, while digging his orchard to plant fruit trees, happened upon a treasure and enjoyed prosperity beyond his hopes.'

Aesop's Fable *98a*
> 'A certain farmer about to come to the end of his life and wishing his sons to gain experience in farming, called them and said, "My sons, I am already departing from life. Search and you will find all the things which are buried in my vineyard." Therefore, after the death of the father, they dug up the entire ground of the vineyard, supposing a treasure buried there somewhere. They did not find a treasure, but the vineyard, having been well-cultivated, produced many times more fruit. The fable points out that labour is treasure to humans.'

Aesop's Fable *98b*
> 'A farmer, about to die and wishing to make his children experienced in farming, summoned them and said, "My children, a treasure lies in one of my vineyards." After his death, they took ploughs and mattocks and dug up all his land. They found no treasure, but the vineyard returned to them many time more produce. The story points out that labour is treasure to humans.'

Cf. *Leviticus Rabba* 5.4.

SELECT BIBLIOGRAPHY
Cerfaux and Garitte (1957: 315); Gärtner (1961: 237–38): Grant with Freedman (1960: 178); Guillaumont *et al.* (1959: 55); Hedrick (1994b: 117–41); Kasser (1961: 117); Layton (1989: 91); Ménard (1975: 73–74); Montefiore (1960/1961: 244); Schrage (1964a: 197); Scott (1991: 392–95); Sieber (1966: 182–83); Wilson (1960a: 93).

Logion 110

Jesus said, 'Whoever has found the world and become wealthy, he should disown the world.'

NHC II 2.51.4–5

ΠΕΧΕ ΙC ΧΕ ΠΕΝΤΑϨ6ΙΝΕ ‾Μ‾|ΠΚΟCΜΟC ‾ΝϤ‾Ρ ‾ΡΜΜΑΟ ΜΑΡΕϤΑΡΝΑ ‾ΜΠΚΟCΜΟC

ATTRIBUTION
Accretion.

INTERPRETATIVE COMMENT
This logion appears to be an encratic reinterpretation of the doublet Kernel saying, L. 81. The meaning of the saying has shifted from Jesus' criticism of the ruling class to the community's criticism of the world and possessions. It reflects a theme characteristic of

the accretions – disdain for the world. It parallels other accretions including L. 21.6, 27, 56, 80, and 111.3. The renunciatory attitude expressed in the logion would have been highly regarded by the later encratic constituency of the Thomasine community. So its accrual in the Gospel can be located between 80 and 120 CE.

SOURCE DISCUSSION

G. Quispel thinks that the author of the Gospel created this saying. It appears to me that the saying represents the opinion of a later Thomasine teacher who took an old familiar Kernel saying (L. 81) and reconfigured it into an encratic teaching. This probably took place during an oral performance in order to provide a new encratic interpretation of Jesus' parable of the treasure. In this case, the teacher was reminding his audience that Jesus was not an advocate for wealth, but rather he commanded his followers to leave behind their wealth and disown the world.

LITERATURE PARALLELS

See L. 81

Acts of Paul 3.5

Paul said, 'Blessed are those who have kept aloof from this world, for they shall be pleasing to God.'

Acts of Peter and the Twelve Apostles 10.14–19

'Peter answered and said to him, "Lord, you have taught us to forsake the world and everything in it. We have renounced them for your sake."'

Pseudo-Macarius, *Hom.* 4.16

'Let us renounce all love for the world.'

Abu 'Ali Miskawayh, al-Hikma, *p. 192*

'Jesus said, "Do you desire the world for the sake of virtuous deeds? It is more virtuous for you to forsake the world."'

Ahmad ibn Hanbal, al-Zuhd, *p. 98 (no. 325)*

'Beware the world and do not make it your abode.'

Abu 'Uthman al-Jahiz, al-Bayan *3.166*

'It is a sign of how trivial the world is to God that only in the world is he disobeyed and only by forsaking the world can his bounty be attained.'

Cf. L. 27

SELECT BIBLIOGRAPHY

Quispel (1981: 265).

Logion 111.1

[1]Jesus said, 'The heavens and the earth will roll up in your presence.'

NHC II 2.51.6–7

[1]ⲡⲉⲝⲉ ⲓ̅ⲥ̅ ⲝⲉ ⲙ̄ⲡⲏⲩⲉ ⲛⲁϭⲱⲗ ⲁⲩⲱ ⲡⲕⲁϩ ⲙ̄ⲡⲉⲧⲛ̄ⲙ̄ⲧⲟ ⲉⲃⲟⲗ

ATTRIBUTION
Kernel saying.

INTERPRETATIVE COMMENT
This saying appears to have originally ended the Kernel Gospel on a prominently eschatological note – the world and its heavens would vanish within the lifetime of the first followers of Jesus. But in the complete Gospel, the surrounding accretions served to reinterpret this logion so that the 'end' of the world is understood to be the result of renunciation
(L. 110), cessation of procreation (L. 111.2), and the mystical recovery of one's true Self,
the lost Image (L. 111.3).

LITERATURE PARALLELS

Isaiah 34.4
> 'All the host of heaven shall rot away, and the skies roll up like a scroll. All their host
> shall fall, as leaves fall from the vine, like leaves falling from the fig tree.'

Hebrews 1.10–12
> [10]'And, "You, Lord, founded the earth in the beginning, and the heavens are the work of
> your hands. [11]They will perish. But you remain. They will all grow old like a garment,
> [12]like a mantle you will roll them up, and they will be changed. But you are the same,
> and your years will never end." '

Revelation 6.14
> 'the sky vanished like a scroll that is rolled up, and every mountain and island was
> removed from its place'.

Pistis Sophia *1.4*
> 'Now it happened when Jesus went up to heaven, after three hours all the powers of the
> heavens were disturbed, and they all shook against one another, they and all their aeons,
> and all their places and all their ranks and the whole earth moved with all who dwelt
> upon it. And all the men in the world were agitated, and also the disciples. And they all
> thought, "Perhaps the world will be rolled up." '

Cf. Mark 13.31; Matthew 24.35; Luke 21.33, John 8.51

SELECT BIBLIOGRAPHY
Gierth (1990).

Logion 111.2

[2]'And whoever is alive because of the Living One, that person will not see death.'

NHC II 2.51.7–8

   [2]ⲀⲨⲰ ⲠⲈⲦⲞⲚϨ ⲈⲂⲞⲖ ϨⲚ̄ ⲠⲈⲦⲞⲚϨ ϥⲚⲀⲚⲀⲨ ⲀⲚ ⲈⲘⲞⲨ

ATTRIBUTION

TEXT AND TRANSLATION ISSUES
I have taken ⲈⲂⲞⲖ ϨⲚ̄ as equivalent to διά and translated it in the causal sense.

INTERPRETATIVE COMMENT

This saying shares vocabulary consistent with other accretions, particularly the expression 'Living One' as a title for God. This saying accrued in the Gospel in response to the delayed eschaton and served to offer a reinterpretation of L. 111.1. The believer who experiences the Living God as the cause of his or her life overcomes death. This appears to be in contrast to unbelievers who mistakenly think that procreative activity is the cause of life. This new encratic hermeneutic suggests that the end of the world, even death itself, occurs with the cessation of procreation. Accrual can be estimated to a time between 80 and 120 CE.

SOURCE DISCUSSION

G. Quispel attributes this saying to the author of the Gospel.

LITERATURE PARALLELS

John 11.25–26

²⁵'Jesus said to her, "I am the resurrection and the life. He who believers in me, though he die, yet shall live, ²⁶and whoever lives and believes in me shall never die."'

SELECT BIBLIOGRAPHY

Quispel (1981: 265).

Logion 111.3

³'Does not Jesus say, "The world does not deserve the person who has found himself"?'

NHC II 2.51.9–10

³ⲟⲩⲭ ϩⲟⲧⲓ ⲉⲓⲥ̅ ⲭⲱ ⲙ̅ⲙⲟⲥ ⲭⲉ ⲡⲉⲧⲁϩⲉ ⲉⲣⲟϥ ⲟⲩⲁⲁϥ ⲡⲕⲟⲥⲙⲟⲥ
ⲙ̅ⲡⲱϣⲁ ⲙ̅ⲙⲟϥ ⲁⲛ

ATTRIBUTION

Accretion.

TEXT AND TRANSLATION ISSUES

For a discussion of the Semitic expression, 'the world does not deserve', see L. 56.

INTERPRETATIVE COMMENT

This saying is an example of an accretion with signs of development of form given the unusual introductory formula ⲟⲩⲭ ϩⲟⲧⲓ ⲉⲓⲥ̅ ⲭⲱ ⲙ̅ⲙⲟⲥ ⲭⲉ. Vocabulary characteristic of the accretions is present, particularly the phrase ⲙ̅ⲡⲱϣⲁ ⲙ̅ⲙⲟϥ ⲁⲛ. The content reflects hermetic wisdom paralleling other hermetic accretions (L. 56 and 80). This accretion appears to have been a late attempt to fuse Hermetic wisdom with the encratic reinterpretation of the original eschatological saying found in L. 111.1. Thus L. 111.1 and 111.2 are combined with a third saying introduced by a late unusual gloss, 'Does not Jesus say'. The words of Jesus here are the words of Hermes, promoting Self-knowledge as the avenue to overcome the world and death. Accrual took place sometime between 80 and 120 CE.

SOURCE DISCUSSION
G. Quispel traces this saying to a Hermetic source.

LITERATURE PARALLELS
See L. 56 and 80

SELECT BIBLIOGRAPHY
Quispel (1981: 265).

Logion 112.1–2

[1]Jesus said, 'Alas to the flesh crucified by the soul! [2]Alas to the soul crucified by the flesh!'

NHC II 2.51.10–12

[1]ⲡⲉⲝⲉ ⲓ̅ⲥ̅ ϫⲉ ⲟⲩⲟⲉⲓ ⲛ̅ⲧⲥⲁⲣⲝ ⲧⲁⲉⲓ ⲉⲧⲟϣⲉ ⲛ̅ⲧⲯⲩⲭⲏ [2]ⲟⲩⲟⲉⲓ
ⲛ̅ⲧⲯⲩⲭⲏ ⲧⲁⲉⲓ ⲉⲧⲟϣⲉ ⲛ̅ⲧⲥⲁⲣⲝ

ATTRIBUTION
Accretion.

TEXT AND TRANSLATION ISSUES
I have taken ⲟϣⲉ to be a form of ⲉⲓϣⲉ whose meaning is usually lost in translation. Since it is the word that is used to describe Jesus' crucifixion by 'hanging' or 'suspension', I have tried to get this meaning across in my translation. See the doublet, L. 87, for comparison and more information.

INTERPRETATIVE COMMENT
This saying coheres to one of the themes characteristic of the accretions, namely its disdain for the body. This saying would have held special importance hermeneutically for the Thomasine encratic constituency since encratic Christians saw 'self-control' as a cure for the predicament of the soul. Accrual can be attributed to a date between 80 and 120 CE. See L. 87 for discussion about the connection with this saying and Alexandrian teachings.

SOURCE DISCUSSION
G. Quispel attributes this saying to a Hermetic source.

LITERATURE PARALLELS
See L. 87

SELECT BIBLIOGRAPHY
Quispel (1981: 265).

Logion 113.1–4

[1]His disciples said to him, 'When will the Kingdom come?'

[2]'It will not come by waiting. [3]It will not be said, "Look! Here it is!" or "Look! There it is!" [4]Rather, the Kingdom of the Father is spread out over the earth, but people do not see it.'

NHC II 2.51,12–18

[1]ⲡⲉⲭⲁⲩ ⲛⲁϥ ⲛ̄ϭⲓ ⲛⲉϥⲙⲁⲑⲏⲧⲏⲥ ⲭⲉ ⲧⲙⲛ̄ⲧⲉⲣⲟ ⲉⲥⲛ̄ⲛⲏⲩ ⲛ̄ⲁϣ
ⲛ̄ϩⲟⲟⲩ [2]ⲉⲥⲛ̄ⲛⲏⲩ ⲁⲛ ϩⲛ̄| ⲟⲩϭⲱϣⲧ ⲉⲃⲟⲗ [3]ⲉⲩⲛⲁⲭⲟⲟⲥ ⲁⲛ ⲭⲉ
ⲉⲓⲥϩⲏⲏⲧⲉ ⲙ̄ⲡⲓⲥⲁ ⲏ ⲉⲓⲥϩⲏⲏⲧⲉ ⲧⲏ [4]ⲁⲗⲗⲁ ⲧⲙⲛ̄ⲧⲉⲣⲟ ⲙ̄ⲡⲉⲓⲱⲧ
ⲉⲥⲡⲟⲣϣ ⲉⲃⲟⲗ ϩⲓⲭⲙ̄ ⲡⲕⲁϩ ⲁⲩⲱ ⲣ̄ⲣⲱⲙⲉ ⲛⲁⲩ ⲁⲛ ⲉⲣⲟⲥ

ATTRIBUTION
Accretion.

TEXT AND TRANSLATION ISSUES
A. Guillaumont argues that the Aramaic נטר (Quispel: חור) is behind the expression ϩⲛ̄ ⲟⲩϭⲱϣⲧ ⲉⲃⲟⲗ, 'by waiting', in *Thomas* and μετὰ παρατηρήσεως, 'with things to be observed', in Luke since it can render both these meanings. He notes that the Syriac ܢܛܪ also has this dual meaning but does not appear in the Syriac versions of Luke 17.20 which have instead ܪ̈ܗܛܐ. So *Thomas*' version cannot have come from Luke, but an earlier Aramaic substratum.

N. Perrin observes, however, that Diatessaronic witnesses also are ambivalent, showing both 'observation' and 'waiting'. This suggests to him that Tatian must have used ܢܛܪ which he thinks the Thomasine author used in turn. But, neither ܢܛܪ (Payne Smith, 11–12) nor אחר (Jastrow, 40–41) has the dual sense Perrin suggests, meaning only 'tarry' or 'delay'.

T. Baarda suggests that there is no need to postulate an Aramaic substratum at all since it is possible that the Coptic expression is nothing more than a tentative rendering of the Lukan text. ϭⲱϣⲧ means 'to see' or 'to look', and with ⲉⲃⲟⲗ, 'to look for, to expect' while παρατηρεῖν means 'to observe' and 'to lie in wait for'. He says that G. Quispel's Aramaism, חור, is actually a Syriacism, ܢܛܪ. He prefers נטר himself. I do not find Baarda's explanation as convincing as Guillaumont's Aramaism נטר because while the latter is linguistically possible, the former requires the postulation of an incredibly clumsy Coptic translation. In fact, we would expect the Coptic translator to have used ⲟⲩϯϩⲧⲏϥ, which we find as the translation of Luke in the Sahidic New Testament.

INTERPRETATIVE COMMENT
This logion has been developed into a dialogue in which the disciples ask Jesus a question concerning the delay of the eschaton. As such, it raises an issue that must have been a major concern of the Thomasine community in the mid-first century. The community's response is heard in Jesus' answer, an answer which serves to reinterpret the original expectation of the community. The Kingdom is no longer to be thought of as a threshold event, rather it has already been established on earth but people do not see it. Accrual can be dated from 60 to 100 CE.

S. Davies goes as far as suggesting that 'Kingdom' *means* the Wisdom of God rather than an apocalyptic Kingdom. But there is no reason to push the interpretation in this direction. Certainly the Kingdom is no longer understood as an imminent event. The dimension has shifted so that the Kingdom has become immanent, already the experience of the Christian community in their present encratic praxis. It is the utopian society they are building within the parameters of their Church.

SOURCE DISCUSSION
See L. 3.1–3

LITERATURE PARALLELS

Gospel of Mary *8.15–19*
> 'Beware that no one lead you astray, saying, "Lo here!" or "Lo there!" For the Son of Man is within you.'

See L. 3.1–3

Cf. Mark 13.21; Matthew 24.23, 26; Luke 17.23; L. 51

AGREEMENTS IN SYRIAN GOSPELS, WESTERN TEXT AND DIATESSARON

Luke 17.20–21 in Mcion a S C P T^P T^A T^T T^v T$^{NL.}$
> will come << was coming

Luke 17.20–21 in a S C P T^A T^{PEP} T^{NL}
> will not come << is not coming

Luke 17.20–21 in A D W Koine Mcion a aur b c d f q r^l S C P T^A T^{L} T aeth
> see here…see there, + see

Luke 17.20–21 in Orig T^V
> but << for behold

SELECT BIBLIOGRAPHY
Baarda (1975: 134–37); Baker (1970: 403); Davies (1983: 57–58); Guillaumont (1981: 200); Perrin (2002: 42–43 and n. 73); Quispel (1958/1959: 288).

Logion 114.1–2

[1]Simon Peter said to them, 'Mary should leave us because women do not deserve life.'

[2]Jesus said, 'Look, in order to make her male, I myself will <<guide>> her, so that she too may become a living spirit – male, resembling you. For every woman who will make herself male will enter the Kingdom of Heaven.'

NHC II 2.51.18–26

[1]ⲡⲉⲝⲉ ⲥⲓⲙⲱⲛ ⲡⲉⲧⲣⲟⲥ ⲛⲁⲩ ⲝⲉ ⲙⲁⲣⲉ ⲙⲁⲣⲓϩⲁⲙ ⲉⲓ ⲉⲃⲟⲗ ⲛ̄ϩⲏⲧⲛ̄
ⲝⲉ ⲛ̄ⲥϩⲓⲟⲙⲉ ⲙ̄ⲡϣⲁ ⲁⲛ ⲙ̄ⲡⲱⲛϩ

²ΠΕΧΕ ΙC ΧΕ ΕΙC2ΗΗΤΕ ΑΝΟΚ †ΝΑϹⲰΚ ⲘⲘⲟϹ ΧΕΚΑΑϹ ΕΕΙΝΑΑϹ
Ν2ΟΟΥΤ ⲰΙΝΑ ΕϹΝΑⲰⲰⲠΕ 2ⲰⲰϹ ⲚΟΥⲠⲚⲀ ΕϤΟΝ2 ΕϤΕΙΝΕ
ⲘⲘⲰΤⲚ Ν2ΟΟΥΤ ΧΕ C2ΙΜΕ ΝΙΜ ΕϹΝΑΑϹ Ν2ΟΟΥΤ ϹΝΑΒⲰΚ
Ε2ΟΥΝ ΕΤⲘⲚΤΕΡΟ ⲚⲘⲠΗΥΕ

ATTRIBUTION
Accretion.

TEXT AND TRANSLATION ISSUES
L. 114.2 contains a strange phrase †ΝΑϹⲰΚ ⲘⲘⲟϹ, literally, 'I will draw her'. This
expression probably represents a translation error going back to the Aramaic or Syriac נגד
which can mean both 'to draw' and 'to lead'. Clearly the meaning of the saying is that
Jesus will be Mary's leader or guide. This translation error is evidence of a Semitic substratum. The same translation error is noted in L. 3.1.

INTERPRETATIVE COMMENT
Secondary development is evident in the dialogue construction and accrual can be dated
from 80 to 120 CE. Peter's statement reflects a late rhetoric that toyed with the idea that
women should be excluded from the community because it was impossible for them to
become the primordial *Man*. This Man was equated with the pre-Fall Adam. He was a
male figure who was envisisoned as 'androgynous' because Eve was still hidden inside of
him. This understanding was the consequence of an interpretation of Genesis 1.26–27 and
2.21–22.

The community appears to have settled on a metaphorical interpretation that served to
maintain women within the community. Women could 'make' themselves 'male', thus
'resembling' the men in the community. J. Buckley thinks that this logion signals that
salvation was a two-step process for women in the community, whereas only a one-step
process for men. In my opinion, the gender refashioning for women would have stressed
encratic behaviour, particularly celibacy and their refusal to bear children. This metaphor
was quite common in antiquity among the early Christians as Meeks, Meyer, and Castelli
have demonstrated.

SOURCE DISCUSSION
G. Quispel thinks that this saying comes from an encratic Gospel source.

LITERATURE PARALLELS
Cf. Philo of Alexandria, *Quaest. Exod.* 1.8; *Quaest. Gen.* 2.49; Clement of Alexandria, *Ex.
Theo.* 79; Hippolytus, *Ref.* 5.8.44; *1 Apoc. James* 41.15–19; *Zostr.* 131.2–10; *Martyrdom
of Perpetua and Felicitas* 10; *Acts of Paul and Thecla* 25 and 40; *Acts of Thomas* 114;
Acts of Philip 44

SELECT BIBLIOGRAPHY
Buckley (1985); Castelli (1991); Meeks (1974); Meyer (1985); Rengstorf (1967).

Subtitle

'The Gospel According to Thomas'

NHC II 51.27–28

ⲡⲉⲩⲁⲅⲅⲉⲗⲓⲟⲛ ⲡ ⲕⲁⲧⲁ ⲑⲱⲙⲁⲥ

Appendix

VERBAL SIMILARITIES BETWEEN *THOMAS* AND THE SYNOPTICS

L. 3.1–3 [1]Jesus said, (('If [[your <<leaders>> [say to you, "Look!] the Kingdom is in heaven", then the birds of heaven [will arrive first before you. [2]If they say,] "It is under the earth", then the fish of the sea [will enter it, arriving first] before you. [3]But the Kingdom [of Heaven] is inside of you and [outside.]))' L. 113.1–4 [1]His disciples said to him, 'When will the Kingdom come?' [2]'It will not come by waiting. [3]It will not be said, "Look! Here it is!" or "Look! There it is!" [4]Rather, the Kingdom of the Father is spread out over the earth, but people do not see it.'	Luke 17.20–21 'The Kingdom of God is not coming with signs to be observed; nor will they say, "Lo, here it is!" or "There!" for behold, the Kingdom of God is within you.'
L. 4.2–3 [2]'For many who are first will be last, [3]((the last will be first)),'	Matthew 20.16 (Qmatt) 'So the last will be first, and the first will be last.' Luke 13.30 (Qluke) 'Indeed, some are last who will be first, and some are first who will be last.' Mark 10.31 'But many who are first will be last, and the last will be first.' Matthew 19.30 'But many who are first will be last, and the last will be first.'
L. 5.1–2 [1]Jesus said, 'Understand what is in front of you, and what is hidden from you will be revealed to you. [2]For there is nothing hidden that will not be manifested.' L. 6.4–5 [4]'(([For everything, when faced] with truth, is brought [to light. [5]For there is nothing hidden] that [will not be manifested.]))'	Matthew 10.26 (Qmatt) 'For nothing is covered that will not be revealed, or hidden that will not be known.' Luke 12.2 (Qluke) 'Nothing is covered up that will not be revealed, or hidden that will not be known.' Mark 4.22 'For there is nothing hidden except to be revealed; nor is anything secret, except to come to light.' Luke 8.17 'For nothing is hidden that will not be revealed, nor is anything secret that will not become known and come to light.'

L. 8.1–3 ¹And he said, 'The human being is like a wise fisherman who cast his <u>net</u> <u>into the sea</u>. He drew it up from the sea full of small <u>fish</u>. ²From among them he found a fine large fish. ³The wise fisherman cast all of the small fish back into the sea and chose the large fish without difficulty.'	Matthew 13.47–50 ⁴⁷'Again, the kingdom of heaven is like a <u>net</u> that was thrown <u>into the sea</u> and caught <u>fish</u> of every kind. ⁴⁸When it was full, they drew it ashore, sat down, and put the good into baskets but threw out the bad. ⁴⁹So it will be at the end of the age. ⁵⁰The angels will come out and separate the evil from the righteous and throw them into the furnace of fire, where there will be weeping and gnashing of teeth.'
L. 8.4 ⁴'<u>Whoever has ears to hear</u> <u>should listen</u>!'	Matthew 11.15; Mark 4.9; Luke 8.8; 14.35 'He who has ears to hear, <u>let him hear</u>.' Matthew 13.9, 43 'He who has ears, <u>let him hear</u>.' Mark 4.23 'If <u>anyone has ears to hear</u>, <u>let him hear</u>.'
L. 9.1–5 ¹Jesus said, 'Look! The <u>sower</u> <u>went out</u>. He filled his hand (with seeds). He cast (them). ²Some fell on <u>the road</u>. <u>The birds came</u> and gathered them up. ³<u>Others fell on</u> the <u>rock</u> and did not take <u>root</u> in the earth or put forth ears. ⁴And <u>others fell among thorns</u>. They <u>choked</u> the seeds and worms ate them. ⁵And <u>others fell on the</u> <u>good earth</u>, and it produced good fruit. It yielded <u>sixty</u> per measure and a <u>hundred</u> and twenty per measure.'	Mark 4.3–8 ³'Listen! A <u>sower</u> <u>went out</u> to sow. ⁴And as he sowed, some seed <u>fell</u> along <u>the path</u>, and <u>the birds came</u> and devoured it. ⁵<u>Other</u> seed <u>fell on rocky ground</u>, where it had not much soil, and immediately it sprang up, since it had no depth of soil. ⁶And when the sun rose it was scorched, and since it had no <u>root</u> it withered away. ⁷<u>Other</u> seed <u>fell among thorns</u> and the thorns grew up and <u>choked</u> it, and it yielded no grain. ⁸And <u>other</u> seeds <u>fell</u> into <u>good soil</u> and brought forth grain, growing up and increasing and yielding thirtyfold and <u>sixty</u>fold and a <u>hundred</u>fold.' Matthew 13.3–8 ³'A <u>sower went out</u> to sow. ⁴And as he sowed, some seeds <u>fell</u> along <u>the path</u>, and the <u>birds came</u> and devoured them. ⁵<u>Other</u> seeds <u>fell on rocky ground</u>, where they had not much soil, and immediately they sprang up, since they had no depth of soil, ⁶but when the sun rose they were scorched. And since they had no <u>root</u>, they withered away. ⁷<u>Other</u> seeds <u>fell</u> upon <u>thorns</u>, and the thorns grew up and <u>choked</u> them. ⁸<u>Other</u> seeds <u>fell on good</u> <u>soil</u> and brought forth grain, some a <u>hundred</u>fold, some <u>sixty</u>, some thirty.' Luke 8.5–8 ⁵'A <u>sower went out</u> to sow his seed. And as he sowed, some <u>fell</u> along <u>the path</u>, and was trodden under foot, and the <u>birds</u> of the air devoured it. ⁶And some <u>fell on the rock</u>, and as it grew up, it withered away because it had no moisture. ⁷And some <u>fell among thorns</u>, and the thorns grew with it and <u>choked</u> it. ⁸And some <u>fell into good soil</u> and grew, and yielded a <u>hundred</u>fold.'
L. 10 Jesus said, 'I have <u>cast fire upon</u> <u>the world</u>. And look! I am guarding it until it blazes.'	Luke 12.49 (L or Qluke) 'I came to <u>cast fire upon the earth</u>. And would that it were already kindled!'
L. 11.1 ¹Jesus said, 'This <u>heaven will</u> <u>pass away</u>, and the one above it will pass away.'	Mark 13.31; Matthew 24.35; Luke 21.33 '<u>Heaven</u> and earth <u>will pass away</u>, but my words will not pass away.'

	Matthew 5.18 (Qmatt) 'For truly I say to you, till <u>heaven</u> and earth <u>pass away</u>, not an iota, not a dot, will pass from the law until all is accomplished.' Luke 16.17 (Qluke) 'But it is easier for <u>heaven</u> and earth to <u>pass away</u>, than for one dot of the law to become void.'
L. 14.4 ⁴'<u>When you enter any district</u> and walk around the countryside, if <u>they take you in</u>, whatever they serve you, <u>eat</u>! The people among them who are <u>sick, heal</u>!'	Matthew 10.8 (Qmatt) '<u>Heal the sick</u>, raise the dead, cleanse the leper, cast out demons'. Luke 10.8–9 (Qluke) ⁸'<u>Whenever you enter a town</u> and <u>they receive you, eat</u> what is set before you. ⁹<u>Heal the sick</u> in it and say to them, "The Kingdom of God has come near to you."'
L. 14.5 ⁵'For <u>what goes into your mouth will not make you unclean, rather what comes out of your mouth</u>. It is this which will make you <u>unclean</u>!'	Mark 7.15 'There is nothing outside a man which by going into him can defile him. But the <u>things which come out of</u> a man are what defile him.' Mark 7.18–23 ¹⁸'Do you not see that <u>whatever goes into</u> a man from outside cannot defile him, ¹⁹since it enters, not his heart, but his stomach, and so passes on?' (Thus he declared all foods clean.) ²⁰And he said, '<u>What comes out of a man</u> is what <u>defiles</u> a man. ²¹For from within, out of the heart of man, come evil thoughts, fornication, theft, murder, adultery, ²²coveting, wickedness, deceit, licentiousness, envy, slander, pride, foolishness. ²³All these evil things come from within, and they defile man.' Matthew 15.11 '<u>Not what goes into the mouth defiles a man, but what comes out of the mouth</u>, this <u>defiles</u> him.' Matthew 15.17–20 ¹⁷'Do you not see that whatever goes into the mouth passes into the stomach, and so passes on? ¹⁸But <u>what comes out of the mouth</u> proceeds from the heart, and this <u>defiles</u> a man. ¹⁹For out of the heart come evil thoughts, murder, adultery, fornication, theft, false witness, slander. ²⁰These are what defile a man; but to eat with unwashed hands does not defile a man.'
L. 16.1–2 ¹Jesus said, 'Perhaps people <u>think</u> it is <u>peace</u> that <u>I have come</u> to cast upon the world. ²And they do not know it is <u>division</u> that <u>I have come to</u> cast upon the earth – fire, <u>sword</u>, war!'	Matthew 10.34 (Qmatt) 'Do not <u>think</u> that I have come to bring <u>peace</u> on earth. <u>I have</u> not <u>come to</u> bring peace, but a <u>sword</u>.' Luke 12.51 (Qluke) 'Do you <u>think</u> that <u>I have come to</u> give <u>peace</u> on earth? No, I tell you, but rather <u>division</u>.'
L. 16.3 ³'<u>For there will be five</u> people <u>in a house</u>. There will be <u>three people against two, and two against three, father against son, and son against father</u>.'	Matthew 10.35–36 (Qmatt) 'For I have come to set a man <u>against</u> his <u>father</u>, and a daughter against her mother, and a daughter-in-law against her mother-in-law. A man's foes will be those of his own household.' Luke 12.52–53 (Qluke) '<u>For</u> henceforth <u>in one house there will be five</u> divided, <u>three</u>

	against two and two against three. They will be divided, father against son and son against father, mother against daughter and daughter against her mother, mother-in-law against daughter-in-law and daughter-in-law against her mother-in-law'.
L. 20.2–4 ²He said to them, 'It is like a mustard seed, ²smaller than all seeds. ⁴But when it falls on cultivated soil, it puts forth a large branch and becomes a shelter for birds of the sky.'	Mark 4.30–32 ³⁰'And he said to them, 'With what can we compare the Kingdom of God, or what parable shall we use for it? ³¹It is like a grain of mustard seed which, when sown upon the ground, is the smallest of all the seeds on earth. ³²Yet when it is sown, it grows up and becomes the greatest of all shrubs, and puts forth large branches, so that the birds of the air can make nests in the shade.' Matthew 13.31–32 (Qmatt) ³¹'The Kingdom of Heaven is like a grain of mustard seed which a man took and sowed in his field. ³²It is the smallest of all seeds, but when it has grown it is the greatest of shrubs and becomes a tree, so that the birds of the air come and make nests in its branches.' Luke 13.18–19 (Qluke) ¹⁸'What is the Kingdom of God like? And to what shall I compare it? ¹⁹It is like a grain of mustard seed which a man took and sowed in his garden. And it grew and became a tree, and the birds of the air made nests in its branches.'
L. 21.5 ⁵'For this reason I say, "If the owner of a house knows that a thief is coming, he will keep watch before he arrives. He will not allow him to break into his house, part of his estate, to steal his furnishings."' L.103 Jesus said, 'Blessed is the man who knows where the thieves are going to enter, so that [he] may arise, gather at his estate, and arm himself.'	Matthew 24.43 (Qmatt) 'But know this, that if the householder had known in what part of the night the thief was coming, he would have watched and would not have let his house be broken into.' Luke 12.39 (Qluke) 'But know this, that if the householder had known at what hour the thief was coming, he would not have left his house to be broken into.'
L. 21.10 ¹⁰'When the grain ripened, he came quickly with his sickle in his hand. He harvested it.'	Mark 4.29 'When the grain is ripe, at once he puts in the sickle, because the harvest has come.'
L. 24.3 ³'There is light inside a person of light. And it lights up the whole world. If it does not shine, it is dark.'	Matthew 6.22–23 (Qmatt) ²²'The eye is the lamp of the body. So, if your eye is sound, your whole body will be full of light. ²³But if your eye is not sound, your whole body will be full of darkness. If then the light in you is darkness, how great is the darkness!' Luke 11.34–35 (Qluke) ³⁴'Your eye is the lamp of your body. When your eye is sound, your whole body is full of light. But when it is not sound, your body is full of darkness. ³⁵Therefore, be careful lest the light in you be darkness.'

	Matthew 5.14–16 [14]'You are the light of the world. A city set on a hill cannot be hid. [15]Nor do men light a lamp and put it under a bushel, but on a stand, and it gives light to all in the house. [16]Let your light so shine before men, that they may see your good works and give glory to your Father who is in heaven.'
L. 25.1–2 [1]Jesus said, 'Love your brother like your soul. [2]Watch over him like the pupil of your eye.'	Mark 12.31 'The second is this, "Love your neighbour as yourself."' Matthew 19.19 'Honour your father and your mother, and You shall love your neighbour as yourself.' Matthew 22.39 'And a second is like it, You shall love your neighbour as yourself.' Luke 10.27 '…and your neighbour as yourself.'
L. 26.1–2 [1]Jesus said, 'The twig in your brother's eye, you see. But the beam in your eye, you do not see! [2]When you remove the beam from your eye ((then you will see clearly to remove the twig in your brother's eye)).'	Matthew 7.3–5 (Qmatt) [3]'Why do you see the speck that is in your brother's eye, but do not notice the log that is in your own eye? [4]Or how can you say to your brother, 'Let me take the speck out of your eye', when there is a log in your own eye? [5]You hypocrite, first take the log out of your own eye, and then you will see clearly to take the speck out of your brother's eye.' Luke 6.41–42 (Qluke) [41]'Why do you see the speck that is in your brother's eye, but do not notice the log that is in your own eye? [42]Or how can you say to your brother, "Brother, let me take out the speck that is in your eye," when you yourself do not see the log that is in your own eye? You hypocrite, first take the log out of your own eye, and then you will see clearly to take out the speck that is in your brother's eye.'
L. 30.1–2 [1][Jesus said], '((Where there are [three people.] [[God is there]]. [2]And where there is one alone, I say, I am with him.))'	Matthew 18.20 'For where two or three are gathered in my name, I am there among them.'
L. 31.1–2 [1]Jesus said, 'A prophet is not received hospitably in his (own) village. [2]A doctor does not heal the people who know him.'	Luke 4.23–24 [23]'And he said to them, "Doubtless you will quote to me this proverb, 'Doctor, heal yourself. What we have heard you did in Capernaum, do here also in your own country.'" [24]And he said, "Truly I say to you, no prophet is received hospitably in his own country."' Mark 6.4 'A prophet is not without honour, except in his own country, and among his own kin, and in his own house.' Matthew 13.57 'A prophet is not without honour except in his own country and in his own house.'

L. 32 Jesus said, 'A city built on a high mountain and fortified cannot fall nor be hidden.'	Matthew 5.14 'You are the light of the world. A city set on a hill cannot be hidden.'
L. 33.1 [1]Jesus said, 'What you ((hear)) in your ears, preach from your rooftops.'	Matthew 10.27 (Qmatt) 'What I tell you in the dark, utter in the light. And what you hear whispered, proclaim upon the housetops.' Luke 12.3 (Qluke) 'Therefore, whatever you have said in the dark shall be heard in the light, and what you have whispered in private rooms shall be proclaimed upon the housetops.'
L. 33.2–3 [2]'For no one lights a lamp and puts it under a bushel basket, nor puts it in a hidden place. [3]Rather the person sets it on a lampstand so that everyone who enters and leaves will see its light.'	Matthew 5.15 (Qmatt) 'Nor do men light a lamp and put it under a bushel basket, but on a stand, and it gives light to all in the house.' Luke 11.33 (Qluke) 'No one after lighting a lamp puts it in a cellar or under a bushel basket, but on a stand, that those who enter may see the light.' Mark 4.21 'Is a lamp brought in to be put under a bushel basket, or under a bed, and not on a stand?' Luke 8.16 'No one after lighting a lamp covers it with a vessel, or puts it under a bed, but puts it on a stand, that those who enter may see the light.'
L. 34 Jesus said, 'If a blind person leads a blind person, both will fall into a pit.'	Matthew 15.14 (Qmatt) 'And if a blind man leads a blind man, both will fall into a pit.' Luke 6.39 (Qluke) 'Can a blind man lead a blind man? Will they not both fall into a pit?'
L. 35.1–2 [1]Jesus said, 'It is not possible for someone to enter the strong man's house and take it forcibly without binding his hands. [2]Then the person will loot his house.'	Mark 3.27 'But no one can enter a strong man's house and plunder his goods, unless he first binds the strong man. Then indeed he may plunder his house.' Matthew 12.29 'Or how can one enter a strong man's house and plunder his goods, unless he first binds the strong man?' Luke 11.21–22 [21]'When a strong man, fully armed, guards his own palace, his goods are in peace. [22]But when one stronger than he assails him and overcomes him, he takes away his armour in which he trusted, and divides his spoil.'
L. 36.1–3 [1](([Jesus said, 'Do not be anxious] from morning [until evening and] from evening [until] morning, neither [about] your [food] and what [you will] eat, [nor] about [your clothing] and what you [will] wear. [2][You are	Matthew 6.25–30 (Qmatt) [25]'Therefore I tell you, do not be anxious about your life, what you shall eat or what you shall drink, nor about your body, what you shall put on. Is not life more than food and the body more than clothing? [26]Look at the birds of the air – they neither sow nor reap nor gather into barns, and yet your heavenly Father feeds them. Are you not of more value than they? [27]And which of you by being anxious can add one cubit

far] better than the [lilies] which [neither] card nor [spin]. ³As for you, when you have no garment, what [will you put on]? Who might add to your stature? He will give you your garment.))'

to his span of life? ²⁸And why are you anxious about clothing? Consider the lilies of the field, how they grow. They neither toil nor spin. ²⁹Yet I tell you, Solomon in all his glory was not arrayed like one of these. ³⁰But if God so clothes the grass of the field, which today is alive and tomorrow is thrown into the oven, will he not much more clothe you, O men of little faith?'

Luke 12.22, 27–28 (Qluke)
²²'Therefore I tell you, do not be anxious about your life, what you shall eat nor about your body, what you shall put on. ²³For life is more than food, and the body more than clothing. ²⁴Consider the ravens – they neither sow nor reap, they have neither storehouse nor barn, and yet God feeds them. Of how much more value are you than the birds! ²⁵And which of you by being anxious can add a cubit to his span of life? ²⁶If then you are not able to do as small a thing as that, why are you anxious about the rest? ²⁷Consider the lilies, how they grow. They neither toil nor spin. Yet I tell you, even Solomon in all his glory was not arrayed like one of these. ²⁸But if God so clothes the grass which is alive in the field today and tomorrow is thrown into the oven, how much more will he clothe you, O men of little faith.'

L. 38.1
¹Jesus said, 'The words that I am speaking to you, often you have longed to hear them. And you have no other person from whom to hear them.'

Matthew 13.17 (Qmatt)
'Truly I say to you, many prophets and righteous men longed to see what you see, and did not see it, and to hear what you hear, and did not hear it.'
Luke 10.24 (Qluke)
'For I tell you that many prophets and kings desired to see what you see, and did not see it, and to hear what you hear, and did not hear it.'

L. 39.1–2
¹Jesus said, 'The Pharisees and the scribes have taken the keys of knowledge. They have hidden them. ²Neither have they entered nor have they permitted those people who want to enter (to do so).'

Matt 23.13 (Qmatt)
'But woe to you, scribes and Pharisees, hypocrites! because you shut the Kingdom of Heaven against men. For you neither enter yourselves, nor allow those who would enter to go in.'
Luke 11.52 (Qluke)
'Woe to you lawyers! for you have taken away the key of knowledge. You did not enter yourselves, and you hindered those who were entering.'

L. 40.1–2
¹Jesus said, 'A grapevine has been planted apart from the Father's (planting). ²Since it is not strong, it will be plucked up by its roots, and it will perish.'

Matthew 15.13
'Every plant which my heavenly Father has not planted will be rooted up.'

L. 41.1–2
¹Jesus said, 'Whoever has something in his hand will be given more. ²And whoever has nothing, even the little that this person has will be taken away.'

Mark 4.25
'For to him who has will more be given. And from him who has not, even what he has will be taken away.'
Matthew 13.12
'For to him who has will more be given, and he will have abundance. But from him who has not, even what he has will be taken away.'

	Luke 8.18
	'For to <u>him who has</u> <u>will more be given</u>, and from <u>him who has not, even what he</u> thinks that he <u>has will be taken away</u>.'
	Matthew 25.29 (Qmatt)
	'For to <u>everyone who has</u> <u>will more be given</u>, and he will have abundance. But from <u>him who has not</u>, even <u>what he has will be taken away</u>.'
	Luke 19.26 (Qluke)
	'I tell you, that to <u>everyone who has</u> <u>will more be given</u>. But from <u>him who has not, even what he has will be taken away</u>.'
L. 44	**Mark 3.28–30**
[1]Jesus said, 'Whoever blasphemes against the Father will be forgiven, [2]and whoever blasphemes <u>against the Son will be forgiven</u>. [3]But <u>whoever blasphemes against the Holy Spirit will not be forgiven</u>, <u>neither</u> on earth nor in heaven.'	[28]'Truly, I say to you, all sins will be forgiven the sons of men, and whatever blasphemies they utter. [29]But <u>whoever blasphemes against the Holy Spirit</u> <u>never has forgiveness</u>, but is guilty of an eternal sin' – [30]for they had said, 'He has an unclean spirit.'
	Matthew 12.31–32 (Qmatt)
	[31]'Therefore I tell you, every sin and blasphemy will be forgiven men, but the blasphemy against the Spirit will not be forgiven. [32]And whoever says a word <u>against the son of man will be forgiven</u>; but whoever speaks <u>against the Holy Spirit will not be forgiven, either</u> in this age or in the age to come.'
	Luke 12.10 (Qluke)
	'And everyone who speaks a word <u>against the son of man will be forgiven</u>. But <u>he who blasphemes against the Holy Spirit will not be forgiven</u>.'
L. 45.1–4	**Luke 6.44–45 (Qluke)**
[1]Jesus said, '<u>Grapes</u> are not harvested <u>from thorn trees</u>, nor are <u>figs</u> picked <u>from thistles</u>, for they do not produce fruit. [2]<u>A good person brings forth good from his treasury</u>. [3]A bad person brings forth evil from his wicked treasury in his heart, and he speaks evil. [4]<u>For from the excessiveness of the heart</u>, he brings forth evil.'	'For <u>figs</u> are not gathered <u>from thorns</u>, nor are <u>grapes</u> picked <u>from a bramble bush</u>. <u>The good man out of</u> the <u>good treasure</u> of his heart <u>produces good</u>, and <u>the evil man out of his evil treasure produces evil</u>. <u>For out of the abundance of the heart</u> his mouth <u>speaks</u>.'
	Matthew 7.16 (Qmatt)
	'Are <u>grapes</u> gathered <u>from thorns</u>, or <u>figs from thistles</u>?'
	Matthew 12.34–35 (Qmatt)
	'You brood of vipers! How can you speak good, when you are evil? <u>For out of the abundance of the heart</u> the mouth <u>speaks. The good man out of</u> his good <u>treasure brings forth good</u>, and <u>the evil man out of his evil treasure brings forth evil</u>.'
L. 46.1–2	**Matthew 11.11 (Qmatt)**
[1]Jesus said, 'From Adam to John the Baptist, <u>no one among those born of women is more exalted than John the Baptist</u> that the person's gaze should not be deferent. [2]Yet I have said, "Whoever from among you will become a child, this person will know <u>the Kingdom</u> and <u>he will be more exalted than</u> John."''	'Truly I say to you, <u>among those born of women</u> there has risen <u>no one greater than John the Baptist</u>. Yet <u>he</u> who is least in <u>the Kingdom</u> of Heaven <u>is greater than he</u>.'
	Luke 7.28 (Qluke)
	'I tell you, <u>among those born of women none is greater than John</u>. Yet <u>he</u> who is least in <u>the Kingdom</u> of God <u>is greater than he</u>.'

L. 47.1–2 [1]Jesus said, 'It is impossible for a person to mount two horses and to bend two bows. [2]Also <u>it is impossible for a servant to serve two masters</u>, or <u>he will honour the one and insult the other</u>.'	Matthew 6.24 (Qmatt) '<u>No one can serve two masters</u>. For either he will hate the one and love the other, or <u>he will be devoted to the one and despise the other</u>.' Luke 16.13 (Qluke) '<u>No servant can serve two masters</u>. For either he will hate the one and love the other, or <u>he will be devoted to the one and despise the other</u>.'
L. 47.3–4 [3]'<u>No one drinks aged wine and immediately wants</u> to drink <u>unaged wine</u>. [4]Also, <u>unaged wine is not put into old wineskins</u> so that they <u>may burst</u>. Nor is aged wine put into a new wineskin so that it may spoil.'	Mark 2.22 'And <u>no one puts new wine into old wineskins</u>. If he does, the wine <u>will burst</u> the skins, and the wine is lost, and so are the skins. But new wine is for fresh skins.' Matthew 9.17 '<u>Neither is new wine put into old wineskins</u>. If it is, the skins <u>burst</u>, and the wine is spilled, and the skins are destroyed. But new wine is put into fresh wineskins, and so both are preserved.' Luke 5.37–39 [37]'And <u>no one puts new wine into old wineskins</u>. If he does, the new wine <u>will burst</u> the skins and it will be spilled, and the skins will be destroyed. [38]But new wine must be put into fresh wineskins. [39]And <u>no one after drinking old wine desires new</u>. For he says, "The old is good."'
L. 47.5 [5]'An old patch is not <u>sewn</u> onto a new <u>garment</u> because a <u>tear</u> would result.'	Mark 2.21 'No one <u>sews</u> a piece of unshrunk cloth on an old garment. If he does, the patch tears away from it, the new from the old, and a worse <u>tear</u> is made.' Matthew 9.16 'And no one puts a piece of unshrunk cloth on an old <u>garment</u>, for the patch tears away from the garment, and a worse <u>tear</u> is made.' Luke 5.36 'He told them a parable also, 'No one tears a piece from a new garment and puts it upon an old <u>garment</u>. If he does, he will <u>tear</u> the new, and the piece from the new will not match the old.'
L. 48 Jesus said, '<u>If two</u> people make peace with each other in the same house, they <u>will say to the mountain, "Go forth!" and it will move</u>.' L. 106.1–2 [1]Jesus said, 'When you make the <u>two</u> one, you will become children of Man. [2]And when you say, "<u>Mountain, go forth!</u>" it will move.'	Matthew 17.20 (Qmatt) 'For truly, I say to you, if you have faith as a grain of mustard seed, you <u>will say to this mountain</u>, "<u>Move</u> from here to there," <u>and it will move</u>. And nothing will be impossible to you.' Luke 17.6 (Qluke) 'And the Lord said, "If you had faith as a grain of mustard seed, you could <u>say</u> to this sycamine tree, 'Be rooted up, and be planted in the sea,' and it would obey you."' Matthew 18.19 'Again, I say to you, <u>if two</u> of you agree on earth about anything they ask, it will be done for them by my Father in heaven.' Mark 11.23 'Truly, I say to you, whoever <u>says to this mountain</u>, "Be taken up and cast into the sea," and does not doubt in his heart, but

	believes that what he says will come to pass, it will be done for him.' Matthew 21.21 'Truly I say to you, if you have faith and never doubt, you will not only do what has been done to the fig tree, but even if you <u>say to this mountain</u>, "Be taken up and cast into the sea," it will be done.'
L. 54 Jesus said, '<u>Blessed are the poor</u>, <u>for the Kingdom of Heaven is</u> <u>yours</u>.'	Matthew 5.3 (Qmatt) '<u>Blessed are the poor</u> in spirit, for theirs is <u>the Kingdom of</u> <u>Heaven</u>.' Luke 6.20b (Qluke) '<u>Blessed are the poor</u>, <u>for yours is the Kingdom of</u> God.'
L. 55.1–2 ¹Jesus said, '<u>Whoever does not</u> <u>hate his father and mother</u> <u>cannot</u> <u>become a disciple of mine</u>. ²And whoever does not hate his brothers and sisters and <u>carry his</u> <u>cross</u> as I do <u>will not be worthy</u> <u>of me</u>.'	Matthew 10.37–38 (Qmatt) ³⁷'He who loves <u>father or mother</u> more than me is not worthy of me. And he who loves son or daughter more than me is not worthy of me. ³⁸And he who does not <u>take his cross</u> and follow me <u>is not worthy of me</u>.' Luke 14.26–27 (Qluke) ²⁶'If anyone comes to me and <u>does not hate his</u> own <u>father and</u> <u>mother</u> and wife and children and brothers and sisters, yes, and even his own life, he <u>cannot be my disciple</u>. ²⁷Whoever does not <u>bear his own cross</u> and come after me, cannot be my disciple.' Mark 8.34 'If any man would come after me, let him deny himself and <u>take up his cross</u> and follow me.' Matthew 16.24 'If any man would come after me, let him deny himself and <u>take up his cross</u> and follow me.' Luke 9.23 'If any man would come after me, let him deny himself and <u>take up his cross</u> daily and follow me.'
L. 57.1–2 ¹Jesus said, '<u>The Kingdom</u> of the Father <u>is like a man</u> who had [good] seed. ²<u>His enemy came</u> at night. He added darnel to the good seed. ³The man did not let them pull out the darnel. He explained to them, "In case you go to pull out the darnel, but <u>pull</u> <u>out the wheat with it</u>. ⁴For on the day of the <u>harvest</u>, the darnel will be discernible, and will be pulled up and <u>burned</u>."'	Matthew 13.24–30 ²⁴'<u>The Kingdom</u> of Heaven <u>may be compared to a man</u> who sowed <u>good seed</u> in his field. ²⁵But while men where sleeping, <u>his enemy came</u> and sowed weeds among the wheat, and went away. ²⁶So when the plants came up and bore grain, then the weeds appeared also. ²⁷And the servants of the householder came and said to him, "Sir, did you not sow good seed in your field? How then has it weeds?" ²⁸He said to them, "An enemy has done this." The servants said to him, "then do you want us to go and gather them?" ²⁹But he said, "No, <u>lest</u> in gathering the weeds you <u>root up the wheat along with them</u>. ³⁰Let both grow together until harvest. And at <u>harvest</u> time I will tell the reapers, 'Gather the weeds first and bind them in bundles to be <u>burned</u>, but gather the wheat into my barn'."'
L. 61.1 Jesus said, '<u>Two people will rest</u> <u>on a couch</u>. <u>One</u> will die. <u>One</u> will live.'	Matthew 24.40–41 (Qmatt) ⁴⁰'Then two men will be in the field. <u>One</u> is taken and <u>one</u> is left. ⁴¹Two women will be grinding at the mill. One is taken and one is left.' Luke 17.34–35 (Qluke) ³⁴'I tell you, in that night there will be <u>two in one bed</u>. One

	will be taken and <u>the other</u> left. [35]There will be two women grinding together. One will be taken and the other left.'
L. 62.1 [1]Jesus said, 'I tell my <u>mysteries</u> to [those people who are worthy of my] mysteries.'	**Mark 4.11** 'To you has been given <u>the secret</u> of the Kingdom of God, but for those outside everything is in parables.' **Matthew 13.11** 'To you it has been given to know <u>the secrets</u> of the Kingdom of Heaven, but to them it has not been given.' **Luke 8.10** 'To you it has been given to know <u>the secrets</u> of the Kingdom of God, but for others they are in parables, so that seeing they may not see, and hearing they may not understand.'
L. 62.2 [2]'<u>Do not let your left hand know what your right hand is</u> going to <u>do</u>.'	**Matthew 6.3** 'But when you give alms, <u>do not let your left hand know what your right hand is doing</u>.'
L. 63.1–3 [1]Jesus said, 'There was <u>a wealthy man</u> who had many assets. [2]He said, "I will use my assets to sow, harvest, plant and fill my granaries with produce, so that I will not need anything." [3]These were the things he was thinking in his heart. But that very <u>night</u>, he died.'	**Luke 12.16–21 (Qluke or L)** [16]'The land of <u>a rich man</u> brought forth plentifully. [17]And he thought to himself, "What shall I do, for I have nowhere to store my crops?" [18]And he said, "I will do this. I will pull down my barns, and build larger ones. And there I will store my grain and my goods. [19]And I will say to my soul, 'Soul, you have ample goods laid up for many years. Take your ease, eat, drink, be merry.'" [20]But God said to him, "Fool! This <u>night</u> your soul is required of you. And the things you have prepared, whose will they be?" [21]So is he who lays up treasure for himself, and is not rich toward God.'
L. 64.1–11 [1]Jesus said, '<u>A man</u> had guests. When he had prepared the dinner, he <u>sent his servant to invite</u> the guests. [2]He went to <u>the first person</u>. He said to him, "My master invites you." [3]He said, "I have some payments for some merchants. They are coming to me this evening. I must go and give them instructions. I decline the dinner." [4]He went to another person. He said to him, "My master has invited you." [5]He said to him, "I have purchased a house and they have requested me for the day. I will not have time." [6]He went to another person. He said to him, "My master invites you." [7]He said to him, "My friend is going to be wed and I am the	[2]'The Kingdom of heaven may be compared to a king who gave a marriage feast for his son, [3]and <u>sent his servants to call those who were invited</u> to the marriage feast. But they would not come. [4]Again he sent other servants, saying "Tell those who are invited, Behold, I have made ready my dinner, my oxen and my fat calves killed, and everything is ready. Come to the marriage feast." [5]But they made light of it and went off, one to his farm, another to his business, [6]while the rest seized the servants, treated them shamefully, and killed them. [7]The king was angry, and he sent troops and destroyed those murderers and burned their city. [8]Then he said to his servants, "The wedding is ready, but <u>those invited</u> were not worthy. [9]Go therefore to the thoroughfares, and invite to the marriage feast <u>as many as you find</u>." [10]And those servants went out into the streets and gathered all whom they found, both bad and good. So the wedding hall was filled with guests.' **Luke 14.16–24 (Qluke)** [16]'<u>A man</u> once gave a great banquet, and invited many. [17]And at the time for the banquet <u>he sent his servant</u> to say <u>to those who had been invited</u>, "Come! For all is now ready." [18]But they all alike began to make excuses. <u>The first</u> said to him, "I have bought a field, and I must go out and see it. I pray you, have me excused." [19]And another said, "I have bought five yoke of oxen, and I go to examine them. I pray you, have me excused." [20]And another said, "I have married a wife, and

person who will be preparing the meal. I will not be able to come. I decline the dinner."

⁸He went to another person. He said to him, "My master invites you."

⁹He said to him, "I have purchased a villa. Since I am going to collect the rent, I will not be able to come. I decline."

¹⁰The servant left. He said to his master, "<u>The people whom you invited</u> to the dinner have declined."

¹¹The master said to his servant, "Go outside on the streets. <u>The people you find</u>, bring them to dine." '

---

therefore I cannot come." ²¹So the servant came and reported this to his master. Then the householder in anger said to his servant, "Go out quickly to the streets and lanes of the city, and bring in the poor and maimed and blind and lame." ²²And the servant said, "Sir, what you commanded has been done, and still there is room." ²³And the master said to the servant, "Go out to the highways and hedges, and compel people to come in, that my house may be filled. ²⁴For I tell you, none of those men who were invited shall taste my banquet." '

L. 65.1–7

¹He said, 'A creditor owned <u>a vineyard. He leased it to some farmers</u> so that they would work it and he would collect the produce from them.

²<u>He sent his servant so that the farmers would give him the produce of the vineyard.</u> ³They seized his servant. They <u>beat him,</u> a little more and they would have killed him.

The servant returned and he told his master.

⁴The master said, "Perhaps [[they]] did not recognize [[him.]]."

⁵<u>He sent another servant.</u> The farmers <u>beat</u> that one too.

⁶Then the master sent his son. He said, "<u>Perhaps</u> they will be ashamed in front of <u>my son.</u>"

⁷Those farmers, since they knew that he was the heir of the vineyard, <u>seized him and killed him.</u>'

Mark 12.1–9

¹'A man planted <u>a vineyard,</u> and set a hedge around it, and dug a pit for a wine press, and built a tower. <u>He let it out to tenants,</u> and went into another country. ²When the time came, <u>he sent a servant</u> to the tenants, to get from them some of <u>the fruit of the vineyard.</u> ³And they took him and <u>beat him,</u> and sent him away empty-handed. ⁴Again he sent to them another servant, and they wounded him in the head, and treated him shamefully. ⁵And <u>he sent another,</u> and him they killed. And so with many others, some they <u>beat</u> and some they killed. ⁶He had still one other, a beloved son. Finally he sent him to them, saying, "They will respect <u>my son.</u>" ⁷But those tenants said to one another, "This is the heir. Come, let us kill him, and the inheritance will be ours." ⁸And <u>they took him and killed him,</u> and cast him out of the vineyard. ⁹What will the owner of the vineyard do? He will come and destroy the tenant, and give the vineyard to others.'

Matthew 21.33–41

³³'There was a householder who planted <u>a vineyard,</u> and set a hedge around it, and dug a wine press in it, and built a tower. <u>He let it out to tenants,</u> and went into another country. ³⁴When the season of fruit drew near, <u>he sent his servants</u> to the tenants, to get <u>his fruit.</u> ³⁵And the tenants took his servants and <u>beat one,</u> killed another, and stoned another. ³⁶Again he sent other servants, more than the first. And they did the same to them. ³⁷Afterward, he sent his son to them, saying, "They will respect <u>my son.</u>" ³⁸But when the tenants saw the son, they said to themselves, "This is the heir. Come, let us kill him and have his inheritance." ³⁹And <u>they took him</u> and cast him out of the vineyard, <u>and killed him.</u> ⁴⁰When therefore the owner of the vineyard comes, what will he do to those tenants?'

⁴¹They said to him, 'He will put those wretches to a miserable death, and let out the vineyard to other tenants who will give him the fruits in their seasons.'

	Luke 20.9–16
	[9]'A man planted <u>a vineyard</u>, and <u>let it out to tenants</u>, and went into another country for a long while. [10]When the time came, <u>he sent a servant</u> to the tenants, <u>that they should give him some of the fruit of the vineyard</u>. But the tenants <u>beat him</u>, and sent him away empty-handed. [11]And he sent another servant. Him also they beat and treated shamefully, and sent him away empty-handed. [12]And he sent yet a third. This one they wounded and cast out. [13]Then the owner of the vineyard said, "What shall I do? I will send <u>my</u> beloved <u>son</u>. <u>Perhaps</u> they will respect him." [14]But when the tenants saw him, they said to themselves, "This is the heir. Let us kill him, that the inheritance may be ours." [15]And they cast him out of the vineyard and <u>killed him</u>. What then will the owner of the vineyard do to them? [16]He will come and destroy those tenants, and give the vineyard to others.'
L. 66 Jesus said, 'Show me the <u>stone</u> <u>that the builders rejected</u>. It is <u>the</u> <u>cornerstone</u>.'	Mark 12.10 'Have you not read this scripture: "The very <u>stone which the</u> <u>builders rejected</u> has become <u>the head of the corner</u>."' Matthew 21.42 Jesus said to them, 'Have you never read in the scriptures: "The very <u>stone which the builders rejected</u> has become <u>the</u> <u>head of the corner</u>."' Luke 20.17 But he looked at them and said, 'What then is this that is written: "The very <u>stone which the builders rejected</u> has become <u>the head of the corner</u>?"'
L. 68.1 Jesus said, '<u>Blessed are you when</u> <u>you are hated</u> and <u>persecuted</u>.'	Matthew 5.10–11 (Qmatt) '<u>Blessed are those who are persecuted</u> for righteousness sake, for theirs is the kingdom of heaven. Blessed are you when men revile you and persecute you and utter all kinds of evil against you falsely on my account.' Luke 6.22 (Qluke) '<u>Blessed are you when</u> men <u>hate you</u>, and when they exclude you and revile you, and cast out your name as evil, on account of the Son of Man.' Matthew 10.22 'and <u>you will be hated</u> by all for my name's sake'
L. 69.2 [2]'<u>Blessed are those who are</u> <u>hungry</u>, for whosoever desires (it), his belly <u>will be filled</u>.'	Matthew 5.6 (Qmatt) '<u>Blessed are those who hunger</u> and thirst for righteousness, for they will be filled.' Luke 6.21 (Qluke) '<u>Blessed are</u> you <u>who are hungry</u> now, for you will <u>be filled</u>.'
L. 71 Jesus said, '<u>I will destroy [this]</u> <u>temple</u>, and no one <u>will build</u> it […].'	Mark 14.58 '<u>I will destroy this temple</u> that is made with hands, and in three days I <u>will build</u> another, not made with hands.' Matthew 26.61 '<u>I will destroy this temple</u> that is made with hands, and in three days I <u>will build</u> another, not made with hands.' Mark 15.29 'You who would <u>destroy the temple</u> and <u>build</u> it in three days…'

	Matthew 27.40 'You who would <u>destroy the temple</u> and <u>build</u> it in three days…'
L. 72.1–3 [1]A man <u>said to him</u>, 'Tell my <u>brothers</u> that they must share <u>with me</u> my father's possessions.' [2]He said to him, 'Mister, <u>who has made me an executor</u>?' [3]He turned to his disciples and said to them, 'Surely I am not an executor, am I?'	Luke 12.13–14 (L or Qluke) [13]<u>Someone</u> in the crowd <u>said to him</u>, 'Teacher, <u>tell my brother</u> to divide the family inheritance <u>with me</u>.' [14]But he said to him, 'Friend, <u>who set me to be a</u> judge or <u>arbitrator</u> over you?'
L. 73 Jesus said, 'Indeed <u>the harvest is plentiful but the workers are few! So ask the Lord to send out workers</u> to the <u>harvest</u>.'	Matthew 9.37–38 (Qmatt) [37]Then he said to his disciples, '<u>The harvest is plentiful, but the labourers are few</u>. [38]Therefore ask the <u>Lord</u> of the harvest <u>to send out labourers</u> into his <u>harvest</u>.' Luke 10.2 (Qluke) He said to them, '<u>The harvest is plentiful, but the laborers are few</u>. Therefore ask the <u>Lord</u> of the harvest <u>to send out labourers</u> into his <u>harvest</u>.'
L. 76.1–2 [1]Jesus said, '<u>The Kingdom</u> of the Father <u>is like merchant</u> who had some merchandise. <u>He found a pearl</u>. [2]That merchant was wise. He <u>sold</u> the merchandise. Then he <u>purchased</u> for himself this single pearl.'	Matthew 13.45–46 (M) [45]'Again, <u>the Kingdom</u> of Heaven <u>is like a merchant</u> in search of fine pearls. [46]On <u>finding one pearl</u> of great value, he went and <u>sold</u> all that he had and <u>bought it</u>.'
L. 76.3 [3]'You too, seek his imperishable and enduring <u>treasure where</u> neither <u>moth</u> draws near to eat nor <u>worm destroys</u>.'	Matthew 6.19–20 (Qmatt) [19]'Do not store up for yourselves treasures on earth, where moth and <u>worm</u> consume and where thieves break in and steal. [20]But store up for yourselves <u>treasures</u> in heaven, <u>where neither moth</u> nor rust consumes and where thieves do not break in and steal.' Luke 12.33 (Qluke) 'Make purses for yourselves that do not wear out, an unfailing <u>treasure</u> in heaven, <u>where</u> no thief comes near and no <u>moth destroys</u>.'
L. 78.1–3 [1]Jesus said, 'Why <u>did you come out into the desert</u>? <u>To see a reed shaken by the wind</u> [2]and <u>to see a man dressed in soft garments</u> [like your] kings and your prominent men? [3]They are dressed in <u>soft garments</u>, but they will not be able to understand the truth.'	Matthew 11.7–8 (Qmatt) [7]'What <u>did you go out into the wilderness to look at</u>? <u>A reed shaken by the wind</u>? [8]What then did you go out <u>to see</u>? <u>Someone dressed in soft robes</u>? Look, those who wear <u>soft</u> robes are in royal palaces.' Luke 7.24–25 (Qluke) 'What <u>did you go out into the wilderness to look at</u>? <u>A reed shaken by the wind</u>? What then did you go out <u>to see</u>? <u>Someone dressed in soft robes</u>? Look, those who put on fine clothing and live in luxury are in royal palaces.'
L. 79.1–3 [1]A woman in the crowd said to him, 'Blessed is the womb that	Luke 11.27–28 (L or Qluke) [27]While he was saying this, <u>a woman in the crowd</u> raised her voice and <u>said to him</u>, '<u>Blessed is the womb that bore you and</u>

bore you and the breasts that nourished you.' ²He said to [her], 'Blessed are the people who have heard the word of the Father and have truly kept it. ³For there will be days when you will say, "Blessed is the womb that has not conceived and the breasts that have not given milk."'	the breasts that you sucked!' ²⁸But he said, 'Blessed rather are those who hear the word of God and obey it!'
L. 86.1–2 ¹Jesus said, '[The foxes have] their dens and the birds have their nests, ²but the human being does not have a place to lay down his head and rest.'	Matthew 8.20 (Qmatt) And Jesus said to him, 'Foxes have holes, and birds of the air have nests; but the human being has nowhere to lay his head.' Luke 9.58 (Qluke) And Jesus said to him, 'Foxes have holes, and birds of the air have nests; but the human being has nowhere to lay his head.'
L. 89.1–2 ¹Jesus said, 'Why do you wash the cup's exterior? ²Do you not understand that He who created the interior is also He who created the exterior?'	Matthew 23.25–26 (Qmatt) ²⁵'Woe to you, scribes and Pharisees, hypocrites! for you cleanse the outside of the cup and of the plate, but inside they are full of extortion and rapacity. ²⁶You blind Pharisee! first cleanse the inside of the cup and of the plate, that the outside also may be clean.' Luke 11.39–41 (Qluke) ³⁹'Now you Pharisees cleanse the outside of the cup and of the dish, but inside you are full of extortion and wickedness. ⁴⁰You fools! Did not He who made the outside make the inside also? ⁴¹But give for alms those things which are within; and behold, everything is clean for you.'
L. 90.1–2 ¹Jesus said, 'Come to me, for my yoke is mild and my lordship is gentle. ²And you will find rest for yourselves.'	Matthew 11.28–30 (M) ²⁸'Come to me, all who labour and are heavy laden, and I will give you rest. ²⁹Take my yoke upon you, and learn from me; for I am gentle and lowly in heart, and you will find rest for your souls. ³⁰For my yoke is easy, and my burden is light.'
L. 91.1–2 ¹They said to him, 'Tell us, so that we may believe in you, who are you?' ²He said to them, 'You <<examine>> the appearance of the sky and the earth, but, he who is in your midst, you do not understand. Nor this critical time! you do not understand how to <<examine>> it.'	Matthew 16.1–3 (Qmatt) ¹'And the Pharisees and the Sadducees came, and to test him they asked him to show them a sign from heaven. ²He answered them, 'When it is evening, you say, "It will be fair weather, because the sky is red." ³And in the morning, "It will be stormy today, because the sky is red and threatening." You understand how to interpret the appearance of the sky, but you cannot interpret the signs of the times.' Luke 12.54–56 (Qluke) ⁵⁴He said to the multitudes, 'When you see a cloud rising in the west, you say at once, "A shower is coming." And so it happens. ⁵⁵And when you see the south wind blowing, you say, "There will be scorching heat."And so it happens. ⁵⁶You hypocrites! You know how to interpret the appearance of earth and sky, but why do you not know how to interpret the present time?'
L. 92.1–2 ¹Jesus said, 'Seek and you will	Matthew 7.7–8 (Qmatt) ⁷'Ask, and it will be given you. Seek, and you will find.

find. ²However, the questions you asked me previously but which I did not address then, now I want to address, yet you do not seek (answers).' L. 94.1–2 ¹Jesus [said], 'Whoever <u>seeks</u> <u>will find</u>. ²[Whoever <u>knocks]</u>, <u>it</u> <u>will be opened</u> for him.'	<u>Knock, and it will be opened</u> to you. ⁸For everyone who asks receives, and he who seeks, finds, and to him who knocks it will be opened.' Luke 11.9–10 (Qluke) ⁹'And I tell you, Ask, and it will be given you. <u>Seek, and you</u> <u>will find</u>. <u>Knock, and it will be opened</u> to you. ¹⁰For everyone who asks receives, and he who seeks finds, and to him who knocks it will be opened.'
L. 93.1–2 ¹'<u>Do not give what is holy to</u> <u>dogs</u>, or they might toss them on the manure pile. ²<u>Do not toss the</u> <u>pearls [to] pigs</u>, or they might make [break] [[them]].'	Matthew 7.6 (M) '<u>Do not give dogs what is holy</u>, and <u>do not throw your pearls</u> <u>before swine</u>, lest they trample them under foot and turn to attack you.'
95.1–2 ¹[Jesus said], 'If you have money, do not give it at interest. ²Rather, <u>give [it] to someone from whom</u> <u>you will not get it (back)</u>.'	Luke 6.34–35 (L or Qluke) ³⁴'And if you lend to those from whom you hope to receive, what credit is that to you? Even sinners lend to sinners, to receive as much again. ³⁵But love your enemies, and do good, and <u>lend, expecting nothing in return</u>. And your reward will be great, and you will be sons of the Most High. For he is kind to the ungrateful and the selfish.'
L. 96.1–2 ¹Jesus said, '<u>The Kingdom</u> of the Father is <u>like</u> <u>a woman</u>. ²She <u>took</u> a little <u>yeast</u>. She <u>buried</u> it in dough. She made the dough into large bread loaves.'	Matthew 13.33 (Qmatt) '<u>The Kingdom</u> of Heaven is <u>like</u> <u>leaven</u> which <u>a woman</u> <u>took</u> and <u>buried</u> in three measures of floor, until it was all leavened.' Luke 13.20–21 (Qluke) ²⁰'To what shall I compare <u>the Kingdom</u> of God? ²¹It is <u>like</u> <u>leaven</u> which <u>a woman</u> <u>took</u> and <u>buried</u> in three measures of flour, until it was all leavened.'
L. 99.1–3 ¹The disciples said to him, '<u>Your</u> <u>brothers and your mother are</u> <u>standing outside</u>.' ²He said to them, '<u>Those here</u> <u>who do the will</u> of my father, they are <u>my brothers and my</u> <u>mother</u>. ³They are the people who will enter the Kingdom of my Father.'	Mark 3.31–35 ³¹'And his mother and his brothers came; and standing outside they sent to him and called him. ³²And a crowd was sitting about him; and they said to him, "<u>Your mother and your</u> <u>brothers are outside</u>, asking for you." ³³And he replied, "Who are my mother and my brothers?" ³⁴And looking around on those who sat about him, he said, "Here are my mother and my brothers! ³⁵Whoever does the will of God is my brother, and sister, and mother."' Matthew 12.46–50 ⁴⁶'While he was still speaking to the people, behold, <u>his</u> <u>mother and his brothers stood outside</u>, asking to speak to him. ⁴⁸But he replied to the man who told him, 'Who is my mother, and who are my brothers?' ⁴⁹And stretching out his hand toward his disciples, he said, 'Here are my mother and my brothers! ⁵⁰For whoever <u>does the will of my Father</u> in heaven is <u>my brother</u>, and sister, <u>and mother</u>.' Luke 8.19–21 ¹⁹'Then his mother and his brothers came to him, but they could not reach him for the crowd. ²⁰And he was told, "<u>Your</u> <u>mother and your brothers are standing outside</u>, desiring to see you." ²¹But he said to them, "<u>My mother and my brothers</u> are those who hear the word of God and <u>do</u> it."'

L. 100.1–4

[1]They showed Jesus <u>a gold coin</u> and said to him, '<u>Caesar's men extort taxes</u> from us.'
[2]He said to them, '<u>Give to Caesar, what is Caesar's.</u> [3]<u>Give to God what is God's.</u> [4]And what is mine, give me.'

Mark 12.13–17

[13]'And they sent to him some of the Pharisees and some of the Herodians, to entrap him in his talk. [14]And they came and said to him, 'Teacher, we know that you are true, and care for no man; for you do not regard the position of men, but truly teach the way of God. Is it lawful to <u>pay taxes to Caesar</u>, or not? [15]Should we pay them, or should we not?' But knowing their hypocrisy, he said to them, 'Why put me to the test? Bring me <u>a coin</u>, and let me look at it.' [16]And they brought one. And he said to them, 'Whose likeness and inscription is this?' They said to him, 'Caesar's.' [17]Jesus said to them, '<u>Render to Caesar the things that are Caesar's, and to God the things that are God's</u>.' And they were amazed at him.

Matthew 22.15–22

[15]'Then the Pharisees went and took counsel how to entangle him in his talk. [16]And they sent their disciples to him, along with the Herodians, saying, 'Teacher, we know that you are true, and teach the way of God truthfully, and care for no man; for you do not regard the position of men. [17]Tell us, then, what you think. Is it lawful <u>to pay taxes to Caesar</u>, or not?' [18]But Jesus, aware of their malice, said, 'Why put me to the test, you hypocrites? [19]Show me the money for the tax.' And they brought him <u>a coin</u>. [20]And Jesus said to them, 'Whose likeness and inscription is this?' [21]They said, 'Caesar's.' Then he said to them, '<u>Render therefore to Caesar the things that are Caesar's, and to God the things that are God's</u>.' [22]When they heard it, they marvelled; and they left him and went away.

Luke 20.20–26

[20]'So they watched him, and sent spies, who pretended to be sincere, that they might take hold of what he said, so as to deliver him up to the authority and jurisdiction of the governor. [21]They asked him, 'Teacher, we know that you speak and teach rightly, and show no partiality, but truly teach the way of God. [22]Is it lawful for us <u>to give tribute to Caesar</u>, or not?' [23]But he perceived their craftiness, and said to them, [24]'Show me <u>a coin</u>. Whose likeness and inscription has it?' They said, 'Caesar's.' [25]He said to them, 'Then <u>render to Caesar the things that are Caesar's, and to God the things that are God's</u>.' [26]And they were not able to catch him by what he said; but marvelling at his answer they were silent.'

L. 104.1–2

[1]They said to Jesus, 'Come. Today, let's pray and <u>fast</u>!' [2]Jesus said, 'What sin have I committed? Or in what way have I been defeated? Rather, <u>when the bridegroom</u> leaves the bridal chamber, <u>then they</u> should <u>fast</u> and pray.'

Mark 2.18–20

[18]Now John's disciples and the Pharisees were fasting. And people came and said to him, 'Why do John's disciples and the disciples of the Pharisees fast, but your disciples do not <u>fast</u>?' [19]And Jesus said to them, 'Can the wedding guests fast while the bridegroom is with them? As long as they have the bridegroom with them they cannot fast. [20]The days will come, <u>when the bridegroom</u> is taken away from them, and <u>then they will fast</u> in that day.'

Matthew 9.14–15

[14]'Then the disciples of John came to him saying, 'Why do we

	and the Pharisees fast, but your disciples do not <u>fast</u>?' [15]And Jesus said to them, 'Can the wedding guests mourn as long as the bridegroom is with them? The days will come, <u>when the bridegroom</u> is taken away from them, and <u>then they will fast</u>.' Luke 5.33–35 [33]'And they said to him, 'The disciples of John <u>fast</u> often and <u>offer prayers</u>, and so do the disciples of the Pharisees, but yours eat and drink.' [34]And Jesus said to them, 'Can you make wedding guests fast while the bridegroom is with them? [35]The days will come, <u>when the bridegroom</u> is taken away from them, and <u>then they will fast</u> in those days.'
L. 107.1–3 [1]Jesus said, 'The Kingdom is like a shepherd who had <u>a hundred sheep</u>. [2]<u>One of them</u>, the largest, strayed. He <u>left the ninety-nine</u>. He sought that one <u>until he found it</u>. [3]After he had laboured, he said to the sheep, "I love you <u>more than the ninety-nine</u>."'	Matthew 18.12–13 (Qmatt) [12]'What do you think? If a man has <u>a hundred sheep</u>, and <u>one of them has gone astray</u>, does he not <u>leave the ninety-nine</u> on the mountains and go in <u>search of the one</u> that went astray? [13]And if <u>he finds it</u>, truly, I say to you, he rejoices over it <u>more than</u> over <u>the ninety-nine</u> that never went astray.' Luke 15.4–7 (Qluke) [4]'What man of you, having <u>a hundred sheep</u>, if he has lost <u>one of them</u>, does not <u>leave the ninety-nine</u> in the wilderness, and go after <u>the one</u> which is lost, <u>until he finds it</u>? [5]And when he has found it, he lays it on his shoulders, rejoicing. [6]And when he comes home, he calls together his friends and his neighbours, saying to them, "Rejoice with me, for I have found my sheep which was lost." [7]Just so, I tell you, there will be more joy in heaven over one sinner who repents than over ninety-nine righteous people who need no repentance.'
L. 109.1–3 [1]Jesus said, '<u>The Kingdom</u> is like a man who had <u>in his field a</u> [hidden treasure], but he did not know about it. [2]And [after] he died, he left it to his [son]. The son [did] not know (about the treasure). He took that field and sold [it]. [3]And the buyer went and ploughed. He [<u>found</u>] the treasure. He started to give money at interest to whomever he wished.'	Matthew 13.44 'The Kingdom of Heaven is like <u>a treasure hidden in a field</u>, which <u>a man found</u> and covered up. Then in his joy he goes and sells all that he has and buys that field.'

Select Bibliography

Primary Source References

Acts of John
Lipsius, R. and M. Bonnet
    1959   *Acta Apostolorum Apocrypha*, II (Hildesheim: Olms).
Elliott, J.K.
    1993   *The Apocryphal New Testament* (Oxford: Clarendon Press): 303–49.

Acts of Paul and Thecla
Lipsius, R. and M. Bonnet
    1959   *Acta Apostolorum Apocrypha*, I (Hildesheim: Olms).
Elliott, J.K.
    1993   *The Apocryphal New Testament* (Oxford: Clarendon Press): 350–87.

Acts of Peter
Lipsius, R. and M. Bonnet
    1959   *Acta Apostolorum Apocrypha*, I (Hildesheim: Olms).
Elliott, J.K.
    1993   *The Apocryphal New Testament* (Oxford: Clarendon Press): 427–30.

Acts of Peter and the Twelve Apostles
Wilson, R.McL. and D.M. Parrott
    1979   *Nag Hammadi Codices V, 2–5 and VI with Papyrus Berolinensis 8502, 1 and 4*
           (NHS, 11; Leiden: E.J. Brill): 204–29.

Acts of Philip
Lipsius, R. and M. Bonnet
    1959   *Acta Apostolorum Apocrypha*, III (Hildesheim: Olms).
Elliott, J.K.
    1993   *The Apocryphal New Testament* (Oxford: Clarendon Press): 512–18.

Acts of Thomas
Lipsius, R. and M. Bonnet
    1959   *Acta Apostolorum Apocrypha*, III (Hildesheim: Olms).
Klijn, A.F.J.
    1962   *The Acts of Thomas* (NTSup, 5; Leiden: E.J. Brill).
Wright, W.
    1871   *Apocryphal Acts of the Apostle, edited from Syriac manuscripts in the British*
           Museum and other libraries (2 vols; London: Williams & Norgate).

Aesop's Fables
Halm, K.
    1852   *Fabulae Aesopicae Collectae* (Leipzig: Teubner).

Perry, B.E.
    1965   *Babrius and Phaedrus* (LCL; Cambridge, MA: Harvard University Press).

Aphraates
Parisot, J.
    1894   *Aphraatis Sapientis Persae Demonstrationes* (Patrologia Syriaca, 1; Paris:
             Firmin-Didot).
    1907   *Aphraatis Sapientis Persae Demonstrationes* (Patrologia Syriaca, 2; Paris:
             Firmin-Didot).

2 Apocalypse of James
Hedrick, C.
    1979   In D. Parrott (ed.), *Nag Hammadi Codices V,2–5 and VI with Papyrus Bero-
             linensis 8502, 1 and 4* (NHS, 11; Leiden: E.J. Brill): 112–49.

Apocryphon of James
Williams, F.E.
    1985   In H. Attridge (ed.), *Nag Hammadi Codex I (The Jung Codex): Introductions,
             Texts, Translations, Indices* (NHS, 22; Leiden: E.J. Brill): 28–53.

Apostolic Constitutions
Funk, F.X.
    1960   *Didascalia et Constitutiones Apostolorum* (repr.; Turin: Bottega D'Erasmo
             [1905]).

Augustine, *C. adv. leg. et proph.*
Migne, *PL* 42

1 Clement
Funk, F.X. and K. Bihlmeyer
    1965   *Die Apostolischen Väter* (Tübingen: J.C.B. Mohr, 2nd edn).
Staniforth, M.
    1968   *Early Christian Writings: The Apostolic Fathers* (New York: Viking Penguin):
             23–52.

2 Clement
Funk, F.X. and K. Bihlmeyer
    1965   *Die Apostolischen Väter* (Tübingen: J.C.B. Mohr, 2nd edn).
Richardson, C.
    1970   *Early Christian Fathers* (Library of Christian Classics Series; Philadelphia:
             Westminster John Knox Press).

Clement of Alexandria, *Eclogae proph.*
Stählin, O. and L. Früchtel
    1970   *Clemens Alexandrinus* (GCS, 17.2, v. 3; Berlin: Akademie Verlag, 2nd edn).

Clement of Alexandria, *Excerpts of Theodotus*
Stählin, O. and L. Früchtel
    1970   *Clemens Alexandrinus* (GCS, 17.2, v. 3; Berlin: Akademie Verlag, 2nd edn).

Clement of Alexandria, *Stromateis*
Stählin, O. and L. Früchtel
    1960   *Clemens Alexandrinus* (GCS, 52, v. 3; Berlin: Akademie Verlag, 3rd edn).

Dead Sea Scrolls
Martínez, F.G. and E.J.C. Tigchelaar
    1997   *The Dead Sea Scrolls Study Edition*, I (2 vols; Leiden: E.J. Brill).
    1998   *The Dead Sea Scrolls Study Edition*, II (2 vols; Leiden: E.J. Brill).

Definitions of Hermes Trismegistos
Salaman, C., D. van Oyen, W. Wharton, J.-P. Mahé (eds)
    2000   *The Way of Hermes: New Translations of the Corpus Hermeticum and the Definitions of Hermes Trismegistus to Asclepius* (Rochester: Inner Traditions).

Dialogue of the Saviour
Emmel, S.
    1984   *Nag Hammadi Codex III,5: The Dialogue of the Savior* (NHS, 26; Leiden: E.J. Brill).

Didache
Funk. F.X. and K. Bihlmeyer
    1965   *Die Apostolischen Väter* (Tübingen: J.C.B. Mohr, 2nd edn).
Staniforth, M.
    1968   *Early Christian Writings: The Apostolic Fathers* (New York: Viking Penguin): 191–98.

Didascalia
Connolly, R.H.
    1969   *Didascalia Apostolorum* (Oxford: Clarendon).
Achelis, H. and J. Flemming
    1904   *Die syrische Didaskalia* (Die ältesten Quellen des orientalischen Kirchenrechts, 2. Buch Texte und Untersuchungen zur Geschichte der altchristlichen Literatur, 25.2; Leipzig: J.C. Hinrichs).

Didymus the Blind, *In Ps.*
Migne, *PG* 39

Ephrem, *Commentary on the Diatessaron*
Leloir, L.
    1954   *Saint Éphrem, Commentaire de l'Évangile Concordant* (Louvain: L. Durbecq).
    1963   *Saint Éphrem, Commentaire de l'Évangile Concordant, Texte Syriaque* (Chester Beatty Monographs, 8; Dublin: Hodges Figgis).
    1966   *Éphrem de Nisibe, Commentaire de l'Évangile Concordant ou Diatessaron* (SC, 121; Paris: Éditions du Cerf).

Epiphanius, *Panarion*
Holl, K.
    1915   *Epiphanius Werke* (GCS, 25; 3 vols; Leipzig: Hinrichs).
    1922   *Epiphanius Werke* (GCS, 31; 3 vols; Leipzig: Hinrichs).
    1933   *Epiphanius Werke* (GCS, 37; 3 vols; Leipzig: Hinrichs).

Epistle of Barnabas
Funk. F.X. and K. Bihlmeyer
    1965   *Die Apostolischen Väter* (Tübingen: J.C.B. Mohr, 2nd edn).
Staniforth, M.
    1968   *Early Christian Writings: The Apostolic Fathers* (New York: Viking Penguin): 159–84.

Epistula Apostolorum
Schmidt, C.
    1967   *Gespräche Jesu mit seinen Jüngern nach der Auferstehung* (repr.; Hildesheim: Olms).
Hennecke, E. and W. Schneemelcher
    1963   *The New Testament Apocrypha*, I (Philadelphia: Westminster Press): 189–226.

Eusebius, *Ecclesiastical History*
Lake, K.
    1965–73 *Historia Ecclesiastica. English and Greek* (LCL; 2 vols; Cambridge, MA: Harvard University Press).

Gospel of the Ebionites
Klijn, A.F.J.
    1992   *Jewish-Christian Gospel Tradition* (VCSup, 17; Leiden: E.J. Brill).

Gospel of the Egyptians
Clement of Alexandria, *Stromateis*
Stählin, O. and L. Früchtel
    1960   *Clemens Alexandrinus* (GCS, 52, v. 2; Berlin: Akademie Verlag, 3rd edn).

Gospel of the Hebrews
Klijn, A.F.J.
    1992   *Jewish-Christian Gospel Tradition* (VCSup, 17; Leiden: E.J. Brill).

Gospel of the Nazarenes
Klijn, A.F.J.
    1992   *Jewish-Christian Gospel Tradition* (VCSup, 17; Leiden: E.J. Brill).

Gospel of Philip
Layton, B.
    1989   *Nag Hammadi Codex II,2–7 together with XIII,2*, Brit. Lib. OR. 4926(1), and P.Oxy. 1, 654, 655*, I (trans. W. Isenberg; NHS, 20; Leiden: E.J. Brill): 140–215.

Gospel of the Saviour
Hedrick, C.W. and P.A. Mirecki
    1999   *Gospel of the Savior: A New Ancient Gospel* (Santa Rosa: Polebridge Press).

Gospel of Truth
Attridge, H.
    1985   *Nag Hammadi Codex I (The Jung Codex)* (NHS, 22; Leiden: E.J. Brill): 82–117.

Gregory of Nyssa, *De instituto Christiano*
Jaeger, W.
    1952   *Gregorii Nysseni Opera*, 8.1: *Opera Ascetica* (Leiden: E.J. Brill).

Hippolytus, *Refutation of All Heresies*
Wendland, P.
    1916   *Hippolytus Werke 3* (GCS, 26; Leipzig: Hinrichs).

Ignatius, *Ephesians*
Funk, F.X. and K. Bihlmeyer
    1965   *Die Apostolischen Väter* (Tübingen: J.C.B. Mohr, 2nd edn).

Ignatius, *Philippians*
Funk, F.X. and K. Bihlmeyer
    1965   *Die Apostolischen Väter* (Tübingen: J.C.B. Mohr, 2nd edn).

Ignatius, *Polycarp*
Funk, F.X. and K. Bihlmeyer
    1965   *Die Apostolischen Väter* (Tübingen: J.C.B. Mohr, 2nd edn).

Ignatius, *Trallians*
Funk, F.X. and K. Bihlmeyer
    1965   *Die Apostolischen Väter* (Tübingen: J.C.B. Mohr, 2nd edn).

Irenaeus, *Adversus haereses*
Rousseau, A.
    1969   *Irénée de Lyon Contre les Hérésies* (SC, 153; Paris: Éditions du Cerf).
    1979   *Irénée de Lyon Contre les Hérésies* (SC, 264; Paris: Éditions du Cerf).

John of Damascus, *De sacra parallelis*
Migne, *PG* 96

Justin, *Apology*
Goodspeed, E.
    1914   *Die ältesten Apologeten* (Göttingen: Vandenhoeck & Ruprecht).

Justin Martyr, *Dialogue with Trypho*
Migne, *PG* 6

Liber Graduum
Kmosko, M.
    1926   *Liber Graduum* (Patrologia Syriaca, 1.3; Paris: Firmin-Didot).

Lucian, *Adv. indoctum*
Harmon, A.
    1969   *Lucian* (LCL, 3; Cambridge, MA: Harvard University Press).

Lucian, *Hermotimus*
Dindorf, G.
    1867   *Luciani Samosatensis Opera* (Paris: Firmin-Didot).

Lucian, *Timon*
Harmon, A.
    1969   *Lucian* (LCL, 2; Cambridge, MA: Harvard University Press).

Mandaean Prayers
Drower, E.
    1959   *The Canonical Prayerbook of the Mandaeans* (Leiden: E.J. Brill).

Mani, Unpublished Letter
Böhlig, A.
    1958–60   'Christiche Wurzeln in Manichäismus', *Bulletin de la Société d'archéologie
           Copte* 15.

Manichaean *Kephalaia*
Schmidt, C.
    1940   *Kephalaia* (Manichäische Handschriften der Staatlichen Museen Berlin, 1;
           Stuttgart: W. Kohlhammer).

Manichaean Psalms
Alberry, C.R.C.
    1938   *A Manichaean Psalm-Book* (Manichaean Manuscripts of the Chester Beatty
             Collection, 2.2; Stuttgart: W. Kohlhammer).

Martyrdom of Peter
Lipsius, R. and M. Bonnet
    1959   *Acta Apostolorum Apocrypha*, III (Hildesheim: Olms).

Mekilta de-Rabbi Ishmael
Lauterbach, J.
    1933   *Mekilta de-Rabbi Ishmael* (3 vols; Philadelphia: Jewish Publication Society).

Midrash Rabbah
Simon, M. and H. Freedman
    1939   *Midrash Rabbah* (10 vols; London: Soncino Press).

Muslim Sources
'Abd al-Gabbar, *Tathbit Dala'il Nubuwwat Sayyidina Muhammad*
Al-Karim 'Uthman, 'Abd
    1966   *Tathbit Dala'il Nubuwwat Sayyidina Muhammad* (Beirut).
Pines, S.
    1966   *The Jewish Christians in the early Centuries of Christianity according to a
             New Source* (Israel Academy of Sciences and Humanities Proceedings, 2.13;
             Jerusalem: Central Press).
Al-Muhasibi
Duval, P.
    1977   *Cahiers Metanoia* 9.32–35.
Kitab Bilankar wa Budasf
Spies, O.
    1975   'Die Arbeiter im Weinburg (Mt 20:1-15) in islamischer Überlieferung', *ZNW*
             66: 283–85.
Abu al-Qasim ibn 'Asakir, *Sirat al-Sayyid al-Masih*
Abu Bakr ibn Abi al-Dunya, *Kitab Dhamm al-Dunya*, in *Mawsu'at Rasa'il*
Abu Hamid al-Ghazadi, *Ihya' 'Ulum al-Din*
Abu Hayyan al-Tawhidi, *al-Basa'ir wa'l Dhakha'ir*
Abu 'Ali Miskawayh, *al-Hikma*
Abu Nu'aym al-Isbahani, *Hilyat al-Awliya'*
Abu 'Uthman al-Jahiz, *al-Bayan*
Ahmad ibn Hanbal, *al-Zuhd*
Al-Raghib al-Isfahani, *Muhadarat al-Udaba'*
'Abdallah ibn al-Mubarak, *al-Zuhd*
'Abdallah ibn Qutayba, *'Uyun*
Muhyi al-Din ibn 'Arabi, *Muhadarat al-Abrar*
Khalidi, T.
    2001   *The Muslim Jesus: Sayings and Stories in Islamic Literature* (Cambridge:
             Harvard University Press).

Odes of Solomon
Harris, J.R. and A. Mingana
    1916   *The Odes and Psalms of Solomon*, I (2 vols; Manchester: The University
             Press).

1920   *The Odes and Psalms of Solomon*, II (2 vols; Manchester: The University Press).

Origen, *Commentary on Matthew*
Benz, E. and E. Klostermann
1935   *Origenes Werke: Matthäuserklärung* (GCS, 10; Leipzig: J.C. Hinrichs).
1937   *Origenes Werke: Matthäuserklärung* (GCS, 11; Leipzig: J.C. Hinrichs).
Benz, E. and E. Klostermann
1976   *Origenes Matthäuserklärung*, II: *die lateinische Übersetzung der Commentariorum series* (Die Griechischen christlichen Schriftsteller der ersten Jahrhunderte; Berlin: Akademie-Verlag, 2nd edn).

Origen, *Contra Celsum*
Koetschau, P.
1899   *Origenes Werke* (GCS, 2; Leipzig: J.C. Hinrichs).

Origen, *Homilies on Jeremiah*
Husson, P. and P. Nautin
1977   *Origène Homélies sur Jérémie* (SC, 238; Paris: Éditions du Cerf).

P. Egerton 2.1
Bell, H.I. and T.C. Skeat
1935a   *Fragments of an Unknown Gospel and other Early Christian Papyri* (London: Trustees of the British Museum).
1935b   *The New Gospel Fragments* (London: Trustees of the British Museum).

Philo, *The Unchangeableness of God*
Colson, F.H.
1930   *Philo Judaeus* (LCL, 3; Cambridge, MA: Harvard University Press).

Philoxemus, *Homilies*
Lemoine, E.
1956   *Homélies [par] Philoxène de Mabboug. Introd., traduction et notes* (SC, 44; Paris: Éditions du Cerf).

Pistis Sophia
Schmidt, C. and V. Macdermot
1978   *Pistis Sophia* (NHS, 9; Leiden: E.J. Brill).

Polycarp, *Phil.*
Funk. F.X. and K.Bihlmeyer
1965   *Die Apostolischen Väter* (Tübingen: J.C.B. Mohr, 2nd edn).

Prayer of the Apostle Paul
Attridge, H.
1985   *Nag Hammadi Codex I (The Jung Codex)* (trans. D. Mueller; NHS, 22; Leiden: E.J. Brill): 8–11.

Pseudo-Clementine Recognitions
Rehm, B. and F. Paschke
1965   *Die Pseudoklementinen. I. Recognitiones* (GCS; Berlin: Akademie-Verlag).
Jones, F. Stanley
1995   *An Ancient Jewish Christian Source on the History of Christianity: Pseudo-Clementine Recognitions 1.27–71* (Texts and Translations, 37; Christian Apocrypha Series, 2; Atlanta: Scholars Press).

Pseudo-Clementine Homilies
Rehm. B. and J. Irmscher
    1969   *Die Pseudoklementinen*, I: *Homilien* (GCS; Berlin: Akademie-Verlag).

Pseudo-Ephrem, *Exposition of the Gospel*
Egan, G.A.
    1968   *St. Ephrem, An Exposition of the Gospel* (CSCO, 292; Scriptores Armenica, 6;
             Louvain: Secretariat du Corpus SCO).

Pseudo-Macarius, *Hymns*
Berthold, H.
    1973   *Makarios/Symeon: Reden und Briefe. Die Sammlung I des Vaticanus Graecus
             694 (B)* (2 vols; GCS; Berlin: Akademie-Verlag).
Dörries, H., E. Klosterman and M. Kroeger
    1964   *Die 50 Geistlichen Homilien des Makarios* (Patristische Texte und Studien, 6;
             Berlin: De Gruyter).
Klosterman, E., and H. Berthold
    1961   *Neue Homilien des Makarios/Symeon aus Typus III* (TU, 72; Berlin: Akadamie-
             Verlag).

Pseudo-Macarius, *Great Letter*
Jaeger, W.
    1954   *Two Rediscovered Works of Ancient Christian Literature: Gregory of Nyssa and
             Macarius* (Leiden: E.J. Brill): 233–301.

Pseudo-Philo, *Liber antiquitatum biblicarum*
James, M.R.
    1971   *The Biblical Antiquities of Philo Now First Translated from the Old Latin Ver-
             sion* (New York: KTAV)

Pseudo-Titus Epistle
Hennecke, E. and W. Schneemelcher
    1964   *The New Testament Apocrypha*, II (Philadelphia: The Westminster Press):
             144–66.

Sayings of the Desert Fathers
Migne, *PG* 65: 71–440.

Sentences of Sextus
Chadwick, H.
    1959   *The Sentences of Sextus* (Cambridge: Cambridge University Press).

Straton, *Gr. Anth.*
Cameron, A.
    1993   *The Greek Anthology, from Meleager to Planudes* (Oxford: Clarendon Press,).

Talmud
Epstein, I.
    1935–52 *The Babylonian Talmud* (34 vols in 5 parts; London: Soncino Press).

Teachings of Silvanus
Pearson, B.
    1996   *Nag Hammadi Codex VII* (NHMS, 30; Leiden: E.J. Brill): 278–369.

Tertullian, *Adv. Marcionem*
Evans, E.
    1972   *Adversus Marcionem* (Oxford Early Christian Texts; Oxford: Clarendon Press).

Testament of Jacob

Box, G.H. with S. Gaselee

    1927   *The Testament of Abraham, translated from the Greek text with introduction and notes with an appendix containing a translation from the Coptic version of the Testaments of Isaac and Jacob* (Translations of Early Documents, Series 2, Hellenistic-Jewish Texts; London: SPCK).

Stone, M.E.

    1972   *The Testament of Abraham: The Greek recensions* (Texts and Translations, 2; Pseudepigrapha Series, 2; New York: Society of Biblical Literature).

Testament of the Lord

Cooper, J. and A.J. Maclean

    1902   *The Testament of our Lord* (Edinburgh: T&T Clark).

Theodoret, *In Psal.*

Migne, *PG* 80

Thomas the Contender

Layton, B.

    1989   *Nag Hammadi Codex II,2–7 together with XIII,2*, Brit. Lib. OR. 4926(1), and P.Oxy. 1, 654, 655*, I (NHS, 21; trans. J. Turner; Leiden: E.J. Brill): 180–205.

Treatise on the Resurrection

Attridge, H.

    1985   *Nag Hammadi Codex I (The Jung Codex)* (NHS, 22; Leiden: E.J. Brill): 148–57.

Turfan Manichaean Fragment

Müller, F.W.K.

    1904   'Handschriften-Reste in Estrangelo-Schrift aus Turfan, 2', *Abhandlungen der preussichen Akademie der Wissenschaften*. Phil-Hist. Kl. Abhandlung.

Untitled Gnostic Text from Codex Brucianus

Schmidt, C. and V. Macdermot

    1978   *The Books of Jeu and the Untitled Text in the Bruce Codex* (NHS, 13; Leiden: E.J. Brill).

Secondary Source References

Akagi, T.

    1965   'The Literary Development of the Coptic Gospel of Thomas' (PhD dissertation, Western Reserve University).

Anderson, G.

    1989   'Celibacy or Consummation in the Garden? Reflections on Early Jewish and Christian Interpretations of the Garden of Eden', *HTR* 82: 121–48.

Arai, S.

    1994   'Caesar's, God's and Mine: Mk 12:17 par. and Gos. Thom. 100', in H. Preiffler and H. Seirvert (eds), *Gnosisforschung und Religionsgeschichte. Festschrift für Kurt Rudolph zum 65 Geburtstag* (Marburg: diagonal-Verlag): 43–48.

Attridge, H.

    1979   'The Original Text of Gos. Thom., Saying 30', *Bulletin of the American Society of Papyrologists* 16: 153–57.

    1981   'Greek Equivalents of Two Coptic Phrases: CG I.1. 65.9–10 and CG II.2. 43.26', *Bulletin of the American Society of Papyrologists* 18: 30–32.

1989   'Appendix: The Greek Fragments', in B. Layton, *Nag Hammadi Codex II,2–7 together with XIII,2*, Brit. Lib. OR. 4926(1), and P.Oxy. 1, 654, 655*, I (NHS, 20; Leiden: E.J. Brill): 96–128.

Baarda, T.

1975   'Luke 12, 13–14: Text and Transmission from Marcion to Augustine', in J. Neusner, *Christianity, Judaism and Other Greco-Roman Cults* (Leiden: E.J. Brill): 107–62.

1983a   'Jesus Said: Be Passersby. On the Meaning and Origin of Logion 42 of the Gospel of Thomas', in *Early Transmission of Words of Jesus. Thomas, Tatian and the Text of the New Testament* (Amsterdam: VU Boekhandel/Uitgeverij): 179–206.

1983b   '2 Clement 12 and the Sayings of Jesus', in *Early Transmission of Words of Jesus: Thomas, Tatian and the Text of the New Testament* (Amsterdam: VU Boekhandel/Uitgeverij): 261–88.

1983c   'Thomas and Tatian', in *Early Transmission of Words of Jesus: Thomas, Tatian and the Text of the New Testament* (Amsterdam: VU Boekhandel/Uitgeverij): 37–49.

1988   '"If you do not Sabbatize the Sabbath…" The Sabbath as God or World in Gnostic Understanding (Ev. Thom., Log. 27)', in R. van den Broek, T. Baarda and J. Mansfeld (eds), *Knowledge of God in the Graeco-Roman World* (EPRO, 112; Leiden: E.J. Brill): 178–201.

1992   'Philoxenus and the Parable of the Fisherman: Concerning the Diatessaron Text of Matthew 13:47–50', in F. Van Segbroeck *et al.*, *The Four Gospels 1992: Festschrift für Frans Neirynck*, II (Leuven: Leuven University Press): 1403–23.

1994a   'The Parable of the Fisherman in the Heliand: The Old Saxon Version of Matthew 13:47–50', in *Essays on the Diatessaron* (Contributions to Biblical Exegesis and Theology, 11; Kampen: Kok Pharos): 263–81.

1994b   '"Chose" or "Collected": Concerning an Aramaism in Logion 8 of the Gospel of Thomas and the Questions of Independence', in *Essays on the Diatessaron* (Contributions to Biblical Exegesis and Theology, 11; Kampen: Kok Pharos): 241–62.

Bailey, K.

1991   'Informal Controlled Oral Tradition and the Synoptic Gospels', *Asia Journal of Theology* 5: 34–54.

1995   'Middle Eastern Oral Tradition and the Synoptic Gospels', *ExpTim* 106: 363–67.

Baker, A.

1964   'Pseudo-Macarius and the Gospel of Thomas', *VC* 18: 215–25.

1965a   'Fasting to the World', *JBL* 84: 291–94.

1965b   'The *Gospel of Thomas* and the *Diatessaron*', *JTS* 16: 449–54.

1965/66   'The "Gospel of Thomas" and the Syriac "Liber Graduum"', *NTS* 12: 49–55.

1970   'Early Syriac Asceticism', *The Downside Review* 88: 393–403.

Bammel, E.

1969   'Rest and Rule', *VC* 23: 88–90.

Bartsch, H.-W.

1959/60   'Das Thomas-Evangelium und die synoptischen Evangelien: Zu G. Quispels Bemerkungen zum Thomas-Evangelium', *NTS* 6: 253–55.

Bauer, J.

1960   'Das Thomas-Evangelium in der neuesten Forschung', in R. Grant and D. Freedman (eds), *Geheime Worte Jesu: Das Thomas-Evangelium* (Frankfurt: Scheffler): 182–205.

1962   'Zum Koptischen Thomasevangelium', *BZ* 6: 284–85.

1964	'The Synoptic Tradition in the Gospel of Thomas' (*StEv* 3; TU, 88; Berlin): 314–17.

Behm, J.
1964	'Γεύομαι', in *TDNT* I: 676–77.

Bethge, H.-G
1997	'Evangelium Thomae Copticum', in K. Aland, *Synopsis Quattuor Evangeliorum: Locis parallelis evangeliorum apocryphorum et patrum adhibitis edidit* (Stuttgart: German Bible Society [15th edition, 1996]), 2nd corrected printing: 517–46.

Betz, H.D.
1995	*The Sermon on the Mount* (Hermeneia; Minneapolis: Fortress Press).

Beyschlag, K.
1974	*Simon Magus und die christliche Gnosis* (WUNT, 16; Tübingen: J.C.B. Mohr).

Bianchi, U.
1967	*Le Origini dello Gnosticismo. Colloquio di Messina 13–18 Aprile 1966. Testi e Discussioni* (Studies in the History of Religions, Numen Supplement 12; Leiden: E.J. Brill).

Blass, F.
1897	'Das neue Logia-Fragment von Oxyrhynchus', *Evangelische Kirchenzeitung:* 498–500.

Brakke, D.
2006	*Demons and the Making of the Monk: Spiritual Combat in Early Christianity* (Cambridge, MA: Harvard University Press).

Brown, Pa.
1992	'The Sabbath and the Week in Thomas 27', *NT* 34: 193.

Bruce, F.F.
1984	'Render to Caesar', in E. Bammel and C.F.D. Moule (eds), *Jesus and the Politics of His Day* (Cambridge: Cambridge University Press): 249–63.

Buckley, J.
1985	'An Interpretation of Logion 114 in *The Gospel of Thomas*', *NT* 27: 245–72.

Bultmann, R.
1961	*History of the Synoptic Tradition* (trans. J. Marsh; New York: Harper & Row).

Callan, T.
1990	'The Saying of Jesus in Gos. Thom. 22/2 Clem. 12/Gos. Eg. 5', *JRS* 16: 46–64.

Cameron, R.
1986	'Parable and Interpretation in the Gospel of Thomas', *Foundations and Facets Forum* 2: 3–39.

Casey, M.
1985	'The Jackals and the Son of Man (Matt. 8.20//Luke 9.58)', *JSNT* 23: 9–15.

Castelli, E.
1991	'"I Will Make Mary Male": Pieties of the Body and Gender Transformation of Christian Women in Late Antiquity', in J. Epstein and K. Straub (eds), *Body Guards: The Cultural Politics of Gender Ambiguity* (New York: Routledge): 29–49.

Cerfaux L., and G. Garitte
1957	'Les paraboles du Royaume dans L'Évangile de Thomas', *Muséon* 70: 307–27.

Cersoy, P.
1898	'Quelques remarques sur les logia de Benhesa [*sic*]', *Revue Biblique* 7: 417–18.

Clarysse, W.
1994	'Gospel of Thomas Logion 13. "The Bubbling Well Which I Myself Dug", in

A. Schoors and P. van Deun (eds), *Philohistôr. Miscellanea in Honorem Caroli Laga Septuagenarii* (Orientalia Lovaniensa analecta; 60; Leuven: University of Peeters): 1–10.

Connolly, R.H.
1934   'A Negative Form of the Golden Rule in the Diatessaron?' *JTS* 35: 351–57.

Cornélis, E.
1961   'Quelques éléments pour une comparison entre l'Évangile de Thomas et la notice d'Hippolyte sur les Naassènes', *VC* 15: 83–104.

Crossan, J.D.
1971   'The Parable of the Wicked Husbandmen', *JBL* 90: 451–65.
1973   *In Parables: The Challenge of the Historical Jesus* (San Francisco: Harper & Row).
1983   *In Fragments: The Aphorisms of Jesus* (San Francisco: Harper & Row).
1985   *Four Other Gospels: Shadows on the Contours of Canon* (Minneapolis: Winston).

Culianu, I.
1992   *The Tree of Gnosis: Gnostic Mythology from Early Christianity to Modern Nihilism* (trans. H.S. Wiesner and I. Culianu; San Francisco: HarperSanFrancisco).

Cuvillier, E.
1992/93 'Marc, Justin, Thomas et les Autres. Variations autour de la Péricope dans Denier à César', *Études Théologiques et Religieuses* 67: 329–44.

Davies, S.
1983   *The Gospel of Thomas and Christian Wisdom* (New York: Seabury Press).
2002   *The Gospel of Thomas Annotated and Explained* (Woodstock: Skylight Paths).

DeConick, A.D.
1990   'The Yoke Saying in the *Gospel of Thomas* 90', *VC* 44: 280–94.
1996   *Seek to See Him: Ascent and Vision Mysticism in the Gospel of Thomas* (VCSup, 33; Leiden: E.J. Brill).
2001a   *Voices of the Mystics: Early Christian Discourse in the Gospels of John and Thomas and Other Ancient Christian Literature* (JSNTSup, 157; Sheffield: Sheffield Academic Press).
2001b   'The True Mysteries: Sacramentalism in the *Gospel of Philip*', *VC* 55: 225–61.
2003   'The Great Mystery of Marriage: Sex and Conception in Ancient Valentinian Traditions', *VC* 57: 307–42.
2005   *Recovering the Original Gospel of Thomas: A History of the Gospel and Its Growth* (Library of New Testament Studies, 286; London: T&T Clark).

DeConick, A.D. and J. Fossum
1991   'Stripped Before God: A New Interpretation of Logion 37 in the Gospel of Thomas', *VC* 45: 123–50.

Dehandschutter, B.
1974   'La Parabole des Vignerons Homicides (Mc. XII, 1–12) et l'évangile selon Thomas', in M. Sabbe (ed.), *L'Évangile selon Marc: Tradition et redaction* (Gembloux: Leuven University Press): 203–19.
1975   'Le lieu d'origine de l'Évangile selon Thomas', *Orientalia Lovaniensia Periodica* 6/7: 125–31.
1979   'La Parabole de la Perle (Mt 13,45–46) et L'Évangile selon Thomas', *Ephemerides Theologicae Lovanienses* 35: 243–65.

Dewey, A.
1994   'A Passing Remark: Thomas 42', *Foundations and Facets Forum* 10: 69–85.

Doran, R.
1991   'Divinization of Disorder: The Trajectory of Matt 8:20//Luke 9:58//*Gos. Thom.*

86', in B. Pearson (ed.), *The Future of Early Christianity: Essays in Honor of Helmut Koester* (Minneapolis: Fortress Press): 210–19.

Dunderberg, I.
1998a ' "*Thomas*" I-Sayings and the Gospel of John', in R. Uro (ed.), *Thomas at the Crossroads: Essays on the Gospel of Thomas* (Edinburgh: T&T Clark): 33–64.
1998b '*Thomas* and the Beloved Disciple', in R. Uro (ed.), *Thomas at the Crossroads: Essays on the Gospel of Thomas* (Edinburgh: T&T Clark): 65–88.

Dunn, J.D.
2000 'Jesus in Oral Memory: The Initial Stages of the Jesus Tradition', *SBLSP* 39: 287–326.

Englezakis, B.
1978 'Thomas, Logion 30', *NTS* 25: 262–72.

Fallon, F.T. and R. Cameron
1988 'The Gospel of Thomas: A Forschungsbericht and Analysis', *Aufstieg und Niedergang der römischen Welt* 2.25.6: 4195–4251.

Fieger, M.
1991 *Das Thomasevangelium: Einleitung, Kommentar und Sytematik* (Neutestamentliche Abhandlungen Neue Folge, 22; Münster: Aschendorff).

Finkelstein, L.
1932 'Review of Ch. Albeck, *Das buch der Jubiläen und die Halacha*', *MGWJ* 76: 529–30.

Fitzmyer, J.
1971 'The Oxyrhynchus Logoi of Jesus and the Coptic Gospel According to Thomas', in *Essays on the Semitic Background of the New Testament* (London: Geoffrey Chapman): 355–433.

Foley, J.M.
1988 *The Theory of Oral Composition: History and Methodology* (Bloomington, IN: Indiana University Press).
1991 *Immanent Art: From Structure to Meaning in Traditional Oral Epic* (Bloomington, IN: Indiana University Press).
1995 *The Singer of Tales in Performance* (Voices in Performance and Text; Bloomington, IN: Indiana University Press).

Fossum, J.
1983 'Jewish-Christian Christology and Jewish Mysticism', *VC* 37: 260–87.
1985a *The Name of God and the Angel of the Lord* (WUNT, 36; Tübingen: J.C.B. Mohr).
1985b 'Gen. 1,26 and 2,7 in Judaism, Samaritanism, and Gnosticism', *JSJ* 16: 202–39.
1989a 'Sects and Movements', in A.D. Crown (ed.), *The Samaritans* (Tübingen: J.C.B. Mohr): 368–77.
1989b 'Colossians 1.15–18a in the Light of Jewish Mysticism and Gnosticism', *NTS* 35: 183–201.
1996 'The Adorable Adam of the Mystics and the Rebuttal of the Rabbis', in H. Cancik, H. Lichtenberger and P. Schäfer (eds), *Geschichte-Tradition-Reflexion: Festschrift für Martin Hengel zum 70. Geburtstag*, I: *Judentum* (Tübingen: J.C.B. Mohr): 529–39.

Garitte, G.
1957 'Le Premier Volume de l'Édition Photographique des Manuscripts Gnostiques Coptes et l' "Évangile de Thomas" ', *Muséon* 70: 59–73.
1960a 'Les "Logoi" d'Oxyrhynque et l'Apocryphe Copte dit "Évangile de Thomas" ', *Muséon* 73:151–72.
1960b 'Les "Logoi" d'Oxyrhynque sont Traduits de Copte', *Muséon* 73: 335–49.

Gärtner, B.
    1961   *The Theology of the Gospel of Thomas* (trans. E. Sharpe; London: Collins).
Gaston, L.
    1970   *No Stone On Another: Studies in the Significance of the Fall of Jerusalem in the Synoptic Gospels* (NTSup, 23; Leiden: E.J. Brill).
Gershenson, D. and G. Quispel
    1958   '"Meristae"', *VC* 12: 19–26.
Gierth, B.
    1990   'Un Apophtegme Commun à la *Pistis Sophia* et à l'*Évangile selon Thomas?*', *RSR* 64: 245–49.
Gieschen, C.
    1998   *Angelomorphic Christology: Antecedents and Evidence* (AGJU 42; Leiden: E.J. Brill).
    2003   'The Divine Name in Ante-Nicene Christology', *VC* 57: 115–58.
Ginzberg, L.
    1947   *The Legends of the Jews* (Philadelphia: Jewish Publication Society of America).
Giverson, S.
    1960   'Question and Answers in the Gospel according to Thomas: The Composition of pl. 81, 14–18 and pl. 83.14–27', *Acta Orientalia* 25: 332–38.
Glasson, T.F.
    1962   'Carding and Spinning: Oxyrhynchus Papyrus No. 655', *JTS*: 331–32.
    1976/77   'The Gospel of Thomas, Saying 3, and Deuteronomy XXX.11–14', *ExpTim* 78: 151–52.
Grant, R.
    1959   'Notes on the Gospel of Thomas', *VC* 13: 170–80.
Grant, R., with D.N. Freedman
    1960   *The Secret Sayings of Jesus* (Garden City, NY: Doubleday).
Grenfell, B.P. and A.S. Hunt
    1897   LOGIA IHSOU: *Sayings of our Lord from an Early Greek Papyrus* (London: Henry Frowde for the Egypt Exploration Fund).
    1904   *New Sayings of Jesus and Fragment of a Lost Gospel from Oxyrhynchus* (London: Henry Frowde for the Egypt Exploration Fund).
Grobel, K.
    1962   'How Gnostic is the Gospel of Thomas?', *NTS* 8: 370.
Guey, J.
    1960   'Comment le "denier de César" de l'Évangile a-t-il pu devenir une pièce d'or?' *Bulletin de la Société française de Numismatique* 15: 478–79.
Guillaumont, A.
    1958   'Sémitisms dans les Logia de Jésus retrouvés à Nag-Hamâdi', *Journal Asiatique* 246: 113–23.
    1960   'Les *Logia* d'Oxyrhynchos. Sont-ils Traduits du Copte?' *Muséon* 73: 325–33.
    1962   'Νηστεύειν τόν κόσμον (P.Oxy. 1, verso, I,5–6)', *BIFAO* 61: 15–23.
    1981   'Les Sémitisms dans L'Évangile selon Thomas essai de Classement', in R. van den Broek and M.J. Vermaseren (eds), *Studies in Gnosticism and Hellenistic Religions, presented to Gilles Quispel on the Occasion of his 65th Birthday* (EPRO, 91; Leiden: E.J. Brill): 190–204.
Guillaumont, A., H.-Ch. Puech, G. Quispel, W. Till, and 'Abd. Al Masih
    1959   *The Gospel According to Thomas: The Gnostic Sayings of Jesus* (San Francisco: Harper & Row).
Haenchen, E.
    1961   *Die Botschaft des Thomas-Evangeliums* (Theologische Bibliothek Töpelmann, 6; Berlin: Töpelmann).

1961/62   'Literatur zum Thomasevangelium', *TRu* 27: 147–78, 306–38.
1962   'Spruch 68 des Thomasevangeliums', *Muséon* 75: 19–29.

Harl, M.
1960   'A propos des *Logia* de Jésus: le sens du mot *monachos*', *REG* 73: 464–74.

Hayward, R.
1981   *Divine Name and Presence: The Memra* (Totowa: Allanhead, Osmun, and Co.).

Hedrick, C.W.
1986   'The Treasure Parable in Matthew and Thomas', *Foundations and Facets Forum* 2: 41–56
1989/90   'Thomas and the Synoptics: Aiming at a Consensus', *Second Century* 7: 39–56.
1990   'On Moving Mountains: Mark 11:22b–23/Matt 21:21 and Parallels', *Foundations and Facets Forum* 6: 217–37.
1994a   'Appendix A: Thomas the Synoptics: Aiming at a Consensus', in *Parables as Poetic Fictions: The Creative Voice of Jesus* (Peabody, MA: Hendrickson): 236–51.
1994b   'The Treasure Parables in Matthew and Thomas', in *Parables as Poetic Fictions: The Creative Voice of Jesus* (Peabody, MA: Hendrickson): 117–41.

Higgins, A.J.B.
1960   'Non-Gnostic Sayings in the Gospel of Thomas', *NT* 4: 292–306.

Hofius, O.
1960   'Das koptische Thomasevangelium und die Oxyrhynchus-Papyri Nr. 1, 654 und 655', *Evangelische Theologie* 20: 21–42.

Horman, J.
1979   'The Source of the Version of the Parable of the Sower in the Gospel of Thomas', *NT* 21: 326–43.

Hultgren, A.J.
1991   'Jesus and Gnosis: The Saying on Hindering Others in Luke 11:52 and Its Parallels', *Foundations and Facets Forum* 7: 165–82.

Hunzinger, L.H.
1960   'Unbekannte Gleichnisse Jesu aus dem Thomas-Evangelium', in W. Eltester (ed.), *Judentum, Urchristentum, Kirche: Festschrift für Joachim Jeremias* (BZNW, 26; Berlin: Alfred Töpelmann): 209–20.

Jackson, H.M.
1985   *The Lion Becomes Man: The Gnostic Leontomorphic Creator and the Platonic Tradition* (SBL, 81; Atlanta: Scholars Press).
1992   'The Setting and Sectarian Provenance of the Fragment of the "Celestial Dialogue" Preserved by Origen from Celsus' Ἀληθὴς Λόγος', *HTR* 85: 273–305.

Jacquart, D., and C. Thommasset
1988   *Sexuality and Medicine in the Middle Ages* (trans. M. Adamson; Princeton: Princeton University Press).

Jeremias, J.
1948   *Unbekannte Jesusworte* (Abhandlungen zur Theologie des Alten und Neuen Testaments, 16; Zurich: Zwingli-Verlag).
1963   *The Parables of Jesus* (New York: Charles Scribner's & Sons, 2nd rev. edn).

Johnson, S.
1997   'The *Gospel of Thomas* 76:3 and Canonical Parallels: Three Segments in the Tradition History of the Saying', in J. Turner and A. McGuire (eds), *The Nag Hammadi Library After Fifty Years: Proceedings of the 1995 Society of Biblical Literature Commemoration* (NHMS, 44; Leiden: E.J. Brill): 308–26.

Kasser, R.
1961   *L'Évangile selon Thomas. Présentation et commentaire théologique,* (Bibliothèque théologique; Neuchâtel: Delachaux et Niestlé).

Kee, H.C.
1963	'"Becoming a Child" in the Gospel of Thomas', *JBL* 82: 307–14.
King, K.
2003	*What is Gnosticism?* (Cambridge, MA: Belknap Press of Harvard University Press).
Klijn, A.F.J.
1962	'The "Single One" in the Gospel of Thomas', *JBL* 81: 271–78.
1970	'John XIV 22 and the Name Judas Thomas', *Studies in John presented to Professor Dr. J. N. Sevenster on the occasion of his Seventieth Birthday* (NTSup, 24; Leiden: E.J. Brill): 88–96.
1992	'Jewish-Christian Gospel Tradition' (VCSup, 27; Leiden: E.J. Brill).
Kloppenborg, J.
1987	*The Formation of Q: Trajectories in Ancient Wisdom Collections* (Studies in Antiquity and Christianity; Philadelphia: Fortress Press).
Koester, H.
1957	*Synoptische Überlieferung bei den Apostolischen Vätern* (TUGAL, 65; Berlin: Akademie-Verlag).
1968	'One Jesus and Four Primitive Gospels', *HTR* 61: 203–247.
1971	'GNOMAI DIAPHOROI: The Origin and Nature of Diversification in the History of Early Christianity', in J. M. Robinson and H. Koester (eds), *Trajectories through Early Christianity* (Philadephia: Fortress Press): 114–57.
1983	'Three Thomas Parables', in A.H.B. Logan and A.J.M. Wedderburn (eds), *The New Testament and Gnosis: Essays in Honour of Robert McLachlan Wilson* (Edinburgh: T&T Clark): 195–203.
1990	*Ancient Christian Gospels: Their History and Development* (Philadelphia: Trinity Press International).
Kuhn, K.H.
1960	'Some Observations on the Coptic Gospel According to Thomas', *Muséon* 73: 317–23.
Kuntzmann, R.
1993	'Le Temple dans le corpus copte de Nag Hammadi', *RSR* 67: 28–29.
Layton, B.
1989	*Nag Hammadi Codex II,2–7 together with XIII,2*, Brit. Lib. OR. 4926(1), and P.Oxy. 1, 654, 655*, I (NHS, 20; Leiden: E.J. Brill).
Leipoldt, J.
1958	'Ein neues Evangelium? Das koptische Thomasevangelium übersetzt und besprochen', *TLZ* 83: 488.
1967	*Das Evangelium nach Thomas: Koptisch und Deutsch* (TU, 101; Berlin: Akademie-Verlag).
Leipoldt, J. and H.-M. Schenke
1960	*Koptisch-gnostische Schriften aus den Papyrus-Codices von Nag-Hamadi* (TF, 20; Hamburg-Bergstadt: Herbert Reich-Evangelischer Verlag).
Lelyveld, M.
1987	*Les Logia de la Vie dans L'Évangile selon Thomas. A la Recherche d'une Tradition et d'une Rédaction* (NHS, 34; Leiden: E.J. Brill).
Liebenberg, J.
2001	*The Language of the Kingdom and Jesus: Parable, Aphorism, and Metaphor in the Sayings Material Common to the Synoptic Tradition and the Gospel of Thomas* (BZNW, 102; Berlin: Walter de Gruyter).
Lightfoot, J.
1997	*Commentary on the New Testament from the Talmud and Hebraica*, III (repr.; Peabody: Hendrickson).

Lord, A.
    2000   *The Singer of Tales* (Harvard Studies in Comparative Literature, 24; Cambridge, MA: Harvard University Press, 2nd edn [1960]).
Lowy, S.
    1958   'The Motivation of Fasting in Talmudic Literature', *JJS* 9: 19–38.
MacDonald, D.R.
    1987   *There is No Male and Female* (HDR, 20; Philadelphia: Fortress Press).
Mahé, J.-P.
    1998   'A Reading of the *Discourse on the Ogdoad and the Ennead* (Nag Hammadi Codex VI.6)', in R. van den Broek and W.J. Hanegraaff (eds), *Gnosis and Hermeticism from Antiquity to Modern Times* (Albany: SUNY): 79–85.
Marcovich, M.
    1969   'Textual Criticism on the *Gospel of Thomas*', *JTS* 20: 53–74.
Markschies, C.
    2003   *Gnosis: An Introduction* (trans. J. Bowden; London: T&T Clark International).
Marjanen, A.
    1998   'Thomas and Jewish Religious Practices', in R. Uro (ed.), *Thomas at the Crossroads: Essays on the Gospel of Thomas* (Edinburgh: T&T Clark): 163–82.
McArthur, H.
    1959/60 'The Dependence of the Gospel of Thomas on the Synoptics', *ExpTim* 71: 286–87.
McDonough, S.M.
    1999   *YHWH at Patmos. Rev. 1:4 in its Hellenistic and Early Jewish Setting* (WUNT II.107; Tübingen: Mohr Siebeck).
McIver, R. and M. Carroll
    2002   'Experiments to Develop Criteria for Determining the Existence of Written Sources, and Their Potential Implications for the Synoptic Problem', *JBL* 121: 667–87.
Meeks, W.
    1974   'The Image of the Androgyne: Some Uses of a Symbol in Earliest Christianity', *HR* 13: 165–208.
Mees, M.
    1970   *Die Zitate aus dem Neuen Testament bei Clemens von Alexandrien* (Rome: Instituto di Litteratura Christiana Antica).
Ménard, J.-É.
    1970   'La Sagesse et le Logion 3 de l'Évangile selon Thomas', *Studia Patristica* 10: 137–40.
    1975   *L'Évangile selon Thomas* (NHS, 5; Leiden: E.J. Brill).
Merkelbach, R.
    1984   'Logion 36 des Thomasevangeliums', *Zeitschrift für Papyrologie und Epigraphik* 54: 64.
    1985   'Logion 97 des Thomasevangeliums', *Bulletin of American Society of Papyrologists* 22: 227–30.
Metzger, B.
    1975   *A Textual Commentary on the Greek New Testament* (New York: United Bible Societies).
Meyer, M.
    1985   'Making Mary Male: The Categories "Male" and "Female" in the Gospel of Thomas', *NTS* 31: 554–70.
    1990   'The Beginning of the Gospel of Thomas', *Semeia* 52: 161–73.
    1992   *The Gospel of Thomas: The Hidden Sayings of Jesus* (San Francisco: Harper Collins).

1998   'Seeing or Coming to the Child of the Living One? More on the *Gospel of Thomas* Saying 37', *HTR* 91: 413–16.

Miller, B. Fordyce
1967   'A Study of the Theme of "Kingdom": The Gospel According to Thomas: Logion 18', *NT* 9: 52–60.

Miller, R.J.
1989   'The Inside is (Not) the Outside: Q11:39 and GThom 89', *Foundations and Facets Forum* 5: 92–105.

Mirecki, P.A.
1991   'Coptic Manichaean Psalm 278 and the Gospel of Thomas 37', in A. van Tongerloo and S. Giversen (eds), *Manichaica Selecta: Studies presented to Professor Julien Ries on the Occasion of his Seventieth Birthday* (Lovanii: International Association of Manichaean Studies): 243–62.

Montefiore, H.
1960/61 'A Comparison of the Parables of the Gospel according to Thomas and the Synoptic Gospels', *NTS* 7: 220–48.

Morard, F.-E.
1973   'Monachos, Moine, Histoire du terme grec jusqu'au 4e siècle', *Freiburger Zeitschrift für Philosophie und Theologie*: 332–411.
1975   'Monachos: une importation sémitique en Egypt? Quelques aperçus nouveaux', in E.A. Livingstone (ed.), *Papers presented at the 6th International Conference on Patristic Studies held in Oxford 1971* (TU, 115; Berlin: Akademie-Verlag): 242–46.
1980   'Encore quelques réflexions sur monachos', *VC* 34: 305–401.

Morray-Jones, C.
1992   'Transformational Mysticism in the Apocalyptic-Merkavah Tradition', *JJS* 48: 1–31.

Morrice, W.G.
1985   'The Parable of the Dragnet and the Gospel of Thomas', *ExpTim* 95: 269–73.
1986   'The Parable of the Tenants and the Gospel of Thomas', *ExpTim* 98: 104–107.

Mournet, T.C.
2005   *Oral Tradition and Literary Dependency: Viability and Stability in the Synoptic Tradition and Q* (WUNT, 2, 195; Tübingen: Mohr Siebeck).

Mueller, D.
1973   'Kingdom of Heaven or Kingdom of God?', *VC* 27: 266–76.

Mussies, G.
1981   'Catalogues of Sins and Virtues Personified (NHC II,5)', in R. van den Broek and M.J. Vermaseren (eds), *Studies in Gnosticism and Hellenistic Religions presented to Gilles Quispel on the Occasion of his 65th Birthday* (EPRO, 91; Leiden: E.J. Brill): 315–35.

Nagel, P.
1960   'Neuer Wein in alten Schläuchen (Mt 9,17)', *VC* 14: 1–8.
1969a   'Erwägungen zum Thomas-Evangelium', in Franz Altheim and R. Stiehl (eds), *Der Araber in der alten Welt* 5:2 (Berlin: de Gruyter): 368–92.
1969b   'Die Parabel vom Klugen Fischer in Thomasevangelium von Nag Hammadi', in R. Stiehl and H.E. Stier (eds), *Beiträge zur Alten Geschichte und deren Nachleben. Festschrift für Franz Altheim*, I (Berlin: de Gruyter): 518–24.

Neller, K.
1989   'Diversity in the Gospel of Thomas: Clues for a New Direction?', *Second Century* 7: 1–18.

Ong, W.
1971   *Rhetoric, Romance, and Technology: Studies in the Interaction of Expression and Culture* (Ithaca, NY: Cornell University Press).
1977   *Interfaces of the Word* (Ithaca, NY: Cornell University Press).
1982   *Orality and Literacy: The Technologizing of the Word* (New York: Methuen).
Otzen, B.
1993   'The Paradise Trees in Jewish Apocalyptic', in P. Bilde, H.K. Nielsen and J.P. Sørensen (eds), *Apocryphon Severini presented to Søren Giversen* (Aarhus: Aarhus University Press): 140–54.

Painter, J.
1999   *Just James: The Brother of Jesus in History and Tradition* (Minneapolis: Fortress Press).

Patterson, S.
1990   'The Gospel of Thomas: Introduction', in J. Kloppenborg, M. Meyer, S. Patterson, and M. Steinhauser, *Q-Thomas Reader* (Sonoma: Polebridge Press): 77–123.
1991   'Paul and the Jesus Tradition: It is Time for Another Look', *HTR* 84: 32–33.
1993   *The Gospel of Thomas and Jesus* (Sonoma: Polebridge Press).
Payne Smith, J.
1998   *Syriac–English Dictionary* (Winona Lake: Eisenbrauns).
Perrin, N.
2002   *Thomas and Tatian: The Relationship between the* Gospel of Thomas *and the* Diatessaron (Academia Biblica, 5; Atlanta: Society of Biblical Literature).

Peterson, E.
1959   *Frühkirche, Judentum, und Gnosis* (Freiburg: Herder).
Peterson, W.L.
1981   'The Parable of the Lost Sheep in the Gospel of Thomas and the Synoptics', *NT* 23: 128–47.

Priest, J.F.
1985   'The Dog in the Manger: In Quest of a Fable', *The Classical Journal* 81: 49–58.
Prigent, P.
1958   'Ce que l'oeil n'a pas vu, 1 Cor. 2,9', *TLZ* 14: 428.
Puech, H.-Ch.
1963   'The Gospel of Thomas', in E. Hennecke and W. Schneemelcher (eds), *New Testament Apocrypha*, I (ET R. McL. Wilson; Philadelphia: Westminster Press): 278–307.

Quecke, H.
1963   '"Sein haus seines Königreiches" zum Thomasevangelium 85.9f.', *Muséon* 76: 47–53.

Quispel, G.
1957   'The Gospel of Thomas and the New Testament', *VC* 11: 189–207.
1958   'L'Évangile selon Thomas et les Clémentines', *VC* 12: 181–96.
1958/59 'Some Remarks on the Gospel of Thomas', *NTS* 5: 276–90.
1959   'L'Évangile selon Thomas et le Diatesssaron', *VC* 13: 87–117.
1960   'L'Évangile selon Thomas et le "texte occidental" du Nouveau Testament', *VC* 14: 204–15.
1962   'Der Heliand und das Thomasevangelium', *VC* 16: 121–51.
1965   'L'Évangile selon Thomas et les Origines de l'Ascèse Chrétienne', *Aspects du Judéo-Christianisme: Colloque de Strasbourg 23–25 Avril 1964* (Paris: Presses Universitaires de France): 37–45.

1967a   *Makarius, das Thomasevangelium und das Lied von der Perle* (NTSup, 15; Leiden: E.J. Brill).
1967b   'The Diatessaron and the Historical Jesus', *Studi e materiali di storia delle religioni* 38: 463–72.
1968   'Jewish Influences on the "Heliand"', in J. Neusner (ed.), *Religions in Antiquity: Essays in Memory of Erwin Ramsdell Goodenough* (NumenSup, 14; Leiden: E.J. Brill): 246–48.
1969   'The Latin Tatian or the Gospel of Thomas in Limburg', *JBL* 88: 321–30.
1971a   'Some Remarks on the Diatessaron Haaranse', *VC* 25: 131–39.
1971b   *Het Evangelie van Thomas ende Nederlanden* (Amsterdam, Brussels: Elsevier).
1974a   'Gnosticism and the New Testament', *Gnostic Studies*, I (Istanbul: Nederlands Historisch-Archaeologisch Instituut te Istanbul).
1974b   'Jewish-Christian Gospel Tradition', *Anglican Theological Review* 3: 112–16.
1975a   *Tatian and the Gospel of Thomas* (Leiden: E.J. Brill).
1975b   'Love Thy Brother', in *Gnostic Studies*, II (Leiden: Nederlands Historisch-Archaelogisch Instituut te Istanbul): 169–79.
1975c   'Gnosis and the New Sayings of Jesus', in *Gnostic Studies*, II (Leiden: Nederlands Historisch-Archaeologisch Instituut te Istanbul): 180–209.
1975c   'Gospel of Thomas and the New Testament', in *Gnostic Studies*, II (Leiden: Nederlands Historisch-Archaeologisch Instituut te Istanbul): 3–16.
1975d   'The Discussion of Judaic Christianity', in *Gnostic Studies*, II (Leiden: Nederlands Historisch-Archaelogisch Instituut te Istanbul): 146–58.
1975e   'The Gospel of Thomas and the Western Text: A Reappraisal', in *Gnostic Studies*, II (Leiden: Nederlands Historisch-Archaeologisch Instituut te Istanbul): 56–69.
1975f   'The Syrian Thomas and the Syrian Macarius', in *Gnostic Studies*, II (Leiden: Nederlands Historisch-Archaeologisch Instituut te Istanbul: 113–21.
1980   'Ezekiel 1:26 in Jewish Mysticism and Gnosis', *VC* 34: 1–13.
1981   'The *Gospel of Thomas* Revisited', in B. Barq (ed.), Colloque International sur les Textes de Nag Hammadi, Quebec, 22–25 *Août* 1978 (BCNH, 1; Louvain: Peeters): 218–66.
1988   'The Gospel of Thomas and the Trial of Jesus', in T. Baarda, A. Hilhorst, G.P. Luttikhuizen and A.S. van der Woude (eds), *Text and Testimony: Essays on New Testament and Apocryphal Literature in Honour of A.F.J. Klijn* (Kampen: Kok): 197–99.
1989   'Hermes Trismegistus and Tertullian', *VC* 43: 188–90.

Reijners, G.Q.
1965   *The Terminology of The Holy Cross in Early Christian Literature, as Based Upon Old Testament Typology* (Græcitas Christianorum primæva, fasc. 2; Nijmegen: Dekker & Van de Vegt).

Reitzenstein, R.
1978   *Hellenistic Mystery-Religions: Their Basic Ideas and Significance* (Pittsburgh Theological Monograph Series, 15; trans. J.E. Steely; Pittsburg: Pickwick Press).

Rengstorf, K.H.
1967   'Urchristliches Kerygma und "Gnostische" Interpretation in einigen sprüchen des Thomasevangeliums', in U. Bianchi (ed.), *Le Origini dello Gnosticismo. Colloquio di Messina 13–18 Aprile 1966* (NumenSup, 12; Leiden: E.J. Brill): 563–74.

Riley, G.
1995a   *Resurrection Reconsidered: Thomas and John in Controversy* (Minneapolis: Fortress Press).

1995b   'A Note on the Text of *Gospel of Thomas* 37', *HTR* 88: 179–81.
Roberts, C.
1970   'The Gospel of Thomas: Logion 30A', *JTS* 21: 91–92.
Robinson, J.
1971   'LOGOI SOPHON: On the Gattung of Q', in J. Robinson and H. Koester (eds),
            Trajectories Through Early Christianity (Philadelphia: Fortress Press): 71–113.
Roques, R.
1960a   '"L'Évangile selon Thomas": son édition critique et son identification', *RHR*
            157: 187–218.
1960b   'Gnosticisme et Christianisme: L'Évangile selon Thomas', *Irénikon* 33: 29–40.
Saldarini, A.J.
1994   *Matthew's Christian-Jewish Community* (Chicago: University of Chicago
            Press).
Sanders, E.P.
1990   *Jewish Law From Jesus to the Mishnah: Five Studies* (Philadelphia: Trinity
            Press International).
Satlow, M.L.
2001   *Jewish Marriage in Antiquity* (Princeton: Princeton University Press).
Saunders, E.W.
1963   'A Trio of Thomas Logia', *Biblical Research* 8: 43–59.
Säve-Söderbergh, T.
1967   'Gnostic and Canonical Gospel Traditions (with special reference to the Gospel
            of Thomas)', in U. Bianchi (ed.), *Le Origini dello Gnosticismo, Colloquio di
            Messina, 13–18 Aprile, 1966. Testi e Discussioni* (Studies in the History of
            Religions, NumenSup, 12; Leiden: E.J. Brill): 552–62.
Schenke, H.M.
1994   'On the Compositional History of the Gospel of Thomas', *Foundations and
            Facets Forum* 10: 9–30.
Schippers, R.
1959   'The Mashal-Character of the Parable of the Pearl', in *Studia Evangelica:
            Papers presented to the International Congress on 'the Four Gospels in 1957'*
            (Berlin: Akademie-Verlag): 236–41.
Schnider, F.
1977   'Das Gleichnis vom verlorenen Schaf und seine Redaktoren', *Kairos* 19: 146–
            54.
Schoedel, W.
1960   'Naassene Themes in the Coptic Gospel of Thomas', *VC* 14: 225–34.
Schrage, W.
1964a   *Das Verhältnis des Thomas-Evangeliums zur synoptischen Tradition und zu
            den koptischen Evangelienübersetzungen* (BZNW, 29; Berlin: Töpelmann).
1964b   'Evangelienzitate in den Oxyrhynchus-Logien und im koptischen Thomas-
            evangelium', in W. Eltester and F.H. Kettler (eds), *Apophoreta: Festschrift für
            Ernest Haenchen* (BZNW, 30; Berlin: Alfred Töpelmann): 251–68.
Schürmann, H. von
1963   'Das Thomasevangelium und das lukanische Sondergut', *BZ*: 236–60.
Schwartz, E.
1932   'Unzeitgemässe Beobachtungen zu den Clementinen', *ZNW* 31: 151–99.
Scott, B.B.
1987   'The Empty Jar', *Foundations and Facets Forum* 3: 77–80.
1991   *Hear Then the Parable: A Commentary on the Parables of Jesus* (Minneapolis:
            Fortress Press).

Sell, J.
    1980   'Johannine Traditions in Logion 61 of the Gospel of Thomas', *Perspectives in
                Religious Studies* 7: 24–37.
Sellew, P.
    1985   'Early Collections of Jesus' Words' (PhD dissertation: Harvard Divinity School).
    2006   'Jesus and the Voice from beyond the Grave: *Gospel of Thomas* 42 in the
                Context of Funerary Epigraphy', in J. Asgeirsson, A.D. DeConick and R. Uro
                (eds), *Thomasine Traditions in Antiquity* (NHMS; Leiden: E.J. Brill, 2006).
Shaw, T.
    1998   *The Burden of the Flesh: Fasting and Sexuality in Early Christianity* (Minne-
                apolis: Fortress Press).
Sheppard, J.B.
    1965   'A Study of the Parables Common to the Synoptic Gospels and the Coptic
                Gospel of Thomas' (PhD dissertation: Emory University).
Sieber, J.
    1966   'A Redactional Analysis of the Synoptic Gospels with regard to the Question of
                the Sources of the Gospel According to Thomas' (PhD dissertation: Claremont
                Graduate School).
Smith, J.Z.
    1966   'The Garments of Shame', *HR* 5: 217–38.
Smith, M.H.
    1990   'Kinship is Relative: Mark 3:31–35 and Parallels', *Foundations and Facets
                Forum* 6: 80–84.
Smyth, K.
    1960   'Gnosticism in "The Gospel according to Thomas"', *HeyJ* 1: 189–98.
Snodgrass, K.R.
    1974   'The Parable of the Wicked Husbandmen: Is the Gospel of Thomas Version the
                Original?', *NTS* 20: 142–44.
    1989   'The Gospel of Thomas: A Secondary Gospel', *Second Century* 7: 19–38.
Spidlik, T.
    1986   *The Spirituality of the Christian East: A Systematic Handbook* (trans. A. Gythiel;
                Kalamazoo: Cistercian Publications).
Stoker, W.D.
    1988   'Extracanonical Parables and the Historical Jesus', *Semeia* 44: 95–120.
    1989   *Extracanonical Sayings of Jesus* (SBL Resources for Biblical Study, 18; Atlanta:
                Scholars Press).
Strobel, A.
    1963   'Textgeschichtliches zum Thomas-Logion 86 (Mt 8,20//Luk 9,58)', *VC* 17:
                211–24.
Suarez, P. de.
    1974   *L'Evangile selon Thomas* (Marsanne: Metanoia).
Tuckett, C.M.
    1988   'Thomas and the Synoptics', *NT* 30: 132–57.
    1991   'Q and Thomas: Evidence of a Primitive "Wisdom Gospel?" A Response to
                H. Koester', *ETL* 67: 346–60.
Turner, H. and H. Montefiore
    1962   *Thomas and the Evangelists* (SBT, 35; London: SCM Press).
Urbach, E.E.
    1987   *The Sages: Their Concepts and Beliefs*, I (Jerusalem: Magnes Press, Hebrew
                University).

Uro, R.
 1998a 'Is *Thomas* an Encratite Gospel?', in *Thomas at the Crossroads* (Edinburgh: T&T Clark): 140–62.
 1998b 'Thomas and Oral Gospel Tradition', in *Thomas at the Crossroads*, (Edinburgh: T&T Clark): 8–32.
 2003 *Thomas: Seeking the Historical Context of the Gospel of Thomas* (London: T&T Clark International).

Valantasis, R.
 1997 *The Gospel of Thomas* (London and New York: Routledge).
 1999 'Is the Gospel of Thomas Ascetical? Revisiting an Old Problem with a New Theory', *JECS* 7: 55–81.

Vermes, P.
 1973 'Buber's Understanding of the Divine Name Related to the Bible, Targum, and Midrash', *JJS* 24: 147–66.

Vielhauer, P.
 1964 'ANAPAUSIS: Zum gnostischen Hintergrund des Thomasevangeliums', in W. Eltester (ed.), *Apophoreta. Festschrift für Ernest Haenchen* (BZNW, 30; Berlin: Töpelmann): 281–99.

Vööbus, A.
 1951 *Celibacy: A Requirement for Admission to Baptism in the Early Syrian Church* (Papers of Estonian Theological Society in Exile, 1; Stockholm).
 1960 *History of Asceticism in the Syrian Orient: A Contribution to the History and Culture in the Near East, Part 2: Early Monasticism in Mesopotamia and Syria* 2 (CSCO, 197, 17; Louvain: Peeters).

Walls, A.F.
 1962 '"Stone" and "Wood" in Oxyrhynchus Papyrus I', *VC* 16: 71–76.

Williams, M.
 1985 *The Immovable Race: A Gnostic Designation and the Theme of Stability in Late Antiquity* (NHS, 29; Leiden: E.J. Brill).
 1996 *Rethinking 'Gnosticism': An Argument for Dismantling a Dubious Category* (Princeton: Princeton University Press).

Wilson, R.McL.
 1958/59 'The Coptic "Gospel of Thomas"', *NTS* 5: 273–76.
 1960a *Studies in the Gospel of Thomas* (London: Mowbray).
 1960b '"Thomas" and the Growth of the Gospels', *HTR* 53: 231–50.

Zoeckler, T.
 1999 *Jesu Lehren im Thomasevangelium* (NHMS, 47; Leiden: E.J. Brill).

INDEXES

INDEX OF REFERENCES

BIBLE

OTHER ANCIENT LITERATURE

INDEX OF AUTHORS